INSTITUTES OF DIVINE JURISPRUDENCE

NATURAL LAW AND
ENLIGHTENMENT CLASSICS

Knud Haakonssen
General Editor

Christian Thomasius

Institutes of Divine Jurisprudence

With Selections from
*Foundations of the Law
of Nature and Nations*

Christian Thomasius

Edited, Translated, and with an Introduction
by Thomas Ahnert

LIBERTY FUND
Indianapolis

This book is published by Liberty Fund, Inc., a foundation established to encourage study of the ideal of a society of free and responsible individuals.

𒂼𒄄

The cuneiform inscription that serves as our logo and as the design motif for our endpapers is the earliest-known written appearance of the word "freedom" (*amagi*), or "liberty." It is taken from a clay document written about 2300 B.C. in the Sumerian city-state of Lagash.

Frontispiece: Portrait of Christian Thomasius by Johann Christian Heinrich Sporleder (1754), oil. Reproduced courtesy of Bildarchiv der Zentralen Kustodie der Martin-Luther-Universität Halle-Wittenberg.

C 10 9 8 7 6 5 4 3 2 1
P 10 9 8 7 6 5 4 3 2 1

Library of Congress Cataloging-in-Publication Data
Thomasius, Christian, 1655–1728:
[Institutiones jurisprudentiae divinae & Fundamenta juris naturae et gentium. English]
Institutes of divine jurisprudence with selections from foundations of the law of nature and nations/Christian Thomasius: edited, translated, and with an introduction by Thomas Ahnert.
p. cm.—(Natural law and enlightenment classics)
Includes bibliographical references and index.
ISBN 978-0-86597-518-7 (hc: alk. paper)   ISBN 978-0-86597-519-4 (pbk.: alk. paper)
1. Law—Philosophy.   2. Natural law—Early works to 1800.   3. Religion and law.   I. Ahnert, Thomas.   II. Thomasius, Christian, 1655–1728. Fundamenta juris naturae et gentium.   III. Title.
KZ2344.A31567 2011
340′.112—dc22   2011013180

LIBERTY FUND, INC.
8335 Allison Pointe Trail, Suite 300
Indianapolis, Indiana 46250-1684

CONTENTS

Book III

Selections from
Foundations of the Law of Nature and Nations

Book I

INTRODUCTION

The German jurist and philosopher Christian Thomasius (1655–1728) published two major treatises on natural law, the *Institutes of Divine Jurisprudence* in 1688 and the *Foundations of the Law of Nature and Nations* in 1705.[1] Thomasius's declared aim in both was to improve and develop the natural law theories of Hugo Grotius and Samuel Pufendorf.[2] Both works have much material in common, a lot of which is standard natural jurisprudential argument, yet Thomasius also used the *Foundations* to reformulate the central principles on which his natural jurisprudence was based. The passages from the *Foundations* in this volume have been chosen because they make clear the key changes in Thomasius's natural law theory that had taken place since the publication of the *Institutes* seventeen years before.

Thomasius was widely regarded as an innovative, even heterodox, thinker during his lifetime, a reputation that he often promoted very vigorously. He boasted, for example, that his decision in the mid-1680s to lecture at the University of Leipzig in German rather than in the traditional Latin had caused great consternation among the conservative professoriate,[3] and in subsequent years he often criticized "pedantry," "dogmatism," and "scholasticism" in university teaching. Thomasius continued to be regarded as an intellectual innovator after his death. In the mid-eighteenth century the historian of philosophy Johann Jacob Brucker

---

1. Christian Thomasius, *Institutiones jurisprudentiae divinae* (Leipzig, 1688), and Thomasius, *Fundamenta juris naturae et gentium* (Halle, 1705).

2. See, for example, Thomasius, *Foundations*, "Introductory Chapter," §1.

3. See Rolf Lieberwirth, "Die französischen Kultureinflüsse auf den deutschen Frühaufklärer Christian Thomasius," *Wissenschaftliche Zeitschrift der Universität Halle* 33 (1983): 63.

praised him as one in a long line of "eclectic" thinkers, who formed their ideas independently and refused to follow blindly the authority of others.[4] Toward the end of the eighteenth century the author Friedrich Gedicke in Berlin presented Thomasius as one of the initiators of the Enlightenment in Germany, describing him as the person "to whom we owe a large part of our intellectual and material happiness."[5] In recent years several studies have reaffirmed his status as a key figure in the intellectual history of the early Enlightenment.[6]

Life of Thomasius

Christian Thomasius[7] was born in Leipzig in 1655, the son of Jacob Thomasius, a respected professor at the university, who taught the young Gottfried Wilhelm Leibniz in the early 1660s. Christian Thomasius entered the University of Leipzig in 1669. In 1672, the year in which Samuel Pufendorf's *On the Law of Nature and Nations* was first published, he graduated with a master's degree from Leipzig, moving to the University

4. Johann Jacob Brucker, *Historia critica philosophiae* (Leipzig, 1744), vol. IV, chap. 9.

5. "Wir alle verdanken ihm einen grossen Teil unserer intellektuellen und materiellen Glückseeligkeit." Quoted in Martin Pott, "Christian Thomasius and Gottfried Arnold," in *Gottfried Arnold: 1666–1714*, ed. D. Blaufuss and F. Niewöhner (Wiesbaden: Harrasowitz, 1995, p. 247).

6. See, for example, Peter Schröder, *Christian Thomasius zur Einführung* (Hamburg: Junius, 1999); Tim Hochstrasser, *Natural Law Theories in the Early Enlightenment* (Cambridge: Cambridge University Press, 2000); Frank Grunert, *Normbegründung und politische Legitimität* (Tübingen: Max Niemeyer, 2000); Ian Hunter, *Rival Enlightenments: Civil and Metaphysical Philosophy in Early Modern Germany* (Cambridge: Cambridge University Press, 2001); Thomas Ahnert, *Religion and the Origins of the German Enlightenment: Faith and the Reform of Learning in the Thought of Christian Thomasius* (Rochester, N.Y.: University of Rochester Press, 2006); Ian Hunter, *The Secularisation of the Confessional State: The Political Thought of Christian Thomasius* (Cambridge: Cambridge University Press, 2007). The foundational work on Thomasius's moral philosophy is still Werner Schneiders, *Naturrecht und Liebesethik: Zur Geschichte der praktischen Philosophie im Hinblick auf Christian Thomasius* (Hildesheim and New York: G. Olms, 1971).

7. On Thomasius's biography, see Rolf Lieberwirth, "Christian Thomasius (1655–1728)," in *Aufklärung und Erneuerung*, ed. G. Jerouschek and A. Sames (Hanau: Dausien, 1994), pp. 29–45.

of Frankfurt on the Oder in 1675, where he received a doctorate in law, before returning to Leipzig in 1679. After an unsuccessful attempt at a legal career, Thomasius began to lecture on natural jurisprudence to students at the University of Leipzig. Within a few years, he was involved in a number of controversies with the university, its theological faculty in particular. His disputation *On the Crime of Bigamy* (*De crimine bigamiae*) in 1685 appears to have led to disagreements with Valentin Alberti, a professor of theology and an opponent of Samuel Pufendorf. Thomasius, in his *Institutes of Divine Jurisprudence* of 1688, was also highly critical of Alberti's natural law theory[8] and defended the main principles of Pufendorf's system. In 1688 Thomasius began publishing a monthly journal, the *Monatsgespraeche* (*Monthly Conversations*), in which he often commented satirically on members of the university. In addition, he plunged into a dispute with the court preacher in Copenhagen, Hector Gottfried Masius, which led to a complaint by the Danish king to Thomasius's prince, the Elector of Saxony.[9] At the same time, Thomasius was associating himself with a quasi-Puritan reform movement within the Lutheran church in Leipzig, the so-called Pietists, who were opposed by the theological faculty at the university. While some clergymen and professors appear to have been sympathetic to the Pietists' general aims, their concern seems to have been that some of the leading Pietists were not qualified theologians and therefore likely to mislead their followers on matters that were essential to salvation.[10] Eventually, pressure from the Lutheran church in Saxony and the Elector forced most of the prominent Pietists to leave the country. Several moved to the lands of the Calvinist Elector of Brandenburg, who

8. For Valentin Alberti's theory of natural law, see his *Compendium juris naturae orthodoxae theologiae conformatum et in duas partes distributum* (Leipzig, 1678), and his reply to Pufendorf, the *Eros Lipsicus, quo Eris Scandica Samuelis Pufendorfi cum convitiis et erroribus suis mascule, modeste tamen repellitur* (Leipzig, 1687). Here the second edition of Alberti's *Compendium*, published in Leipzig in 1696, has been used.

9. Frank Grunert, "Zur aufgeklärten Kritik am theokratischen Absolutismus: Der Streit zwischen Hector Gottfried Masius und Christian Thomasius über Ursprung und Begründung der summa potestas," in *Christian Thomasius (1655–1728): Neue Forschungen im Kontext der Frühaufklärung*, ed. Friedrich Vollhardt (Tübingen: Max Niemeyer, 1997), pp. 51–77.

10. See Ahnert, *Religion and the Origins of the German Enlightenment*, p. 13.

welcomed them, in part because he believed that they would be useful allies against his territory's Lutheran church, with which his relationship was strained.[11] In 1690 Thomasius also left Saxony, having been forbidden to teach, publish, and conduct academic disputations, and moved across the border into the territories of the Elector of Brandenburg. There Thomasius first taught at an academy for noblemen in Halle. Very soon, however, he joined others in urging the foundation of a full university in Halle.[12] Their efforts were successful, and in 1694 the new University of Halle was opened, which soon became one of the leading academic institutions in the early German Enlightenment. Thomasius was appointed a professor in Halle and remained there until his death in 1728.

Institutes of Divine Jurisprudence (1688)

Thomasius first published the *Institutes* in Leipzig in 1688 as a textbook to accompany his lecture course on natural law. At that time he did not hold a university post but taught students in private seminars, so-called *collegia*. The *Institutes* was intended as a vindication of the main principles of Pufendorf's natural jurisprudence against critics such as Valentin Alberti. Yet Thomasius's work was more than a repetition of Pufendorf's ideas. In Pufendorf's theory, for example, the notion of human weakness (*imbecillitas*) had played a central role, which it did not have in Thomasius's *Institutes*. Pufendorf argued that, unlike other animals, single humans in a state of nature were weak. They lacked teeth, claws, fur, speed, and the other natural attributes that allowed wild beasts to survive without assistance from others. This *imbecillitas*, according to Pufendorf, drove humans to form societies. It also made it clear that God must have wanted them to

11. On the relationship between the Hohenzollerns and Pietism, see the classic work by Carl Hinrichs, *Preußentum und Pietismus: Der Pietismus in Brandenburg-Preußen als religiös-soziale Reformbewegung* (Göttingen: Vandenhoeck & Ruprecht, 1971), and Mary Fulbrook, *Piety and Politics: Religion and the Rise of Absolutism in England, Württemberg and Prussia* (Cambridge: Cambridge University Press, 1983).

12. On Thomasius's proposal for a new university in Halle, see Friedrich de Boor, "Die ersten Vorschläge des Christian Thomasius 'wegen Auffrichtung einer Neuen Academie zu Halle' aus dem Jahre 1690," in *Europa in der Frühen Neuzeit: Festschrift für Günther Mühlpfordt,* ed. E. Donnert (Weimar: Böhlau, 1997), 4:57–84.

do so, because he would not have created humankind only for it to perish immediately.[13] The argument from *imbecillitas,* however, was susceptible to accusations of "Hobbesianism," because it seemed to turn individual necessity into the foundation of natural law.[14] It is perhaps for this reason that Thomasius did not emphasize the argument from *imbecillitas* in his natural law theory but replaced it with another that relied on less selfish grounds to account for the origins of society. Humans, Thomasius wrote, had been created capable of reasoning. That was a fact of which each individual was aware. Reasoning, however, was impossible without words, and words were terms imposed on the world by mutual agreement among several humans. The use of words and language, therefore, depended on the existence of human society and relationships, and the rational nature of humans was thus evidence that God had intended them to live in societies together.[15]

In most other respects Thomasius's argument was similar to Pufendorf's. The laws of nature were divine commands that could be known from the observation of human nature and reflection on it. They were grounded in the divine will, just as laws in general were based on the will of a superior, that is, someone who had the right to impose an obligation on others. Without these commands, physical nature had no intrinsic moral value, either good or bad. All moral values were impositions on a morally indifferent, physical nature by a superior. Moral and physical qualities, therefore, were strictly distinct from each other.[16] Thomasius also argued, like Pufendorf, that the human will was free in the sense of being "indifferent"; that is, it was able to choose freely between any of the

13. Samuel Pufendorf, *On the Duty of Man and Citizen,* ed. J. Tully, trans. M. Silverthorne (Cambridge: Cambridge University Press, 1991), bk. 1, chap. 3, §11, p. 36; see also Pufendorf, *The Whole Duty of Man, According to the Law of Nature,* trans. Andrew Tooke, ed. Ian Hunter and David Saunders, with *Two Discourses and a Commentary by Jean Barbeyrac,* trans. David Saunders (Indianapolis: Liberty Fund, 2003), bk. I, chap. 3, §11, p. 57. On Pufendorf's natural law theory, see Knud Haakonssen, *Natural Law and Moral Philosophy: From Grotius to the Scottish Enlightenment* (Cambridge: Cambridge University Press, 1996), pp. 35–43.

14. See Alberti, *Eros Lipsicus,* p. 13.

15. Thomasius, *Institutes,* bk. I, chap. iv, §§51–55.

16. Ibid., chap. i, §85.

various courses of action that presented themselves to it at a particular time. If that were not the case, the will could not be held morally responsible for its decisions. This freedom of the will was a key difference between humans and beasts. It meant that the former were moral agents, while the latter were not, though Thomasius also believed that following the fall from grace the human will was not always able to exercise its freedom unimpeded. Ever since original sin, the human passions interfered with the operations of the will and distorted its choices. But this interference was never so strong that humans ceased to be responsible for their actions.[17]

God's commands in natural law were not arbitrary, but his reasons were not fully evident to humans. It was only clear that, having created human nature as it was, God must have wanted humans to act according to the principles of natural law, as they were known from the empirical observation of humankind. Thomasius placed great emphasis on the inscrutability of God's mind to human understanding. This was one important respect in which he distinguished his natural law theory from that of opponents such as Valentin Alberti. Alberti believed that the content of natural law was not the product of divine commands but founded on eternal truths in the mind of God.[18] The moral principles of natural law were not identical to these truths, but they were derived directly from them and, therefore, were just. They were not known to humans on the basis of empirical observation and reflection but were innate and part of the so-called *imago divina,* the divine image that God had implanted in humans when he created the world.[19] Yet Alberti also said that these moral principles had been present in their full strength and clarity only in the state of innocence, before original sin. Following the fall from grace, they were blurred and obscured, and humans depended on divine revelation to supplement their imperfect knowledge and understanding of them. In particular, it was the Decalogue, given by God to the Israelites after their exodus from Egypt, that summarized the central precepts of natural law.[20]

The first of Thomasius's main objections was that Alberti's theory of

17. Ibid., chap. ii, §§39 and 42.
18. See Alberti, *Eros Lipsicus,* p. 67.
19. Ibid., p. 14.
20. Ibid., p. 284; see also Exodus 20:1–17; Deuteronomy 5:6–21.

the *imago divina* and the derivation of natural law from eternal truths implied a continuity, which did not exist, between human understanding and the mind of God. The two differed in kind, not just in degree, and the distance between them was insuperable.[21] Humans should therefore not dare to speculate about the ideas in God's mind. The grounds for God's decisions are inscrutable, and humans must not assume that their moral reasoning and that of God's are comparable and based on similar principles. The precepts of natural law were binding because they were known to be the commands of God, who was the rightful superior of humankind, not because they conformed to particular eternal truths. Thomasius also argued that Alberti's theory of eternal rational truths appeared to subordinate God's will to an external standard of morality: it implied that there were rules independent of and superior to God, which God had to adhere to, thus restricting his freedom and power.[22] Alberti replied that this standard according to which God acted was part of his own intellect, and thus it constituted no external restriction on him. To say that God acted according to principles that were part of himself, and not arbitrarily, did not imply that his freedom or his power was limited.[23]

Thomasius's natural jurisprudence in the *Institutes* was thus largely, if not completely, Pufendorfian. Yet natural law formed only one-half of the "divine jurisprudence" referred to in the full title of his work. The other half was divine positive law, and one of Thomasius's main concerns in the *Institutes* was to clarify the relationship between natural and positive divine law. As we have seen, Valentin Alberti argued that the main example of divine positive law, the Decalogue, was a republication of the laws of nature, which had been erased or at least obscured by the effects of original sin. Thomasius's view in the *Institutes* was that divine positive law was not needed to reconstruct and understand the main principles of natural

21. Thomasius, *Institutes*, bk. I, chap. iii, §§49–62.
22. Ibid., chap. ii, §72.
23. See Alberti, *Compendium*, 2nd ed. (Leipzig, 1696), p. 197. The debates between Thomasius and Pufendorf on the one hand and Alberti on the other were, to some extent, a continuation of the earlier controversies between realists and nominalists. On Pufendorf's relationship to realism and nominalism, see Alfred Dufour, "Pufendorf," in *The Cambridge History of Political Thought, 1450–1700*, ed. J. H. Burns with the assistance of Mark Goldie (Cambridge: Cambridge University Press, 1991), p. 567.

law. It was, however, important for other reasons, in particular because it provided guidance on certain temporal matters on which natural law was silent.

The most significant temporal matter, judging by the space devoted to it in the *Institutes,* was marriage.[24] Thomasius had examined the relevance of natural law for marriage in his disputation *De crimine bigamiae* of 1685, where he had concluded that the prohibition of bigamy had to be based on divine positive law because natural law did not offer any clear arguments against it.[25] In the *Institutes* Thomasius discussed at length the laws banning the different forms of polygamy and limiting marriages between relatives. Thomasius's conclusion there, too, is that these restrictions rest on divine positive law, not natural law, which is insufficient to explain them.[26] To the extent that divine positive laws are directed toward the affairs of temporal society, they stand in no need of interpretation by theologians. Jurists are capable of understanding and applying them, like the precepts of natural law or human positive law, and in so doing do not need to seek the advice of theologians.[27] This right of jurists to interpret Scripture on matters relevant to temporal law was part of Thomasius's argument against clerical authority more generally, which he continued and expanded in the following years, especially after he moved to the territories of the Elector of Brandenburg and began to teach at the University of Halle.[28] Here Thomasius also began to rethink his natural jurisprudence, a process that led to his second main work on natural law, the *Foundations of the Law of Nature and Nations,* published in 1705.

Foundations of the Law of Nature and Nations (1705)

An important change in Thomasius's natural jurisprudence concerned the relationship between moral and physical qualities. In the *Institutes* he

---

24. See Thomasius, *Institutes,* bk. III, chaps. ii and iii.

25. Christian Thomasius, *De crimine bigamiae* (Leipzig, 1685).

26. See Thomasius, *Institutes,* bk. III, chap. iii, §1.

27. Ibid., bk. II, chap. xi, §3.

28. See the collection of writings by Thomasius in *Christian Thomasius: Essays on Church and State,* ed. Ian Hunter, Thomas Ahnert, and Frank Grunert (Indianapolis: Liberty Fund, 2007).

had argued that these two types of qualities were distinct and separate: whether a particular action or condition was deemed morally good or evil depended on the moral value imposed on it by a superior, not on its physical attributes. In the three books of the *Foundations* Thomasius changed his mind and argued that moral value was not something that was attached by an act of will to a morally indifferent nature. Instead, moral qualities were a species of natural qualities, and moral philosophy itself formed part of natural philosophy, or "physics."[29] In particular, actions were morally good or bad, depending on their natural effects. Moral actions tended naturally to further the well-being and happiness of the agent and others, while immoral actions caused infelicity and ill health. This was so because God had created nature in such a way that its ordinary course reinforced moral conduct.[30]

These natural advantages and disadvantages in temporal life could be considered a form of divine rewards and punishments, though Thomasius said that they were not comparable to the sanctions threatened by a human legislator.[31] In particular, they were not sufficiently obvious to deter humans from breaking the law of nature, because "every [human] punishment must be inflicted visibly, but the evils which God has ordained for the transgressors of natural law come secretly, in such a way, that the connection of the evil with the sin is not evident, even if the evil itself is evident."[32] The natural consequences of moral and immoral actions were thus more similar to advice than to coercion.[33] God had no reason to compel humans to act morally by threatening them with punishments, because he derived no advantage from their obedience. Also, if the disadvantages of immorality were so clear and powerful that they deterred everyone from violating natural law, there would be no merit in being virtuous. A human legislator, on the other hand, had a clear interest in forcing his subjects

29. Thomasius, *Foundations,* bk. I, chap. i, §§59–60.

30. Ibid., chap. v, §§33–40.

31. On the question of punishments in natural law theory, see Thomas Ahnert, "Pleasure, Pain and Punishment in the Early Enlightenment: German and Scottish Debates," in *The Development of Moral First Principles in the Enlightenment,* ed. S. Byrd, J. Hruschka, and Jan C. Joerden, Jahrbuch für Recht und Ethik 12 (Berlin: Duncker und Humblot, 2004), pp. 173–87.

32. *Foundations,* bk. I, chap. v, §39.

33. Ibid., §34.

to be obedient, regardless of whether they did so only out of fear. Related
to this new idea of punishments was another change in the *Foundations,*
Thomasius's rejection of the notion of a divine positive law: because God
was not comparable to a human legislator, who enforced his laws with
punishments, the concept of a divine positive law, which was analogous
to human positive law, made little sense. Divine positive law, according
to Thomasius, had been the invention of self-interested clergymen, who
had tried to use their authority in questions of scriptural interpretation
to exercise influence on temporal matters, such as legal cases concerning
marriage.[34]

Thomasius also completely changed his notion of the freedom of the
human will and its relationship to the human intellect. His previous idea
of an "indifferent" will, he now argued, was wrong, for if the will was
equally indifferent to all available courses of action, it was impossible to
explain why it chose one rather than the other.[35] The human will was
free, but not in the sense of being "indifferent." It was free insofar as it
was "spontaneous," that is, insofar as the external actions of the agent corresponded to the intentions of his or her will and were not frustrated by
external circumstances and accidents.[36]

The degree of this "spontaneity" also determined the extent of an agent's
moral responsibility. A person, for example, who aimed a gun at a bird and
shot a friend by mistake could not be said to have acted "spontaneously"
and to be guilty of murder, since the person had not intended any harm
to the other.[37] The choices of the will, however, were not free in the sense
that the agent could have chosen to will something different. The will was
not an ability to choose but was best described as a passion, desire, or love
that provided the motive force and direction of human actions.

This love always had a determinate aim, though this aim could vary

---

34. Thomasius, *Foundations,* "Introductory Chapter," §§16–17. Thomasius's rejection of divine positive law then forced him to revise his explanation of the laws against
polygamy and incest by referring to the rules of *honestum* and *decorum.* See Thomasius,
Fundamenta juris naturae et gentium, reprint of 4th ed. [1718] (Aalen: Scientia, 1979),
bk. III, chap. ii. The English title *Foundations* in used to refer only to that material
from the *Fundamenta* included in this book.

35. Thomasius, *Foundations,* bk. I, chap. i, §56.

36. Ibid., §§67–70.

37. For various examples, see Thomasius, *Fundamenta,* bk. I, chap. ii, §§112–14.

from person to person and according to external circumstances: some, for example, loved sensual pleasures; others, wealth or honors.[38] The direction of this will-as-love or will-as-passion could not, however, be influenced by the other main faculty in human nature, the intellect (or reason), because conclusions of the intellect did not have the power to motivate actions. They only informed the will how to achieve its ends, not which ends were or were not desirable. As David Hume would later put it, reason was the slave of the passions and ought to be nothing else.[39]

In defining the will as love or passion, Thomasius was drawing on a rich intellectual tradition to which he had been attracted since at least the late 1680s.[40] This was predominantly French and had emerged from the revival of interest in the thought of St. Augustine, following the posthumous publication of Bishop Jansen's *Augustinus* in 1640. Its central feature was a deeply Augustinian attempt to explain virtue and vice as the respective products of different varieties of love or desire.[41]

"Reasonable love" (*amour raisonnable*) described that form of desire directed toward virtuous ends. Opposed to it were various kinds of corrupt love that drove humans toward pursuing selfish and immoral ends. From the early 1690s Thomasius had similarly begun to explain moral and immoral action as the product of "reasonable" and "corrupt love," respectively.[42] He also began to argue that the change from "corrupt" to "reasonable" love could take place only as the result of religious and spiritual regeneration, an argument that subjected him to charges of religious "enthusiasm" and caused him to somewhat modify his views around 1700.[43]

38. The three main passions, according to Thomasius, were ambition, lust, and avarice, a triad that was derived from a combination of Aristotle's *Nicomachean Ethics* 1095a and 1 John 2:16. See Schneiders, *Naturrecht*, p. 212, and Thomasius, *Fundamenta*, bk. I, chap. ii, §§68–70.

39. David Hume, *Treatise of Human Nature* (Oxford: Oxford University Press, 1978), 2.3.3.4, p. 415.

40. See Schneiders, *Naturrecht*, p. 172.

41. Augustine, *The City of God Against the Pagans,* ed. and trans. R. W. Dyson (Cambridge: Cambridge University Press, 1998), bk. XIX, chap. xiv.

42. See Christian Thomasius, *Einleitung zur Sittenlehre,* "Unterthänigste Zuschrift" (Halle, 1692).

43. On this, see Thomas Ahnert, "Enthusiasm and Enlightenment: Faith and Philosophy in the Thought of Christian Thomasius," in *Modern Intellectual History* 2.2 (2005): 167–70.

Yet it is arguable that Thomasius's notion of "reasonable love" continued to be closely tied to a particular and rather heterodox form of Christianity, which I have discussed elsewhere.[44]

Thus, reasonable love was the foundation of true virtue and of a life fully conforming to natural law. Thomasius was, however, convinced that the majority of humans would never be guided by reasonable love but would continue to follow their corrupt desires. The human legislator was powerless to change them: threats of punishment could influence external actions but not turn corrupt into reasonable love, since sincere love could never be the product of coercion. Human society could nevertheless function tolerably well because it did not require the complete conformity of its members to natural law. In particular, Thomasius distinguished between three levels of natural law, not all of which depended on the presence of reasonable love.[45]

The first was the *iustum* (the just), which was summarized in the negative precept not to do to others what you would not have them do to you.[46] The *iustum* marked the lowest degree of conformity to natural law, but it was also the one most essential to human society, which would disintegrate without it. Obedience to the negative precepts of *iustum* did not require reasonable love in the agent but could be enforced through threats of punishment and fears of revenge.

The second level was the *decorum* (the decorous). Its main principle was the command to do to others what you would have them do to you.[47] It covered, for example, acts of benevolence or politeness toward others. Unlike the negative precept of the *iustum,* the main precept of *decorum* was positive and therefore could not be binding on everyone at all times. For, while it was possible to abstain from harming any other person at all times, one could not perform acts of benevolence or kindness toward all other people in every single moment. Some acts of *decorum* might be commanded by the legislator and enforced with threats of punishment, though they were then not usually the expression of reasonable love but of fear.

---

44. Ibid. and Ahnert, *Religion and the Origins of the German Enlightenment.*
45. Thomasius, *Fundamenta,* bk. I, chap. vi.
46. Ibid., §42.
47. Ibid., §41.

The third level of obedience to natural law was the *honestum* (the honest), which demanded that humans rid themselves of corrupt passions and be guided by reasonable love, for the sake of their own happiness and well-being. Thomasius summarized the main command of the *honestum* as "Do unto yourself what you would like others to do to themselves."[48] The *honestum* represented the highest degree of conformity to natural law, though its violation also represented the smallest evil, compared to the violation of the rules of *iustum* or *decorum,* which were more important to social life. Those who fulfilled the precepts of the *honestum,* however, also observed those of the *decorum* and *iustum,* because they acted out of reasonable love, while obedience to the rules of *decorum* and *iustum* might be founded on motives other than reasonable love and thus did not automatically imply obedience to the precepts of *honestum.*

This emphasis on passions, love, sentiments, and related terms in moral theory became a prominent theme in Enlightenment thought. It was, for example, characteristic of the new genre of didactic "sentimental" literature, which was produced for the growing reading public of the eighteenth century.[49] Moreover, Thomasius's arguments about the passions were central to discussions by various German moral theorists in the eighteenth century, men such as Nicolaus Hieronymus Gundling, Johann Friedrich Hombergk zu Vach, and Johann Jacob Schmauss.[50]

There are also striking parallels between the evolution of Thomasius's natural jurisprudence toward this greater emphasis on the passions and the broader development of moral thought in early-eighteenth-century Europe. A member of the St. Petersburg academy of sciences, Frédéric-Henri Strube de Piermont, commented that natural law was based on "the passions insofar as they conform to nature."[51]

48. Ibid., §40.

49. On this connection, see Friedrich Vollhardt, *Selbstliebe und Geselligkeit* (Tübingen: Max Niemeyer, 2001).

50. Nicolaus Hieronymus Gundling, *Ausführlicher Discours über das Natur- und Völcker-Recht* (Frankfurt and Leipzig, 1734); Anon. [Johann Friedrich Hombergk zu Vach], *Dubia juris naturae* (Douai, 1719); Johann Jacob Schmauss, *Neues Systema des Rechts der Natur* [1754], ed. M. Senn (Goldbach: Keip, 1999).

51. "[L]es passions entant qu'elles sont conformes à la nature" (Frédéric-Henri Strube de Piermont, *Ébauche des loix naturelles* [Amsterdam, 1744], p. vii). Strube de Piermont also referred to Thomasius in his work.

There is a very similar emphasis on passions and sentiments in the moral philosophical literature of the Scottish Enlightenment, ranging from Francis Hutcheson's *Essay on the Nature and Conduct of the Passions and Affections* (1728) to David Hume's *Treatise of Human Nature* (1739–40) and Adam Smith's *Theory of Moral Sentiments* (1759). Thomasius does not seem to have directly influenced these later debates in the Scottish Enlightenment; the similarities are, however, remarkable, and they strongly suggest that the changes in Thomasius's natural law theory between the *Institutes* and the *Foundations* exemplify a more general development in the natural jurisprudence of the early European Enlightenments: a transition from a focus on laws and commands, which had been characteristic of Pufendorf's voluntarist natural jurisprudence, to a moral psychological emphasis on passions and sentiments as the true springs of virtue.

NOTE ON THE TEXT

The translation of the *Institutes* is based on the 1688 Leipzig Latin edition. The translation was then compared to the seventh Latin edition of 1730 (reprinted by Scientia Verlag, Aalen, in 1994) and the contemporary German translation (not by Thomasius himself) of 1709, reprinted by Olms Verlag, Hildesheim, in 2001. The translation of the chapters from the *Foundations* is based on the text of the first Latin edition of 1705. The fourth Latin edition, published in 1718 and reprinted by Scientia Verlag, Aalen, in 1979, has also been used. This later Latin edition contains some additions to the 1705 text, which have not been included in the translation, though some of the information in the additions has been incorporated into the footnotes. The translation was then checked against the contemporary German translation of 1709 (reprinted by Olms Verlag in 2003). The aim here has been to produce a usable and accessible text, not a full critical edition; the few significant discrepancies between the different editions used for translation have been pointed out in the footnotes. Complete reference information is given in the bibliography.

ACKNOWLEDGMENTS

I am especially grateful to Knud Haakonssen for inviting me to contribute this translation and edition to the Natural Law and Enlightenment Classics series. I should also like to thank Michael Lurie in Edinburgh for helping me to identify the sources of some Latin quotations. Finally, I should also like to record my gratitude to Diana Francoeur and her colleagues at Liberty Fund for their superb work in preparing the manuscript for publication.

Some final changes to the text were made during a period of research at the Institute for Advanced Study in Princeton in 2010–11. My membership at the Institute was funded by Rosanna and Charles Jaffin, Friends of the Institute for Advanced Study, and the Herodotus Fund. I am deeply grateful for their support. Any inaccuracies or other shortcomings that remain are my responsibility.

INSTITUTES OF DIVINE JURISPRUDENCE

Introductory Dissertation,
Addressed to My Audience

§1. It is customary for the authors of books to preface the treatises they publish with a discourse in which they either recommend the work or discuss various other matters for the reader. I will not inquire here whether these discourses are useful or irrelevant, nor am I concerned with their title, whether they are more properly called a *prooemium,* a *praefatio,* or an *antefatio,* which is a term I have seen some people prefer. I believe that this should be left to the judgment of each individual and that the common proverb "everybody prefers his own way" is very appropriate here.

§2. I have various reasons for prefacing my *Institutes* with an introductory dissertation. First, I want you to have a clearer idea of my intention; second, I want to defend myself against the accusation of literary plagiarism and render the authors I have used in this work their proper due; third, to clarify certain opinions, which have been expressed a little obscurely and could expose me to slander, and to fortify them against objections; and finally, to say something about amendments to some passages.

§3. But I address you, my beloved audience, not only because I produced these *Institutes* of public law for your sake, and it is thus your immediate concern to know what is relevant to understanding them. It also seemed to some extent to be in my interest to justify my teaching and my studies to you, you whose fees and love by the grace of God sustain me, and who have encouraged me to be diligent and to contemplate true philosophy, since I had no opportunity to abuse public funds in order to be lazy or to profess a false wisdom, which rests on authority rather than reason.[1]

§4. So, I would have wasted my time and my efforts, if I had seized my quill to refute those who examine my writings insidiously and anxiously, not for the sake of learning, but with the intention of putting obstacles in the way of my honest endeavors, and of ensnaring my words. Yet I live under an obligation to those people who are free from passion when they read my *Institutes* or the present dissertation and believe that I, too, can put forward opinions which may not always and directly discover the truth, but which can nevertheless be of some use in inquiring about it and finding it, and who believe that one should not ask who says something, but what is said, and that often even the vegetable gardener makes appropriate comments.

§5. Thus, when I moved from school to university, I did not immediately enter one of the higher faculties, as our young people, unfortunately, often do. Instead, I first spent a number of years studying philosophy.[2] There I had the opportunity to hear my blessed father[3] lecturing on Grotius's books *On the Rights of War and Peace;* and even though I did not understand very much at that time, nevertheless the dignity and elegance of the doctrine captivated me. Soon I was seriously devoting myself to understanding it better than others and of absorbing it into my very flesh and blood. I also remembered that my father had in his lectures often referred his audience to the theologians, who drew attention to Grotius's errors in religion, and to the jurists. It was to the latter that Grotius's work was mainly relevant. My father himself declared in his prolegomena that he had chosen this treatise to support the noblest part of jurispru-

---

1. At the time of writing the *Institutes* Thomasius did not hold a university position but depended on the income he received from private teaching of university students.

2. The higher faculties were usually law, medicine, and theology. All other subjects, such as ethics, logic, metaphysics, and natural philosophy, were taught in the lower faculty of philosophy.

3. Jacob Thomasius (1622–84), professor of rhetoric and moral philosophy at the University of Leipzig.

dence. I therefore thought it necessary in my private studies to add two of Grotius's commentators to my reading of him. One of them is a jurist, who is very learned in divine and human affairs and is the ornament of the University of Wittenberg, Caspar Ziegler;[4] the other is a theologian in Tübingen, whose many publications have made him well known, Johann Adam Osiander.[5] Of these two the first dispelled in short but succinct observations on Grotius the clouds of obscurity on many points. The other has repeated most of what Ziegler has said, even though he does not mention him, thereby helping me to memorize the arguments better. Apart from that, he warned me to beware of the heterodox opinions of Grotius, and at the same time introduced me to the moral philosophy of the Scholastics.

§6. Then appeared the books on the law of nature and nations by the illustrious and incomparable Samuel Pufendorf.[6] I read these avidly, not only because his *Elements*[7] had given me a certain foretaste, though I had only inspected them cursorily, but also because I was very taken by his clear and perspicuous style. I noticed there that most of the subjects which Grotius had neglected were explained very lucidly, and that he also clarified many of Grotius's more obscure passages. And yet, I was not pleased with some of his opinions which contradicted the common belief in God's eternal law, its conformity to divine sanctity, the existence of a standard of morality prior to the divine will, and similar matters. At that time I did not know how to separate theological questions from philosophical ones, and there was nobody who could teach me these things. I had also realized that in Osiander's commentary on Grotius[8] and especially in another

---

4. Caspar Ziegler (1621–90), poet and jurist at the University of Wittenberg, author of *In Hugonis Grotii De jure belli ac pacis libros, quibus naturae & gentium jus explicavit, notae et animadversiones subitariae* (Wittenberg, 1666).

5. Johann Adam Osiander (1622–97), professor of theology at the University of Tübingen.

6. Samuel Pufendorf (1632–94), jurist and philosopher, author of the highly influential *De jure naturae et gentium libri octo* (Lund, 1672).

7. Samuel Pufendorf, *Elementa jurisprudentiae universalis* (The Hague, 1660).

8. Johann Adam Osiander, *Observationes maximam partem theologicae in libros tres De jure belli et pacis H. Grotii* (Tübingen, 1671).

book by that author titled *Typum legis naturae*[9] these doctrines were defended strenuously. Thus I thought that he who even dared to doubt their truth was in danger of eternal damnation. Although it was not clear to me how Pufendorf's objections could be met, and the replies of the learned, with whom I discussed this when there was an opportunity to do so, were entirely unsatisfactory, nevertheless the authority of so many venerable men prevailed. I therefore blamed the dullness of my own mind, rather than suspecting there to be anything wrong with the common doctrine.

§7. In the meantime my love of natural law had led me, with the consent of my father, to choose jurisprudence among the three higher faculties. My intention was to remedy the shortcomings of philosophy in that area [i.e., natural law]. For among other things, the commentary of the learned Boecler on Grotius[10] showed that they who attempted to define and explain natural law without jurisprudence found it very difficult to do so only on the basis of the philosophy that is taught at the universities. Thus, I developed a basic understanding of it as well as I could and, since I had no guide who prescribed a method to me, I did the usual thing and listened now to one person, now to another, and thus acquired some understanding of it, which was, however, confused, fragmented, and incoherent, rather than true wisdom. Matters did not improve when I was sent by my family to Frankfurt an der Oder to complete my study of jurisprudence. This was not the fault of my teachers, who were excellent men and each of whom was highly deserving of praise. It was rather the widespread method of learning, according to which young students were usually taught by several doctors, who often disagreed among each other and drew on diverse principles. This was hardly suitable for producing anything solid. Also, as tends to happen, friends and conversations with fellow students wasted many hours which could have been spent on studies and attending lectures.

9. Johann Adam Osiander, *Typus legis naturae* (Tübingen, 1669).

10. Johann Heinrich Boecler (1611–72), professor of law at Strasbourg and author of *In Hugonis Grotii Jus belli et pacis commentatio* (Strasbourg, 1663–64).

§8. I rapidly became aware of this, however, and, putting that common proverb "we learn by teaching" into practice, I tried to fill the gaps and connect my different studies, which had often been interrupted. Thus, once I had graciously been granted a license to teach by the university authorities, I lectured a little on the *Institutes of Justinian*[11] to some of my fellow students. To others I explained the questions of Jan Klenck on the books of Grotius[12] in order to make an attempt at understanding this most noble discipline, to see what I could manage and what progress I would make by reading Grotius and Pufendorf.

§9. Until then I had been an assiduous defender of the doctrines of the Moralists,[13] and though in all other respects I liked Pufendorf very much, I set aside those aspects that were considered heterodox. In this opinion I was strongly confirmed by the "index of novelties," a highly dangerous document, especially as it was received with applause by numerous people.[14] There were further writings like this, which attacked Pufendorf as a common enemy. I was extremely pleased about their appearance, because I hoped that I would be able to learn from them how to reply to Pufendorf's arguments. I noticed many arguments which begged the principle or were circular, yet I selected some with which I believed I would be able to strike or avert the blows for the sake of the common cause. I profusely thanked those authors, who were inspired by the love of orthodox truth to take up arms; and at the same time the multitude of syllogisms, which were often prolix and difficult to understand, excited my admiration. I believed that if Pufendorf were confronted with these arguments he would succumb to their enormous weight, and would not even dare to open his mouth to contradict such great men.

11. These *Institutes,* compiled under the direction of the emperor Justinian (ruled A.D. 527–65), were a short manual of Roman law.

12. Jan Klenck, *Institutiones juris naturalis, gentium, et publici, ex Hugonis Grootii De jure belli ac pacis libris excerptae* (Amsterdam, 1665).

13. That is, scholastic moral philosophers and jurists.

14. Nicolaus Beckmann and Josua Schwartz, *Index quarundam novitatum, quas Dominus Samuel Puffendorff libro suo De jure naturae et gentium contra orthodoxa fundamenta Londini edidit* (n.p., 1673).

§10. I was, however, mistaken, for soon afterward the apologia of Pufendorf became available to us.[15] When I read this I sensed that my weapons were inadequate to ward off his blow. At about that time I was beginning to dispel some of the clouds which had until then shrouded my understanding. For I had previously imagined that everything defended by the common opinion of the theologians was a proper part of theology, and that a good man should beware of listening to any heretic or innovator, two terms which were considered synonymous at the time. Yet, more careful meditation on the difference between theology and philosophy and a more diligent examination of the writings of authors on politics and public law had taught me that many views were upheld by the unanimous opinion of theologians and were generally held to be theological matters, although they did not belong to theology but to moral philosophy or jurisprudence. This was so because philosophers were content with their Aristotelian catalogue of eleven virtues and jurists with their glossators and so gave the theologians, first the papal theologians and then ours, the opportunity to seize the noblest part of wisdom, which was neglected and without a guide. This scrutiny had also taught me that the power to declare someone a heretic did not pertain to private persons, even though they might enjoy a lot of authority, but to the prince. And finally, it had taught me that the accusation of heresy did not necessarily imply the crime of heresy, and that this and the term *heretic* were very widely abused. I saw, however, that Pufendorf had demonstrated precisely these opinions to his adversaries and that their hopes of victory had rested to no very little degree on their erroneous principles.

§11. Thus I began to doubt the moral doctrines of the Scholastics. For I had never been disposed to adhere to preconceived opinions so rigidly that I could not be torn away from them when the truth became evident. I saw more than once my father setting a laudable example by abandoning his earlier opinions, if the following day showed him something else to be

15. Samuel Pufendorf, *Apologia pro se et suo libro, adversus autorem libelli famosi, cui titulus Index quarundam novitatum, quas Dominus Samuel Pufendorf libro suo De jure naturae et gentium contra orthodoxa fundamenta Londini edidit* (Germanopolis, 1674).

closer to the truth. But what had held me up in my pursuit of the truth had been above all the education in sectarian philosophy and the vain and unjust fear of suffering from a bad reputation if I diverged from the common opinion. When I noticed, therefore, that my judgment had gradually matured, and I reminded myself that I was a rational being like other humans, I became aware at the same time that I was sinning against the benignity of the Creator if I allowed myself to be led wherever it pleased others, like cattle wearing a muzzle. Therefore I closed the eyes of the mind, so that the brightness of human authority would not blind them, and cast aside all consideration of who or how great a person had written what I was reading. I examined only the arguments on either side and considered what this person asserted, that person criticized, another proved, and yet another replied. But above all I firmly impressed on myself the state of the controversy and noted how tenacious one person was, how another twisted and turned like an eel in order to elude his adversary and confuse him, until I concluded that I had to unlearn a lot and sensed that I had known nothing and that my knowledge was nothing but a confused chaos and a heap of many things, which were mixed with each other without any order.

§12. But when I had thought about this carefully and managed to reduce the chaos to some order, I unintentionally became a deserter, in the sense of someone who having fled from a tyrant invading the liberty of a commonwealth takes up arms in defence of liberty against this tyrant. For clear reasons had triumphed over the otiose subtleties of scholastic moral philosophy. I was also ashamed of any longer taking the side of those who had been full of boasts as long as there was no enemy and had been the first or among the first to sound the signal for battle, but, when their veterans had at their encouragement attacked the enemy and perished miserably, and they themselves had been honestly summoned to battle and had been challenged several times, hid behind their walls and thus indicated either their fearfulness or the injustice of their cause. Finally I was horrified, because I saw that egregious injustices were committed under the pretence of Christian benediction by some whose duty it was to guide the flock of Christians. They interfered in battle, without being called to it or being equipped with appropriate arms, and, like blindfolded gladiators, cut down anything which they encountered. I also noticed that they could not bear it if the smallest word of theirs had been ignored, as if a minister of the word enjoyed a privilege of inflicting injury and as if their holy office gave them immunity against enemies and allowed them [the ministers] to betray their office and provoke these enemies without a reason. Then I remembered a story which I had read, I know not where, of a beggar who had visited a bishop and had first asked for substantial alms; when these were denied he asked for a smaller amount, and when he failed to obtain these he asked for a very small amount. When all his requests had been in vain, he asked for a benediction. The bishop gave him that. The beggar, however, returned it to the bishop, saying that his benediction was not worth a penny, since he could not obtain a penny from the bishop before, in spite of his persistent requests.

§13. From this time on, after shaking off the yoke of sectarian philosophy, I took great care to preserve the liberty I had once acquired. Thus, even though I did not consider it unbecoming to struggle for truth under an illustrious leader, even in the last ranks, I always acknowledged him as a leader, not as a ruler, although a good leader differs little from a ruler, insofar as he diverges from the truth only very rarely and then only unintentionally. Although I thought at first that once I had reduced the doctrine to some system I would be able to keep it forever, I sensed that like any other person who reduces a confused heap of things to a particular order, I too had to correct the order several times and improve it. For I continually detected new errors to be corrected, which are just an indication of human weakness.

§14. In the meantime I perceived the rich fruits of cultivating such a noble doctrine. I ceased teaching it for a while, as soon as I sensed that the ideas I had previously believed rather than understood did not cohere with each other. Yet, when I returned home and there, having shaken off the original torpor, simultaneously devoted my efforts to civil jurisprudence, I noticed while I was teaching that with the help of natural jurisprudence I was able to explain the Pandects quite adequately. This was so although I had never previously studied them in their entirety. And, apart from other matters, if there were any laws which contradicted natural jurisprudence, I tried in the preparation to see whether I could find a means of reconciling these with each other using the rules of sound interpretation drawn from Grotius and Pufendorf. I then consulted other authors and if I found them agreeing with me I was confirmed in my opinion; if they disagreed I compared them with my exposition and with each other and again applied these same rules of interpretation, always banishing the prejudice in favor of authority. Thus, I sometimes rejected a solution even if it stemmed from Bachovius[16] and approved another, even if it was by Manzius.[17]

§15. Natural jurisprudence, however, helped me not only in the theoretical interpretation of laws. When I turned to legal practice, to try to apply law to individual facts (without which theory is a cadaver destitute of a soul), I became aware that it was of even more use, since very often the infinite variety of circumstances, which characterizes matters of civil law, produces a case and a situation which is either not covered by civil laws at all or to which several conflicting laws apply. Thus, if someone cannot draw on common principles or the rules of extending or restricting laws, he must often laboriously use the many myriads of advisers, respondents, and people who make decisions, from Germany, France, Italy, Spain, and almost the entire world, until he finds a case at the very end, as they say.[18] And even then, when an appropriate case has been found, it is still unclear whether the judges to whom the decision of the case pertains favor the same opinion as the author of the decision. He who provides a good definition of the general foundations of law inscribed on the hearts of humans can easily master this Herculean labor. At the same time he can easily avoid this danger by other means which we shall not discuss here.

§16. Yet, after a few years I withdrew from legal practice, since I believed that I had done my part in scrutinizing the application of civil law to the

---

16. Reiner Bachof von Echt (1575–ca. 1640), jurist at the University of Heidelberg.

17. Caspar Manz (1606–77) converted to Roman Catholicism and became a jurist at the University of Ingolstadt.

18. Thomasius is referring to the many collections of legal decisions (*consilia, responsa*) that were published for jurists to help them in resolving a case.

affairs of humans and the benefits and disadvantages of legal practice. I also knew that man was meant for civil life rather than a solitary life, and that jurists in particular had the hope, held out to them as a prize, that once they had studied Roman law and acquired experience in legal practice they would be promoted to high offices in the commonwealth. And yet I felt there to be as great a difference between the law court and the court of the prince as that between night and day. For even if I leave aside count-less other matters which I could mention here, one needs a mind willing to suffer mob rule to bear patiently the tedium of the law court; but since I did not find this quality in myself (since though I very gladly bear all burdens imposed by the prince, God's representative on earth, I am a little less patient when it comes to putting up with the tedious affairs of the general population) I sought leisure in domestic study which would bring with it the tranquillity I was hoping for. And since I was persuaded that my thoughts were now in such an order that young students would benefit from having those thoughts communicated to them, and since some asked me for my opinions, I began to devote myself to you, my dearest listeners.

§17. Above all I made an effort to restore the universal foundations of law, derived from natural law, which students at this university have neglected for long enough. Nor were my efforts without success, thanks to the help of God. I first lectured on this most useful doctrine, according to the work of Hugo Grotius, seven years ago. Your attendance in large numbers, which I had not expected, encouraged me. But immediately after finish-ing the first book, you left me alone with Grotius, although I had had a full room the day before. The fear of the plague had driven you away from Leipzig. I had almost despaired (such little confidence do the minds of humans have in divine benevolence) of having another opportunity of this kind; but once the situation had improved and you returned to me with-out fear, I picked up the thread which had been interrupted for two years. You then attended my lessons diligently until I finally completed the task with the help of God. I then compared Grotius with Pufendorf and with all of his commentators, always following the principle of the freedom of philosophizing by adding my opinion whenever there was a controversial matter. But above all I tried to clarify the ambiguities in Grotius's text and not to leave aside a single word which could occasion obscurity.

§18. My doctrine had not displeased you, just as your diligence could not but please me. Soon after I had completed the course on Grotius there were some who desired a repetition. I agreed, but instead of the work by Grotius I proposed that most elegant little book by Pufendorf *On the Duty of Man and Citizen.*[19] Apart from other reasons, you yourselves realized how many hours were previously devoted to the investigation of the ideas of Grotius—time we could save by looking at a perspicuous author and which we could direct to more useful ends. Yet, because you demanded a fuller history and knowledge of the principles for which this illustrious man has been criticized and still is being criticized, I began with a more elaborate discussion of these same matters over the course of several months and presented them for teaching purposes as a consideration of jurisprudence in general. I acted openly toward you and sincerely: I put forward arguments on both sides of the controversy, and before I submitted my resolution, I took first this side, then that, in order to accustom you to paying more attention to the reasons than the authors of opinions. I demonstrated the sources and the origin or occasion of doctrines and the connection of conclusions with the first principles, which varied according to different hypotheses, and I took great care that in my hypotheses (mine, however, were those on which Pufendorf himself had constructed his discipline) I always proved my assertions through necessary inferences from the first practical principle, which had previously been demonstrated according to analytical rules. Then I turned to Pufendorf's text and, following his method step by step, never ceased to recall the hypotheses of either side to you in the particular controversies and to show the connection of even the remote conclusions with them. Sometimes, though rarely, I even indicated how the difficulties of contrary opinions could be avoided

19. Samuel Pufendorf, *De officio hominis et civis* (Lund, 1673). This was a condensed presentation of the arguments Pufendorf had developed at greater length in the *De jure naturae et gentium* of 1672.

by other means, or which weighty reason drove me to make use of my liberty and, resting on common hypotheses, to incline toward an opinion different from that of Pufendorf.

§19. I did not write down what I had discussed but communicated to you whatever the memory of my meditations before the individual lectures suggested to me. And as I saw some of you avidly taking notes on my lectures, I hoped that it would be possible for me to ask you for them, so that I would be able to refresh my memory later. But this did not really work. For after comparing three or four examples of your efforts with each other, I observed that few of you had fully understood my arguments, and some, whose miserable condition and lack of judgment I greatly deplored, had attributed fictitious opinions to me and very often combined contradictory opinions in one sentence. I therefore pondered how I could remedy this defect in future and assist your understanding of the material.

§20. I had also noted already some time before that in the common division of divine laws into moral, ceremonial, and forensic, the term *moral laws* usually mixed divine natural law and divine positive universal law with each other, as if moral law and natural law were synonyms, and as if there were no other kind of divine positive law than the ceremonial and the forensic. Yet, in the absence of some universal law which is also positive, it would be necessary either pitifully to abandon the orthodox opinions on the turpitude of polygamy and the prohibition of incest, etc., in the face of their adversaries, or to abstain from a decision of these very grave and important controversies. And while Hugo Grotius explained this distinction within divine law clearly enough, he not only mixed several errors into his statement on universal positive law, but in some cases also confused this law with natural law. Among our people, however, as far as the gentlemen in theology are concerned, I have noticed no one who has properly set out this distinction between natural law and universal positive law, or who has explained universal positive law appropriately and said which principles were relevant here, even though I went through very many authors, especially modern ones, who published works on moral theology. As far as the jurists are concerned, there is a complete silence on this matter among them, with the exception of the most learned Kulpis in his *Collegium Grotianum*.[20] There he examines the question of polygamy and promises to show in a separate treatise that there is such a universal positive law [against polygamy]. I eagerly awaited this treatise, since I hoped for many erudite insights from this famous man on the basis of my reading of his precise *Collegium Grotianum,* insights which could have illuminated me or helped me a lot in my meditations on this divine positive law. This most noble man, however, delayed fulfilling his promise, no doubt because of the pressure of other urgent business, and so I thought that I would not be committing a sin if I dared to drag this universal positive law, if not from darkness, at least from twilight, even though I am neither a theologian nor a jurist; I am, however, wholly devoted to divine laws and jurisprudence. I do this in the hope that, even if I do not present everything completely accurately, other equitable people will draw on my attempts and use them to examine more accurately this difficult subject, which is worthy of both theologians and jurists in equal measure.

§21. Hence, as some of you asked me last year to repeat the course on natural law, and to communicate to them in writing in individual points what I had previously taught to others orally about the confirmation of Pufendorf's hypotheses, and about my observations on the little book by Pufendorf *On the Duty of Man and Citizen,* I then took the opportunity and began to work on the present *Institutes of Divine Jurisprudence.* My aim was twofold: *first,* after presenting the general principles of jurisprudence, to explain the controversies over Pufendorf's hypotheses, according to the method which I thought most suitable for you, and to defend these hypotheses as if they were my own, and to show clearly in chapters on the single natural law the connection of the conclusions with the hypotheses and first practical principles, according to Pufendorf's opinion and rarely according to my own, and so to give you some introduction to reading the well-developed and learned work by this illustrious man *Of the Law of*

---

20. Johann Georg von Kulpis (1652–98), jurist and politician, author of the *Collegium Grotianum, super Iure belli ac pacis: Anno 1682 in Academia Giessensi 15. exercitationibus primum institutum,* 2nd ed. (Giessen, 1686).

Nature and Nations and profiting from it, so that his adversaries and their writings can no longer cause you difficulties. *Second,* the aim is to show more distinctly the differences between universal positive law and natural law, and to illustrate the precepts of the former, insofar as their interpretation pertains to jurisprudence, concerning the doctrine on marriage and the chapter on punishments.

§22. Above all, it seemed necessary to me to reason consistently and to quote no authors, especially no modern authors, in the text, not even the great Pufendorf himself. For I knew well how preconceived opinions have the habit of becoming an obstacle in the acquisition of truth, and among these opinions none does more harm than the prejudice in favor of established authority. I therefore thought that it would be very useful for you if I abolished this prejudice to make sure that you did not ignore the arguments of Pufendorf's adversaries just because Pufendorf's authority had already inclined you toward his opinion; alternatively, if these [arguments of the adversaries] should prove attractive, you might block the well-argued responses and reasons based on human nature. Moreover, I wanted to stimulate your industry and persuade you to read Pufendorf's work carefully, in the belief that if I did not quote passages, you yourself would read it with all the more care and would compare it with my *Institutes.* And since I often had to depart from the common opinion of great men, or from the opinion of a particular man of great authority, and it was yet my intention to inquire into unadorned truth, without regard to persons, and to struggle with opinions, not people, I did not want to detract from the reverence owed to the people with whom I disagree by referring to them.

§23. As far as other methods of teaching are concerned, I know that much is said in schools concerning the synthetic and the analytic methods, but these debates are otiose rather than useful. I believe there is only one good method, that is, to progress from the easier to the more difficult, from the known to the unknown, and that everything else depends on each individual's judgment. It is correct to say that method must be a matter of individual judgment. And since all our erudition consists of the science of demonstrating true propositions and showing the connection between them and since the truth of propositions presupposes knowledge of the terms, it seems impossible to deny that the most natural method is the so-called mathematical one, which progresses from definitions to axioms and develops observations from them. Pufendorf arranged his *Elementa* according to that method. But each proposition has only two terms, and it would therefore be tedious if the definitions of all terms are listed in a continuous series, and it seems that the connection between the different propositions could not be shown very clearly if many axioms were presented successively. I believed, therefore, that I would best be able to avoid these two disadvantages if I mixed definitions and axioms and prefaced the individual propositions with definitions of the subject and the predicate, or added these definitions immediately after the proposition, and if I clearly linked the axioms themselves by starting from some first principle and deriving everything else from that by way of conclusions.

§24. I have divided these *Institutes* into three books. In the first of them I have presented a definition of divine jurisprudence and the doctrine of the first practical principle, as well as the first principle of natural law and universal divine positive law. To that I have added a proof that the duty of man toward God is not part of divine jurisprudence. In the second book I list the precepts of natural law that concern humans living in any kind of society. In the third, however, I list those precepts of natural law which direct the duties of man with respect to particular societies, that is, conjugal, paternal, domestic, civil, those based on treaties, and the society of nations. The beginnings of the chapters will show their connection with each other, and in the second and third books I mostly followed the order adopted by Pufendorf in his book *On the Duty of Man and Citizen*. I say mostly, for a look at these will easily show what I have changed here and there.

§25. Since I had Pufendorf's work and the other writings published in his defense in mind throughout the *Institutes,* you will not be surprised at finding that often entire points have been borrowed from him and have not been changed by a single word. For my project, which I have ex-

plained to you, required me to do so. But there are in these *Institutes* some
arguments of my own, which I continually mixed with the ideas of others.
Thus, inevitably the incomparable man himself was linked to me without his intending to be. I do not know whether he will accept this with
equanimity. He may rather desire his possessions to be clearly separated
from mine. Yet he will not need to do so, since I am prepared, without the
intervention of a judge, to divide my *Institutes* so that I leave to him only
what is well said, even if it is mine, because his writings and hypotheses
led me to investigate them. Those arguments, however, that are found to
be incoherent and improper I shall take upon myself.

§26. Yet I will happily admit that I have sometimes borrowed the ideas
of other learned men to whom must be rendered what is due to them,
and I must indicate to you those authors whom you should add to the
reading of my *Institutes*. For book 2, chapters 6, 7, and 8, I carefully examined Uffelmann's *Treatise on the Obligation of Man,* which is the result
of an oration that was held not many years ago in the Academia Julia;[21]
from this I transferred to chapter 6, "On the Duty of Persons Forming
an Agreement," §64, some arguments criticizing Pufendorf's opinion on
the lack of obligation in an agreement with highwaymen. In the following passages, however, I have showed how easy it is to defend Pufendorf's
opinion. But in chapter 7, "On the Duty of Man Concerning Speech,"
and similarly in chapter 8, "On the Duty of Those Taking an Oath," I
have adopted many arguments from the said book by Uffelmann, though
I reserved the freedom of presenting them differently and disagreeing with
them. In the final chapter of the same book, "On the Interpretation of
Divine and Human Will," I also found most helpful the very accurate discussion of the interpretation of obscure law which was publicly presented
under the most learned Rebhahn as *praeses* at the Academy in Strasbourg
in 1671.[22] In book 3, in the second chapter on the duties in marriage, an

---

21. That is, at the University of Helmstedt. The treatise to which Thomasius refers
is the Helmstedt disputation *De jure quo homini homo in sermone obligatur* (Helmstedt,
1667) by Heinrich Uffelmann (1641–80).

22. Johann Rebhahn (*praeses*), Johann Daniel Stalburger (*respondens*), *De interpretatione juris obscuri* (Strasbourg, 1671).

occasion for more profound meditation was often provided by the studies of Lambert Velthuysen on natural modesty and human dignity and on the principles of justice and propriety. These treatises are to be found in his works, published in 1680 in Rotterdam.[23] These are to be compared especially with my comments in the said chapter 2, §153 following. The third chapter of book 3 was based on my recollection of the famous controversies which were conducted in the writings of various people concerning divine law on conjugal duties, that is, on polygamy, the works of Sincerus Warenberg, Theophilus Alethaeus, Athanasius Vincentius, and Daphnaeus Arcuarius, who wrote in favor of polygamy; for writings against polygamy, see Musaeus, Christian Vigilis, Sluter, Feltmann, Brunsmann, Diecmann, etc.[24] For the various legal opinions concerning the marriage of eunuchs, see the collection published by Hieronymus Delphinus two

23. See Lambert van Velthuysen, *Opera omnia* (Rotterdam, 1680). The specific works Thomasius is referring to are Velthuysen's *Epistolica dissertatio de principiis iusti et decori, continens apologiam pro tractatu clarissimi Hobbaei, De cive* (Amsterdam, 1651) and the *Tractatus moralis de naturali pudore et dignitate hominis in quo agitur, de incestu, scortatione, voto caelibatus, conjugio, adulterio, polygamia et divortiis, etc.* (Utrecht, 1676).

24. Sincerus Warenberg, Theophilus Alethaeus, and Athanasius Vincentius were all pseudonyms of Johannes Lyser (1631–84), who published a series of works on polygamy. These included Sincerus Warenberg, *Alethophili Germani discursus inter polygamum et monogamum de polygamia* (n.p., 1673) and the *Polygamia triumphatrix, id est discursus politicus de polygamia* (Lund, 1682), published under his pseudonym of Theophilus Alethaeus, with notes by himself written under another pseudonym, Athanasius Vincentius. Daphnaeus Arcuarius was the pseudonym of Lorenz Beger, who wrote *Daphnai Arcuarii Kurtze, doch unpartheiisch- und gewissenhafte Betrachtung des in dem Natur- und Göttlichen Recht gegeründeten heyligen Ehstandes* (n.p., 1679). Johannes Musaeus, *Dissertatio de quaestione controversa, an coniugium, primaeva eius institutione salva, inter plures, quam duos, esse possit?* (Jena, 1675), was a response to Lyser's *Discursus politicus de polygamia* (Freiburg, 1674). Christian Vigilis (a pseudonym for Friedrich Gesenius), *Ad Sincerum Warenbergium Suecum epistola seu dissertatio super polygamia simultanea* (Germanopolis, 1673), was also a reaction to Lyser's writings. "Sluter" is Severin Walther Schlüter, author of *Theologische Gedancken von der Polygynia, oder Von dem nehmen vieler Weiber* (Rostock, 1677), also a response to Lyser. Gerhard Feltmann (1637–96), German jurist, published a *Tractatus de polygamia* (Leipzig, 1677). Johann Brunsmann, *Monogamia victrix: sive orthodoxa ecclesiae christianae sententia, de unius duntaxat eodem tempore concessis christiano nuptiis, a criminationibus vindicata quibusvis* (Frankfurt, 1678). Johann Diecmann, *Vindiciae legis monogamicae* (Stadae, 1678), was also directed against Lyser.

years ago;[25] on divorces, see Selden *The Jewish Wife,* book 3, chapter 18 and the following chapters,[26] and Strauchius in the fragment on the *Institutes of Public Law,* title 35;[27] on incest with the sister of the deceased wife, see the work by Havemann, Tabor, Strauchius, Buchholz, and the editor of the *Acta Oettingensia;* there are also works by Samuel Bohlius and his adversaries on the incest of stepchildren, etc.[28] My blessed father's disputation on paternal power needs to be read together with the fourth chapter of the third book §§14ff., because there I intended to defend the opinion of my father that paternal society cannot be derived from consent. Chapters 9 and 10, on the duties toward legates and toward the dead, should be compared with Grotius, book 2, chapters 18 and 19, and his commentators, and with my father's disputation on the inviolability of legates.[29]

§27. I believed at first that my good intentions, which I have just explained to you, would be treated fairly by all those who love studies and good scholarship and seek the truth. Yet I realized that I lived in a century in which there were not a few to be found who considered it their duty to obstruct free philosophical argument, to build walls and throw up barriers, to enclose it within limits which no human prudence could tear down, because they sensed quite rightly that this liberty of philosophical

25. Hieronymus Delphinus, *Eunuchi conjugium* (Halle, 1685).

26. John Selden, *Uxor Ebraica* (London, 1646); *On Jewish Marriage Law,* translated with a commentary by J. Ziskind (Leiden: Brill, 1991).

27. Johannes Strauch, *Institutionum juris publici specimen* (Frankfurt, 1683).

28. Michael Havemann, *Adsertio responsi Mosis, contra matrimonium cum defunctae uxoris sorore* (Frankfurt and Bremen, 1660). Havemann and Johann Otto Tabor were arguing against Christoph Joachim Buchholtz, a jurist at the University of Rinteln, who had published a defense of marriage with the sister of a deceased wife (*Pro matrimonio principis cum defunctae uxoris sorore contracto* [Rinteln, 1651]). Buchholtz replied to Havemann and Tabor in his *Adsertio responsi iuris pro matrimonio principis cum defunctae uxoris sorore: Adversus argumenta Johannis Ottonis Taboris ICti & Michaelis Havemanni theologi* (Rinteln, 1659). On Strauchius (Johannes Strauch), see note 27 on this page. Samuel Bohl, *Tractatus contra matrimonium comprivignorum* (Rostock, 1637). Jacob Thomasius (*praeses*), Johann Jordan (*respondens*), *Dissertatio politico-oeconomica, de societate paterna* (Leipzig, 1654).

29. Jacob Thomasius (*praeses*), Johann Adam Preunel (*respondens*), *Legatus inviolabilis* (Leipzig, 1667).

argument severely damaged the authority of the sectarian philosophers. For at one time the lecterns of the philosophers were protected by the authority of Aristotle or of some similar member of the original wise men, such as Albert, Thomas, Scotus, etc.,[30] against those who philosophized freely. Now, however, the fortress of Aristotelianism has been taken, and so it seems there is a need for new trickery to defend the royal doctrines of the old masters. And since they do not have any real arguments with which to strengthen their fortress, they believe that their cause is advanced best if they persuade the people under the pretext of religion that, whatever they do, they act with God's guidance and they struggle in defense of piety, and if they accuse their adversaries of being atheists, heretics, impious people, and careless innovators. Apparently they forget what the *Apology for the Augsburg Confession,* article 4, page 286, says about hypocrites, namely that they are guilty of impiety and of vices of all kinds far more than those they slander as impious.[31]

§28. I was not surprised, therefore, when I heard at the time of the publication of my first book of these *Institutes* that various criticisms of it were disseminated in public. And, as you know, the common claim was that I had based it on principles, which led you to atheism, heterodoxy, and I know not what impiety, and which all smacked of some new-fangled philosophy which threatened the commonwealth. This calumny was so widespread that discussion of it was even common among women visiting those who were in childbed. But I derided this open slander with high-minded contempt, and although one of you then told me that there were a few who were planning to lay a trap for me in this affair, I was nevertheless calm in the midst of all the uproar and lived secure in my conscience concerning both my conduct and my opinion, since I knew well that I lived under the rule of a just prince who was able and willing to protect the innocent. I was not even curious to find out the author of this horrid calumny, just as I am not keen to know this now, but rather wish

---

30. These are medieval Scholastic philosophers: Albertus Magnus (ca. 1200–1280), Thomas Aquinas (1225–74), Duns Scotus (ca. 1265–1308).

31. See Philipp Melanchthon, *Apologia Confessionis Augustanae* (1531), translated into German and edited by Horst Georg Pöhlmann (Gütersloh: G. Mohn, 1967).

sincerely that everything may turn out well for him, whoever it might be; for not only does Christianity order me to do so, but the zeal for sound philosophy to some degree tells me to, as do the examples of others who philosophize with moderation and without aggressiveness. Among these I mention above all René Descartes, whom the author of the first objections against his *Meditations* calls a hugely ingenious and very modest man.[32] And indeed whenever I read the books by Gisbert Voetius, otherwise a man of great erudition, which he wrote against Descartes, and again compare the letter written in reply by Descartes to Voetius, I always have the impression (I am speaking of the style, not the subject matter) of two very dissimilar men, one of them a theologian, who is, however, not impartial and speaks badly of others, the other a politic person, but one who is extremely peaceful and accepts most criticisms generously.[33]

§29. Usually it is Zoilus and Momus[34] who come under attack in prefaces, even where there is no Momus. I too had an excellent opportunity to spit bile at the Zoiluses, if I had not always believed that such invectives were a sign of an unsound, or at least of an undisciplined, mind. Moreover, these calumnies directed against me soon vanished; lies cannot persist for long. They are like snowballs which can grow to an enormous size when they are formed by humans, but which are rapidly reduced to nothing once they are exposed to the rays of the sun. Finally there seemed to be no need for invective, since my *Institutes* are sold publicly and themselves refute this calumny. I submit these *Institutes* to the scrutiny of all the learned,

32. René Descartes, *Meditationes de prima philosophia* (Paris, 1641), to which was appended a set of six "objections raised by several men of learning" together with Descartes' answers; translation in *The Philosophical Works of Descartes,* vol. 2, trans. E. S. Haldane and G. R. T. Ross (Cambridge: Cambridge University Press, 1982). The first objection was by the Dutch Catholic priest Johan de Kater; see p. 66 of the English translation.

33. Gisbert Voetius (1589–1676), Dutch theologian and critic of Descartes. A reply by Descartes to Voetius was published in *Epistola Renati Descartes ad celeberrimum virum D. Gisbertum Voetium in qua examinantur duo libri, nuper pro Voetio Ultrajecti simul editi, unus de Confraternitate Mariana, alter de Philosophia Cartesiana* (Amsterdam, 1643).

34. These are semimythical figures and usually appear as classical personifications of the hostile critic.

but only those who are truly such, for I scorn the censure of the others, who have no learning or know nothing beyond school and the seven liberal arts, even though they are filled to the brim and swollen up with their faith in a false philosophy.

§30. Yet I believe it to be in your interest, my listeners, that you who are, so to speak, caught between both sides know what responses I would want to be given in these controversies, whenever these matters happen to come up in familiar conversation, as they do. However, I wish you could avoid these occasions as much as is possible and not provide an opportunity for these kinds of quarrels, since nothing is more pedantic and nothing renders humans less suitable for civil life than being a disputatious animal in daily conversation and being unable to tolerate dissenters; just as he on the other hand suffers from the same vice of pedantry who stands at the lectern set up for the sake of public disputation and will not tolerate objections which are put forward according to the rules of the art, but to which he cannot reply, and yet is too embarrassed to admit an error. But as it is not always in our power to avoid quarrels completely, even among those we are familiar with, or to avoid hearing the thoughtless comments of one or the other person, your basic interest and the need to prevent you from being confused about the ideas you received from me demand that I say a little more about this matter.

§31. Thus, as far as the vice of atheism is concerned, I only ask my adversaries to look at the arguments I list in the first book, chapter 3, §§85ff., where I show that atheism is directly contrary to the principles I demonstrated. Concerning heresy, however, I should be much obliged to that person who will show me a thesis in these *Institutes* which is contrary to Holy Scripture and the articles of faith we profess. Moreover I appeal to you, who have heard me expound jurisprudence and philosophy on a daily basis, whether I have ever professed any opinion which contradicted the sacred mysteries of our faith and whether I did not rather devote all my efforts to preserve the strict limits which separate sacrosanct theology and human wisdom from each other and to show to you from the history of philosophy in all ages what great unrest the mixture of philosophy with theology has caused within the church. But why do we need long discussions? Do you believe that the venerable theologians of our university, or any others who are entrusted with the inspection of doctrines, be they private or public, will allow that heterodox doctrine to be spread and to corrupt your minds? Far from it. Yet I do not deny, and have demonstrated to you several times, that there are many questions and assertions which theologians commonly use, but which, if you examine them carefully, are properly speaking not theological, but philosophical or juristic. The fact that these matters are generally regarded as part of theology is mainly due to scholastic theology, which has done enormous damage by mixing philosophy with theology contrary to the admonition of Paul, and has created a confused and disorderly mass, in one word, a kind of amorphous chaos. But it is also the fault of philosophers and jurists who neglected letters[35] before the Reformation and so gave the papal theologians the chance to seize what was left derelict. That is what happened to natural jurisprudence, as I say in the *Institutes* themselves, since the law of nature and nations and theology are entirely different. This I prove in book 1, chapter 1, §§163ff., and chapter 2, §§137ff. The news from the capital of Spain has recently brought us an excellent illustration of my opinion: "One suspects that the Dutch extraordinary envoy will receive satisfaction against the Inquisition for the insolent acts committed in his house in the case of Mr. Chares. These acts were condemned without exception by all high-ranking ministers, especially as Mr. De Lyra himself said that the inquisitors were people who understood theology, but not the law of nations, and thus did not know what was due to a public minister."[36] Nor do I conceal my belief that the power to declare a heretic does not pertain to either private persons or the clergy, but is a regalian right and pertains to the prince's right in sacred affairs, even though this regalian right must be exercised according to the standard of the divine word. I see that this is how it has been observed in the primitive church and in the first ecumenical councils, and the genuine principles of political science teach me the same. I believe also that it belongs to the duty of a good citizen in the Holy

35. The Latin term here is *studia elegantia,* that is, for example, history, philology, and literature.

36. It is not clear which incident Thomasius is referring to here.

Roman Empire, not to speak disparagingly either in public or in private about the religions that are tolerated in the Empire, because this is what the peace treaty of Westphalia teaches me. I believe furthermore that the rules on the duties of the good citizen also apply to the clergy and that this doctrine does not contradict the word of God. I believe that the prince makes proper use of his right if he coerces those with just punishments who are refractory and driven by some intemperate zeal: I believe that gentleness does more to convert adversaries in the church than harsh methods full of verbal abuse, etc. If there is anything heterodox in any of this, I will most willingly suffer correction by those to whom this power belongs.

§32. I turn to impiety; I hear that the supposed sign of this is that I strongly disagree with my late blessed father. From this someone inferred that I did not care about divine laws, but wanted all of them to be purged from sacred Scripture. This is certainly a cheeky argument, and one that is in many ways contrary to logic. I confess that I sometimes dissent from my father, but the Catechism does teach me that I may do so with a clear conscience and without violating the fourth precept [of the Decalogue]. If someone wanted to extend this to the point of saying that the honor and reverence owed to parents also included some sort of adulatory denial of truth, though truth is guided not by authority, but by right reason, I fear that this person would be hissed and booed even by the catechumens, who are still learning the Catechism. It is not true and even a lie to say that I think harshly of my father. I appeal to all of you to say whether I ever uttered a single little word which could be interpreted as disparaging my father, whenever I indicated to you my disagreement with him. As I have pointed out above, it is possible for me not to mention the name of my father or of others to whom I owe reverence without damaging the reliability of the information. It is true that I did not think highly of some doctrines of the Peripatetics, because I noticed that they did not rest on any firm reason; it is also true, and I acknowledge it, that I sometimes referred to the philosophical writings of my father on this in my lecture, since he was, to my knowledge, the best interpreter of Peripatetic philosophy, whose ideas I developed further. But then there was no more of a disagreement between my father and myself than there is in a court of law between a plaintiff and the lawyer of the accused, especially as my blessed father himself diverged from common opinion in many ways, since he had better reasons, not only in his published writings but also in hitherto unpublished manuscripts (as we will show in an example in the following passages), thus setting a praiseworthy example to me.

§33. There remains the accusation of being an innovator. The disciples of true wisdom do not take this very seriously, since it is to be considered a matter of pride not to want to see everything with the eyes of others, but to find out something that has been overlooked by others, on the basis of one's own reasoning powers. And that is the specific characteristic of Eclectic Philosophy, which I have adopted. Its superiority over sectarian philosophy is demonstrated in an erudite dissertation by Johann Christoph Sturm, which preceded a treatise on Eclectic Philosophy that appeared in the previous year:[37] But none of the Sectarians or none of those who worship antiquity as if it were a deity will refute this [eclectic philosophy], nor can they refute it, as I have shown to you on another occasion.[38] Thus I embrace many new ideas and I reject many new ones. Many new ideas I introduce myself by making use of my liberty of philosophizing and by being guided by reason which accepts new and old ideas equally. If a reply were required, I could fittingly use the sharp-witted epigram of a man among us who is both an excellent theologian by virtue of his life and his doctrine, as well as a most elegant poet—an epigram with which he recently honored participants in a public disputation:[39]

> Whoever, in oral debate, wants to protect the errors of the ancients
> And boasts that everything he teaches is ancient
> He, while he mocks the others by the name of innovators
> Will graduate in the class of the obsolete.

37. Johann Christoph Sturm (1635–1703), natural philosopher and mathematician at the University of Altdorf, near Nuremberg. The work referred to here is his *Philosophia eclectica, h.e. exercitationes academicae, quibus philosophandi methodus selectior, ea nempe, quae ex plurimis diversa sententium cogitatis optima quaeque modeste seligit* (Altdorf, 1686).

38. Presumably a reference to Thomasius's *Introductio ad philosophiam aulicam* [1688], ed. W. Schneiders and M. Schewe (Hildesheim: Georg Olms, 1993).

39. It is not clear whom Thomasius has in mind here.

I know that it is not easy to introduce something new in theological matters because the peace within the church must not be disturbed, though
novelty can be defended if it is put forward properly. But I deny having
introduced any novelty in that sense and have submitted my *Institutes* to
public censorship.

§34. Yet these calumnies allowed me to see that some had taken the concise brevity which I used in the first book as an opportunity to distort
my words. I therefore not only expressed my meaning in the second and
third books more elaborately than I had originally intended to, but also
conferred privately on the matters in the first book with some friends,
men whom I revere for their supreme zeal for piety which is the true
theological virtue. I asked them to warn me in time if they detected anything there which was contrary to the articles of faith, or might seem to
be so, or could be interpreted in a bad sense because it was ambiguously
expressed, or which promoted some novelty dangerous to sacred doctrine.
And they were very happy to do so, discussing various objections with me
in a peaceful manner. I accepted these gratefully, and in order to explain
what is expressed rather obscurely in the first book and to reaffirm what
is doubtful, I can only communicate to you the ideas which came into
my mind as a result and from my own rereading of that book. Insofar as
possible, I do this very briefly and according to the rule that I either teach
you how to avoid an objection through an appropriate interpretation of
my intention or that I show that the opinion I defend, even if new, is not
theological, and not even so new, but resting on the authority of men who
are above suspicion, and often on that of our own theologians, even if this
opinion is not commonly accepted.

§35. In chapter 1, §§3ff., I set out a much improved and corrected classification of faculties, and in §22 of the same chapter I assert that the common
doctrine of the Peripatetics in this matter is full of endless errors. And I do
not change my opinion on this matter now. However, this doctrine is certainly not theological, nor even new. For while I believed at the time that
I had been the first to detect these errors, since I only remembered one
error that my father pointed out in his history of metaphysics, published

together with his metaphysical questions,[40] namely that the Scholastics described their metaphysics as wisdom, when it was nothing other than a dictionary of terms, many of which do not serve wisdom, but sophistry. Another error he pointed out in his annotations on practical philosophy was that intelligence was listed among the theoretical faculties. Yet, while doing something else recently, I noticed an elegant meditation in the manuscripts of my blessed father, which showed that the other observations I had made on the common division of qualities were already made by him around 1660. On this account I congratulated myself on the similarity of my thoughts with those of my father. This discussion is a little too long to be inserted conveniently into this preface. Yet my point will become clear if I offer a summary of his intention and his procedure in the division of the qualities. He says:

> There is on the one hand intellectual virtue, on the other the virtue of the will; among the intellectual virtues one is simple, that is, intelligence, which belongs equally to theoretical and practical principles, while the other is composite. This composite intellectual virtue is either theoretical—that is, wisdom and science—or practical—that is, prudence, the guide in moral affairs, and diligence, which is the guide in matters of art. The virtue of the will is either moral, the secondary subject of which is the sensitive appetite of desire or anger; or it is artificial, that is, art, the secondary subject of which is the locomotive power of the mind as well as the body.

§36. However, as far as I know, this observation is my own, for in the same chapter 1, §23, I disclose a blatant error, contrary to Christian theology, on the difference between theoretical and practical faculties: it is illuminated by dissertations 5 and 6 of the Platonic philosopher Maximus Tyrus.[41] There you will discover many arguments which he formulated on the superiority of theoretical over practical philosophy and which smack of the pagan hypothesis that the essence of God consists in contemplation

---

40. Jacob Thomasius, *Erotemata metaphysica pro incipientibus: Accessit pro adultis historia variae fortunae, quam metaphysica experta est* (Leipzig, 1670).

41. Maximus of Tyre, *The Philosophical Orations,* ed. and trans. M. S. Trapp (Oxford: Oxford University Press, 1997), Orations 15 and 16.

and that the approach of man to God is through theoretical contemplation. I remember that among the speeches of my blessed father there was
one, the 21st,[42] in which he himself defended the superiority of a life of
theoretical contemplation. But it is not true that he disagrees with me;
in fact, he confirms my opinions in many respects. The purpose of this
speech is to demonstrate the superiority of the theoretical life based on the
prerogative of the first table of the Decalogue over the second. We do not
deny this prerogative, but we do deny that the first table pertains to a life
based on theoretical contemplation, and so we disagree in the definition
of the terms. For the entire Decalogue regulates human duties, and these
are the subject not of theoretical philosophy, but of practical philosophy,
and the duties of man toward God will always concern practice, not mere
theory. Our blessed father's statements concerning pagan opinion on the
superiority of theoretical philosophy over practical at the beginning of the
said speech do, however, amply confirm what we have posited in the said
chapter 1, §§24ff.

§37. What requires some explanation, however, is my statement in §24,
toward the end, that "it is a false opinion of the pagans that God's essence consists in contemplation"—that is, pure contemplation—and one
which does not have any action as its end. You must therefore beware of
mocking my words, perhaps by inferring that I declare God's essence to
consist in external action and so avoid Charybdis by being wrecked on
Scylla and adopt the error of those pagans who say God is necessarily
joined to prime matter from all eternity. For, leaving aside other matters,
this argument would apply only if God were human. But as God's essence is infinitely superior to that of humans, you would not even be able
to infer that (if I had denied completely that God contemplated, which,
however, you see I have not done) because contemplation is not the essence of God; it must be action. Similarly you would not be able to infer
that if someone says a stone cannot see, he concludes the stone to be blind.
For just as there is something in between seeing and being blind—that is,

42. Jacob Thomasius, *Orationes, partim ex umbone Templi Academici, partim ex Auditorii Philosophici cathedra recitatae, argumenti varii* (Leipzig, 1683).

not seeing—which can be predicated of the stone because of its imperfection, so I believe that there can be a third term between contemplation and human action in God which I do not know because of his supreme perfection. For, based on Scripture, I know nothing of God's essence; but I admire it, and without philosophical knowledge I believe those things which Scripture has revealed to me about it. Now if it is permissible to speak in the human way of God's infinite essence, then my father's words in the said speech, pages 504ff., will be found to be very pleasing:

> God is happy not only in contemplation, but also in action. For even if he undertook infinite tasks in one moment they would not burden this supremely powerful and pure being. God's beatitude is derived from himself, not from elsewhere. We by contrast owe whatever we have that is good to God, not to ourselves. What worms we are when compared to the divine majesty.

§38. In the same chapter 1, §29, I say that "Law is always binding, pacts are not." Of course the consent of two or more parties produces an obligation (Scripture tells us so repeatedly and confirms that we are bound by promises). I discuss this in detail in chapter 6, book 2, on preserving faith; but I want the obligation that follows from the pact not to be the product of the consent itself, but of the will of the legislator who commands the keeping of promises. Thus I immediately subjoin that "a law is binding if there is a pact." But I have done this in order to contradict more firmly some people who ultimately derive the power of obligation from a pact. Among these the foremost, if I am not mistaken, is Hobbes.[43] At the same time I contradict Grotius, who asserts that the laws of nature would be binding even if we assumed that there were no God, etc.[44] Yet, even if you preferred to replace the phrase that "law is sometimes binding because of a pact" with the statement that "a pact is binding because of a law" I will not contradict you, because I believe that these two phrases are compatible,

---

43. See, for example, Thomas Hobbes, *Leviathan,* ed. R. Tuck (Cambridge: Cambridge University Press, 1996), part II, chap. 17.

44. Hugo Grotius, *The Rights of War and Peace,* vol. 1, ed. Richard Tuck (Indianapolis: Liberty Fund, 2005), "The Preliminary Discourse," §xi, p. 89.

since either suggests that a law can be binding in the absence of a pact but not without a legislator.

§39. In §31 of the same chapter I say that the eternal law is a scholastic fiction. By that I do not mean the thing denoted by that term, whether they mean divine justice or the entire order of nature established according to God's will and decree. For who but the most blatant atheist would claim that these are the product of nothing? I declare, however, that the use of the term *law* by the Scholastics in explaining their concept is most improper and a fiction: Thus it follows that God does not act according to a law. You may think this is a harsh way of putting it, since what is poorly expressed is entirely different from a fiction, and fictions are not what is expressed in inappropriate words, but what does not exist outside the mind of the author of the fiction or of those who accept it. I would reply that a distinction needs to be made between different kinds of unsuitable expressions. For some of these expressions are such that they are held to be improper even by those who use them; others are such that those who use them claim that the predicate, which is applicable to the subject only in a very improper fashion, can be applied to it properly. I admit that it is not accurate to call the former inappropriate expressions fictions; but as far as the latter are concerned, these are real fictions, because the improper predication, while it is claimed to be proper, does not exist as such outside the conception of the author of the fiction, but he invents it entirely by saying that it is proper. Thus, if someone presented a portrait of somebody as the person himself, or wanted Herod to be a fox in the proper sense of the word, or the meadows to be smiling in the literal sense of the word, he would without doubt be inventing this. But it is evident that most of the Scholastics defended the idea that eternal law is a law in the proper sense of the word. On this basis they initiated wide-ranging controversies concerning the definition of this law, all in order that this general definition of law could be adapted better to God. Mr. Osiander discusses these at greater length in his *Typum legis naturae.*

§40. The doctrine that beasts are without sense perception clearly does not belong to theology. And if the interest of religion is mixed up with this controversy, the argument for the lack of sense perception of animals even triumphs over the contrary opinion. The words of the true and genuine critic Pierre Bayle on this matter are elegant; compare the *Excerpts from the Republic of Letters,* March 1684, pages 26ff.:

> Religion comes to be involved in this cause because the anti-Cartesians hope thereby to undermine the machines of Descartes; but they are not able to see the benefit which the philosophers' followers have derived from this. For they believe they have shown that in attributing a soul capable of cognition to animals, all proofs of the natural immortality of the soul are overthrown. They have shown that their opinion has no more obstinate enemies than the godless and the Epicureans, and that there is no better way of attacking these philosophers than by robbing them of all their false arguments, when they bring up the soul of beasts and claim that there is no difference between the soul of beasts and that of men, except that the former have a little less, and the latter a little more soul. It is certain that there are no more godless people than those who say that beasts come very close to the perfection of humans. This is how the Cartesians have used religion for the purposes of their philosophy. But they are not content with this reason. They have examined divine nature to find arguments against the rationality of beasts, and one can say that they have found many good things there.[45]

And his entire, highly erudite dissertation, which he proposed on the occasion of the treatise of Darmanson, *La beste transformée en machine,* pages 19–34,[46] is worthy of being read by you. To put it briefly, the whole doctrine can be summarized in these few points: (1) The Peripatetics, I believe, concede that the soul of man cannot be conceived as anything other than a faculty for thought. (2) They concede that the internal senses perform acts of cognition. (3) Either it must be conceded that all cognition occurs as a result of thought, or it must be confessed that those who attribute cognition to the senses do not know what they are saying. Thus, (4) the conclusion follows naturally: Animals lack internal senses because they lack reason. Therefore animals must either be granted reason or they

---

45. Thomasius is quoting in French from Pierre Bayle, *Nouvelles de la République des Lettres* (Amsterdam, 1684).

46. Jean Darmanson, *La beste transformée en machine, diversée en deux dissertations prononcées à Amsterdam* (n.p., 1684).

must be deprived of both reason and sensation, or perception, or cognition, or whatever word you want to use here. But this doctrine is not so new that it has to be traced from the age of Descartes. Sturm says in the first dissertation of his *Eclectic Philosophy,* page 54:

> the first was Gomez Pereira, who asserted that animals lacked all cognition or perception,[47] and Willis in *De anima brutorum,* chapter 1, page 6, testifies that he [Pereira] was followed in the present century by Descartes and Digby.[48] Morhof in his dissertation on the paradoxes of the senses[49] says that Gomez, a Spanish philosopher and physician, devoted a lot of effort to this, and in Methyna in 1554 published a book he had worked on for thirty years, which was named the *Antoniana Margarita* after his parents.[50]

Add Bayle in the work cited, pages 20ff., where he shows that this opinion perished soon after Pereira, and so the glory of inventing it should not be denied to Descartes. There has even been an anonymous author who reminded Bayle that already at the time of Augustine there were debates on this matter, and to prove this he quotes the words of Augustine from *De quantitate animae,* chapter 30: "But it seemed to you that there was no soul in the body of living beasts, although this may seem absurd, and there has been no lack of highly learned people who adopted this opinion, and I believe there is no lack of them now." See Bayle, *Nouvelles de la République des lettres,* month of August 1684, page 2,[51] and Rondelius in a particular letter, a fragment of which Bayle published in the month of October of the same year, page 290,[52] points out to him that more than three hun-

---

47. On Sturm see note 37 in this chapter. Gomez Pereira was a Spanish philosopher who published a medical work, the *Antoniana Margarita, opus nempe physicis, medicis ac theologis non minus utile, quam necessarium* (n.p., 1554).

48. Thomas Willis (1621–75), *De anima brutorum quae hominis vitalis ac sensitiva est exercitationes duae* (London, 1672); Sir Kenelm Digby (1603–65), English natural philosopher and courtier.

49. Daniel Morhof, *Dissertatio de paradoxis sensuum* (Kiel, 1676).

50. See note 47 on this page.

51. See Augustine, *The Greatness of the Soul; The Teacher,* trans. and ed. J. M. Colloran (Westminster, Md.: Newman Press, 1950).

52. A reference to a piece in the *Nouvelles* by Jacques de Rondel, author of a life of Epicurus (*La vie d'Epicure* [Paris, 1679]).

dred years before Augustine, at the time of the Caesars, the Stoics doubted whether beasts had a sensitive soul; another three hundred years before them Diogenes the Cynic did the same, even though the anonymous author soon retracted his opinion because in studying Augustine he had noticed that in the words quoted from Augustine the question did not concern the doctrine of Pereira. The learned Bayle therefore suspected that perhaps passages quoted by Rondelius did not clearly prove his intention; see the month April 1685, page 425, which is a question we perhaps will discuss in greater detail elsewhere.

§41. The arguments which I put forward on the imputability of moral actions in chapter 1, §66, are almost all taken from the writings of Mr. Pufendorf, *Of the Law of Nature and Nations,* book 1, chapter 5, and *On the Duty of Man and Citizen,* book 1, chapter 1. Yet I believe that the Peripatetics pretty much agree with me on these rules and that they are generally taught by them in their books on ethics, especially the principle which I state in §69, that facts cannot be morally imputed to a person when he has no influence over their presence or absence. But I understand all these rules to refer to the human court [*forum*], because in the entire *Institutes* I discuss jurisprudence, which has as its ultimate end the preservation of temporal peace through the execution of laws and the administration of justice, and so I do not contradict the theologians and their doctrine of the imputation of original sin in the divine court. The fact that I composed a treatise on divine jurisprudence is no hindrance, though it might lead a reader to believe, according to the laws of sound method, that these general rules are to be taken in such a wide sense that they apply not only to the human but also to the divine court. But it will be clear to anyone from what I say at the end of chapters 1 and 2 that jurisprudence, even when it is called divine and is concerned with divine laws, is not concerned with the divine court, but leaves this entirely to the theologians. I wanted, however, to add an explanation of my opinion because I wanted to avoid causing scandal to others.

§42. In chapter 2, §2, I state that certain divine laws have the well-being of humans in this life as their purpose. And by that I mean their immediate purpose, for this is what I say expressly in the same chapter, §§125 and 138. Thus I do not deny that every divine law which has eternal salvation as its purpose also simultaneously has well-being in this life as its purpose. I do deny, however, that this is its immediate purpose.

§43. In §3 of the same chapter I said that I disapproved of the common division of divine law into moral, ceremonial, and forensic. Yet I deny that I have thereby committed an impiety or a crime against sacred theology. I have put forward my reasons for this disapproval in a public disputation *On the Crime of Bigamy,* §§8 and 20.[53] Many who use this division treat moral and natural law as identical, and argue that the Decalogue everywhere inculcates precepts of natural law, or they defend the view that outside of the Decalogue there are no moral precepts in Scripture. They do this although it is evident that the moral law is broader and comprehends within it positive universal law, and that the Decalogue also inculcates universal positive laws, for example in the ninth and tenth precepts; finally there are moral precepts outside the Decalogue, for example in Leviticus 18.[54] As far as the first point is concerned, Mr. Osiander agrees with it in his *Typum legis naturae,* page 117, §15, where he says lucidly that "the moral and the natural law are based on different reasons." The late Dorscheus said in his first *Disputation on Moral Theology,* §10:[55]

> divine positive law was superadded to natural law and communicated to humanity. It was put forward by Moses more fully and restricted to the government of the Israelite people, which was more ancient than the laws of all nations and also provided all first legislators with the origins of their laws. This is clear from the testimony of the pagans, on which Eusebius comments in book 1, *Praeparatio evangelica,* chapter 9;[56] from the fact that they trace the origin of all laws to Egypt, which, according to Joseph

53. Thomasius, *De crimine bigamiae.*

54. Chapter 18 of Leviticus lists a series of divine commands concerning relationships by blood and marriage.

55. Johann Georg Dorsche, *Theologia moralis: Ex MSSto edita, & publicae sententiarum collationi in Academia Wittebergensi exposita* (Wittenberg, 1685).

56. Eusebius (A.D. ca. 264–340), bishop of Caesarea. His *Praeparatio evangelica* (*Preparation for the Gospel*) is a collection of statements that are drawn from pagan authors and appear to support the truth of Christianity.

Psalm 105.22, owed its habitation to the ancient pious Israelites;[57] from the comparison of Roman and Hebrew laws by Justus Calvinus in his *Themis Ebraeo-Romana,* William Velrot in his *Parallels of Jewish and Roman Law,* Molinaeus in his *Comparison of Roman and Hebrew Laws,* and others. Add Diodorus Siculus, book 1 of his *Bibl.,* chapter 5, page 43.[58]

Then he [Dorscheus] adds in §11 that the written moral law, which was transmitted by Moses, was known already before the time of Moses, and he proves this, according to the order of the precepts of the Decalogue, with various scriptural passages. Finally he says in §13: "It is clear from the divine illumination of the Patriarchs and God's proclamations in Genesis 3, 4, 6, etc., that moral laws which were known before the time of Moses were not only to be ascribed to natural reason but were also positive laws, and thus promulgated by God." Add to these the blessed Scherzer in his *System of Theology,* locus 9, §9, page 266: "From this foundation emerges the distinction between the natural moral law and the positive law (which is better than the common distinction between primary and secondary natural law)."[59] On the second point, concerning the ninth and tenth precepts, we will soon say more. Concerning the third, what we have just noted from Dorscheus can suffice. Add to this what I discuss in great detail in the *Institutes* themselves in book 2, throughout chapter 3.

§44. The question concerning government within marriage in the state of innocence, which I touch upon in §§29ff. of chapter 2, is, I believe, not a properly theological question, the affirmation or denial of which implies heterodoxy or breeds scandal in the church. Thus, just as I do not demand

---

57. See Josephus, *Jewish Antiquities* (vols. 4–9 of Josephus, *Josephus,* trans. H. St. J. Thackeray, 10 vols., Loeb Classical Library [London: Heinemann, 1926–81]).

58. Justus Calvinus, *Themis Hebraeo-Romana: Id est, iurisprudentia Mosaica, et iuris tum canonici, tum civilis, Romana, invicem collata, & methodice digesta* (Hanau, 1595); Diodorus Siculus, *Diodorus of Sicily,* ed. and trans. C. H. Oldfather, 12 vols., Loeb Classical Library (Cambridge, Mass.: Harvard University Press, 1933–67). This appears to be a reference to bk. 1, chaps. 28 and 29 in the Loeb edition. It has not been possible to identify the works by Velrot and Molinaeus, though the latter is presumably the French Catholic theologian Pierre du Moulin (1568–1658).

59. Johann Adam Scherzer, *Systema theologiae, 29 definitionibus absolutum* (Leipzig, 1680).

that the learned esteem my opinion, so do I not believe there to be any need to search in the commentaries of our theologians to see whether one or the other supports my opinion. I confess that there are several whom I have seen embrace a different opinion from my own. However, if we have to act on the basis of authority, I oppose to all of these the words of Luther on Genesis, chapter 3:[60] "But if Eve had remained in the state of innocence, she would not have been subject to the rule of the man but would have herself been his companion in government, which is now a matter for men alone"; but if we want to argue on the basis of reason [rather than authority], I refer to those arguments which I discuss in more detail again in book 3, chapter 3, §§35ff., where I have also taken up this question.

§45. In chapter 1, §51, I state the common axiom: "Nothing is in the intellect which was not previously in the senses," and this I declare to be true without limitations. But in chapter 2, §39, I say that the human intellect in the state after the fall from grace is like a clean slate, which is suitable for receiving various impressions: and in the same chapter, §§66 and 67, I declare that right reason is part of man from birth as a potential faculty capable of exerting its powers once the ideas have been formed previously by the intellect from sense impressions. I consider the doctrine of the Scholastics far too subtle; they teach that even infants have certain first practical principles by nature in the form of some kind of faculty with which they are born, etc. All these I add here because one follows from the other. And first, concerning that principle "Nothing is in the intellect . . ." this is so trite and widespread that it is to be found in all Peripatetic works on physics, so that I need not fear that this might be an assertion that does not conform to theology; see my blessed father's *Physics,* chapter 49, questions 66ff., pages 263ff., and Zeidler's *Posterior Analytics,* page 231, thesis 31, and page 572, §8.[61] Concerning the other argument, it must be pointed out briefly that Plato and Aristotle disagreed over the way in which cognition works in our minds: Plato claimed this is the result

60. See M. Luther, Luther's Works, vol. 1: *Lectures on Genesis,* chaps. 1–5, ed. J. Pelikan (St. Louis, Missouri: Concordia Publishing, 1958), p. 203.

61. Jacob Thomasius, *Physica* (Leipzig, 1670); Melchior Zeidler, *Analysis posterior, sive De variis sciendi generibus et mediis eo perveniendi libri tres* (Königsberg, 1675).

of remembering, while Aristotle said it occurs through the reception of external sense impressions by the intellect. Plato therefore compared the human intellect to a slate that has been wiped clean, Aristotle to a bare one that has never been written on; see Zeidler, *Posterior Analytics,* page 391, thesis 4, and page 586, thesis 1. You should not however need to believe that when I mention a clean slate I have run over to the side of Plato. The previous principle, "Nothing is in the intellect . . . ," proves that this is not what I mean. This is directly opposed to Platonic philosophy, as I shall demonstrate to you elsewhere. I used the term *clean* [*rasa*] according to the common manner of speaking, in which *clean* [*tabula rasa*] and *bare* [*nuda*] are often used interchangeably. I am, however, happy for this term to be exchanged for the other in order to remove any cause for ambiguity. Finally, concerning the third point, I here have the consent of erudite men above all suspicion, and not only from other universities, but from our own. I refer again to Melchior Zeidler from Königsberg, who in his frequently cited treatise, book 2, chapter 3, §2, and in many following chapters shows in great detail that human reason from the time of birth is only a potential, and that ideas are innate only as mere possibilities, but not as actual qualities [*habitus*]. I also appeal to Conrad Horneius from Helmstedt, who in book 4 of his *Moral Philosophy,* chapter 2, §6, page 559, shows quite clearly that first principles, both theoretical and practical, require a previous knowledge of the terms and cannot be understood by infants.[62] I also refer to Johannes Zeisold from Jena, who in the years from 1651 in four public disputations on natural ideas demonstrated our opinion from basic principles and strengthened it against the objections of Sperling at the University of Wittenberg.[63] From our doctrine I refer you back to that of my blessed father, who, according to the judgment of our much revered Alberti in his oration on my parent,[64] was a Christian phi-

62. Conrad Horneius, *Philosophiae moralis sive civilis doctrinae de moribus libri IV* (Frankfurt, 1634).

63. Johannes Zeisold, *Disputatio physica de notitiis naturalibus* (Jena, 1651–52); Johannes Sperling (1603–58) taught at the University of Wittenberg.

64. This speech ("Philosophus Christianus in viro celeberrimo, Dn. Jacobo Thomasio, die IX. Septembri Anno M.DC.LXXXV, in anniversariam ejus memoriam") was delivered by Valentin Alberti (1635–97) on the occasion of the first anniversary of Jacob Thomasius's death. Alberti was professor of theology at the University of Leipzig and author of an anti-Pufendorfian work on natural law, the *Compendium juris naturae*

losopher (a title he aspired to throughout his entire life, and which is commonly applied to those people who do not contradict sacred theology by philosophizing, nor defend any opinions which are contrary to Scripture and could disturb theology. But if someone wanted to distort the meaning of this elogy and imply that this blessed man confused the disciplines of philosophy and theology, which are most clearly distinct, and that he attempted to demonstrate theological theses from principles of reason or philosophical theses from hypotheses of revelation, then he would do my blessed father a great injustice, since he would never have dreamed of confusing the two). My father therefore put forward these same principles which we have taught concerning natural knowledge, even concerning the knowledge of God himself; see his *Physica,* questions 68ff., page 284:

> This rule is valid (nothing is in the intellect, etc.), but only concerning those ideas which are in the intellect in the form of an act, or an intelligible species, but not concerning those that are there in the form of a potential or a habit. A.: Prove it. B.: There are in our intellect certain innate ideas of the first principles, but they exist in the form of a potential, even if no sense perception of these principles preceded them. A.: I thought, however, that there are some intelligible species in our intellect, without having entered through the senses. For is not God (to leave aside other examples) in our intellect, although he cannot be grasped by sense perception? B.: Hear therefore another qualification: there is nothing in the intellect, which did not previously exist in the senses, whether in itself, or through something else. Thus I grant that God is not himself an object of sense perception, but I deny that he does not become such an object through something else.[65]

§46. These passages will show you that my opinions on these matters are neither new nor particularly heterodox because they were defended by men who have never been suspected of heterodoxy. Those who disagree, however, as well as those who generally defend the opinion of the Scho-

---

orthodoxae theologiae conformatum (Leipzig, 1678). Alberti's speech also appeared in a work by the Leipzig theologian Johann Benedict Carpzov: *Christi Thomaslection von der Jacobsleiter, bey Christlicher Leichbestattung des . . . Herrn Jacobi Thomasii, . . . in damahliger Leichpredigt . . . den 14. September, . . . Anno 1684. in der Pauliner-Kirchen erklaeret von Jo. Benedicto Carpzov* (Leipzig, ca. 1685).

65. Jacob Thomasius, *Physica* (see note 61 in this chapter).

lastics point to Romans 2, verse 15, where it is said that the law of nature is inscribed on the hearts of men. That is why the *Index of Novelties,* n. 19,[66] also claims that the illustrious Pufendorf denies the law of nature to be something implanted in human nature and an innate faculty. But the illustrious man makes a fully satisfactory reply to this in his *Apology,* pages 46ff.,[67] where he shows very clearly, and by using other, parallel passages of Scripture, that the phrase *writing on the hearts of men* means something other than an innate faculty of this kind. And Zeisold in his entire fourth disputation already tried to show the view that our opinion was not contrary to religion, and gave a satisfactory reply to many contrary arguments by Sperling and pointed out that already in his time our famous philosopher and theologian Jacob Martinus had attacked that doctrine of the Scholastics.[68] Sperling therefore, in his *Anthropologia,* book 1, chapter 3, question 8, pages 186ff., insisted on the passage from the Apostle as a proof for innate ideas by writing:

> For this the Apostle said: "For when the Gentiles, which have not the law, do by nature the things contained in the law, these, having not the law, are a law unto themselves: Which shew the work of the law written in their hearts, their conscience also bearing witness, and their thoughts the mean while accusing or else excusing one another."[69] Here it is possible to form the following conclusion: Whatever is inscribed on the hearts of pagans is not acquired but innate. The work of the law of nature is inscribed on the hearts of the pagans. Therefore the work of the law of nature is not acquired, but innate.[70]

Among other things he cites the response of Martinus from the *Partitiones metaphysicae,* section 3, question 4, page 321, where he writes as follows:

> The response to the authority of the Apostle is at hand: a distinction needs to be drawn between the inscription itself and the means of inscription. When natural [innate] knowledge is denied, this does not mean that

66. Beckmann and Schwartz, *Index quarundam novitatum.*

67. See notes 14 and 15 in this chapter.

68. Jacob Martini (1570–1649), professor of theology at Wittenberg from 1623 until his death. On Zeisold and Sperling, see note 63 in this chapter.

69. Romans 2:14–15.

70. Johann Sperling, *Physica anthropologia* (Wittenberg, 1647).

pagans do not have the law of God inscribed on them by nature, since they do what is required by God's law; but what is denied is the form which some insist on, namely, that it is inscribed at birth: that cannot be demonstrated from the saying by Paul referred to. Attention should be paid to the intention of the Apostle, and then the matter will be clear. He argues thus: either the reason for works in the cause of justice is the same for Jews and for Gentiles, or God regards the person. God does not, however, regard the person. Therefore the reason for both is the same. The minor premise is proved, or, rather, is contained within verse 11.[71] For God does not regard the person. The proof of the major premise and the connection is contained in the following verses and can be summarized in this syllogism: all those who sin equally cannot, as far as their sins are concerned, be judged differently before God. Jews and Gentiles have sinned equally, therefore. . . . The Apostle proves the minor premise in verse 12.[72] For whoever has sinned without a law (that is, pagans) will also perish without a law: and those who have sinned against the law (the Jews) will be damned by the law. Having argued thus, the Apostle proceeds to verses 14 and 15[73] (in which the entire core of the objection that was raised resides) and shows that his statement that Gentiles had sinned without a law was not to be understood simply and absolutely, but in a certain sense. Pagans lacked the external promulgation of the divine law (these are the words of Mr. Mylius on this passage), which was made to the Israelites in the Sinai desert. That is what Paul means when he says they have no law. In the meantime, he says, nature provided what was required by the law and they therefore were a law to themselves; that is, they had within themselves and in their entire nature the means to balance this defect to a certain degree. Will therefore the law insofar as it is revealed be opposed to natural law?[74]

Among the modern theologians I mention Mr. Osiander, who in the *Typum legis naturae,* page 158, where he speaks of the nature of the human intellect, calls it an "indifferent and indeterminate power, according to Ar-

71. Romans 2:11.

72. Romans 2:12.

73. Romans 2:14–15.

74. Jacob Martini, *Partitiones et quaestiones metaphysicae, in quibus omnium fere terminorum metaphysicorum distinctiones accurate enumerantur & explicantur* (Wittenberg, 1615).

istotle, a bare slate," since on the same page he adds a reference to that passage of the Apostle, but see also pages 129ff., where he argues against those who deny that there is a natural law and insist that humans introduced all laws for themselves on grounds of utility. He first refutes this opinion by referring to the same passage from Paul; then he argues against those people on the basis of reason and adds a reference to natural ideas and says that "Reason is by nature instructed with certain theoretical principles which are so evident that they are evident even to an infant if the relevant terms are put forward, for example, what a whole is, what a part is . . . and so it is to be understood that the knowledge of these terms is pre-existing and based in the mind." Thus this venerable man says quite clearly that these ideas are mere possibilities until the terms are understood. Finally, the fact that even the smallest infants are credited with faith by the theologians is no obstacle, although faith requires some knowledge, and this knowledge has to be actual [i.e., not potential]. For faith is not the work of nature. But we are here concerned with a natural effect that can be demonstrated with the light of reason, and that need not be explained through obscure and meaningless words. Therefore, just as a physician who denies that a virgin can give birth does not in that respect contradict a theologian who says that the virgin Mary did give birth, so the philosopher, when he denies that there is natural knowledge from birth, does not contradict the theologian who asserts that faith is awakened in infants by supranatural means from birth. Rather, this philosopher, if he is a Christian and sees Scripture telling us that infants have faith, does not allow himself to be drawn into the debate of the Scholastics, whether this children's faith is an act or a potential or an ability, but will think roughly as follows:

> Holy God, you have said in your word that you have not manifested the mysteries of faith to the wise of this world, but to the foolish and those who believe that all of wisdom is of no use in understanding even the smallest point of the mysteries of faith; you have through your elected vessel reminded humans that in matters of faith they should not allow themselves to be deceived by philosophy. See, almost the entire world has come to the point that it wants to measure the incomprehensible mysteries of faith with some sort of Scholastic theology, which is nothing other than a chaotic mixture of reason with your revelation. But help me

to prefer the authority of your word to the authority of humans, however great they may be, and if I see in matters pertaining to faith your words before me, which are either wholly clear or can be interpreted by reference to other parallel passages, help me to believe these by simply assenting to them, even though I do not understand how the predicate is connected to the subject, and not to try to express your ineffable mysteries with metaphysical distinctions or other useless subtleties of this kind. Therefore, if your word teaches me that infants, who do not have the use of reason, believe in Christ, I believe this, even though I cannot form a distinct concept of this for myself, because I know that your word does not lie. But I do not know what this "faculty" [*habitus*] is which the Scholastics, who want to explain Scripture from philosophy, intruded into Scripture, and which they insist is neither a potential nor an act. And so, while they want to be understood clearly, the effect is that they themselves do not understand what they want, and nor do others who hear them. . . .

§47. In the same chapter 2, §65, I aim to prove that divine positive law must be derived from divine revelation and I refer to the passage by the Apostle, Romans 7:7: "I would not have known that concupiscence is a sin if the law had not told me: thou shalt not desire." This passage I interpreted to mean that the Apostle here professes that he, if left to the devices of his natural reason, would not know that concupiscence is a sin unless the divine positive law had told him: thou shalt not desire. But later I noticed that not all of the theologians shared that opinion, that this law, "thou shalt not desire," is positive law, but some considered it to be natural. Based on this opinion one could argue against my doctrine as follows: the law on concupiscence rests on creation itself, and this requires from us that we are as we have been created, and that is without any desire for evil; therefore this precept is such that if God's justice and truthfulness are to remain intact he cannot do anything other than demand that man is such as he in his holy counsel had destined him and made him to be. For the law on which creation rests is natural, not positive. From what has been said it follows that the difference we looked for between natural and positive law in §64 does not cover the whole question, because the knowledge of natural law must be sought from right reason, positive law, however,

from revelation. This would be valid if our reason itself had not been obscured: while it recognizes and detests the more obvious vices, it does not
extend to the deeper and more subtle ones, which it would, however, have
recognized equally well in the state of innocence, even though we would
have known the positive laws only from revelation. And therefore it is the
result of the corruption of nature, which the Apostle himself deplores,
that he does not even realize his own illness except from the renewed
promulgation of the law, etc. But though I placed this periphrasis of the
passage from Paul into my *Institutes,* I did not do so without consulting
our theologians, and above all I looked to the words of the late Scherzer
in his *Systema theologiae,* locus 7, §9, page 154: "Innate concupiscence is
prohibited in the Decalogue; therefore it is a sin. In Romans 7:7, concupiscence is discussed, the lawlessness of which cannot be recognized on
the basis of the law of nature."[75] And if you compare these words of the
blessed Scherzer with my *Institutes* or my exegesis of this passage, I am
certain that I will not have diverged from his meaning in the least way, and
that this doctrine is one that will not cause any unrest in the church, even
though other theologians favor a contrary opinion. I do not want to argue
with them, but it does seem to me that—leaving other things aside—this
disagreement can be easily resolved by distinguishing between the law of
nature in the primordial state and that in the state after the fall, so that
the objection against our opinion is relevant to the former, but we, following the blessed Scherzer, speak of the latter. And I believe that with
this distinction the dispute can be resolved better than if you distinguish
as follows: it is one thing for something to be prohibited by natural law,
another for the prohibition to be recognized by reason alone in its present
state. For, first, Scherzer not only says that the sin of concupiscence cannot be recognized by reason, but he says notably that it cannot be known
from the law of nature. Second, I suspect that this distinction can be attacked on the basis of the passage from Paul, Romans 2, verses 14 and 15.
While this testifies that the laws of nature are inscribed on the hearts of
all nations, this passage according to the common interpretation means
that the pagans also knew the law of nature after the fall, without the aid

75. See note 59 in this chapter.

of revelation, and that therefore natural law at this time is nothing other than that which can today be known by humans from the light of reason, be it through certain ideas present from birth or through acquired ideas. Nor will the fact that the law of nature is unchanging and does not admit dispensation remove the distinction between the law of nature of the state of innocence and that after the fall, as long as you make the following distinction: the variation of the law itself, in which there is a proposition representing the intention of the legislator, is one thing, and another is the variation of the degree of knowledge of the same law, inculcating the same proposition in the state of innocence and in the state of corruption.

§48. I think the matter is clear, but to make sure you do not believe that I, who am not a theologian, have improperly tried to judge a dispute among theologians, I cannot but cite Osiander. Though he is a little long-winded, he will not only confirm my argument, but will absolve me from the accusation of introducing theological innovations. This eminent man says in his *Typum legis naturae,* pages 167ff., §§44 and 45:

> The law of nature considered in the state of innocence and that of corrup-
> tion after original sin are quite different from each other by their nature,
> condition, and effects. . . . For the law of nature in the primeval state
> requires the rectitude of all faculties, which tolerates no crookedness; it
> looked toward the divine image and was founded on justice, sanctity, and
> truth. For God created man morally good, not with infantile imperfec-
> tion, as Josephus claims,[76] and not just simple and free from evil, as the
> Photinians[77] believed, but positively morally good in terms of the intel-
> lect, the will, and the passions. . . . See the passage in Deuteronomy 9,
> verse 5. Thus Augustine in his sermon on the truth of the Apostle, chap-
> ters 2 and 14,[78] says that man is made just and that nature has been cre-
> ated good by God. But the law of nature in the state of corruption is but
> a shadow of the primeval rectitude and a vestige of the divine image,

76. Josephus, *Jewish Antiquities* (see note 57 in this chapter). Book I, chapters 33–51, are on the Creation.

77. The Photinians were a Christian heresy of the fourth century.

78. Augustine, *Sermons,* 11 vols., trans. and notes by E. Mill, ed. by J. E. Rotelle (Hyde Park, N.Y.: New City Press, 1990–97), vol. 1.

faded letters from a clear type, because it exists with the completely corrupt condition of all faculties, the blindness of the intellect, the perversity of the will, the depravity of the passions, on which see Ephesians 2, verses 1, 2, 3. Second, the primordial law of nature forbade all concupiscence; it showed that all discord between the faculties was bad, and not only obliged a person to an active justice, as Molinaeus[79] believes, but even nature itself to intrinsic rectitude, as creation itself teaches us. See the passage in Genesis 1, verse 31, and compare Genesis 2, verse 25, and Genesis 3, verses 6 and 7. Augustine said correctly that the first man was created without guilt or vice in his nature (sermon 11 on the Apostolic Truth, chapter 2).[80] The law of nature after the fall, however, does not eradicate concupiscence, nor does it draw attention to this profound evil in the innermost fibers of the mind, so that the Apostle himself says in Romans 7, verse 7, that he had not recognized sin without the help of the law—that is, the Mosaic law—which prohibits concupiscence. For although he acknowledged, as a Pharisee, that concupiscence which leads to evil external actions is a sin, he believed that the inner stirrings were not to be given this despicable name. Although he was able by the light of reason and natural law to come to realize that the inner stirrings, produced with the concurrence of the will, were reprobate fruits, he still could not penetrate to the evil root and recognize the evil of habitual concupiscence without divine law. Thus he says further in verse 14: "We know that the divine law is spiritual; but I am carnal, beholden to sin." The Decalogue therefore or the divine law is spiritual, but man, as he is, remains carnal even with the law of nature: for if a regenerate person calls himself carnal, regardless of the fact that the spirit of renewal is dominant within himself, how much more carnal is an unregenerate person, even though there is a little of this spirit in him. Third, the law of nature in the first man included the love of God and of our neighbor and was a pure and perfect faculty, with which he could produce truly good works, which pleased God. And when this law was observed, it culminated in eternal beatitude. For he who acts thus will, according to Moses, live in them (Leviticus 18, verse 5). This is why Augustine also declared that Adam had been created as a blessed being, endowed with a good will. For the joy, he said, which is born from the acquisition of this good, is called the blessed life since it elevates the mind peacefully, quietly, and

---

79. Presumably Pierre du Moulin (see note 58 in this chapter).
80. Augustine, *Sermons* (see note 78 in this chapter).

constantly—unless you believe that to live blessedly is something other than to enjoy what is truly and certainly good. See book 1 of the work *On Free Will*, chapters 12, 13, and 14, *On the City of God*, chapter 20.[81] But the law of nature in corrupt man does not know what this love of the true Deity—the Father, the Son, and the Holy Ghost—is, nor does it know this sincere and perfect love of our neighbor; it does not give birth to truly good works, but—if you consider the evil within the soul—only to the appearance of virtue, nor does it lead to eternal beatitude. Otherwise pagans could, by constantly observing the rules of external honesty, aspire to the goal, the ultimate end, which exceeds all of nature after the fall of Adam and all the natural powers [i.e., eternal life]. That would also be contrary to the explicit words of Christ in Mark 16, verse 16. It is the case, therefore, that the law of nature in the state of innocence is not the same as the law of nature in the state of corruption, since the former draws attention to a more sublime dominion and binds humans to it; the latter, however, exists in an inferior sphere: it does, of course, take care that humans do not degenerate into beasts, but does not in any way stimulate the search for and the veneration of God. It is also the case that the law of nature which had informed the mind of Adam was repeated in the Decalogue which corresponded to it exactly; it required that perfection which shone forth in Adam and demanded the highest and most extensive love of God and one's neighbor, as interpreted by Christ, Matthew 22, verse 37.

§49. In §§125ff. of chapter 2[82] I stated that the divine positive laws, which direct the duty of man concerning the worship of God, have eternal beatitude as their immediate purpose, and I immediately related ceremonial law to this. Yet I sensed later that there were some theological arguments which could be put forward against me on that matter. One is that the ceremonial law did not have eternal beatitude as its aim in the sense of being a means to acquiring it, so that whoever rigorously observed the Decalogue would achieve salvation. The ceremonial law was also imposed after man had become corrupt and incapable of being saved through a law, and

81. Augustine, *De Libero Arbitrio: The Free Choice of the Will* (Philadelphia: The Peter Reilly Company, 1937); Augustine, *The City of God Against the Pagans*, ed. R. W. Dyson (Cambridge: Cambridge University Press, 1998).
82. In book 1 of the *Institutes*.

divine wisdom would never have imposed a law for a purpose that could never be achieved. The purpose of this law was rather that the Israelite people and the church, from which the Messiah was to be born, should be distinguished from other nations and that the law should be a guide to this end for those people who were subject to it and had that particular promise. The ceremonial law as law therefore did not save anyone, even if it was adhered to rigorously, but it did contribute to salvation, insofar as it furthered belief in the Messiah. For it cannot be denied that the sacrifices and the other sanctions of the law relate to the faith in Christ, but that the law and its sanctions are one thing, the faith they encourage is another. God, therefore, did not have either temporal well-being or eternal salvation in mind when he framed the ceremonial law, in the sense that it would be obtained through this law. But he prescribed a form of worship which on the whole led humans toward faith and the Messiah and directed them toward him, so that they might achieve salvation through him and by these means. If God intended something with a law, this would be obtained by adhering to the law. In that case God would have done better if he had not given corrupt human nature any law at all and had tried to bring about their salvation without a law, because the honor of saving humans, according to his own order, is due to his grace and to faith alone, etc. What do we reply? To put it briefly: We agree completely that, by observing the ceremonial law, humans cannot acquire eternal beatitude, but we deny that therefore it cannot be said that God intended the eternal beatitude of man in this law. We argue, rather, that because God in imposing this law wanted to provide guidance toward faith in Christ, he thereby intended to save humans. We believe it also has to be said that in the very imposition of this ceremonial law God intended the salvation of man, not immediately, but eventually, insofar as it contributed toward faith. Therefore we note that this phrase that "God had a purpose in the law" is to be understood in two ways: first to refer to an intention, which supplies the law as an immediate means to achieve this end; second, it is understood to refer to an intention, which looks to achieve an end in such a way that the law itself does not supply the means, but only leads us to the means to achieve the end. The former meaning is that used in the objection, but we are concerned with the latter sense in our *Institutes*. I will illustrate through a simile that the latter sense is not inappropriate. Thus it is not inappropriate for me to say that he who studies physic because he wants to later devote his efforts to medicine intends to cure the human body, even when he learns in physic the imperfections to which the body is subject. This is so even though the knowledge of these imperfections is not the means to achieve this cure, but only leads to another discipline which does show the cure, namely, medicine. Yet I can forgive someone who has skimmed my *Institutes* or read them superficially and then raises this objection, because I realize that my choice of words encourages it. For I had said that in the laws which concern the worship of God, including the ceremonial law, God immediately intended the eternal beatitude of humans. How did God intend this salvation in a law if the law itself is not a means to achieving it? The ceremonial law and all the other laws that were published after the fall do not dictate beliefs that are to be held, but actions to be performed, and regulate some matters concerning divine worship. We admit that they look toward eternal life only in the last instance and to the extent that they offer guidance toward faith. But we thereby clearly assert that these same laws are concerned mediately with eternal beatitude. If this is the case, surely, one of the main principles on which our *Institutes* rest would be overturned. Thus, in order both to support my principles and to put to rest this grave doubt, it is all-important that I resolve another ambiguity which is contained in the phrase "to intend something immediately." The word *immediate* is taken either in an absolute sense as a negation of any other means, or conditionally as a negation of certain means. If someone wants to examine accurately what we have discussed in our *Institutes* in the said chapter [2 of book I], §§125ff., it will be clear to him that when we say that "laws regulating divine worship have eternal beatitude as their immediate end," it is not our intention to deny all means, such as faith, but to deny only that these laws concern eternal salvation via temporal well-being, or that they concern temporal well-being and the tranquillity of humanity in the first instance and eternal life in the second. We will explain our meaning again with a simile. If I compare the study of nature with ethics I say correctly, and certainly not inappropriately, that the immediate aim of ethics is the care for the mind; the study of nature, however, has as its immediate end the care of the body. Apart from this comparison, however, or if I compared the study of nature with medicine, it would necessarily follow that the care of the body through the study of medicine is mediated by medicine even though the study of nature would have this care of the body as its immediate aim through the mediation of medicine.

§50. At the end of chapter 2 I discuss the exact difference between jurisprudence and theology and the true boundaries between these two university faculties. I argue there that the explanation of divine laws concerning the duties of men toward their fellow men also belongs to jurisprudence and that this doctrine is shared by jurists and theologians; see §§137, 141, and 142 in that chapter [2]. But in order to remove any remaining doubts on that, I appealed (1) to the common practice in the territories of the Protestant princes, for it is known that in matrimonial cases (and the divine positive law, which also pertains to jurists, applies particularly in these cases) when there is any doubt concerning a prohibition in divine law, opinions are sought not only from the theologians, but from the faculties of law. And this is because the doctrine on marriage among Protestants is part of ecclesiastical jurisprudence, which Carpzov at our university and Brunnemann and the excellent Stryk in Frankfurt an der Oder have explained in greater detail in entire treatises.[83] And in these treatises they also cite opinions of faculties of law on matrimonial cases. Thus from the response of such a faculty of law emerged the controversy between Buchholz, Havemann, and Strauch concerning the case of a marriage with the sister of a deceased wife.[84] Bucholz listed various testimonies of our theologians to prove that matrimonial cases are a secular matter, because matrimony, according to our belief, is not held to be a sacrament; see the responses of the Rinteln jurists, etc., numbers 9 and 10, pages 27ff.[85] (2) The practice of the consistories[86] shows the same, because usually half

83. Benedict Carpzov, *Jurisprudentia ecclesiastica seu consistorialis* (Leipzig, 1649); Johann Brunnemann, *De jure ecclesiastico tractatus posthumus* (Frankfurt an der Oder, 1681). This work was edited by Brunnemann's son-in-law, the jurist Samuel Stryk, who added extensive annotations to the text.

84. See note 27 in this chapter.

85. On Buchholtz see note 28 in this chapter.

86. A *consistory* was a board of officials appointed by the prince to supervise ecclesiastical affairs.

their members are theologians and half are jurists, for no other reason than that spiritual matters concerning eternal salvation pertain primarily to the theologians, while secular matters, which directly concern temporal tranquillity, are the business of the jurists. And in order to show that this is not a gratuitous comment, I appeal (3) to the principal Constitution of the Elector Augustus, the Saxon Elector, in the Regulations of the Leipzig and Wittenberg Consistories, title 1:

> Since not only cases of conscience, but also secular cases must be brought before these consistories and dealt with there, concerning matrimonial cases, the goods and salaries of church employees and schoolmasters, the life and conduct of teachers and congregation, none shall be staffed exclusively with either theologians or secular officials, but in equal measure with persons from both estates, that is, with two learned and pious, upright and honorable theologians, and with two secular officials. Title 8. The opinion or judgment, however, should be formulated and pronounced according to holy Scripture and the laws that are commonly accepted and in general use in our territories. And since a number of eminent theologians, [such as] Luther and Phillip [Melancthon], drew conclusions from Scripture, which concern cases of marriage and other similar matters but are incompatible with the common laws, so the members of our consistories shall pay heed to these, too, and insofar as these have been hitherto observed in our territories and have been accepted through the practice of the consistories, shall formulate their judgments and decisions on that basis.

Therefore, I concluded in §140 of chapter 2 that in this respect jurisprudence is privileged in comparison to medicine and philosophy, because these two must not draw their principles of demonstration from theology. There is no doubt in the case of medicine; nor do the physicians pretend to have the right to do so. In the case of philosophy I recently gave you conclusive proof of this. That is what the venerable Faculty of Theology of our university referred to recently in the program for the ninth Sunday after Trinity this year, displayed in public, which said that "nobody in our university should be permitted to explain the mysteries put forward in Scripture, or to derive what is just and unjust from revelation, which is the duty of moral theology, or to hold classes on the fathers of the ancient church, the dogmas, heresies, rites, and whatever else ecclesiastical history examines, unless he has obtained the right and the privilege of teaching these matters from us after a thorough examination."

§51. In chapter 3, §§65ff., I touch on the mixture of philosophy with theology, which was the worst possible thing introduced by the Scholastics, and in the following paragraphs I include Pneumatics[87] in that. This goes against the authority of many men who enjoy great respect in many matters, so in order that my opinion may not appear too harsh or new to you, I draw on the authority of the illustrious Seckendorff in his *Christen-Staat*,[88] book 3, chapter 7, §2, pages 514ff.: "Our Messiah did not reject the use of the Jewish schools, but rather pointed to them and called them the chair of Moses. What he did reject, however, was the abuse, that is, the mixture of God's word with human opinions and interpretations and the formation of different sects: for it is from the disputes of the schools that the factions of the Pharisees and Sadducees developed, about which much can be read in the New Testament." See also, in the same work, chapter 7, §4, pages 518ff.:

> One does not hear it said that Paul had a philosophical manner of speaking or arguing according to the terms of the art of logic, topical argument, metaphysics, or apodictic argument, which were already in existence by then. He was perfectly capable of forming rational and concise conclusions and using ornate expressions supplied by reason and practice without the artful books and teachings of the Greeks, and he kept the Holy Spirit as an instrument for preaching the word. These are the elements that are left over from the good light of nature and which he purged and sanctified. Thus, when he began to dispute with the sects of the Epicureans and the Stoics in Athens and could adapt himself well to people, becoming, as he himself says, all things to all people, he did not need the philosophical wisdom of the schools, but only proclaimed the gospel of Jesus and the resurrection to them [the sects], regardless

---

87. *Pneumatics* was the science of spiritual being. It usually included the human soul, angels, demons, and God. It was part of philosophy but was directly relevant to the discussion of theological questions. Thomasius was always very critical of this discipline because he believed that it confused theology and philosophy.

88. Veit Ludwig von Seckendorff, *Christen-Stat* (Leipzig, 1685). Seckendorff (1626–92) was a Lutheran politician and political writer. He was also appointed the first chancellor of the new University of Halle but died before it was formally opened.

of how incoherent it seemed to them. And since he spoke publicly (in the *Areopagus*[89]) on the square where executions took place, he did have a great opportunity to start talking on, for example, being as such, the divine nature, or the condition of the world, just like the philosophers who came up with these topics and could conduct nit-picking arguments over them with each other. Yet he did not do it but set aside all such art and artful words and began from a point that seemed the worst possible and made them ignorant idiots: that is, from the altar of the unknown God. He then moved on to the foundation of the word of God, without considering it worth examining or refuting their theology and idolatry in detail, or disputing *de natura deorum,* that is, the nature of God and his properties in metaphysical terms. Instead he began with the article of the Creation and the right knowledge and reverence for God that followed from this: he accused them of idolatry and ignorance. And, leaving aside all their countless and subtle books, he put forward the single testimony of a poet which confirmed Creation, namely, that humans were a divine race or came from God. Thus he left their whole philosophy and subtlety aside, admonished them only to convert by holding up to their eyes the threat of the last judgment and the glorious opportunity, which the judge of the world (Christ risen from the dead) offered through faith.[90] Thus it is evident how this incomparable Apostle or messenger of God, who was directly instructed by heaven, taught Christianity even among the most learned people of that age (these were in Athens which had the most famous school of philosophy). He did this without philosophical art and did not use any tools provided by the learning common at that time, unless he found something in a well-known book that conformed to the article of faith concerning Creation. One also finds that he first taught from the Old Testament in the Jewish schools and then used this to prove that Jesus of Nazareth was the Messiah prophesied in it. He directed his two dearest and best disciples and followers (who became wonderful and holy bishops), that is, Timothy and Titus, to Scripture and to reading and repeating it diligently, just as he warned them to abstain from worldly cleverness and school quarrels.[91] He warned Christians in general of this, as he did in these words to the Colossians: "Beware lest

89. That is, the public council of Athens.
90. Acts 17:15–33.
91. See Paul's letters to Timothy and Titus.

anyone spoil you through philosophy and vain deceit, after the tradition of men, after the rudiments of the world, and not after Christ."[92]

See also chapter 8, §1, page 531: "Very erudite people have already observed that as soon as the philosophers or the learned pagans adopted Christianity and introduced their doctrines and manner of teaching into the church, the quarrels of the schools, of which Saint Paul had warned, increased. Most of the heresies emerged from these, for the same learned men brought their previously held opinions into the church and wanted to judge of the articles of faith according to the rules and modes to which each was accustomed." And §2, pages 534ff.:

> When, however, the old books of the pagan philosophers fell into the hands of the clerics, especially the monks, then Scholastic Theology broke loose, doing more harm than good. It seems to me as if the good monks and priests who first laid their hands on these books were driven by great curiosity and at first made a big secret out of it. They also wanted to be seen to be able to speak and chatter of other things than holy Scripture and the Fathers or the legends and saints' histories, which is what they almost exclusively fed the laity, both high and low. Their action would have been Christian and good if they had burned the recovered pagan books immediately, rather than using them. . . . For unfortunately it seems that they learned to grasp the meaning of God's word with the help of these arts. They acted like someone who wants to furnish a palace according to the example of some random old farmhouse. And if one compares the dignity of holy Scripture with worldly wisdom, then they have mixed gold with copper and lead, pure wine with murky water, by beginning to measure and examine articles of faith according to the standards of philosophy. Then they wanted to know how to talk about God, Christ, the holy sacraments according to the *praedicamenta* and the *predicabilia*, then *substance, accident, quality, quantity, act, potential, moral cause, abstract, concrete,* and other such terms, far more nit-picking than those the pagan philosophers had ever produced, and with invented barbaric expressions that had to be applied to the mysteries of faith, which then had to be examined and weighed according to them. Among other countless terms and their distinction were *otherness, thisness, identity, individuation, whatness, supposite, whereness, voluntariness, eminently,*

92. Colossians 2:8.

formally, entitatively, concomitantly, radically, intentionally, primary and secondary, numeric, precise, reduplicative, and many other similar ones. . . . And since this art has taken over almost the entire clerical estate, it was no longer possible to subdue it. Instead it became as necessary as some others, for once one had gone beyond God's word it was necessary to disprove the errors which developed from this with equal subtlety. This developed in the manner described in the learned proverb concerning the northeasterly wind, which they call *Caecius,* which tends to produce great waves it cannot disperse. . . . And so scholastic theology became a system which nobody could ever finish learning. On the contrary, the quarrels increased to such an extent and arguments were conducted with so much deceit that it was almost impossible to distinguish any longer the true and well-founded opinion or at least rarely possible to form a definite conclusion about it.

See also the additions to chapter 7, §2, page 299:

> Johann Gerhard in his *Theological Method,*[93] final chapter, makes the following comment on the Scholastics: the blessed Luther took the well-founded and salutary decision to ban Scholastic theology, which he called ignorance of the truth and inane fallacy, from our schools, and where one tried to re-introduce it, it was as if one wanted to have acorns instead of bread as food. For, he said, the Scholastics had confused philosophy and theology concerning the principles of disputation. Hence Erasmus compared Scholastic theology, especially as it was practiced at the Sorbonne in Paris, to the centaurs, who according to the poets were half human and half horse.[94]

Thus you will not be surprised that in chapter 3, §61, I reject that term *eminenter,* which the Scholastics use in discussing the divine attributes, because you see that the illustrious Seckendorff in the passages cited above reckoned this, too, among the barbaric terms and distinctions.

§52. In chapter 4, §§35ff. I believe I showed through genuine arguments that it is possible, without damaging Christian religion, to use a fiction concerning something that God has revealed to us as being different. And

---

93. Johann Gerhard, *Methodus studii theologici* (Jena, 1620).

94. A reference to the humanist Desiderius Erasmus (Erasmus of Rotterdam, ca. 1466–1536), a frequent critic of Scholastic theology.

in order that the argument not be conducted in vain, I defined in §38 what I meant by a fiction, namely, the first part of a hypothetical proposition which neither affirms nor denies anything, but which only infers the second part as a consequence from this fiction. This description is appropriate for the incident that gave rise to this controversy. When the illustrious Pufendorf was about to publish his work on natural law, he assumed that one had to abstract from the state of innocence and, when arguing with a pagan, assume the present state of man. On this basis, that is, the hypothesis of the pagan who knows no other state, the pagan must be persuaded of the truth of the natural precepts, however he conceives the origin of humanity. But this is nothing else than to infer a necessary connection between the second part—that is, the precepts of natural law—and the first part of the hypothetical proposition, which the pagan considers true, but the doctor of natural law neither affirms nor denies. The argument that among others is usually advanced against Pufendorf's doctrine is that a Christian must not invent anything. I could not contradict this opinion any more strongly than by showing that a fiction defined in that sense is not contrary to religion and, moreover, differs from a lie, which I define in book 2, chapter 7. Yet, if someone refused to be satisfied by my argument, I would ask him, before he picks a fight with me, to propose his own definition of a fiction and to show that I have not defined it correctly. If he uses the term *fiction* in another sense than I do and refuses to explain his meaning of the term by offering an unambiguous description, nobody can blame me if I abstain from a struggle that would be inglorious, like that of blindfolded gladiators who make the audience laugh but are useless at finding the truth, which should be the purpose of all disputation. He may tell me that hypothetical propositions could not be used against him; for example, that in the trite inference "if an ass flies, he has feathers," the logician does not pretend that the ass flies or has feathers, but only shows the consequence, by which one follows from the other. He may repeat this a hundred times, but I will still uphold my definition of a fiction until he has supplied me with another and better one. Indeed, thinking further on this matter, I can see no way how anybody can deny that in this proposition the prior part *if an ass flies* is a fiction, unless it is that the term *fiction* was not expressly used here. Yet the principles of determining equally strong arguments show clearly that it is one and the same whether you say, "If an ass flies, he has feathers," or you explain your intention thus: "Imagine that an ass flies, then he will have feathers"; just as, again, it does not matter whether you say: "Imagine a person; no matter by what means he has been set in this world, he is nevertheless a social being," or: "If a person is placed in this world, no matter by what means this comes about, he is nevertheless a social being." The arguments that are derived from the definitions of things are normally apodictic, and the description I have provided of the fiction shows that it is not contrary to religion, even if we invent something that has been revealed to be otherwise in Scripture or invent whatever pleases us. It is clear from this that it is a gross violation of the rules of learned debate to accept my definition of the term *fiction* but at the same time criticize the use of fictions and hypothetical propositions, which I used only for the sake of explanation, wishing to show that the reason for the difference is that nothing was to be invented in an argument if the contrary has been revealed by Scripture. For nowhere have I used an argument from analogy, against which otherwise the proof of a disparity would carry a lot of weight. Thus I do not infer that if the fiction "if an ass flies" is valid, then it must also be all right to come up with the fiction that man has been placed in this world, by whatever means, or that there are two kinds of humans in this world, which is a fiction I put forward in §31. So that you do not think I need an argument from analogy, I ask: Do you believe it to be a sin against orthodox religion, if an arithmetician speaks thus: "Let us pretend that there were twelve pots in Canaan in Galilee, of which each held three measures; it follows then necessarily that they were filled with thirty-six measures in total." But here something is invented which Scripture revealed to us differently, namely, that there were only six pots. And I am convinced everybody will say that this fiction of the arithmetician is close to being a lie, because he invented something contrary to revealed truth. And if that is not said, this will not protect him against the accusation that his argument is absurd, even if he put forward as a proof that truth, especially divine truth, is simple, and that therefore what is contrary to it is a lie. Apart from the fact that here a moral lie is confused with a logical error, how is it possible to say that if our definition of a fiction is assumed and holds up, a fiction which neither affirms nor denies anything is contrary to truth? I believe that all remaining doubts concerning my opinion and its orthodoxy will now have been lifted from your minds. I will add a few comments on its novelty. I do not fear being accused of that, because I am convinced that fictions are accepted by scholars in all faculties. I would even be prepared to bet that, even in their dreams when fantasy strays more widely, none of our people would have thought of asserting that a Christian cannot invent something that is contrary to scriptural revelation. Rather, if someone wanted to examine the writings of the theologians more closely, he would undoubtedly be able to collect several examples of such fictions. So far I have not had the leisure to do so carefully, but I will offer you one, which is very clear and based on the authority of a theologian who is absolutely orthodox, that is, our venerable Mr. Alberti. For I read in part 2 of his *Compendium of Natural Law Conforming to Orthodox Theology*,[95] chapter 7, §21, page 139: "Imagine the following impossible situation: that there existed at that time [when Adam distributed a part of his goods among Cain and Abel, so that the former owned all immovables, that is, the fields, the latter the movable possessions, that is, the cattle] so great a number of humans as would have been required to possess the entire globe; then Adam would have had to grant each individual some part of it, because he had received some for each person."

§53. In the same chapter 4, §64, I conclude that sociality is the foundation of the law of nature. I do not want to put forward any new argument to prove this assertion, but will refer to a passage from the illustrious Seckendorff, which will, so to speak, make it obvious to you that our opinion already flourished before the birth of Christ, and that it is therefore older than the doctrine of the Scholastics, who derive natural laws from divine sanctity, and older than the very recent opinion of those who look for it in the state of innocence, and that this illustrious man proved our conception of human sociality. This is contained in the *Entwurff oder Versuch von dem allgemeinen oder natuerlichen Recht*, which is added to his German speeches, pages 442ff., §§10 and 11:[96]

95. See note 64 in this chapter. Valentin Alberti was one of Thomasius's main critics.
96. Veit Ludwig von Seckendorff, *Teutsche Reden* (Leipzig, 1686).

It is not difficult to see what the real characteristic and formal nature of this right is, namely, that it instructs the nature and reason of man and regulates his sociability with other human beings, or rather presupposes it. For because all humans have a creator and are the descendants of one man (a fact which the pagans suspected, but we know as a certain truth from God's word), and have been created by God in such a way, both in their body and soul, that one human being cannot live without another, so the entire nature of man is such that he forms societies with others, not only in the conjunction of man and woman (for this is characteristic also of animals) and not out of a pure instinct, the way herds gather, but with deliberation and rational thought. Therefore, it must be posited that not just need, but the nature and reason of man, which are derived from the divine order, demand sociality and a form and just manner of dealing with each other in such a society. This is evident from, among other things, the fact that if it occurred from mere need, a man who had everything he required for his sustenance and comfort would not desire the company of other humans. He desires it zealously, however, unless he is deprived of natural reason or corrupted by deeply rooted sinful habits or bad education. So, like others, Cicero the learned Roman proves that such a desire is inborn, general, and a work of nature. Thus he says: "Humans are born for the sake of other humans, so that they can be useful to each other and help each other." 1. *Off.*[97] "Next to God it is man who can be most useful to man." 2. *Off.*[98] "Nature requires that one human being advise and help another, whoever he may be, for no other reason than that he is human." 3. *Off.*[99] "Nature drives us to want to help many people, especially in order to instruct them and make them wise. For this reason it is not easy to find someone who would not happily teach another what he knows. Thus we are not only eager to learn, but to teach others." 2. *De finib.*[100] We differ from animals mainly in that we speak with each other and can communicate our opinion to each other. In another passage he provides a parable by an old philosopher and says:

97. Cicero, *On Duties* [*De officiis*], ed. M. T. Griffin and E. M. Atkins (Cambridge: Cambridge University Press, 1991), bk. I, chap. 22, p. 10.

98. Ibid., bk. II, chap. 11, p. 67.

99. Ibid., bk. III, chap. 27, pp. 109–10.

100. Cicero, *On Ends* [*De finibus bonorum et malorum*], trans. H. Rackham, Loeb Classical Library (Cambridge, Mass.: Harvard University Press, 1999).

If it were possible that a man were elevated to heaven and there saw the glories of the stars and other beautiful things, and then returned to earth, this would no longer give him any pleasure and joy, if he did not find or meet anybody with whom he could talk of the things he had seen and heard.

It can easily be concluded from this that if God had not commanded this sociality, humans would not require any other right in this life than what we see in animals, who have an instinct for self-preservation and seek to satisfy their lust.

And although some favor the opinion that this means of demonstrating sociality achieves little among pagan nations and barbarians, we nevertheless oppose to this the words of the illustrious author, ibidem, page 440, §6:[101]

The fact that we who are Christians and have specific and detailed civil laws speak about, teach, and inquire after this general divine or natural law has this reason and purpose in particular, among others: (1) that we recognize all the more our beatitude which we receive from the revelation of the divine word and can judge on good and evil all the better. For this reason we also believe the law of God and nature exists in order to discipline us, to direct us to Christ. Thus we do not only realize our faults and errors more readily, but also live all the more in a holy and just manner, because we are bound to it with twofold, even threefold ties. For we are under an obligation to do what is right, on the basis of nature and reason insofar as we are human beings and inhabitants of this world, on the basis of the laws of the magistrate insofar as we are citizens and members of our fatherland, and on the basis of God's word insofar as we are believers and Christians. (2) that God's word may not be accepted by all nations, and our civil and territorial law is even less accepted by strangers, but the rules and general reasons of natural right are valid in all human affairs. Even infidels or those outside the church, that is, those who are strangers and not subject to our government, must conform to these, since they must understand and allow themselves to be guided by the teachings of nature and reason, right and wrong, especially in matters of peace and war and in commerce and trade, even though

101. Seckendorff, *Teutsche Reden.*

they neither respect nor recognize either the foundations of our religion or our civil laws.

Furthermore, Boecler in the Prolegomena to Grotius's *On the Rights of War and Peace*[102] pointed out that according to the most ancient philosophers the origin of law and justice had to be derived from the principle of sociality. Mr. Schilter proves this opinion in his *Philosophy of Law*, chapter 3, §6, page 84.[103] Add Augustine, *On the City of God*, book 19, chapters 5, 13, and 14.

§54. So far I have supported those opinions that might seem either doubtful or ambiguous in the first part of the *Institutes*. In the remaining two books this sort of explanation did not seem necessary because there I put forward what I meant in a little more detail in order to avoid obscurity. But you should not think that I defend my opinions out of sheer pertinacity and a perverse, instinctive self-love, rather than a desire to find out the truth. And in order to set you an example to follow, and so that you do not think it shameful to abandon your previous opinion after you have been taught something better, I will also indicate some passages which I later believed required some correction. I have already pointed out most of these in the discourse itself. In chapter 1, §53, page 18, the last words are to be deleted: "although the locomotive power of beasts differs from this, since it is devoid of thought." In the same chapter 1, §75 as a whole is to be corrected as follows: The actions somebody performs under the influence of great fear, such as a promise, are sometimes imputed and sometimes not imputed, whether the action is contrary to the laws or not. This will become clear from the full discussion in the chapter on the duty of man concerning promises. In chapter 2, §116, you should correct the words contained there as follows: "Moreover we believe that the use of this distinction is adequate, because affirmative precepts of divine law always allow for an exception in cases of supreme necessity, while negative precepts do not." In the same chapter the paragraphs 127, 128, 129, and 130 should

102. Boecler, *In Hugonis Grotii Jus belli et pacis commentatio.*
103. Johann Schilter, *Manuductio philosophiae moralis ad veram, nec simulatam jurisprudentiam* (Jena, 1676).

be deleted. In chapter 4, §59, write as follows: "And to be precise, the pleasure of the senses will be very rare and practically nonexistent outside society"; and remove the subsequent words of this paragraph, "Through induction . . ." until the end. In book II, chapter 1, §164, following the words: "I do not think so," put these in their place after deleting the others: "For the law of nature, which forbids killing a person, has itself a tacit exception of necessity, whenever this does not principally have the violation of the law as its object and there is no means of evading it by a natural instinct, as is explained in the examples listed." Thus, the later paragraphs 165, 166, 167, 168, 169, 170, 171, 172, and 173 should be removed.[104]

104. In the 1688 edition of the *Institutes* this paragraph is followed by another with a list of errata. These have been silently corrected in the present edition.

BOOK I

∞ CHAPTER I ∞

On Jurisprudence in General

§1. The term *jurisprudence* involves two concepts, prudence and right [*jus*].

§2. There is no better way for us to understand prudence than by going over the different faculties [*habitus*][1] in a little more detail.

§3. A faculty is either *infused*, that is, one which man possesses without previous knowledge, or *acquired*, for which labor and effort are necessary.

§4. The *acquired* is gained either through *supernatural* or through *natural* powers.

§5. The faculty which is acquired through *natural* powers is either *intellectual*, if it is based in the intellect and is acquired through acts of the intellect, that is, affirmation and denial, or it is *voluntary*, if it is based in

---

1. The term *faculty* (*habitus*) is used here in a technical philosophical sense that is ultimately derived from Aristotle's *Nicomachean Ethics*, 1103a, and describes the principles of action in human nature. H. Rackham translated the *Nicomachean Ethics* for the Loeb Classical Library (Cambridge, Mass.: Harvard University Press, 1947).

the will and is acquired through acts of the will, that is, the desire for or aversion to something.[2]

§6. The *intellectual* faculty has as its object either *principles,* which may be theoretical or practical, in which case it is called *understanding,* or *conclusions* from these.

§7. In the latter case, concerning conclusions, this faculty is either *theoretical* and aims to understand the creator and creation, or *practical* and aims to understand human actions.

§8. The *theoretical* has as its subject either *being as such* and is called *ontology* (nowadays usually *metaphysics*), or certain *species of being.*

§9. And this ontology either considers the *creator*—this is called *wisdom* [*sapientia*], and once used to be called *metaphysics,* but today is termed *the first part of pneumatics*—or it considers *corporeal creatures* and is called *science.*

§10. Science, however, examines corporeal creatures either with respect to their essence and qualities, which is what *physics* does, or with respect to quantity, which is the subject of *mathematics.*

§11. We now turn to the *practical* faculty. Its synonym is *prudence,* which takes on different names according to the diversity of human activities. If these actions are those of people living in a *civil society,* it is called *political prudence;* if they are the actions of those living in *domestic society,* it is called *economic prudence.*

§12. Each of the two is concerned with *future* and *past* actions. The former is *advisory* in a broad sense; the latter is *judicial* in the broadest sense.

§13. Advisory prudence is occupied either with one's own actions or with those of others.

---

2. Paragraphs 3 to 5 are modified and expanded in later editions.

§14. And it is occupied with the actions of *superiors,* or *equals,* or *inferiors.*

§15. The last of these is given the special name *legislative prudence,* which is the noblest part of *jurisprudence* in a broad sense. The other forms retain the title of *advisory prudence,* and that part which advises the superior in legislating or acting according to the norm of the divine laws is the other part of jurisprudence in the *broad* sense.

§16. Moreover, the actions of men, both future and past, are *honest,* that is, they conform to a law and are predicated of man insofar as he is rational; or they are *pleasant,* that is, they delight the external senses and concern man considered as an animal; or they are useful, that is, they are directed to the *preservation of the individual.* In the last case man is considered as a living physical being.

§17. That *prudence* which is concerned with honest actions in general is jurisprudence in the broad sense, and that which is concerned in particular with the honest actions of others in the past is judicial prudence in the *strict* sense, or jurisprudence in the strict sense, or the third part of jurisprudence in the broad sense.

§18. But that prudence which has as its object the pleasant or useful actions of men is prudence in the sense of skill [*ars*].

§19. If man directs these, as he should, toward honest actions, this is good and he remains prudent; if he does not do so, he is said to be astute or cunning.

§20. If he is obviously without prudence in skill, he is termed *imprudent.*[3]

§21. The faculty of the will remains. This is acquired by actions that are prescribed by law and in that case is a *moral virtue,* or by actions prohib-

3. Paragraphs 11 to 20 are modified in later editions.

ited by law, when it is called a *moral vice,* or, finally, by actions permitted by law, when it is nothing more than *skill.*

§22. These points had to be presented in a little more detail, because the common doctrine of the Peripatetics on the division of the faculties and the various kinds of intellectual virtues is full of countless mistakes, which anyone who has compared their teachings with what has been said so far will easily detect.

§23. We cannot but point out here a little more fully that according to general opinion the difference between theoretical and practical intellectual faculties is that the latter also have action as their object, but the former have contemplation as their ultimate end.

§24. Now this error is not only contrary to right reason, since all theoretical faculties have practical ends, as can easily be shown empirically. It also conflicts with true religion and is the result of the false opinion of the Gentiles, who believed that the essence of God consisted in contemplation.

§25. Various comments by the great Aristotle, whom they follow, are relevant here: "That beatitude based on contemplation is nobler than that based on practice; that the former is accompanied by a more sincere pleasure than practice; that theoretical contemplation joins humans more closely to God than practice does"; similarly: "That prudence serves wisdom . . ."[4]

§26. Instead of these trifles we prefer the saying of Paul, the wise Apostle who above all contemplation preferred love that is born from prudence.[5]

§27. This is all we have to say concerning the term *prudence.* The term *right* is understood in several ways. Above all, it is understood either as *law* or as *an attribute of a person.*

---

4. See, for example, Aristotle, *Metaphysics* 1072b 24–30, trans. Hugh Tredennick, Loeb Classical Library (London: Heinemann, 1933–36), vol. 2, bk. XII, chap. VII, p. 151.

5. Presumably a reference to 1 Corinthians 13.

§28. *Law* is defined in one way by Grotius, in another by Aristotle, and in yet another by jurists. The Scholastics, however, labor over this question in ways that are strange and inept at the same time. We define it thus: "A law is a command by a ruler obliging subjects to guide their actions in accordance with this command."

§29. According to this definition, a law differs from advice and from a pact in various ways. And that is not controversial. You should, however, note the following in particular, because it is not commonly accepted: "A law is always binding, even without a pact; a pact never without a law," though a law sometimes obliges via a pact. Then the pact is only the occasion for the obligation, just as opening the doors is the occasion for letting light into the room.

§30. The author of a law is always a *ruler* [*imperans*]. We would rather use this term than the term *superior,* as others do. For apart from the superiority associated with rule there are other superiorities, of order, for example, or of dignity, as well as superiority based on beneficence. Here we are not concerned with these.

§31. It follows that God does not act according to a law and that the eternal law is a fiction of the Scholastics.

§32. He on whom the law is imposed is the *subject* or the *person obeying.* This presupposes reason, and as brutes lack reason, they are not bound by law.

§33. Thus *man* remains. Therefore law is commonly termed a norm of human actions. But the action of man in conformity to law is, in one word, called *duty.*

§34. But there are different kinds of human actions. Some are specific to man, others are common to him and to animals and plants. Therefore, we must determine which ones law can regulate. And here we first need to form a clear idea of *man himself and his essence* and must rid ourselves of certain prejudices.

§35. *Man* is a rational animal. This is how man is commonly defined. Nor does the *scala praedicamentalis* of substance in the books on logic allow any other definition, even though it neither corresponds to the intention of Aristotle nor is to the taste of Porphyrius, the inventor of this scale.[6] But the same definition is subjected to a variety of criticisms by Chrysostomus, Cardano, van Helmont, Antoine le Grand, and others.[7] We will retain it but add the necessary explanation.

§36. We do not believe an *animal* to be a living body with powers of sensation, but a living body endowed with locomotive powers. Indeed, as the most acute philosophers have shown us, animals lack sensation—that is, internal sensation—without which the external senses do not deserve the name of senses, and they are not moved in any other way than clockwork, except that the more subtle particles of air sometimes strike those animal organs which are the seat of the external senses in man and thereby cause internal movements.

§37. I know that this hypothesis will not please those who measure the truth of assertions by their antiquity. Yet, even if I could make no other reply to them, I would at least urge them to tell me, if, as I hope, they do not attribute powers of reasoning to beasts, what the difference is between [on one hand] basic sensation, the imagination and memory, which they attribute to beasts, and [on the other] human reason.

§38. Therefore, just as man has life in common with plants, he has the powers of locomotion in common with beasts. What remains is covered by the term *rational*. But human reason is nothing other than thought.

6. The *scala praedicamentalis* was a schematized overview of the different kinds of being and their attributes ("predicates"). The most famous example was the tree of the Neoplatonist philosopher Porphyry (A.D. 233–ca. 305), which starts out with "substance" at the top and includes in descending order such items as "corporeal," "living," "animal," and "man."

7. St. John Chrysostom (A.D. ca. 347–407), Syrian churchman and a doctor of the church; Girolamo Cardano (1501–76), Italian mathematician, physician, and astrologer; Johann Baptista van Helmont (1579–1644), Flemish chemist, physiologist, and physician; Antoine le Grand (1629–99), French Catholic theologian and philosopher.

See Descartes' wise statement: "Man when he understands something, thinks; when he wills, thinks; when he feels, thinks."[8]

§39. It follows automatically that the two functions of our reason that are usually listed, namely, the *intellect* and the *will,* need to be supplemented by a third, namely, *sensation,* which is distinct from locomotion but includes the sensitive appetite.

§40. *Sense* is commonly divided into *internal* and *external.* Vision, hearing, smelling, taste, and touch usually represent the external senses, to which some add sexual lust as a sixth; others add a seventh and eighth to all of these, thirst in the mouth and hunger in the stomach. The internal sensations are reduced to three kinds: basic sensation, imagination, and memory.

§41. All external senses, however many they are, are passions of the body, not actions of the soul. But insofar as there is a simple apprehension of these things, the result is a sense perception which we can accept being described as *basic sensation,* just as *imagination* is used to describe the sensation by which man forms ideas for himself from these passions or when he is prompted by them. Finally, *memory* is the term for the sensation by which man remembers a sense impression, while *reminiscence* is the term used if this act of remembering takes place by means of ratiocination.

§42. The Peripatetics, however, say and teach that all senses perceive sensible objects, the external senses passively, the internal actively. But just as passive perception is a fiction, so I do not understand how active perception can exist without thought; and so they who teach this must concede that the internal senses are identical to the power of perception of the rational soul, or else they themselves have no idea what they are teaching.

8. René Descartes, "Principles of Philosophy," Principle IX, in *The Philosophical Works of Descartes,* vol. I.

§43. Furthermore, the *sensitive appetite,* as it is described in the schools, is nothing other than a will which approves of the object that delights the body. And if this desire is not contrary to the law, it is fine; if not, the will of man is perverted. Yet such a perversion of the will does not mean that it can be treated as part of a sensitive soul that is common to humans and beasts any more than perverted reason can. For in either case man still thinks, even when he reasons perversely and desires perversely.

§44. Intellect and will are left. If we disregard the ancient fables of some intellect acting outside man, *intellect* is understood either in a broad sense which includes intellective memory, or in a strict sense that is opposed to it. Indeed the intellect of man either apprehends the objects of the external senses *directly,* by forming a proposition on their nature or goodness from the accidental properties affecting the sense organs and delighting the body, or by forming unclear ideas of objects which it has perceived through the senses previously; or it *reasons* by meditating further on the truth of these propositions, the goodness of the object and on the ideas of it.

§45. The prior faculty retains the title of *intellect,* while the other is commonly described as *intellective memory.* We will call the former the first operation of the intellect, the latter the second, which can, however, be varied in infinite ways depending on whether it does more or less. If you want to call the first operation *reason* and the second *ratiocination,* we will not object either.

§46. Thus, we do not need to agonize over the widespread controversy whether there are three, four, or however many operations of the mind, especially as the first operation of the mind that is taught in the schools does not exist, and our division is more useful, about which I will say more soon.

§47. Therefore, among the internal senses the one which is called *basic* pertains to the first operation of the intellect; *imagination* and *memory* pertain to the second.

§48. It is common to divide the intellect into *theoretical* and *practical*. But apart from the fact that this division seems to have been invented once upon a time in order to show the difference between the reason of brutes and that of humans, and that there is the same snake in the grass which we detected above when we were discussing theoretical and practical faculties, I also do not know whether this distinction would be of much use to us, even though we may tolerate it with respect to the object of intellectual activity.

§49. But just as the intellect judges on the nature of things and their relationship to man, so the will determines what is to be done by man. And this decision of the will follows immediately from either the first operation of the intellect or the second. The first of these desires *directly;* the *latter* chooses. You could thus describe the former as *appetite,* the latter as *choice* or as *will in the strict sense.*

§50. The first motions in the *sensitive appetite,* as it is commonly described, concern the simple appetite, while the other motions of the sensitive appetite, as well as the whole rational appetite, pertain to choice by the will.

§51. The ordinary process of reasoning and of the actions of man is therefore as follows. After external objects have affected the external senses, there follows the first operation of the intellect. This is received by the appetite, which either directly commands the locomotive power or passes the matter on to the second operation of the intellect to be considered, and after that chooses and impels the locomotive force, etc. From this it is clear that the axiom "Nothing is in the intellect which was not in the senses" is true without limitations, as is the following: "There is no desire for something that is unknown."

§52. Since, therefore, man lives, is nourished, grows, moves from one place to another, feels, understands, and wills, it must be determined which human actions are subject to a law. In sum, those that are subject to the decision of man. But these are not the actions usually attributed to the vegetative soul, nor are they the passions of the external senses, the first operation of the intellect, or the first motions of the appetite. The remaining actions, therefore, which are controlled by the decision of man are the passing on of a decision to the second operation of the intellect, in some sense the second operation of the mind itself, and the choice following it, as well as the locomotive powers.

§53. Yet the common statement that "the sensitive appetite is subject to the command of the will" does not hold true for its first motions, just as the common argument that the locomotive power always depends on the decision of man is not true. The exception here is the locomotive force which man uses instinctively to ward off imminent harm to the body, although the locomotive power of brutes also differs from this, since it is devoid of thought!

§54. But just as it is certain that in our intellect and especially in its second operation there is a natural rectitude which, given the requisite attention, will not allow us to be deceived in moral matters, so man's will in the strict sense is entirely free. It is also a true axiom that the will cannot be coerced, although it always desires what is good in general and often is inclined by a peculiar disposition of character, the temperament of the humors, the nature of the climate and soil, the semen, age, diet, health, occupation, etc., as well as by the shape of the organs of the body, habits, passions, and some diseases, and also by the external actions of others; but he must always be guided by the obligation imposed on him by his superior.

§55. Because of this liberty of the will, actions are imputed to man; that is, man is rightly held to be their author and is required to be answerable for them, and the effects of these actions are attributed to him. Therefore, we like the opinion of the illustrious Rachel very much, that there is one beginning of human actions—namely, choice—not four, as is commonly argued—namely, conscience, volition strictly speaking, deliberation, and choice.[9]

9. Samuel Rachel, *Dissertatio moralis de principiis actionum humanarum* (Helmstedt, 1660).

§56. Furthermore, just as human actions are called *moral* in relation to a law, so the judgment on these actions by an intellect imbued with the knowledge of the laws is called *conscience*. This is either *antecedent* to human actions or *subsequent*.

§57. The *antecedent* conscience judges either correctly according to the law or erroneously. Therefore, another division of the conscience is into *right* and *erroneous*.

§58. *Right* conscience either knows how to demonstrate its judgment from certain and undoubted principles or draws on commonplace arguments. Therefore, right conscience (for erroneous conscience can only be probable) is generally subdivided into *right conscience* properly speaking (we will call this demonstrative) and *probable* right conscience.

§59. The Scholastics added the notion of a *doubtful conscience,* that is, when the judgment of the intellect is undecided and cannot discern whether something is good or bad and so whether it is to be done or omitted. But this is not a form of judgment. It is the suspension of judgment and therefore not a form of conscience.

§60. More relevant here would be the *scrupulous* conscience, which is close to doubt, [namely] when the judgment of the intellect is accompanied by anxious fear that the thing which somebody considered good might be bad, and vice versa. This belongs more frequently to the erroneous conscience than to the right conscience.

§61. The rules, however, which the learned have formulated as guidance for the states of conscience we have talked about either follow automatically from what has been said above or else they are obscure and doubtful.

§62. *Subsequent* conscience, insofar as it approves correctly what has been done or condemns wrongdoing, is subdivided into *tranquil* and *restless,* or, as we say in German, a good and a bad conscience.

§63. Opposed to the voluntary actions of man, which are also called *spontaneous*, are the actions performed against his will. These are so partly because of a deficiency of the *understanding*, partly because of a defect of the *will*.

§64. To the *understanding* are opposed *ignorance* and *error*. Either of these defects is *vincible* or *invincible*, and it is either *efficient* or *concomitant*. All these points are clear from the standard books on ethics.

§65. Opposed to the *will* are *coercion* and *fear*. Fear is described in various ways, depending in part on the person causing it (whether he has the rightful power to instill fear or not) or on the person suffering fear (whether he is a constant man or not).

§66. The above allows us easily to formulate a response to particular questions concerning the imputability and morality of human actions and the degree to which they can be subject to laws. (1) Actions that are committed by one person, as well as operations of other matters of whatever kind and events of whatever kind, cannot be imputed to another person, except insofar as he can and is obliged to influence these or insofar as he has anything to do with them.

§67. He has something to do with the actions of others if he furthers them, commands them, consents to them, gives the persons performing the action a guarantee, or participates in their profit, gives advice, praises, assents, does not forbid, or hinder, or dissuade, and does not make known when he is obliged to do any of these things.

§68. Thus the actions of others can be imputed to these people, although it is imputed to the former primarily, to the latter secondarily. More on that in its proper place.

§69. (2) If it is not in the power of a particular person to determine whether what is in him or is not in him is there or is not there, this cannot be imputed to him, unless he did not apply the obligatory diligence in ridding himself of defects and introducing what is free of defects instead.

§70. (3) He who does not have an occasion to act and is not responsible for it will not be blamed for his failure to act.

§71. (4) Those deeds that are perpetrated as a result of invincible and efficacious ignorance or error are not imputed. But where ignorance or error is only concomitant or vincible the action is imputed. One example is the ignorance of laws that have been properly published.

§72. (5) The error of a third person, be it vincible or invincible, cannot be blamed on another who is not guilty of the error of the third person. In such a case it is more equitable for the erring person to be blamed.

§73. (6) Those actions that are beyond the powers of a person are not imputed, except insofar as he is responsible for the fact that they are impossible actions. Here the rule applies that *nobody is bound to perform impossible actions.*

§74. (7) Those actions to which a person is coerced are not imputed.

§75. (8) The actions somebody performs under the influence of great fear, such as a promise, are sometimes imputed and sometimes not imputed, whether the action is contrary to the laws or not. This will become clear from the full discussion in the chapter on the duty of man in relation to himself and in the chapter on the duty of man concerning promises.[10]

§76. (9) The actions of men lacking the use of reason are not imputed to them.

10. This paragraph reflects Thomasius's own revisions in later editions of the *Institutes* (see, for example, the German edition printed in Halle in 1709). These revisions were incorporated here because the precise meaning of this paragraph in the first edition of 1688 is not entirely clear.

§77. (10) In a human court it is very rare for actions committed in sleep or in dreams to be imputed.

§78. The author of law is either God or man. The former exercises his command by virtue of his right of creation independently of the consent of man. Man acquires the right to command either immediately through a divine concession or via the consent of another human. From this follows the first division of law into *divine* and *human.*

§79. Opposed to laws is their *modification* when the command itself is abolished either wholly or in part, and *dispensation* when one or the other of the subjects is exempted from a law which otherwise would pertain to him and from its obligation while the law remains in force for all others.

§80. Therefore, those people are mistaken who confuse *dispensation* with *restrictive interpretation.*

§81. Only the person who can pass a law can change it and grant dispensation from it.

§82. Right, understood as an attribute of a person, is an active moral quality conferred by a superior, which enables this person either rightfully to receive something from some other person with whom he or she lives in a society, or to do something.

§83. That is called an *active* moral quality which extends the liberty of man, even though it is sometimes used to describe a passive physical experience, for example, the right of a beggar to receive alms. It is opposed to a *passive* moral quality which restricts the liberty of man, which is what an *obligation* does, even though this restriction often denotes a physical action, for example, the obligation of the rich man to give alms.

§84. In explaining the origin of right the learned are either silent or disagree in strange ways; some argue that nature produces right, others say that it is law; some say it is property, others consent, and others again say that it is one of these two.[11]

§85. We must first of all distinguish the right of God and that of humans. The former is a right only by analogy and is very different from the right of humans. For God has this from himself through Creation. But the right of humans must ultimately be derived from the will of God, and in general from the will of a superior, which produces a right insofar as it increases liberty and, insofar as it restricts it, is called a law and is the origin of obligation. Consent on both sides is only an occasional and nonessential cause. Nature considered physically is irrelevant here, as is property, which is already a form of right.

§86. Right pertains to a person. A person here denotes a human being considered in his state [*status*]. A *state* is a quality which affects man and according to which his right varies.

§87. A *person* is either *simple,* that is, a single human individual, although he may participate in several states, or *composite* and formed by the union of several individuals in a particular state. The latter is called a college, society, university, etc.

§88. Thus, we will not discuss the right of God and of angels because that is not relevant here.

§89. By the word *something* in the definition of a right I mean a corporeal creature in general, be it human or inferior to man, be it a substance or an accident, something which is traded or which is not traded. Thus, again, neither God nor angels are relevant here.

§90. This right is demanded from another human with whom one lives in a society. For man alone is the immediate and primary object of right.

11. It is unclear what Thomasius means by "one of these two."

§91. A *society* is a union of several humans for a certain end.

§92. Nevertheless, the term *society* is understood so broadly that it includes the society between God and humans in an analogical sense.

§93. Society in this broad sense is divided into *unequal,* which is that between persons who are different in kind and one of whom commands the others; *equal,* which differs from unequal societies in both respects [i.e., they are between persons of the same kind, none of whom commands the others], and *mixed,* which exists between persons of the same kind, one of whom commands the others.

§94. The only unequal society is that between God and man. Human societies are either equal or mixed.

§95. Human society is either *natural,* toward which man is led by divine command or by the concern for the utility of all humans, or *conventional,* which humans enter into for the sake of a particular benefit.

§96. Since these forms of particular benefit vary in infinite ways, *conventional* societies, therefore, are *infinite* in number. *Natural* societies are divided into *simple* (that is, *conjugal, domestic,* and *paternal*) and *composite.*

§97. Simple societies are the direct components of the house or the family. Several families compose a *village,* a *district,* a *city,* or a *commonwealth.* What consists of several villages is called a *commonwealth* or a *province.* Finally, a society composed of several commonwealths is a *society of nations.*

§98. Among the natural societies this last one is the only *equal* society [in the time] after original sin. Among conventional societies there are several examples of equal and of mixed ones.

§99. These points had to be made because of the various disagreements among the learned. Some of them clearly ignore the first division of society [into equal, unequal, and mixed]; some confuse unequal with mixed societies; some consider divine society to be a form of equal society, while others deny that it is relevant for civil life. Some consider all societies to be unequal; others consider all to be equal. Some ignore the other division of societies [into natural and conventional], while others either reject natural society or do not describe it correctly. And some define the village and the commonwealth differently or say something different about the society of nations.

§100. I return to the definition of right and put forward the following axioms: (1) Outside a society there is no right.

§101. (2) In every society there is right.

§102. (3) In an unequal society right lies only with the superior. In an equal or mixed society right is common to both sides.

§103. The terms *to have* and *to do* in the definition of right are related to the division of right into perfect and imperfect, even though others are of a different opinion.

§104. First, *right*[12] is of course divided into *perfect,* which Grotius calls a *faculty,* and *imperfect,* or an *aptitude,* as he has it. The former is the power by which I can coerce another who does not want to fulfill his obligation to render what is due. The latter is a different matter. Here the fulfillment of the obligation is left to the shame and conscience of the person who has the obligation corresponding to this right.

§105. The means of enforcing a right is called *war,* if it takes place among those who live in the state of nature. Among those, however, who live in civil society, it is called *punishment or legal action.*

§106. The point of this division, according to Grotius, is that strict justice corresponds to faculty and attributive justice to aptitude. But just as

---

12. This enumeration of characteristics of right is continued in §114 of this chapter.

this great man was wrong in presenting his strict justice as identical to commutative justice and his attributive justice as identical to distributive justice in Aristotle's sense, so we would feel more comfortable without this Grotian division of justice [into strict and attributive], even though we could tolerate it. For it is not useful to us in any way and does not add anything to our division of right, and we would feel even happier if we could do without the Aristotelian division of justice, which is more suited to torturing minds than to educating them.[13]

§107. We would rather like to look for the particular usefulness of perfect and imperfect right by asking what violation of a right should lead to a legal action in a civil society and above all by determining by what right the prince may take up arms against someone who is inflicting harm on him.

§108. Therefore, we must briefly explain the signs indicating the two rights [perfect and imperfect], for Grotius does not discuss these. These signs, however, vary according to the different kinds of societies. (1) In an unequal society the only superior, that is, God, has a right over man and this right is perfect.

§109. (2) Among those living in an equal society the right that is part of natural liberty and which gives rise to agreements, and in general every right except that concerning the duties of humanity, is perfect.

§110. (3) In a mixed society the right of the superior over his subjects is always perfect, even with respect to the performance of the duties of humanity.

§111. (4) On the other hand, the right of subjects over superiors as such, even if it is based on pacts, is normally imperfect.

---

13. That is, the division of justice into distributive and commutative (see Aristotle, *Nicomachean Ethics,* 1130b).

§112. I said "as such" to avoid the objection that a wife, children, and servants sometimes have the right to legal action against the *paterfamilias.*

§113. I also said "normally." In extraordinary cases the prince grants his subjects the right to a legal action against himself, though these are legal actions only in an improper sense. They are certainly not coercive remedies.

§114. Second, with respect to the source from which right is derived it can be divided into *connate,* which man has immediately from God without the consent of the person who is placed under an obligation (the power of parents, for example), and *acquired,* which belongs to him on the basis of an agreement with another, such as sovereignty.

§115. Third, a division of right, or rather of faculty in particular, derives from the object. For the object of right is either the *actions* of others or the *things* belonging to others—actions insofar as I direct them (which is called authority [*imperium*]) or insofar as they do not interfere with me.

§116. I say "insofar as they do not interfere with me." This refers either to my personal actions and is called liberty, or to the use and disposition of my physical possessions, which is called property.

§117. The things of others are the object of right in that either the thing itself is the principal subject of consideration and the other person the secondary subject or the person is the principal subject of consideration while the thing is the secondary subject. We will call the former a right in a thing, the latter, credit.

§118. The thing is the principal subject of consideration when the person, whoever it is, possesses this particular thing and is under an obligation to me. The person is the principal subject of consideration when a certain individual is required to give me a thing, whether he owns it or not.

§119. In other cases the terms *authority, liberty,* etc., are understood in a different sense. For the term *authority* is also taken in a broad sense and is applied to property. Thus Grotius granted the authority over the sea to a commonwealth. Likewise, we speak of authority over a territory, etc.

§120. *Liberty* is also understood as a natural ability of humans to do what their physical powers allow them to do, without consideration of other humans. And then it is not a form of right, but sometimes even its opposite.

§121. It will be more appropriate to discuss the various meanings of *property, right in a thing,* and *credit* in connection with Roman jurisprudence.

§122. Fourth, the faculty of those living in civil society is either *common* or *eminent.* The *common faculty* is that of the subjects, the *eminent* that of him who holds power in the commonwealth over the things and persons in that commonwealth.

§123. This distinction can be applied to the above. For liberty is either *eminent,* which is otherwise described as *liberty of the ruler* and coincides with sovereignty (unless you wanted to say that liberty concerns the prince himself, sovereignty the relation of the prince to those below him), or it is *common* liberty, which is also called *personal* liberty.

§124. Concerning the distinction of authority into eminent and common, I do not think there can be any doubt what kind of power of command the head of a household enjoys.

§125. However, disputes have arisen over eminent property rights. We do not see a sufficient reason for abandoning the division of property rights into eminent and common.

§126. It is the same with the right over a thing and credit.

§127. The usefulness of this distinction is evident from the following rule: "whenever common right conflicts with eminent right, the former must invariably give way to the latter." This is clear from what has been said about perfect and imperfect right, and can easily be demonstrated by inductive argument from examples of liberty, authority, etc.

§128. We should finally [fifth] add that division according to which *right* is either *natural* or that *of nations* or *civil*. But in truth this is the same as the division of right into connate and acquired, apart from the fact that it has three elements.

§129. For the right that takes its origin immediately from the will of God is usually called *natural right* [*ius naturalis*]. That which is produced by an agreement between different nations is called *the right of nations* [*ius gentium*]. Finally, what is derived from the will of a human sovereign is termed *civil right* [*ius civilis*].

§130. Accordingly, liberty belongs to natural right. Property, contract, and servitude are matters of the right of nations. Legally binding promises and in some sense the power of the head of household are said to belong to civil right.

§131. Yet we must beware of confusing these meanings of the term *right* with the division of law [*lex*] into natural law, the law of nations, and civil law, especially as this confusion is not uncommon among jurists and moral philosophers.

§132. This observation is of use in many questions, as will be shown in its proper place. The particular reason for avoiding the confusion [between right and law] is that the right of humans, insofar as it is a faculty, can be changed completely by a superior, even if it is a natural right or part of the right of nations. We will explain below that the opposite is true of natural law and the law of nations.

§133. Related to this observation is the well-known rule that "everybody can renounce his right," though I believe that this must be qualified as follows: "unless this right is a necessary means of fulfilling an obligation."

§134. The correlate of right is obligation. *Obligation* is a passive moral quality, imposed on a person by law and restricting his liberty by forcing him to give something to or do something for another person with whom he lives in a society.

§135. This definition can be explained largely with the comments we have made about right. Yet it has to be noted that the restriction of liberty, which is the essence of an obligation, is nothing other than an act of reasoning that is based on knowledge of a law prescribed by a superior and informs a person of the anger of this superior and the punishment that will follow if the law is broken.

§136. This makes it clear that there can be no obligation without a superior, and least of all one without God. Whence again it follows that obligation does not properly speaking have its origin in agreements.

§137. Giving and acting differ as follows. To give is to transfer property. Acting comprehends all other actions and the failure to perform an action.

§138. There are as many types of obligation as there are types of right.

§139. For in correlates, what applies to one also applies to the other. Thus it follows necessarily that all obligation toward a human being is mutable, be it a natural obligation, an obligation of nations, or a civil obligation.

§140. Obligation is changed in some cases by the will of a superior, if he abolishes the right of the person to whom the obligation is owed, and in some cases by this person's spontaneous renunciation of his right.

§141. Beware, however, of confusing a law that imposes an obligation with the obligation which is the result of the law. For even if the latter is mutable, the law can still be immutable.

§142. Grotius adds a third meaning of right to the two we have mentioned so far. He argues that it is also applied to the *attributes of an action.* But this meaning pertains more to what is right in a particular case than to the concept of right.

§143. An *action*, however, is *right* [*actio justa*] in general if it is either commanded by a law or is permitted; and it is permitted either because a person has a right to it or because there is no punishment for it.

§144. For a just or honest action is, to use Grotius's expression, just in the *positive* sense if it is commanded by the laws, or *permitted,* that is, just in the *negative* sense, when it is not prohibited by the laws.

§145. A *permitted action* is either *perfectly, fully, ethically, and internally* permitted when it is based on a faculty pertaining to a person, or *imperfectly, not fully, politically, and externally* permitted when it is contrary to law, but not punished in a human court.

§146. These just actions can be compared with each other with respect to the law: an honest action is one that is *according* to law; an action that is tolerated, but not fully permitted, is *contrary* to law; and a fully permitted action is *not contrary* to law. Or they can be compared with respect to the legislator. No action is incompletely permitted to God, though this can be the case with regard to the prince.

§147. This meaning of a just action is compatible with the preceding two meanings of the term *right* because it comprehends each of these two [that is, law and the faculty of a person] within itself. It differs, however, insofar as the term *right* there is discussed in an abstract sense and directly, while here [i.e., in the case of a just action] it concerns a specific case or is discussed indirectly; it also differs insofar as the meaning of a just action is less strict and includes an action that is tolerated, which pertains neither to a law nor to a faculty.

§148. But just as the term *a just action* is taken in a threefold sense, so the expression "an honest action" is sometimes predicated of an action that is fully permitted, so that the term *a permitted action* is often extended to an honest action.

§149. And although the terms *permitted* and *authorized* are almost synonymous, the scope of permission is wider than that of authorization.
Permission is either a matter of fact, which only indicates the removal of
an impediment but has no effect on the rightfulness and does not lead
to an authorization; or it is a matter of right, which guarantees a secure
conscience, or at least freedom from punishment. It is then either a full or
an imperfect authorization.

§150. The opposite of a just action, the unjust action, can be taken in a
broad sense to describe everything that is contrary to law. It then includes
any action that is not fully permitted. Or it is taken in a strict sense and
is distinguished from this action, which is then said to be dishonest, despicable, and not permitted, though the terms "dishonest" and "not permitted" are subject to the same ambiguities we have pointed out in our
discussion of honest and permitted actions.

§151. An unjust action is also described as an *injury,* but an action tends
to be described as *unjust* with reference to the legislator and as an *injury*
with reference to the victim. This is the origin of the rule that "a person
does not suffer an injury if he agrees to it." And an action can be unjust
even if there is no injury.

§152. In other cases the term *injury* is either understood *very broadly* as
anything that is not done rightfully, even by those who have no intention of harming, or *broadly* as the denial of any right, either perfect or
imperfect, or it is understood *strictly* as the denial of a perfect right, or *very
strictly* as a personal insult.

§153. Finally, not only the action but also the human being is called *just*
and *unjust.* An action is called just or unjust depending on whether the
external actions of a person conform to law. A person, however, is characterized as just or unjust depending on the intentions behind his actions.

§154. Which of these many meanings of *right* is relevant to jurisprudence?
All of them, in some sense. Jurisprudence not only instructs us how laws
are to be passed, explained, and applied, but also explains the nature of the

faculty belonging to any particular person by right and provides means of protecting and preserving it. It also gives advice on how actions are to be undertaken according to law so that they turn out just, and it judges those that have been undertaken to determine whether they are just or not. And it does all this with the intention that men may become just.

§155. At the same time it is evident from what has been said that the principal object of jurisprudence is the laws and that the other meanings are applicable only secondarily and with reference to the laws.

§156. Thus jurisprudence in its widest sense is nothing other than an understanding of the laws.

§157. When laws are to be passed, or actions to be initiated according to them, jurisprudence is described as *legislative* or *advisory*. But when laws are to be applied to past actions, it is called *judicial*. Giving advice on actions which are to be directed according to laws and judging on actions that happened in the past presuppose the interpretation and understanding of laws.

§158. *Legislative* jurisprudence is not relevant to our purpose. *Advisory* jurisprudence bears some relation to our aim, but we will mainly discuss *judicial jurisprudence* since this also presupposes the advisory variety.

§159. Judicial jurisprudence, therefore, is the prudence required in explaining laws concerning the well-being of man in this life and applying them to the actions of humans.

§160. This definition is clear from the above, but you must note that *jurisprudence,* which is an intellectual faculty [*habitus*], must not be confused with the actual explanation and application of laws. If these actions are based on prudence, they are classified as habits of the will and are to be considered partly skills and partly moral virtues. They may even be considered a vice when they are used to harm other people.

§161. There are, therefore, two parts of judicial jurisprudence: *the interpretation of laws,* which you could for the sake of distinguishing it term the jurisprudence of professors and doctors of law; and the *application of laws,* which is the jurisprudence of *advocates and judges.* Here we are referring to both, but in these *Institutes* we are concerned primarily with the former. The latter we will examine when discussing the resolution of controversies that are taken from ancient and modern history.

§162. There will, however, undoubtedly be as many *kinds* of jurisprudence as there are kinds of law. Therefore, we will be correct in dividing jurisprudence into *divine* and *human.* The former tells us how to explain and apply divine laws, the latter how to do so with human laws.

§163. To avoid meddling in holy theology, we added a limitation to the definition of jurisprudence, saying that it pertained to the laws concerning the temporal well-being of man. We need to expand on this in a little more detail.

§164. I am assuming that our academies at present are usually divided into four faculties, that is, theology, law, medicine, and philosophy, though a fifth or even sixth faculty has been added to this in some places.

§165. I assume, moreover, that philosophy, which now constitutes a separate faculty, is understood in a far narrower sense than it once was among the Greeks and Romans. There it was indeed the knowledge of divine and human affairs, that is, the contemplation of all those things which could be derived from sound reason, which meant that it embraced medicine, jurisprudence, and a large part of pagan theology.

§166. The point of this observation is mainly that we should not confuse the properties of ancient philosophy, which acted as the queen, with present-day philosophy, which is left with nothing but the function of an honest servant. See, for example, that well-known phrase of Plato that commonwealths will be happy when philosophers rule or rulers philosophize, etc.[14]

14. Plato, *Republic,* bk. V, 473d. One translation is that of T. Griffith, ed. G. R. F. Ferrari (Cambridge: Cambridge University Press, 2008).

§167. Thus it seems most appropriate to explain the distinctions between these four faculties as follows. The faculties are either subordinate [*instrumentales*], that is, philosophy, or principal [*principales*], that is, the remaining three.

§168. The principal faculties either have as their object the body of man and aim for its health, which is what medicine does, or they strive to care for the human soul and its happiness.

§169. That is, its *temporal* happiness, which is the object of *jurisprudence,* and its *eternal* happiness, which is that of *theology.*

§170. Yet, the main means of obtaining human happiness, as the philosophers generally admit, are laws. It is, therefore, obvious that the explanation of laws, depending on the kind of happiness which they serve, pertains sometimes to the *jurist,* sometimes to the *theologian.* This will be discussed more clearly in the following chapter.

§171. From this follow the order and the ranking of the four faculties, as this has been accepted among us and defended in published writings. Hence it will be easy to respond to those who want to start a controversy with jurisprudence on that account.

§172. Those who are competent at jurisprudence are called *jurisprudents* or *jurisconsults.* Whether there is a difference between them and the *jurisperiti*[15] is the subject of acrimonious debate,[16] but that debate does not seem important enough to detain us.

---

15. Literally: "those experienced in law."

16. This is discussed in Amadeus Eckholt's commentary on the title *De origine juris* in *Compendiaria Pandectarum tractatio,* 2 vols. (Leipzig, 1680).

CHAPTER II

On Divine Jurisprudence

§1. *Divine jurisprudence* is the prudence that is required for explaining the divine laws concerning the well-being of humans in this life and for applying them to the actions of humans.

§2. All of this is obvious, as long as we explain which divine laws have the temporal well-being of man as their object. But that will be clear from the *division of divine law.*

§3. It is generally taught that divine law is *moral* or *ceremonial* or *forensic.* We have said elsewhere why we are dissatisfied with this division.[17]

§4. We say that *divine* law is either *natural* or *positive.* The others say so, too, but in doing so they mean something different.

§5. The paramount question here is, in what respects are these two kinds of divine law *similar* and in what are they different? The following points will elucidate our opinion.

§6. (1) Divine positive law agrees with natural in that God is the author of each of the two, or, if we want to be more precise and speak of God in human terms, the divine will is its author.

---

17. Thomasius, *De crimine bigamiae,* §§8 and 20.

§7. We do not accept the argument that natural law took its origin from the sanctity of God antecedently to his will while positive law did not. For everything that is in God exists there simultaneously.

§8. Man is not permitted to form a conception of God since such a conception involves imperfection.

§9. Thus we cannot speculate about God, mainly because of our imperfection, and it is therefore impossible to consider our ideas of God to be true or to acknowledge them as a foundation on which conclusions in a factual discipline, such as jurisprudence, should rest.

§10. (2) Natural law and divine positive law converge with respect to the *condition of man* to which they apply. For each binds man in the state of innocence and after the fall.

§11. For the first division of the state of humans is that between man in the state of innocence and man after original sin. It will not be fruitless to examine each of the two a little more carefully because the usefulness of this meditation will soon become apparent.

§12. We will begin, however, with the state of innocence since it is prior in terms of chronological order and more excellent, if we are allowed to do so. For we need to beware of meddling in theology. We explain jurisprudence as a faculty [*habitus*] that is to be acquired by our natural powers, as we have said above. Whatever we know about the state of innocence, however, we know from Sacred Scripture.

§13. Therefore, we either have to stop here or we must see how we can extricate ourselves from this difficulty. What if we said that this state of perfection was known to pagans, too? Indeed, there are countless testimonies of Greek and Latin philosophers and poets to this effect.

§14. Yet I fear that this will not be enough. Pagans knew of the state of innocence but only had a very confused notion of it. They knew about it, not from the dictate of reason, however, but from their contacts with the Jews.

§15. Therefore, we need to try another approach. Perhaps we Christians are privileged over the pagans. They were not allowed to interfere in theology because they only taught jurisprudence. But we go further, for what we teach is Christian jurisprudence.

§16. But here again the theologians guarding the borders of their discipline will tell us to retreat and not to climb over the fence that separates our discipline from theology. The term *Christian jurisprudence* will be suspect to them, because if by this we mean a discipline that borrows its principles of proof from theology, it will be vain for us to try to cover up our trespassing with a few slogans, especially as far as natural jurisprudence is concerned. But if we restrict our proofs to theological matters, our Christian jurisprudence will not deserve its name any more than, for example, arithmetic is a Christian arithmetic because its principles allow us to calculate how many measures of wine filled the vessels at Canaan.[18]

§17. Therefore, we halt, especially as we know a way of avoiding this problem. For just as arithmetic, for example, does not encroach on theology, even though it applies its own principles to examples from sacred history, so we will not sin if we apply our principles to the state of innocence. It is one thing to borrow principles of demonstration from another discipline, another to apply these principles to an object taken from another discipline.

§18. And this is especially true of history, which, whether it is sacred or profane, is used by all four faculties.

§19. Thus, it is permitted to talk about man's state of innocence, but only on the basis of sacred history, for the traditions of the pagans or the rabbis in that respect are mere trifles.

18. See John 2:1–11.

§20. This state of innocence was perfect since in it man was created in the image of God. Therefore, the miseries which accompany the corrupt state today were absent.

§21. The human body was certainly endowed with the same members as a healthy person is today, and there was the same distinction of the sexes. And the members of the body would have been directed by the soul, immediately from creation in the case of Adam and immediately from birth in his children. We are not really concerned about the size of humans in the state of innocence since that adds nothing directly to human perfection.

§22. Moreover, man would never have died or fallen ill. He would always have enjoyed the most wholesome food and drink. Digestion would have been excellent. Poison would not have harmed. Whether man would have eaten meat in that state is an idle rather than a useful question. I believe he could have but cannot imagine that he would have wanted to.

§23. The sense organs were, as far as we can imagine, perfect and completely reliable. There would have been the pleasures of the senses, but subject to laws. Thus, there would have been the pleasure derived from touch in that it can be based on physical causes and anatomical principles, but not the kind of pleasure that causes man to lose self-control and is called lust. Humans would have enjoyed powers of locomotion immediately from birth, and these would not have been disturbed or impeded [by illness].

§24. Concerning his intellect, man would not only have been so perceptive in natural matters that he would have recognized at first sight the natures, qualities, and forms of created beings, which today are concealed from us or are barely perceived even after the most laborious research. In moral matters, too, man would have possessed supreme prudence in understanding law and its significance for his actions. Thus we must criticize the belief, defended by Grotius and others,[19] that the Protoplasts were

19. See Grotius, *The Rights of War and Peace*, bk. II, chap. ii, §xvii, p. 422.

simple-minded and ignorant of vices rather than being endowed with the knowledge of virtue. This belief would also be an insult to God.

§25. And I do not see any reason why I should think differently about infants. They would indeed have been able from birth to reason with their parents on any subject whatsoever and would only have required a very brief period of time to be informed of the meaning of words which had their meaning from the imposition of man, not from the nature of the thing itself.

§26. The will enjoyed a great degree of liberty. Man could choose between sinning and not sinning but was more inclined to not sinning.

§27. Moreover, man in the state of innocence was not for one moment outside a society, but was joined immediately in a society with God, which was unequal but in which there was greater love and trust than can today exist in any paternal society.

§28. Man, however, by his nature desired something similar to himself, but did not find this similarity in God, because divine perfection was too distant from him, and thus it was not good that he was alone. Therefore God, in his supreme benignity, created a female companion for Adam, that is, Eve, whom he created from his rib (which yet was not superfluous in Adam, and its removal did not mutilate his body) and gave to Adam in matrimony.

§29. This society in the state of innocence was supremely equal, for only after the fall the power to command was transferred by God to the husband in order to punish the wife, and before the fall the common cause of subjection, imperfection, could not be attributed to Eve.

§30. The Apostle teaches that it does not befit wives to rule over their husbands, and he uses the argument that Adam was created earlier than Eve.[20] But one cannot infer from this that in the state of innocence Adam commanded Eve because Eve could not command Adam.

20. 1 Corinthians 11:8; 1 Timothy 2:11–13.

§31. The argument put forward by others, that the husband is superior to the wife in dignity and power because God intended to create the wife to complement the husband and not vice versa, establishes a priority of order but not a superiority of dignity or power, as can easily be shown with the example of a society of merchants.

§32. Such was the society of the state of innocence; would it have continued to exist if man had not lost his integrity? Some have thought so and denied that paternal society would have existed in the state of innocence. This has recently been argued among the English by Thomas Hobbes, who made bad use of his intellect, and among the Dutch by that horrible author Adriaan Beverland.[21]

§33. We not only defeat those authors with the words of the divine benediction: "go forth and multiply," but rout them by pointing out the shape of the human body and the members destined for procreation.

§34. We believe, however, that this society too would have been equal, but would have differed from conjugal society in that children would have had to show reverence toward their parents not so much because of a priority of order, but because they received the benefit of procreation from them.

§35. For the debt of reverence does not presuppose the imperfection implied by subjection, and the cause of paternal rule, as will be shown in its appropriate place, would have been absent in the state of innocence.

§36. But the domestic society of masters and servants [servi] would certainly have been absent from the state of innocence. For the economic need, which introduced this society both on the part of the master and the slave, would not have existed in the state of innocence, not to mention the division of property.

21. Thomas Hobbes (1588–1679). Thomasius has in mind chapter 32, paragraph 10, of the *Leviathan* (1651; modern ed. by R. Tuck [Cambridge: Cambridge University Press, 1996]), as well as Adriaan Beverland's (1654–1712) *Peccatum originale kat exochen sic nuncupatum* (Eleutheropolis, 1678).

§37. And would there have been a commonwealth? That will become clear if we consider the structure of the commonwealth. It consists of the power to command, which is directed to preserving public peace and the sufficiency of all things. We have already shown that there was no political power in the state of innocence. And power would not have been necessary to obtain either peace (since there would have been no fear) or sufficiency (since there would have been no lack of anything).

§38. But they who argued for the existence of a commonwealth in the state of innocence confessed almost unanimously that they did not mean a society with power in the proper sense. Thus, some distinguished between directive power and coercive power. But by doing so they admitted that there was no power [in the state of innocence], because a directive power is like a cold fire.[22]

§39. Then follows the state of fallen man. Here many things were altered. The organs of the body required some time before they were able to exercise their powers of locomotion and to be guided by the soul. Death enters the world; various diseases precede and further it; digestion is often poor; man must beware of poison; food must be prepared with various artifices so that it does not inflict harm; the sense organs of humans frequently deceive; the intellect has become much less acute. In infants it is like a clean slate, suitable to receiving any impressions whatsoever. The will of man has lost much of its liberty and is inclined almost wholly to evil, because the passions very frequently rise up and make man lose control of himself and in any case are perpetually straining at the leash.

§40. We believe that these changes in man have been so great that it is absolutely impossible for man to correct these imperfections in the present life by natural means.

§41. If he could do so, it would be in his power to rid himself of original sin or to evade divine punishment. Either of these, however, is absurd.

---

22. That is, a contradiction in terms.

§42. Insofar as the intellect is concerned, however, perfection did remain to the extent that man could recognize the common rules and precepts, above all those of the law of nature that are relevant to the will, which was inclined toward evil, but in such a way that it retained at least the liberty of constraining external actions effectively.

§43. Moreover, if we look at the changes with respect to societies, in divine society today there is no longer the face-to-face conversation with God, nor is God only loved as a benign father; he is also feared as a just judge. Conjugal society has been turned from an equal into a mixed society, as a punishment for original sin. The power to command was introduced into paternal society for the sake of education. The curse on the soil and the resulting division of property produced the society of masters and servants, and the fear of external violence led to the foundation of cities and commonwealths.

§44. The state of innocence is also called the state of right nature [*natura recta*], and the state after the fall from grace that of corrupt nature. Yet we must note that here by corruption we do not mean moral corruption with respect to external actions, since that description pertains either to the physical corruption of man or, at least, to the moral corruption of the internal actions that strongly incline to sin against the laws.

§45. Thus the postlapsarian state is still right to some extent, and the sinful external actions in that state do not reflect the defects of the state but of the humans living in it.

§46. Hence, you should also note the following ambiguity: *corruption* is opposed either to the *state of innocence* or to the *postlapsarian state,* to the extent that this latter state is still uncorrupt; in that case it refers for example to the condition of thieves, etc.

§47. There are many more different meanings concealed in the term *natural state.* We know of the distinction between the *natural* and the *legal* states of man, which is explained in different ways by different authors but is usually interpreted to mean that the natural state was that of man flourishing in the state of innocence; the legal state, however, that of corrupt nature. And this distinction is commonly applied not only to individual humans, but also to human societies, above all to civil society. And apart from that its use in solving several political controversies is often emphasized.

§48. We have done so, too, in another place.[23] But now we have changed our opinion, in part because the natural state [in this sense] presupposes the existence of a civil society in the state of innocence, and we have just demonstrated the opposite; in part because those [political] controversies can be solved, if not better, then equally well, if we direct our attention exclusively to the legal state.

§49. Almost any beginner will know how much political theorists have criticized the natural state of Hobbes, which he insisted to be a war of all against all, and how much he opposed the social state to this. Pufendorf's comments in various places against this state of war deserve to be read here.

§50. The state of man after the fall from grace can be described as natural in many respects. This will be clear from the following distinctions. The natural state initially describes a condition common to all humans that distinguishes them from the beasts also after the fall from grace, namely, that they are able to reason and to acknowledge a supreme legislator and direct their external actions according to his precepts. This state is opposed to the life and condition of beasts or to the life of humans abusing this state and following the dictates of their corrupt reason in every way.

§51. This natural state can, second, be subdivided conveniently into a natural state and a social state, the former understood as the condition of humans that would obtain if man, after the fall, from birth had been

23. Christian Thomasius (*praeses*), Georg Reichard Emme (*respondens*), *Philosophiam juris ostensam in doctrina de obligationibus et actionibus . . . sollenniter proponit Georg Reichard Emme* (Leipzig, 1682).

left to his own devices and not enjoyed the help of other humans; and the latter, the social state, understood as the condition of humans living a life that is improved by the efforts of others.

§52. And this natural state and social state are not to be confused with the natural state and the social state of Hobbes. Even though we may be using the same terms, the substance is very different. For in his theory of the natural state Hobbes considers man to be in opposition to other humans, and he wants this to be a state of war of all against all, none of which fits with our natural state.

§53. The social state is, third, either *natural,* that is, the condition of humans living in an equal society who do not have a common lord and in which no one is subject to another, or *civil,* which is the state of those who live in a civil society and in the other minor societies comprehended within a civil society.

§54. The natural state in this sense must not be confused with that of Hobbes. Hobbes's state is one of war and opposed to the social; ours is peaceful and social.

§55. And, fourth and finally, the civil state is either *natural,* that is, a condition which man has by nature and without any human action (for example, being a man, being an infant, etc.) or it is *adventitious,* that is, a condition which man has as a result of human imposition (for example, being a consul, a nobleman, a peasant, etc.).

§56. Yet we believe that it is justified to apply the term *natural state* to all these meanings. In the first meaning the term is based on the essence of man, in the second on the misery accompanying the nature of postlapsarian man, insofar as he is left to himself; in the third it rests on the natural liberty and equality of humans, and in the fourth on the properties, mainly the physical properties, which man has by nature.

§57. Yet if someone wanted to call the first type of a state of nature *the state of humanity,* that of the second *the condition of solitary life,* and that of the third the state of equality, we will accept that, since we do not want to argue over words.

§58. These four natural states can be compared with each other with respect to their actual existence. The first exists or at least should exist in all humans. The second is not common, but it can exist, for example, if a single man is cast ashore on an uninhabited island after surviving a shipwreck; and it exists, for example, in the case of infants exposed by parents. The third is very common, for example, among nations in their mutual relations. About the existence of the fourth, however, there can be no doubt.

§59. Thus, those people err who believe that the state of nature of the second kind is a fictitious state or that the misery which we said accompanies that state is fictitious.

§60. But we had a reason for presenting this fourfold meaning of the natural state. The first will be useful in deriving the duties of man toward God, the second in demonstrating the need for a society, the third in comparing diverse precepts of natural law with each other and elsewhere. The fourth belongs to jurisprudence, especially human jurisprudence.

§61. We now return to the argument. We have said that in either state of man, that of innocence and that after original sin, both forms of divine law, natural and positive, had a place. Concerning natural law, perhaps, there is no doubt. Positive, revealed law in the state of innocence was that which prohibited eating from the forbidden tree, as well as the prohibition of polygamy and divorce when marriage was originally established. In the state after the fall from grace there are various positive laws, about which more will be said later.

§62. We are, however, trying to explain the divine laws to the extent that they are relevant to jurisprudence. I therefore believe it is evident that we are primarily concerned with those laws which govern the postlapsarian state. For jurisprudence must explain the laws which are to be applied to human actions subsequently [to the state of innocence]. We are not, I believe, judging our first ancestors [that is, Adam and Eve], we are not their lawyers, and we are not concerned with their actions, but with humans of this age who retain only remnants of the original felicity. If only they can preserve these, that is enough for tranquillity in this life.

§63. Now let us see the differences between these two laws. Usually authors look for the difference in the fact that natural law binds all humans, while positive law binds only the Jewish people. But it will be clear from the following that this is not sufficient.

§64. (1) For a start natural law and divine positive law differ in their principles of knowledge: in natural law this is right reason; in divine positive law it is divine revelation.

§65. The proof of this difference is derived from the second difference. The Apostle Paul recognized this difference exactly, and this is clear in part when he said that those nations that did not have the positive law did by nature what was according to natural law, and in part because he declared that he would not have known from reason alone that concupiscence is a sin, unless the divine positive law had said, "Thou shalt not covet."[24]

§66. By *right reason* I here mean a natural faculty of reasoning or deriving true conclusions from true first principles. But as is obvious to anyone, man has this faculty from birth as a potential. This is suitable for exercising his powers if, with the input from the senses, the ideas have first been formed by the intellect and the same potential has later been exercised in human society.

§67. Therefore, we cannot but laugh at the excessively subtle meditations of the Scholastics, who teach that infants have certain practical principles by nature that have the form of a kind of innate faculty, and these tell them what is to be done or omitted according to the law of nature.

24. Romans 2:14–15 and Romans 7:7.

§68. Each practical principle is a proposition. Every proposition indicates whether a predicate does or does not conform to the subject. Yet infants are destitute of the knowledge of terms, especially moral terms, since even adult, erudite humans barely agree on their meaning. Who would, therefore, believe that infants, for example, know that murder is to be shunned and that agreements are to be kept, since they do not know what an agreement is, what murder is, etc.

§69. The Scholastics themselves are unsure whether this innate faculty is only a potential in infants or is already present in them. Some have reached the point of saying that this faculty is neither of the two, but is somewhere between being actually and potentially present. Thus, we have a particularly felicitous solution whereby something is put forward which can both be and not be at the same time.

§70. Even if positive law is derived from divine revelation, it is not permissible to argue as follows: This act, which is commanded or prohibited in Scripture, is recognized as honest or despicable by pagans, too. Therefore, it is part of natural law. For these pagans are either Greeks or Romans. The Romans took their laws from the Greeks. The philosophers of the Greeks borrowed much from Moses. Solon similarly introduced many laws from Egypt to Athens. The Egyptians, however, took the rudiments of their laws from the Hebrews.

§71. (2) These laws differ in that natural law is concerned with actions that either conform necessarily to the common rational nature of man or are contrary to it; positive law is concerned with actions that are neither.

§72. For since it is apparent from natural reason that God wanted man to be rational and also for his actions to be subject to a particular kind of norm, it follows necessarily—to avoid contradiction—that God wanted to command the actions which necessarily further the rational nature of man and to forbid those which are contrary to it. But since there are many actions by which, when they are committed or omitted, the essence of man is neither violated nor furthered as such, man will not be able to know how these are regulated. Here the promulgation of a whole other law is required.

§73. I speak of a necessary conformity of an action with reason whenever the omission of an action by humankind would necessarily cause it to perish, and of repugnance to reason whenever humanity would perish as a result of this action being committed.

§74. This difference is interpreted differently by the Scholastics and indeed in various ways. For sometimes they say that what pertains to natural law is actions that are *in themselves and by their nature, even antecedently to the divine will, honest or despicable,* while indifferent actions pertain to positive law.

§75. Sometimes they say that *obligation in natural law flows from the object to the precept;* in positive law, however, from the precept to the object.

§76. Yet none of these definitions are that good. You could say that actions determined by natural law are honest or despicable as such [*per se*] with regard to their immutability. But they apply this expression "as such" to imply that this is antecedent to the act of commanding natural law.

§77. However, they contradict themselves when they say that certain acts are *by their nature honest* or *despicable.* In a human action you can consider either its nature or its morality in relation to a law: its nature insofar as it is abstracted from moral circumstances, and morality insofar as the moral circumstances are examined.

§78. Moral circumstances are covered in the common phrase *who, what, where,* etc.[25]

25. Various versions of this list existed in early modern philosophy and legal argument. One example was *quis, quid, ubi, quibus auxiliis, cur, quomodo, quando* ("who, what, where, by what means, why, in what manner, when").

§79. But beware of thinking that, where one or another of these circumstances is present, there is immediately a moral circumstance.

§80. For otherwise you would have the absurd consequence that no action could be considered as a natural phenomenon, since every action certainly involves one of these circumstances.

§81. Thus these circumstances are called moral insofar as a law commands or prohibits a particular action because of these.

§82. And so he who calls certain actions honest or despicable by their very nature says that certain actions are by their nature moral. But he who says so does in fact declare that certain actions, if abstracted from their moral circumstances, by virtue of this abstraction involve moral circumstances.

§83. Further, an honest action is one which is commanded by a law, a despicable action one which is prohibited by a law. A law, however, is the will of the legislator, and the source of all laws is the divine will.

§84. So they who want certain actions to be *honest* or *despicable antecedently to the divine will* also want certain actions to be commanded or prohibited by a law that is prior to law.

§85. I know indeed that a distinction is made between honest actions considered materially and formally; they claim that laws are defined materially by us, but that those actions are honest or despicable formally which conform to the dictate of right reason.

§86. Yet I also know that the distinction between material and formal, when applied to moral affairs, is either obscure or superfluous, and in most cases unsuitable. I know that in this respect *good* in the sense of useful is confused with *good* in the sense of honest. I know that they define law as a dictate of reason and stick to that error. I know finally that the

Apostle who defined *sin* as the transgression of the law knew very well the formal characteristics of a despicable action.[26]

§87. Finally, how, without contradiction, could *obligation diffuse itself from the object to the precept,* since the efficacy of every obligation depends on reverence and fear of the legislator?

§88. Thus, are not all actions by their nature indifferent? They are indeed; that is, all physical actions abstracted from their moral circumstances are neither commanded nor prohibited.

§89. Yet you will say that blasphemy and theft, for example, by their nature are not indifferent. I say, however, that these are not terms for action considered with respect to their nature. For blasphemy involves a concept of deliberate choice, that somebody utters certain words expressing disrespect for God. Theft involves the concept of fraudulent removal. And because of these circumstances blasphemy and theft are already prohibited by an eternal law.

§90. If you abstract from these circumstances these actions will no longer be despicable. They will not even be blasphemy or theft. The physical action in blasphemy is the uttering of words which are blasphemous. A witness, for example, when he repeats these words in giving evidence, does not commit blasphemy. In theft physical action is seizing something that belongs to someone else, etc.

§91. Thus, in order to explain briefly what I mean: the Scholastics confuse the *natural aspect of an action,* that is, an action considered physically, with the *moral nature of an action,* that is, an action considered morally.

§92. But perhaps we are contradicting ourselves by refuting others. Is it not the same whether you say that the object of natural law is an action which

26. See 1 John 3:4.

is honest or despicable antecedently to the divine will, or you say that there are actions which have a necessary connection with or are repugnant to the rational nature of man? For if we declare that God commanded or prohibited these actions because of such a conformity or repugnance, do we not by that very fact concede that these actions are honest or despicable prior to the divine will? Do we not admit that obligation flows from the object to the precept?

§93. There is, however, no danger of that. It can indeed be inferred from our assertion that those actions that are the object of natural law are by their nature good or bad.[27] Yet it cannot be inferred that they are honest or despicable. These actions harm or promote the utility of humankind, even if you abstract from the divine will, but as long as you remain with that abstraction, they are not commanded or prohibited by law, and they do not obligate humanity to anything.

§94. Thus it is certain that particular medicines are very useful for ill people, and some foods on the other hand are highly harmful to them. Yet these medicines or foods do not obligate the sick person to do anything, if you abstract from the will of the legislator. Remove the legislator and it will be true without exception that every person is the sole guardian of his own utility.

§95. Ah, you will cry, I have caught you! When fools avoid one vice they fall into another. According to your opinion, therefore, *utility itself is the mother of justice and equity; nor does nature know just from unjust.*[28] And this is what Carneades declared, what the herd of Epicurean swine has taught, and Hobbes, the Epicurean, has largely warmed up and reheated. Thus there is no natural law or justice, or if there is any, it will be supreme foolishness, because by taking care of the well-being of others, one's own utility will suffer. If this is not introducing the poison of atheism by deceit, what is?

27. That is, useful or harmful.
28. Horace, *Satires*, I.III.98 and 113, in Horace, *Satires, Epistles and Ars Poetica,* trans. H. Rushton Fairclough, Loeb Classical Library (London: Heinemann, 1926). Carneades (ca. 213–129 B.C.) was a skeptical philosopher and head of the Academy in Athens.

§96. Yet I cannot imagine anyone would be so impudent as to accuse us of such a belief when we have tried so strenuously to prove the existence of this very law and of natural justice and its differences from other laws. This is so especially since the *utility of individual humans,* which the above-mentioned philosophers turn into the origin of universal law, is quite different from the *utility of all of humanity.* Thus, just as public utility is the proper norm of private utility in a commonwealth, so too is common utility the norm of particular utility in the society of humanity as a whole. To put it briefly: not everything that is useful is honest, but everything that is honest is also useful.

§97. Thus natural law is divine law inscribed on the hearts of all men, obliging them to do what necessarily conforms to the rational nature of man and to omit that which is contrary to it.

§98. We will inquire in more detail into this conformity with the rational nature of man in the following sections,[29] but the main feature of *natural law,* its *immutability* and the impossibility of *dispensation,* follows automatically from our definition, because the rationality of man is indeed immutable and does not allow for dispensation.

§99. There are various well-known objections, especially with regard to dispensation. One example concerns the removal of the Egyptians' silver vessels commanded to the Israelites by God, the killing of Isaac, the lie of the Egyptian midwives, etc.[30] Jurists have come up with an almost infinite variety of distinctions, which are all unnecessary, since clearly no dispensation took place there: these acts were commanded or recommended by God and thus were not theft, homicide, or lying, as prohibited by natural law. And so those who disagree with us confuse the change of the subject matter with a change in the law.

29. See *Institutes,* bk. I, chap. iv.
30. Exodus 12:35–36; Genesis 22:2; Exodus 1:18–20.

§100. Yet you might argue that the very fact that these actions are not theft, homicide, etc., means God gave dispensation from the law of nature, since dispensation is a declaration by the superior that a law does not apply to a particular action. I would then respond that this confuses restrictive interpretation with dispensation, which is precisely what we warned against.

§101. Natural law can be divided quite conveniently with respect to natural human societies. Some precepts of natural law concern the *common society of all humans,* living among themselves in a state of nature, or, as we have said above, in a state of equality. Now that commonwealths have been introduced this is called the society of nations; others direct the duties of humans living *in a commonwealth* and in societies that form part of a commonwealth, such as households.

§102. The former is usually called the *law of nations.* You could, therefore, call the former natural law in the strict sense, for the sake of distinguishing it from the latter.

§103. Elsewhere the term *law of nations* is understood in different ways, either (1) as an attribute of a person or a *faculty,* which nations exercise with the permission of nature; (2) as the *moral customs* of several nations, when they tend to make use of their right unanimously and in the same manner (in this sense, possessions, wars, servitudes, commercial ties, etc., are said to be matters of the law of nations); (3) as a *law,* and in fact as *natural* law in general, because this does obligate all nations; (4) as the *civil* law of many nations (here private persons' means of acquisition, which are said to be of the law of nations, are relevant); or (5) as *the law of nations in the proper sense,* which describes the duties of nations *qua* nations toward each other.

§104. It will, however, be quite apparent that in the controversy *whether the law of nations is a species of divine law or of human law,* it is necessary to pay attention to the ultimate meaning. If we take this into account we can easily respond to those people who join Grotius in turning the *law of nations into a form of conventional* and *human law.* For they are talking either of the moral customs of nations or of right understood as the attribute of a person.

§105. In sum: The nations are equal among each other, and they do not acknowledge a superior among men. Therefore they cannot be under an obligation from human law.

§106. But, you say, they are bound by a lawful agreement; that is, they are bound by their own will. I repeat, however, that an agreement is not a law, nor is the agreement itself binding, but in every case a law binds via an agreement. We have already said this above.

§107. Thus the nations are (all) under no obligation to each other from an agreement. For where and when was an agreement of this kind established?

§108. The notion of a tacit agreement will not help you out, as if nations bound themselves by imitating each other and by continuing to use certain actions which were initially undertaken by a few. I do not admit the existence of such a universal and continued imitation of this kind and I deny that imitation alone implies a tacit pact.

§109. Perhaps the manners and customs of those who use this law mean that the law of nations is unwritten. But perhaps they do not. There is no unwritten law outside of a commonwealth. For custom is law because of the tacit approbation of the prince. When that is lacking, the custom is called *de facto*. Yet where among nations do we find the tacit approbation of a prince?

§110. The Scholastics, moreover, divide precepts of *natural law* into *affirmative* and *negative*. That is easy to understand and applies to all laws, but the usefulness of this distinction is exiguous.

§111. "No," says the Scholastic; "it is a hugely useful distinction. Affirmative precepts are *always* binding, *negative precepts always and at all times.*"

§112. "Nonsense," I reply; "what poppycock. Let us speak in such a way that we understand each other."

§113. Both types of precepts are *always* binding; that is, they are eternally true. But affirmative precepts are not binding *at all times;* that is, they do not bind all humans, nor do they bind in every single moment. Examples are the command to honor your parents, give alms, etc. But the negative precepts bind everyone and at all times. An example is the command not to insult anyone.

§114. So do the precepts "Obey a superior," "Live honestly," "Render everyone his due" not bind all humans at every time? And does the command "Do not commit a crime of lèse majesté" bind all humans and, for example, the princes and sovereigns themselves?

§115. You see that these effects do not depend on the affirmation or the negation, but are to be derived from elsewhere. The laws of nature either impose duties on humans living in any society whatsoever, or they impose duties that are peculiar to particular societies. Likewise, man can omit a thousand entirely different actions in one and the same moment, but he cannot perform these several different actions in one moment.

§116. Those are the subtleties which anyone can understand without pretty formulae. Moreover, we do not believe it is right to use this distinction to say that *affirmative* precepts of natural law always allow for an *exception in cases of supreme necessity, and negative precepts do not.* That will be clear from what is to be said in its proper place.

§117. Divine positive law is divine law publicized to humans through divine revelation and directs those actions that do not have a necessary connection with the rational nature of man.

§118. Thus, it is evident that this divine law is mutable and admits dispensation, but only by God, not by the pope or any prince. Yet the will of God is not therefore changeable.

§119. Positive law is divided into *universal* and *particular*. There is no doubt concerning the latter, but the *existence* of the former is denied by some and defended by others. I think that the question *what* it is needs to be examined before the question *whether* it exists, if this can be done while preserving peace with the Scholastics.

§120. We speak of *universal* law with respect to all of humanity, *particular* with respect to a certain people. This distinction can, however, be taken in a twofold sense, either in relation to *publication* or in relation to *obligation*. Either meaning is relevant here, but publication is more important.

§121. Thus *universal divine positive law* is that *which has been publicized to all humans or to certain persons representing all of humanity*. The *particular law* is that *which was given to the Jewish people*.

§122. The Jews not only affirm all too confidently that this universal law was given to Adam and Noah, but they also describe it in their own way, mixing as they are wont to do false statements with true and augmenting natural law with positive law, mainly from their rabbinic traditions, whose opinion Selden, that ornament of Britain, explained in more detail in a work devoted to this particular question.[31]

§123. We have set aside all these traditions and look only toward Scripture, and so choose the middle way: we cannot deny the existence of such laws. For not only was Adam given the precept concerning the forbidden tree, and on avoiding polygamy and divorce, when marriage was first established, but Noah too was ordered to punish homicide as a capital crime and to avoid eating blood, etc.

§124. It is clear that these are positive laws because the relevant actions do not have a necessary connection with the rational nature of man.

---

31. John Selden, *De jure naturali et gentium iuxta disciplinam Hebraeorum* (London, 1640). Another edition appeared in Strasbourg in 1665.

§125. We will survey the forms of this positive law in their proper place. We should only note this in advance, that these positive laws direct the duty of man either with respect to the worship of God or with respect to other humans. In the former case they have eternal beatitude as their immediate object. The latter have temporal well-being as their immediate object.

§126. *Divine particular law* is either *ceremonial* or *forensic*. The former concerns the regulation of divine worship, the latter the decision of court cases among the Jews. In the forensic law God aimed at the particular temporal well-being of the Jewish people, in the ceremonial at the eternal beatitude of all of humanity.

§127. Therefore, ceremonial law for the greatest part (that is, insofar as proselytes too were bound to its observance) binds all humans.[32]

§128. Thus, *ceremonial* law is, so to speak, in between forensic law and that law which we have called universal law. Universal law is such by virtue of its universal publication and obligation. Forensic law is particular in both respects. But ceremonial law is particular in its publication, universal in its obligation.

§129. For all precepts concerning religion are universal in terms of their obligation, for there is only one religion which cares for eternal salvation. They who neglect it are punished eternally.

§130. Nor should you be distracted by the common rule that "a law which has not been publicized is not binding." This actually means that the (positive) law is not binding *before* it has been published. It does not mean that it binds only *those to whom it has been actually publicized.* For this would lead to many limitations, including, without doubt, the following: unless the subjects to whom it has to be publicized are at fault and do not admit the publication, for example, if they are rebels.

---

32. Paragraphs 127–30 are removed in later editions (see, for example, the German edition of 1709).

§131. *Forensic* law has been extinct since the Jewish commonwealth has been extinct and the Jews have been dispersed over the entire globe. *Ceremonial* law expired with the advent of Christ, who having first fulfilled the law introduced new sacraments and a new religious worship, either by himself or through his apostles. This obligated all humans, in the same way, as once the Jewish law did, as we have said. About this there is all the less doubt, as the apostles were ordered to preach the gospel to all nations.

§132. However, Christ should not be called a new legislator because of that. For those who use that phrase imply that Christ also changed something in those precepts which concern the duties of humans to each other and required a more perfect obedience from Christians in the New Testament. But that would obviously contradict the infinite wisdom of God the Father, and it is also refuted at length by the theologians.

§133. So, does the particular Mosaic law and especially the forensic law have no use today? Grotius claims it has a threefold use: one is to show that the commands of those laws are not contrary to the law of nature. Another is to show that Christian magistrates may now pass laws that are similar to those given through Moses, unless maybe they are ceremonial or Christ ordered something to the contrary. Third, [it shows] that whatever has been commanded by the Law of Moses and belongs to the virtues Christ demanded of his disciples must also be fulfilled by Christians now, perhaps even more fully than before.[33]

§134. We agree with the first of these uses, but we have already refuted the second and third uses added by Grotius. We also deny that the second use suggested by Grotius concerning forensic laws applies to other cases as well. For in these laws God had in mind the well-being of the Jewish commonwealth, but the individual Christian magistrates must have the utility of their commonwealths before their eyes, which can be different from the utility of the Jewish commonwealth.

33. Grotius, *The Rights of War and Peace,* bk. I, chap. i, §xvii, pp. 175–79.

§135. For example, the forensic law punishes theft by requiring the culprit to restore double or quadruple the amount stolen. This was sufficient for the punishment of thefts among the Jewish people. Thus, if in any commonwealth these punishments are sufficient, the prince will do well if he adopts them. But if he cannot obtain his end and thefts continue to multiply, the prince commits a sin if he does not increase the punishments together with the growth in crimes.

§136. They clearly err, however, who believe that divine forensic law prescribes a norm to princes, to which they must adapt the laws of their commonwealths, and that they sin if they issue a regulation which is not determined by these forensic laws or is contrary to them. On this basis, for example, they criticize the hanging of thieves.

§137. It is clear from the division of divine laws that divine jurisprudence has as its object natural law, and among the divine positive universal laws those that concern the duties of humans toward other humans.

§138. For these laws, as well as natural law, have the temporal well-being and tranquillity of man as their object—not principally, I should say, but still directly.

§139. We believe that this doctrine conforms to common practice in the territories of Protestant princes, and among us to the practice of the consistories and the regulations issued by the princes.

§140. Thus, our jurisprudence can be called *Christian* with regard to its positive laws because not only is the object of demonstration here taken from sacred Scripture, but the first principle of demonstration is derived from revelation, which the other parts of jurisprudence, as well as medicine and philosophy, do not do, and indeed must not do.

§141. Therefore, jurisprudence also differs from theology, partly because of its object, but properly because of its end. Indeed, only jurisprudence is concerned with human laws, because these are accommodated to the temporal well-being of man. The precepts of religion pertain to the theologians, and the doctrine concerning these bears the name theology in the strict sense, which explains the articles of faith.

§142. The divine laws, however, which regulate the duties of humans toward humans are common to theologians and jurists. They belong to the former insofar as they are, according to the intention of the legislator, subordinated to eternal salvation, or insofar as the gospel cannot be explained properly without the law. They are relevant to the latter insofar as God in them has immediate regard for the tranquillity and decorous order of this life.

§143. And therefore, when the theologians interpret these precepts, they do not simply call their treatises theology, but *moral theology*, which explains what actions are to be performed.

§144. You could also draw the following distinction between moral theology and divine jurisprudence. Moral theology inculcates the moral law [i.e., the Ten Commandments], which binds all humans without distinguishing between natural law and positive universal law; moral theology always uses sacred Scripture as its foundation, which is why moral theologians generally treat the moral law and natural law as synonyms. Divine jurisprudence, however, separates natural law from divine, and proves the former from the dictate of right reason, according to the doctrine of the Apostle Paul, but seeks the latter from revelation alone. This distinction is immensely useful in controversies, which are otherwise extremely difficult, concerning the obligation of the prince with respect to precepts of this kind and his power of granting dispensation and of legislation, etc.

§145. Therefore, it is correct to divide divine jurisprudence into natural and the divine positive universal law that inculcates the duties of humans toward each other. The latter we shall from now on for the sake of brevity simply call divine, and the laws with which it is concerned, divine laws. We will make an effort to do what has not been done before, that is, to keep them apart in the individual chapters, though we do not consider these two species in isolation from each other.

CHAPTER III

On the Interpretation of Divine Laws in General and on Practical Principles

§1. Every variety of jurisprudence teaches the interpretation and application of laws. For these are the means of introducing general tranquillity. And if jurisprudence neglected to teach the means of implementing the laws and remained content with saying what they are, it would not deserve the name of prudence.

§2. Interpretation must precede application, according to the rules of good teaching.

§3. *Interpretation is the explanation of the will of another person when the intention is not clear.* For the kind of interpretation that is called *authentic* is, properly speaking, no interpretation, but either a new law or a new agreement. That is not relevant here.

§4. This *will* is either that of a *superior* or that of an *equal.* Therefore, interpretation is either that of *laws* or of *agreements,* similarly of last wills, scholarly arguments, etc.

§5. *Laws,* however, are either *inscribed in the hearts of men* or are *published* through *revelation.* In the former case, interpretation uses *demonstrations.* In the latter, interpretation makes use of *conjectures* or probable arguments.

§6. Either interpretation rests on certain rules and axioms, which are derived from first principles.

§7. *First principles,* however, are propositions formed by the intellect, beyond which the intellect cannot go in its reasoning.

§8. For since the intellect of man is finite, it cannot in its demonstrations ascend to the infinite, but is forced to stop at some point.

§9. According to the difference between theoretical and practical intellectual faculties [*habitus*], however, the *first principles* are divided into *theoretical* and *practical*.

§10. Many have written a lot on the theoretical principles. The practical have clearly been neglected, or taught in a confused fashion, or are even now sought for laboriously.

§11. Our only aim, after the glory of God, is the zeal for truth, and so we will contemplate the matter objectively, as it is, without looking for approval from anyone or flattering anyone, because we will not slavishly follow any particular author. Nor will we fear anybody's hate, because we will not mention those we disagree with, nor will we fight with insults, but by reasoning.

§12. But we shall have to examine the matter in a little more depth. I presuppose (1) that the *intellect,* whichever way you define it, *is one thing,* and that the theoretical and practical intellects in reality are identical.

§13. (2) Our intellect either contemplates the *essence of things,* or their nature, character, accidents, or whatever you want to call this, or it contemplates the *proper actions* of humans.

§14. (3) All things are *distinct* from each other, but there are also shared characteristics, so that there is no being which does not have something in common with another in relation to a third term.

§15. (4) When the intellect, therefore, contemplates the nature of things, it either contemplates their *shared characteristics* or their *differences*. Thus, every definition is based on this twofold concept, that is, of similarity in the genus and dissimilarity in the specific difference.

§16. (5) He who is able to draw out the similarities of things is said to have a powerful *mind;* he who accurately discerns differences has *judgment.*

§17. (6) Moreover, by contemplating the essence of things and their nature the intellect either conceives them as they really are or combines them with each other by some fiction, as they are not. And this act of the intellect is called imagination.

§18. By comparing all those things we have surveyed so far with each other we arrive at the supreme and first proposition, that is, the one to which all others can be referred, but which itself cannot be derived by means of demonstrative proof: *anything either is or is not.* Or, *it is impossible for something to be and not to be at the same time.* Or finally, *mutually contradictory things cannot be true simultaneously.* For these all mean the same. And this is generally called the *first theoretical principle.*

§19. Among those things, however, that are proper subjects for contemplation, man also finds himself. And when he contemplates his nature he sees that he was created not only for the sake of speculation, but for action as well.

§20. But when he compares his actions with his essence, he realizes that his nature does not allow him to be free of law and to regulate his actions without any norm.

§21. From this follows the definition of law. It also leads to the concept of a ruler and that of obligation since these are implied in the definition of law.

§22. When he finds that there are a variety of laws, he compares them with each other and looks for their differences. The upshot of these contemplations, or the conclusion, which is the first law and to which all others must be related, is called the *first practical principle.*

§23. From what has been said it is clear that the *first practical principle* is not the first in an absolute sense, but is subordinated to the *first theoretical principle.*

§24. For the first theoretical principle is the sum of all contemplations on the essences of things and nature. The practical is on the essence of one thing in particular, that of law. The species, however, is contained within the genus.

§25. The practical principle, therefore, already presupposes the knowledge of various things and above all of man and of human actions. And thus it also presupposes the theoretical principle.

§26. Thus they are mistaken who believe that the first practical principle is not subordinate to the theoretical.

§27. For it would follow that the theoretical principle would be false if there were anything in my mind which neither is nor is not.

§28. And so they who teach this deny in fact the first principle of the intellect.

§29. Or they make two distinct entities out of the human intellect.

§30. I will not mention that they themselves admit there is no point arguing against someone who denies first principles. We happily accept this in the case of the first theoretical principle. For nobody will readily deny this if he is human and no peasant.

§31. But if we assume the same in the first practical principle, we will not escape controversy, since the most erudite men disagree over this with each other, each of them surrounded by a crowd of his pupils.

§32. If they all kept on contradicting each other, saying that there is no point arguing with someone who denies the first principles, except by resorting to physical violence, then a war would in fact break out, if not of all against all, certainly of most of the learned with each other.

§33. Therefore, the first practical principle must be demonstrated immediately from the theoretical.

§34. If I be permitted to do so, I can express this principle in a few words: "Obey him who has the power to command you."

§35. I prove this first from *the definition of him who commands.* He who commands is one who has the power to bind another. If there were no need to obey him he would not have this power, but it is impossible for something to be and not to be at the same time.

§36. *From the definition of law:* Law is the command of a ruler binding subjects, etc. If there were no need to obey him who commands, the law would therefore not be law.

§37. *From the definition of obligation:* we have explained this above. There would be no obligation if there were no need to obey him who commands.

§38. This axiom deserves to be called a *first* practical principle because, for one thing, all particular laws must be related to it which can easily be proved through inductive argument from examples.

§39. It also deserves this name because it cannot itself be demonstrated using another law, since it follows from the definition of law in general.

§40. You could therefore call the principle the *object of jurisprudence in general.* For all forms of jurisprudence presuppose it.

§41. But since we have divided jurisprudence into divine and human, we must see what the *first principle of divine jurisprudence* is.

§42. Its nature rests on the fact that all divine laws are referred to it, and that it itself is, however, demonstrated immediately from the first practical principle, mediately from the first theoretical principle.

§43. It will be the following: "Obey God."

§44. The immediate proof is that this is true because God is a ruler.

§45. The mediate demonstration of this is that this is true because otherwise God would not be God.

§46. Either proof will be developed a little more fully since here it is simply supposed that there is a God and that he is a superior.

§47. Even the most barbarian nations have acknowledged and continue to acknowledge that there is a God. Many have even demonstrated it, especially those who wrote on natural theology or argued against the atheists.

§48. And here various arguments can be put forward. The most powerful is taken from the order of the causes of things. Whatever we see in this terraqueous globe does not exist out of itself, but is dependent on something else; yet we also see that those things on which they are dependent do not exist out of themselves, and so on. Thus we have to stop at some first cause, because the progress ad infinitum is repugnant to the intellect. This first cause is God.

§49. But our intellect cannot know perfectly what God is, even if it is assisted by the light of revelation, because of the infinite distance of human nature from the divine. The light of reason on its own is even less capable of understanding these mysteries.

§50. Thus, it is quite evident from what has been said about the existence of God that his essence is nobler than that of humans, who, as nature tells us, are in all other respects the most perfect among the sublunary creatures and are consequently longer lasting than those entities which we see around us, etc.; in one word, that he transcends our intellect, since our intellect can only understand what is equally or less perfect than ourselves.

§51. Yet there is a need for more subtle demonstrations if you want to prove from the light of nature that God is not one of the celestial bodies, since most humans do not know their changes, and I fear that even the most erudite would not be able to do so if they set aside revelation. When the Apostle, therefore, argues from the light of reason against the pagans, he attacks mainly those who regarded humans or beasts or inferior sublunary creatures as God, not those who worshipped the sun or celestial bodies.[34]

§52. Thus, at the same time, the wisdom of God is to be admired: among the nations that had ignored his most holy revelation, he allowed those who wanted to be considered the most rational to lapse into more absurd forms of idolatry than the barbarian nations. For these usually worshipped celestial bodies or invisible powers. But what is more absurd than the idolatry of the Egyptians, Greeks, and Romans?

§53. There will be the same difficulty if you want to argue on the basis of natural reason alone with those who say that *nature* or a *soul of the world* is God, or who defend the error that the *world is eternal.* For I do not believe that a pagan can be firmly held in check, even if you reply to him that he who asserts an eternal world denies that there is any cause of it, and so denies God. I can easily predict what he will say, namely, that this inference does not follow necessarily, for he who denies a cause of the world can declare that the world itself is God, or certainly that the world is coeternal with God since it is known that the pagans asserted two coeternal principles, God and prime matter.[35]

---

34. Romans 1:18–25.

35. The wording of this paragraph is changed in later editions to imply that natural reason is, in fact, sufficient to refute these pagan arguments.

§54. Thus I dislike the plan of the scholastic philosophers, who devote great efforts to investigating the divine attributes with the light of reason by two means, which they call those of *perfection* and of *negation:* the perfection which is in man they say is present *eminently* in God, and the imperfection which is in man is absent in God. For this is subject to infinite perplexities and qualifications. It is certainly not really suitable to be a proof, which is what they aim for, or at least should be aiming for in a theoretical discipline.

§55. To argue on the basis of perfection will be misleading if human perfection presupposes some imperfection; negation will also be misleading if the perfection opposed to human imperfection is at the same time joined with the imperfection, or if human moral imperfection is held to be such because of the physical imperfection of man.

§56. Thus, it is an imperfection of man that he cannot fly, but should you, like the pagans, invent a winged Mercury because of that?[36] I do not think so. For this perfection of birds is combined with the imperfection that they are corporeal.

§57. How would you know that this imperfection (of a bodily nature) does not apply to God, if Scripture had not revealed that God is a spirit? For if among those who acknowledge sacred Scripture there are wise men who imagine that God is corporeal, it is not surprising that the Stoics, the wisest philosophers among the pagans, defended the same doctrine.

§58. So it is a moral imperfection in man if he rejoices over the pain of another, even if this person suffers deservedly, for he who rejoices in this fashion is called *cruel.* But God himself testifies that he wants to laugh at the misfortune of the godless. Do you, therefore, believe that God is cruel? Far from it! So what is the difference? It is that this moral imperfection in man presupposes a physical imperfection, and that even

36. Mercury, the messenger of the gods and himself the god of thieves and merchants, was traditionally depicted with winged shoes.

a human being distinguished by the greatest dignity is equal in essence to the lowest beggar. Yet in comparison to God all humans are only dust and shadows.

§59. Thus virtue is not the smallest among the human perfections, and among the virtues justice is preeminent. These virtues, however, cannot be conceived without imperfection. For virtue is the habit of living according to laws; justice is the habit of rendering everyone their due. I will not insist here that the term *habit* is not applicable to God, for there might be objections to that, but I do say that there is no law that is prescribed to God and that man has nothing which he could also attribute to God.

§60. Therefore, I would not dare to apply the title *virtuous and just* to divine majesty if I did not see that his infinite wisdom in the revealed word had not rejected these terms for our imperfect perfections. When I see this, however, I am filled with humble veneration because God decides to speak to me in human terms, and at the same time I confess most willingly that the genuine and most exact sense of these expressions exceeds my intellect and so pertains to the mysteries of faith.

§61. And so I believe I do better by freely confessing my ignorance than by concealing it, like the Scholastics, and pretending some sort of great wisdom and trying to cover my ignorance with a cloak of hollow clichés. For what, I ask, is this term *eminently* which they use? It is either the same as *primarily*, or they use it to describe that which is the case *improperly*. The first meaning pertains to what is analogous, the latter to what is equivocal.

§62. If, for example, they claim that *virtue and justice are in God eminently, as in the most noble analogous case,* they may be providing me with a definition of *virtue and justice* which can be applied primarily to divine justice and secondarily to human justice. Yet we will expect this in vain, for these two forms of justice do not differ in degree but, properly speaking, fundamentally and are as distant from each other as heaven and earth.

§63. And if they decide that divine and human perfections cannot be comprehended in a common definition, they thereby confess that they predicate these *improperly* of God. That is, they do not know how these properties can be predicated of God.

§64. What does philosophy gain from these trifles? Who would not laugh if someone tried to demonstrate the perfections of man from the perfections of the flea and asserted nothing other than that the perfections of the flea were present to an eminent degree in man. Yet the distance between man and God is greater than that between the flea and man.

§65. But those are the fruits of Gentile philosophy, or rather their abuse, that the Scholastics set about deriving mysteries of faith from philosophy and turned philosophy into the norm of theology, contrary to the precept of the Apostle, who warned the Colossians not to allow themselves to be deceived by philosophy and vain fallacy and, contrary to the aim of the Fathers, who sometimes used philosophy in theological matters, to reveal the absurdities of the pagan philosophers.[37]

§66. Among this abuse I reckon almost all of the Scholastics' *pneumatics,* or their philosophy of spirits, such as God, angels, and the soul of man separate from the body. For everything they have taught on this matter and the arguments they have laboriously assembled will never convince a pagan, if revelation is set aside (with the exception of a few points concerning the existence and providence of God). But once you acknowledge Scripture, there is no need for all their ridiculous little books.

§67. Yet we believe there is a difference between God and the other classes of spirits in that the *existence of God,* as we have shown, can be investigated with the light of reason, but we cannot know (I say, "know") anything about angels and the soul separate from the body, not even that they exist, without the word of God.

§68. This absurd plan of the Scholastics, however, bred all the more absurdities, so that they even applied place and time, which are used as physical

---

37. Colossians 2:8. According to Thomasius he was here drawing on the arguments in Seckendorff's *Christen-Stat,* bk. III, chaps. 7 and 8.

measures of bodies, to spirits, although they cannot be measured, at least not in the way bodies can. The result is this golden, priceless mystery that, for example, the entire soul is in the entire body and is present in every part of the body in its entirety. If someone can prove this to me conclusively within a hundred years, may he carry away the prize of victory!

§69. Thus, you say, does reason show me nothing about God other than his existence and that he is the first being? It does certainly, but for the most part in a confused fashion: that he is *independent,* that he is *omnipotent,* etc. For he who calls God an independent being does not so much affirm something particular as deny his dependence. But he who calls God omnipotent does say that God can do everything, which does not involve a contradiction. Yet on the basis of the light of reason man only knows what is contradictory in an absolute sense, but not everything that implies a contradiction with respect to God, that is, that conflicts with his attributes as they are revealed in Scripture.

§70. Yet reason informs us clearly that God holds power over man and that God wants to exercise this power actually.

§71. God holds power over man because he is his creator.

§72. But I will demonstrate from the most solid proofs that God wants to exercise this power over man and that he wants at the same time to take care of the affairs of men. These proofs are all based in the first principle that it is impossible for something to be and not to be at the same time.

§73. (1) God is the creator of man. This assertion depends on the definition of God since we have demonstrated his existence above.

§74. (2) God therefore wanted man to be a rational animal. This is evident from the definition of man.

§75. (3) This means that God wanted man to live according to some norm, or law. This, again, flows from the definition of man, because it does not conform to the rational essence of man, to live without a law.

§76. (4) Furthermore, God wanted man to act with love and fear according to a prescribed norm or law. I prove this from the definitions of law and obligation which I have provided above.

§77. Thus, God also wanted to take care of the affairs of humans. This flows from the definitions of love and fear, because someone who is not concerned with my affairs would be feared and loved in vain.

§78. I believe there can be no room for doubt here and there is no need for further explanation, since I have said that "a rational animal cannot live without a law."

§79. Because beasts do not have a law, it does at first seem to contradict the excellence of man that he lives bound by a law, since it is inappropriate to restrict the freedom of a more excellent creature, but to concede liberty in every way to a less noble one.

§80. Yet the matter is obvious concerning beasts. They do live according to a norm infused into them by the supremely wise creator, but they cannot act according to an external norm because they are destitute of all liberty of action.

§81. Thus, when natural liberty is predicated of beasts, it does not denote a faculty of action implanted in them, but a part of the earth granted to them by nature and without consideration of human ownership, in which they exercise the locomotive powers of their bodies.

§82. Yet man has free will and is therefore able to direct his actions according to an external norm.

§83. But it is clear that he must put this ability into practice if he compares his nature with that of the other animals with respect to the body and the soul.

§84. Concerning the body he detects a greater weakness, when it comes to preserving himself without the help of other humans, than in brute animals. This weakness is so great that he would necessarily perish if other humans were not under an obligation to come to his help.

§85. Concerning the soul, insofar as he is corrupt in this state after the fall, he sees a greater depraved tendency to harm others. This is the result of several effects which are absent in beasts, even according to the opinion of the Peripatetics. If these people were not coerced by the fear of a greater evil, humankind would perish.

§86. But more than anything else, if man considers his *soul,* insofar as it is still *right* in this imperfect state, he will notice that he does not have a soul implanted in him only for the purpose of preserving the body (as are the souls of beasts), but one which consists of faculties that are stimuli to a fear of the Deity and to a social life. He notices that among humans there is a huge diversity of talents and inclinations which does not exist among beasts, and that this not only requires direction by a law to prevent the disturbance of peace by it, but that it [law] requires some sort of order and norm insofar as it helps to bring about peace and tranquillity among humans.

§87. Those who deny the principles that have so far been put forward concerning God are called theoretical *atheists;* you can divide these into *crass* and *subtle.* The former I call those who claim that there is no God. The latter are those who either claim that God does not care about the affairs of men or who say that he cares about them in such a way that they leave man no liberty of action, that is, who invent a sort of Stoic fate.

§88. For just as he who denies the existence of God destroys the foundation of all morality, so are all moral precepts similarly in vain if you accept those two last assertions.

§89. For if God does not take care of the affairs of humans, there is no ruler, and there will be nobody who must be obeyed.

§90. And if everything is directed by fate, there will be no obligation and no fear.

§91. For if by fate we mean God himself, it is in vain that he is feared and loved if I cannot acquire his love or avoid his anger.

§92. If by fate we mean something other than God, he is feared and loved in vain because he cannot make me happy and cannot punish me.

On the Interpretation of Divine Laws in Particular, That Is, on the First Principles of Natural Law and Positive Universal Law

§1. The structure of our argument demands that we learn about the main points of natural law and of divine positive law. And we shall start with natural law.

§2. By the first principle of natural law we should not understand the first practical principle, or the first principle of jurisprudence or of jurisprudence in general, insofar as it is distinct from natural and revealed jurisprudence. For by this first principle we mean, or certainly should mean, a proposition that comprehends all other precepts of natural law under a common axiom—one, so to speak, which presupposes the two other, more general axioms, that God and a ruler [*imperans*] must be obeyed.

§3. Thus, there will be three requisites, according to which, like a touchstone, we shall examine a principle of this kind. These are that it is (1) *true,* (2) *adequate,* (3) *evident.*

§4. I say *true;* that is, it must not contain any false proposition.

§5. *Adequate;* that is, this proposition truly contains all precepts of natural law within itself, and no other precepts than those of natural law.

§6. *Evident;* that is, it can be shown from the first practical principle, abstracting from revelation, that this is the divine will, and the link between it and the conclusions is evident and tangible.

§7. Perhaps you are laughing at such a circumstantial apparatus, and secretly you are delighted because you think you have with little effort found what we are looking for. What, you think, is this other than *Do that which necessarily conforms to the rational nature of man, and omit that which is repugnant to it.* We have already inserted this into our definition of natural law above, deriving it from the principle of noncontradiction. Thus its truth is clear, as are its adequacy and its evidence.

§8. But restrain your joy. You should have remembered that I had earlier promised a more detailed discourse on the conformity with the rational nature of man. I had in mind this chapter. In fact everyone makes a lot of noise about right reason, but when they are asked what right reason is and what the conformity with the rational nature of man is, then they are stuck. The connection of this principle with the first practical principle is indeed evident, but the connection of the conclusions with the principle itself is obscure. My complaint about the circumscription that everybody gives, however, is that truth is hidden away and thus, together with truth, adequacy and evidence are concealed.

§9. This was the subject of controversy for a long time among *philosophers, jurists, theologians,* and I almost added *physicians,* too, since someone discussed the laws of nations concerning headaches in a public disputation at a Catholic university.[38]

§10. The disputations of the *ancient philosophers* on the *supreme good* are relevant here. For Polemon the Platonist philosopher said, and Zeno and the Stoics, who received this opinion from him, taught everywhere, that

---

38. It has not been possible to identify this disputation, but Thomasius indicates that it was defended at Prague in 1687.

the supreme good is to live according to nature. Plato taught the same, as did Aristotle.[39]

§11. So far the ancient philosophers agreed on the matter itself. The aim of all of them was to teach *that a peaceful life of man with others* is the supreme good. When they should have clarified this and taught the means of acquiring it, they quarreled over inane matters, which were irrelevant to the question. Do you believe that someone who says that the supreme good consists in an *act of virtue* becomes better able to acquire the supreme good than he who says that it is a *habit of virtue* or he who wants it to be a *pleasure of the mind?* Do you not believe that those people who argue over whether money consists in the physical object, the quantity, or the aptitude to buy other things are unable to make a profit, while in the meantime others are carrying out commercial transactions?

§12. Thus, we leave all of them to their mad wisdom. Justinian claimed that there were three precepts of right: "Live honestly," "Harm nobody," and "Render everyone his due."[40]

§13. In fact, his generosity is a little overwhelming. We are looking for one proposition, and he gives us three instead. Let us pick the best one.

§14. The precept "Do not harm anyone" has to my knowledge not met with universal approval, maybe because it was too narrow. The other two have found some adherents.

§15. You may see some arguing vigorously that in the precept "Honest actions are to be performed, despicable actions are to be omitted" the sum of all natural wisdom is concealed. We do not object to that, but we would like some *evidence.* What is honest? No matter whether you call that honest which conforms to a *law* or that which conforms to *reason,* we are still not

---

39. Polemon was head of the Academy in Athens from 314/313 to 270/269 B.C. Zeno (335–263 B.C.) was a pupil of Polemon and the founder of the Stoic school.

40. Justinian, *Digest,* ed. Alan Watson (Philadelphia: University of Pennsylvania Press, 1998), I.1.10. [Hereafter this work is referred to as *Digest.*]

enlightened. For we shall then ask, "What is that which conforms to reason and law? You explain something obscure with something equally obscure."

§16. Yet we fear above all that we will be ridiculed by the entire world if we attempt to put forward the idea of *innate principles* against those who deny the perspicuity of this axiom and if we wanted to censure them for denying the very first principle.

§17. But as far as the third precept is concerned, "Render everyone his due," we see no reason why we should glory in it as if it were a newly discovered continent after the jurist had already mentioned this in his time in the definition of justice. If this precept really were *evident,* it would be surprising why none of the many ancient glossators, who studied the same with such great diligence, ever arrived at a clear idea of it.

§18. I think something similar ought to be said of another slogan of Roman law, that "everyone should live by the same law he uses to settle the legal cases of another person." A similar rule is "What you do not wish to have done to you, do not inflict on another." All of this is true; these are pious sayings, but they are not *evident,* nor are they *adequate.* They do not apply to relations between unequal persons. They cannot be applied to the duties of man toward himself.

§19. We almost forgot Hobbes. He put forward the following fundamental law of nature: "Seek peace, where it can be had, and where it cannot, resort to war."[41] Not bad indeed, if only Hobbes had meant what he said, and if only by peace he had meant the peace of all. A little earlier he had said that the first foundation of natural law is that "everyone should protect his life and limbs as much as he can."[42] Many scholars have already shown that this is false. That norm regulates the instincts of brutes. The excellence of man requires a different rule.

---

41. Thomas Hobbes, *On the Citizen,* ed. R. Tuck and M. Silverthorne (Cambridge: Cambridge University Press, 1998), chap. 2, §2, p. 34.
42. Ibid., chap. 1, §7, p. 27.

§20. Until now we have easily cleared the field of lightly armed soldiers and fresh recruits who had little support. But now we need to resort to heavier weapons. The enemies attack in droves; their bold leaders march ahead of them: *Sanchez, Rodriquez, Vasquez,* names bound to instill terror.[43] What then shall we do? Shall we flee? Shall we fight? The former is shameful. The latter is audacious. Either is prudent. We will flee, since even a Horace flees.[44]

§21. Therefore, having placed ourselves outside the battlefield we expect their approach. What need, they say, is there to search laboriously for a norm of reason? Man is created in the image of God, and it therefore must be the case that in the state after the fall the rays of divine sanctity and justice, which are, so to speak, relics of the divine image, shine forth in man. Thus, since God did everything according to the norm of his divine sanctity, goodness, wisdom, and justice, and so imposed on himself out of his own free will a quasi-eternal law, it has to be the case that natural law is also based on this archetype, and therefore to conform to right reason is the same as *conforming to divine sanctity and justice.*

§22. What do we say to that? Let us examine whether this proposition, "whatever conforms to divine sanctity is commanded by natural law, whatever does not conform to it is prohibited by natural law," conforms to the above requirements. I will not comment on its *truth.* For we have already shown above[45] that this eternal law is a fiction of the Scholastics and that God is not subject to a law, except in a very improper sense.

§23. Let us then consider the *adequacy.* And this norm seems to us *wider* than what is regulated by it, and in another respect *narrower.* For do you

---

43. These are Spanish Catholic scholastic philosophers.

44. According to Roman legend the rivalry between the cities of Rome and Alba Longa was decided by combat between three representatives of each side. When the Albans had killed two of the three Romans, the third Roman, Horatius, fled, with the three Albans in pursuit. Horatius then succeeded in killing all of the Albans one by one, as they caught up with him.

45. See *Institutes,* bk. I, chap. I, §31.

not believe that *divine positive law* is also based on its conformity with sanctity and justice? But we are already seeking the axiom from which we could derive the conclusions of natural law.

§24. If you respond that positive law is founded in conformity with the divine will, natural law in conformity with its sanctity, antecedently to the divine will, I will return to the comments I have already made above on this improper notion of divine attributes.

§25. But it is also *narrower.* Natural law dictates *gratitude.* But how do you deduce this virtue from the archetype of divine justice? Who ever did God a favor in order to have it returned?

§26. But above all we miss *evidence.* I will not repeat that virtues and justice are predicated of God in human terms and improperly. You should only consider this: natural reason provides no or only very confused notions of the image of God and its sanctity, but Scripture must here do its best. Hence, if a pagan asks why homicide, for example, is contrary to divine sanctity, or why keeping agreements for example is according to his justice, we shall either not have a reply or we shall have to draw on sacred Scripture and so meddle with it.

§27. I believe, however, that this belief of the Scholastics in the conformity of natural law with the divine essence owes its origin to pagan philosophy. For Augustine and Clement of Alexandria[46] mention that Plato defined the supreme good and the essence of virtue as man becoming similar to God. The ineptitudes of the Stoics, who compared their wise man to God, are widely known.

§28. We therefore remember the saying of the apostle and do not seek the norm of natural right outside of man, but in man himself, in whose hearts

---

46. Augustine of Hippo (A.D. 354–430) and Clement of Alexandria (ca. 150–ca. 215): fathers of the Christian church.

it is inscribed.[47] Let it be the case that there is in human reason an image or some remnant of the divine image, yet why do we not look at this reason of man in itself rather than in relation to something outside itself? Human reason is indeed something that exists in itself, not a mere relation the essence of which only consists in the fact that it is related to something else.

§29. Thus, we believe that the condition itself of humanity or the state of all of humanity is the norm of natural law. And why should we not think that? Indeed, natural reason itself, which almost everybody speaks about, is a condition of this kind. Indeed, it automatically follows from the definition of a state provided above, that every state is in its way a norm of law.

§30. But I believe that here I am being warned of violating the first practical principle when I am occupied with trying to demonstrate everything from it. For I said above that *law is the norm of human actions.* And now I say *that the condition of humans is the norm of law.* Will the law therefore simultaneously be the norm of humans and humans the norm of law? Thus, the same thing is and is not a norm at the same time.

§31. I will try to extract the response to this objection from you. Let us pretend that there are two kinds of humans in this world who are not known to each other by any intercourse and conversation, one with an erect and robust body, the other endowed with a weak body and a misshaped hump on the back of the neck, the head bowed down toward the earth. Imagine a diet was to be prescribed to each kind of humans by a physician, or that a garment was to be made by the tailor, so that each of the two is held upright and does not creep on the ground like a quadruped. Well then, do you think the prescribed diet or the specially designed garment will not be rightly called a norm for living, or a norm for walking?

§32. Moreover, do you not think that the physician in prescribing the diet and the tailor in making the garment must also study the nature of the

47. Romans 2:15.

bodies to which these norms are to be applied? Indeed, the physician will ban more kinds of food for the person with the weak body than for the robust person and will also supply medicines in smaller doses. And when the tailor is making the garment for the crooked people, he will have to leave space for the hump. And while in the garments of the former that material is sufficient which gently prevents them from bending down, in the latter case there is need for stiff metal strips which suppress their inclination to walking hunched over.

§33. But how does this concern me, you will ask. In these examples the norm and what is regulated by the norm are in no way the same. The condition of the body is the norm of the diet and the garment. But the diet and the garment are not the norm of the body, but of the corporeal actions. These are different things.

§34. I will respond that it is the same with law and a particular state. *The state is the norm of the law; the law, however, is the norm of actions,* which humans living in this state must perform.

§35. Leave me alone, you say, with your silly comparisons. You will not extricate yourself from my objection like that. This is all fictitious. *But it does not suit him who professes the true religion to invent such things, which God revealed to us differently.* Nor will you be able to protect yourself by appealing to philosophical freedom, since your philosophy must not conflict with the precepts of true religion.

§36. Yet I do not remember sacred Scripture prohibiting a fiction, and I do not remember the Augsburg Confession prohibiting that we argue from fictitious cases. Theologians often invent many things. The jurists make up a lot. Logic teaches how the young should argue from fictitious cases in an erudite fashion. But should, therefore, the treatise on fictions be eliminated from jurisprudence as a heresy? Should the books on logic be purged as heretical, which put forward this example of a hypothetical proposition: if the ass flies, he has feathers? I do not think so.

§37. There can be no doubt that a *lie* is one thing, a *fiction* another. Granted that a lie is contrary to religion, yet a fiction is something fundamentally different.

§38. We shall say nothing here of fictions in Roman law, but a fiction, as we have used it, is nothing other than the first part of a hypothetical proposition which neither affirms nor denies anything, but only infers from the fiction the second part as a consequence. From this the axiom is known that a condition does not assume anything to exist. Similarly, it is not necessary for examples to be true.

§39. Therefore, the assertion stands that the norm of laws of nature is to be derived from the common state and condition of humanity. The comparisons we have used to propose this thesis remain intact, and we will use them in future to demonstrate related claims.

§40. For as we have deduced above that the state of man is twofold, that of innocence and that after the fall, therefore order demands that we see *which state* we must turn to in deriving the law of nature. But here I ask that you yourself reply to me.

§41. Let us assume that a physician lives among humans who are furnished with a weak body and poor health and is himself weak and must prescribe a general rule for staying healthy to his countrymen. Do you believe that he should look to the constitution of robust men, after he has gained some confused knowledge about them from a travel book, or after he has found out from the writings of some other physician what means such people tend to apply to preserve their health? And when he realizes that he cannot achieve this state of health among his own people, do you believe that he must look to an idea of health that is formed from the constitution of robust people and must devote his efforts to preserving or bringing about such a state of health?

§42. But—and this is the main point here—we have already shown very clearly that man, with his natural powers, cannot in this life recover the perfection of the state of innocence even to the smallest degree but must be content with what is left over.

§43. And why do we need to say any more about it? Paul, one of God's elect, complained bitterly of this misery and that man *cannot rid himself of this inclination to evil,*[48] and he is a witness greater than any other.

§44. I cannot accept this cliché, which all Peripatetics would approve of, that he who teaches a particular discipline *must form an idea for himself of a most perfect state,* even if such a state does not exist and cannot exist, given the present condition of humans.

§45. I do not criticize this view for having its origin, apparently, in pagan and especially Platonic philosophy. I criticize it because it is obviously not suitable for civil life. We are dealing not with abstract ideas of men, but with actually existing humans. Thus, the remedies to be used are those that will preserve them. Nor do I believe that someone will earn thanks who refers to More's *Utopia* when a prince asks him about securing the utility of the commonwealth.[49]

§46. Moreover, there was a positive law in the state of innocence, too. If, therefore, the conformity with this state were the foundation of natural law, it would follow that positive laws would also be the norm of natural law.

§47. There are also many things today which did not exist in the state of innocence and would not have developed, not only particular societies but also specific states of humans and their offices, such as those of executioners, midwives, warriors, tailors, surgeons, almsgivers, etc. Not to mention the fact that there were or were going to be many things in the state of

---

48. Romans 7:15.

49. Thomas More's (1478–1535) *Utopia* (1516) was a fictitious account of a well-regulated commonwealth. For a modern edition see Thomas More, *Utopia,* ed. G. M. Logan and Robert M. Adams, revised ed. (Cambridge: Cambridge University Press, 2002).

innocence that have no place today, such as the nudity of the first humans, marriages between brothers and sisters, and similar matters.

§48. Finally, if we look for an evident principle, the requirements of the doctrine of the Apostle will not be met because he wanted to refute the pagans on the basis of the light of nature. For if you ask why homicide is contrary to the state of innocence and the keeping of pacts conforms to it, Scripture will have to supply the missing answer in either case. There also remains an almost infinite number of controversies concerning the state of innocence, in which either side can be defended because Scripture tells us very little about this state.

§49. We shall, therefore, primarily consider the nature of man as it is: it is corrupt indeed, but (so that you do not quibble over the idea of a corrupt law) right in its own way. Since we are writing among Christians, we will on the basis of the same principle confirm and illustrate our opinion later by showing that the same principle of ours also obtained in the state of innocence.

§50. For man in the state of innocence and man after the fall do not differ in kind, just as humans with a robust and with a weak body do not. The conclusions vary in either case, but the general principles are the same in both. These principles cannot be learned just by recognizing the difference between the two states, yet a good physician must be able to cure both the robust and the weak men on the basis of the same general principles, applied in different ways.

§51. Thus man differs from beasts in that he is rational. If only our intellect were powerful enough to have complete knowledge of itself a priori! Yet we are forced to inquire into the nature of reason in a roundabout way.

§52. The reason of man consists in thought. To think is to connect one term with another and one proposition with another. The latter is called reasoning. But we can only reason with words, which we either retain in our mind or utter aloud. Therefore, λόγος [speech], according to the Greeks, is either ἐνδιάθετος [uttered within] or προφορικός [put forward/ uttered aloud]. Words, however, as we shall see below, are imposed on things by humans living in the same society.

§53. Moreover, whatever the Cartesians say, infants do not think from the very first moment after birth, but are endowed only with an aptitude for thinking. Without the company of other humans this aptitude cannot be actualized. For the reports we read about humans brought up by wild beasts say that humans of this kind were almost identical to beasts, or that by living among the beasts this aptitude for thought was developed only to a very small degree.

§54. To summarize briefly: *there is no reason without speech, there is no use for speech outside society, nor is reason active outside society.* Thus we will not go wrong in saying that this aptitude, which exists in humans before the exercise of reason, is nothing other than an inclination to reason with other humans. Indeed, every aptitude tends toward an action as its end.

§55. Thus, when we call man rational, it is the same as if we say that he is social. Sociality, however, is a common inclination, infused into humanity by God, by the force of which he desires a happy and peaceful life with other humans. But why peaceful? Because in a state of turbulence we do not exercise our reason.

§56. This peaceful life, put into practice, is called *society.* The contrary of that, as the Peripatetics themselves confess, is *conflict.*

§57. But we prove our opinion *a posteriori,* because man outside society cannot be happy. I will not even mention here that great misery in which infants find themselves if they are destitute of human company. Even for adults life would be miserable if there were no other humans who would minister to their needs.

§58. What then? I appeal to everybody's own conscience: even if we pretend that someone enjoyed the kind of felicity the poets attribute to *Psyche*, yet, if he were deprived of all human society, would he not rather wish to live in human society and do without these delights of the senses?[50]

§59. And to be precise, there can be no pleasure of the senses outside of society. It would be prolix to try to prove this by induction here. We demand that you come up with a counterexample.

§60. Even misanthropes would be miserable without human society because they would have nothing to hate.

§61. Even those bookworms and those people who never consider themselves more alone than when they are not alone would be miserable without books. But where would they get their books from if there were no human society? Assume that all other humans would be annihilated; what use would books be if they cannot show others what displeases them in this or that author, etc.

§62. If you wanted to confirm our argument with evidence from the history of the state of innocence, we have divine testimony, which is greater than all prudence, even that of Solomon. Adam was very happy in general, but he lacked a companion. Divine wisdom pronounced that it was not good for man to be alone.

§63. Thus, the conclusion remains unshaken that the rational nature of man is identical to his social nature. And therefore what is understood by conformity with rational nature is conformity with the sociality of man.

---

50. Psyche became Cupid's lover and wife. The story of Psyche is told in books 4–6 of Apuleius, *The Golden Ass,* trans. W. Adlington, rev. S. Gaselee, Loeb Classical Library (London: Heinemann, 1947).

§64. We, therefore, declare that the sum of natural law is contained in this principle: "Do that which necessarily conforms to the social life of man and omit that which is contrary to it."

§65. Thus, no doubt remains concerning the truth of this principle. Its adequacy is not only clear from the fact that all special precepts of natural law are to be derived from that source, but also from the fact that it does not depend on any precept of positive law.

§66. Its evidence finally is demonstrated as follows. First, if God had wanted man not to act according to his sociality, he would not have wanted him to be rational. An irrational human being, however, would be a contradiction in terms.

§67. Then the connection of conclusions with this first principle is also evident. For whenever I ask, for example, how homicide, thefts, etc., are contrary to sociality, I respond clearly that this is because they disturb the common peace of all humankind.

§68. Similarly, when I ask how, for example, the keeping of agreements necessarily conforms to sociality, the response is evident: because, if this were not preserved, this same peace would be disrupted.

§69. You see, at the same time, that an action necessarily conforming to sociality is one the omission of which disturbs the common peace of humanity, and that action which does not conform to sociality is one the performance of which disturbs the common peace of humanity. For this omission or performance would lead to war, a war of all against all, which could extinguish all of humankind.

§70. Yet there is no lack of arguments against the adequacy of our principle. Some believe that it is possible to derive rather different conclusions from this source. Thieves, for example, also act according to their society and its purpose. This objection questions the truth of our axiom at the same time.

§71. But these theorists obviously confuse society with sociality. Society is rightly constituted only if it does not conflict with sociality.

§72. And so that you do not wonder how a society can conflict with sociality, since society is named after sociality, remember that there is no question that the reasoning of a thief conflicts with reasonableness.

§73. Several people believe, however, that only the duties of man toward other men can be deduced from our principle, but not the duties of man toward God, toward himself, and toward beasts.

§74. We readily admit this to be the case with respect to the duties of man toward God insofar as these refer to external worship. That, as we will soon show, is part of Christian jurisprudence, not natural law.

§75. Even if by duties toward God you mean a general obligation toward God, you will not be able to object to our argument because the command to obey God is not a precept of natural law but its presupposition. We have shown that this precept pertains to divine law in general.

§76. The duties of man toward himself, properly speaking, do not exist. Nobody can be under an obligation to himself and therefore cannot owe a duty to himself. The duties that carry this name are, in fact, duties either toward God or toward other humans, insofar as man is under an obligation to either of them with respect to himself. In the case of the former we will derive these duties from Scripture; in the case of the latter from sociality, in the appropriate place.[51]

§77. Finally, there are no duties of man toward beasts, just as there is no society of man with beasts, although the harsh treatment of beasts violates sociality or divine positive law, as we shall explain when there is a convenient occasion to do so.[52]

---

51. See *Institutes,* bk. II, chap. ii.
52. Ibid., chap. ix, §27.

§78. Thus far on the first principle of natural law. The first principle of divine positive law is this: "Do that which God revealed to you in Scripture you should do and omit the doing anything contrary."[53]

§79. With regard to universal positive law in particular, we identify three requisites as far as the principles of knowledge are concerned. Two are held in common with any positive law; a third is specific to it: namely, (1) that Scripture indicates an action to be commanded or prohibited, (2) that this action cannot be derived from sociality, (3) that Scripture indicates this law of God to apply to all humans.

§80. From these two sources we shall derive all conclusions of particular precepts like rivulets. And there is no need to say anything more about the interpretation of natural law. For in putting forward the conclusions we will use the same method of demonstration and the same kind of reasoning as before. In positive law, however, we have another kind of interpretation, which uses conjectures or probable arguments instead of demonstrations. For positive law is not inscribed on the hearts of humans.

§81. It thus has to be explained in certain general rules how these probable arguments are to be formed. But this discussion has to be deferred until we have explained the nature of agreements and the duties concerning them.

§82. For God, in his supreme benevolence, accommodated himself to the capacity of the human understanding when he revealed positive law by using human speech, and so here the same rules are to be observed as in the interpretation of agreements. Thus, we cannot examine it [positive law] before looking at the rules concerning speech and agreements. Moreover, scholars agree almost unanimously on the interpretation of the divine law that is relevant to the duties discussed here.

53. Later editions add "in addition to the requirements of sociality" to the beginning of this sentence.

⚶ CHAPTER V ⚶

On the Duties of Man Toward God

§1. By a duty of man toward God we here do not mean some theoretical principle, but a practical one. And this principle does not regulate internal actions only, but mainly external ones. It is, however, not a first practical principle, but a specific one which can be demonstrated by way of a conclusion from the first principle of natural law or positive law.

§2. It is contained in this one precept: "Worship God according to the manner revealed by himself."

§3. What we mean by God is evident from the preceding passages; by worship we mean an external human action, consisting in speech, deed, or gesture, which signals the attention and reverence that is due to another.

§4. Divine worship is sometimes divided into internal and external, yet internal worship is in fact not worship in the absolute and most proper sense, but only a presupposition of external worship.

§5. Thus, those matters which tend to be referred to internal worship— that man should honor and revere God, or that he should admire his supreme power and goodness; that he should love him as the author and giver of all good; that he should place his hope in him, as all our future happiness depends on him; that he should acquiesce in the divine will which does everything according to his goodness in the best possible way; that he should fear him as being all-powerful and the one whose displeasure can cause the greatest evil; finally, that in all matters he should most humbly obey him as creator, lord, and best and greatest ruler—all these, I say, insofar as they can be demonstrated from natural reason we already assume to be included in the first general principle of divine jurisprudence, "Obey God."

§6. Thus, the external worship of God, that is, the worship of God in the simple sense, or the religious worship of God, is either *general* and thus common to most, if not all, nations, or *special.* The former, it seems, can be considered mainly in relation to three elements: the invocation of God, praising him, and showing gratitude.

§7. I call *special external worship* the different kinds of invoking, praising, and thanking God, which vary between nations. Among Christians, for example, this concerns the usual practice (or what should be the usual practice) of appealing to God in the name of Christ, with a mind free of vengefulness, in public, by extending one's hands, baring the head, even toward one's enemies, through music, fasting, and listening to the word of God. The sanctification of the Sabbath and the use of the sacraments, etc., also belong here.

§8. And while I know very well that many people tend to derive the external worship of God from the dictate of right reason, we must proceed differently here.

§9. It is certain that it is appropriate for God to be worshipped by humans, and this is above all evident from the arguments of those who have attempted to demonstrate divine worship on the basis of natural reason.

§10. It is also most just that man should worship God whenever God demands it. This follows from the first principle of divine jurisprudence, "Obey God."

§11. But that is the question, or at least should be the question: *Can un-aided human reason prove that God demands worship from humans?* We say that this is very difficult to prove.

§12. For if you look at God, he does not need this external worship. The philosopher Demonax used this as an excuse when he was accused of impiety and sacrilege because he had never sacrificed to Minerva.[54] He replied that he had not offered Minerva any sacrifices so far because he believed that she had no need of his offerings.

§13. As far as man is concerned, however, the sociality of man or a peace-ful life, or whatever you want to call his temporal happiness, is not directly harmed by this omission of external acts of worship as long as there is internal worship.

§14. Thus, I do acknowledge that blasphemy and contempt of God and whatever is contrary to internal worship, be it retained within the mind or declared in external actions, is contrary to right reason because it conflicts with the internal worship commanded by the precept "Obey God."

§15. I also acknowledge that external worship is one of those things that are permitted to an eminent degree: it is not only not repugnant to the natural reason of man, but also far better, if God is worshipped than if this worship is omitted.

§16. Yet all this is not enough to prove the need for external worship. It is legitimate for human reason, left to its own devices, to argue that it does not matter whether prayers are spoken aloud. For God, who knows our hearts, can hear our [unspoken] sighs, and he, as my creator and preserver, knows what I am in need of even without my prayers.

---

54. See Pierre Ayrault, *Rerum ab omni antiquitate iudicatarum Pandectae, recognitae a Philippo Andrea Oldenburgero* (Geneva, 1677), bk. I, title 2, chap. 5, p. 10. The story of Demonax was originally told by Lucian (see Lucian, "Demonax," p. 151, in Lucian, *Lucian,* trans. A. M. Harmon, vol. 1 [London: Heinemann, 1913]).

§17. Thus human praise adds nothing to divine eminence and majesty, and right reason even tells us that whenever a person praises God without reverence or fear, this person sins gravely, for he intends to deceive God through the use of external signs. But if man inwardly glorifies God, reason considers external praise superfluous.

§18. The same should be said of rendering thanks. Rendering thanks is necessary among men, in order to show another that a favor is accepted by myself and that I am prepared in turn to serve the other, as will be shown later.[55] But with regard to God, my thoughts alone are enough to show this.

§19. In sum, prayers, praises, rendering thanks, are necessary external signs among humans because man does not know the thoughts of another man. God, however, does.

§20. And I do not care if you say that the external worship of God is necessary not because of God, but because of humans themselves, since the felicity of commonwealths could not survive without external worship, and there is no commonwealth in which there was not some form of external worship of God. You may add that even pagans place great emphasis on external religious worship.

§21. These arguments may seem pretty good, but we have already pointed out above that it is not possible to use the testimonies of pagans (quite apart from the question whether they are talking about external or internal worship) as definitive proof that something is part of natural law. And so the common practice of pagans can only provide an illustration, not a proof.

§22. But as far as the felicity of commonwealths is concerned, we must beware that we do not substitute the secondary purpose of divine worship for its primary purpose. Reason can understand that the happiness of commonwealths is supported by external worship if one citizen indicates

55. See *Institutes,* bk. II, chap. v, §50.

to another through external signs his internal reverence for the Deity, which is the foundation of all obligation. This further increases the trust of the members of society toward each other. Yet these external signs are very often deceptive, and their omission does not necessarily disturb the happiness of the commonwealth.

§23. Moreover, if the happiness of commonwealths were the real purpose of divine worship, the generally accepted rule of philosophers (that is, that the end determines the means) would necessarily imply that religious worship would have to vary according to the variety of commonwealths and that the utility of individual commonwealths would regulate divine worship. That would be very impious.

§24. In fact, virtually everyone professes that the true end of religious worship is the eternal beatitude of man, but reason on its own knows nothing of that end. How then could it arrive at the knowledge of divine worship as a means to that end?

§25. These observations suffice concerning the so-called general religious worship of God. With regard to particular forms of worship there are as many arguments for our opinion as there are circumstances and varieties of such worship. There seems to be no need to explain these individually in detail since particular worship presupposes the general, the necessity of which, as we have shown, is not evident to reason.

§26. Thus, you see how ignorant our reason is with regard to this most noble duty of man, and to what extent the light of reason without the light of revelation is shrouded in darkness, and how dangerous it is to try to understand the holiest mysteries of God by the standards of reason, which is so weakened by the fall. And so you understand why, in the precept directing man's duty in this regard, I would add: "God must be worshipped according to the way revealed by himself."

§27. If we study sacred and ecclesiastical history, it will be clear that worship invented by human reason never pleased God, but that the Deity, from the very beginning of the world, wanted true worship to be guided by the standard of divine revelation.

§28. The true church is more ancient than false religions, and the devil has been the perpetual ape of God. Thus, it seems more probable that they are right who believe that the Egyptians and the other nations of the first centuries [of humankind] borrowed a lot from (or rather retained a lot of) what had been established by God in the beginning; it seems less likely, as some argue, that God drew on the precepts of the Egyptians or the Zabians when he passed his positive laws, especially his ceremonial laws.

§29. It is also evident from the above what is to be said about the common division of religion into natural and revealed.

§30. We have just now noted that the term *religion* is used in different meanings. It is understood as the action of the intellect concerning God and divine matters, that is, as knowledge of God; as the action of the will, and then either as internal worship or external worship; as knowledge of God together with internal worship; as external and internal worship; or as knowledge and both kinds of worship together. For different authors use the term *religion* in different ways.

§31. Those who by religion mean "knowledge of God" are certainly right to subdivide it into natural and revealed, though they commonly attribute more to this natural knowledge than is appropriate. Thus, the detailed comments we made above on this matter are also relevant here.[56]

§32. Those who use the term *religion* to refer to internal worship are not wrong either since we have just shown that this is derived from the principles regulating human action.[57]

---

56. Ibid., chap. iii, §49.
57. See §5 in this chapter.

§33. And I am convinced that they are right in considering this natural religion in the first and second sense a part of true religion.

§34. This opinion is attacked by a number of people on the grounds that natural knowledge of God and of internal worship is not enough to achieve salvation. Yet I do not believe that this argument is conclusive since being true and leading to salvation are two different things.

§35. Thus true natural religion and revealed religion differ in that the latter is salvificatory, while the former is directed only to the temporal well-being of man.

§36. And how could it be otherwise since natural religion is far less perfect than revealed and rests on purely human faith, which is based on natural reason?

§37. They, however, who by "natural religion" mean some kind of external divine worship known on the basis of natural reason are wrong. All external worship is based on revealed religion.

§38. We have already shown this. Also, it is impossible to name any religion in the entire world which does not claim to be based on some revelation. We depend on the revelation of the true God; all heretics either distort the interpretation of sacred Scripture or proclaim revelations peculiar to themselves, which is what the Jews do. The Turks believe the revelations of their pseudo-prophets; pagans, from the beginning, mixed diabolical revelations with divine and even today either allow themselves to be deceived by the lies of the devil or believe the fallacies of his ministers, such as the Brahmins and similar people.

§39. In that respect [i.e., external worship] revealed religion, therefore, is either true or false. But external worship based on natural religion has to be a fiction or a form of false religion.

§40. And we must not be expected to derive particular conclusions concerning the duty of man toward God from the principle concerning the worship of God which we have posited above. For that is the business of theologians.

§41. We shall therefore omit to explain the precepts of Christian religion [on the basis of natural religion], as well as those religious precepts that were made known to humanity at the time of Adam or Noah.

§42. The many questions concerning sacrifices and their origin, which have been argued over a lot, are relevant here.

§43. It is the same with several controversies over the Sabbath and its observance, especially the question what part of this precept is moral and what is ceremonial.

§44. Similarly, there are the controversies concerning the prohibition of eating blood and parts of a living animal and its present-day use after the decree of the Apostolic convention on this matter was imposed on converted pagans in the early church.[58]

§45. Thus, we could have dispensed with this chapter, because it is about another kind of jurisprudence, if we had not had to respond to the opinions and reasons of those who disagreed with us.

THE END OF THE FIRST BOOK

---

58. Acts 15:20.

BOOK II

I undertook this work trusting not in eloquence, but in truth. This work may be greater than can be accomplished with my powers alone, but truth itself will complete it.[1]

—Lactantius, "On False Wisdom," chap. 1

∞ CHAPTER I ∞

On the Duty of Man Toward Himself

§1. Like beasts, man has a physical body, which is usually described as a form of animal life; and both [i.e., humans and beasts] have a desire for self-preservation as a natural instinct that is distinct from reason.

§2. The locomotive power of beasts, which lack reason, follows no other guide than this instinct [for self-preservation].

§3. Man, however, is rational and thus social, and therefore he must free his locomotive power from being governed by this instinct and subordinate it to sociality.

---

1. See Lactantius, "On False Wisdom," 1.4, in Lactantius, *Divine Institutes,* trans. and ed. Anthony Bowen and Peter Garnsey (Liverpool: Liverpool University Press, 2003), bk. 4, p. 168.

§4. Thus the Stoics and, following them, other philosophers who discussed the duty of man were wrong when they explained this duty by referring to the first and second impressions of nature.[2]

§5. What they call the first principle of nature is nothing other than the instinct implanted in this body-machine, an instinct which is irrelevant to the moral duty of man and which is beyond the pale of law, insofar as man shares it [this instinct] with beasts.

§6. The care for oneself must take precedence before the particular duties toward others, insofar as someone who does not take care of himself is unable to benefit others. And the more difficult it is to correct self-neglect or prejudices, the more should man be concerned about this care of self.

§7. You could, therefore, formulate the following general precept concerning man's duty toward himself: "Aim to preserve yourself in such a way that you further a peaceful life with others."

§8. Thus, man must make use of those means of self-preservation that are necessary for encouraging sociality.

§9. Man cannot preserve his life using those means [of self-preservation] that disrupt peaceful relations with others.

§10. Those means which neither further nor disrupt these relations may, according to natural law, be used or omitted (unless divine law commands something else), but there are different degrees of permissibility, depending on the extent to which these means tend to contribute more to encouraging or disrupting social peace, even if they do so incidentally.

§11. As man consists of a soul and a body-machine, we must now consider what his duty is with respect to each of the two.

---

2. Thomasius here refers to Grotius, *The Rights of War and Peace,* bk. I, chap. i, §§1–2.

§12. This duty is summarized by the precept: "Know thyself." For he who does not know himself cannot properly judge what means are suitable for furthering sociality.

§13. Yet this precept pertains not only to the soul, as Cicero argues, who follows the mistaken belief of pagan philosophers that the soul alone is the essence of man. It pertains to man as a whole.[3]

§14. Insofar as the soul is concerned in particular, man knows it is his noblest part since it distinguishes him from beasts. It follows that the former must perform the function of a guide, while the latter is a servant or tool. From this is derived the specific precept: "Prefer the cultivation of the mind to that of the body."

§15. We have also shown above that man was created not just for the sake of theoretical speculation, but also for action. Hence this other precept follows: "Prefer the cultivation of the will to that of the intellect."

§16. These precepts state nothing other than that the moral good of the mind is to be preferred to its natural good, and that each of these must be preferred to those goods that only benefit the body.

§17. The so-called goods of fortune are required partly to cultivate and encourage both goods of the mind [that is, intellect and will], and partly to sustain the well-being of the body. Their use is to be regulated according to the above rules.

§18. I pass over the spiritual and eternal goods of the soul, even though the authors on natural law sometimes have a habit of discussing their cultivation. For I do not see how the eternal beatitude of man and the immortality of the human soul, which this beatitude presupposes, can be demonstrated by the light of reason.

---

3. Thomasius is here drawing on Pufendorf, *De jure naturae et gentium*, bk. II, chap. iv, §5.

§19. We also avoid interfering with theology here. For we have shown that the discussion of this beatitude is to be left to theologians alone.

§20. Possibility here needs to be distinguished from actuality: of course, reason recognizes that the immortality of the soul is not impossible for God, for there is no logical contradiction in believing that a creature will exist forever.

§21. Yet I deny that it is possible to prove philosophically that the soul is actually immortal and that God wanted to turn this possibility into an actuality.

§22. And that is so because every proof must ultimately be derived from the definition of a thing. But the soul has no complete idea of itself. Although it feels, so to speak, that it is a thinking being, there is no necessary connection between thinking and eternal duration.

§23. Thus, man may examine his soul or its properties throughout his entire life, but he will not find out anything substantial without the help of sacred Scripture. This doctrine, therefore, belongs to the mysteries of faith and to the prerogatives Christians have before pagans.

§24. For as far as those pagans are concerned who asserted the immortality of the soul, it is quite certain that in some cases they adopted this belief from others, as several [pagan] authors have hinted; in others they based their argument on the consensus of nations or constructed their opinion on obscure and quite improbable arguments.[4] And in other cases they used proofs that were based on a false and heterodox hypothesis.

§25. In general, pagan philosophers assumed two coeternal principles, God and prime matter.

---

4. See Seneca, *Ad Lucilium epistulae morales,* trans. R. M. Gummere, Loeb Classical Library (London: Heinemann, 1953), "Epistle CXVII," 3:341. Aristotle, "On the Soul," in Aristotle, *On the Soul; Parva Naturalia; On Breath,* trans. W. S. Hett (Cambridge, Mass.: Harvard University Press, 1995), 423a, p. 171.

§26. As far as the souls of humans are concerned, however, some believed these to be produced by the power of matter and thus to be mortal, which is what the Epicureans argued.

§27. Others, such as the Platonists, believed that human souls were effluvia of the divine essence, and that they were all created at the same time in order to exist separately [from matter], but (because of some strange idea about matter) deserved to be imprisoned in physical bodies. Thus, they argued, the essence of man consisted only in the soul, which was a divine particle and thus immortal, or at least very long-lasting.

§28. I move on to the body. If man considers its structure, he will notice that the mind is supported by the body and that if the latter is in a poor shape the mind will not be able to do anything remarkable either. Among the goods of the body, however, life is the most important; bodily health comes second, followed by sound limbs. If life ends, the union of body with soul is dissolved; if the health of the entire body is ruined, the soul is disturbed in most of its external functions; and if particular limbs are damaged, those functions cease for which the soul requires this limb.

§29. From this follows the precept: "Prefer life to health, health to sound limbs."

§30. Yet all the precepts we have put forward so far are subject to a limitation. The goods of the mind are to be subordinated to the preservation of common peace, and life, health, sound limbs, wealth, and the other minor goods take second place to it.

§31. This is where the contemplation of the whole, that is, of the union of body and soul, leads man, as we have argued repeatedly. Moreover, the same thought process shows man that he is a finite substance with respect to the powers of his mind and the strength of his body, and that there are many things which are not within our power and which it would be useless and therefore stupid to strive for.

§32. Another precept follows from this: "You must not strive for something beyond your powers."

§33. I believe that all conclusions concerning the duty of man with respect to himself can be conveniently related to these rules, and that controversial questions can be easily resolved on their basis.

§34. These [conclusions] are, for example, that man should use what is within his power well and according to reason.

§35. That man, where there is scope for human prudence, should not trust to blind chance.

§36. That man should not measure his own or others' prudence and justice by the outcome of actions.

§37. That man should not allow himself to be distracted from a proposed action that is good by either fear or the desire for pleasure.

§38. That he should adapt to matters that he cannot change.

§39. That he ought to avoid carelessness in present affairs and excessive curiosity about the future.

§40. That he should avoid arrogance when he is fortunate, and desperation in adversity.

§41. That he ought to preserve by all means the reputation of a good man and, insofar possible, to restore it to its previous brightness if it has been damaged by calumny.

§42. That he should seek fame only from outstanding deeds which benefit mankind.

§43. That he should use honor to benefit others.

§44. That he should abstain from arrogance and vainglory, especially in matters of little value.

§45. That he should maintain equanimity, if he has no opportunity to put his ability into action.

§46. That he should be satisfied with his lot and regard the rest as irrelevant to himself.

§47. That he ought to be innocently industrious in acquiring material goods.

§48. That he ought to be satisfied with little.

§49. That he should use his acquisitions as a means to satisfy his own necessities and to benefit others.

§50. That he should train the mind to avoid despair if material goods are lost.

§51. That he should distribute his goods with moderation and not dissipate them unreasonably.

§52. That he should abstain from pains that are not necessary.

§53. That he ought to enjoy delights of the senses with moderation.

§54. That he should control his passions.

§55. That he should not feel joy over the misfortunes of others or silly things.

§56. That he ought to rid himself of sadness, except insofar as he requires it for compassion and repentance.

§57. That he should love a worthy and honest object in such a way that other duties are not impeded and that the loss of this object does not result in illness.

§58. That he ought to be free from hate for other humans and from envy.

§59. That he should not exhaust himself in vain by hoping for various uncertain and impossible things.

§60. That he should resist fear and anger with every effort as passions that are inimical and very damaging to the human mind.

§61. That he should choose an appropriately honest form of life, depending on his inclination, aptitude of body and mind, family, goods of fortune, parents' advice, the command of the civil authorities, and opportunity or necessity.

§62. That he should not reject the study of letters on the grounds that they render men unable to perform the affairs of peace and war, but rather to perfect the talents he is born with.

§63. Yet that he should not waste time on useless studies, but to devote it to useful and elegant ones.

§64. That he should engage in studies that are useful for human life, not to immerse himself in them to pass the time while neglecting other duties.

§65. That he ought to follow reason rather than authority and to suppress the stubborn desire to defend false opinions.

§66. So far nearly all learned men agree. Now we must look at the controversial questions. First, concerning the power of man over his own life.

§67. No sane person would deny that it is not only permitted, but far more honorable to choose the likelihood of a shorter life in order to serve others, rather than seeking an inglorious life staying at home in order to reach an extremely old age.

§68. There is also no doubt that a person can be rightfully commanded by his superior to risk his life for the sake of others.

§69. Even without this kind of command, all other things being equal, a person can undergo this danger for the sake of others.

§70. Suicide, however, requires a more careful examination. It is clear from the above that it is an offense toward God and human society to take one's own life arbitrarily.

§71. The same holds if someone kills himself because he is weary of inconveniences, feels indignation at common evils, or is afraid of pains, when by bearing them patiently he could benefit others by his example.

§72. Nor is he to be excused if he uses the help of another.

§73. Far less are civil laws to be approved that command or even permit citizens who have committed no crime to throw their lives away.

§74. However, if someone saw that he would live in infamy before God, or realized with certainty that an enemy or tyrannical prince would soon kill him with intolerable cruelty, or, even if he is innocent, is commanded by the prince to bring about his own death because of a supposed crime, or is allowed to bring about his own death in order to avoid the shame of an execution—then it will be extremely difficult to convince him on the basis of human reason alone that he must abstain from suicide in these cases, since it is morally certain that these humans can benefit neither themselves nor others by preserving their lives.

§75. I do not want to include those here who commit suicide in order to avoid some sort of groundless shame (which is also why the examples of Socrates and Cato are very dissimilar, in spite of what Cicero says).[5]

5. Cicero, *Tusculan Disputations*, trans. J. E. King, Loeb Classical Library (London: Heinemann, 1927), I.xxx.74.

§76. It does not hold for young men or women who by committing suicide prevent the violation of their chastity, though these are more deserving of being excused.

§77. If someone believes that it is always better to be alive, even under the most severe pains, then he has perhaps been misled by the experience of some sharp pains which do not, however, exceed the common patience of humans, or he has forgotten the story of Job, a man who otherwise was most patient.[6]

§78. Yet you will say that Scripture teaches us that all those who committed suicide are indiscriminately damned to suffer eternal punishment. That is fine, I say, if Scripture teaches that suicide is incompatible with eternal beatitude. But we are only concerned with the dictate of reason and the temporal happiness of man.

§79. Therefore, I leave the dispute to be resolved by the theologians, whom we will not contradict any more than a physician would who says that a virgin cannot give birth.

§80. Moreover, let us examine self-preservation in cases when we are forced at the same time to repel violence inflicted by another, that is, defend ourselves. That is undoubtedly permitted if it is done without harming him who is planning to inflict evil on us.

§81. However, insofar as it is linked to the ruin of the person inflicting the harm it may seem contrary to the tranquillity and utility of human society.

§82. But this only seems to be so because in fact it is not. Rather, reason tells us that a ban on this kind of violent self-defense would lead not to peace but to the ruin of humankind.

---

6. See the book of Job in the Old Testament.

§83. Christian religion presents no obstacle to that. It is argued that the attacker is in danger of going to hell if he is killed, and several authors therefore believe that it is more praiseworthy to allow oneself to be killed rather than kill the attacker, or that the attacked will commit an injustice if he intends to repel the smaller harm to himself by inflicting greater harm on the aggressor. Yet there are many reasons with which to reply to this objection.

§84. But the distinction whether he who is attacked is a more useful person to society than the attacker, so that a violent defense is permitted in the former case while it is not in the latter—that is clearly inappropriate here, if you look at it in these general terms.

§85. Another question is if violent self-defense, which we have shown to be permitted, is also commanded to man. Some say so without reservation, claiming that he who neglects to defend himself in fact commits suicide.

§86. Others use the above distinction to argue that self-defense is not only allowed but obligatory if others have an interest in the survival of the person who is attacked.

§87. But if somebody only lives for himself, this violent self-defense is only permitted [and not obligatory], especially if the attacker's life is beneficial to many others and it is probable that he will be subject to eternal damnation if he is killed.

§88. Now, to kill two birds with one stone, we think that it should above all be taken into account whether the attacker holds [rightful] power over the attacked or not. In the former case, if the power is that of supreme political authority, I believe that the attacked is not only not obliged to defend himself by violence, but is obliged to abstain from doing so.

§89. Indeed, the peace of all commonwealths would be disturbed if the subjects were given the power to resist the prince and his servants by means of violence.

§90. And it will be no excuse for the attacked if he says that the prince abused his power and attacked him unjustly, since the justice and injustice of actions are not suitable criteria for resolving controversies among those who are bound together only by natural law—such as princes and their subjects, when they come into conflict with each other.

§91. If the attacker has a power which is less than supreme authority, I would not say that the attacked acts in a particularly praiseworthy fashion if he allows himself to be killed, but this [lesser] power means that the attacked can be excused if he allows himself to be killed by his lord, father, etc.

§92. Nor does he deserve to be considered to have committed suicide or to be compared to a person who killed himself with the help of another. For the latter desires and commands his own death; the former sincerely abhors it and shuns it, but does not resist it. The question is whether this nonresistance is a sin.

§93. If, however, supreme political authority conflicts with lesser power— when, for example, a soldier is attacked by his father, who is on the side of the enemy—then I believe violent self-defense is not only permitted, but, other things being equal, an obligation.

§94. If the attacker lacks authority over the attacked, though he commands others, and if the attacked lives only for himself (which he should not do), I believe the attacked is obliged to defend himself even if this means the death of the attacker, because the attacker, in attacking, evidently violates the principle of sociality, and it is very uncertain whether he will change. The attacked, however, is obliged to advance the future utility of others insofar as that is in his power. But he cannot do so without defending himself by force.

§95. In order for this self-defense to be considered just, however, some of its conditions need to be examined. These are summarized under the title of *innocent self-protection.* Many authors wrote a lot on this: the commentators on Roman civil law often did so in a confused fashion and Catholic theologians did so with impiety.[7] The matter cannot be resolved without the distinction between the state of natural equality and that of civil subordination.

§96. The difference between these two states, insofar as innocent self-defense is concerned, is mainly based on three aspects: (1) the injury caused, (2) the time that has elapsed since it occurred, (3) the duration [of the injury].

§97. Those who live in the state of nature have the right to repel any injury, even the smallest, by means of violence and, if they cannot evade it by any other means, by killing their adversary.

§98. I say they have the right to do so, and I will therefore not spend time on the distinctions drawn by others between impunity [that is, freedom from punishment] and impeccability [that is, freedom from all wrongdoing], or between that which actually occurs among humans and that which should occur if nature were interpreted rigorously.

§99. For even in the state of nature these axioms remain intact: "The person injured by an enemy enjoys unlimited right over him (as long as he remains in a state of hostility). Likewise, until the person who has violated and thus broken the band of society is prepared to return to a state of peace with me he has no right to demand the fulfillment of the duties of sociality from me."

---

7. According to Thomasius, Roman civil lawyers did not distinguish accurately between the natural and the civil state, while scholastic theologians held it permissible to kill someone who was thought to be preparing to give false testimony. Thomasius is here drawing on Pufendorf, *De jure naturae et gentium,* bk. II, chap. v, §§3 and 7.

§100. The contrary argument, that the law of nature demands equality in resistance, too, lacks all foundation. If conscience is opposed to these rules, it must be considered erroneous.

§101. Moreover, just as no injury would have had to be feared in the state of innocence, so it is also impossible to contradict our opinion on the other questions concerning self-defense by arguing from the state of innocence.

§102. In the civil state, however, the liberty to defend oneself seems to be restricted insofar as it only permits the defense of one's life or another good which would suffer permanent damage.

§103. Thus, in the state of nature moderate self-defense begins when it is clear that another person is planning to inflict injury on me, even if he has not yet fully executed his attempts. Hence, it will be permitted to attack someone preparing to harm me.

§104. In the civil state, however, the right to self-defense begins when the attacker makes it clear he wants to inflict injury on me, is armed with the powers and means of harming me, and is in a place from which he can actually inflict harm, taking into account that time which is required if I want to anticipate him rather than being anticipated.

§105. Because of the presumed perturbation of the mind a modest excess in [the use of violence] by the attacked is excusable.

§106. If the attacked is not to blame, then he will not be obliged to flee if he is on open ground, unless he can do so easily.

§107. That both sides should be equally well-armed is one of the dreams of moral philosophers.

§108. Finally, in the civil state the defense lasts until the danger of suffering an injury has ceased.

§109. But in the state of nature it is also permissible to take revenge for an injury which has been inflicted. I shall say more about this later.

§110. On the basis of these distinctions, especially the first, the controversies over the defense of those goods that are less important than life can easily be resolved.

§111. In the state of nature their violent defense is clearly permitted; therefore, the question only concerns the civil state.

§112. Thus, I have the right to protect the integrity of my limbs by killing my adversary since his actions threaten my life.

§113. If it is therefore argued that the danger of mutilation is no sufficient justification as long as it is certain that one's life is not threatened, that is as if I said that an elephant could fly if only it had wings.

§114. Chastity is a trickier question. If you consider it physically, it is possible to receive compensation for its loss. But if you consider it from a moral perspective, it cannot be taken away from me against my will because it is a state of mind.

§115. I used to believe that the justification for the defense of chastity by force could be based on the fact that the virgin ran the danger of experiencing, even if only for a moment, pleasure from the illicit intercourse with another and that this just fear of participating in the other person's sin qualified as irreparable damage since she could not undo it and money cannot compensate for this kind of guilt.

§116. Having considered the matter more carefully, however, that argument does not seem sufficient either. Apart from the fact that it is not true that every time there is a violation of chastity the victim feels pleasure, this momentary pleasure of the victim cannot on the basis of reason alone be shown to be a sin, even if it is one.

§117. Yet if we wanted to see what usually happens and form a conjecture on that basis about the presumed will of princes, I would say that in cases of doubt the prince is assumed to have permitted this kind of defense. In examples from history those who held political power have usually, if not always, praised such self-defense and approved it, sometimes even bestowing a reward on it.

§118. It is, however, repugnant to reason and universal custom to be allowed to avert a box on the ear or another person's false testimony by killing the person from whom we fear this: a box on the ear is not irreparable, and false testimony has nothing to do with violent attacks.

§119. The same is true for the defense of honor and esteem.

§120. The defense of material goods is regulated as follows. When the stolen goods can be recovered with the help of the magistrate, it will not be allowed to go so far as to kill the attacker, unless the person who comes to rob our property cannot be brought before a court. In the latter case it is permitted to kill robbers or nocturnal thieves.

§121. For my self-defense to be blameless, however, it is not necessary either in the state of nature or in civil society for the attacker to be plotting my death by insidious means. This is because the same applies to the person who attacks me by mistake even if the mistake is genuine. For, leaving aside other arguments, we have already shown above that it is more equitable to blame an error on the person erring than on a third party [that is, the unintended victim].

§122. At the same time it is clear that this blameless self-defense does not deserve to be punished since it is lawful and a form of accidental homicide. The chastisements that have sometimes been imposed on accidental homicide are, therefore, not punishments in the proper sense.

§123. It is evident from what has been said that man is not only driven to avoid danger to his life by a natural instinct, but enjoys the right to do so on the basis of reason. If there is only one way in which this danger to one's life can be resisted, it is usually termed necessity.

§124. Thus, of the three types of necessity distinguished by some, the first of which is for the sake of what is honorable, the second for that of safety, the third for that of convenience, only the second is relevant here.

§125. The Scholastics divide necessity into supreme necessity, which is what we have described, and great necessity, which we can evade by means of two or more remedies, of which one is usually inconvenient and the other illegal. In fact, however, great necessity is not relevant here, but is a form of necessity based on convenience.

§126. The following rule exists concerning our kind of necessity: "Necessity hath no law."

§127. I say our kind of necessity. The Scholastics often extend this mistakenly to necessity based on convenience when they are resolving particular controversies. It is enough to point this out once.

§128. It cannot apply to necessity based on what is honorable since that is derived from a law, but our necessity has no law.

§129. Although this axiom is used by everyone and many have commented on it, the distinctions put forward by the learned (we leave aside the follies of the Scholastics and the papal moralists) do not answer all the questions concerning its meaning. At the very least they require some further explanation.

§130. Thus the question is whether necessity creates a tacit exception in laws, so that a legislator is not presumed to have wanted to force a subject to observe a law when observing it endangered the subject's life.

§131. There is no controversy with regard to human laws. There necessity regularly creates exceptions, since general utility consists of the utility of individuals, and the preservation of individuals normally contributes more to common utility than observing human law.

§132. That is, unless the legislator explicitly ordered something to the contrary. That limitation is evident.

§133. Or unless the nature of the matter—war, for example, the conduct of others, etc.—requires a different behavior.

§134. The examination of divine laws is extremely difficult. It seems best there if we progress from what is better known to what is unknown and if we form an idea of the general rule on the basis of examples.

§135. A divine law is "The Sabbath must be observed." There is no doubt here that I do not violate the Sabbath if I stay at home because of a severe illness or because I have to prepare food.

§136. On the other hand, there is no question that if an idolatrous prince commands the profanation of the Sabbath with actions that are prohibited on that day, one should rather suffer death than obey.

§137. Finally, I believe that someone who is banned by a tyrant from public worship on pain of death is certainly not obliged by divine law to risk his life by attending a service. For the examples of the martyrs are heroic and presuppose a special divine impulse.

§138. It was divine law that the laity (if they can be called that) were not allowed to eat consecrated bread, and nobody should eat pork. David, however, was allowed to eat the bread when he suffered extreme hunger. Yet it was not permitted to the Jews to eat pork when pagans commanded them to do so, threatening them with the most severe torments.

§139. And since the same reason applies, I conclude that David was not allowed to eat the consecrated bread if Saul, for example, had ordered him to do so on pain of death, but that the Jews were allowed to eat pork during the siege of Jerusalem.

§140. You have here an example of negative precepts, in which necessity sometimes allows for an exception and sometimes does not. Now take an example which never admits an exception.

§141. This is, "You must not have sexual intercourse with your mother."

§142. Why is this different? Perhaps a distinction needs to be made between divine positive laws and natural laws in that positive laws commonly allow for an exception in cases of necessity. But that would be contrary to what we have said about the profanation of the Sabbath, the eating of pork by the Jews, and committing incest with one's mother.[8]

§143. We shall see whether we can make any progress in the following way. Divine laws are either affirmative or negative. Affirmative laws, by their very nature, presuppose the opportunity, material, and ability to act in order for someone to be bound by them. That is understood to be lacking when I cannot act without perishing. It does not matter how this necessity comes about though it must not be my fault.

§144. As far as positive laws are concerned, we can repeat what I have said about the sanctification of the Sabbath. As far as natural laws are concerned, the same reason holds, no matter whether they are precepts directed toward an imperfect obligation, which requires the performance of the duties of humanity, or a perfect obligation, such as keeping promises.

§145. In the case of negative precepts various distinctions are necessary. First, the question is whether the necessity has its origin from God or from the malice of other humans; then whether the main malicious intention of other humans is to cause death or whether they primarily seek to transgress the law; finally, whether the means of evading this is supplied by natural instinct or, again, by human malice.

---

8. That is, the prohibition of incest is based on positive law, but it allows no exception.

§146. If necessity is the product of human malice and is intended to cause death, and natural instinct supplies a means of evading it, then it will be allowed to make use of this means, even if it is otherwise prohibited by God, because God is not presumed to want to encourage human vileness by applying a rigorous interpretation of his laws. In addition, the instinct to apply this means is given by God since it is natural.

§147. Thus, a Jew would have been allowed to preserve his life by eating pork if another person wanted to starve him to death for no just reason. And a Christian will be allowed in a similar case of necessity to take food against its owner's wishes. Here again you have examples from positive and natural law.

§148. If, however, the means of escape is provided by human malice, it will not be permissible to use it because he who proposes this means offends God. The acceptance of this means usually implies a denial of God's existence because it is assumed that God will compensate the loss of this present life with a greater good.

§149. So if an infidel had offered pork to a Jew whom someone else was trying to starve to death, the Jew must abstain from eating the meat. Similarly, if a mother promises to release her son who has been unjustly imprisoned on condition that he commit incest with her or, to take an example from natural law, if he kills an innocent person, then this offer must not be accepted.

§150. It is even less permitted to evade necessity by violating divine law if the person who has caused this necessity is trying to bring about an illegal action. This is so because the same reasoning applies as above.

§151. And this is true no matter whether the means to do so is supplied by a new form of malice—if, for example, a tyrant wants to force someone with death threats to abjure true religion and this person is then promised freedom in exchange for acts of lewdness or homicide.

§152. It is also true if natural instinct impels me to save my life. For then life takes second place to the offense caused to God, just as when a pagan orders nothing but pork to be offered to a Jew who refuses to abjure his religion.

§153. But if the necessity takes its origin from God and the means to escape it is provided by a purely natural instinct, it will be permitted to make use of it because the means is from God and because the action does not imply atheism.

§154. Thus, it would have been permitted to Jews to eat pork in times of famine, and it will be allowed to still hunger in times of famine by eating food that is owned by others.

§155. It is another matter if human malice provides the means of escaping necessity because that constitutes an affront to God.

§156. One example is if someone promises bread during a famine in exchange for committing acts of lewdness or homicide.

§157. If we take these distinctions into account, I believe that it is easy to reply to various particular questions on the right of necessity.

§158. There is no doubt that it is permitted to sever a limb to save one's life.

§159. To feed on the flesh of human cadavers in times of famine is deplorable, but not a crime.

§160. It is even deplorable rather than unjust in such a case to decide on the death of one person or a few by drawing lots, in order that several others be saved.

§161. This is true all the more if two people are exposed to an immediate threat to their lives, in which each would perish—in a shipwreck, for example, or in battle. Then one person will be allowed to save himself by bringing about the death of the other, who would perish in any case. He is, for example, allowed to push him off the plank, which is too small for both, or to leave him in mortal danger by closing the city gates.

§162. There is even less doubt that one person is allowed to expose another to the danger of death or great injury indirectly, such that it is not his intention to harm him, but only to defend himself by this action, which will probably cause great harm to another. An example is if a lame man, a child, or someone else impedes a person fleeing down a narrow alley.

§163. The reason in these three cases is the same: the necessity comes either from God or from humans who endeavor to kill me. The means of escape, however, is supplied by the natural instinct to preserve my life.

§164. But, you will say, does this not result in homicide, which is prohibited by natural law? I do not think so. For the law of nature, which prohibits homicide, does not refer to any killing of humans, but only to the treacherous murder of an innocent person.[9]

§165. I shall not argue that the killing in the above cases is not treacherous, for that is debatable. But I deny that in those cases the killing constitutes murder.

§166. "What must I hear?" you say. "Do you not know that even the Gentiles say that to murder is the same as being the cause of death?"

§167. Fine, but I deny that in the above cases the person defending his life is the cause of death.

§168. Insofar as moral imputation is concerned, the primary intention is taken into account, so that, depending on whether this intention is licit or illicit, accidental effects and secondary intention can be judged on this basis.

---

9. This paragraph is altered, and the following paragraphs from 165 to 173 do not appear in the 1709 German edition.

§169. Thus, if someone intends to kill another, but misses with his sword and cuts open [and heals] a deadly ulcer instead, he will not be able to claim the reward for this beneficial deed.

§170. Similarly, if someone intends to correct a servant, but by mistake strikes a friend, he will not be held responsible for the injuries.

§171. Also (so you do not say that in the above examples this is true only because the beneficial deed in the first case and the harm in the second had not been intended), if someone increases the height of his building for the sake of convenience, and only incidentally wants to deprive the neighbor of daylight, he does not do the neighbor an injustice.

§172. For it is a secondary intention whenever I desire, from a purely natural instinct, a means to achieve an end, a means that I would not desire if I could achieve the end in some other way.

§173. Thus, to return to our cases, the intention there is primarily the defense of one's life, and only secondarily the killing of another person, which in these cases often does not happen necessarily even if it is quite likely. Thus, they who defend their life are to be called the accidental causes of another person's death, or they are the physical but not the moral cause of death.

§174. I believe it is different for someone who is commanded by a tyrant to kill an innocent man unless he wants to lose his own life, because the origin of the necessity comes from man, who intends to bring about an action contrary to law by providing a means to escape this necessity.

§175. It is no use distinguishing whether the prince commands his subject to perform an action which is the subject's own, or only the execution of an action which is, properly speaking, that of the person commanding it. As if, in the latter case, the murder of an innocent person cannot be imputed to the subject any more than to the sword or the axe.

§176. While this comparison of man with a sword is in many ways inappropriate because they are different in many respects, I also doubt that it can be called a mere execution if a person, at the command of someone else, kills another human being whom the person obeying the command knows to be innocent. I also doubt that it can be compared to the commanded reading of a speech full of lies (which is no more a crime than when a scribe at court records blasphemous words). If you really wanted to describe the murder of an innocent person as the mere execution of another person's will, I would like to ask what the difference is between the death of a human being and the command to commit incest with one's mother. Everyone acknowledges that doing so is such an awful and despicable deed that it is considered noble-minded to want to die rather than perpetrate this crime. While the prohibition of incest is based on positive law, as we shall show later, homicide is banned by natural law.[10]

§177. It remains for us to see whether necessity confers the right to take away other people's possessions or whether this amounts to theft. Different authors have different opinions on this. Some believe that it is theft, but is not to be punished. This seems to involve a contradiction since they call something a crime which does not deserve a punishment.

§178. Some believe that in this question there is no case of necessity, but this view does not rest on a firm proof.

§179. Some deny it to be theft and look for a way out in the various definitions of theft. Some claim that it is not the appropriation of another person's property since in these cases [of necessity] the original communion of goods is revived. Others affirm that the owner had no right to be unwilling [to part with his possessions]. Others believe that it is no fraudulent appropriation. We agree with this last argument.

§180. Indeed, in cases of extreme necessity duties required by humanity are transformed into perfect duties. Others have already put this forward

10. See *Institutes*, bk. III, chap. iii, §99.

in more detail, together with the required limitations. It will also be clear from what is to be said in its proper place.[11] Thus, even those who contradict concede that an indigent person should approach the magistrate to indicate that there is a perfect obligation [to allow him to take food].

§181. To sum up, they who believe that theft is being committed in this case do not know the definition of theft.

§182. Finally, if we are subject to supreme necessity through no fault of our own, this allows us to cause the loss of the possessions of others which are less precious than our own. We are, however, responsible for part of the loss and must offer restitution for part of it to the other person. On this is based the equity of the Rhodian law on loss.[12] I am also allowed to tear up nets in which my ship has been caught.

§183. It is more difficult to judge whether necessity justifies causing the loss of the possessions of others when there is a risk of losing our property. This cannot be considered supreme necessity unless it is linked to danger to my life. Some conclude from this that he who wages a just war is allowed to occupy a territory that is at peace if there is a clear danger that the enemy will invade it. Though cautions are usually added to this, nevertheless this pertains more to those matters where it is possible to allow an exception rather than those that can be defended on the basis of natural law.

§184. Among those who live in a civil state, it can be justified more easily—for example, if the political authority commands or allows the destruction of buildings during a fire, or if someone provides a surety for damage that has not yet been done or grants right of way to my piece of land, which is surrounded by the land of my neighbors, and similar cases.

---

11. Ibid., bk. II, chap. v, §20.
12. See *Digest* 14.2.0 ("De Lege Rhodia de jactu").

On the Duty of Man Toward Others, in Particular on Preserving Equality Among Humans

§1. Now I shall discuss the duties of man toward other humans. These either guide humans living in a particular society or concern humans no matter what form of society they live in.

§2. Common duties derive either immediately from God, independently of any human consensus, or they presuppose pacts and agreements among humans.

§3. You could call the former absolute, the latter hypothetical. We shall not protest if you call the former innate, the latter acquired, since innate obligation corresponds to absolute, and hypothetical obligation to acquired.

§4. This distinction seems to have been invented for teaching purposes since it does not contribute a lot to resolving controversies.

§5. It is said that the main difference between obligations imposed by a superior and those that take their origin from mutual agreement seems to be that the latter are no longer binding as soon as the other person deviates from the agreement, while the former continue to be binding even if one person ceases to fulfill his duty. The argument here is that the author of the obligation can compensate the person who suffers a loss. But this seems rather confused.

§6. It is also confused to say that the obligation to perform the duties of natural law, which are commanded by God, is comparable to an obligation based on an agreement, because one person's breaking of the agreement means he can no longer demand the performance of these duties from the other, and the other person also has the right to compel him to provide compensation.

§7. But if (as it seems) the meaning here is that I am never under an obligation toward another person who first violated these duties, but am under a special obligation toward a superior on the basis of absolute precepts, then there are several possible objections to that.

§8. It is true, a superior can force me to pardon an offense by someone even if he does not offer compensation. In the state of nature I would not be obliged to do so [that is, to pardon the offense] as long as the other person did not make amends. Yet the superior is not presumed to do so normally and without a specific declaration of this will, and this applies not only in absolute precepts but in hypothetical ones, too.

§9. For who would deny that God or any other superior can force a subject, other things being equal, to keep faith with someone who has broken the terms of a contract, or to pardon someone who refuses to offer restitution of his property, etc.?

§10. Moreover, the argument that I am not bound to perform a reciprocal duty toward someone who has harmed me unless the superior has specifically commanded me to do so is only true for obligations among equals, or those that superiors have toward inferiors. But unless we want to follow Monarchomach principles, it is not true for the obligation which inferiors are under toward superiors, no matter whether this obligation is based on a hypothetical or an absolute precept.[13]

13. That is, superiors are not obliged to fulfill their obligations toward inferiors if the latter do not fulfill their obligations toward their superiors, but inferiors may not cease to fulfill their obligations toward superiors, even if the superiors fail to perform their duties toward their inferiors.

§11. The first absolute precept, however, seems to be that based on the condition of humans which above we have described as the condition of humanity.

§12. Since this prevails among all humans, universally, be they rulers or subjects, it creates some kind of equality among us.

§13. And this equality can be explained in different ways, on the basis of a dictate of reason or by resorting to revelation. In the former case this equality reflects either man's right nature or his corrupt nature.

§14. For if you first consider the essence of man and his existence, by virtue of which he is an animal, all humans trace their origin to the same roots and are propagated the same way: they are born, die, expel what is superfluous to nature as filth, are all subject to the vagaries of fortune, etc.

§15. But this natural equality is something humans have in common with beasts, and it is not a suitable foundation for rules according to which to live one's life. What is more important here is the equality of right, insofar as they are humans, because everybody must perform the duties of natural law toward others, however much they excel others in terms of the goods of the mind, the body, or fortune, just as everybody expects the performance of these duties from others. Nor does anybody have a greater right to inflict injury on others. For they who lack abundant goods of the body, fortune, and the mind are not inferior to others when it comes to enjoying the law that is common to all.

§16. Moreover, when we examine the corrupt state of man [that is, after original sin], we shall also notice an equality of malice, in that adults are all equally capable of hurting others and causing them harm, if not with violence, then by cunning and fraud.

§17. You should, however, beware of overemphasizing this latter form of equality as Hobbes does, since it is more of an appendix.

§18. Among Christians, however, there is also Christian equality, which is derived from the light of Scripture. This says that the friends of God must not be esteemed according to their nobility, power, or wealth, but according to the sincerity of their piety, to which all are obliged. And in the last judgment and in the rewards and punishments after death no attention is paid to those things with which mortals try to distinguish themselves before others in this life.

§19. These forms of equality, and especially the equality of right, lead to the general precept that guides all duties among humans: "Treat another human equally as a human being."

§20. The general validity of this precept is evident not only from the conclusions that are based on it. It is also demonstrated by that saying of our savior, who taught us the essence of the law directing our duties toward others: "Love your neighbor as you love thyself."[14]

§21. Thus, our formula converges with that of Christ, and these other paraphrases of the same precept are close to both: "What you do not want to be done to yourself, do not do to another," and "Every person should apply the same law to others as to himself," although these are not as self-evident, and the latter was used in a much narrower sense in Roman law.

§22. We must not, however, confuse the equality of liberty or power with the kind of equality we have been discussing so far. The equality of power means that all humans are understood to be equal by nature in such a way that in the absence of a previous human deed or agreement nobody enjoys any power over another, but each person is master of his own actions and powers.

§23. That equality [of liberty or power] does not apply to all humans, but only those who live in the state of nature.

§24. Yet, while its opposite, inequality, is found mainly among those who live in civil society, as we have said above, not every inequality is introduced after civil states were established. In part, inequality emerges in a

---

14. See, for example, Matthew 19:19.

society ruled by heads of families, which precedes political societies, as will be shown later.[15]

§25. It follows automatically that our precept [to preserve equality] is valid even among those who are unequal with respect to their liberty, for they too are equally humans in relation to each other.

§26. It must be noted, however, that our precept in most cases imposes a perfect obligation on those who live in the state of nature, but among those who live in civil society it obliges those who hold power only imperfectly.

§27. In civil society the duties of citizens that follow from this precept are often limited by the ruler, according to the utility of the commonwealth.

§28. To develop a better understanding of this precept to preserve equality, let us divide it into four particular precepts, two negative and two affirmative.

§29. For he observes equality who gives himself neither more nor less than others, but gives each side equal amounts.

§30. Therefore, the first negative precept is that I should not give myself more than another, which would reflect pride.

§31. The other negative precept requires me not to give another person less than myself, which would be a form of harm.

§32. The first affirmative precept is that in the absence of an agreement I should give another person as much [as I would give myself]. This is based on the duties of humanity.

§33. The second is that I should grant another as much [as I would grant myself] if a corresponding agreement has been formed. This is based on the duty to keep promises. Now I shall examine each in turn.

15. See *Institutes*, bk. III, chap. v.

CHAPTER III

On Avoiding Pride

§1. In the first negative precept, "Avoid pride," it is easy to recognize what pride is. For the meaning of our precept is that nobody who does not enjoy a special right should arrogate to himself more than others but should allow others to enjoy the same right as he does.

§2. Thus pride is a vice by which someone grants himself more than another, without just cause.

§3. While those people are most suitable for society who happily grant the same to others [as to themselves], those people are clearly unsociable who consider themselves to be superior to others and at the same time want everything to be permitted to themselves and find excuses for all their actions, yet they forgive others nothing. They also claim honor and a special role before all others, although they have no particular right to that, and are like rough and many-cornered stones, which are useless for building.

§4. Pride shows itself in two ways in humans: either without or with external signs of contempt for others, that is, in deeds, words, facial expression, laughter, a gift, a picture, etc.

§5. Each of these, but especially the first, either rests on certain reasons and pretexts which may not be just, but are at least plausible and are based on properties of the body and mind, honor, and wealth. Or there is not even that.

§6. These forms of pride differ in their degree. That which has pretexts occupies the lowest degree. It does not render humans obviously unsociable and is often, other things being equal, accepted among humans. You could call this common pride for the sake of distinguishing it from the others.

§7. The kind of pride that is unfounded but does not involve contempt is placed in the middle; this is, when someone does not believe he has any particular merit for which he should be esteemed, but believes that esteem is based on usurpation, as if he who demands more esteem also gets more of it.

§8. This mistake is so absurd that it would be hard to believe there are people who prostitute themselves in this fashion were there not many who flattered them and by their vain praise encouraged them in this pride. For it is foolish if someone esteems himself highly for no good reason, and this same person treats others as fools if he thinks that they would esteem him for no good reason.

§9. This form of pride, therefore, cannot be excused as easily as the previous kind, yet among humans it is not punished, because they who are affected by this vice harm themselves more than others. They seem to deserve pity rather than disdain and attract the derision rather than the anger of others. They often serve for the amusement of others. You could, therefore, call this foolish pride.

§10. Yet that pride which, in addition, looks down on others is an intolerable injury because it provokes feelings of anger and lust for revenge in others. There are many who would rather expose their life to immediate danger or disrupt peaceful relations with others than suffer great disgrace. This is because the intention behind this pride is to undermine the esteem of another person, which, if it is intact and vigorous, constitutes the entire joy of the mind.

§11. Since this form of pride is a just cause of war, it is rightly subject to punishments in political society. It comes as close as is possible to being an insult (which we will discuss in the following chapter) and is generally described as the particular crime of disgrace or injury by [the different] nations.

§12. If you abstract from civil laws, however, you could conveniently distinguish that form of disgrace which occurs without reproaching another person for a defect (when, for example, someone mocks another person by pulling faces, by making gestures, and by other physical forms of expression) and that form which reproaches another person for certain defects either in words or deeds—in his behavior, for example, or in a picture.

§13. The latter reproaches another person either for natural defects or moral vices.

§14. These three forms of pride differ in their degrees, the first being serious, the second more serious, and the third the most serious.

§15. It is also clear that physical injury, beating, or killing pertain to the following chapter, since they do not necessarily detract from a person's reputation or esteem.

§16. The fact that Roman jurists regarded these [forms of pride] as a type of injury may be due to the fact that there is no ordinary way to estimate the damage these cause a free man, and it would therefore not seem to square with a legal action based on the Lex Aquilia,[16] the purpose of which is to provide a true and generally accepted valuation of goods. Therefore, they considered it an action applicable to injuries, since this allowed a person bringing a lawsuit to estimate the value of his reputation, which is not part of commercial exchange, and hence it did not seem inappropriate if something similar were granted to the person bringing a lawsuit for harm caused to his health and the soundness of his limbs.

16. The Lex Aquilia (see *Digest* 9.2) regulated compensation in case of wrongful damage.

§17. The belief of the ancient Greeks that certain humans were slaves by nature must therefore be rejected. It is contrary to the natural equality of humans and to common peace in that they who consider themselves naturally free and wise claim power over natural slaves on the grounds that they are stupid and barbarian.

§18. Opposed to pride is humility, the constant companion of true generosity, which is based on our awareness of the weakness of our nature and our errors, which we may have committed or may commit, and which are as great as those which may be committed by others.

§19. The result is that we do not prefer ourselves to anybody else because we believe that others are just as able to use their free will as we are since they are endowed with it as much as we are. The legitimate use of this free will is the only thing that man can truly consider his own and on the basis of which he can either esteem or despise himself.

CHAPTER IV

On Not Harming Others
and on Compensating for Harm
That Has Been Done

§1. The other negative precept that is based on the general condition of humankind and on the precept concerning the observation of equality is "Do not harm anybody."

§2. This precept is extremely broad in its scope and, at the same time, very easy to observe. It is also highly necessary because without it human social life cannot exist in any sense.

§3. The term *harm* is ambiguous. It describes first the denial of any sort of right owed to another, even if this is based on an imperfect obligation. But this is an incorrect use of the term.

§4. Second, it is understood as the denial of a perfect right, whether this is owed on the basis of an agreement with the person denying it to us or without such an agreement. Thus, it is used in the case of contracts.

§5. Third, it is taken as the denial of a right which is owed to me even without an agreement with the person who harmed me, no matter whether this denial was directed at goods which cannot normally be taken away by unjust force, such as my honor and reputation, or those that are susceptible to unjust harm. Thus, he who insults me also harms me.

§6. Fourth, it is understood as the harm caused to goods which are of the latter kind, be they physical goods or those of good fortune. Thus, physical injury is an example of harm.

§7. Fifth, and finally, it can stand for the harm caused to goods of fortune, for example, if someone kills my sheep, spoils other things, or steals them.

§8. The first meaning is not relevant here, not only because it is based on a misunderstanding but also because we are here looking for a particular precept, not a general one, and because it is more relevant to the following chapter.

§9. The second meaning is not relevant here either, for the harm that occurs in cases of contract concerns the precept on keeping promises.

§10. The third, however, is not the concern of this chapter either, as our comments in the previous chapter make clear.

§11. Thus, we turn to the fourth, which does belong here. The meaning of our precept, therefore, is as follows: You must not spoil or steal another person's goods of the body or of fortune if he owns them independently of any agreement with you, and you must not prevent him from making use of these.

§12. Note that I say "if he owns them independently of any agreement with you." This precept not only protects the rights that nature itself granted to us directly, such as life, the body, limbs, chastity, and liberty, but extends itself to all institutions and conventions by which something is acquired for a human being, as is the case with material wealth, as long as they are not owned only on the basis of an agreement with the person causing the harm.

§13. But what is the use of the fifth meaning? I added this because of the Lex Aquilia of the Romans, which concerned only material wealth. It is obvious from the preceding chapter why this is not extended to the other goods, to those of the body and to chastity.

§14. Harm, however, results in damage, which here means a lack of some good because of the illegal actions of another.

§15. All negative precepts, however, imply an affirmative precept, and so the consequence of our precept is: "Compensate for the damage you have done."

§16. For if someone has actually been harmed and must put up with the damage without compensation, while he who caused the harm can enjoy the fruits of his crime safely and without offering restitution, then the precept not to harm others would be vain and entirely useless.

§17. There are several kinds of damage. It is first either positive, if I take away something that belongs to somebody else (if, for example, I commit theft or burn down somebody's home), or it is privative, if I prevent a gain that another had reason to expect.

§18. Second, damage either produces some gain for the culprit, as in the case of theft, or it does not produce any gain, as in burning down a building.

§19. Third, damage is inflicted either directly on the thing itself, or as a consequence, for example, in the fruits of things, etc.

§20. Fourth, damage is either the result of malice (that is, of choice) or of fault (that is, the failure to apply the required diligence).

§21. And fifth, it is inflicted either by an act of commission, as in the case of theft or when I lay fire to the property of someone else, or by an act of omission, if I do not extinguish the fire or contain it when that is what I should have done.

§22. Sixth, as far as the act of commission is concerned, either I harm another person immediately by using the physical powers of my body—if, for example, I break another person's property with my hand or tear it up—or I cause harm using the mediation either of natural causes, such as a sword, a cudgel, or fire, for example, or of humans—if, for example, I order another person to be harmed by my emissaries.

§23. Seventh, I cause harm either on my own or as an associated cause.

§24. Eighth, this associated cause is either the principal cause, or a minor cause, or an equally important cause [to the others].

§25. All these forms of damage are relevant here and are included in the precept concerning damage and compensation for it.

§26. The sense of this precept is as follows: That he should offer the person who has been harmed some compensation for the damage, no matter how this has been done. He should do so either by the restitution of the thing itself or, if this is not possible, of its value together with all interest.

§27. This illustrates another difference to legal action based on the Lex Aquilia. For that [the Lex Aquilia] does not cover privative damage unless this damage is a consequence, that is, insofar as it presupposes a positive damage.

§28. It [the Lex Aquilia] also does not apply if the damage produces a gain for the person inflicting it. For there the person who has suffered the damage has already been provided for with a special legal action concerning theft, robbery, and the prohibition of unjust force.

§29. To return to the meaning of our precept: concerning the damage that is inflicted by consequence, it has to be noted that the compensation needs to be paid only if I would otherwise probably have received the good that I desire. Thus, if someone has made a servant his heir, and this servant is then killed by someone else in the lifetime of the testator, then the killer will not be required to pay the value of the inheritance to the master. Yet he would be required to do so if he did this after the death of the testator.

§30. Similarly, it must be considered here whether the damage by consequence is my fault. Thus, a person who steals grain will normally not be obliged to compensate a master for the servants who died of hunger because of the lack of grain.

§31. The lack of either requisite is clear in the example of the fisherman whose nets are stolen and who demands an estimate of the value of the fish which he would have been able to catch had his nets not been stolen.

§32. But if damage is inflicted with malice and cunning, a culprit living in the state of nature is obliged to give the person who has been harmed a security; in civil society he will be obliged to suffer the punishment imposed by the prince.

§33. In the state of nature, however, if the culprit offers compensation and asks for forgiveness, one should accept it and pardon him.

§34. If damage is caused by my fault and there is no contractual obligation, I am nevertheless obliged to offer restitution for the damage, whatever the nature of my fault.

§35. If I withhold something that I owe on the basis of a contract, then I am only obliged to offer compensation to the extent that is specified in the contract. Thus, if by my negligence I damage something that is deposited with me, I will not be required to offer compensation if by the same act of negligence my own property was lost at the same time.

§36. For I am not culpable here because in the case of something deposited with me I am not required to be more careful with other people's property than my own things.

§37. There is no compensation for an accident, however, if damage is the result neither of choice nor of negligence. As the proverb says, the owner suffers the loss.

§38. Thus, it is unnecessary to add the qualification introduced by the learned that I am required to compensate for an accident that was preceded by my fault or my deceit—if, for example, I transfer something deposited with me to another location against the will of the owner and it is stolen from there by thieves. For here the owner suffers a loss not by accident but by my fault, for I should not have transferred the object to another location.

§39. If a rich man harms a pauper by accident, it will be an appropriate act of generosity to console the poor man with some favor. But this obligation pertains to the following chapter.

§40. In order for someone to be held responsible as an associated cause, he must really be a cause of the damage and have contributed to the total damage or part of it.

§41. Thus, if a person did not contribute anything substantial to the act that led to the damage, did not do anything beforehand to set this act in motion, and did not benefit from it, he will not be required to compensate for the damage, even if he has committed some transgression. This refers, for example, to those people who are delighted by the misfortunes of others, who praise damage that has been perpetrated, who excuse it, who wish for it before it occurs, and who, while it happens, favor it or approve of it.

§42. Among those who are responsible to various degrees for the damage, those who were the principal cause of it are obliged to offer compensation first. If they are not available, then those who went along with it are.

§43. So first those are held responsible who incited the deed by commanding it or by some other means of compulsion. If the perpetrator of the shameful deed could not refuse his services, he will be treated only as the instrument. He who is an accomplice without having been compelled will be held primarily responsible. Then follow all others who contributed something to the deed.

§44. If the same action was committed by several persons, all of whom are culpable to the same degree, each will be held responsible for everything in the case of those actions that are collective, such as laying fire, breaching a dike, and similar actions; in actions which can be divided [among several people], such as bodily injury, each person is responsible for what he did, no matter whether they perpetrated this crime after conspiring to do so or if they did so without a conspiracy.

§45. If, however, I receive full compensation for the damage from one of the persons who were held responsible to varying degrees or who were individually held responsible for an entire action, then the others are free of all obligation, for I am demanding the value of my property, and once I have received it I cannot ask for it another time from another person.

§46. Thus, there are many differences between an obligation to compensate for damage and a punishment since what I have said so far does not apply to punishments. People who praise or approve of a crime, for example, can be punished, and very often those who are responsible for damage to varying degrees are given the same punishment; finally, the punishment of one person does not liberate the others from punishment, which I shall discuss further in its proper place.[17]

§47. Our precept, therefore, prohibits all kinds of crimes by which others are harmed, such as murder, injury, beating, robbery, theft, fraud, force, and, in its own way, rape and adultery, to the extent that chastity is violated and the husband is burdened with the education of another person's child. This is so even though it can easily be argued that most of these cases are not covered by the Lex Aquilia.

§48. A person who has committed manslaughter is required to pay the physicians and to pay the expected support to those to whom the deceased owed maintenance. The profit which the deceased could have made had he lived, but which was entirely uncertain, will not be taken into account here, just as the life of a free man will not be (though that of a slave is).

§49. He who has mutilated another will be held similarly responsible for paying the medical expenses and for compensating the mutilated person

17. See bk. III, chap. vii.

for the reduction in his gains. Though here too, to be precise, if you abstract from civil laws one must not estimate future gains, which are uncertain, but provide the person injured with the means of living if he has been prevented by his injury from caring for himself in future.

§50. An adulterer and an adulteress must compensate the husband for the cost of raising the child of the adulterous woman. They are not however, I believe, required to pay the legitimate children for the loss of part of their share of the inheritance to the illegitimate child, even if we abstract from the rules of civil law concerning the succession of children from an adulterous relationship to the goods of their parents. This is so partly because they do not suffer damage from the adulterer, but from the will of the parents, partly because thereby legitimate children are deprived of a future gain, which is largely uncertain.

§51. He who has sexual intercourse with a virgin by force or fraud is required to compensate her with the equivalent of what she, having been deflowered, has lost from an expected marriage. This is the case if he marries her or furnishes her with a dowry. She who consents to intercourse must impute the effects to herself. If someone has persuaded a virgin to sleep with him by promising her marriage, he will not be required to marry her, but by the standards of the state of nature already has married her.

§52. A thief and a robber are obliged to return what they have stolen, together with the natural increase and the consequent damage and probable loss of profit, even though they are also compelled to suffer the punishment for theft and robbery in addition to that.

§53. Concerning damages that are caused by our servants or animals without our fault, the Roman laws allowed claiming compensation. This is not derived from our precept, but it is not therefore to be considered a pure invention of civil law. It rests rather on the equity of performing the duties of humanity. I shall discuss these now.

On the Various Duties of Humanity

§1. The third particular precept derived from the condition of humanity and the law for the preservation of equality is the first among two affirmative precepts: "Promote the utility of another human being as much as you conveniently can."

§2. For it is not sufficient for sociality if you only abstain from injuring another and if another person does not suffer. Life is happy and peaceful if we take care of each other so that we are well.

§3. The preservation of equality, however, is the main means to achieving this. Man desires not only that without which he cannot subsist, but needs other goods to live a comfortable life, and he cannot acquire these without the help of other humans. He might also require the help not only of some particular humans but of any humans whatsoever, even lowly ones. Thus, he would sin against equality if he were not prepared to give to others what he himself demands from them.

§4. I have, however, considered this precept to be absolute. You must not be confused by the fact that most of these particular questions presuppose property rights, although every obligation that follows from the division of property belongs to the hypothetical precepts, as we shall explain below.

§5. In any case, it is certain that our precept originally was applicable immediately after the fall from grace, even before the emergence of property rights. The subsequent division of property led to new conclusions, but ones that are to be derived from the same principles as before.

§6. The convenience of another person is promoted either by my possessions or by my deeds.

§7. And this is either with regard to his possessions, so that they are increased or preserved by my efforts.

§8. Or it is without regard to his possessions, if I come to his help against violence from others or if I assist him in correcting his own faults.

§9. These are either faults of the body (when I give advice on sustaining bodily health) or of the mind (when I teach something he does not know, come to his help in other ways by remedying the imperfections of his intellect, restrain him from sins, or correct him in a friendly fashion if he is guilty of a sin).

§10. It is quite clear that these duties of humanity, when the convenience of another person is promoted by my efforts, regardless of his possessions, were already applicable before the division of property.

§11. In the postlapsarian state, therefore, this precept was always very useful, but it is not immediately evident whether this would have applied in the state of innocence.

§12. For I think that the duties which require me to come to the help of another and preserve or increase his possessions with my possessions or my efforts—these duties, I believe, did not exist in that state of innocence, in which the sublime friendship among all meant that there would always have been a community of goods, as will be demonstrated later.[18]

---

18. See *Institutes,* bk. II, chap. ix, §72.

§13. From the above examples it is clear that the other duties that require me to come to the help of another in matters other than his possessions presuppose a physical imperfection, or a moral imperfection, either in the person to whom the duty is owed or in others. Such imperfections, however, would have been entirely absent from that state of perfection [before the fall from grace].

§14. That is, unless you wanted to resort to duties the desire for which does not involve any great imperfection, such as showing the way to someone who is lost, allowing him to light his fire with mine, etc. But these are to be considered further elsewhere.[19]

§15. But the efficacy of our precept is different among those who live in the state of nature and those who live in civil society.

§16. Among the former it normally produces only an imperfect obligation, and thus it differs from the other precepts. Hence, the person who violates this precept is usually called inhumane rather than unjust.

§17. For this precept usually only commands promoting the utility of another person, not meeting his necessities; this is, moreover, a utility, the lack of which could easily be met by others if one particular person did not want to do so. Thus, there was no need for individual humans to be placed under a perfect obligation, but it was more glorious and more appropriate for eliciting the love of others and declaring one's own love to leave the performance of these duties to human decency and not rely on coercion.

§18. Those duties that involve our labor or some disadvantage to ourselves do not necessarily require us to prefer the convenience of someone else to our own. Instead, this common rule usually applies: true charity begins with oneself. In the state of nature each individual is the best judge of his own convenience; and therefore, whenever anyone demanded such a

19. Ibid., §34 of this chapter.

duty from another who refused it and appealed to his own utility, it was impossible to grant a right of coercion without causing great disturbance to all of mankind.

§19. And what else remains to be said? The preservation of equality itself shows that this precept only imposes an imperfect obligation. All humans are equally obliged to perform such duties on the basis of the common condition of humanity. Therefore, this equality would be violated if a person in need of something tried to force someone else before all others to perform these duties of humanity in a matter that is common to all and without a sufficient reason.

§20. That is what normally takes place. For it could also happen that among those living in a state of nature an obligation to perform the duties of humanity becomes a perfect obligation. But when is this the case? There is a ready response: if those reasons cease which render this obligation ineffective [i.e., imperfect].

§21. There are three conditions for someone to be under a perfect obligation. (1) He who demands the performance of a duty of humanity would perish if he did not receive it. (2) He cannot receive what he desires equally well from others. (3) The person from whom he demands this does not have an identical need. And this is what we have said above, namely that supreme necessity transforms the duties of humanity into perfect rights.

§22. Take one example. Let us imagine that two heads of family from different nations, who are not related to each other in any particular sense and are joined only by the bond of humanity, are shipwrecked in a barren region, and that at the same time the possessions of one of them, which are sufficient to sustain his life and that of his fellow, are washed up on the shore. In that case, he is under a perfect obligation to help his fellow with his abundant supply of goods.

§23. And this concerns the state of nature. In the civil state, however, what I have said does not apply universally. Here superiors can demand the performance of these duties from inferiors on the basis of a perfect right, although, to be accurate, they are then no longer duties of humanity because they are not based on the common condition of mankind but on the particular state of subjection, which usually presupposes a particular pact, and are thus required by the right of command.

§24. Concerning the relations of subjects to each other, these duties continue to be valid, but in such a way that the ruler can for the sake of common utility introduce a law that grants a legal action to him to whom these duties are owed or can by some other means force the person who owes these duties to perform them. Then, however, they again lose the character of duties of humanity.

§25. Finally, the duties of humanity that subjects demand from the ruler qua ruler do indeed retain the nature of an imperfect obligation. In that respect, however, they are no different from the ruler's other duties, since subjects qua subjects do not have any powers of coercion against rulers.

§26. So much on the duties of humanity in general. We have described their division above, but only in passing and in another connection. There is another division which is not very dissimilar to the previous one and merits a more careful examination. The duties of humanity are either performed without a definite object, that is, without regard to certain humans, or with a definite object, if they are directed toward the utility of certain people.

§27. A person promotes the convenience of others without a definite object if he cultivates his soul and body in order that actions useful to others are possible or if, by his ingenuity, he makes discoveries which benefit human life.

§28. Those, however, violate this duty who learn no honest trade and consider their soul to be nothing but some kind of salt which prevents their body from rotting; they do nothing but eat, drink, sleep, go for walks, and consume the fruits of the earth, and are nothing but idle burdens on the earth.

§29. Also, nobody must envy those who try to achieve merit with human-kind or obstruct their praiseworthy endeavors. If there is no way of matching their achievements, they should preserve their fame and their good reputation, which is the main reward of these labors.

§30. We serve the utility of others in a definite sense either without disadvantage or burden to ourselves or with effort and labor. The former is called common humanity, the latter a favor.

§31. Concerning common humanity, the following axiom should be noted: "He who refuses common humanity to another or envies it is considered exceptionally evil and inhumane."

§32. This means that he renders himself unworthy of being the recipient of the duties of humanity again.

§33. But when you hear the term *exceptionally evil*, beware of thinking that even in the absence of a case of necessity you can go to war against someone who refuses this common humanity in the state of nature. For this is repugnant to the principles we have taught concerning the duties of humanity in general, even though this kind of inhumanity can be punished in civil society, as is clear from the above.

§34. The duties that are thereby performed are usually called matters that are without disadvantage to ourselves [*res innoxiae utilitatis*], such as giving directions to someone who is lost, lighting another person's fire with my own, allowing someone to draw water from a well, leaving something which I cannot consume on my own to others, etc.

§35. On these observations depends the resolution of various controversies which have been much debated by authors on natural law. (1) Concerning the passage through our territory, both on land and on sea: it is obviously extremely harsh to deny this to individual humans and small groups who seek this passage for a just reason. But if it is a large army, or some other large number of people, the matter is more controversial.

§36. Yet it seems that the dispute is conducted with more subtlety than usefulness. For the examples produced in this question refer to cases which do not presuppose extreme necessity. Thus, even if this passage had been refused, contrary to the precepts of humanity, to those who sought it, they would have had no [just] cause to go to war as long as this refusal was not accompanied by insults.

§37. Those who deny it cannot be accused of inhumanity if they claim that this passage will not be harmless, because the guarantees that are usually supplied are not sufficient.

§38. (2) Concerning the passage of goods of others through our lands: this case is similar unless these goods are indispensable for sustaining life; then it is just to go to war if someone denies passage.

§39. The right of storage is a different matter. It means that goods passing through our territory can, without violating the duties of humanity, be compelled to stay in our lands even if there is no necessity for it, etc.

§40. (3) As far as customs and their justification are concerned, it is obvious why customs can be levied on the goods that are transported by land across our territory. The reason for raising the usual taxes in rivers is also evident. But in the case of sounds the matter is more difficult.

§41. Although quite substantial reasons can be produced [for raising taxes in sounds], it must be confessed that this kind of maritime tax is far more odious than all others, and so has to be levied with moderation and without greed. It is also easy for one or the other person to claim exemption from this tax.

§42. I cannot automatically consider all those to be inhuman who (4) deny seafarers the right to land on shore and remain there for some time, or who (5) do not want to admit foreigners [into their territory] and extend hospitality to them, as long as they do not expect similar hospitality from foreigners. In either case, there may be good reasons for denying this to them.

§43. Even less (6) can those be accused of inhumanity who refuse to shelter people who have been expelled from their homes, even if these people offer fair conditions, because receiving them is not a matter of common humanity but a favor. This [shelter] cannot be demanded on the basis of strict law, nor can another person's territory be entered without paying respects to its ruler, even if the land is uncultivated.

§44. Nor (7) can it be considered a violation of the duties of humanity if someone prohibits trade with another people, whether he prevents them from buying those goods from him which are not necessary for life, or he does not want to buy from them and does not permit them to offer goods for sale in his territory.

§45. Nor (8) does he deserve to be called inhumane who does not want to confirm friendship with a private person or with an entire nation through marriage. Therefore, the refusal of marriage alone will never be a just cause of war unless it has been accompanied by insults.

§46. But (9) it is highly implausible to derive some common right, and thus an obligation for everyone, from the fact that something has been generally permitted to all foreigners and to conclude that it is an insult if one person is then excluded from this permission. Yet it cannot be denied that it is more prudent to explain the reasons for such a refusal, or at least to temper the words of the refusal so that no hidden insult is implied in them.

§47. A favor is when someone gives something to another for free, either out of a particular feeling of benevolence and generosity, or out of some particular affection, or out of pity for someone else's condition. This favor consists in payments or labor which meet the other person's needs or are particularly useful to him.

§48. Others have already discussed what must be observed in the dispensation of favors with respect to the person giving and the person receiving and with respect to the way in which this is done and other circumstances. This cannot be subjected to exact rules because the variety of circumstances is too great.

§49. However, while humans are generally obliged to perform the duties of humanity toward each other, the degree of obligation is greater for him who has experienced not a general act of humanity but a favor. For then it is a matter of gratitude and is the counterpart to a favor.

§50. Gratitude, however, is when he who accepts the favor shows that it is accepted by him and favors the giver for this reason and seeks an opportunity to do the same or more to the extent that he is capable of doing so.

§51. The need for this virtue is so great that if it did not exist, all kindness and trust among humans would disappear, as would all benevolence; nor would anyone do anything for free or make any attempt at gaining another person's benevolence.

§52. Although, therefore, an ungrateful mind in itself does not cause an injury, the ungrateful person is considered more loathsome and detestable than the unjust person because he cannot be persuaded by favors, which soften even wild beasts, to conceive feelings of humanity.

§53. Ingratitude, however, is twofold. One is minor, which only denies the duties of humanity; the other is major ingratitude, which in addition causes harm to the benefactor.

§54. Minor ingratitude is a refusal to perform either the common duties of humanity or favors. We shall call the former singular, the latter common ingratitude.

§55. Major ingratitude is a cause of war, and there is no doubt that it is a cause for legal action in civil society or aggravates a legal action that has already been initiated.

§56. It is asked whether legal action is possible on the basis of minor ingratitude, which is not a cause for war. I believe that such action should not be allowed easily. But there is no doubt it can be allowed and among some nations has been allowed.

§57. That is, if this minor ingratitude is singular. In a case of common ingratitude, however, such an action is not really possible.

§58. But you should note the following: if a legal action is allowed in a case of singular ingratitude, then it is no longer gratitude to perform the common duties of humanity by granting a favor.

On the Duty of Persons Forming
an Agreement

§1. The fourth particular precept derived from the state of humanity and the second of the affirmative [precepts] is: "Keep your promises."

§2. The necessity of agreements among humans is clear from the fact that the duties of humanity and their fulfillment are not suitable for everything that humans can usefully expect of each other. This is partly because of the condition of him who should perform the useful action, partly because of the condition of the other person who asks for it, and partly because of the thing that is desired.[20] Moreover, once conflict has erupted among humans in the state of corruption, this cannot be settled by any other means than agreements.

§3. Agreements, however, are mainly concluded in order for one person to impose a perfect obligation on another, who would otherwise be under only an imperfect obligation, based on the need to perform the duties of humanity, and we enter these agreements indiscriminately with all kinds of humans. Thus, I say, it is obvious that the peace of mankind,

20. That is, as Thomasius explained in later editions, if the person who was expected to perform the duty needed the good or labor himself, or the other person refused to be the recipient, or the object that was desired was very precious (see Christian Thomasius, *Göttliche Rechtsgelahrheit* [1709], reprinted with a preface by Frank Grunert [Hildesheim: Georg Olms, 2001]).

and in particular the preservation of equality, require that faith is kept in promises.

§4. An agreement is the consensus of two people on the decision either to give or do something.

§5. And this is either gratuitous, if only one person places himself under an obligation, or mutual, if both do so.

§6. The immediate cause of an agreement is consensus, namely mutual consensus, even if the agreement itself is not mutual.

§7. On the part of the person placing an obligation on himself it is called a promise, on the part of the other an acceptance.

§8. A promise is either perfect or imperfect.

§9. A perfect promise is a declaration that I want to be bound in such a way that the other person may demand what has been promised to him as something that is owed to him from me.

§10. The promise is imperfect if I declare that I want to be bound in such a way that the other person cannot demand the fulfillment of the promise from me, as is the case in the promises of patrons.

§11. These [that is, perfect and imperfect promises] must not be confused with a bare statement, when I tell another person about my current intention of furthering his well-being, but do so in such a way that I do not want to oblige myself to it. That is clearly not relevant here.

§12. Thus, a promise is required to produce an obligation, for without it nobody can restrict the liberty of an equal against his will. Likewise, there is no agreement without an acceptance by the other side, because nobody can impose [his promise] on an unwilling person.

§13. Thus, if a promise is not accepted, the person who gave the promise loses none of his right over what he offered, because he who sets up an agreement does not intend to leave his property derelict.

§14. If a request preceded the promise, this request will be considered to continue until it is expressly revoked. In that case, an acceptance is understood to have been made in advance.

§15. But this is so only if the offer corresponds to the request. For if the offer either exceeds or falls short of this request, an express acceptance is required, because my needs often are not satisfied unless I receive as much as I have asked for.

§16. And this is undoubtedly true in mutual promises. We believe, however, that the same holds for gratuitous promises, though Roman law disagrees, based on the incongruous idea that the smaller sum is included in the larger.[21]

§17. Each side in an agreement makes known its will either in words or in deeds. The consensus and the agreement based on it are therefore divided into express and tacit.

§18. An express agreement is not difficult to understand: it is one where consensus is indicated by words. But concerning tacit agreements we need to draw some distinctions.

§19. Although tacit consent is one that is declared in deeds, and writers treat tacit and presumed consent as synonyms, presumed consent in fact differs from tacit, according to Roman law. We should therefore take

21. See *Digest* 45.1.1.4 and 45.1.83.3: the argument there was that if someone promised a sum of ten when the other demanded twenty, then a valid promise to give ten had been made because ten was contained within twenty. Thomasius is arguing that an obligation is formed only if both parties agree on the sum promised.

particular care to avoid confusing them, especially since they are often conflated.

§20. Permitted actions which humans use are either signs that are accepted by the common consent of mankind as means of declaring our will, such that any reasonable person who hears of this action immediately infers that I wanted to indicate something specific and determinate by it; or they are not signs accepted by the common consent of mankind for declaring the will, but natural equity requires that an obligation should accompany these actions and follow from them.

§21. The consent that rests on actions of the first kind is tacit, while the consent that is based on an action of the latter kind is called a presumed consent in Roman law, because whoever is a good citizen is presumed to agree to the rules of natural equity.

§22. Thus, a nod shows tacit assent; a signature declares, other things being equal, that I want to release the debtor from his debt; and the demand for food and drink from an innkeeper implies that I also want to pay for it.

§23. On the other hand, conducting a business, entering on an inheritance, and in general all actions that are included in the quasi-contracts of Roman law[22] do not imply direct consent to paying the damages caused to the owner of a business, to paying a legacy to the legatees, etc. The rules of natural equity, confirmed by civil laws, create a presumed consent here.

§24. Moreover, presumed and tacit consent differ (1) with regard to the person. He who cannot express his consent expressly cannot do it tacitly either. Thus, the nod of a madman, his signature, demand for food will not produce the said effects.

---

22. A *quasi-contract,* as permitted by law, is the act of a person by which he obligates himself toward another, or by which another binds himself to him, without any formal agreement between them.

§25. Yet madmen are placed under an obligation on the basis of presumed consent when, for example, their affairs are conducted for them.

§26. Indeed, (2) tacit consent binds only those who have declared their consent by their actions. But presumed consent also binds people who have not done anything. Thus, the owner of a business is generally obliged to pay the manager for the costs he has incurred in establishing it even if he does not know [yet] that the business has been established.

§27. Moreover, (3) either of these two kinds of consent is very different from express consent. Concerning tacit consent there is this rule: "It is in vain that we look for tacit consent when the opposite express consent is evident." The reason is that words are the normal signs of declaring one's will; actions, however, are extraordinary or supplementary ones.

§28. Thus, if I say that I do not want to assent, do not want to forgive your debt, do not want to pay the innkeeper for his food, then the nod, signature, and demand for food would have no effect.

§29. Presumed consent is an entirely different matter. Even if the manager of a business or an heir immediately and publicly solemnly declare before a notary and witnesses that they do not want to be put under an obligation by conducting the business or accepting the inheritance, this express declaration will be in vain. Thus, here the common axiom applies: A protestation that contradicts the action has no effect.

§30. You see, therefore, (4) that even the unwilling are bound by presumed consent, but only the willing are bound by tacit consent.

§31. Thus, (5) in presumed consent the obligation will come directly from the law; in tacit consent the law operates by means of a consensus.

§32. To put it briefly, (6) tacit consent is truly a form of consent. Presumed consent is improperly called consent. Thus, tacit consent produces true contracts according to Roman law, presumed consent only quasi-contracts.

§33. You should not, however, believe that this only exists in Roman law. For then it would be only a matter of human jurisprudence. Yet it also has some use in divine jurisprudence, which will become particularly clear below when we will examine the duties of children toward parents.

§34. They who lack a will cannot make a promise. These are children, madmen and the mentally confused, and very drunk people.

§35. This does not prevent drunks from being responsible for their transgressions and obliged to suffer punishments. For this obligation, as we shall explain later, comes directly from the law and binds even those who did not act willingly. But the type of obligation discussed in this chapter requires an agreement as an essential condition.

§36. Madness and drunkenness can indeed be easily proved, but there are no accurate universal rules that determine the duration of infancy. Thus, there are good reasons why its determination is left to civil law, which also has the task of providing guardians for adolescents, who are older than infants but whose will is not yet fully formed.

§37. Moreover, there are two parts to consent: understanding and will. Opposed to understanding are error and fraud. The former is when I do not know something (for this is taken in a broad sense and includes ignorance) or think it is different without being deceived by another person; fraud is when my error originates from the deceit of another person or this deceit is at least related to my error.

§38. Roman law has turned the issue of errors in contracts into a complex question, partly because this material does not have its own chapter [in the Corpus Iuris], though it is of everyday importance. Instead, the relevant rules are carelessly scattered among various chapters. In part this is also because the jurists who compiled the *Digest* often disagreed with each other. This produced a multitude of distinctions between an error concerning the persons and the object of a contract, between the matter and the form of the subject of the contract; also, if something consists of two materials, the question arises whether these are united, so to speak, through confusion or exist separately, or can easily be separated; finally, there is the distinction between the essential nature of the agreement and its contingent features, etc.

§39. But here is not the place to explain Roman law, and, leaving aside civil laws, I also think that it is according to natural equity to reiterate the above rule that an error, when in doubt, should always harm the person who errs.

§40. For everybody must reveal his intentions to another when making a promise, but the cause of the contract, its object, and the person with whom I form a contract generally do not contribute anything to the essence of an agreement. Therefore, there is no reason why my error should be imputed to the other party rather than myself if he did not further it by fraud or guilt. Moreover, if my error causes a disadvantage to another person, there would be ample scope for mental reservations, which, as has been shown in more detail by others, undermine all agreements and promises.[23]

§41. I nevertheless limit this axiom as follows: unless that circumstance in which I erred has been expressly added to the promise as a condition. For then the other person with whom I have made the agreement has no just occasion to complain about me.

§42. The learned tend to distinguish between gratuitous promises and mutual agreements. Concerning gratuitous promises the following rule

23. *Mental reservations* were unspoken qualifications by a person making a promise or statement. They were regarded as examples of insincerity and were associated especially with Jesuit casuistry. Thomasius is arguing that there would be fewer inhibitions to appeal to mental reservation if the person who made a false statement or promise did not suffer any consequences from doing so.

is formed: When I postulate something as a condition without which I would not have made the promise, the promise naturally will have no effect without it, because the person promising has not consented absolutely, but on condition. And if this condition is not fulfilled, the promise is nullified.

§43. But if the person making the promise keeps this condition to himself, we do believe that he is responsible for not making it clear. Thus, even if I have been falsely informed that my business has been conducted successfully by you, and I promised you something on that basis, I am bound to it, even after I have detected this lie, as long as you did not lead me by fraudulent means to make my promise. For then this case clearly does not apply.

§44. Just as the case of the soldier who believed a false messenger reporting the death of his sons and instituted another heir in his testament is not relevant here because the interpretation of last wills is different from that of promises.

§45. In mutual promises a distinction is drawn, depending on whether someone has been led by an error to form a contract or whether the error concerns the matter that is the subject of the contract. Concerning the first it must be considered whether the subject [of the contract] is still intact (that is, if no part of the contract has been fulfilled yet) or not (if, for example, what has been promised has already been accepted). In the former case it is fair to be granted an opportunity to withdraw, especially when I have made clear what led me to enter into this agreement. But if the subject is not intact, the person erring cannot insist on the rescission of the contract unless the other person permits it on the grounds of humanity.

§46. We believe, however, that even if the subject is intact, the erring person cannot withdraw. An example is if a head of household is told that his horses at home have perished, tells this to a horse dealer, and buys others from him. Even if the buyer realizes he has been misinformed before the horses are handed over and the money is paid, he must adhere to the contract. The false message was relevant to the cause that led him to enter the contract, but it is not part of the transaction itself unless it was added to the agreement as a condition. After all, a head of household can buy horses, whether he owns others already or not.

§47. Finally, it is a little opaque to say that the agreement is null and void if there is an error concerning the subject of a mutual promise, because the laws for making an agreement were not observed, and not so much because of the error itself. For it is not clear how these laws of an agreement that are referred to here are distinct from the error.

§48. Nor does this point seem necessary for discussing the relevant examples. True, if I stated that I wanted to buy a slave who was an experienced cook and the slave turned out to have no idea of cooking, then the contract is invalid even if the seller is not to blame. The same is true if I bought Davus, yet the vendor, through no fault of his own, gave me Syrus. But here the cause is apparent, because the circumstance in which the error occurred formed a condition of the promise.

§49. Let us continue with fraud. There a distinction must be drawn between fraud by him with whom we entered into a contract and fraud by a third party. In the latter case the agreement is valid, but the third party, who is guilty of fraud, is obliged to compensate us. In the former case it will be up to the victim whether he wants the promise, be it gratuitous or mutual, to be declared null and void, or whether he wants to leave the agreement intact and demand payment for damages.

§50. Nor do we make a distinction whether the fraud was the cause of the contract or incidental to it. That distinction is an invention of Roman law and is intended to illustrate the difference between contracts in good faith and those under strict law, a distinction that is unknown to natural jurisprudence.

§51. Also, according to Roman law the injured party could not declare a contract null and void because of fraud [though he had a right to demand compensation].

§52. Violence and fear are opposed to the will. It is hardly conceivable that someone can be forced by pure violence to promise something. Words cannot be extracted against a person's will in the way that limbs can be brought to do something by violence against their will. But if someone forces me to write, or, for example, pushes down my head, the promise will undoubtedly be void according to the general rules concerning the principle of moral actions.

§53. Fear can be considered in two ways. First, insofar as it is a probable suspicion that we will be deceived by another, either because of his vicious behavior or his declared bad intentions in a current affair. Note the following rules on this matter.

§54. If such fear was present at the time the promise was made, I acted imprudently by making a promise. The promise, however, is valid, nor can it be rescinded on that pretext.

§55. If I have become fearful after making the promise, because of signs that are either new or were previously unknown to me, I will not be compelled to fulfill the promise before the other person has provided adequate protection against fraud.

§56. Another form of fear is the extreme terror of the mind that is a response to a threat of serious harm when we do not want to make a promise or enter an agreement.

§57. If a third party inflicts this fear, the agreements that have been made with the other person because of this fear remain valid.

§58. The promise will even be valid if unjust fear is inflicted on a third party and I, out of pity, promise something concerning this third party to the person inflicting the fear.

§59. If he to whom I make the promise uses fear to force me to make it, then the promise will be valid as long as he does this because he has the authority to command me.

§60. But if someone who has no authority over me extracts this promise by entirely unjust force, it is a serious question whether this promise entails an obligation.

§61. Some believe that an obligation follows because fear does not remove all consent, but that the person inflicting the fear is nevertheless obliged to make restitution because he has committed a wrong by inflicting fear.

§62. This is not that different from the principle of Roman law that grants him who caused the fear the right to a legal action [to enforce the promise or agreement], but at the same time allows the other person to defend himself against this action on the grounds that the promise was motivated by fear.[24]

§63. Others believe that this produces no obligation: obligation in agreements is not the result of my consent alone when the other person is prohibited by natural law from accepting my promise; and any obligation that exists must also be balanced against the obligation of the person inflicting the fear to compensate me for the damage I suffered.

§64. Finally, others believe that he who made a promise to the person inflicting the fear is firmly obliged to keep it because natural law dictates that agreements must be kept. The above reasons are no obstacle. Even if he who inflicts fear has no right to do so, he does nevertheless have the right to accept my promise. And so his right, which he has accepted from the agreement with myself, corresponds to my obligation. There can also be no case for compensation, since it must be presumed that he who, for example, promises a highwayman a hundred thaler[25] has at the same time renounced his right to compensation against the thief on the basis of the injury. Why should he otherwise make a promise to the highwayman?

§65. Among these various opinions I like the first least because it rests on useless subtlety and was used by the Romans mainly to distinguish

24. On these questions see *Digest* 4.2 ("Quod metus causa gestum erit").
25. A currency unit in early-modern Germany.

the offices of the praetor and the judge. Even in Roman law, however, there is a well-known saying by a famous jurist that it makes no difference whether someone has no right to a legal action or whether an exception is made on the grounds of fear.

§66. Between the two others, however, there is a middle way that pleases me. We have already said above that agreements in themselves do not produce an obligation, but are only a means or a necessary cause of an obligation, and that an obligation derives all its force from law. The law which already forbids inflicting force and fear on another person also prohibits the person inflicting the fear from acquiring a right as a consequence. Nor should it be assumed that the law wants to bind the person who made the promise while benefiting him who has broken the law. Thus, it will be easy to respond to the reasons for the third opinion.

§67. In order that our opinion be better understood, we posit (1) that it is morally certain that he who causes the fear did not have the right to do so; (2) that the fear is of a present danger, that it is strong enough to influence a steadfast man, and that it can be avoided only by making this promise; (3) that the promise made out of fear has not been confirmed after the fear has ceased either by express words or by actions that imply subsequent consent.

§68. We can, therefore, easily infer that we are talking about promises that have been made, for example, to (1) a highwayman, (2) who is acting as such, (3) under the influence of fear. For if you make an agreement with a highwayman without the fear of present danger, or when this danger is over, there can be no doubt that there is an obligation because of the lack of the second and third prerequisites.

§69. You will also be under an obligation if you have entered into an agreement with someone who defeated you in war. This is not so much because the second requisite is usually absent, but mainly because of the lack of the first requisite. For even if the defeated side, for example, was convinced of the justice of its struggle, only that which can be demonstrated to others is said to be morally certain, since not being [just] and not appearing to be just are here virtually the same.

§70. The victor, however, will never lack pretexts having some appearance of justice and will draw other nations to his side. Among equals, therefore, justice and injustice are unsuitable remedies for resolving controversies, so war was invented as a sort of extraordinary remedy for restoring peace. The belligerents, as a compromise, leave the decision to the luck of war.

§71. Nevertheless, this compromise rests not so much on their tacit as on their presumed consent, and on the necessity of natural law. For unless war is ended by agreements of this kind, sociality and the peace of humankind would be disturbed forever. What do I say? The war between two parties would eventually lead to a war of all against all.

§72. It is undeniable that he who offers a peaceful agreement instead of the war sought by the other side, who deplores war, and who is then forced to accept unfair conditions of peace is not prohibited from protesting on the grounds of fear before the peace has been signed, or from seeking redress for the injury later when there is an opportunity to do so. But this must be done cautiously: the peace must be palpably unfair, and the two other conditions mentioned above must be present.

§73. But what shall we do about public enemies, who are often promised immunity or even more than that by princes in order to prevent civil wars? Princes who break the peace are generally in bad repute; yet the cause of the public enemy is without question and evidently unjust since we have often said that in a society of unequal members the inferior never has the right of coercing the superior through war, even if he has suffered an injustice from him.

§74. But it is easy to reply that the thief and the public enemy are completely different matters. The former cannot produce even the slightest legal pretext. But the public enemy can often claim that the prince has done either him or the commonwealth an injustice. And so he is often not destitute of all right, but only chooses the wrong means to exercise his right. Also, it is often unclear whether the state is purely monarchical or whether only the form of administration is monarchical.[26] Thus, it will not be obvious which of the two belligerents in such a war is the superior and which of them the inferior.

§75. That is perhaps what Cicero was referring to when he said that it was no fraud not to pay robbers the money they had been promised in return for sparing their victim's life.[27] For the pirate is not a public enemy, but the common enemy of all. No faith needs to be kept with him, nor common oath. We shall discuss oaths later.

§76. If this reason by itself is not sufficient, you could add that in those promises that are made to public enemies, there is usually no fear of an immediate danger, which may even affect a steadfast man, but of a war the outcome of which is still uncertain, etc.

§77. Thus, I should think that if a public enemy suddenly attacks his king without previously waging war and forces him under threat of death or something similar to come to an agreement, then this agreement produces an obligation no more than the promise made to a pirate does. So much on consent.

§78. Yet we can only promise those things that are within our power and subject to our will, and this promise tends to produce an obligation which usually presupposes this rule.

§79. It follows then (1) that nobody can oblige himself to something impossible with his promise. He who makes such promises and he who ac-

---

26. In a monarchical state the monarch was the sovereign. In a monarchical form of administration sovereignty was held by an individual or group other than the monarch. This distinction was drawn by Bogislaw Philipp von Chemnitz (alias Hippolitus a Lapide) in *Dissertatio de ratione status in Imperio nostro Romano-Germanico* (n.p., 1640).

27. Cicero, *On Duties*, bk. III, chap. 107, 141.

cepts them both show signs not of sound understanding, but of extreme foolishness.

§80. That is, unless he to whom the promise is made did not know that the promise was impossible to fulfill, and the person making the promise did know it was beyond his power.

§81. For some things are impossible for all humans, such as flying or touching the sky with a finger. Some are impossible for a few people only, such as procreating or giving a thousand or a hundred thaler, etc. The above qualification applies to the latter cases.

§82. The person making the promise will not be released from all obligation if he promises something possible which later becomes impossible, either through the fraud or fault of the person promising or even by accident, though the degree of obligation varies depending on the kind of guilt or accident.

§83. Thus Hobbes's opinion is not universally true, but subject to many limitations: agreements do not oblige actually to fulfill a promise, but only to make the best possible effort to do so.[28]

§84. Is it impossible for someone to promise not to resist the infliction of mortal injuries? It will be more appropriate to discuss this below when we talk about punishments.

§85. (2) Nobody can bind himself by an agreement to do something prohibited by the laws. The legislator does not contradict himself, and if he already has commanded a certain action, he cannot approve the contrary decision by the contracting parties without contradicting himself. Therefore, this kind of agreement is not permitted, even if it is not beyond the natural powers of the parties.

---

28. Hobbes, *On the Citizen,* chap. 2, §14, p. 38.

§86. For that reason nobody is required to fulfill a promise to do something despicable, not only when nothing has happened yet. Even after the other party has perpetrated the shameful deed, the person who made the promise is not bound to pay him the reward or an indemnity.

§87. But if you have already paid the reward for the shameful deed, no matter whether the deed has been done or not, you will not be able to demand it back from the person who accepted the promise. For in an equal cause the condition of the possessor is the stronger, and the person who made the promise bears the responsibility for his turpitude.

§88. Unless, that is, the turpitude is that of the accepting person alone, even leaving aside Roman law. In that case, the above reasons no longer apply.

§89. (3) Nobody can promise what belongs to someone else. For these things are not subject to our will, nor is it within our power to give them.

§90. The promise to give another person's possession is not valid. But there are some contracts concerning other people's possessions, those that regulate their administration, safekeeping, use, and similar matters.

§91. (4) It is the same with other people's actions when these are not subject to our direction. If they are subject to our direction, then they are treated like our possessions as far as agreements are concerned.

§92. Thus, he who promises that another person will do something will not be bound by that promise unless circumstances show the meaning of the promise to be that he will make an effort to ensure that the other person fulfills what has been promised. Then he will be bound to make every morally possible effort that the promise be fulfilled.

§93. If he promises to make a third party do something for me, he will be considered under an obligation to render any payment which the third party has failed to make.

§94. (5) Finally we cannot form valid agreements concerning our actions or possessions over which another person has already acquired a right. For these are exempt from our will.

§95. Unless, perhaps, the other person's right has expired. The person making the promise, however, should not wish for such a case if it is shameful to do so. Thus, it is valid to promise to do work for someone on condition that work for another person has been completed, just as it is valid to promise to rent out our buildings once the present tenancy has ended. But it is shameful to promise subjection for as long as the commonwealth, to which there already is an obligation, does not suffer from a civil war or perish by some other way.

§96. Thus, conditional agreements concerning marriage which one spouse makes during the lifetime of the other are declared invalid among Christian princes—not without reason—and punishments have been decreed for those who form such agreements.

§97. This is also why, in Roman law, the promises of a free man and of a commonwealth would be invalid if they were made on condition that he become a slave or it [the commonwealth] become private property.[29]

§98. We shall now turn to the form of the promise: this is either pure, or for a certain time, or on condition. The first grants a full right, the second an incomplete right, until the relevant date arrives; the last grants not even an incomplete right, but only a hope that he will be required to fulfill it. The only effect is that the person who makes the promise cannot withdraw before the condition is met.

§99. The difference, therefore, between the two latter forms of promise lies mainly in this: he who fulfills his part of the promise by mistake before the condition of the promise is met can demand that this be reversed. But

---

29. See Justinian, *Institutes,* trans. Peter Birks and Grant McLeod (London: Duckworth, 1987), bk. 3, title 19 "De inutilibus stipulationibus," §2.

this does not apply to him who fulfills his part of a promise before the deadline.

§100. A promise for a certain period and a conditional promise differ in that a date is a future point in time and it is certain that and when it will happen. In the case of a condition, however, it is uncertain whether and when it will come about; at least, it is uncertain whether it will happen.

§101. Therefore, a promise is made on condition when the validity of the promise is linked to an outcome, depending on a specific event.

§102. Those conditions that are tacitly included in all promises, even pure ones, are not properly called conditions—for example, I will give you a hundred thaler if no greater force prevents me, if the world still exists, etc.

§103. Likewise, the conditions referring to the present or the past [are not real conditions] unless the tacit meaning here is "if that, which refers to the present or the past, is found to be the case."

§104. Also conditions which will necessarily be met, for example, "if there will be a day tomorrow."

§105. And since the same holds true for the contrary, impossible conditions are also not true conditions.

§106. Yet there is the following difference between these and the other improper conditions: the latter usually create a pure promise; in the case of an impossible condition, however, what we have said about impossible promises applies here too.

§107. Nor do we distinguish between promises and last wills if we leave aside the rules of civil laws, though these have decided, quite rightly, that these [impossible conditions] are not considered to be valid in last wills, to prevent humans from being mocked by pointless actions.

§108. Shameful conditions, however, when they depend on an uncertain outcome, cannot be considered improper conditions, and they are not a form of impossible conditions, as jurists have argued, for they have not properly understood a law in the *Digest*[30]—though here the same is true concerning their effectiveness as in the case of illicit promises.

§109. Thus, a condition has to be possible to be valid. This the doctors of civil law unanimously divide into conditions that are within the powers of a person, those depending on chance, and those that are mixed.[31] I doubt, however, whether this distinction will be of much use outside civil law.

§110. For as we have shown elsewhere, the mixed conditions and those within the powers of a person differ little, even according to ancient jurists; and the differences between the conditions depending on chance and the conditions within the powers of a person are partly mere subtlety, and partly imply the rule that the condition within the powers of a person is considered to be fulfilled if the person who was meant to fulfill the promise can do no more to fulfill it.

§111. But this axiom is not only subject to many qualifications by the Roman jurists concerning its particular applications (it even gave rise to a remarkable controversy).[32] It will also hardly work even if you leave aside civil laws, because the question of whether the person who made the promise and added the condition was referring mainly to the will of the person responsible for fulfilling the promise or to a contingent event, which is always part of such conditions, must be determined from other circumstances. For if he referred to the contingent event, then this axiom would not be applicable.

30. Thomasius is referring to Justinian's *Digest* 28.7.15.

31. See Justinian, *Codex Justinianus*, ed. Paul Krueger (Berlin: Weidmann, 1877), 6.51.1.7.

32. See Christian Thomasius (*praeses*) and Peter Johann Oehnsen (*respondens*), *Disputatio juridica de filio sub conditione, si se filium probaverit, herede instituto, ad l. Lucius 83. de cond. & demonstr.* (Leipzig, 1686).

§112. If the condition does not depend on the pure will of the person making the promise, but on a case which presupposes the will of the person making the promise, then an obligation only emerges when this case has come into existence. The person making the promise will not be under an indiscriminate obligation to do anything that is morally acceptable to fulfill the promise.

§113. A place is usually added to the promises, an addition that also produces an incomplete right, until enough time has elapsed for this place to be conveniently reached.

§114. We also promise something either directly to a particular person or through others, whom we use as messengers and interpreters of our will. Jurists call these mandataries and procurators.

§115. If these act in good faith and do not exceed the clear limits of their mandate, they place us under a firm obligation toward those with whom they have formed an agreement in our name.

§116. But ministers whom I have chosen to make promises in my name must not be confused with those whose function is only to signify a promise, such as, for example, couriers who have been entrusted with a letter explaining our will. For if the minister dies before he has signified our will to the relevant person, we can revoke our promise, even if the other party found out about our promise from a third party and accepted it. This is not the case when a courier dies and he receives the letter from someone else.

§117. There is another difference: if I have used a courier, my revocation is valid as long as I revoke my promise before it has been accepted by the other party, even if the courier knew nothing of the revocation. But if I have used a mandatary, then the revocation will be invalid unless it has been made known to the mandatary.

§118. But I think that here various cases need to be distinguished, especially whether the revocation is directed to the mandatary or to him to whom the promise was made. Also, whether this revocation reached the person with whom the agreement was made before the acceptance of the promise.

§119. There is also another question: can I accept a promise in the name of another person, who has given me no mandate? You cannot remove all scruples just by drawing the following distinction, whether the promise is made as follows: "I promise with you as a witness to give this to Sejus"; or like this: "I promise to you that I will give this to Sejus." But in the latter case a distinction needs to be drawn, whether he to whom the promise was made in this fashion did or did not have an interest that the third party should receive his due. The Roman jurists did not neglect this distinction.[33]

§120. But this is less doubtful: if the person the promise was made to dies before he has accepted the promise, the acceptance cannot be made against my will by his heirs, even if it is certain that the contracting parties are normally assumed to have wanted to care for their heirs.

§121. There follows the division of agreements. The passive division, which created trouble for Roman jurists and their interpreters, is that between pacts in the strict sense and contracts. But since either of these two kinds of agreement presupposes the division of properties and the existence of prices, their discussion will have to be postponed until later.

33. See Justinian, *Institutes,* bk. 3, title 19 "De inutilibus stipulationibus."

CHAPTER VII

On the Duty of Man Concerning Speech

§1. We will now turn to hypothetical precepts, which have this name not only because they presuppose concomitant agreements and laws on keeping faith but mainly because it is easy to derive them from the general precept concerning the preservation of human equality and its four rivulets, like theses from a hypothesis.

§2. Thus, you will not be surprised if here and in the other chapters where the reasons for axioms will be provided, I will often only briefly draw attention to the above or just apply these precepts to particular conclusions. At the same time, in the individual chapters I will mainly pay attention to the purpose of the particular matters which are discussed because this is of the greatest importance in moral matters.

§3. Concerning speech, however, we need first to say something about its definition and origin, before we provide the precepts concerning the duty of humans in speaking.

§4. Speech is an articulate sound by which humans communicate their thoughts to each other and reason among themselves.

§5. Speech is, however, described as an articulate sound, to distinguish it from voice in general and from sound. Sound is whatever the ears hear as a result of the collision between material bodies. Voice is a sound uttered by animals. Speech is proper to humans. Beasts, however, usually have an inarticulate, very rarely an articulate, voice or rather a voice that is halfway between articulate and inarticulate—parrots, for example, etc. But speech is always articulate.

§6. I leave aside the distinction between voice as a signal of something pleasant and unpleasant and speech as a signal of something useful and harmful, honest and despicable. This is already implied by the previous distinction, although I would prefer it if the good and the useful were omitted here or extended to voice as well as speech.

§7. Thus, speech is specific to humans. It distinguishes them from beasts and reflects humans' use of reason, as even Aristotle agrees. Cicero's words deserve to be noted. Nature persuades humans by the force of reason to unite with each other, to use a common language and live in a society.[34] Moreover, the bond of society is reason and speech, which by teaching, learning, communicating, discussing, and judging unites humans with each other and joins them in a kind of natural society.[35]

§8. You see here that reason, speech, and society are linked to each other by Cicero. Our observations above on the explanation of sociality illustrate this further.[36]

§9. When Paul, the teacher of the Gentiles, turns them away from lies and urges them to accept the truth, he produces no other reason than that humans are united by their fellowship with each other, not physically, of course, but morally and socially.[37]

§10. The primary aim of speech, therefore, is to allow humans to reason with each other; reasoning, however, requires tranquillity. The general

34. See Cicero, *On Duties* [*De officiis*], ed. M. T. Griffin and E. M. Atkins (Cambridge: Cambridge University Press, 1991), bk. I, chap. 12.
35. Ibid., chap. 50.
36. See *Institutes,* bk. I, chap. iv, §§52ff.
37. Ephesians 4:25.

precept concerning the duty of speakers, therefore, is: use speech and the other signs of the mind to further common tranquillity.

§11. But there is no doubt about that. You surely desire more specific axioms, which I shall provide immediately by showing the difference between speech and the other signs of the mind. This difference is to be found in the term *voice*.

§12. The signs of things are either natural or arbitrary. The former are derived from natural properties of things and pertain to natural philosophers or medics. Thus, smoke is a sign of fire, dawn of the coming day, pallor of disease or love, etc., flight of fear.

§13. Arbitrary signs are those having meaning on the basis of human decisions that are not made by individuals in isolation but are based on general consent.

§14. The purpose of all these signs is to communicate the thoughts of one person to another. But man cannot look into the mind of another man, and the natural signs of the mind are very few. They are also often suppressed by those who are skillful deceivers. Sociality then would not have been provided for if anyone could have imposed whatever meaning he wanted to on signs. Humans, therefore, had to agree on this by mutual consent.

§15. But these arbitrary signs are either common to several nations or specific to some.

§16. Each is derived from the use of a great variety of different things,[38] and in particular from the use and variation of the human voice.

§17. These latter signs based on the use of speech are especially suitable for preserving sociality. Without speech there can be no, or only a very crude form of, society, peace, and discipline among humans.

---

38. Thomasius is referring, for example, to the use of drums or trumpets to transmit signals and also to gestures such as bowing before another person.

§18. And imagine two humans being forced by some necessity to be together although neither is versed in the language of the other. Beasts of
different kinds are more easily united in sociable relationships than they
are, even though they are humans. The great similarity of their nature will
not help them at all in associating with each other if they cannot communicate the meanings of their mind only because of the diversity of their
languages. Man will rather spend time with his dog than with another
man who speaks a different tongue.

§19. This is not to mention the countless inconveniences that cannot but
result from equivocation caused by other signs or differences in language.
An Italian, for example, who was unable to bear the hot water in a bath,
shouted "caldo"[39] and was nearly boiled to death when the German bath
keeper thought he was complaining about the cold and poured hot water
over him. Similarly, a German in a remote province who displayed his
teeth and made pitiful sounds asking for some food had his teeth extracted because his host thought he suffered from a toothache.

§20. Moreover, while Gentiles, who do not have the benefit of the history
of Creation, have said various things about the origin of speech, we know
from Scripture that God implanted it into the first humans at the very
beginning. Those born from them then learned it by hearing it until the
construction of the tower of Babel gave rise to the diversity of languages.
Here the pagans agree, saying that speech has its power of meaning not by
nature or from some intrinsic necessity, but purely by human agreement
and establishment.

§21. Unless, perhaps, you wanted to object on the basis of the contrary
arguments of Cratylus reported by Plato, which are, however, vain and
have already been refuted by others in greater detail.[40]

---

39. *Caldo* is Italian for "hot"; *kalt* in German means "cold."

40. See Plato, "Cratylus," in Plato, *Cratylus; Parmenides; Greater Hippias; Lesser Hippias,* trans. H. N. Fowler, Loeb Classical Library (London: Heinemann, 1926), p. 7.
Thomasius here also draws on Pufendorf, *Of the Law of Nature and Nations* (Oxford,
1703), bk. IV, chap. i, §4, and Heinrich Uffelmann, *De jure quo homo homini in sermone
obligatur liber unus* (Helmstedt, 1676).

§22. But just as the meaning of other signs of the mind rests on human convention, so speech too derives its meaning from the same source.

§23. But this convention is either general, and applies to an entire people using the same language for matters that are commonly known or used, or it is special, used by experts and erudite people discussing matters that are popularly unknown and remote from everyday life.

§24. But although we are here concerned mainly with the duties of speech (as the chapter title indicates), what we have said shows that this is also applicable to the other signs of the mind. Therefore, we have joined these to speech in a general axiom.

§25. Letters occupy a kind of intermediate position between these two, and for this reason civil law sometimes considers them words, sometimes deeds. However, letters are closer to words and speech, of which they are the image, just as speech is an image of the mind.

§26. Having said this, I see a threefold classification of the special precepts which are part of man's duty concerning speech. The first of these concerns the act of speaking, the second the choice of signs, the third the conformity of the mind with the signs.

§27. Because speech discloses the mind, three questions follow from this: (1) whether my thoughts are to be revealed to another, (2) whether in declaring these thoughts we should use signs invented by others, and (3) whether signs must correspond with thoughts.

§28. We shall answer these three questions most easily by drawing on the four particular and absolute precepts and the general precept which we have derived from the purpose of speech.

§29. This leads to the following negative precept concerning the first question: "Be silent if by your speech others are offended or suffer undeserved harm, or if humanity, an agreement, or peace in general demand it."

§30. This precept covers verbal insults, as well as boasting, adulation, and buffoonery, but above all garrulousness.

§31. While these are to be avoided by everyone, public servants, military commanders, legates, councilors, etc., must be particularly averse to them.

§32. The corresponding affirmative precept commands the following: "Speak whenever humanity or an agreement obliges you to do so, or if silence exposes another person to contempt or harm, or disturbs the peace."

§33. Others add: "Speak whenever the honor of God requires it." But this limitation is to some extent already tacitly included in our rule, insofar as all precepts of natural law presuppose the inner reverence for God as their first principle. Thus, we abstain from adding this limitation expressly because these people are mainly concerned with religious worship and with solving the extremely difficult question: when is a confession of faith necessary, and when is it not? As this goes beyond the remit of jurisprudence, we leave this decision to the theologians.

§34. They, however, sin against this precept who are silent about dangers to the commonwealth, a fellow citizen, or their neighbor; who, having acquired information, do not report it accurately; and who do not chastise those entrusted to their care whenever it is necessary.

§35. Although we assume two particular precepts concerning the first question, we will be content with a single, negative one in the second: "Do not use words in another meaning than that agreed upon."

§36. The reason for the difference is that taciturnity, even if it does not benefit sociality more than speech, [in this case] benefits it in equal measure. It is different if someone wants to use words in a particular meaning which has not been agreed upon.

§37. Others can easily be offended if a word is used in this particular meaning, and the utility of humankind would then not be furthered.

And, as is clear from the above, it constitutes a violation of the express or tacit agreement on which all speech rests.

§38. I am aware that nobody (least of all philosophers) has been deprived of the power to create new words. But this license is irrelevant to our rule since it, too, rests on an express or tacit agreement. We will explain elsewhere how far this license extends.

§39. There remains the third question. The affirmative precept there is "Speak your thoughts if humanity, an agreement, or common peace requires you to."

§40. Opposed to this is the negative precept: "Abstain from lying whenever someone is hurt or suffers contempt as a result and peace among humans is disturbed."

§41. Indeed, I am bound to reveal my thoughts to another and speak what is in my mind whenever the person I am dealing with has a perfect or an imperfect right to it. But this occurs when one of these four absolute precepts requires it.

§42. And as speech has been invented for our sake, I will be allowed to form my speech in such a way that it expresses something different from what I have in my mind when it is of some considerable use to me and nobody else's right is violated.

§43. And if we intend to further the utility of others whom we would harm by speaking the truth, then it will be allowed to use fiction and oblique phrases. For he who wants to and must benefit another person should not do this in a way that would prevent him from achieving that aim.

§44. Even if nature wants speech to be the interpreter of the mind, it wants this to be done with prudence and, other things being equal, also wants mutual and indeed common welfare to be provided for. And since the latter is the primary purpose of speech, by which the other [purpose] is measured, the intention to deceive cannot be against the law of nature, when it directly tends toward this end [that is, common welfare].

§45. Moreover, philosophers agree that truth requires us to give every person his due by speaking the truth. Thus, on the other hand, it only prohibits that falsehood by which another, innocent person is deceived.

§46. But, you say, everyone has a perpetual right not to be deceived by another. Thus, lying will always be despicable.

§47. Yet I shall deny the universality of this objection as readily as you defend it. Others have also responded to the arguments by those who disagree.[41]

§48. It is clear from what has been said what truth is, insofar as it is a virtue, and what the vice opposed to it is, which is called mendacity.

§49. Metaphysical truth is different from logical truth and ethical truth. The first concerns the state of being, insofar as it refers to existence. The second concerns the state of a proposition, insofar as that which is asserted or denied about a subject is true independently of human cognition. Opposed to the former is metaphysical falsehood, a state of nonbeing (or, to be more precise, *nothing* is opposed to metaphysical truth, since nonbeing has no predicates). Opposed to the latter is a false proposition.

§50. Moreover, just as logical truth consists in the conformity of a proposition with its object outside the mind, so, too, ethical truth consists in the conformity of external signs, particularly speech, with the mind.

---

41. See, for example, Samuel Pufendorf, *On the Duty of Man and Citizen,* ed. J. Tully (Cambridge: Cambridge University Press, 1991), bk. I, chap. 10, §§9–10; and Pufendorf, *The Whole Duty of Man, According to the Law of Nature,* ed. Ian Hunter and David Saunders, trans. A. Tooke (Indianapolis: Liberty Fund, 2003), bk. I, chap. 10, §§9–10, pp. 122–23.

§51. But beware of immediately equating ethical truth with moral virtue. Ethics also deals with indifferent actions, not just honest or despicable ones.

§52. Therefore, this truth deserves the appellation of virtue only insofar as this conformity of words with the mind renders everyone his due. With this addition, this kind of truth can be called truth in justice.

§53. The Peripatetics have generally used this addition in order to distinguish this virtue from homiletic truth,[42] which we have deliberately omitted because many commentators consider the homiletic virtues to be either nonessential or an ornament of virtues rather than actual virtues.

§54. Homiletic truth, in particular, seems to be one of the virtues of the intellect, rather than [one of] the moral virtues. Therefore, according also to Aristotle's judgment, a braggart is useless (μάταιος) rather than evil (κακός).[43]

§55. The braggart sins not so much because he tells falsehoods about himself (except to the extent that this speech causes injury to another, which is opposed to truth in justice), but because he talks a lot about himself, whether what he says is true or not.

§56. Hence, it is evident that it is not accurate to define homiletic truth as the virtue of preserving the right measure when speaking the truth about oneself in everyday conversation. It should have been said that it preserves the right measure in speaking of oneself in general.

§57. Or rather, the term *truth* has been incongruously imposed on this virtue, since its essence does not consist in conformity of signs with the mind.

---

42. That is, truthfulness in social intercourse and conversation.

43. Aristotle, *Nicomachean Ethics,* trans. H. Rackham, Loeb Classical Library (London and Cambridge, Mass.: Harvard University Press, 1947), 1127b10.

§58. False speech is opposed to ethical truth generally speaking. False speech consists in the disagreement between the speech and the mind of a person who intends to deceive another.

§59. Opposed to truth in justice is mendacity, which deserves this name if this discrepancy [between speech and mind] and the intention to deceive lead to the violation of another person's right.

§60. Therefore, it is clear that *false speech* and *mendacity* are not synonyms. All mendacity is despicable, while false speech is sometimes morally indifferent.

§61. So they who consider any discrepancy between signs and the mind to be mendacity improperly extend the term of the species to that of the genus. And when they consider this mendacity always to be a vice, they mistakenly apply the properties of the species to that of the genus.

§62. Moreover, it is clumsy to say that a veracious man can be mendacious but cannot deceive. For *to deceive* and *to be mendacious* are synonyms. But mendacity and false speech are different.

§63. Also, the lies that are commonly called courteous and humorous are not mendacity in the proper sense. Already Luther observed this, saying that polite lies were a particular virtue and form of prudence.

§64. Finally, the fact that some related faithfulness to truthfulness, perfidy to mendacity, is typical of colloquial speech rather than philosophical argument.

§65. It is true that he who keeps promises is commonly said to speak the truth; he who is perfidious, to have lied.

§66. But in philosophical terms faithfulness and perfidy differ from truth as a general concept, since their essence consists in the conformity or disagreement of subsequent actions with the preceding signs of the mind.

§67. For he who spoke the truth at first can become perfidious later, and he who lied can repent and be faithful.

§68. Closely related to false speech, but not to be confused with it, are simulation and dissimulation. These generally differ from falsehood because the latter is expressed in speech, the former by a deed which is nonverbal.

§69. Like false speech, simulation and dissimulation have the purpose of deceiving and tricking another person.

§70. But simulation and dissimulation differ in that the latter consists in an omission, such as silence, the former in a positive act, the use of other signs apart from speech in such a way that they do not agree with the mind of the person using them.

§71. Since, therefore, simulation is closer to lying, dissimulation closer to the refusal to speak the truth, it is also clear that nothing new is to be expected concerning the justice of either. What we have said above about silence must here be applied to dissimulation; what we have said about lying must be applied to simulation.

§72. It is evident at the same time what is to be thought about the division by jurists of deceit into good and bad, which has been attacked by many and poorly understood. As they defined *deceit* as "fraud," they wanted to include lying, simulation, and dissimulation in this term.

§73. And since we have shown that lying can be permissible, as can simulation and dissimulation, there will, therefore, also be a good form of fraud.

§74. Thus, the question concerning the permissibility of deceiving others has been resolved on the basis of the above, more easily and more clearly than if you had distinguished, as others do, between lying and withholding truth (or partial truth), or between lying and ambiguous speech (or some tacit restriction).

§75. For in part these distinctions conceal an impious and criminal opinion (mental reservation, for example). Others, which look for an excuse in notions of withholding truth and ambiguous speech, are unsuitable to resolving controversies and are subject to the same limitations which we applied to lying. Other authors have discussed this in more detail.

§76. We can easily resolve more particular questions on the basis of the preceding arguments. (1) It is forbidden to lie indiscriminately to children and fools as if they were not free to judge our speech. Since they are as human as we are, we may use fiction and fables only if they benefit from them to a greater degree than from the truth and to the extent that they are incapable of understanding the bare truth.

§77. The same reason offers an excuse for lying if someone (2) uses fiction in speaking to adults for a good purpose and for their own or the common utility when open speech cannot achieve this—if, for example, an innocent person has to be protected, an angry person placated, a sad person consoled, a timid person encouraged, a fastidious person persuaded to take medicine, obstinacy overcome, or an evil plot prevented—as long as everything else is in order (if, for example, this is done without offending God).

§78. (3) Thus, it is permissible to promote the welfare of the commonwealth by using fiction to conceal its secret affairs of state and councils, which it has an interest in keeping from others, or to express an opinion in doubtful and obscure matters that does not reflect what I believe to be true if doing so will help to get at the truth.

§79. What we cannot accept is the belief (4) that it is never a lie when we address a fictive speech to someone who is not deceived, though a third person derives a false opinion from it. The argument here is that I have nothing to do with this third person.

§80. But that opinion is not always true. In daily social intercourse I am usually assumed to have something to do with all those who are present, even if my speech is addressed specifically to one person in the company.

And even if we accepted that reasoning, this kind of action, nevertheless, would still be susceptible to the accusation of vice, since lying is not the only sin that is related to speech.

§81. We must, therefore, take great care here that there is no violation of the prohibition concerning the first question above. Thus, we need to add many qualifications here which have already been explained with great precision by others.[44]

§82. Above all, if someone wants to deflect the irritating and harmful curiosity of others, he must take care that other innocent persons do not suffer as a result, and that he who is unrestrainedly curious is afflicted with a small and moderately unpleasant evil rather than with real harm.

§83. But (5) since we may harm enemies by open force, we may also mislead them with stories or a fictive speech, as long as this is not done in pacts entered into with the enemy; for in concluding these we move away from the state of hostility to some degree, even if not completely.

§84. This limitation also applies to those other cases in which we said lying was permitted. As we just pointed out, the precept to keep faith is different from that to speak the truth.

§85. It is more difficult to determine whether (6) an accused can deny a crime he is accused of, or extricate himself by using false arguments, without being guilty of lying. I believe he cannot, not only if this concerns the payment of a debt or compensation, but also if the main issue is the imposition of a punishment.

§86. For it is generally accepted that the judge has the right and the ability to extract the truth from the accused by any means. Thus, it automatically follows (from the above argument on speaking the truth, whenever the person I am dealing with has a right to it) that the accused is under

---

44. Thomasius is referring to Pufendorf's *Of the Law of Nature and Nations,* bk. 4, chap. i, §18.

an obligation to tell the judge the truth. Moreover, right and obligation, as was shown at the beginning of these *Institutes,* are correlates, neither of which can exist without the other.

§87. So I do not understand the common argument that not every right that concerns the exercise of some action has a corresponding obligation, especially if its object is a human being, as in the present case.

§88. This is so especially as the judge has the right to extract this truth from the accused—not just the right not to be prevented from doing so by others. This right relates, above all, to the accused himself.

§89. And indeed the commonwealth would suffer too much harm if delinquents did not feel the pinpricks of conscience that urged them to confess their crimes. Otherwise, punishments would achieve their purpose very rarely, since witnesses and other forms of proof are usually lacking in these kinds of actions, which are commonly hidden, and the use of torture, supposing this hypothesis to be true, is entirely impermissible.

§90. The assertion, however, that the commonwealth has little interest in punishing a crime that has not been noticed after compensation has been paid for the damage, and that it can be covered up and excused—I doubt whether this conforms to good politics. The main purpose of punishment is the correction of others, which presupposes knowledge of the crime. However, even if the crimes are not known to the judge, they are usually known to accomplices or other citizens; and even if their statements are insufficient for a trial, they are sufficient to cause a lot of nuisance [to the criminal].

§91. I also do not understand (it must at least happen extremely rarely) how the crime cannot be considered known once compensation has been paid. Either someone confesses to the crime by paying for the damage, or he refuses restitution entirely by denying the crime.

§92. It is no objection to our assertion to say that because nobody is bound to offer himself up for punishment or indict himself the denial of a crime is no sin. Apart from the fact that the antecedent clause merits further discussion, the consequence does not seem to follow from it.

§93. For the rule, put forward by others, that I am allowed to present something in a different light for the same reason that I am allowed not to say anything about it at all, and on the other hand that I cannot conceal whatever cannot be presented other than the way it really is—this rule has been repeatedly challenged. It has also often been emphasized that speaking and speaking the truth belong to different precepts. In general, there are many things you must not refuse to disclose if you are asked for them, even though you are not obliged to disclose them voluntarily.

§94. Moreover, it is argued that a punishment must be inflicted on someone who does not want to suffer it. We must, however, voluntarily accept that to which we are obliged. Yet man by nature abhors punishments; that presupposes that the delinquent does not have an obligation to suffer punishment. This must be discussed later when we shall examine this question in particular.

§95. Yet the advocate hired by the defendant acts in his interest and must use the same means of defense as the defendant. It is therefore evident that he cannot legitimately produce false legal opinions or fictitious verdicts in criminal cases or instruct the defendant to deny the crime, or even take on his case with a clear conscience if the defendant has secretly confessed the crime to him.

CHAPTER VIII

On the Duty of Those Taking an Oath

§1. If man had remained honest there would have been no need for an oath. For this has only been introduced as a crutch for corrupt nature, because in the present state of sin there is no other means by which to suppress fallacy or perfidy in a person who asserts or promises something, or to remove doubt and disbelief concerning our intention in someone with whom we have business.

§2. For when an omnipotent and omniscient witness and avenger is invoked as a witness, there is a strong presumption of truth and faithfulness. Nobody is easily believed to be so impious that he would dare to bring down the most severe wrath of God on himself.

§3. If, therefore, we attempted to derive the duties concerning oaths from the state of innocence, it would be as foolish as trying to draw water from fire.

§4. But we must not believe that an oath is a corrupt invention of corrupt nature. We have no reason to do so, and in Scripture oaths are commanded more than once and used by the most holy men.

§5. Contrary arguments from Scripture, designed to show that oaths are prohibited, have been refuted by others some time ago.[45]

---

45. Thomasius is referring to Uffelmann, *De jure quo homo homini in sermone obligatur liber unus.*

§6. We define an oath as the deliberate invocation of God as a witness and guarantor, to confirm a statement or a promise.

§7. The purpose of every oath on the part of the person who has an oath sworn to himself is to place others under a firmer obligation to speak the truth or keep a promise, using their fear of an omnipotent and omniscient God, whose wrath they draw upon themselves if they knowingly deceive in an oath. This is done if the immediate fear of humans is not strong enough, because they do not respect their power or hope to be able to escape or to deceive them.

§8. Therefore, if the doctrine of atheism is contrary to any precept of divine law (though it is contrary to all, as is clear from the first book), it is directly contrary to the rules that we have established concerning the duty of oath takers.

§9. But on the part of him who takes an oath the purpose of an oath is certainty and faith, to reassure the other person involved concerning the truth of what has been affirmed or denied, or to affirm that the person taking the oath will fulfill what he has promised.

§10. The apostle expressed this elegantly when he said that an oath for confirmation is to them an end of all strife.[46] In any case he who accepts the oath is reassured because his doubts are settled. That is, unless you wanted to say that the apostle was referring in particular to the oath that is used to resolve controversies, which is called a *litis decisorium* [decision of a controversy].

§11. The categorization of an oath is based on its purpose. Certain things are added to promises and pacts to make sure they are observed with even greater reverence. But some are used to support a statement concerning an unknown fact. The former oath is called promissory, the latter assertory.

---

46. Hebrews 6:16.

§12. The promissory oath is used to guarantee future events, the assertory oath past events.

§13. All types of oaths based on the distinctions by the ancient Roman jurists can be reduced to these two types. For example, [Roman jurists distinguished] the oath of a witness who swears an oath about somebody else's action and an oath that concerns his own affairs and resolves a disputed question. And this could be done with the agreement of the other side, either outside court (that is, voluntarily) or in court (that is, under compulsion); or it could be done by command of the judge, which is called judicial. The particular forms of that are the purgatory oath and the suppletory oath.[47] But all these kinds of oaths are forms of assertory oaths.

§14. At the same time, the purpose of oaths tells us that oaths are accessory speech. This already presupposes another assertion or promise, which it confirms. The usefulness of this observation will become clear in many ways and should therefore be carefully noted.

§15. If we abstract from civil law, therefore, there is little use for the division of oaths into confirmatory, which is added to a separate promise, and promissory, when something is directly promised to the person the oath was made to. For it is obvious from what we have said previously that each of these two oaths is promissory, and each confirms another obligation, whether it precedes it or accompanies it.

§16. Nor is an oath superfluous if it has been added to an already firm obligation. Even if all nonatheists believe that God punishes the violation of promises, including those that are not supported by an oath, it is still useful to remind them that someone who directly provokes God's wrath

---

47. A *purgatory oath* is an oath required from the defendant to clear himself from an accusation if the evidence is insufficient for a conviction but doubts remain about the defendant's guilt. A *suppletory oath* is an oath required to confirm and supplement evidence that is insufficient or uncertain.

and deliberately cuts himself off from God's grace and mercy will be punished even more severely.

§17. We have said that the purpose of an oath is affirmation. We, therefore, must not believe that an oath makes those acts binding that were previously uncertain, that were not obligatory, or that produced no obligation. Rather, everything we have said above concerning promises and speech in general is relevant here too.

§18. Thus, oaths concerning illicit matters are not valid. And an existing valid obligation cannot be avoided by a subsequent oath, nor can a right based on this obligation be annulled by an oath. It is, for example, pointless to swear not to repay a debt.

§19. It is absurd to invoke divine anger if you have not done anything that God has forbidden and threatened to punish. To do so is to turn the reverence for God into a sort of mockery.

§20. Grotius goes beyond the previous argument and says that even if an oath does not involve something that is not illicit itself, the oath is invalid if a greater good is prevented by it. Nearly all of the examples he produces, however, concern illicit matters. An example is someone who swears never to do another person any good, etc.[48]

§21. For even if an obligation to perform certain duties is imperfect, it is a grave sin to refuse categorically to follow this imperfect obligation.

§22. In order to understand the meaning of Grotius's extension [of the concept of oaths] let us suppose a case that did in fact occur: a person was so angry that a relative married a woman of lower rank that he swore not to attend their wedding celebrations and never to invite them to his house. The oath was about something that was not itself illicit, but it pre-

---

48. See Grotius, *The Rights of War and Peace,* bk. II, chap. xiii, §vii, p. 780.

vented a greater moral good (namely, deeper friendship, which is greatly encouraged by intimate conversation).

§23. In such cases, however, I find it more plausible to adopt the view of those who believe that this oath should be kept, especially if someone declares that by this oath he did not intend to refuse to perform the other duties of daily life and charity toward another person, nor to turn away someone who appears spontaneously and without an invitation at his house.

§24. Likewise, an oath concerning something impossible is not binding.

§25. And, generally speaking, the addition of an oath does not change the nature and substance of a promise or a contract. Nor does an oath turn a conditional promise into an unconditional one, and it does not make a promise binding after the basis on which the promise was made to the other person no longer exists.

§26. Formal acceptance is also required in promises backed by an oath, and so the person to whom the promise was made can choose not to insist on it.

§27. Moreover, leaving aside civil laws, a contract supported by an oath can be rescinded if the reasons for doing so are such that they are also sufficient for rescission in the state of nature. Nonage alone is no such reason.

§28. Also, just as in promises a deliberate intention is required on the part of the person making a promise, so the same is necessary on the part of a person taking an oath. Thus, an oath is not binding if someone just quotes an oath or recites it to another using the first person.

§29. Furthermore, just as a promise extracted by deceit is not binding, so an oath that another tricked me into taking does not impose an obligation on my conscience.

§30. A simple error is a different matter unless the subject of the error was included as a condition for the oath. We have also discussed this above in the case of simple pacts.[49]

§31. If a robber extracted an oath through fear, this would have no other effect than that which results from a promise made to a pirate without an oath, as we have shown above.

§32. Oaths taken on the soul of another person are not entirely to be rejected. In matters allowing for an agent (not, therefore, when giving testimony) they bind the person by whose soul the oath was taken as firmly as pure contracts do. I fear, however, that these [oaths] do not fulfill the purpose of oaths as well as those which are taken by the person actually making the promise.

§33. Civil laws can, however, determine that certain oaths which would be invalid in the state of nature because of an offense caused to the person taking the oath remain valid in the civil state. Such laws assume that everybody can renounce something done in his favor and the person taking the oath will therefore have thought seriously whether the subject of the oath is to his advantage or not.

§34. Some people assert the validity of similar oaths, such as those extracted by deceit or fear, on the grounds that the oath includes a promise to God and promises toward God have to be kept, even in the state of nature. Others, however, argue quite rightly that this is incompatible with the nature of oaths.

§35. It is one thing to promise God that I will pay a robber, for example, quite another to make a promise to a robber and invoke God in doing so.

§36. For the presumption is that the most holy God will not have accepted an invocation that favors a godless rascal who violates every duty of sociality.

49. See *Thomasius,* book II, chap. vi, §39.

§37. So we have gradually been led to a discussion of the form of oaths, which depends on the purpose we have explained above.

§38. This form is either the one required according to the opinion of all nations, namely, that God is invoked as a witness and avenger; or it is something added to this by individual nations in order to strengthen the authority of oaths by solemn rituals and symbols.

§39. I have no objection if, for the sake of teaching, you call the latter the accidental, the former the essential form of an oath.

§40. The latter [the accidental form] mainly pertains to civil law. The former, however, is one we need to analyze further. It contains two elements. God is, first, invoked as witness of the truth and then as an avenger—of lies in assertory oaths and of perfidy in promissory oaths.

§41. Both are necessary for the purpose of an oath. Invoking God as a witness would, on its own, not be sufficient to instill the fear of God that is required for producing trust and certainty in the other person. God also has to be feared as the avenger of perjury, and he could not be feared as such if he were not believed to be a witness.

§42. It is not necessary for both elements to be explicit in the oath. Each tacitly implies the other. When the most just God is invoked as witness, the person invoking him also fears his vengeance; and when the person swearing implores God as omniscient punisher, he is also convinced that he is a witness.

§43. We often find it mentioned that pagans invoked created beings in oaths. They were presumably misled by a vain belief that such created beings were God. For example, you read of pagans swearing by the stars.

§44. Or they may have believed that people, when swearing, tacitly asked God to seek revenge for perjury on the things dearest to them. Examples are oaths taken on one's own head, one's soul (which was common then and still is), the health of a son, or the ruler's head, protective deity, or welfare, as was common usage among the ancients.

§45. You can, therefore, divide oaths into express and tacit. The former applies if you swear to God directly; the latter if you invoke divine revenge against a created being that you do not consider divine.

§46. But if we see oaths taken on the most insignificant created beings, these are to be considered jokes rather than true oaths, since many people adopted the bad habit of using oaths as an ornament and supplement to speech. Examples are Socrates' oaths taken on his dog, his goose, his plane tree, and Zeno's oaths on his caper bush, etc. They did not swear by these in order to swear by the gods, but in order not to swear by the gods.

§47. We have now come to the effects of swearing an oath. Insofar as we are dealing with affirmative oaths, the effects are the same as those we discussed in the previous chapter concerning speech. Insofar as oaths are promissory, they are the same as those discussed above concerning keeping faith. As we noted above, this follows from the fact that oaths are mere additions to speech. Therefore, if we disregard civil laws, oaths do not produce any new or special obligation.

§48. It is, therefore, quite true that all deceit and caviling or fraudulent interpretation must be kept out of oaths. But the main reason is not so much that this is the effect of invoking God, whom nobody can deceive and whom nobody mocks with impunity. For cavil must be absent from any assertion and promise. And the examples used by Doctors [of Law] in this matter all show that such cavilers have sinned even without the addition of an oath to their speech.

§49. It is no peculiar feature of oaths that they are not always to be explained in a wide but sometimes in a strict sense, if the subject matter seems to require it. We will emphasize the same rule below, in the general discussion of interpretation.

§50. But I do not accept the argument that oaths should be interpreted strictly when the oath is to the disadvantage of another and is added not so much to a promise as to threats (on the basis of which nobody acquires any right).

§51. Various cases of this rule are put forward. For example, the Israelites had sworn that they would not give their daughters to the Benjaminites, but they allowed these [the daughters] to be kidnapped by them. Athanaricus had sworn to his father that he would not step onto the Romans' soil, but then met them in the middle of a river. The Achaeans were bound by an oath not to annul their decrees, but asked the Romans to change them as they saw fit. The emperor Aurelian, having sworn that he would not allow even the dogs to live after conquering a city, sent out his soldiers to kill all dogs [and not the inhabitants]. Themison, having promised to execute the commands of the Etearch, had the latter's daughter thrown into the sea, as her father had ordered, but then pulled her out again immediately, unharmed. Timoleon swore to Milarch that he would not accuse him in Syracuse, but then ordered him to be killed instantly, etc.[50]

§52. Yet I fear it is possible to reply in all these cases that these are caviling interpretations, which do not reflect the intention of those who took the oath when they took it, let alone that of those to whom the oath was made.

§53. In any interpretation we must take into account the time at which the promise or the statement was made. But concerning an oath in particular,

50. See Judges 21. On Athanaricus, see Ammianus Marcellinus, *Ammianus Marcellinus,* trans. J. Rolfe, Loeb Classical Library (Cambridge, Mass.: Harvard University Press, 1971–72), vol. 3, XXVII.v.9, p. 35. The story of Etearchus and Themison is told by Herodotus in his *Histories* (see Herodotus, *Herodotus,* trans. A. D. Godley, Loeb Classical Library [London: Heinemann, 1928], vol. 2, bk. IV, 154, p. 355). The story of Aurelian's command to his soldiers to kill the dogs in a conquered city is from Vopiscus's life of Aurelian in the *Historia Augusta,* a name given in the early seventeenth century to a collection of biographies of Roman emperors (see *Histoire Auguste,* ed. and trans. André Chastagnol [Paris: Laffont, 1994], "Divus Aurelianus," chaps. xxii–xxiii, pp. 992–94). Timoleon was a military and political leader of Syracuse in the mid-fourth century B.C.

that meaning must be considered valid which is assumed by the person swearing the oath.

§54. Yet I do not believe that we should therefore label all the deeds we have listed above, or indeed similar deeds, unjust. It seems that we should rather proceed as follows in determining whether they are just or not. The oaths concern either a licit or an illicit matter. If it is the former, this cavilling interpretation does not absolve the persons who took the oath from their obligation. If it is the latter, this [caviling] interpretation is to be considered superfluous rather than illicit, for if they neglected to do what they were required to do according to the oath, they should not be considered to have broken their word. For the oath they swore and did not keep concerned an illicit action.

§55. Thus, the oath of the Israelites, for example, was made from just zeal and should have been kept, rather than rendered void by caviling—that is, unless you wanted to argue that they were not allowed to exterminate the tribe of Benjamin by keeping this oath. But there are several possible replies to this objection.

§56. Similarly, Aurelian could have omitted the killing of the dogs, Themison the submersion in the sea, since Aurelian's oath concerned an illicit action, that is, the destruction of a city following his victory, and Etearchus had demanded an unjust action from Themison.

§57. For it is observed, quite rightly, that an oath, like promises backed by an oath, includes tacit restrictions and limitations which flow from the nature of the matter itself. Thus, if I have granted someone the right to demand whatever he wants, I am not bound by this oath if he asks for something absurd or unjust. These considerations can easily be applied to the oath of Themison.

§58. So, you will say, an oath has no specific effect of its own? I think it has none, unless perhaps you wanted to say that the invocation of God suggests that he who commits perjury must expect a harsher punishment than those who lied in other circumstances or deceived without having taken an oath.

§59. An oath does, however, differ from pure promises in the following way. The latter bind the heirs of a person who made a promise—even more so with a promise backed by an oath before men (it is another matter if the promise was in the form of a vow). The oath clause itself, however, and the invocation of God's name do not extend to any person other than to him who took the oath. The heir, therefore, cannot be considered to have committed perjury if he does not keep the oath made by the deceased.

§60. The effect of oaths, however, as of all promises, is annulled by relaxation or dispensation. We use the general definition [of dispensation], namely, that it is an action by which either the superior of the person who took the oath declares the oath to be void because of an inability to fulfill it or the superior of the person to whom the promise was made waives the obligation on specific grounds.

§61. For as we have said above, nobody is required to do something impossible. If, therefore, someone who is subject to another person's power takes an oath, this is always with the tacit condition that the right of the superior must not be violated.

§62. He [the superior], however, will commit an injustice if he grants a dispensation when neither his rights nor the rights of the society over which he presides have been violated.

§63. And so does he who, without just cause, deprives his subject of a right based on an oath. A crime committed by the person to whom the promise was made and the public interest are considered just causes.

§64. Moreover, he who is the superior neither of the person who took the oath nor of the person to whom the oath was made cannot grant dispensation. From this alone it is evident whether the Roman pope does or does not have the right to grant dispensation concerning the oaths of kings and princes.

§65. An entreaty has some affinity with an oath. This is an act whereby a person appeals to God or something else that is very dear to him and highly revered, and beseeches another to speak the truth. An example is the high priest who adjured Christ to say truthfully whether he was the son of God.[51]

§66. This action must not be confused with calling to witness, which is also related to an oath and by which a person affirms, through comparison with something dear to himself, that the truth is no less close to his heart than what he has named. Joseph, for example, did this by referring to the life of the pharaoh, Elisha to the life of Elijah.[52]

§67. Finally, there are certain promises that are not oaths, and yet have the same effect as oaths among humans. This is either because of the person making the promise (e.g., if a prince promises "by his princely word") or it is because of the special custom of a certain people. Thus, among the Persians, if the parties sealed a promise by giving each other the right hand, this created the firmest kind of obligation.

§68. And that is enough concerning the theory of oaths. It remains to list the precepts on the duty of humans concerning oaths. Now, we consider an oath insofar as it is either an addition to normal speech or based in a particular clause in which there is a formalized appeal to the name of God.

§69. In the former case the general precept for both promissory and assertory oaths (but especially the latter) is: "Speak the truth"; that is, take care that external signs are an accurate reflection of your mind.

---

51. Matthew 26:63.
52. Genesis 42:15; 2 Kings 4.

§70. Moreover, even if there is no oath, whenever we respond to the question of another person or make a formal declaration at his request, our response or declaration is related to his question or request. Therefore, our response should not be separated from the mind and the intention of the person making the demand or posing the question.

§71. Therefore, it is urgently necessary in oaths that we understand the words of the oath in the sense in which we think the other person to whom the oath was made would probably understand them. Thus, ambiguity of wording must be avoided to the extent that this is possible.

§72. For we do not speak or take oaths to ourselves but to others with whom we interact, and thus we speak in order to be understood and swear in order that another person can be all the more assured of our sincerity.

§73. Therefore, it is up to him to whom the oath is made to formulate the oath and to declare how he wants its words to be understood.

§74. A specific precept that only pertains to promissory oaths is "Keep the promises you have made."

§75. Each of the two precepts bans perjury, which in a broad sense includes lying under oath, as well as the violation of an oath through perfidy.

§76. This more extensive meaning [of perjury] is accepted in modern usage, although perjury was once used by some to describe only perfidy in a strict sense, while certain papist writers used the term *perjury* for mere lies.

§77. False testimony is an example of lying under oath. It is the same if someone swears and nevertheless has no intention of considering himself under an obligation as a result.

§78. The violation of an oath through perfidy occurs not only when someone refuses directly to fulfill an obligation based on an oath. It also takes place when the person making the promise implores the superior of the person to whom the oath was made to release him from his obligation.

§79. An example is if someone has sworn to observe the statutes of a university, but later pleads with the superior to be granted a dispensation from them.

§80. This kind of dispensation may be accepted without the taint of perfidy if the superior freely grants it. But the person who made the promise does not have the right to ask for this dispensation because it is obviously contrary to the intention of him to whom the promise was made.

§81. I also believe that those people are not exempt from the charge of perjury who have sworn to fulfill their duty faithfully, but have then willfully neglected some part of it, even if subsequently they submitted themselves to punishment. A thief is a thief even if he has suffered a beating.

§82. Those who have sworn an oath concerning a particular action, but then act contrary to it, are even greater perjurers.

§83. This is so unless someone in his promise expressly reserved the right to either fulfill his promise or pay a fine for acting contrary to it.

§84. Or if those who prescribe the formula of the oath either interpret it themselves or allow it to be interpreted publicly in such a way that it allows acting contrary to it without the taint of perjury as long as the guilty person accepts the punishment. This is the usual interpretation of the students' oath, promising that they will not take revenge for injuries inflicted on them but will appeal to the magistrate for help.

§85. Two precepts deserve to be noted concerning the latter case,[53] according to which an oath consists in the invocation of God: (1) "Do not swear casually," and (2) "Swear only by God."

---

53. See §68 in this chapter.

§86. The former follows directly from the purpose of the oath, the latter directly from its form.

§87. The assertory oath was introduced to make it possible to reach a decision on an unclear fact that cannot be demonstrated in any other way. Therefore, an oath is careless when no proof is required, when the matter can easily be demonstrated by other means, or when there is no suitable object of proof.

§88. In questions of right and wrong, therefore, oaths are not permissible, and it would be inappropriate and careless to use an oath to prove the truth of a legal doctrine.

§89. It is a serious violation of this precept to use an oath as a mere rhetorical ornament, and to treat it only as an expression, without intending to confirm one's words with this oath. Thus, Hobbes says quite rightly that these solemn declarations are not oaths, but an abuse of the name of God and the result of a bad habit, when their only purpose is to state something especially emphatically.[54]

§90. We have shown above that lies may sometimes be justified. In those cases he who adds an oath to such a lie is not to be considered a perjurer. He does, however, seriously violate the precept about avoiding carelessness because there is no reason to combine such lies with an oath.

§91. The first precept concerns assertory oaths. But it also applies to promissory oaths. For he who swears to do something impossible swears carelessly. A relevant example here is someone who swears to do something he knows has been prohibited by his superior.

§92. The other precept, insofar as it is to be derived from natural law, means nothing other than that one should swear by God to the extent that he can be known from natural law.

54. Hobbes, *On the Citizen,* chap. 2, §20.

§93. But insofar as universal positive law inculcates the belief in the true God and his worship, it compensates for the defects of natural reason. This law says: "Do not swear by any other than the true God."

§94. Therefore, it is contrary to natural law to swear by something one does not consider to be God because this does not meet the purpose of an oath; and it is contrary to divine law and the precepts of religion to swear by a false God whom one considers to be the true one. This is enough for now since further discussion of religious worship in the form of oaths is a matter for the theologians.

§95. The precepts of natural law concerning oaths must not be confused with religious precepts since an oath is a form of divine worship, and for that reason divine worship is sometimes also described as an oath.

§96. Moreover, he who swears by something that he does not believe to be God is swearing a false oath rather than committing perjury, but he who swears by a false God whom he believes to be true swears a valid oath, and therefore commits perjury if he swears falsely or insincerely.

§97. Similarly, a person is, for example, guilty of lèse majesté if he plans to murder his prince and by mistake injures his [the prince's] sworn enemy.

§98. The answer to the question whether it is possible to swear by creatures depends on what has been said. Either these are used in entreaties[55] or in calling upon someone as a witness. These are not relevant here because they are not oaths.

§99. They [the creatures] may be mentioned in the oath as something by which God must punish us. Then it will be a tacit oath.[56]

55. See §§65–66 in this chapter.
56. See §44 in this chapter.

§100. Or they are believed to have something divine about them. Then divine revelation forbids a Christian to take such an oath because it would imply idolatry.

§101. They may also be attributed some divine quality, not on the basis of what they are but by virtue of some relationship to God, because they are consecrated or belong to God. For example, one might swear by a temple, an altar, etc. Or one might swear by something that represents the Creator, such as the heavens. These formulas do not excuse the person who uses them and are therefore better avoided. But if they are used, then he who deceives by using them is to be considered a perjurer.

§102. It is a different matter with a formula that is commonly used among us: So help me God, and his word, or the sacred gospel. That is neither impious nor unjust.

§103. The precepts we have discussed so far, and that are to be observed by the person taking an oath, conform to the three commonly accepted companions of an oath: namely, truth, that no lie be told; justice, that faith be kept, and that one swear only by God; and judgment, to prevent frivolous oaths.

§104. But he to whom the oath is made also needs to be admonished: "Do not demand an oath for no good reason." For that would again be contrary to the purpose of an oath and to the reverence owed to God, which is the foundation of all divine laws, as we have shown above.

§105. Are we, therefore, allowed to accept an oath from someone who we know will commit perjury? Usually a distinction is drawn between a judge and a litigant: it is said that the former is allowed to do this because it is part of his job, but if the litigant does it he sins.

§106. I would accept this opinion since the carelessness is entirely on the side of the person accepting an oath from someone who will certainly commit perjury. It is pointless to demand it. But first it needs to be asked whether the question itself is in fact appropriate.

§107. For I deny that there can be certain knowledge of another person's future perjury. Not only is there no certain knowledge of future events, but it is also impossible in particular for a human, who cannot see into other people's hearts, to know those things that depend on the decision of another.

§108. It is not enough if the person concerned has already often committed perjury, for he could now reform himself.

§109. If he openly confesses that he will commit perjury, he does not provide a reliable indication since these threats may be used to avoid having to take an oath.

§110. I would, therefore, rather treat this question as curious, but useless, except in some special cases (e.g., what if he who has to take an oath openly professes atheism? But that is not likely).

§111. Another question is more fruitful: is it permissible to demand an oath from an infidel when he swears by false gods? Quite a few argue that such an oath can be accepted, but not demanded from an idolater.

§112. Yet I believe it can even be demanded as long as the oath is correct in all other respects. For the formula of the oath must always be adapted to the religious conviction favored by the person taking the oath.

§113. This follows from the purpose of an oath. For it is pointless to force someone to swear by a God in whom he does not believe and whom he therefore does not fear.

§114. Thus, since the law of nature presents no obstacles, this opinion can be defended until it is shown that the precepts of religion require something else, which has not been shown so far. Other authors have responded to the objections to his view.

CHAPTER IX

On the Duty Concerning Things and Their Ownership

§1. Having discussed speech, we must now continue with ownership [*dominium*]. Its most important effect is that on the power to use things, and we will first have to make a few general comments on that.

§2. Now, this power can be considered with respect to the Creator, with respect to things, or with respect to other humans.

§3. As far as the two former concepts are concerned, authors on morality are usually concerned with justifying this capability to use created things on the basis of a divine grant and with defending the killing of beasts in particular against objections by others.

§4. We think the matter can be most easily resolved if we separate, first of all, the light of reason from that of revelation and consider the nature of this power more carefully.

§5. It is clear, however, from the hypotheses we have demonstrated before that this power does not deserve to be called a right with respect to God, over whom man has no right at all.

§6. Thus, we need not show with what right man exercises this power. That would be a foolish question. But it is sufficient if there are no objections that undermine this power.

§7. For there is no reason why something should not be considered permissible if it is not prohibited by any law.

§8. Since man, therefore, has the natural power to use other created things, this power is to be regarded as indifferent until a restriction is put forward on the basis of either nature or revelation.

§9. In addition, divine permission can also be demonstrated to some degree from reasoning. For at present man needs the other creatures to feed himself and to defend himself against the evils that threaten to destroy him physically. Thus, it follows that God also wants to grant humans the right to use these things, without which life, which is God's gift, cannot be preserved.

§10. But that is limited proof and only concerns that use which is necessary to man. However, since man very often uses other creatures for his pleasure and a more convenient life, it will be difficult to progress along the line of argument that places the burden of proof on us.

§11. For man does not need all creatures. And the opinion of Aristotle, Lucian, and other pagans does not deserve praise.[57] According to them other things would have been created in vain if man were not allowed to use them. For, so they say, the machine of the world could have been adorned far more sparingly if only those things had been created which were of some use to man.

§12. So let us rather stick with the argument of natural liberty, especially since we see that the revelation of sacred Scripture does not contradict this opinion. It is possible, rather, to prove from it, on very firm grounds, that such a special concession has been made to man allowing him to use created things.

57. Aristotle, *Politics,* ed. S. Everson (Cambridge: Cambridge University Press, 1990), bk. I, 1256b, p. 11; Lucian (ca. A.D. 115–after 180), Syrian satirist writing in Greek. It is not clear which passage Thomasius has in mind here.

§13. And these include not only the bare necessities (which, in the state of innocence, were far fewer and restricted to nourishment, since defense against the other evils now threatening physical well-being was superfluous) but also those things required for convenience and pleasure.

§14. As we have noted before, this grant, however, does not have the force of a precept but only confers a privilege that one can use freely. Man is not compelled to use it by all means. For otherwise man would sin against the divine law if he left any animal at liberty or neglected an opportunity to capture it. No sane person would argue this.

§15. From our general comments on the duties of man toward God follows a negative precept: "Do not use creatures to insult the Creator." For this use would conflict with the internal worship of God which is the foundation of all laws of nature.

§16. This precept punishes above all the abuse of creatures when these are destroyed pointlessly and frivolously. It implies contempt, in the human sense, of the most benign Creator if I destroy his gift for no purpose.

§17. You could mention here that God wanted to extend the peace of the seventh day to beasts as well. But this refers to the precepts of [revealed] religion, and so should be left to the theologians.

§18. With respect to the created things which humans use, this use does not deserve to be termed a right because man and the other creatures do not share the same law.

§19. Yet, the term *wrong* does not apply either because man is under no obligation to other creatures.

§20. This is true no matter if they are plants or created beings that are inferior to plants [e.g., stones], about [both of] which there is no doubt, or if they enjoy locomotive powers as beasts do.

§21. Even if there are many objections in the case of beasts, we do not need to spend time refuting them. In part these [objections] are directed against the arguments with which others wanted to prove a right to kill these [creatures]. As you see, we do not take it upon ourselves to prove this. And in part they also rest on the false hypothesis of philosophers who attribute reason to beasts and at the same time apply the precept not to harm others to beasts. But we have banished reason from beasts to such a degree that we have not even left them with sense perception, properly speaking, which would presuppose some form of cognition and thus thought.[58]

§22. It is clear that God does not suffer an injustice if beasts are killed, because God is the author of this relationship between men and beasts, which is devoid of right.

§23. I would, therefore, not want to compare the state of man in relation to beasts with that of a state of war. Even if there is some similarity between these two states, there are, nevertheless, many respects in which they are different. For one thing, wars among humans are neither universal, nor perpetual, nor do they grant unlimited freedom. Moreover, war is an extraordinary state that has its origin in the violation of a right. The state between humans and beasts, however, is an ordinary one and does not presuppose any violation of a right since there is no community of right between them.

§24. We must now continue with a consideration of the power humans have of using creatures in relation to other humans. Here it is worth noting that the person using this power is under an obligation toward others, and other humans are under an obligation to this person.

§25. The obligation of the person using others is either indirect—that is, mediate—and reflects the degree to which man owes his preservation to

---

58. According to Thomasius, proper sense perception involves mental activity. Animals, however, respond quasi-mechanically to external stimuli.

sociality, or it is direct and extends to the degree that man is under an immediate obligation to others.

§26. The indirect obligation is contained in this precept: "Use other creatures in such a way that by using them you do not ruin the endowments of your mind and body." This follows from what we have said above concerning the duties of man toward himself.

§27. As far as the moral endowments of the mind are concerned, we must take care that the killing of animals, for example, does not accustom the mind to cruelty. Plutarch and others observed that humans who had become used to killing beasts went on to murder humans and wage war.[59] It is also worth noting that Scripture describes Nimrod as a hunter.[60] The Pythagoreans, by contrast, urged gentleness toward beasts as well as the contemplation of love and compassion toward humans.[61]

§28. It is, therefore, not without reason that the Athenians punished the person who had skinned a ram alive, and the Spartans did the same to someone who gouged the eyes out of quails and then released them.[62]

§29. He who abandons or weakens his rational faculties through excessive food or drink sins with respect to the natural goods of the mind.

§30. Finally, as far as the goods of the body are concerned, we must abstain from various kinds of intemperance.

---

59. Plutarch, "The Eating of Flesh," II.4, p. 573, in Plutarch, *Moralia,* vol. 12, trans. H. Cherniss and W. C. Helmbold, Loeb Classical Library (Cambridge, Mass.: Harvard University Press, 1957).

60. Genesis 10:9.

61. *Pythagoreanism* was the philosophical and religious school allegedly derived from the teachings of Pythagoras (born mid-sixth century B.C.). One of their rules prescribed a form of vegetarianism based on the doctrine of the transmigration of souls.

62. The case of the Athenians who punished a man for flaying a ram alive is referred to by Plutarch in "The Eating of Flesh," I.7, p. 559. See note 59 on this page.

§31. Thus, Pythagoras, when he forbade killing animals, wanted, among other reasons, to accustom his disciples to a better diet, which would improve bodily health and intellectual acuity.

§32. The direct obligation of man toward others is as follows: "Use creatures in such a way that you preserve the equality with other humans." That is, you should not abuse these creatures for the sake of pride; you should not harm others by their use; you should serve others by using them; you should keep promises related to this. These injunctions can be easily understood on the basis of the above discussions.

§33. I now pass over in silence the particular interest of the commonwealth to which man has to adapt himself. For it is in the interest of the commonwealth that nobody uses his property badly. Often an interruption in the use of something furthers the utility of the commonwealth.

§34. The obligation of others toward the user is contained in the precept that nobody should prevent another from making use of creatures.

§35. Corresponding to this obligation is the right of the user by virtue of which he can make use of creatures without being disturbed. This right is called a common ownership insofar as it admits others to the use of the same thing. Insofar as it gives the right to prevent others from using the same thing, it is called dominion. We shall say more about that now.

§36. In order to avoid debating like blindfolded gladiators, we have to start by explaining the relevant terms. It is clear from what has been said that by *dominion* we understand a right extending only to things, insofar as the word *thing* is distinguished from legal actions that only concern persons, but this concept does not completely capture the essence of *dominion*.

§37. It is, therefore, more accurate to say that it is a right by which a thing is specific to a particular person. *Property* is when the substance of something belongs to someone in such a way that it does not belong to anyone else.

§38. For *property* and *dominion* here are synonyms even if authors sometimes understand them in different ways.

§39. *Property* or *dominion,* however, in something is either that of a single person or of more than one person. The former is called *dominion* in the simple or strict sense, for example, in the sense that Titius is the owner of his house. The latter is usually termed *common dominion* or *common ownership.* Thus the heirs of Titius have common ownership of the house.

§40. *Common ownership* is when the substance of something belongs to someone as much as it belongs to another.

§41. It is either negative, when the thing belongs to several people in such a way that in effect it is not the exclusive property of anyone (neither a single person nor several individuals). Thus, according to Roman law, wild beasts are in common ownership.

§42. Or it is positive when the thing belongs to several people in such a way that it is the property or dominion of several people jointly. See the example of Titius's heirs.

§43. Thus, *dominion* in the simple sense is the purest form of dominion because it excludes all common ownership, and *negative common ownership* is the purest form of common ownership because it excludes all dominion.

§44. But *positive common ownership* and *common dominion,* as you can see, are identical so that they are illustrated by one and the same example and differ only in the concepts used. For when the two heirs of Titius are considered in relation to each other and individually, their inheritance is in common. When they are considered jointly and in relation to others who are not heirs, their inheritance is their property.

§45. Things themselves, however, are described in different ways, depending on these three rights. They are either owned by an individual, or held in common, or nobody's property.

§46. It appears, therefore, that the terms *property* and *common ownership* involve relations of one person to another person. It follows that if there were only one human being in the world and he could use created beings according to his whim, neither the term *dominion* (since there would be nobody whom he could prevent from using these) nor *common ownership* (since there would be nobody who would be able to use these at the same time) would be applicable.

§47. And how else could it be? *Dominion* and *common ownership* are forms of right. Above, however, we have shown that humans have no right unless there are other humans.

§48. For even if you relate this single human being to God, it would not be appropriate to use the term *dominion,* not only because in this respect God is the owner of all creatures, but because man has no right toward God.

§49. If you consider the relation to beasts, the situation is similar because there is no common right or obligation between humans and beasts.

§50. I prefer calling a spade a spade rather than terming this power of one man to use other creatures a kind of dominion that is not unlimited in the formal sense but, as the result of concession, a potential rather than actual dominion.[63] Even if this expression, properly explained, is acceptable, still there is no doubt that the term *dominion* is applied improperly here, and the doctrine of dominion, it seems, can be explained more perspicuously without it.

63. See Pufendorf, *Of the Law of Nature and Nations,* bk. 4, chap. iv, §3.

§51. Even if there are several people, you will not be able to use the term *dominion* in either the simple sense or in that of common ownership if there is no other person whom the owners could justifiably exclude from the use of a certain thing.

§52. The inheritance of Titius, for example, is the [common] property of two heirs when, as I have said, they are considered in relation to others. If these heirs were alone in the world, there would no longer be a common dominion, but the inheritance would only be common to both of them. So a positive common ownership would become a negative common ownership.

§53. Some people distinguish between common and private ownership. But it is clear from these descriptions that this is the same division as ours, according to which we say that dominion is either simple or common. That is, unless they, by applying this distinction, confuse common ownership and negative common ownership.

§54. Thus, some do not understand what is meant when those who describe the two forms of dominion in strange ways declare that Adam was granted common dominion by God and that this dominion pertained to the entire human race and was at the same time private, that is, mine, yours, etc.[64]

§55. For since the entire human race consists of myself, yourself, etc., it is not clear here how private dominion differs from common unless someone wants to take refuge in that sublime controversy over the existence of universals outside the operations of the mind, and to interfere in the bloody war between Nominalists and Realists.[65]

64. Thomasius is referring to Alberti's *Compendium*, chap. 7, §14.

65. "Realists" believed that universal concepts existed independently of the particular things they stood for. "Nominalists" argued that they did not. These two schools of thought originated in the later Middle Ages but continued to be of importance in university teaching of Thomasius's time.

§56. Moreover, as dominion in the simple sense and common dominion are mutually exclusive, it is too subtle to say that each of the two forms can be present in one subject, though some have used such subtlety.[66]

§57. Thus, they formed concepts without knowing jurisprudence (for it is there that the terms *dominion* and *common ownership* primarily belong) when they believed that this right according to which I can acquire the property in something is dominion in the proper sense, and therefore divided *dominion* into potential and actual, though the term *potential dominion* is like light without illumination.

§58. Having made these comments on the origin of dominion, let us now examine whether in the primeval state of humans there was dominion or common ownership, and if the latter, whether it was positive or negative.

§59. You will, however, notice immediately that this question, like all other controversies concerning the origin of things or rights, is a historical question. And should you want to discuss this without drawing on revelation at all, you have to form conjectures and argue in a roundabout way, though others who are very erudite have already shown how this controversy would be resolved in the case of a dispute with a pagan who had a different idea of the primeval state. The conclusions they reach are the same as ours, or are different only in minor respects.

§60. We, however, are writing in the company of Christians, and we have already shown above that statements of historical fact can be taken from sacred history without mixing up the different disciplines, even when we are developing arguments on natural law. Thus, we shall not hesitate to look for our definitions in divine revelation, but we shall at the same time observe the rules of sound interpretation which right reason provides us with.

---

66. Thomasius is referring to the views of the jurist and polyhistorian Heinrich Boecler (1611–72), as they are quoted in Pufendorf, *Of the Law of Nature and Nations,* bk. 4, chap. iv, §12.

§61. God spoke to the first parents: Subject the earth to yourselves and rule over the beasts. Thereby they accepted the power to subject inferior creatures to themselves, with the effect that they knew God would not oppose their use of other creatures for their own purposes. But this power is only improperly known as dominion, no matter whether you say that it was granted by God to Adam before the creation of Eve, or to Adam and Eve simultaneously.

§62. For it does not deserve to be called a right, let alone dominion or common ownership, with respect to beasts or other inferior creatures. Similarly, as long as Adam was alone, it could only be called a potential future right with respect to other humans, but this is not the proper meaning of the word as such.

§63. When Eve had been created, however, right in the proper sense emerged. But you cannot infer from this that there was therefore also dominion, because common ownership is also a right.

§64. Thus, I do not remember anyone declaring that Adam would have had any just reason to prevent Eve from using creatures, or that Eve would have required special permission from Adam to exercise this right. It would, therefore, be inept if we wanted to describe Adam's right at that time as dominion in the strict sense. But there must have been common ownership, and as long as Adam and Eve were alone this was not positive but negative.

§65. Moreover, although the first humans did not produce children in the state of innocence, undoubtedly they would have. Thus, perhaps common dominion might have evolved from the negative common ownership of the first parents.

§66. Or perhaps not. For the usual opinion is that the first humans represented their descendants with respect to the divine grant. Therefore, the children would have had the same right as their parents immediately from birth.

§67. There would also have been no reason why God in this state should have given the parents a prerogative right before the children, since they [the children] were to be born in the same state of perfection. It is instead probable that the benefits conferred on the parents would have pertained to the children, too, since they also partook of the punishment [for original sin].

§68. I think we have also shown that in the state of integrity no paternal government was to be expected. Thus, there was no reason to expect a restriction of the children's right in using things.

§69. Therefore, the negative common ownership in this state would not have changed as the result of procreation and the increase of the human race, but would only have been extended to other persons.

§70. Whether humans would have remained in this state of common ownership if Adam had not fallen from grace is an interesting question. We do not think it at all likely that this [common ownership] would have been abandoned in favor of a distinction of dominions.

§71. It is a trite proverb that friends share everything. The greater the degree of friendship (and it was the greatest possible), the more likely was common ownership. Thus, we read that there was an analogous situation in the primitive Christian church.

§72. Moreover, there would have been the greatest possible equality, but the distinction of dominions greatly promotes inequality among humans. The distinction of dominions would certainly have created rich and poor.

§73. Nor were there any reasons for doing so [that is, distinguishing dominions]. The earth produced everything spontaneously. Labor was not a burden then. Nature was content with little. Luxury did not exist. There was no quarrel and no envy.

§74. They err, therefore, who look for the distinction between dominions in the state of innocence because of its perfection, arguing that just as all order conforms to right reason, so would the most beautiful way of possessing things conform perfectly to this state.[67]

§75. That is as if one said that the present state of the church was more perfect than that of the primitive church, because as charity has declined common ownership has also disappeared.

§76. Nor should one believe that there was complete confusion because of this common ownership in the state of innocence, as if this common right to everything meant that nobody was allowed to use particular things, available to all, for their own benefit, and to use them in such a way that no other person had the right to take these things away after they had been appropriated. Rather, in this negative common ownership there was a certain kind of property, namely, with respect to fruits, the use of which consisted in consumption: if someone wanted to use such fruits as food or drink, they became his property as soon as he had seized them.

§77. It may seem self-contradictory to say that there is property in a state of common ownership, especially negative common ownership, which excludes property.

§78. But it is not. For negative or positive common ownership can remain in place for the whole or its more important parts (that is, what bears fruit), even though there is property in the subordinate parts (that is, the fruits themselves).

§79. Thus emerges the distinction of each kind of common ownership into absolute and modified. I call absolute common ownership that in which there is no property at all; modified, where that is not so.

67. Again, a reference to Boecler's views as cited by Pufendorf in his *Law of Nature,* bk. 4, chap. iv, §13 (see note 66 in this chapter).

§80. Before the first parents consumed any fruits, there was an absolute common ownership. As soon as one [fruit] had been taken for consumption, modified common ownership began.

§81. Beware of using the term *absolute* to signify a form of common ownership in which there can be no property. For this is impossible. In that respect all common ownership is modified. But with regard to the actions of humans, absolute common ownership has lasted a certain period of time, even if that is very short.

§82. But I have emphasized that in the primeval state dominion emerged from the appropriation of something fungible,[68] not through the appropriation of just anything. For if this were something that is not fungible, be it mobile or immobile, then appropriation alone would not confer dominion, but only a momentary use-right for the time of the possession. When this use ceased, others would have an equal right over it, or would have had the right to make use of this thing for their own purposes.

§83. But this momentary right does not deserve to be called property, nor has it, to my knowledge, ever been called that by jurists.

§84. If, for example, Adam lay beneath the shadow of a tree or played with some wild animal, he still did not therefore have the right of property over this tree or beast even if Eve could not have removed him from his place or taken the animal away from him without committing a grave injustice. But if he went away spontaneously or stopped playing, she had the right to take over his spot or the animal.

§85. Thus, if Eve plucked an apple for the sake of eating it, Adam would have had no right to take it away from his wife. He would have had to find another one, and so Eve after taking the apple could have said with

---

68. That is, this fungible thing can be replaced by an equivalent when someone gains an exclusive right to it; for example, one fruit can be replaced with another.

every justification that the apple was in her dominion, because she could exclude her husband from its use in perpetuity.

§86. So even though we have called it common ownership when the substance of something pertains to one person in the same way that it pertains to another, and even though common ownership implies an equal right to use a common thing, all of this is to be understood in such a way that the right of individuals over what is held in common does not produce the sort of Hobbesian right of everyone to everything which leads to the deadly state of a general war of all against all.[69]

§87. It follows that if we abstract from every human agreement and argue on the basis of the general precept to preserve sociality and the common peace of mankind, there can be no such common ownership in which one person can disturb a fellow human being in the use of something that cannot be consumed, or take away something which can be consumed and which the other wants to consume.

§88. The particular precept about preserving equality inculcates the same. For it would undoubtedly be a violation of this precept if someone wanted to drive away another from a spot on which he lay, or wanted to deprive him of something consumable, just so that he could rest on this spot or use this thing.

§89. Finally, this licence cannot but produce extreme confusion and war. For once this is admitted, then equals are allowed to do equal things, and it would follow automatically that if Eve used the said licence to take away an apple from Adam, he could take the same apple away from Eve with as much justification, and so on forever, until he who is stronger eats the apple. It would be the same in all other matters. You would have a war of all mankind among the first humans.

69. Hobbes, *On the Citizen*, chap. 1, §12.

§90. Thus, although some have argued eruditely that occupation, which is the cause of dominion, receives its force from a tacit agreement between the first humans, this opinion is undoubtedly limited with respect to consumables, which have been taken for immediate consumption. This is partly because all common ownership, as something involving common use, would be pointless without the right of appropriating what you had taken; and this common use would be pointless if others had the right to deprive me of what I want to use for the purpose of necessary consumption. And this is so partly because they themselves very eruditely refuted this Hobbesian right.

§91. As for the objection of others that, given this primeval right of humans over things, it is not clear how the bare physical act of a single person, such as occupation, can prejudice the rights of others unless they give their consent—that is, unless there is an agreement—that objection can be easily removed.

§92. For in the beginning occupation, which is a physical act, does not establish property rights; but the law of sociality on preserving equality, together with this physical act, excludes others from the use of something consumable that someone else has already taken.

§93. They who raise this objection obviously regard pacts as the source of all obligation. However, we have supposed a law, which often produces an obligation without a pact, while a pact never produces an obligation without such a law.

§94. If you wanted to use the term *tacit agreement* so broadly that it includes a presumed pact, then the dispute is about words rather than the matter itself. For we have shown above that this presumed pact is not an agreement in the true sense.

§95. We must not neglect to say, however, that there is a reason why we have mentioned immediate consumption. It was to indicate that we are not of the opinion that the occupation of consumables with the intention of setting them aside for future use produces dominion, even in the absence of a pact. Just as the purpose of common ownership and the precept about preserving sociality and equality do not necessarily make provision for such an appropriation, so too are we unable to conceive of its existence in that most perfect state [before the fall from grace]. For where there was to be a supreme abundance of things and the perpetual equality of supreme friendship, no reason could exist for setting aside consumables for one's own use. There this setting aside would undoubtedly have interfered with the precept about preserving equality.

§96. Let us move on to the postlapsarian state. Here matters are changed. The field brought forth weeds rather than fruits. Labor became a burden for the human body, but without it fruits were rarely to be hoped for. The human body had need of huts, clothes, etc., against the inclemency of the weather, and these could not be made or built without some labor and effort. Beasts could not be taken and captured without trouble. Their maintenance required additional effort. The mutual love among humans, the firmest support of common ownership, had weakened greatly.

§97. Still, this change did not bring about the actual distinction of dominions. Nor did God after the fall from grace divide the dominion over things afresh between Adam and his children. Instead, the primeval divine grant remained in place and was only limited and restricted in its effects.

§98. Thus, it followed that the common ownership of that most happy state was no longer compatible with the peace of humankind. For even if there had been no other reasons for the further division of dominions, it would have been enough that quarrels had to emerge from the difference between labor performed and the benefit received if humans labored on common things, contributed to what was owned in common, and were maintained from the common store. And it would be inhumane if others were permitted to claim the use of huts or clothes when they had contributed nothing to making them.

§99. It should not however be assumed that all humans abandoned common ownership simultaneously and in one single act. Most probably, it seems, there was an initial agreement concerning consumables to the effect that whatever someone had taken from the common fruits that grew spontaneously and had set aside for future use was his rightful property. Similarly, that those items which could not be consumed and which he had occupied, be they movable or not, in order to live in them, cultivate them, and reap fruits from them, be considered his property together with the fruits produced by them.

§100. Thus, since there were few humans in the beginning, and the world was vast, it is clear that few things were then occupied and subject to dominion. Most remained in common ownership until the human race had increased, and most of these things, though not all, became property as a result of occupation.

§101. This occupation in the postlapsarian state does not seem to preclude the possibility of a pact completely. For even though natural reason suggests that the dominions over things are distinguished from each other, and that occupation is the most convenient way of ending disputes, it [natural reason] still does not declare positively that we acquire dominion by seizing something physically. For there is an enormous difference between taking something that can be consumed in an instant and taking other things.

§102. Thus, it is plausible that following the increase in the number of humans, they divided certain things among themselves by mutual consent to avoid quarrels and introduce good order, and that everyone was assigned his portion; and that this was done with the added agreement that those things left over after this division were to become the property of the person who had first claimed them by taking them.

§103. First occupation [of something] implied use, from which others were not allowed to prevent me according to the rules of common ownership. But this kind of use is not compatible with the nature of the thing unless I am able to exclude others from it. But in the occupation of other things it is possible for me to derive some use from them, though not so conveniently, even if I do not keep others from sharing these things.[70]

§104. It is thus very true that the distinction of dominions in these matters emerged in the postlapsarian state, mainly in order to prevent quarrels. Still, because of the corruption of the human race, very often wars do still arise over what is mine and yours.

§105. Sacred history fully confirms what we have said, or at least does not contradict it, no matter whether you take the sons of Adam or the progeny of Noah in the restoration of the human race after the flood.

§106. Concerning Adam's children, sacred history mentions only that Abel was made a shepherd and Cain a farmer. This does not exclude the possibility of prior occupation and even presupposes it. There are, however, many reasons not to assume that Adam was ordered by God to distribute dominions over things among his children in the state of innocence, but could not put this into practice because he spent such a short period of time there; nor that he therefore did it after the fall from grace, by distributing a part of his goods between Cain and Abel, so that the former owned the immobile goods—that is, fields—and the latter the mobile goods—the herds, etc.

§107. For apart from the fact that this divine precept about the division of the different parts of the earth does not exist in Scripture, but is the product of wishful thinking, we have also shown above that this division of goods contradicts the perfection of the state of innocence.

§108. Holy Scripture also says nothing about the division of Adam's goods between Cain and Abel, nor does it say that they were not allowed to seize other things which were free from possession, in addition to those assigned to them by their father.

70. The order of paragraphs 102 and 103 is reversed in later editions.

§109. For even if we do not deny the paternal power of Adam, yet if we abstract from civil laws, this power does not imply power over the goods of his children; and in the case of adults, such as Cain and Abel, this paternal power expired automatically, as we shall explain below.[71]

§110. The statement that Abel received the mobile goods, Cain the immobile goods, is no more than pleasant speculation. As if Cain did not need an ox to pull the plough; as if he ate nothing but grain; and as if Abel had not needed a pasture for his sheep, or had not consumed bread as food! That is, unless you want to say that Adam at the same time introduced relationships of commerce, barter, and hire, etc., between the two brothers, or unless you make up more reasons to defend such contemplations in spite of the fact that Scripture does not mention them and even pretty much contradicts them.

§111. As far as the age of Noah is concerned, God used the same formula of benediction here as he did for the first parents.[72] Therefore, we have to interpret it in the same way as that other [formula] to the extent that the changes in the human condition following the fall allow us to do so. Certainly it does not prove the introduction of private dominion.

§112. And, to make this even clearer, Scripture says that when God made this benediction and granted the power of subjecting all other creatures, he did not address Noah alone, but his children, too. This was in order to indicate that they had acquired the same right as their father.

§113. Thus, it is highly probable that dominions over things gradually emerged among the descendants of Noah as the result of occupation, since sacred history does not mention a division made by their father.

§114. The words of Scripture would have to be greatly distorted if someone wanted to interpret these to mean that Noah distributed the nations and islands among his sons, that each of them should own his portion in peace.

71. See *Institutes*, bk. III, chap. iv, §53.
72. See Genesis 9:1.

§115. For even if Philastrius is so sure this distribution occurred that he considers denying it to be a heresy, we will not fear this heresy maker any more than jurists fear Baldus [de Ubaldis], or whoever of the ancient glossators declared that it was heresy to deny that the Holy Roman Emperor was the lord of the entire world.[73]

§116. This bugbear did not deter Bochart from disagreeing.[74] And others have observed that the traditional belief in this division by Noah belongs to the fables of that fictitious character Berossus.[75]

§117. And how could Noah divide the nations among his sons? There were no nations except for those which sprang from Noah's children. Were they already entire nations at the time of this supposed division? Did Noah take the children of one son and transfer them into the power of another? Or did certain nations survive the flood, which Noah then assigned to his children?

§118. Thus, we have to be very cautious: when we look to our private interest, we must not invent something to confirm a new and hitherto unheard-of hypothesis and thereby betray the common interest of Christianity to the so-called Pre-Adamites, who make every effort to show that the great deluge was not universal but only affected the lands of the Jews.[76]

§119. It is therefore clear what is the meaning of this precept not to disturb another in the use of creatures. It is twofold and concerns either common ownership or dominion. In the former case a person is under an obligation

73. Philastrius was bishop of Brixen in the second half of the fourth century A.D. and the author of a book on heresies (see Philastrius, *Diversarum hereseon liber,* ed. F. Marx, Corpus Scriptorum Ecclesiasticorum Latinorum, vol. 38 [Prague, Vienna, Leipzig: Tempsky, 1898]). Baldus de Ubaldis (ca. 1327–1400) was an influential medieval jurist whose commentaries on Roman law were used well into the early modern period.

74. Samuel Bochart, *Geographiae sacrae pars prior: Phaleg seu de dispersione gentium et terrarum divisione facta in aedificatione turris Babel* (Caen, 1651), bk. I, chap. xvi, p. 71.

75. Berossus, a priest at Babylon in the third century B.C., wrote a history of Babylon in three books in Greek, of which only quotations survive.

76. See Christiaan Schotanus, "De prima mundi aetate," p. 168, in *Bibliotheca historiae sacrae per duas aetates & duo annorum milia, ab Adam ad Abraham* (Franeker, 1660).

to allow another person to enjoy an equal right to the use of something as long as this person does not seek to acquire property rights in it through occupation or some other means of acquiring dominion.

§120. In the latter case, however, a person is obliged not to try to use something which is in the dominion of another person against the owner's will, always excepting the case of extreme necessity.

§121. Also, from the reasons for introducing dominion and from its definition another special precept follows which is relevant to common ownership: that man should allow something which is of inexhaustible utility and which human effort cannot prevent others from using to remain in the state of primeval common ownership.

§122. The purpose of all property is that someone acquires a good for himself alone which is not sufficiently abundant to be used by all or which gives rise to quarrels if it remains in common ownership, and that he does so in such a way that he can prevent others from using it in future. It is, therefore, evident that there are three prerequisites in the thing that is to be subjected to dominion.

§123. (1) First, that this thing can be of some use to humans, either indirectly or directly, either in itself or through its connection with something else. It would be superfluous and silly to want to claim something useless, though it may perhaps be difficult to come up with an example of something that is totally useless.

§124. (2) It must not be possible for all humans to use this thing sufficiently without the danger of strife. Otherwise, a person would sin against the precept to preserve equality and especially to avoid pride if he wanted to exclude others from using these sorts of things.

§125. Certain things can be used by humans within such tight limits that their use cannot be shared with several others. For the sake of peace, it is of the greatest interest that these things become private property.

§126. Other things, however, offer various kinds of uses and can be consumed in certain ways while they are abundant in other respects. In the former respect they can become property; in the latter respect the law concerning the duties of humanity requires that their use be shared with others.

§127. Among these are the light and warmth of the sun, air, rivers, and similar things. Thus, it is not inhuman and malevolent if someone claims these things as property, but it would be inhumane to deny others the innocuous use of these things.

§128. But if things are sufficient for all possible uses by all humans, it would be absurd to want to divide them.

§129. I have, however, added—importantly—that this is only so if a thing, by its nature, has uses the exercise of which does not give occasion for strife.

§130. It is thus evident that the earth could not remain in common ownership although the extent of the entire earth is such that it is sufficient for any kind of use by all peoples. This is because after the fall from grace human industry in particular was required in order to benefit from this usefulness. Moreover, if humans had not been allowed to occupy parts [of the earth], there would have been occasion for strife, even concerning those uses which do not require human effort.

§131. But you may want an example of a thing that by its very nature offers some use to all humans without the danger of strife. I will give you one. Consider the vast ocean spread between the great continents of Europe, Africa, Asia, America, and the unknown southern territory.[77] Whatever benefits man derives from this, they are sufficient for all of humanity and do not require industry or cultivation. Moreover, they do not give rise to strife since they are not so frequent that there is a danger humans would compete over the use of the ocean.

77. That is, Australia.

§132. (3) For something to be suitable for dominion it must be possible for the thing itself to be seized and guarded to some degree. For as property includes the right of keeping others away from this thing, it would be useless unless it could be put into effect against these others, and a person would claim something as his property in vain when he cannot by any means prohibit others from partaking in it against his will. This would mean a sin against the duty of man toward himself, which commands that one should not strive for something beyond one's powers.

§133. The more narrowly something can be enclosed and defined, the easier it is to secure the effects of property against others. Thus, the more suitable something is for keeping others from seizing it unjustly, the more securely property rights over it can be guaranteed.

§134. A thing is not immediately exempt from property rights just because others cannot be conveniently kept away from it. But if that thing is so diffuse that protecting it completely is impossible, or if the costs of guarding it are excessive, then one should not assume that anybody wanted something that is so difficult to guard to be his property. And if someone did want it, he had no right to do so.

§135. Again, take the example of the vast ocean.

§136. You see, therefore, what should be declared concerning the well-known controversy over the dominion of the sea. To put it briefly, those parts of the sea which are not part of the vast ocean can be subjected to dominion through occupation, but there is no right to do the same to the ocean. Others have explained the matter at great length and eruditely.[78]

§137. Moreover, once dominion was introduced, physical occupation alone was no longer sufficient to acquire property since occupation is effective

78. See Pufendorf, *Of the Law of Nature and Nations*, bk. IV, chap. v, §5. The question of whether dominion of the sea was possible was a long-standing controversy originating with Hugo Grotius's *Mare liberum* of 1609 (see Hugo Grotius, *The Free Sea*, ed. David Armitage [Indianapolis: Liberty Fund, 2004]).

only until something that did not belong to anybody has become the property of somebody. Thus, the necessity and utility of the human race required there to be other forms of acquisition aside from occupation.

§138. For teaching purposes you can divide these forms as follows on the basis of reason and insofar as they are commonly accepted among nations independently of their civil laws: some are principal, which have their own rules; others are accessory because they draw on the rules of the other forms depending on circumstances, but do not have different rules of their own.

§139. A principal means of acquisition is either original or derivative. By means of the former property in something is first introduced. By means of the latter existing dominion is transferred from one person to another.

§140. The only original means now is occupation. This, however, involves seizing something which does not belong to anybody with the intention of establishing property rights over it. From this follows the commonplace rule that whatever does not belong to anyone becomes the property of the occupier.

§141. The ways of seizing different things, however, vary as much as the things themselves. Mobile goods are seized with one's hands, immobile goods with one's feet, by entering them.

§142. Another difference between the two is that bodily contact is sufficient to occupy something immobile, but in the case of mobile goods it is also necessary to remove them from their location and transfer them to our place or custody. It could perhaps be said, though, that in respect to mobile goods it is enough to seize these without moving them as long as this seizure can be proved.

§143. Similarly, mobile goods and especially self-moving goods are occupied with the help of various instruments, such as javelins or a trap, etc.

However, it has never been common among the nations for immobile goods to be seized by using javelins, for example.[79]

§144. Moreover, since mobile goods usually have clearly defined limits, there is no doubt that I acquire the entire thing if I seize one end of it.

§145. Immobile goods, however, are naturally connected to one another. We must, therefore, draw a distinction here. They either allow certain limits to be defined by human industry or not. In the case of the former (buildings, for example) it is also assumed that the whole thing is acquired if one part has been seized physically—if, for example, someone has entered a house. Here, however, it is necessary to use other physical signs to declare my intention of occupying these immobile goods.

§146. Such signs, for example, are the setting of boundary stones, maintaining them, etc.

§147. Finally, if we abstract from particular statutes, immobile goods are never acquired through the occupation of mobile goods, since mobile goods are added to immobile goods, not the other way round. But acquiring property in an immobile good usually means that the mobile goods belonging to it are acquired at the same time.

§148. Accessories, however, are all those things that do not belong to anybody and are contained in immobile goods, or which cannot be used without immobile goods. This is so, no matter whether they can be moved, such as inanimate objects, or whether they move themselves, such

---

79. A reference to a story told by Plutarch in his *Greek Questions,* 30: two representatives of the inhabitants of Andros and Chalcis ran toward the gates of a deserted city, each to claim it for his respective people. The Andrian, sensing that he was being outrun, hurled his spear at the gate of the city, where it stuck before the Chalcidian had reached it. The Andrian then claimed that by this act he had taken possession of the city for Andros (see Plutarch, *Moralia,* vol. 4, ed. and trans. F. C. Babbitt, Loeb Classical Library (London: Heinemann, 1936), pp. 211–13). See also Pufendorf, *Of the Law of Nature and Nations,* bk. IV, chap. vi, §8.

as beasts, and whether they are above the earth, such as the air, or beneath it, such as a buried treasure.

§149. And it is so, whether they are such that I could use them immediately as I wished or whether they require some special and laborious mode of appropriation in order to use them.

§150. And whether I know where I can get them or not.

§151. There is another difference between self-moving things and things moved by something else, in that the dominion over things moving themselves (among which I include the air) is only momentary and lasts only as long as they do not move themselves outside this immobile thing unless we have a special way of appropriating them. If these move themselves elsewhere, without human assistance, then our dominion ceases because they are then the accessories of something else.

§152. It is another matter with passively mobile things. Because these are normally only moved by humans, moving them does not deprive me of my dominion, and those moving them do not acquire dominion by taking them because they already were somebody's property.

§153. But if a person who has become the owner of an immobile thing by occupation in a separate act seizes self-moving things,[80] then they remain in his dominion even if they later transfer themselves to another location.

§154. Moreover, just as things which have been acquired cease to be in our dominion as a result of dereliction and return to their primeval condition, so there can also be no doubt that dominion over them has to be sought again through occupation.

80. That is, animals, whether tame or wild.

§155. On this basis we can easily reply to the thorny questions of jurists concerning the acquisition of wild beasts and their loss, the acquisition of precious stones found on the seashore, and the present-day right of the prince over these, that is, whether this right is to be considered dominion and whether subjects hunting contrary to the prohibition of the prince are committing theft. It also helps us to answer the questions whether the acquisition of a treasure is an example of occupation and whether the acquisition of things that are sent to us is another example, etc.

§156. But since the utility of a thing also depends on the fact that I cannot be forced to keep it against my will, but can hand it over to another whenever I wish, it follows that we have to examine the derivative forms of acquisition. All of these, if we abstract from the laws, depend on the will of a prior owner and the will of the person to whom dominion has been transferred. For there is nothing more natural than that the will of owners to transfer their property to someone else is effective.

§157. Only rarely are there disagreements about the will of the person to whom the property is transferred. The will of the previous owner, however, is either express or tacit.

§158. It is express either on the basis of words only—for example, if someone formally declares that he renounces his property in something in favor of someone else, who then accepts it.

§159. Or it is express, based on words that are linked to the act of transferring the property. This form is usually called a handover.

§160. The spoken word, however, is ephemeral; it admits of various conflicting interpretations even when it has been written down and uttered in the presence of witnesses. The use of goods, however, requires possession, and the actual transfer of possession is not subject as much to disputes. Thus, it is clear that the transfer of dominion by means of a handover is much more clear-cut.

§161. Thus we can quite easily respond to the question whether a hand-over is really required for the transfer of dominion or whether this is an invention of Roman law alone. Similarly, on what grounds did the Romans allow the transfer of dominion without possession in certain transactions, especially in last wills? Finally, why were several forms of fictive or symbolic transfer invented in Roman law?[81] Etc.

§162. Also, the transfer of dominion through words alone is the effect of actions among the living and of contracts, or the result of a last will or testament.

§163. Therefore a testament here is nothing other than a verbal declaration of what a person wants to happen to his goods after his death.

§164. This limited consolation for mortality is certainly accepted, if not among all, then among most nations, that a person, during his lifetime, can transfer his goods to the person he loves most in the event of his death.

§165. Moreover, it seems to have been common usage in ancient times to name heirs publicly when death was imminent and to hand estates over to them physically. Later, many nations for important reasons adopted a different form of testament, by allowing a person to indicate or put into writing his last will at whatever time he wanted. This he could change according to his whim, and on this basis the heirs who were named or listed in writing acquired a right when the person who had made the testament passed away.

§166. Although such last wills may deservedly enjoy great favor, they have to be modified to the extent that necessity and the utility of commonwealths require it. They [that is, commonwealths] are accustomed to stipulate legally how each person should set up his testament. Whoever ignores these rules cannot complain that his will was not observed.

81. That is, the transfer of ownership by a symbolic act rather than the handing over of the actual goods.

§167. But it is often inexpedient to transfer my property entirely to another person, and instead it is better to grant a use right and benefit, which another person needs, while I retain my property rights. Thus, nations commonly transfer such benefits through words alone, or by means of a handover, or in a last will.

§168. This transfer occurs in such a way that only a personal obligation is intended and no burden is imposed on the good that confers this benefit— as does happen, for example, in the case of lending, hiring, etc.— or in order that someone acquires some right over a good with respect to its use while our property right remains intact.

§169. And in this case a certain particle of our property, though one that is dependent and inferior to our property right, is transferred to another person together with the power of using and enjoying it. This is the origin of the distinction between *dominium directum* [outright ownership] and *dominium utile* [use right]. The forms of the latter are the emphyteutic right,[82] the *jus superficiarium*,[83] and the rights of vassals to a fief. Or, alternatively, the entire property right remains with us.

§170. The purpose of this is either to act as a guarantee for the person who grants us the use, to make sure he does not suffer damage. This is called a right of pawn or a security. Or it is some other use right and is called a servitude.

§171. If this use primarily concerns someone else's person, it is called personal servitude—for example, usufruct, use, lodging, the work of servants, etc.

§172. If it primarily concerns the use of another person's land, it is called real servitude.

---

82. A perpetual right in a piece of land that is the property of another.
83. The right to use the surface of a piece of land (e.g., by building on it) without a transfer of ownership in the land.

§173. And if this concerns the use of buildings in the city, then it is called urban servitude. If it is about the use of rural areas, that is, farming and grazing, it is called rural servitude.

§174. The forms of urban servitude are the obligation to allow one's own house to sustain the weight of the neighbor's wall; to let the neighbor seat his beams in our wall; to allow his timbers and roof to overhang our land; to allow the rainwater from the neighbor's drip and gutters to flow onto our land; to build higher or lower because of smoke, waste water, or light (in order not to block light from the neighbor's property); the obligation not to obstruct a neighbor's view, etc.

§175. Examples of rural servitudes are the right to walk on a path, drive livestock, drive a cart on a certain path, channel water, draw water, lead herds to the water, graze them, have a lime kiln, dig for sand, quarry for clay or stone, chop wood, press grapes, etc.

§176. Roman jurisprudence is largely concerned with explaining these rights because these kinds of transfers take place very frequently among private persons. Because of their equitability and because Roman jurists very often based their decisions on the dictates of right reason, the European nations largely tend to follow Roman jurisprudence when it comes to public agreements. But the extent to which [Roman law] resolves these questions on the basis of purely civil reasons can be shown more easily elsewhere.[84]

§177. Let us, therefore, return to the subject. We do not want to neglect the sort of transfer of dominion that, as we have said, occurs tacitly. This applies mainly to intestate successions and to the acquisition of ownership as a result of uninterrupted possession.

84. See Christian Thomasius (*praeses*), Hieronymus Winckler (*respondens*), *Dissertatio juridica de servitute stillicidii, vom Trauff-Recht* (Leipzig, 1689).

§178. Intestate succession takes place if a person has not left a last will, or if the heir named in the testament refused the inheritance or is incapable of being an heir.

§179. It is thus common custom among nations for possessions left after a person's death not to be considered derelict; they, therefore, do not have to be granted to the first person to occupy them. In part this is so because it tends to be assumed that someone was prevented by death [from making a will] or that he was deceived in the hope he had formed concerning a friend.

§180. Therefore, it is generally decided on the basis of the deceased person's tacit will that he who was the closest friend of the deceased at the time of his death should receive the goods of the deceased.

§181. Determining who is a friend, however, requires conjectures. These are all the more difficult as human friendships fluctuate greatly.

§182. Friendship rests either on natural causes—that is, blood relationships—or is freely chosen and based on specific reasons. The latter case seems less appropriate for the matter at hand because of the extreme difficulty, indeed impossibility, of definition. Moreover, this difficulty was not unknown to the deceased, and he could have easily resolved it by making a will. Having neglected to do so, he himself seems to have indicated that no attention should be paid to such friends.

§183. There remains the first form of friendship. This is presumed to be the stronger the closer the blood relationship was. Thus the nations in deciding cases of inheritance usually followed the rule that the person who is closest on the basis of blood relationships must acquire the inheritance.

§184. Whenever a rule is based on conjectures, there are exceptions. So the nations have added other conjectures to these prior forms of friendship and made certain exceptions from this rule. For the purposes of teaching you can divide these into common exceptions, which are based on a circumstance common to all humans, and specific ones, which concern the circumstances of one or several particular nations.

§185. Each of these two exceptions rests on the common distinction of relatives into three types: descending, ascending, and collateral.

§186. Descendants — that is, children — create the following universal exception from the said rule: whatever degree they are, they are preferred to ascendants and collaterals because of the universal affection of parents, which is always greater for descendants than for ascendants.

§187. In addition to this there is in many cases (and especially when the children are not yet adults who are able to take care of wealth themselves) a natural duty, by which parents are obliged to take care of their children's maintenance. Thus, it was believed all the more that parents who had died without a testament had wanted to provide for their children as generously as possible and to leave to them whatever they had owned.

§188. But as far as the ascendants and collaterals are concerned, it is not so obvious which of the two is to be preferred to the other, since there are probable conjectures on either side. You might argue that brothers are to be preferred to parents according to the more ancient Roman law; or you might value brothers less highly than parents according to Saxon law;[85] or you might consider brothers and parents to have equal rights, according to Justinian's laws.

§189. To avoid giving occasion for intractable court cases, these disputes had to be resolved in advance either by laws or by agreements. Therefore, there is no commonwealth or province which does not observe either written or unwritten laws in intestate successions.

85. See Eike von Repgow, *The Saxon Mirror: A* Sachsenspiegel *of the Fourteenth Century,* trans. M. Dobozy (Philadelphia: University of Pennsylvania Press, 1999), bk. I, 17, pp. 73–74.

§190. These [laws] thereupon lay down rules for the prerogative of legitimacy based on gender, age, family relationship, and the right of representation.[86]

§191. Prescription is the next case. This is when someone has acquired possession of something and has held on to it peacefully and without interruption for a long time. For then it is to be regarded as full ownership, to such an extent that the present owner can repel his predecessor should he attempt to reclaim his property.

§192. This applies to relations between different nations and to those between private individuals.

§193. In either case the shared and final aim is the peace of humankind, for the sake of which dominions should be clearly defined, and no occasions should be created for wars by allowing us to reclaim something that once belonged to us or to our relatives.

§194. But the specific reasons for either form of prescription vary greatly. In the prescription of nations only there is the tacit dereliction by the previous owner, who is considered to have left something derelict when he did not reclaim it for a very long period of time and did not declare his intention of reclaiming it. This argument is based on common human custom.

§195. Thus, the only requisite of this form of prescription is undisturbed possession by another for a very long period of time, which cannot be defined rigidly because of variations in circumstances. Generally speaking, however, only so much time is required as is necessary for showing that the previous owner knew someone else possessed his good and that he had not lacked an opportunity to protest.

---

86. The *right of representation* (*jus representationis*) refers to the right of the testator's grandson to be considered the legitimate heir, even if the testator's son has died before the testator.

§196. A hundred years is undoubtedly such a period.

§197. If, therefore, somebody has, in some sense, protested in all seriousness against the possessor within this period, the prescription will not be accepted among nations.

§198. It is thus accepted that the claim to the title is by itself sufficient to interrupt the process of prescription.

§199. Among private individuals, however, civil laws are not primarily concerned with tacit dereliction when they allow something to be acquired by prescription. Their purpose, rather, is to punish subjects' negligence.

§200. Therefore, they have set down a definite and shorter period of time, which varies according to the kinds of things to be acquired through prescription—one year, two years, three years, ten years, twenty years, thirty years, etc.—and within which the prescription can be completed, even if the previous owner did not know all this time where his property was or protested frequently outside of court.

§201. To avoid conceding too much thereby to unjust possessors, civil laws also require good faith and a just title from the person who wanted to take possession, and, with respect to the good itself, that it should be regularly accessible to private individuals and not held by means of theft or force.

§202. From this follow many conclusions concerning prescription by private individuals which are unknown to prescription as defined by the law of nations. That is why jurists list prescription among the private means of acquisition according to civil law.

§203. A relevant case is when the law transfers dominion over things against the will of the previous owner as a form of punishment, that is, when the condemned have all their goods, or a part of them, taken away from them because of their crimes and these are handed over to the public or the victim.

§204. For among nations there is no means of depriving an owner of his property against his will.

§205. Even if in war something is taken away by an enemy through superior force, against the will of the owner, and becomes the property of this robber, the previous owner does not lose the right to use equal force to regain his possessions until he has renounced all claims to these losses in subsequent peace treaties.

§206. We still need to say something about the accessory means of acquisition, which is also called accession. This is summarized in one rule: "What is accessory follows ownership of the principal good." Therefore, nothing new is to be expected here. No matter whether the principal thing is acquired through occupation or through a derivative mode of acquisition, the accessory thing is acquired on the same legal basis.

§207. We have already provided an example of occupation above. Likewise in the case of a handing-over, the person the building is sold to or handed over to is considered to have acquired the accessory goods of the building at the same time.

§208. Still, when it comes to the application of the rule, controversies arise over what is to be considered principal and what accessory.

§209. It seems uncontroversial to regard fruits as accessories because they are part of the [principal] thing.

§210. It follows that ownership of the offspring of an animal belongs to the owner of the female animal since it is a part of her.

§211. Those who believe that the owner of the male animal is entitled to part of the offspring appear to be resting their case on a dubious hypothesis (apart from the fact that others have already given an adequate response to these people), namely, that the offspring is an accessory of the male although it is not part of him, or that begetting is a means of acquisition, which is nonsense.

§212. Greater controversy surrounds other accessions—for example, if a picture must follow ownership of the canvas, writing that of the paper, the external form that of the material. To me it seems to be as follows.

§213. When two things (and by that I also mean labor) occur together or are connected in some other way, each of them may be mine. In that case there is no doubt that they are also mine jointly. This is the case, for example, when I make a plaster with my medicines or a cup from my silver.

§214. It is also possible that one of them does not belong to anybody while the other belongs to me. Then, once I have become the owner by seizing the first thing, it remains mine after the two things have been joined to each other. This is so, for example, when I prepare food from the meat of a wild animal.

§215. Or one of them belongs to someone else. If, in that case, I do not have any clear knowledge of the identity of the other owner—that is, if the previous owner cannot prove his ownership—then natural reason suggests it belongs to the person to whose thing it is attached. Examples are flotsam, [buried] treasure, etc.

§216. If, however, ownership of this thing can be proved and we abstract from civil laws, then it is more likely that no new acquisition takes place, but that we both have ownership of this thing, and that the thing thus is held in communal ownership pro rata.

§217. A union of two things has come about by accident, or through the will of each party, or through the will of one person, or as a result of the action of a third party.

§218. But if neither of us wants our property to be held in common, another question arises: who decides how common property is to be divided?

This does not pertain so much to the forms of acquiring property as to the office of the judge and arbiter.

§219. And this is what the Roman jurists and Justinian primarily had in mind when they resolved controversies over *specificatio*,[87] a painting, a piece of writing, soldering with lead or copper, etc.

§220. It is not our purpose to discuss their opinion at great length, but it may perhaps be useful to make the following points.

§221. If the two things that are joined to each other are easily separated, then they are separated and each person has his property restored.

§222. If they cannot be easily separated and the joined object is fungible, then the person joining the two must give something as compensation to the other person, who has no reason to complain since no particular affection is directed to fungible objects.

§223. If the other person's thing is not fungible, then the duty of the judge cannot be set out in general terms since the circumstances here can vary too much.

§224. For even if you wanted to argue that that should be considered the principal object without which the other cannot exist, this can hardly be considered a universal norm for judging such controversies.

§225. For one thing, there are many cases where this rule could be applied to either person's property, as in the case of *specificatio:* form cannot exist without matter, and matter cannot exist without form.

§226. Also, very often attention must be paid to the price of things. The result is that the owner of the more precious parts prevails. Justinian fol-

---

87. That is, if one person makes something out of material belonging to another. See Justinian, *Institutes* 2.1 ("De rerum divisione").

lowed this rule in the case of paintings,[88] while our laws do so in the case of written texts.

§227. We also need to take into account the neediness of the previous owner, which works in his favor. If, for example, someone has by a genuine mistake sown on someone else's field and grain prices rise, then it would be inequitable to deny him the grain, etc.

§228. In such cases, therefore, the matter has to be entrusted to the prudent opinion of an arbiter. It is in the interest of the commonwealth that the decision of matters [like these] is not left to the arbitrary equity of judges.

§229. Thus, it is better if the prince prescribes certain axioms to judges (as Justinian did in the case of *specificatio*) based on what usually happens, even if these fail in some cases.

§230. From what we have said so far about ownership and the relevant precept it is clear that the essence of the duty of other humans toward the owner can conveniently be summarized as follows. Either something remains with the owner, or it has been passed to a third party. In the former case any person whatsoever is required to allow him to enjoy his possessions peacefully and may not destroy them by force or fraud, embezzle them, or appropriate them. This follows from the precept that prohibits harming others.

§231. If something has passed to a third party, then he holds it either in bad faith or in good faith. The possessor in bad faith is required to restore the thing itself or its price, together with all its fruits and all interest. This principle is based on the heading concerning compensation for damage.

§232. The possessor in good faith holds the thing either on the basis of a contract with the owner, such as a contract for hire, or rent, or a deposit.

88. Justinian, *Institutes* 2.1.

He is required to restore the thing to the owner, according to the law on contract. This conclusion is based on the principle concerning keeping faith.

§233. Or the possessor has held something in good faith with the aim of keeping it, not knowing that someone else is the rightful owner. In that case either the thing itself still exists or it has been consumed.

§234. In the former case, the possessor in good faith is required to do whatever he can to make sure that the thing is returned to the legitimate possessor or owner.

§235. In the latter case, if another person's property that has been acquired in good faith has been consumed, the possessor needs to restore as much wealth to the owner as he has derived from it.

§236. These two assertions appear to be derived in part from the precept concerning the duties of humanity, in part from the precept that prohibits harming others, especially insofar as a possessor in good faith loses his good faith once he knows who the rightful owner is.

§237. We shall not protest if you want to add the universal agreement of primeval mankind to these reasons and to derive the obligations of the possessor in good faith from it.

§238. We will not, however, detain ourselves with the specific conclusions which the learned have formulated to describe the duty of the possessor in good faith. In part this is because others have already explained them extremely well, in part because they tend to be discussed in greater detail in Roman law, and in part because quite a few of them seem to occur rarely among the nations.

On the Duty Concerning the
Prices of Things

§1. After dominions over things had been introduced, humans began to engage in commerce with each other. Commerce is nothing other than the mutual exchange of things (by which I also mean labor). For not every part of the earth produces everything, and therefore nobody has everything he needs or delights in. Thus, it was necessary to seek from another person those things that were lacking. And since it was not possible to demand everything gratis it was necessary to offer the other person something in return that would be of use to him in the future.

§2. The person who did not want to give a thing or labor to another for free usually wanted to receive some equivalent in return for it. But very often the things that were exchanged were different in kind. The spontaneous result of this was that by some convention humans imposed on things some measure for their esteem, whereby even things with disparate natures could be compared to each other and weighed against each other.

§3. This weighing against each other, however, implies the comparison of several things with each other in terms of their quantity. And this is either according to their mathematical quantity, that is, on the basis of the three spatial dimensions, or according to their moral quantity, that is, their value. We are here concerned with the latter, which is called *price*.

§4. Thus, the price is the value of things and actions that are exchanged commercially, insofar as they afford humans some use and pleasure.

§5. You see, therefore, that the peace of humankind demanded that a price be established. In particular, the preservation of equality and the precept concerning the duties of humanity demanded it since anybody can engage in commerce with anybody else and the exercise of commerce is in part also to the advantage of others.

§6. Moreover, the price is either common, when certain objects and works are compared to each other directly, or it is eminent, when the common prices of all other things are measured by it and it represents these common prices in a virtual sense. This is called *coin* or *money*.

§7. In an exchange, for example, the common price is appropriate. In a purchase the eminent price is used.

§8. The common price is more ancient than the eminent and appears to have been used for as long as humans lived in their primeval simplicity. The simpler the population (that is, the more it was content with the basic necessities of life), the longer was it content with the direct reciprocal exchange of objects and labor.

§9. The eminent price originally seems to have been produced in part by luxury, in part by the desire to increase the riches of the commonwealth.

§10. For after humans had begun to desire a whole variety of different things for their convenience or pleasure, it was no longer easy for anyone to possess exactly those things which another wanted to have in exchange for his possessions, or which were of equal value to them.

§11. Moreover, those commonwealths that wanted to appear cultivated and more civilized than others (which they described as barbarian) had to divide the citizens according to their different occupations. Many of these estates could not live without luxury and the eminent price, or at least could have done so only with difficulty.

§12. We have said that humans were obliged to determine the prices of things because of the command to preserve equality; and the determination of the price, if we abstract from international treaties and civil laws, should be based on the following precept: "When you compare your thing to that of another do not consider him to be unequal to yourself without just cause, do not deceive him, and do not neglect the duties of humanity." The first is based on the injunction to avoid pride, the second on the precept prohibiting harming others, and the third on the law concerning the performance of the duties of humanity.

§13. So, for example, it is a violation of the first precept when someone values his commodity—that is, his grain, wine, or property, for example—more highly than another person's equally good grain, wine, or property.

§14. It is a violation of the second precept if someone knowingly and falsely attributes a particular quality to a thing and also if he says nothing about a defect.

§15. It is contrary to the third precept if, for example, someone demands a higher price from a poor person than from a wealthy person.

§16. But as we have said above, the precepts to avoid pride and perform the duties of humanity do not always produce a perfect right, and the performance of the duties of humanity requires many other circumstances that are not that obvious. Thus, among those living in the state of nature no further specific rules on the determination of the price can be defined, and further inquiry has to be left to every individual's conscience.

§17. Because the contracting parties in this state [of nature] remain equal, it follows here that both sides can choose above all the price they prefer. That is, if you consider their external freedom, each seller may in an exchange demand a large sum of money for his good, while the buyer may offer a far lower price.

§18. This is what the Romans appear to have had in mind when they say that the contracting parties in a sale are naturally allowed to circumvent each other. A relevant example is that of the Greek comedian (if I am not mistaken) who, having promised the people that he would reveal the desires of everybody, said, quite truthfully, that all want to buy cheaply and sell dearly.

§19. Thus, there will be no place among those who live in this state [of nature] for the rescission of a contract because of damage by more than half [of the fair price].[89]

§20. If one of the contracting parties was guilty of deceit, then the rescission will be applicable on the basis of the deceit even if the damage was far less than half [of the fair price].

§21. If there was no deceit and each party knowingly entered into the contract, then there is no reason to rescind the contract, not even on the basis of civil law.

§22. If each contracting party errs and is ignorant, then we do not need to look for half of the fair price, because among those who value their good as it pleases them there is nothing by which you could measure what is half of the fair price. Instead, we need to refer to that which we stressed above concerning error in contracts.

§23. Yet in this case everybody will estimate the degree to which the law on the duties of humanity imposes an obligation, admittedly imperfect, on him.

§24. But commerce is not greatly encouraged by this form of valuation, and equality is preserved more effectively among those who are equal if individuals submit themselves to the judgment of several people. Thus, it is common practice among nations, for good reasons, that each of the contracting parties turns to the judgment and opinion of similar people in similar

89. This was a so-called *laesio enormis*. See Thomas Ahnert, "Roman Law in Early Enlightenment Germany: The Case of Christian Thomasius' *De Aequitate Cerebrina Legis Secundae Codicis de Rescindenda Venditione* (1706)," *Ius commune* XXIV (1997): 153–70.

transactions, and they consider that agreement to be fair in which this kind of estimate was used and that to be unfair in which it was ignored.

§25. Therefore, with respect to this custom, you can distinguish between the common preferred price and the preferred price in the strict sense.

§26. I call something a *common preferred price* when a person in commercial exchanges involving his possessions uses the customary estimate of others.

§27. A *preferred price* in the narrow sense is when someone values his own thing more highly than others commonly do.

§28. But even this price is sometimes not considered unfair, namely, if there are special circumstances which are not very common but because of which others are also accustomed to value their things more highly.

§29. We, therefore, need to explain briefly the foundation of each of these two prices, which are generally accepted among the nations.

§30. As far as the common price is concerned, those people are certainly mistaken who look for it in the nobility of the substance and the excellence that one thing has in relation to another.

§31. For if this were the case, then the price for a bad serf would have to be greater than that for an excellent horse, that of a flea greater than that for a highly salubrious plant, that of parsley greater than that for precious stones or very expensive pearls, which is absurd.[90]

§32. And how would different human labors be valued in relation to each other since they have no substance?

---

90. That is, the substance of human beings is nobler than that of beasts, that of beasts nobler than that of plants, and that of plants nobler than that of inanimate matter, such as precious stones.

§33. I would not look for the foundation of this price in the suitability of a thing or labor for contributing indirectly or directly to the necessities of human life or toward making it more comfortable and pleasant.

§34. It is of course true that the necessity, convenience, or pleasure of something leads the contracting parties to make an acquisition, but these considerations do not guide them in determining the price.

§35. Therefore, I say, quite rightly, that useless things have no price. And it is also for the most part true if I say that things with some utility for humans have a price. I cannot say, however, that things, when they are compared with each other, have a greater, lesser, or equal price, depending on their respective utility.

§36. If this were the case, then something that is necessary to humans would always have to be valued more highly in commercial exchange than something that is merely convenient, and the latter more highly than something merely pleasurable. But how often is food sold for less than a precious stone or pearl!

§37. In addition, there are many things that are extremely useful for human life and that have no price, either because they must not have an owner (as is the case with the upper reaches of the air, the ether and the celestial bodies, or the vast ocean); or because they are unsuitable for exchange and therefore excluded from commerce, such as a free man; or because in commercial transactions they are never considered anything other than an accessory of something else, such as sunlight, clean air, a pleasant view, wind, shade, etc. (although these too increase or reduce the price of farms or estates); or because divine or human laws have prohibited these from being traded commercially, such as sacred acts, the administration of justice, etc.

§38. What, therefore, shall we say? Scarcity is usually the most important consideration in the prices of things, whether these are necessary for man, or only useful, or pleasant. Hence the common saying that everything that is scarce is dear.

§39. Thus food is cheap where it is abundant, more expensive where it is scarce, extremely dear and often priceless at the time of famine.

§40. And thus the human desire for luxury has produced enormous prices for things that are not necessary, and that human life could easily do without, because of their scarcity and because they are imported from remote locations, such as precious stones, pearls, and tulips, when these were very rare, etc.

§41. In works of art the subtlety and elegance of the skill, the fame of the craftsman, the difficulty of producing the piece, the small number of craftsmen, and similar considerations are all about scarcity.

§42. It is the same with works and actions. Their price is linked to their difficulty, the skill required, the utility, necessity, scarcity of agents, dignity, and finally the reputation of the art itself, whether it is esteemed to be noble or base.

§43. At the same time it is evident from this why nations have generally adopted rare metals for [measuring] the eminent price. Apart from the fact that these substances are very compact, so that they cannot be easily destroyed or broken into small pieces, their scarcity has the effect that they can be treated as the equivalent of many other things and can measure these things by means of an eminent price.

§44. The foundation of a price based on preference [in the narrow sense] is a desire that is not very widespread, but that is approved by a number of people. For example, the person from whom a thing has come to us is highly esteemed by ourselves and the thing has been given as an expression of his affection, or we have become used to it, or it is a reminder of something significant, or we have averted a great evil with its help, or it has been made by ourselves, etc.

§45. These principles prevail in the state of nature. In commonwealths, however, considerations of utility do not allow subjects to enjoy such freedom in determining prices. Therefore, examples of prices based on preference are very rare here; its only use, as one might expect, is in cases concerning compensation for damage, and even here it is not always applicable.

§46. The common price is often used with respect to the market value, where apart from the scarcity of things the labor and the costs of the merchants who convey and handle them are usually taken into account, as is the question whether goods are bought in great or small quantities. The common price is also changed abruptly by the abundance or lack of buyers, money, or goods. It is also relevant whether a good is seeking a buyer or whether a seller who would otherwise not sell continues to receive offers. Finally, it is relevant whether someone offers immediate payment or defers payment to a later date.

§47. In these matters in which the aforementioned circumstances need to be taken into account, the prince cannot decree specific laws on prices because there is such huge variation in these circumstances. Instead, the determination of this price has to be left to the common judgment of contracting parties.

§48. Because this judgment is subject to a lot of variation, such a price cannot be reduced to a single point, but allows for some flexibility. If a person bought something for two coins, for example, another person in the same commonwealth might buy it for two and a half, while another might pay one and a half. All three are to be regarded as having acquired the thing for a fair price.

§49. However, to prevent this flexibility from being limitless and thus conniving at the damage inflicted by some on others, three degrees of the common price are usually distinguished: the lowest (or pious), the medium (or moderate), and the highest (or harsh). As long as one remains within this range, something can be bought or sold for more or less.

§50. This is what Roman law was concerned with, when it granted the right to rescind a contract (in cases where it was not possible to prove fraud by the other party) if someone had suffered damage of more than half the just price. As I understand this, this is the case when someone has paid more than twice the amount of the lowest price or received less than half that of the highest price. For people who are experienced very rarely tend to exceed these limits, even if they disagree over valuations.[91]

§51. This law does not please everyone since this limit often involves some iniquity in the case of large acquisitions—for example, if someone has bought for five thousand thalers a house which is generally valued at a minimum of three thousand thalers and a maximum of four thousand thalers. Yet, it seems, it can be said in defense of the justice of the Roman laws that these were intended to come to the rescue of those who bought something of small value, where it is not expedient to inquire at greater length about the price; the person, on the other hand, who is so negligent in matters of great importance that he suffers a substantial loss seems to have been considered unworthy of the support of the law.

§52. In addition, in cases of such great importance it is easier to prove the other person's fraud, which brings about a restitution of the property even if the damage is less than half.

§53. But if the prince sees that he himself can determine the prices of things, which usually happens in the case of fungible goods and domestic products and in common services, then it is best if he does so in order to prevent quarrels.

§54. The result is a new kind of price, which is unknown to those who live in the state of nature and which is commonly called the legitimate price.

§55. This is not flexible, but consists in a single point, such that the smallest deviation from it constitutes an injustice.

91. See Justinian, *Codex* 4.44.2 and 4.44.8.

§56. This goes so far that it is not only forbidden to accept more [than the legitimate price], but often even to pay more, especially in those cases when the price has been set down not so much for the benefit of individuals as for the sake of public benefit and in the form of a sumptuary law.

§57. It will not be allowed to accept less [than the legitimate price], especially if the determination of the price is intended for the prohibition of monopolies [of buyers] or has been introduced for the general benefit of merchants.

§58. Having talked about dominion and price, the order of things leads us now to a discussion of contracts, which presuppose the separation of different dominions and the invention of prices and the distinction between contracts and pacts.

§59. Now, to be frank, divine jurisprudence does not recognize this distinction between pacts and contracts, which, insofar as it exists, owes its origin entirely to the Romans.

§60. Indeed, the ancient Romans wanted to take care that subjects were not harmed by an excessive willingness to enter into promises, no matter whether these were gratuitous or mutual. They, therefore, decreed that no effective obligation resulted from mere promises without a transfer, unless someone promised something to another in the form of a solemn stipulation.

§61. Thus, in the most ancient times stipulation was the only form of contract, while all other promises seem to have come under the description of simple pacts.[92]

---

92. That is, so-called *pacta nuda,* which were not themselves actionable though they were not entirely ineffective or invalid. See Reinhard Zimmermann, *The Law of Obligations: Roman Foundations of the Civilian Tradition* (Oxford: Clarendon Press, 1996), p. 508.

§62. Finally they gradually exempted certain transactions from this rule that a simple pact [*pactum nudum*] could not be enforced by law, either because the pact was followed by a payment, or because of the frequency of these pacts or their necessity for the encouragement of commerce and the daily benefit of citizens, or for the sake of adherence to contracts or some singular consideration of equity that was entirely contrary to the original intention.

§63. Hence the division of pacts into simple [*pacta nuda*] and nonsimple [*pacta non nuda*], and of the latter into legitimate and adjunct. The adjunct are divided into I do not know how many subspecies, which have been the cause of countless quarrels among jurists.

§64. From this developed the distinction of contracts into named and unnamed, and the division of the latter into real, verbal, by letter, and through consent—though these are not so controversial, except for the fact that another division of contracts, into those of strict law and of good faith (which originally stemmed from the distinction between the offices of the praetor and the judge), and the excessive subtleties concerning the formulae of legal actions and their titles had made the teachings concerning pacts and contracts more complicated, etc.

§65. These difficulties in Roman law were only increased by the clumsy rhapsody of Tribonian, and they then took hold of almost the entire Christian world, partly because the popes kept a lot of the material about contracts in their Decretals,[93] rejecting only a small part of it, and partly because some centuries ago the study of law began to revive in Italy and Germany, and the law of Justinian was at the same time introduced to universities and the law court. There Roman law was interpreted by men who were enormously diligent, but devoid of any interest in letters and history.

---

93. The *Decretals* were the collection of papal responses to particular questions concerning cases in ecclesiastical law. Some decretals became general church law by decree of the pope.

§66. Thus it happened that the current Romano-Germanic private law is an amorphous chaos, which cannot be reduced to an art by means of rules which one could safely trust.

§67. At the same time the doctrine of contracts and pacts in natural jurisprudence has so far been examined largely according to the principles of the Romans. This is partly because Christian kings almost unanimously accepted Roman law, at least to some degree, by reason of the many rules of equity contained in it, and observed these [rules] in contracts in their relations with each other.

§68. In part it is because the Scholastics and papal theologians, who a long time ago, before Grotius, had taken control of the doctrine of natural law, which had been abandoned by the jurists, suffered from a fault that is very common in that kind of person: they interfered in other people's business and used the pretext that they were writing about justice and law in order to meddle excessively in matters of Roman law and to scrutinize its minutiae according to the rules of their fictitious equity.

§69. Grotius was more modest in this respect, as were those other wise men who followed him: he was the first to reclaim successfully for the jurists what had been seized by others through force, or subterfuge, or doubtful means. They demonstrated eruditely to what extent the doctrine of contracts in Roman law conformed to natural equity, and so we do not think it necessary to reinvent the wheel, but will reserve what needs to be said about that for our private lessons on Romano-Germanic private law.

§70. We also refrain from discussing the means of dissolving obligations, such as payment, the substitution of obligations, compensation, and release, since these tend to be discussed in greater detail by the commentators on Justinianian law. And in those matters this law puts forward a wealth of equitable rules, which are not that obscure.

On the Interpretation of Divine and Human Will Insofar as It Is Expressed in Words

§1. We could therefore finish the second book and move on immediately to the particular duties of man in different societies had we not remembered that the discussion of interpretation above was interrupted for certain reasons, and its last part was postponed until after the doctrine of pacts.[94]

§2. For I said above that the interpretation of natural laws was one matter and that of revealed laws another. Either presupposes certain rules and axioms, which depend on first principles. But natural laws rest on uninterrupted chains of argument even in their remote conclusions, while conclusions in revealed law are to be derived from a general axiom by means of conjectures and probable arguments. There the same rules apply that legal practitioners use in interpreting human laws and pacts.

§3. Above all, it must be emphasized that we are speaking of positive laws that concern the temporal well-being of all humans. For whether the interpretation of the mysteries of faith is based on common rules of good interpretation or whether this requires special assistance and illumination by divine grace is not our concern here since we believe that theology is best left to the theologians.

94. See *Institutes,* bk. I, chap. iv, §82.

§4. Now, in a human court everybody is obliged to do what the legislator wants him to do, or what he obliges himself to do by his own will. The will of the legislator, however (excepting the law of nature), and of the person making a promise can only be inferred by others from the signs they use to declare their will. It is thus clear that the genuine standard and measure for the interpretation we are talking about is the determination of the intention on the basis of the most probable signs.

§5. Among the signs, however, by which an intention is declared, the more important are those that are in the form of speech. Therefore, we shall here be concerned mainly with the interpretation of a will that has been expressed in words, especially since the rules we will relate here can be applied in almost the same way to a will that has been expressed in deeds, which is the origin of tacit consent.

§6. Moreover, since words are signs of the mind, it is a universal truth that words are to be subordinated to the intention, not vice versa.

§7. In every law or pact, therefore, we need to look first at the words, but at the same time check whether the legislator or contracting party wanted to indicate something other than he said.

§8. Sometimes, indeed, we use words very precisely to express our meaning, so that we say what we think. But sometimes words only reflect part of our meaning, and we say less than what we mean. And sometimes the words are more extensive than what we have in mind, and we say more than we mean.

§9. The result of these different ways of speaking are three forms of interpretation: declarative, which explains what others mean in accordance with their words; extensive, which broadens their more restrictive meaning in such a way that they cover another case, which was included in the intention; and restrictive, which informs us that not everything covered by the words was intended by the speaker.

§10. These three forms differ in that the declarative mainly concerns the proposition that is declared in words, while the extensive and the restrictive look to something else, which is not expressed in the words themselves, namely, the reason [*ratio*] that impelled a person to speak these words.

§11. The words with which declarative interpretation is concerned are, therefore, considered either as simple terms or as propositions or entire speeches.

§12. But while every good interpreter begins with the meaning of the simple terms, there can be no doubt that he has to understand what these mean as part of a composite whole, since laws and pacts are, at the very least, propositions.

§13. For composition often has the effect that words mean something different than when they are used on their own.[95] And this is commonly called the idiotism of language.

§14. Both verbal expressions (that is, terms as well as propositions) are either vulgar (that is, common), or technical (that is, terms of art).

§15. Each of these is either perspicuous or obscure. I call those perspicuous that clearly and distinctly reveal the mind of the speaker to those who are experienced in a particular language or discipline. Obscure words are those that experienced people understand only with difficulty or not at all.

§16. As far as perspicuous words are concerned, these are obscure to those who are not experienced in the relevant discipline or language (which is why philosophers have distinguished between subjective and objective obscurity), but this obscurity can be easily remedied, partly by trusting those who teach languages to inform you reliably, partly by learning the

95. For example, "to bite the dust."

principles and rules of a discipline from its practitioners and consulting lexica and dictionaries, which exist for this purpose.

§17. Yet, he who wants to be an autodidact will not progress far in understanding either [perspicuous or obscure words]. And he who has not learned the language or discipline must refrain from interpretation, in part to avoid exposing himself to ridicule and in part to avoid meddling, either by fraud or by force, in the affairs of others.

§18. Thus, the explanation of terms that theologians use in talking about the mysteries of faith are to be left to them by the jurists and physicians. And similarly, the Lex Aquilia, the Senatusconsultum Velleianum et Macedonianum, the *dominium bonitarium et Quiritarium,* territorial overlordship, vassalage, etc.,[96] are no business of theologians and physicians. Likewise, *alkali* and *acid,* as well as the countless terms for illnesses and symptoms, are no business of theologians and jurists. The explanation of any of these is no concern of philosophers, etc.

§19. Obscure words either suffer from an obscurity that can be removed or they are so obscure that nobody can understand what the speaker meant. The first is what we are talking about here, as we shall show more fully in this chapter.

§20. Obscurity, however, is partly the result of the external form of letters, and partly that of the internal meaning of words.[97]

---

96. The Lex Aquilia (*Digest* 9.2) regulated the amount of compensation for damages; the Senatusconsultum Velleianum (*Digest* 16.1.2.1) prohibited women from incurring liability for others; the Senatusconsultum Macedonianum (*Digest* 14.6.1) ruled that a lender who had given money to a son who is still under the rule of the father should have no legal right to reclaim his money, even after the death of the father; the *dominium bonitarium* and the *dominium Quiritarium* referred to two different kinds of ownership transfer.

97. Thomasius is here drawing on Rebhahn, *De interpretatione juris obscuri,* theses 23 and 24.

§21. The external form of words is shaped either by language or by writing.

§22. That which is shaped by speech is called sound. And unless the sound is totally inarticulate, it deserves to be interpreted. For even he who speaks with difficulty must be considered a speaker. This is particularly appropriate if someone in the instant before death expresses his last will, which he will never do again, in words that are not fully intelligible—for example, if someone said, "My servant Cratinus shall be free," and he only has a servant called Cratistus.

§23. Insofar as this kind of obscurity is to be remedied through interpretation, it is subject to much the same rules that we will put forward concerning the clarification of internal obscurity.

§24. The obscurity that stems from writing or from those features that are extrinsic to written text can occur if a person's handwriting is unclear and messy. This fault is common to many scholars, so that it has become proverbial to say that we learned men write poorly. Take the famous example of the physician who wanted to prescribe parsley [*apium*], but who had formed his letters in such a way that the pharmacist read "opium" instead.

§25. Or the writer has used obscure signs and notes and puzzling abridgments, which we call abbreviations. It is not without reason, therefore, that Justinian severely prohibited using these in formulating laws. Thus, an ignorant cleric once misread "Otto, by the grace of God," etc.[98]

§26. Or the copyist made a mistake in transcribing the words.

§27. Or the written text has been altered so much by erasures, insertions, and additions, or by some other means, that it can no longer be read clearly.

---

98. The abbreviation for *gratia* (by the grace of) could be misread as "gram."

§28. Or the writing has been mutilated. That can be the result either of the original carelessness of the scribe or of the passage of time.

§29. Or the text is correct as far as the letters go, but suffers from poor punctuation, or a lack of punctuation creates ambiguity, as is the case in the well-known verse: "remain open door at no time be closed to an honest man," etc.[99]

§30. Even if the rules we shall soon discuss are of some help in these and similar obscurities, it nevertheless cannot be denied that the most powerful assistance is to be sought from natural prudence and a singular faculty of judgment, in which some excel before others. Thus, those people who are particularly adept at this kind of interpretation are commonly called critics by the learned.

§31. Thus, I move on to the obscurity that affects laws and agreements as the result of the internal meaning of the words. This occurs when the speaker has used words that are (1) obsolete, whether they were clear and common at the time they were used, as in the case of the Laws of the Twelve Tables and the laws of the Lombards and the other ancient tribes of Germany;[100] or they were antiquated at the time in which they were used, as is the case in that response by a learned man: *Rebare te fari scio,* etc.[101]

§32. (2) Words that have been coined recently are also often the cause of obscurity, since terms tend to be based not on the opinions of individuals but on common use. This happens if someone, on his own, gives words a new meaning—for example, if someone commonly uses the term *suppellectile* for silver tableware, cloaks, or robes. Or it happens if someone

---

99. That is, this is either an appeal to the door to remain open at all times and not be closed to an honest man, or an appeal to remain open at no time and to be closed to an honest man, depending on whether a full stop is placed after or before "at no time."

100. The Laws of the Twelve Tables originated in the mid-fifth century B.C.; the medieval Consuetudines Feudorum of the Lombards were codified in the seventh and eighth centuries A.D.

101. "You thought you spoke to someone who knew."

forms new terms through combining others, in order perhaps to express the peculiar terms of another language or for some other reason. Or something altogether different may be created. A relevant example here is perhaps someone who calls soldiers "those who speak with bombard-sword and deadly pike-flame," or the Scholastics' *perfectihabeam*.[102]

§33. (3) Obscurity can arise easily if someone makes use of foreign words in speech. Thus, it is best to avoid this obscurity by adding a suitable paraphrase. Roman laws have followed this rule diligently when they talk about *scopelismon*[103] and *chomata*.[104] Similarly, obscurity is increased if these foreign terms are used incorrectly by inexperienced people and have their meaning changed, which is something familiar to our Gallo-Germans.[105]

§34. (4) Above all, however, it is ambiguous words that cause obscurity. These are constituted in such a way that they mean two or more things. We must not join those foolish skeptics who claim that everything that exists and, even more, everything that is expressed in words is ambiguous and uncertain; but at the same time Diodorus's opinion, which he defended against Chrysippus, has been exploded: he argued that no word was ambiguous, but there are more things than words and there is an enormous number of things without names, which we cannot signify by their own names, but by borrowing terms from elsewhere.[106]

§35. But if a word means several things, either one of the meanings is proper and the other improper, or both are proper. Thus, *library* properly stands

102. A combination of two words, *perfecti* and *habeam*.

103. A crime that involved placing stones on another person's field as a threat not to cultivate it (see *Digest* 47.11.9).

104. *Chomata* were irrigation channels to direct the water of the Nile. *Digest* 47.11.10 regulates the punishments for interfering with these.

105. That is, Germans who use fashionable French expressions.

106. See Aulus Gellius, *The Attic Nights of Aulus Gellius,* vol. 2, trans. J. C. Rolfe, Loeb Classical Library (London: Heinemann, 1948), bk. XI, chap. xii, pp. 325–27; Lucius Annaeus Seneca, "On Benefits," bk. II, chap. xxxiv, pp. 119–21, in Lucius Annaeus Seneca, *Moral Essays,* vol. 3, trans. J. W. Basore, Loeb Classical Library (London: Heinemann, 1935); Quintilian, *The Orator's Education,* vol. 3, ed. and trans. D. Russell, Loeb Classical Library [Cambridge, Mass.: Harvard University Press, 2001], bk. 7.9.

for the place where books are kept; improperly and as a trope it stands for the books kept there. Thus, *arms* properly refer to the tools that we use in war; improperly they mean armed men. *Iron* in the proper sense means a certain kind of metal, but used as a trope it stands for iron weapons.

§36. If each of two meanings is proper, then either one is contained in the other, or neither contains the other.

§37. The former occurs either when the name of the genus is distinguished from that of a particular species—for example, when *women* are distinguished from *virgins;* also, when the terms *adoption* and *family relationship* are understood differently; or when the name of the species is used for an individual, as is the case, for example, when the reference is to a man, a horse, etc.; or when one particular proper name is common to several individuals—for example, if someone who knows several people called Stichus has bequeathed something to Stichus; or when the masculine term includes the feminine (*man* and *horse* are examples); or when a term in its technical sense has a broader meaning than it does in common usage—*death,* for example, etc.

§38. Yet there are an infinite number of cases where there are two different meanings for one term, and neither contains the other. One example is when *gallus* stands for a bird and a human being,[107] *jus* for a food or a certain location,[108] etc. Thus the meaning of *mine* and *yours* is ambiguous in the verse of the poet: "Paulus bought the songs, Paulus recited his songs";[109] "Fabulla swears that the hair she bought is hers."[110]

§39. Sometimes there is also ambiguity in joined words and in the context of speech. This usually is the result of excessive brevity, when the words

---

107. The Latin word *gallus* can mean either "cockerel" or "Frenchman."

108. The Latin word *jus* can mean a particular kind of soup as well as a law court.

109. That is, he claims the songs are his by virtue of his purchase, although they are not his in the sense of having been written by him (Martial, *Epigrams,* vol. 1, trans. W. C. A. Ker, Loeb Classical Library [London: Heinemann, 1930], bk. II, §xx, p. 123).

110. Martial, *Epigrams,* vol. 1, bk. VI, §xii, p. 365.

that made the meaning clear have been left out. For example: "my heir should give a hundredweight of the silver vases chosen to my wife. You will receive a hundred thalers when it is convenient."[111]

§40. Yet, a speech that is burdened and encumbered by abundant and superfluous words can also render the meaning of the words ambiguous or obscure. An example is, if someone bequeathed the estate, as he had been taught to do, and added: "with furnishings and slaves"; or if after the furnishings have been bequeathed, he should superfluously name certain kinds of furnishings out of inexperience; or if someone in making a promise says: "I sing of arms and the man[112] and I pledge."

§41. (5) Muddled speech produces obscurity when interpretation suggests either meaning to be false. But this perplexity can have its origin in the words alone, for example, if someone determines his heirs by saying: "If Titius will be heir, may Sejus be heir. If Sejus will be heir, then may Titius be heir."

§42. Or obscurity stems from chance circumstances. For example, the law says that a woman who has been raped may either choose the rapist's death or to be married to him. A man has ravished two women, of whom one chooses his death, the other marriage. Or let us assume there is a law that a brave soldier should have the right to demand something as a reward. But then there are two brave soldiers who demand the same young woman. Or let us assume there is a law that he who begins an uprising has to suffer punishment, while he who ends it may ask for a reward. The same person began and ended an uprising and seeks a reward. A person making his last will had said: "I legally bequeath my estate to Titius, if the Lex Fal-

111. In the first sentence it is not clear who will choose the silver vessels. The second does not specify whose convenience the conditional clause refers to. The first example is from Quintilian's *Institutio oratoria,* bk. 7.9 (see Quintilian, *The Orator's Education,* vol. 3, p. 285).

112. This is the first line of Virgil's *Aeneid* (see Virgil, *Virgil,* trans. H. Rushton Fairclough, rev. G. P. Goold, Loeb Classical Library [Cambridge, Mass.; Harvard University Press, 1999], p. 263).

cidia does not apply in the case of my last will."[113] This estate was worth a hundred gold coins, but apart from that he had already bequeathed three hundred, and when he died he had less than four hundred. Another person said: "I leave to Titia all my weavers, except for those which I have already bequeathed to someone else; to Plotia I leave all my serfs, except for those that I have already left to someone else." There were, however, servants who were both serfs and weavers.

§43. (6) The incompatibility and conflict of two statements is another cause of obscurity. This incompatibility, however, is first detected in the application of different laws, which do not contradict each other in their wording, to a particular case, which is such that neither law can be applied at the same time. For example, one law says that a statue of the person who kills a tyrant should be put up in the gymnasium. Another law says that there should be no statue of a woman in a gymnasium. Now a woman has killed a tyrant. Another law says: "He who killed a tyrant may demand whatever he wants from the magistrate, and the magistrate should grant it." Another law states that, when the tyrant has been killed, the magistrate should kill his five closest relatives. The tyrant was killed by his own wife, who asks for her son, whom she had with the tyrant, to be spared as a reward. A law says "Nobody should walk about in public bearing arms on a holiday." Another: "Nobody should remain at home once he has heard the signal indicating a public disturbance, but should be at the disposal of the magistrate in the marketplace with his arms." Then a disturbance occurs on a holiday, etc.

§44. As is evident from these examples, this form of incompatibility is particularly close to the previous, final kind of complexity; thus, if we examine the nature of each more carefully, they are perhaps best not considered examples of the obscurity of words and declarative interpretation, for the sake of which we discussed this doctrine in advance. Instead, they are to be considered either cases of subjective obscurity or a matter for another form of interpretation, above all, restrictive interpretation.

113. The Lex Falcidia (Justinian, *Institutes,* 2.22) imposed a limit on the amount of legacies.

§45. This kind of obscurity occurs in particular (and with some frequency) when there is a conflict between two precepts of natural law that have been either republished by God or formulated by human theorists of natural law; or it occurs because of external circumstances that render the meaning of a particular law unclear. A law says that one should give alms. Another, that theft must not be committed. Now, someone has committed a theft in order to give alms. It is said that a favor deserves a favor in return. Your father and a patron who has bestowed immense favors on you are present at the same time, but your affairs are such that you will have to give preference to one over the other, etc.

§46. What is more relevant here is that kind of incompatibility when two propositions appear to be mutually contradictory, even without reference to a particular case, such that one affirms what the other denies (though this seems to be a form common to declarative and restrictive interpretation). This is so if this incompatibility occurs in a single context (for example, if the testator in the same will at times declares someone an heir unconditionally, and sometimes on certain conditions, or if he bequeaths something and then takes it away again; or when Ulpian says somewhere[114] that the father must first name an heir, then appoint a guardian for his son and must not change the order in which this is done, and soon he [Ulpian] adds that the appointment of the guardian is nevertheless valid if someone first appoints a guardian for this son and then names an heir, even though this is the reverse order). Alternatively, this incompatibility may occur in different locations. There are infinite examples of contradictions of this kind in Roman law.

§47. We then need to consider the sources of the conjectures we need in order to remove the obscurity of words. This obscurity is such that it either can be removed with the help of the rules of sound interpretation or does not allow for any remedy.

114. See *Digest* 28.6.2.4 and 28.6.2.5.

§48. In the former case we need to take into account (1) the matter itself
and its nature, with which the legislator or the contracting parties are
concerned. Hence the rule that words are to be understood according to
the underlying subject matter. Related to this is the following principle
of the logicians: predicates have to be compatible with their subjects. Yet
our formulation is broader: we not only judge the predicate according to
the nature of the subject, but sometimes the subject is determined by the
predicate, for example, if we say: "The *canis* sparkles"[115] or "The *gallus*
flies."[116]

§49. The use of this rule, however, extends to all kinds of obscure meaning. We can often quite effectively guess the meaning of words that are
difficult to hear or are written in poorly legible script by taking into consideration the subject matter. So, if I am unsure whether a person I am
speaking to, or who has written to me, wanted to say *merx* [good/com-
modity] or *merces* [wages], we need to assume the former whenever it is
about a sale and the latter if we are discussing a particular job. And if I do
not know whether someone wanted to write *evictum* [evicted] or *edictum*
[edict], the presumption is in favor of the former if it is about trade. But if
the debate concerns the faults of something that has been sold, then it may
well be the case that he wanted to talk about an *edictum*.[117]

§50. Moreover, in the case of obsolete, new, or foreign words the subject
matter sometimes helps to shed some light. Thus, people who learn languages as adults, when they have no teacher and searching in dictionaries
would be very tedious, successfully guess the meaning of an unknown
word from their knowledge of the adjacent words. Thus, for example,
when an author who writes in German, but is used to mixing in French
words, has written: "A person who has married an old but rich woman
for her money, diverts himself with Cato at home." The underlying material indicates he meant that this person was amusing himself with some

115. The Latin word *canis* means both "dog" and the "Dog Star, Sirius."
116. *Gallus* means both "cockerel" and "Frenchman."
117. That is, in this case, a law regulating the sale of goods.

young woman in the household. It does not mean, as someone ineptly and circuitously tried to interpret it, that he amused himself at home by adopting a grim, sulking expression typical of [the ancient Roman statesman] Cato.

§51. Moreover, the subject matter often resolves ambiguity. Thus, if a *library* has been bequeathed, *library* must be presumed to stand for books; if the construction of a *library* has been ordered, *library* must refer to a building. And thus those who have been commanded to put down their *irons* have met this demand when they have laid down their iron weapons. Thus, if someone has been prohibited by a treaty from carrying *arms* into the territory of a third party, this refers to soldiers; if enemies are ordered to hand over their *arms,* this refers to the instruments of warfare.

§52. Sometimes the subject matter also indicates whether someone intended to use a word in the broader or stricter sense. For example, in feudal matters the term *heir* stands for the male heirs, not for any allodial heirs, etc.[118]

§53. If it is said, therefore, that a Frenchman [*Gallus*] conquered a province, it is clear that we are speaking about a human being, not the bird. So, when I have said, "Here is my book," there is no doubt that I have acquired ownership of it. But if someone speaks of "his hair," this usually means that he has not acquired it elsewhere, etc.

§54. Thus, in the above example[119]—my heir should give a hundredweight of the silver vases chosen to my wife—the extreme brevity of the expression (which the testator could have avoided if he had said "which he" or "which she had chosen") has caused obscurity; the subject matter and the purpose of the inheritance, among other things, show that the decision should be made in favor of the wife, not the heir.

---

118. Allodial ownership is absolute, unlike feudal ownership.
119. See §39 in this chapter.

§55. The subject matter is also important if ambiguity is caused by an abundance of terms. If, for example, someone has promised the furnishings and at the same time lists certain kinds [of furnishings], but not all, I would think that (abstracting from all other circumstances) only the furnishings that are listed are owed—if the promise is gratuitous; but if the promise is onerous, in exchange for something, then [it is to be assumed that] the other furnishings are owed too.

§56. We shall now have to think about further examples, where this rule helps in interpreting muddled or contradictory speech. What we have put forward so far will be sufficient evidence.

§57. There is another rule that is related to this first one and appears to be included in it. The learned usually refer to it separately; they say that it is based on the context of the relevant passage: "in the interpretation of every speech one must pay attention to the preceding and subsequent passages; what lies between them is assumed to be adapted to and to relate to these." Here Celsus's warning is pertinent: it is harsh to judge or respond unless we take into account the entire law; we must not draw on one small snippet of it.[120]

§58. For the context is to be taken into account, so that it is clear what the underlying subject matter is.

§59. If we think about this a little further, it will be evident that a conjecture based on the subject matter is only similar to a conjecture based on related passages; the two are, however, not identical, since the rule concerning the subject matter can apply even when there are no preceding or subsequent passages; and the rule concerning context can be used even without taking the subject matter into account. Take, for example, the case when either of two meanings of an ambiguous term squares with the underlying subject matter or if the text does not seem to make any sense at all.

---

120. *Digest* 1.3.24. Celsus was a Roman jurist in the second century A.D.

§60. An example of the former is when I say: "The *gallus* is cooking"; and an example of the latter, if for example the legal text of a stipulation declares that the second person gave a pledge promising the first person some grain. In the preface, however, it is mentioned that the transaction between the contracting parties concerned ten bushels.

§61. Therefore (2) there is this general rule, which is based on the use of context: "Obscure phrases are to be explained using the statements of the same author that are clearly expressed elsewhere or in the same place, that is, in the preceding or subsequent passages (which are linked by their proximity) or in other passages by the same author which are formulated at another time." These are described as linked by their common origin. An example is if I left someone a third of my house in my will and then wrote in the codicil: "I bequeath to Titius one hundred coins, apart from the share in the house."

§62. I believe that the usefulness of this rule extends to any kind of obscure meaning, including obsolete, new, foreign, cryptic, and conflicting words, whenever they can be explained. I believe this principle also applies to the following rules, and it is enough to have said so once.

§63. (3) Another rule is based on the effect of the words. This states that words are to be explained in such a way that their effect does not undermine the matter at hand, and that the effect they have does not lead to some absurdity. This would, for example, be the case if the explanation conflicted with human or divine law.

§64. Thus the Athenians caviled when they promised in a treaty to give up the lands of the Boethians and then denied that the lands were those of the Boethians since they [the Athenians] had occupied them with their army. Similarly, when the law threatens harsh punishments to anyone who draws blood in the street, it would be absurd for a barber to be punished for opening another person's vein in the street. The same rule serves to resolve the controversy between Protagoras and Evathlus in favor of

Protagoras.[121] The case of the person who wanted to free Cratinus when he only had a slave called Cratistus is relevant here too.[122]

§65. (4) The disposition of the person is also very important in interpretation. From this is derived the rule that obscure words are interpreted on the basis of the disposition of each person. If, therefore, someone established Titius as his heir, and there are several persons called Titius, then that Titius will be the heir whom the deceased evidently loved most.

§66. (5) Related to this preceding rule is the conjecture that is derived from the quality of the person. For very often words are to be explained according to the condition or rank of the person who is speaking or to whom the speech is addressed.

§67. Thus, if a scholar left someone all his papers, that includes the books, though normally books are not included in the term *papers* in the proper sense. If someone promised a dowry or left another person an income, this will have to be determined according to the condition and rank of the person to whom this was left or promised.

§68. (6) Above all, the reason for the law or agreement must be taken into consideration. Therefore, that interpretation of a law should be adopted

---

121. Evathlus was a disciple of the Athenian orator Protagoras. They made an agreement that Evathlus should pay Protagoras a certain sum as soon as Evathlus had learned enough to win a case in court. After a certain time Protagoras judged his pupil to have reached that level and demanded the agreed-upon sum. When Evathlus refused, Protagoras took him to court, saying that Evathlus would have to pay him, no matter what the outcome of the case: If Protagoras won the case, he would be paid the agreed-upon sum; if he lost, then Evathlus would have won a court case and would thus be obliged to pay the fee to Protagoras. Evathlus replied that, on the contrary, Protagoras would certainly not be paid: Either the judges would find in favor of Evathlus, in which case Evathlus would not feel obliged to pay; or if Evathlus lost his case, he would not be obliged to pay the agreed-upon sum because the condition of the contract had not been met. The case is mentioned in Diogenes Laertius, *Lives of the Philosophers,* bk. IX, chap. 56 (see Diogenes Laertius, *Lives of Eminent Philosophers,* vol. 2, trans. R. D. Hicks, Loeb Classical Library [London: William Heinemann, 1925], p. 469).

122. See §22 in this chapter.

which accords with the reason of the law, and that which is out of tune with it must be rejected.

§69. Moreover, the reason for the law is twofold: one is the reason that caused the legislator to make a law; the other reason is his intention in making the law.

§70. The intention of the legislator is usually, if not always, directly contrary to the cause that impels him to make this law. And so it is obvious that we must look to both when applying this rule.

§71. When farmers, therefore, were prevented from gathering the harvest because of their duties in law courts, this provided the Romans with the occasion for introducing holidays at harvest time; the intention was that these impediments should cease.

§72. Similarly, the high price of food, or the prince's fear of it, may cause him to ban the export of grain; the intention is to prevent high food prices.

§73. The fact that a law is often applied to a case that has nothing to do with the occasion for the law is no obstacle. Thus, the holidays at harvest time also benefit those who have nothing to do with the harvest.

§74. You have to remember that in this and the other rules we are speaking of conjectures about the tacit will of the legislator. These conjectures cease to apply whenever the express words of the law state something different, as in the above matter concerning the holidays during harvest time.

§75. There may be other circumstances which suggest that we need to go beyond the intention of the legislator or the occasion for the law when we interpret it. This might be in order to avoid the increase in lawsuits or for whatever other similar reasons there may be. Such circumstances are not to be neglected; one conjecture must be balanced against another.

§76. Thus, usufruct was invented so that bequests would not be destroyed, but after it had been invented, it was not inappropriate to believe that it could also be established among the living by way of agreement.

§77. But this is also clear from the fact that Roman law rules that a deficient cause of a legacy does not automatically render the legacy null and void; and yet there are cases in which the same laws have allowed a legacy to be rendered null and void because of a deficient cause. To remove this apparent conflict, or rather to show the difference between these two [cases], most learned jurists propose a rather clever distinction between an impulsive and a final deficient cause, implying that the absence of the latter, but not the former, undermines the legacy. But there are other, very different reasons to be put forward here.

§78. The testator, for example, might say: "I give Titius one hundred because he took care of my affairs." Imagine that this is a case of a deficient cause.[123] Then what will you achieve with the help of this distinction? Will the legacy be valid to a greater or lesser degree? For if the cause had been true, then taking care of his affairs would have been the impulsive cause, while the reward for doing so was the final cause. And thus in similar cases these two types of causes occur simultaneously.

§79. However, we must not confuse these two reasons for laws and pacts with the reasons that jurists use in demonstrating particular conclusions on the basis of more general laws—for example, when the reason for saying that the child of a female servant is not a fruit [of slave ownership], because fruits are created for the sake of other humans, or as is said more correctly and circumspectly elsewhere, because female servants are not bought in order to bring forth children, etc.

§80. For (1) we are at present concerned with the reason of a law or pact that requires interpretation, not with the reason justifying an interpretation that has already been put forward. (2) We are concerned with an

---

123. That is, Titius did not take care of the legator's affairs.

interpretation that rests on topical and probable arguments, not with an interpretation that is, so to speak, demonstrative and derives particular conclusions from a general axiom (for example, that usufruct is established in order for the usufructuary to benefit from all fruits, for the sake of which something is usually acquired).

§81. If, therefore, the reason for a law or pact has been inserted into the law or pact itself, then the interpretation will not be that difficult. But very often this reason will be concealed. Hence, new conjectures are necessary to elicit the reason before an appropriate interpretation is possible.

§82. It does not appear to be possible to use rules to identify these conjectures because of the infinite variety of circumstances that occur here and because the variety of these conjectures is also infinite.

§83. Examining them successfully requires political prudence when the interpretation of public laws and pacts is involved. When the agreements of private persons are concerned, it requires great economic prudence, or, if we may say so, commercial prudence in the interpreter. This prudence cannot be acquired in academies and schools, but is the result of polite and familiar social intercourse with those who know about these matters.

§84. A great help in interpreting public and private pacts is, above all, erudition that is based on the diligent reading of histories, as well as specific knowledge of what preceded particular pacts or treaties. It is, therefore, in the interests of the parties to a treaty, who sign, for example, a peace treaty in good faith, to make the terms of the peace settlement publicly known.

§85. This is enough on declarative interpretation: we must not neglect the other two forms of interpretation, namely, extensive and restrictive interpretation. As far as extensive interpretation is concerned, the first five rules we provided for declarative interpretation will rarely, if ever, be applicable, while the rule we have just explained, concerning the reason of the law, is common to all three forms of interpretation.

§86. If we are discussing the means of removing any kind of obscurity, we need to retain the meaning of the obscure word or phrase that conforms most closely to the reason for the law.[124] This is especially useful if a term has two meanings, one broader, the other stricter. Hence, if, for example, the prince has banned the export of grain, the term *grain* covers either all types of cereals or only wheat or some other kind of grain. That depends on whether a high price, which was the prince's reason for making this law, is feared for all or only some kinds of grain.

§87. Yet even if the words of a law or pact are perspicuous and not ambiguous, then very often new cases emerge that may or may not be covered by the words of the laws, but concerning which there may be reason to doubt whether the law should be applied to them or not.

§88. Here we must draw almost exclusively on the reason behind the law. Extensive interpretation, therefore, usually rests on this rule: "Where the reason is the same, there the same law applies." Or: "The effect of identical reasons is that the law and the pact must be applied to similar cases that are not explicitly included in their wording."

§89. It must, however, be the same reason, not just a similar one. This is so even if the new cases are only similar but not identical to the cases covered by the wording of the law.

§90. But there is often more than one reason for passing a law, and according to the established opinion of philosophers a single thing can have several purposes, which either are all equally important, or one of which is the primary purpose while the others are secondary. It is, therefore, not universally necessary for the reason on which the extensive interpretation is based to be the only reason for the law.

§91. That will only be the case when the legislator had only one end in view.

---

124. This sentence was added in later editions (see German edition, Halle, 1709).

§92. If a single law has several reasons and these are equally important, it follows that all are to be considered together in extending the law, to avoid the mistake of separating them from each other. This is no different from natural phenomena, where all causes are required for a certain effect to be produced.

§93. But if one of these is the most important, I should think it is enough, if it alone is applicable to a similar case.

§94. In one word: the cause that justifies the extension of the law must be valid, and the legislator must have considered this cause in its general sense, so that he would have wanted to apply it to the present case, too, if he had foreseen it or thought of it. And this is so because otherwise the law would be useless or unfair.

§95. Thus, if a law prohibits accepting a plough as a surety, it will not be permitted to accept a ploughshare either. If the law commands that he who killed his father be sewn up in a leather sack, then he who killed his mother will be sewn up, too. If it is not allowed to drag someone away from his house before a court of justice, then it will not be allowed in the case of tents either. If an agreement exists between neighboring peoples not to surround a location within a certain distance with walls, then they cannot fortify this location with a rampart either if the reason for the ban is that this location should not be suitable for defense against military force. And if someone orders in his last will that Titius be his heir, if his posthumous son (whom he expected to be born) dies, then Titius will be heir even if it happens that no posthumous son was born to the testator.

§96. The elegant problem proposed by Lucian is relevant here. The law says that the murderer of a tyrant receives a reward. Someone entered the castle to kill the tyrant. He did not find the tyrant, but only his son, whom he killed, leaving the sword in the wound. Soon afterward the tyrant came and saw his son had been murdered. Out of grief he killed himself with the assassin's sword. And so he who had killed the son of the tyrant claimed the reward due to a tyrannicide.[125]

§97. Lucian defended the case of the person seeking the reward with an argument that deserves to be taken seriously—that generally the same reasoning is held to apply to the person who killed and the person who caused death.

§98. But Erasmus of Rotterdam, in a speech for the opposing side, came up with an argument that implied the injustice of the demand. This is not as concise as Lucian's, but the erudite exposition of various rules of good interpretation which are applicable to the present matter can easily compensate for the tedium that is the result of prolixity.[126]

§99. His [Erasmus's] opinion is more pleasing, especially because he demonstrates at greater length that this deed of the pretended tyrannicide is not to be regarded in any way as the true and moral cause of the tyrant's death.

§100. You see from the above examples that extensive interpretation has a place in both affirmative and prohibitive laws. Their main use is in preventing caviling and fraud, which are used by wicked people in order to evade the rules of law.

§101. Thus, a jurist drew a useful distinction by saying that a person acted against the law if he did that which was contrary to the words of the law (and the reason corresponding to these words); whereas he who acted contrary to the intention of the legislator, but did not violate the letter of the law, committed fraud in relation to the law.[127]

---

125. See Lucian, "The Tyrannicide," p. 445, in Lucian, *Lucian,* vol. 5, trans. A. M. Harmon, Loeb Classical Library (London: Heinemann, 1936).

126. See Erasmus of Rotterdam, "The Tyrannicide," in Desiderius Erasmus, *The Collected Works of Erasmus,* ed. E. Fantham and E. Rummel, with the assistance of J. Ijsewijn (Toronto, Buffalo, London: University of Toronto Press, 1989), 29:77–123.

127. This is the ancient Roman jurist Julius Paulus (flourished ca. A.D. 210). See *Digest* 1.3.29.

§102. In general, however, the doctors of law distinguish between four kinds of fraud. The first is the result of exchanging one thing for another—if, for example, the law forbids lending money to the son of the family but the usurer lends him grain, wine, etc., and, similarly, if the prince forbids exporting grain or wool and someone exports flour or sheep. The second is based on substituting one person for another—if, for example, spouses, who are not allowed to present gifts to each other, substitute other persons, who then present gifts to the spouses. The third is the result of substituting a different contract—for example, if the same spouses [rather than presenting gifts to each other] sell each other precious objects for a single coin, or if a lender sells something to the son of the family when he is supposed to lend it. The fourth, finally, is the result of changing the form of a contract—if, for example, a woman who is not allowed to be a guarantor even when she is willing to act as such for someone else takes out a loan on behalf of this other person. This form, however, seems little different from the third, and we need to think further if there are not more ways to be found in which the law can be violated through fraud.

§103. Restrictive interpretation remains. Grotius says that this is to be sought in a defect in the original intention or a new case that conflicts with this intention.[128] He claims that the first is the result of an absurdity, a failure of reasoning, or a fault in the subject matter. The latter occurs either because of some natural reason—for example, if equity or humanity requires us to diverge [from the letter of the law]—or because of some other indication of intention. This is evidently so if words elsewhere appear to conflict with the present law or pact in a particular case, etc.[129]

§104. We do not on the whole disagree with these conclusions themselves, but the method and the reasoning seem a little obscure, and in a certain respect to produce confusion. All interpretation must be based on the probable intention of the person who spoke, and that is not the intention

128. Grotius, *The Rights of War and Peace*, bk. II, chap. xvi, §22.
129. This paragraph is shortened and modified slightly in later editions.

he had some time before or may have some time after speaking. It follows automatically that restrictive interpretation must always be founded on a defect in the original intention, not on the subsequent incompatibility of a new case with the intention (to the extent that this is distinct from a defect in the original intention).

§105. Restrictive interpretation implies that the legislator said more than he meant and did not consider the case in question. Thus, it always presupposes a new case opposed to the intention of the speaker, and again I do not see how the original defect in the intention can be different from the incompatibility of a new case with it. We shall, therefore, see whether the question cannot be set out more conveniently.

§106. Extensive interpretation only takes into account the reason for the law or agreement. Restrictive interpretation, however, also allows for the other rules of interpretation. So (1) what we have said above concerning the underlying subject matter also applies here, since the speaker is always believed to have had this in mind, even if the words appear to be more widely applicable.

§107. Thus, if a fief has been granted to someone and his male descendants, then this is not taken to include his grandchildren from his daughter because that contradicts the nature of such a fief, which clearly excludes women and their descendants.

§108. And when a patron is banned from forcing a freedman to swear not to marry, then the underlying subject matter shows that this is to be understood of a freedman who can have children. Therefore, a patron who has demanded this oath from a castrated freedman is not punished.

§109. Then (2) the rule we pointed out above, that words are not to be interpreted in such a way that they have either no effect or an absurd and inequitable effect, has its uses even in restrictive interpretation. For nobody of sound mind may be thought to have intended something absurd.

§110. Take the following law: "A courageous man may have what he demands." If someone who has achieved feats of courage demands the land of a fellow citizen, who, however, after some time demands his land back as a reward for his courage, then the need to avoid absurdity implies that the law be explained in such a way that courageous men may not have their rewards taken from them.

§111. That is also the basis for resolving the controversy between Protagoras and Evathlus: the latter, after being condemned by the judges to pay [Protagoras's] wages, could not have protected himself by appealing to the agreement. According to this it had been agreed that the teacher was owed the wages when the student's law case was not successful. It would be absurd for someone to have agreed to something which would have made it more difficult for him to obtain what was owed to him on the basis of that agreement.

§112. The interpretation of law according to equity is relevant here. This is the correction of law when it is deficient because of its universality, and when it is shown on the basis of natural reason that a certain particular case is not comprehended in a universal law, because if you followed the letter of the law precisely then it could contradict natural and divine laws. That is deservedly considered absurd, since nobody can be obliged to something like this.

§113. Thus, a law may command that a foreigner who has climbed onto the city walls be punished with death, and then a foreigner climbs onto the city walls during a siege and repels the enemy who is scaling the ladder. Or a law orders that women are to be kept away from a certain place on pain of death; then they [women] enter this place in order to extinguish a fire. All punishment will then cease because the law of nature says that a good deed deserves a reward, not punishment.

§114. Grotius argues that this is also true even when it is not totally illicit to stick to the words, but when doing so seems too grave and intolerable to someone who examines the matter fairly—either by considering the condition of human nature in an absolute sense or by comparing the person and the matter in question with the actual purpose of the action.[130]

§115. Thus, he who lent another something for a certain number of days could demand it back earlier if he should have great need of it. If someone promises to help an ally, he will be excused if he is threatened at home and requires his troops. The concession of immunity from taxes and tributes is to be understood of payments that are made every day or annually, not those that supreme necessity demands and without which the commonwealth cannot exist.

§116. Yet I should think that these conclusions could be derived more clearly from the rule concerning the underlying subject matter. Indeed, Grotius himself tried to explain them on the grounds that the nature of beneficial acts is such that one should not assume anyone to have wanted to bind himself to suffer a great inconvenience.

§117. A case that can be more conveniently related to the point in question is if words from a different passage do not perhaps directly conflict with the relevant law or agreement, but cannot be observed at the same time as the law or agreement because of some circumstance at that particular moment. Then one will have to be restricted for the sake of the other. Otherwise, neither would have any effect, which would be absurd.

§118. But the question is which of the two must give way to the other. Generally it seems that the following rule must be observed because laws restrict human liberty and one does so to a greater degree than the other: "That law which binds the human will more closely should be preferred to that which imposes a less strict obligation."

§119. The specific rules listed by the doctors of jurisprudence are relevant here. (1) A permission gives way to a prohibition. The reason is obvious

---

130. Grotius, *The Rights of War and Peace,* bk. II, chap. xvi, §26.

because what is permitted clearly does not impose an obligation. We already noted at the beginning that permission is not properly speaking an effect of law.

§120. So if a law says that every Roman citizen is free to have a concubine, and another law declares that a soldier is not allowed to have a woman with him in a military camp, it is evident that the permission in the first law does not apply to the soldier.

§121. (2) What is commanded gives way to that which is prohibited. For the freedom of the human will is restricted within narrower bounds by negative precepts than by affirmative precepts, as we have shown above. For what is forbidden can be avoided at all times, but what is commanded can be put into action only at certain times.

§122. Thus, it reflects a preposterous sense of duty to steal leather and then give shoes to paupers instead of alms, though this example is more relevant to the fourth rule. You will get a more suitable example if you change it slightly as follows: "It is forbidden to steal in order to repay your creditor."

§123. The reason we referred to in the previous rule is also applicable in cases other than the conflict of a negative with an affirmative precept. Therefore (3) that which must be done at a certain time is to be preferred to that which can be done at any time.

§124. Thus the observance of the Sabbath takes precedence before daily duties. The reason again is that a precept relating to a certain point in time is more strictly binding at that time than another.

§125. If, however, two duties conflict so that either both must be fulfilled at that time or neither of the two can be postponed easily, then (4) the imperfect obligation gives way to the perfect obligation. For since a perfect obligation is greater in degree, it is also believed to bind our freedom more strongly.

§126. Thus, the repayment of debts takes precedence over the giving of alms.

§127. If each of two obligations is perfect, then (5) the more ancient obligation takes precedence over the newer since my liberty was already restricted by the older obligation at the time that the new obligation was imposed. Thus, an older debt should be repaid first.

§128. That is, unless a perfect obligation is linked to another, imperfect obligation with respect to the same person to whom I have the obligation, for then (6) the twofold obligation triumphs over the simple and more ancient obligation because of the rule, which everybody knows, that a twofold obligation binds more strongly.

§129. Thus, a more recent debt to a poor man is to be paid before another, older one to a rich man.

§130. If either obligation is imperfect, then (7) the law of beneficence gives way to the law of gratitude, because, as we have said above, in the latter case a person is under an obligation to show gratitude on two grounds: common humanity and the acceptance of a favor. Thus, here too there is a twofold obligation.

§131. Thus, if you have to choose between a poor patron and another poor person, even a relative, then the patron must take precedence.

§132. But this is only the case if both are poor. For if a wealthy patron wants a present from me and the beggar asks for alms, then the beggar takes precedence before the patron because the greater the poverty of the person who requires me to perform the duties of humanity, the closer does my obligation come to being perfect, as we have said above. In that case, therefore, we need to return to the fourth rule.

§133. It is, therefore, clear what is to be done if my father and my son come to me at the same time to ask for maintenance. For I decide as follows: as long as the son is not yet grown-up, he is to be preferred to the father, because I am under a perfect obligation toward him but under an imperfect obligation toward my father. If, however, the son is already grown-up, he is to take second place to the father, because the father is owed gratitude, etc.

§134. But if several people who have not granted me any favors demand a favor from me, then (8) the closer the relationship we have with another person, the more do the duties we owe to them outweigh the duties to others. The reason again is contained in the thesis: the wife takes precedence before the brother, the brother before the uncle, etc.

§135. In general, the rules we have listed so far appear to be limited by the following: (9) in the case of laws that are made by subordinate powers, the law of the inferior power gives way to that of the superior power wherever it is impossible to meet the requirements of both. Thus, God is to be obeyed rather than humans, and the commands of kings outweigh those of heads of families.

§136. (10) Other things being equal, the law that is more specific and more closely related to the matter at hand is preferred to the more general, since general precepts are directed to something by specific precepts.

§137. (11) A law is preferred to another insofar as its subject matter is superior to that of the other on the grounds of its nobility, utility, or necessity. For it is silently understood that the inferior obligation is to be fulfilled only if it is compatible with the more important obligation.

§138. Let us assume there are two laws. One says that nobody should carry arms in public on a holiday. Another states that nobody should stay at home if there is an alarm but should present himself armed to the magistrate in the market square. If there is an alarm on a holiday, then the latter law represents an exception to the former, of the following kind: "Nobody should carry arms in public on a holiday unless he is called out by the magistrate because of an alarm."

§139. Grotius lists several similar rules. Yet these are not as obvious, and there are reasons to have some doubts about them. One example is the following: "The prohibition that includes a penalty is to be preferred to that without a penalty, and that which carries a greater penalty is to be preferred to that which has a lesser."[131]

§140. For just as a prohibition without a threat of punishment seems pointless, so the rule that of two evils the lesser is to be chosen is not applicable to moral evils.

§141. Thus, Grotius's statement that if two agreements, one upon oath, the other not, clash and interfere with each other, then the former shall be preferred to the latter, reflects his belief that an oath adds a new obligation to a promise, a belief which we have already refuted above.[132]

§142. Finally, when he concludes that what was said last must prevail,[133] that is not a matter for restrictive interpretation and a case where two laws only seem to be in conflict, but a case when all interpretation ceases and there is a true antinomy.[134]

§143. The rules on avoiding absurdity and iniquity in restrictive interpretation are sufficient to show this. (3)[135] Finally, the reason for the law is of great importance in restricting the general words of a law. Hence the common axiom: "If the reason for the law ceases, so does the effect of the law itself."

§144. As in the case of extensive interpretation above, so here too we need to distinguish whether there are one or several reasons for a law or agreement. If there is only one, then there is no doubt that the law must be restricted when that reason ceases.

---

131. Grotius, *The Rights of War and Peace,* bk. II, chap. xvi, §29.
132. Ibid.
133. Ibid.
134. That is, a contradiction between two equally binding laws.
135. Points (1) and (2) are found in §§106 and 109 in this chapter.

§145. But when there are several reasons for a law and one of them ceases, the others do not immediately expire and are not necessarily less able to sustain the efficacy of the law: sometimes, however, the law is restricted if only one reason is lacking.

§146. There can be no question that if a law or agreement has several reasons, each of which is equally essential, it will be enough if only one of them does not apply: the law will then have to be restricted.

§147. It is, therefore, likelier that right reason will suggest a narrow rather than an extensive interpretation. Indeed, as in all matters, it is enough for one cause to be missing for an effect not to be produced; and for the effect to occur, all causes have to be present together. In actions that produce an obligation it is therefore enough if one essential cause is missing for the interpretation to be restricted, whereas all causes have to be present to permit an extension [of the obligation to another case].

§148. If one out of several reasons is the principal reason and the others are secondary, then the interpreter must not refrain from restricting the applicability of the law if only the former ceases to be true, even if some of the latter can be applied to the case in question. But if one of the latter ceases, then there will be no need for a restrictive interpretation, as long as the principal reason is still valid.[136]

§149. The following will provide an example of restrictive interpretation on the grounds that the reason of the law does not apply. A law says that they who have deserted a ship because of a storm should lose everything [i.e., that they left on board]; those who remained on board become owners of the ship and everything on it. Assuming that because of the strength of the storm the entire crew deserted the ship and climbed into the rowboat, except for one person, who was so ill that he could not escape. By accident the ship is carried into a port unharmed. The sick man is in possession of the ship, but the original owner demands that it be returned.

---

136. This sentence is not in the first edition of the *Institutes* but was added later.

§150. Here the reason for the law was that he who risked his life to save the ship should be rewarded in some way. The sick man cannot pretend to have done so, since he did not stay on board for that purpose and did not contribute anything to saving the vessel.

§151. We should, however, note a few limitations to our rule. (1) It often happens that the reason for a law is not only unknown, but also such that some general rule of equity appears to suggest something different. If, however, the will of the superior has made itself clear on that matter, then it is right that subjects be ordered to accept this will as a reason that is sufficient to produce an obligation, until the prince who alone has the power to do so corrects the law on the basis of equity.

§152. (2) Finally, our rule [that a law ceases when its reason ceases] will only apply if its reason ceases to be true universally, that is, in other similar and common cases, not in specific, very rare instances.

§153. For example, a law says that a person under a certain age may not draw up a last will. The reason is that he lacks the required judgment. Let us assume that there is someone who has sufficient prudence before he has become an adult. The question is whether he is allowed to draw up a testament. The answer is no.

§154. Another example: a law says that the goods of minors may not be alienated unless there is a necessity to do so, and this has been introduced to protect them from being deprived of their possessions without due care. There is a case in which it is useful but not necessary for the minor to sell something. The question is whether the judge may be allowed to do so. The answer is no.

§155. Closely related to the previous observation is the following: (3) The reason for the law does not necessarily cease if its actual consequence ceases; if the potential consequence is still there, that is enough to prevent a restrictive interpretation.

§156. That is, a law or agreement in which the legislator or the contracting parties have a particular reason in mind (say, the avoidance of a danger or some inconvenience) is not only valid in those cases when this [i.e., the danger or inconvenience] would actually follow, but also in those in which it is believed that this danger or inconvenience is likely to occur or could at least occur without great difficulty.

§157. Thus, if the law says that nobody should walk through the streets at night with torches, it is no excuse if someone claims he will use them with such circumspection that nobody will suffer any harm.

§158. And if a treaty between two nations says that an army or fleet may not be led to a certain location, and the purpose is to prevent actual harm being done to someone, then it will not be permitted to lead an army or fleet to that location even if there is no intention of causing harm. For it is enough that the person who is at this location could easily inflict harm on the other.

§159. We nearly forgot to mention the rule which is very widely used and commonly believed to be very far-reaching, and which therefore has a place in every kind of interpretation: that is, the rule resting on the division of matters into favorable and disagreeable.

§160. As far as declarative interpretation is concerned, nothing is better known than the common saying that what is favorable is to be interpreted more broadly, what is disagreeable more strictly.[137]

§161. This is quite similar to the rule that what is favorable is to be interpreted broadly, what is disagreeable narrowly, without making this a case of extensive and restrictive interpretation.

---

137. See Grotius, *The Rights of War and Peace,* bk. II, chap. xvi, §10, and Pufendorf, *Of the Law of Nature and Nations,* bk. V, chap. xii, §§12ff.

§162. I do not know, however, whether this rule is as useful as it is commonly believed to be, and whether it is not more appropriate if we stick to the existing rules and do not complicate matters unnecessarily.

§163. For if you first examine the foundation of this rule, it depends on the classification of the subject matter we are talking about. So there is no reason why you should not be able to refer this to the rule concerning subject matter, namely that words are to be understood according to the underlying subject matter.

§164. If you then ask what is favorable and what is disagreeable, you will notice that the opinions of the learned vary rather a lot. Grotius distinguishes three kinds of promises: favorable, disagreeable, and mixed or middle ones.[138]

§165. He calls those favorable that involve an equal exchange and that take into account common utility. The greater and the more obvious this utility is, the greater, he says, is the benefit contained in the promise. Therefore, the benefit contained in those promises that are made for peace is greater than in those made for war, and the benefit involved in a war for the sake of protection is greater than that in a war undertaken for other reasons.

§166. He declares those to be disagreeable that burden one party more than the other, impose a punishment, render actions void, or detract something from what went before.

§167. If it is mixed—for example, if a person changes an earlier promise, but does so for the sake of peace—then this is to be considered either favorable or disagreeable depending on the magnitude of the good and the change. Other things being equal, however, the benefit is to be considered more important.

---

138. Grotius, *The Rights of War and Peace,* bk. II, chap. xvi, §10.

§168. Also, given that Grotius uses this distinction in the case of promises, it may seem doubtful whether it applies to the interpretation of laws, too. Indeed, Grotius's statement about equality and inequality cannot be applied to laws, which are always imposed on inferiors [i.e., subjects]. And yet there is nothing more common than for jurists to extend this rule to laws, for example, when they argue that favors conferred by the prince are to be interpreted broadly, penal laws narrowly, and statutes and all laws that derogate a general law only admit a restrictive interpretation.

§169. Second, you will not be able to find any human affairs that you could call entirely favorable or disagreeable, since these terms do not describe the essential nature of a thing, but its relation to the benefit or harm that humans receive from it; but what is harmful to one person may be useful to another. And if one and the same thing were beneficial to several people, then no conflict would arise between them, and there would be no need to interpret the law or agreement in order to remove such a contradiction.

§170. Third, although Grotius was concerned with providing specific rules on distinguishing the favorable from the disagreeable [in agreements], I fear that these are not very weighty if you abstract from the rules that we have provided above. Take the rules on what is favorable: what if it is agreed in a peace treaty to return captives of either side, and one side, which holds far more captives, wants to exchange captives individually while the other wants to exchange all captives on one side for all on the other. Then, based on Grotius's comments, the latter claims that the exchange is a favorable matter since it is intended to make peace, and that therefore the formulation is to be interpreted broadly. The former, however, will insist that this would be an unfair treaty because it burdened one side more than the other and therefore was not beneficial.

§171. Then let us imagine there is a law that prohibits the export of grain and decrees a severe punishment for any exporter, and someone has exported flour. If someone wants to apply the rule concerning what is favorable and disagreeable, it is easy to see that according to it the exporter should not be punished because this law is to be considered disagreeable according to Grotius's opinion. This is so not only because it restricts the previous freedom [to export], but also because it contains a punishment. Yet it is clear that this law is applicable to the present case because its reason is relevant.

§172. It is well known that in Roman law the solution of ambiguous cases was often based on the benefit involved; examples are cases concerning personal liberty or dowries. But here either one of the preceding rules is taken into account, or this [favorable] decision is made on the basis of civil law, which defines what is to be considered favorable. If it had not done so, the matter could not have been resolved. We, however, are concerned with rules of interpretation that are only derived from right reason.

§173. Fourth, Grotius's rules on the use of what is favorable, in sum, are as follows: (1) In matters that are not disagreeable, that is, as I understand it, in those that are mixed, words are to be understood in their most common meaning. (2) In favorable matters, if an expert is speaking, the words can be understood in the sense peculiar to experts, but not in a contrived sense, unless this is to avoid absurdity and iniquity. (3) In disagreeable matters figurative speech is admissible to some degree for the sake of avoiding onerous implications. Grotius only produces one or two examples for each of these, which is not sufficient evidence for saying that they are universally true. There are many instances when these rules are not sufficient to clarify expressions with doubtful or obscure meanings; or even if the application of these rules does not conflict with right reason, it is possible to solve the problem without these rules concerning the underlying subject matter, effect, reason, etc.

§174. Thus while Roman law granted a legal action to someone who was deprived of his possessions, Grotius is right to say that this also applied to someone who was prevented by force from taking possession of his belongings. However, this is not on the basis of the first rule, concerning matters that are not disagreeable, but on the basis of the reason for the law, because Roman law thereby wanted to restrain all use of illegitimate force by private persons.

§175. Caligula,[139] for example, denied the right of citizenship to the grand-children of those people who had acquired it for themselves and their descendants, and claimed that only the first generation of descendants had been included. In this case there is no need to resort to Grotius's first rule to demonstrate the iniquity of Caligula. It is enough to point out that the term *descendants* is clear, and Caligula lacked all reason for a restrictive interpretation.

§176. Similarly, I would not want to defend the deed of Aurelian by referring to the final rule concerning what is disagreeable; when he went forth to wage war in the East, he promised the people crowns weighing two pounds if he returned victorious. On his return, however, he gave everyone crowns made of bread.[140] For that was a clear case of caviling, though the people cannot be excused for their stupidity in hoping for gold crowns.

§177. What we have said so far applies to the kind of obscurity that can be overcome and explained in a legitimate way by applying the art of correct interpretation. In other cases, which are so obscure that they leave the human intellect no possibility of discerning the meaning, the interpreter's efforts will be wasted.

§178. If, for example, someone evidently says something without any meaning at all, or if what has been written is not legible, then it is impossible to examine it or understand what it means.[141]

---

139. Roman emperor from A.D. 37 to 41.

140. See the life of Aurelian in the *Historia Augusta* ("Divus Aurelianus," xxxv.1, p. 1006, in *Histoire Auguste*).

141. Rebhahn, *De interpretatione juris obscuri*, thesis 43; see also *Digest* 33.10.7; 21.1.9; 28.4.1; 34.8.2.

§179. It is a similar case if no conjecture concerning the will is possible: if, for example, the person making a will gave his children Titius as a guardian, but there are two persons called Titius, father and son, and it is not apparent whom he meant, then neither will be guardian. Or if someone said, "If Stichus will not be the heir, then he should be free and the heir," then this substitution [of Stichus for himself] will not be valid.[142]

§180. Or if the will of the speaker cannot produce any result, as is the case in truly muddled cases such as the one above concerning Stichus's replacement by himself.

§181. Thus, Julian wrote that it was useless, because muddled, to say "if Titius will be heir, then may Seius be the heir; if Seius will be heir, let Titius be the heir," since the condition could not be fulfilled.[143]

§182. However, pace Julian, it seems to me not that the person making the will wanted neither of the two to be the heir, as Julian understood it, but that he wanted neither to be the heir without the other, just as if he had said, "Titius and Sejus are to be heirs; if one of them will not be heir, then the other one should not be heir either."

§183. For since the formulation admits of this interpretation, we think it is to be preferred to the exposition by Julian, because it conforms more closely to the rule concerning the effect, which we have emphasized above.

§184. What appears to be more relevant here is the famous example of the agreement between Paris and Menelaus. The agreement was that Helen be given to the victor. When this agreement was repeated before the fight, it was said that he who killed the other should have Helen. Paris succumbed and saved himself by fleeing. Menelaus demanded that Helen be granted to him as victor, but Paris contradicted him, saying that he was still alive. The question was whether the repetition explained the earlier ambiguous

142. See *Digest* 26.2.30 and 28.6.10.7.
143. *Digest* 28.7.16.

agreement or whether the reference to the death of one of the combatants was only by way of an example. There are plausible conjectures for either opinion, and, it seems to us, they are evenly balanced.[144]

§185. Similarly, if there are evident contradictions within a particular speech, then interpretation ceases, because nobody could have wanted mutually contradictory things at the same time. Hence Roman law stated that where there are mutually contradictory statements in a last will, neither is valid. Also different passages that undermine each other but are uttered by the same party have no validity.[145]

§186. That is, unless one statement is more recent than the other. For what was agreed upon last by two parties overrides any previous agreement, and where two laws contradict each other, the more recent overrides any previous ones.

§187. Yet there is a serious, but very common violation of this last principle concerning contradictions, when interpreters of Roman law assert that there are no antinomies in the laws of Justinian.

§188. I am speaking of those jurists who labor to reconcile by whatever means possible a law that has been abrogated in one part of the Justinianic law with the law abrogating it, or different laws in the same part of the text that obviously contradict each other.

§189. I wish that the jurist who is otherwise very famous for disputing against Wissenbach had left out passages like the following more often: "We must try to resolve any antinomies by drawing more precise distinctions."[146]

144. See Homer, *The Iliad,* vol. I, trans. A. T. Murray, Loeb Classical Library (London: Heinemann, 1930), bk. III, vv. 253–55 and 276–83.

145. See *Digest* 50.17.188 and *Codex* 14.21.14.

146. Thomasius is referring to the jurist Johannes Strauch, whose *Dissertationes undetriginta ad universum jus Justinianum privatum* Thomasius published with annotations in 1682. Johann Jacob Wissenbach (1607–65) was a jurist at the University of Franeker.

§190. Indeed, that is a fine solution, which is rightly considered a violation of the rules for a good disputation, when someone does not try to understand the intention he is trying to interpret, but instead twists the intention of the other person to fit his own will.

§191. We will discuss this at greater length elsewhere. You, however, must learn that it is impossible for anyone to become a jurist by doing that; it leads away from the path of correct interpretation, to sophistry and caviling.

§192. Before we move on to another subject, we must stress that you must not apply the above indiscriminately to interpreting the divine will. For even though we said that the same rules of interpretation are used in explaining human speech and divine laws, yet we should not assume that everything we have said concerning the obscurity of words and the different kinds of obscurity is relevant to the divine will.

§193. For Scripture continues to be perspicuous even if one or the other passage is difficult to explain. There the rules of good interpretation are to be used, partly to remove our ignorance, partly to avoid caviling over the words of Scripture.

§194. Between the obscurity of the divine will and that of the human will there are many differences, some of which we will touch upon very briefly.

§195. (1) The obscurity of the divine will has more to do with the human intellect than with the words of God. In declarations of the human will the fault more often lies with the written text and the words, not the interpreter.

§196. (2) The difficulty of understanding Scripture confuses only the unlearned and sophists.[147] The obscurity of the human will, however, has more than once caused problems for the most learned and wise people.

147. A reference to 2 Peter 3:16.

§197. Therefore, (3) if you apply the rules of interpretation and, especially, apply the principle concerning passages that have a common origin, you can easily avoid this difficulty in the case of divine precepts. The obscurity of the human will, however, is often inexplicable.

§198. (4) For you will not detect any confusion in divine laws, but you will do so in the laws and agreements of humans.

§199. (5) You will also not be able to show a genuine contradiction in the precepts of God, but an infinite number can be shown to exist in human laws, whatever a Tribonian[148] may protest to the contrary, etc. As far as the rest is concerned, ask the theologians.

END OF THE SECOND BOOK

---

148. Tribonian was the main architect of the emperor Justinian's codification of Roman law in the sixth century.

BOOK III

O how difficult is truth for the ignorant, and how easy
to those who know!¹

—Lactantius, *De orig. error.*, chap. 5

To the most noble and excellent Mr. August Heiland, etc.,
patron and most honored relative,
member of the aulic council of justice of
the most serene and lofty prince and lord,
George William, duke of Brunswick-Luneburg, etc., etc.,
Christian Thomasius,
who is about to rid himself of his lazy torpor
and embark on a most amiable exchange of letters,
and at the same time
is about to congratulate heartily
his most noble excellence
on his marriage
to a very select young woman,
dedicates
this third book of the *Institutes,*
which is mainly concerned with marriage
with all required reverence.

1. Lactantius, "On the Origin of Errors," chap. 5.16, pp. 131–32, in Lactantius, *Divine Institutes,* ed. and trans. A. Bowen and P. Garnsey (Liverpool: Liverpool University Press, 2003).

CHAPTER I

On the Duty of Man Toward
Fellow Humans in General

§1. So far we have considered the duty of humans generally, living in any kind of society. Now we must turn to the precepts guiding particular societies.

§2. At the beginning we explained what a society is and how many different forms there are.

§3. At the same time we reviewed the natural forms of societies, conjugal, paternal, master-servant, household, village, province, commonwealth, and finally the society of nations.

§4. Some of these, such as the society of nations, are called natural because man is placed in them by nature, even without his choice. Some, however, are called natural because nature leads man to them by a special instinct, which impels humans to choose to enter these societies voluntarily.

§5. And this instinct to form a society is either common to both states, namely that of innocence and that following original sin, as in the case of conjugal society or paternal society, or it is specific to the postlapsarian state, as in the case of the relationship between master and slave, the village, municipality, province, and commonwealth. We have discussed both of these at the beginning of this work.[2]

2. See *Institutes*, bk. I, chap. i, §§95ff.

§6. You could describe the first instinct as internal since God created it together with man, the latter as external because it is mainly the product of need and the fear of danger.

§7. We will discuss the latter at greater length below, when we examine civil society, and sacred history does not allow us to doubt the former.

§8. We would be insulting the divine will and the history of the state of innocence if we wanted to argue that a corrupt appetite is the reason why humans desire conjugal society more than civil society, as if this were about the pursuit of pleasure rather than something honest.

§9. Even Aristotle recognized this, although he was a pagan. Man, he said, is by nature made to a greater degree for marriage than for civil society, because the household is prior to and more essential than civil society, and because the procreation of children is common to every kind of living being [not just humans].[3]

§10. But the most important reason in moral matters is based on the purpose of something, and so societies are distinguished from one another mainly according to their purposes, and certainly ought to be distinguished from each other on that basis.

§11. There is no doubt concerning the purposes of the three simple forms of society: conjugal society is introduced for the sake of procreation, paternal society for the sake of educating the offspring, and the master-servant relationship for the sake of producing the material goods that are necessary for life.

§12. Composite societies need to be examined more carefully. As far as the household or the family is concerned, we shall not inquire in detail whether paternal society is necessary for that or not. More precisely: a

---

3. Aristotle, *Nicomachean Ethics*, bk. 8, chap. 12, §7 (1162a). Thomasius is using the edition by Samuel Rachel, published in Helmstedt in 1660.

complete family requires a threefold combination of a paterfamilias with a wife, children, and servants. If one of these is missing, it becomes a more or less incomplete family, depending on how essential the missing member is.

§13. The purpose of the household is defined by the normal activities of the paterfamilias, and thus it either has the same purpose as the master-servant relationship, or, more probably, combines the purposes of the three simple societies: for you could quite appropriately describe the procreation of children and their education as the normal activities of the paterfamilias.

§14. Thus, the creation of a household in fact involves no new purpose that is different from the purposes of the simple societies [that compose it].

§15. Next comes the village or country district. These two are said by some to differ in that the village is defined by the proximity of inhabitants, who do not, however, have their own magistrate or leader, while the country district is based on a certain form of government. And yet, according to the common usage of philosophers these two terms are used interchangeably, so that depending on the hypothesis a village may be credited with a form of government, while a country district is not.

§16. The Peripatetics say the purpose of the village is to provide a benefit that is not needed every day (such as protecting flocks of sheep from wolves, driving away a nocturnal burglar, extinguishing fires, putting up fences that have been blown down by the wind, etc.).

§17. Civil society is said to have two purposes; one is the ultimate end, which is εὐδαιμονία, that is, the true beatitude associated with civil society, not for one person alone but for the entire population; the other is a subordinate end, namely αὐτάρκεια, or the sufficiency of external goods and defenses, which is such that we live with more refinement than in a country district and are able to drive away not only a petty burglar at night but also a large band of robbers.

§18. The discrepancy between these two purposes leads to a difference in the respective material foundations of villages and civil societies. The material of a village is an undefined number of families (though there has to be more than one) that is sufficient for providing the essential benefits that are not needed every day. A civil society, however, consists of several villages, since it requires more families than a village does. This is necessary for the first purpose, because it is not possible to have a range of magistrates and laws cannot be enforced unless there is a fairly large number of people. It is also necessary for the second purpose, because in addition to peasants which are sufficient for a country district, there is a need for merchants, artisans, and soldiers.

§19. Yet when we examine this opinion more carefully, it seems that there are some doubts about it. First, this difference of ends is not described accurately by the terms, because there is no doubt that autarky [αὐτάρκεια] can also refer to less-frequent benefits for humans, so that the purpose of a country district differs from that of civil society in degree rather than in kind.

§20. You then might want to reply that there is still a huge difference in that the only purpose of a village is to offer these less-frequent benefits, while autarky is only the secondary purpose of a civil society and that we therefore need to place greater emphasis on true beatitude as the ultimate end of a civil society; this end cannot be obtained in a village, because no village as such is based on an agreement according to which one neighbor turns another from being a bad man into a good one. Yet here, too, there are many grounds on which we can reply.

§21. Second, beatitude in civil society can only mean peace and common tranquillity. And whatever circumlocution you use, this tranquillity is guaranteed mainly by establishing a defense against violent attempts to disturb it. That defense I would consider part of happiness rather than autarky. Yet in a sense this tranquillity is obtained in a village, though the degree is different: it is said that repelling a nocturnal thief is one of the purposes of a village, while it is that of a civil society to defend itself against a powerful band of robbers.

§22. Moreover, it does not seem contrary to the agreement on which a village is based for one neighbor to turn another from a bad man into a good one. For those who insist on the opposite assume that the nature of a village requires neighbors to be equal, so that none has the right to punish the other.

§23. But that argument not only begs the question but is opposed by Aristotle himself, who insists that the country district is above all a settlement established by households. And while the household is ruled by the oldest person in it, settlements are ruled on the basis of kinship.[4]

§24. Third, concerning the examples the Peripatetics use to explain the less-frequent benefits provided by a village, you will see that here too some list things that leave no or very little difference between a village and a civil society: they include buying, selling, fighting, plowing, trading, etc., all of which activities contradict the above statement that for a country you only need peasants.

§25. Fourth, the above examples are not enough to distinguish the village from the family, especially if the latter is not reduced to the minimal number of people. For why should a paterfamilias with a couple of servants not be able to drive away a wolf, repel a nocturnal thief, extinguish a fire (under normal circumstances), put up a fence, etc.?

§26. Moreover, fifth, turning to the basis of a village and that of a civil society, just as the Peripatetics do not dare to specify the minimum number of families required for the constitution of a country district, so, sixth, it is not universally true that a civil society must have several villages.

4. Aristotle, *Politics,* bk. 1, chap. 1, 1252a.

§27. For what would prevent a large number of families from being as-sembled in one village in which some heads of families act as magistrates, others as peasants, merchants, artisans, and soldiers?

§28. The Roman Republic is an example: in the beginning it consisted of only one village. He who argues that this is no civil society denies the existence of a civil society where there is a republic—that is, he denies the essence of a thing although its form is present.

§29. Hence we have said above that a civil society sometimes consists of several families, sometimes of several villages, and sometimes of several provinces. Villages and provinces therefore differ from civil society not so much in kind or in terms of their ends, but in the way that parts differ from the whole.

§30. For just as a civil society is large or small, it has more or fewer parts. Sometimes, therefore, you can divide it into several provinces, provinces into several villages, villages into several families; and sometimes, if the territory is more extensive, provinces can be divided into lordships or dis-tricts, and these in turn can be divided into several villages.

§31. And perhaps that is the reason why Aristotle in his *Politics* first ex-amines the three simple societies and then immediately goes on to discuss the commonwealth. He refers to households and villages only briefly, in passing, and never talks about provinces and the other possible parts of great states, because these societies lack a specific purpose that is different from that of civil society.

§32. Thus, all you can expect from us is an assessment of the duties of humans in the three first societies. Following that we will immediately move on to the state.

§33. And this is where the Peripatetics usually stop, because they do not go on to the society of nations, even though it is one of the natural socie-ties, as will soon become clear. Their argument is that civil society is the most perfect of all societies because its end is civil beatitude, which is not obtained in societies that are greater than civil society.

§34. Nevertheless, we will go on searching, partly because the Peripatetics' argument does not seem very reliable, and partly because it is still unclear whether civil society is always the most perfect form of society.

§35. For even if we were happy to admit that the perfections of civil society are greater than those of the common society of nations, as we will explain shortly, civil society, nevertheless, is not to be preferred automatically to all larger societies. At the very least it does not deserve to be preferred to a society that is formed by the confederation of several commonwealths.

§36. For treaties are usually concluded for the sake of either commerce or military aid. The former are intended to preserve autarky, the latter happiness. Either purpose makes it evident that states by themselves are often incapable of achieving their ends and therefore are not the most perfect kinds of societies.

§37. Thus, while a society formed by allied states is not natural, but artificial, and it is not directed toward a new purpose that is different from that of the state, a society formed by allied states often fulfills the ends of a state better than the state does and comes as close as is possible to being a natural society, even though it is artificial. We will, therefore, need to say something about treaties (after having talked about civil societies).

§38. And following our discussion of treaties, we shall not neglect to examine the duties in a common society of nations, even if this society does not achieve the perfection of civil society. That argument [that the society of nations does not achieve the perfection of civil society] is not sufficient [to justify not examining the duties in a common society of nations].

§39. For otherwise there would be nothing to say about simple societies either [because these too do not achieve the same perfection as civil society].

§40. The argument that it is enough for someone in the state of nature to progress to the most perfect condition possible presents no obstacles. For we have already refuted the opinion of the Peripatetics that he who teaches a discipline must first form some idea of perfection.[5]

§41. What is more likely to persuade us to refrain from discussing this kind of society is the fact that it does not appear to have a purpose different from that of the state; it is only directed toward tranquillity or happiness [like the state].

§42. But that is no problem. Happiness in civil society is not the same thing as the common happiness of humankind.

§43. Yet we cannot deny that particular precepts which occur in all other societies are not to be expected in the society of nations, because the purpose of this society provides a standard for all other ends in its constituent societies. Therefore, the general axioms which will hold true here necessarily apply to the other societies, too.

§44. These, however, will be nothing other than what we have already been concerned with in the previous book.

§45. Yet a discussion of the duty of nations toward each other will not be futile, since two important subjects from the law of nations, on the inviolability of legates and the right of burial, will provide an excellent opportunity to form particular conclusions from these general precepts.

§46. But, you will say, all this discussion will be in vain if there is no society of nations. That is true, but there is a society among the nations, because the whole of humankind is united by a particular purpose.

§47. We have already spoken about this purpose, which is general peace and tranquillity. The union of all humans toward this end, however, can

5. See *Institutes,* bk. I, chap. iv, §44.

be demonstrated from the fact that there is a shared right among all humans to obtain this end.

§48. Clearly, if nothing else holds this society of nations together, certainly the precept about preserving equality, and the four duties derived from it, does, which we have pointed out in the previous book.

§49. Since these are absolute and predate all human convention, they show at the same time that the society among nations is entirely natural and not artificial. Grotius very appropriately called this the society formed by reason and speech,[6] and we have so far described this as the natural state in the simple sense, insofar as it is opposed to the civil state.

§50. Camillus, in Livy's history, recognized this when he said that he was associated with the Falisci by a natural society.[7] Among the philosophers Cicero often stressed the universal society of mankind.

§51. But we must not confuse this society with a world society, which the pagan philosophers, and especially the Stoics, discuss more than once. They believed this to be wider than the society of nations and to include the gods as well as humans. This is wrong, and insofar as divine jurisprudence is concerned we have already made a few comments about the society of man with God and have explained these at greater length elsewhere.[8]

§52. We also believe that it is not appropriate to describe this society of nations as a universal commonwealth of all humans. There is no commonwealth without sovereign political power [*imperium*], yet the society of nations lacks human sovereignty, and is the only natural society after the fall from grace that is a society of equals.

---

6. Grotius, *The Rights of War and Peace*, bk. III, chap. xix, §3.
7. Livy, "From the Founding of the City," bk. V, chap. xxvii (see Livy, *Livy*, vol. 3, trans. B. O. Foster, Loeb Classical Library [London: Heinemann, 1924], pp. 93–95).
8. See *Institutes*, bk. I, chap. i, §§92ff.

§53. And that is why the society of nations is less perfect than civil society. The society of nations is alluring because it is free and impervious to any kind of subjection, but in comparison to political society it has several inconveniences attached to it in this corrupt state of humanity, because the security of individuals receives too little attention in it. There [in the society of nations] everybody is protected by his own strength, while in political society he is protected by the strength of all others. There nobody can be certain of the fruits of his industry, whereas here they enjoy all of them. There passions, war, fear, ignorance, and savagery rule, whereas here you find the rule of reason, peace, security, knowledge, and benevolence.

§54. It is not true that there is no society among those who do not know each other personally, or by reputation, or by some other means, as we, for example, do not know the inhabitants of Novaja Zemlja.[9]

§55. For this objection only suggests that in this society there is not such a close friendship as in others. It cannot be inferred that there is no society at all.

§56. For if there is a single society between the citizens of an empire, such as the Saxons and the Bavarians, between the citizens of a principality, such as the inhabitants of Leipzig and those of Dresden, and among the inhabitants of a town, as is clearly the case, the fact that there is no close friendship does not mean there is no society at all, even if not everybody knows everybody else.

§57. Having said this, we must now briefly inquire more closely into the precepts that guide the duties of allies in general. There is no doubt, I believe, that all and each of the precepts we have demonstrated at greater length in the previous book also apply to individual human societies.

§58. Apart from that we must examine the basic kinds of society. As we have explained above,[10] a society is either mixed or equal (the only purely

9. A remote archipelago in the Arctic Ocean.
10. See *Institutes,* bk. I, chap. i, §93.

unequal society is that between God and humans, and that is not relevant to this book). In an equal society, the society of nations, these precepts are enough.

§59. All other natural societies are mixed, and in such a mixed society, insofar as it includes political power [*imperium*], there is an additional, particular precept that pertains to inferiors and subjects: Obey the person who holds political power in such a society.

§60. This follows not only from the first practical principle which we demonstrated at the very beginning of this treatise.[11] It also follows from the definition of a mixed society, which would not be mixed if the person holding political power did not have the right to demand obedience from the others.

§61. It is also based on the preservation of sociality, because the peace and tranquillity of humanity would be greatly disturbed if the inferiors in particular human societies did not obey their superiors: if that were the case, it would be impossible in the present state of corruption to obtain the purpose of most societies, about which I shall say more soon.

§62. The command to keep agreements also often reinforces this obedience, because political power is in most cases introduced on the basis of an agreement.

§63. I say "in most cases." We need to avoid two extremes here. One is the belief that all political power has its origin in agreement; the other is the opposite belief that all power has its immediate origin in the divine will, without human agreement.[12]

---

11. Ibid., chap. iii, §34.

12. Thomasius associates the former opinion with the political theory of Thomas Hobbes, the latter with that of Johann Friedrich Horn (see, for example, Johann Friedrich Horn, *Architectonica de civitate,* Editio Novissima [Leyden, 1699], bk. 2, chap. 1, §iv, p. 170).

§64. We believe that political power is to some extent produced immediately by God, and to some extent is based on an agreement (in the way
that an agreement sometimes contributes to producing a right or obligation, as we have explained above). The matter will be made especially clear
when we discuss the individual types of societies.

§65. Here we must note, however, that the origin of a law, which orders
obedience to the holder of political power, must not be confused with
the origin of political power itself. The former law is entirely natural,
and is evident from ratiocination, without either divine or human revelation. But ratiocination is not always enough to understand that political
power in a particular society belongs to this or that person. Sometimes it
is necessary to be aware of an agreement in order to know on whom this
agreement has conferred political power. That is the case in civil society.
Sometimes this knowledge even presupposes divine revelation and universal positive law, as is the case in conjugal society.

§66. As we have shown, the three main varieties of mixed societies are
characterized by specific ends, as is the commonwealth, which is a form
of composite society. Thus there is an additional, very specific precept of
natural law for these: "Do what necessarily furthers the purpose of each
society, and avoid that which necessarily disturbs it."

§67. Otherwise a society would not be a society because its purpose defines its essence.

§68. It would also be a violation of the first principle of divine jurisprudence, that God, the author of human society, must be obeyed; of the
precept concerning keeping agreements insofar as societies are based on
an agreement; and of one of the specific precepts in the previous book, for
example, those concerning the duties of humanity, insofar as the purpose
of a society rests on such a precept.

§69. But one thing can have several purposes, and one purpose may also
be the principal purpose of a society, while the other or others are second-

ary. Right reason tells us that our rule applies to the primary purpose, because this is what gives a society its specificity.

§70. This will, therefore, always take precedence over secondary purposes.

§71. With regard to establishing a society there is the following rule: "If it is certain that the primary purpose of a society cannot be obtained by the people who want to enter this society, then there will be no society, nor must this society be permitted even if a secondary purpose could be attained that would not be possible outside this society."

§72. I say: "if it is certain." For if there is a hope that people who are temporarily prevented from doing so are capable of achieving the primary purpose by natural means, at least to some degree, then such a society is permissible, even if it is better for them to refrain from it.

§73. Let us turn to the foundation of societies. Let us assume that some people who were capable of entering a society have done so. Then this society will not be dissolved immediately if one or the other of the people involved have become incapable of living in this society and there is no hope that they will recover their ability to do so. It will not be permissible then for one person to withdraw from the society against the will of the other, and sometimes a command of the superior prohibits a person from withdrawing even if both sides agree.

§74. The use of these observations is evident in various societies, and above all in conjugal society.

§75. Insofar as natural jurisprudence is concerned, you need to expect nothing more there than that we apply precepts that so far have been presented in summary form, in part by forming particular conclusions on that basis, in part by resolving certain controversial questions.

CHAPTER II

On the Duty of Man with Regard to Conjugal Society

§1. Let us start with simple societies, because civil society is composed of these. Among these, conjugal society is the most natural, because all humans generally feel an instinctive desire within themselves to enter such a society.

§2. It is difficult to explain what everyone's duty is in that regard, because the matter has been greatly complicated by the controversies of theologians, jurists, and philosophers, who have often argued with more acrimony and subtlety than perspicuity and clarity.

§3. Yet it seems that the main reason for this difficulty is that divine laws were often mixed with human laws; ignorance led to the confusion of natural law with universal positive law, or their separate discussion was sometimes neglected because of the purpose or the argument of the work.

§4. In truth, God has reinforced no other society of human beings with as many particular precepts as conjugal society. We shall therefore make every effort to separate these precepts from the law of nature, although we shall start with the latter. We shall thereby be better able to explain later what revelation adds to reason.

§5. But first I repeat the following, based on the hypotheses I have demonstrated so far: (1) By natural law we mean nothing other than the law we have defined above, and the foundation of which, as we have shown, lies in the necessary conformity and nonconformity with the social, that is peaceful, nature of man.

§6. (2) The conclusions or questions that occur here are to be examined according to the axioms listed in the preceding chapter, which all derive from this source [i.e., natural law].

§7. (3) It automatically follows that the justice or injustice of the actions we are dealing with must be decided on the basis of these rules and that actions they clearly do not refer to are to be considered permitted, if we leave aside divine revelation.

§8. (4) Yet we must take care to note that the term *permitted action* is not absolute, but stands in relation to a law, and describes that which is neither commanded nor prohibited by that law. When you find the term *permitted action* in the earlier part of this chapter you therefore must not assume that this action must be permitted under divine law. There we are only speaking of the law of nature. But there are many things forbidden by positive law that are not covered by natural law.

§9. (5) Furthermore, even if what is called permitted lies somewhere in between precepts and prohibitions, this middle is not to be understood as a single point, but allows for some leeway: it is sometimes closer to a prohibition, and sometimes closer to a command. That is similar to the way in which the Peripatetics use the concept of the mean in explaining their concept of virtue.[13]

§10. For those actions that further sociality or the purpose of a society by accident, but not necessarily, are closer to being commanded. On the other hand, those actions that disturb this purpose by accident are closer to being prohibited. If, therefore, we abstract from divine revelation, it

13. See Aristotle, *Nicomachean Ethics*, II.vi.4 (1106a).

is more laudable to do the former and refrain from the latter. We shall, therefore, here add a degree of permissibility.

§11. (6) Thus you must not be surprised if the final part of this discussion will show that some actions that on the basis of natural law seem closer to being commanded are prohibited by divine positive law. For divine prudence cannot be measured by the standards of human prudence, and it must be sufficient for us to know that these kinds of actions are not essential to sociality, especially as it may often be the case that several circumstances occur in one action at the same time, one of which tends to further sociality, while another tends to disturb the public peace. Thus, if we had no divine revelation, our reason would often be unsure whether it is more laudable to perform or refrain from such an action.

§12. (7) Also, we must not ignore what we stressed above, that the following argument is not valid: actions that are commanded or forbidden in sacred Scripture are considered honest or despicable by heathens; therefore, they are part of natural law.

§13. Thus there is a reason why Grotius is criticized by his commentators: he believed that to prove natural law you had to use the testimonies of philosophers, historians, poets, and orators, even if he does not claim this argument to be demonstrative or say that it should be used indiscriminately.

§14. Grotius states: "When many men of different times and places unanimously affirm the same thing for truth, this ought to be ascribed to a general cause; which in the questions treated by us, can be no other than either a just inference drawn from the principles of nature, or an universal consent. The former shows the laws of nature, the other the law of nations. The difference between which is not to be understood from the testimonies themselves, but from the quality of the subject."[14] This merits several comments.

14. Grotius, *The Rights of War and Peace,* "The Preliminary Discourse," bk. I, §xli.

§15. First, it seems very unconvincing when he says that a common assertion by many people in different times and places must have its origin in some universal cause. By "many people," the philosophers, historians, poets, and orators he appeals to, he obviously means Greek and Roman writers. If there are no other arguments to explain their consensus, no reason will persuade us that it must be ascribed to some universal cause, because these nations were separated from one another by no great distances; they could easily form a tacit consensus on certain matters as a result of constant commerce, the affairs of war and peace, and a certain similarity of life and manners.

§16. So, when Grotius lists the universal causes that are evident from the testimony of nations, he lists too few of them. He only appeals to the dictate of right reason and common consensus. He evidently has forgotten that at the beginning of his erudite work, among the universal laws binding all of humankind and the nations, he himself had also included some form of law based on the divine will, which he had not derived from the principles of nature or the consensus of nations.

§17. And as we have shown above, this was more than once the cause behind the statements of pagan philosophers.[15]

§18. At the same time, we dismissed the idea that the law of nations properly speaking differs from natural law in kind. It is therefore not necessary to put forward any more arguments against that which Grotius adds here concerning consensus and the law of nations.

§19. Finally, Grotius himself admits that the question what is and is not natural law must be determined not so much on the basis of the testimonies of pagans as on the basis of the nature of the matter. Thus it is evident that it would be safer to leave aside this argument from the common opinion of pagan philosophers.

15. See *Institutes,* bk. I, chap. ii, §70.

§20. And this will have to be emphasized more strongly. For when the authors who have tried to explain conjugal duties resolve the more intricate controversies, they often claim that some action is prohibited by natural law, but they do not provide a reason for the prohibition. Instead, they present the testimony of some pagan philosopher instead of a reason, as if this were a splendid thing to do.

§21. Let us turn to the matter at hand. Any human being contemplating his nature, without the aid of revelation, will detect within himself some secret propensity and strong desire prompting him to join with an individual of the opposite sex. If he examines these inclinations, he discovers that God has implanted this as a mutual affection in each of the two sexes.

§22. He also realizes that the origin of these desires is in the constitution of the body rather than the mind, not only because man often senses these desires while thinking of some other thing, or notices that they pre-empt and stimulate his thoughts. It is also because one finds similar desires in beasts. Hence, there is an opportunity to compare human nature with the constitution of beasts.

§23. It is noticeable that animals are forced by these desires to copulate at certain times in the year, and that this copulation is intended by nature for the purpose of procreation. Once this has happened, however, the male often deserts the female, and the latter alone bears the burden of giving birth and feeding the offspring.

§24. But he [man] feels that his desires are not limited to certain times of the year but are in some sense perpetual. He realizes that the parts of his blood are more agile [than those of beasts] and his spermatic vessels are stronger. They are, however, also designed for the purpose of procreation.[16]

16. Thomasius is drawing on Richard Cumberland's *De legibus naturae* of 1672 (see Richard Cumberland, *A Treatise of the Laws of Nature*, ed. J. Parkin [Indianapolis: Liberty Fund, 2005], "A Philosophical Inquiry into the Laws of Nature," chap. II, §xxviii, p. 450).

§25. Furthermore, he recognizes that this inner inclination is linked to a feeling that is unknown to beasts, namely love. Under its influence he believes that, even without physical contact, a greater part of his own happiness depends on the benevolence of a certain person rather than on the benevolence of other people; he is saddened if he is hated or disliked by that person, and is more deeply affected by this person's delights than his own, and shares this person's pains.

§26. Moreover, while beasts do not distinguish between individuals, man detects within himself a variety of instincts, the causes of which he often does not know, so that he may feel no love or even the opposite of love toward one particular individual, which then directs him toward one rather than the other person.

§27. Moreover, men feel a strong affection for the offspring that has been conceived and born from a woman.

§28. Finally, humans of either sex generally feel a desire for sexual intercourse, even if they cannot produce offspring—for example, if the woman is already pregnant, or if for reasons related to civil society or peaceful coexistence they cannot form a union for the sake of begetting children. Even then they feel a particular pleasure in the act of intercourse, which is the main cause of this desire in the first place. Those who consider the matter carefully see that in beasts it is a different matter.

§29. For it is only with difficulty that a mute animal engages in intercourse after conception. And since arguments related to civil society or peaceful coexistence do not apply to beasts, these cannot be the reason why they do not follow their natural instinct for begetting offspring.

§30. Properly speaking, beasts feel no pleasure in copulation, because, as we have said above, they lack all reason and internal sense, yet some sort of appearance of reason and of this kind of pleasure is evident in beasts.

§31. Anybody can on the basis of his own, inner experience realize that pleasure is a form of thought that is either immediate or joined with reflection on a pleasure that is either present, or past, or future. You cannot predicate either of a beast, because it does not think or reflect in any way.

§32. There is a difference between these three forms of pleasure: present pleasure, more than any other, affects man in strange ways and leaves a particular impression on his imagination and memory. When he thinks more carefully about past pleasure, he is often stimulated by renewed desire, even if its object is absent, and he is inclined toward lengthy meditations on future pleasure.

§33. Should you want to compare the pleasure felt by man with the appearance of pleasure in beasts, you will notice that the action producing this pleasure is common to man and beasts, even to the extent that man tries to shake off the rule of reason (which otherwise separates man from brutes), and very often succeeds in doing so.

§34. For beasts are driven so vehemently by the desire for procreation that, whenever they feel it particularly keenly, they can barely be restrained with beatings and superior force, which is otherwise sufficient to suppress their other inclinations. Likewise in humans the idea of the moment of immediate pleasure presents itself so appealingly to man that in that instant he cannot conceive any greater good, even if reason, once it is free from these charms, soon shows him that the opposite is true.

§35. For that reason humans sometimes lose their self-control, if their desire for copulation is frustrated for a long time, and perpetrate deeds they would otherwise never commit.

§36. For even if the excess of other passions pushes humans toward actions that are incompatible with the dictate of reason, the reason for this can be attributed either to poor education, or habit, or some specific circumstance which man could easily repress some time before the excess occurred.

§37. But the frenzy of lust (which is what we have been speaking about so far) is common to all humans and sometimes draws even well-educated and reasonable people away from the path of reason, to such a degree that their behavior hardly differs from madness.

§38. The origin of this tendency is unknown to humans without divine revelation. Therefore, if he wants to use [natural] reason alone, he cannot but infer that the cause of the lust as of the madness is natural.

§39. When he believes that madness is the result of more particular factors, while lust is inherent in the nature of all humans, he will necessarily compare the two and consider madness to be nonnatural or even contranatural and accidental, while lust is a natural passion.

§40. Now, since he knows that man does not get his nature from himself, he can construct an argument, based on an absurd assumption, leading him to conclude that the creator of man instilled this passion in him.

§41. So you see how blind our reason is without the light of Scripture. Thus it is easy to anticipate whether you can expect any reliable conclusions from comparing the preceding reflections, the truth of which will be evident to anyone from experience, with the precepts and rules of natural law we have explained so far.

§42. If you first consider the duty of man to enter marriage, your natural reason, insofar as it is correct, will not deviate greatly from the divine will. Reason will tell you that the difference between the sexes and the natural ability given to humans to procreate through physical union reflects the will of the Creator that we should fulfill this natural possibility.

§43. This is all the more true because man realizes that the mutual attraction between the sexes is greater than among beasts, as is the affection toward his offspring. He sees that one reason for this, among others, is to prevent him from neglecting this important duty, out of carelessness or because of the burdens associated with giving birth or educating children, and because children are often the cause of hardship and cares. For without this care humankind would not survive.

§44. Natural law has written into the human heart the precepts for other actions which humans are driven to by a natural appetite, such as self-preservation or the love of offspring and its upbringing. Similarly they feel that they are under a kind of obligation to procreate.

§45. For one should not believe that there is no need for a law in these and similar actions, just because instinct and sensual appetite are enough to impel man to such actions. The reasoning should rather be turned on its head: nature wanted these duties to be performed very thoroughly because they immediately help to preserve humankind; and because nature lacked confidence in the dictate of reason she ordered that it be supplemented with an instinct so strong that man can resist it only with great difficulty.

§46. But here we need to distinguish between different instincts, in case someone claims that we want to measure man's obligation indiscriminately by his instinct. We are not talking about those instincts that are not directed to the safety of humankind, that have their origin in some forbidden deed, or that violate the law of nature we have already demonstrated. Thus, you will contradict us in vain by pointing to the instinct of a mother to kill her [illegitimate] child out of fear and in order to avoid infamy.

§47. The first precept, therefore, that directs the duties of man with respect to marriage is this: "You should marry."

§48. Its general reason is the preservation of sociality. For since matrimony is the foundation of a social life, humans will also be obliged to enter marriage, just as they are required to do all other things that are necessary for that end [of sociality].

§49. But the precept to preserve equality also produces this obligation. For one pair of humans is not enough to live peacefully in the current condition: the increase of humankind is necessary to obtain that end, and our parents were induced by this obligation to beget us (whoever we are and however many we are). Our concern for equality also leads us to take care of ourselves and our companions, as well as of future companions. Otherwise, as one person dies after the other, it can easily happen that the longest-lived lead the most miserable life of all.

§50. Yet at the same time this reason shows us what type of precepts (apart from the general axiom that equality must be preserved) our precept belongs to: the law commanding the duties of humanity, because by producing a child we benefit others in general and without an explicit agreement.

§51. And we do not only benefit those who are joined with us in some form of society, but also our descendants, who at present exist only in our loins. For they too are to be considered as if they were already born, whenever we consider their well-being.

§52. The reasons offered indicate that our precept belongs to the group of the indefinite and indeterminate precepts, which do not bind individuals necessarily and at all times.

§53. Such affirmative precepts not only require an appropriate opportunity for their fulfillment. We must also repeat what we have emphasized above, concerning the performance of the duties of humanity: they place us under an imperfect obligation, which is to our own advantage.[17]

§54. Hence, the appropriate time for contracting marriage depends not only on age or the suitability for procreation. There also has to be a decent livelihood, the ability to maintain a wife and the children that are to be born. The husband also has to be suitable for taking on the role of a head of household. And sometimes present conditions and current duties do not permit considering marriage.

§55. Therefore, it is not only unnecessary, but stupid, for young men to think about wives when they cannot guarantee anything but hunger for

17. See *Institutes,* bk. I, chap. i, §109.

themselves and their dependents, will fill the state with beggars, and know little more than boys do.

§56. They act correctly who delay marriage in order to cultivate their mind during celibacy and learn to perform outstanding services to human society. This is something that married men are not able to do to the same degree, because of the customs of civil society or the dispositions of women.

§57. Nor should those people be criticized who realize that they are able to remain continent and lead a celibate life, and that they can benefit humankind or their civil society to a greater degree by remaining celibate than if they were married. We must not believe that they are obliged by nature to allow feminine charms to put a brake on their glorious pursuits.

§58. Far less do those have to fear criticism who have children from a previous marriage and do not want to impose the burden of a stepmother or stepfather on them, even though second marriages are not to be considered illicit in themselves since they do not always mean that children from the first marriage will be badly cared for.

§59. All this is to be understood in the sense that [the duties of] humanity should not be disturbed just to avoid disturbing the purposes of marriage.

§60. It is appropriate that we examine these now. It is not enough to know that there is a command to enter marriage unless we also know what marriage is. Its essence, however, as we have said in the case of other societies, depends on its purpose.

§61. It is evident that the term *marriage* is commonly used among the nations to describe that society which is formed for the sake of cohabitation. Thus it follows that whatever nature determines as the purposes of cohabitation are also to be considered the purposes of marriage.

§62. But as we have already said above, human beings are led to desire a union for two reasons, procreation and the suppression of lust.

§63. Left to his own devices, man regards both of these as natural: the former because he sees that there is no use for the human seed other than producing a child; the latter because experience teaches us that generally all humans are driven by an internal instinct to enjoy this kind of pleasure.

§64. It follows that man in that case regards these as the two true purposes of matrimony.

§65. But it often is the case that, if there is more than one true purpose, then one is more important, or should be more important, than the other. The first of these is then termed the principal end, the latter the secondary. We therefore must inquire into these two purposes of marriage.

§66. If the matter were to be decided on the basis of a casual comparison of human nature with that of beasts, one might conclude that the extinction of lust is the primary purpose of marriage, because we have noted above that the procreation of children is common to man and beasts, but the stimulus of lust is specific to humans.

§67. Yet we will not allow this cloud to obscure the light of truth. We also showed at the beginning that even though beasts do not experience lust in the proper sense, there is an appearance of it that is very similar to lust.

§68. We argued there that this appearance of lust is similar to lust in humans, in that lust overthrows the rule of reason. Also, that which is greatly contrary to reason cannot be the primary end of a society.

§69. On these grounds it is common for the more egregious, or even all, forms of intercourse motivated by lust to be designated by the term *bestiality*, not only in Latin, but also in the languages of other nations.

§70. Finally, in resolving questions of natural law we must first look not to the secondary and accidental differences between the essences of man and beasts, but to the primary difference, which is reason; reason consists in sociality, sociality in tranquillity, and that is based on the general precepts we have discussed earlier.

§71. All these concern the common utility of humanity, which should be the basis for the utility of individual humans. It necessarily follows that the procreation of children is the principal end of marriage, the suppression of lust its secondary aim.

§72. For the former is intended to benefit all of humanity, the latter only particular individuals.

§73. Add to this the fact that the procreation of children simultaneously extinguishes lust, but it is not true that every suppression of lust leads to procreation. Therefore, the former act is more natural than the latter, since in it common and individual utility are linked to each other.

§74. Apart from these two purposes of marriage there is a third, according to the common consent of the learned: mutual assistance. In order to understand this more accurately, it must be noted that marriage can be considered either in itself, without regard to other societies, or in relation to a family, of which it is a part.

§75. In the former respect it is covered by these two purposes. In the latter it is also directed toward mutual assistance within the family.

§76. But here too you can divide mutual assistance into ordinary, which is that within a family, and extraordinary or subsidiary, which remedies the failings of another form of society.

§77. Ordinary assistance is when the wife helps the husband in educating the children, directing the servants, and acquiring and preserving material goods.

§78. Extraordinary assistance takes place when the head of the family is too poor to pay for male servants and maids. Then, the absence of a society of master and servants means the husband will have to do the work of the male servant, the wife that of the maid.

§79. But I think it is clear from the above that each of these two forms of mutual assistance belongs to the secondary purposes of marriage, the former because it concerns the external relationships of the married couple, the latter because it presupposes a deficiency.

§80. Incidentally, you should note that by mutual assistance writers generally mean something that is distinct from the first two ends.

§81. Since, therefore, human societies are defined by their primary purposes and it has been demonstrated that procreation is the primary purpose of marriage, it is easy to formulate the following axiom (leaving aside revelation): "Marriage is the society that is entered into for the sake of procreation." Similarly, a society that does not have procreation as its aim is not to be considered a marriage.

§82. Therefore, before we move on to the precepts that spouses ought to observe, we have to show the conclusions that can be derived from the two principles by rigorous argument.

§83. As far as the affirmative [principle] is concerned, it was obvious at the beginning from the teachings about society in general that the essence of marriage does not begin with the fulfillment of the purpose and the act of conjunction itself. Here the common rule applies that the purpose is what is intended first and put into practice last. And so the marriage is valid as soon as consent has been given to achieve its purpose.

§84. And this is where the common argument of jurists is relevant: consent, not sexual intercourse, makes a marriage. By that is meant not only what we have just said, but also that sexual intercourse without an agreement to be married cannot be considered a marriage, because it is not clear whether this was done for the sake of procreation or only for that of satisfying lust. We will see more about this in the explanation of the latter, negative principle.

§85. Moreover, what we have noted above concerning consent and the nature of agreements in general needs to be repeated here when we are talking about consent in entering a marriage. For that reason the contracting parties need to have sufficient command of their reason, and there must be no unjust fear caused by either side.

§86. It is the same with fraud: if we abstract from divine revelation and the specific customs of various nations, we do not distinguish between a fraud that occurs with respect to an essential part of the marriage and one that relates to what are called accidental features—for example, if someone persuades the other that he or she is rich, noble, a virgin, etc. For while there is no doubt in the former case that there is no marriage, as far as the latter is concerned, the rule we have just explained leads us to the same principle,[18] that fraud must never benefit the guilty party, but that it is left to the discretion of the damaged party whether he or she wants to rescind the contract or force the other party to offer compensation for the damage.

§87. We do not change anything in cases of error either, insofar as that is distinguished from fraud. For we said that, if in doubt, an error must always harm the person erring, unless the circumstance concerning which he erred was added to the promise explicitly as a condition.

§88. From this we infer that error concerning a person, if there is fraud on the part of one of the contracting parties, does render a marriage void, which is what happened to Jacob.[19] But if this is not the case, the marriage remains valid—for example, if someone promises Titia to marry her when he thinks she is Caja, [it is valid] as long as he does not say that he wants to marry her as Caja.

§89. Also, an error concerning virginity does not prejudice a marriage if the spouse did not mention it in the marriage vows.

18. Ibid., bk. II, chap. vi, §49.
19. Genesis 29:16–28.

§90. It is different if there is an error concerning the sex or the ability to beget children, because then the purpose of a marriage cannot be obtained, and these two qualities must be part of the promise as a condition.

§91. If there is an error concerning beauty, nobility, wealth, etc., and a person made no explicit agreement concerning the dowry, for example, but used up the wealth of his spouse on the basis of an unspoken hope, he will not be allowed to dissolve the marriage or refuse its consummation if it has been properly agreed.

§92. But if a person has inserted these as a condition into the marriage agreement, then there will be no obstacle in natural law to reversing this agreement if the error is detected—for example, if someone said, "I shall divorce you if you do not bring the agreed dowry."

§93. Thus, if someone explicitly added a clause that he would only have a particular woman as a wife if she was noble or if she brought a certain dowry with her, then he will not be bound to conclude the marriage before this condition has been met.

§94. Even if someone failed to check whether this condition had been met and concluded the marriage, he will not be considered to have renounced this condition tacitly. If what had been hoped for then fails to materialize, I should think that constituted sufficient grounds for a divorce.

§95. For a divorce is usually a disagreeable matter and should not be undertaken lightly, and among equals negligence cannot deprive a person of a right that normally pertains to him, especially if this [negligence] was induced by the fraud of another person, which must be the case if these conditions were added to the agreement.

§96. It is also no obstacle if in the given case there was no agreement as follows: "I shall divorce you if you do not bring along a certain dowry," but an agreement like this: "I shall not marry you." The latter is sufficient, because in that way the consent will be lacking if she does not bring along the dowry.

§97. But, you say, he has nevertheless concluded the marriage when he had sexual intercourse. I reply that this was not a true consummation because, as we noted, sexual intercourse without a valid marriage agreement does not constitute marriage.

§98. Moreover, agreements through which we enter a particular society have no other essence than that which depends on the society's purpose, because that fulfills the essence. It is therefore clear that once marriage is entered into among humans in a natural state of equality and liberty, the woman may desire offspring no less than the man, and she has a right to that. To that end it is necessary that man and woman form an agreement concerning physical intercourse.

§99. If this agreement is simple and only concerns the procreation of offspring, does not involve an agreement about continued cohabitation, and does not grant one party power over the other, then neither will have any right over the other except for that of physical intercourse for the sake of procreation.

§100. From this it follows that if you take natural law alone it is not essential for the marriage agreement that the woman promises to the man not to allow anyone apart from himself access to her body.

§101. You may want to argue that anyone examining the condition of human nature more carefully would believe it is more consistent with the character of either sex for the marriage agreement to be initiated by the man, so that the man asked the woman, not vice versa. It would follow that the man seeks to have his own child, not one that is supposititious or the product of adultery. But I fear that what has been said about men initiating marriage cannot be demonstrated from the nature of the sexes and must rather be attributed to the customs of nations, the education of women, or other causes, which are to be derived from revelation.

§102. I also do not believe that the essence of the connubial agreement naturally requires the wife to promise the man uninterrupted cohabitation or to leave the choice of domicile to him, which would mean that the wife could not under the marriage agreement go abroad or sleep apart from her husband against his will.

§103. This argument depends to some extent on the previous hypothesis, that by nature it is the man who brings the woman into his family, of which he is the head and guide, not vice versa; and apart from that, the husband is the head of the family not by nature, but on other grounds.

§104. We do not deny that a roving and inconstant life, without a fixed home and without a basis for one's fortunes, is greatly inconsistent with decorum; that the education of common offspring can be arranged most conveniently by the combined efforts of both parents; and that, moreover, continuous cohabitation is the source of great pleasure among spouses that are well matched with each other. Yet, all this only shows that the agreement where these things are promised is superior to the other, simple agreement. It does not show that this simple agreement is contrary to nature. Thus, the man not only cannot insist on cohabitation against the wishes of his wife; he should also know that he is assumed to be aware of this.

§105. Finally, if we take the pure law of nature, the principal agreement of a complete marriage does not, properly speaking, result in the husband's power over the wife, even if we conceded that the wife is obliged by nature to promise to her husband to allow no other man access to her body, and to cohabit with her husband on a permanent basis.

§106. For a person is not automatically subject to the power of another if this person is bound to follow the other person's will with respect to particular kinds of actions. Thus, while the wife is required to obey the will of her husband in matters that are specific to marriage, he does not necessarily exercise power over her with respect to other actions.

§107. And then, the purpose of matrimony is not, as that of states, the defense and security of humans. The latter cannot be obtained without political power, just as states cannot be understood without political power. The purpose of marriage is the propagation of the human race, which, it seems, can be achieved by means of agreement and friendship alone, without power.

§108. If we argued that the wife is obliged by nature to the above, it would follow that the conjugal agreement is by nature an unequal agreement, in which the wife above all owes the husband obedience, while he owes her protection.

§109. But we have already refuted that idea [that the wife is obliged by nature to the above]. We therefore affirm that this inequality is not the result of nature, but (leaving aside revelation) depends on the free will of the contracting parties.

§110. It is not allowed here to appeal to a natural prerogative of the male sex. For even if there were such a thing, it would only be a reason for saying that the man was more suitable to receive obedience. It would not impose an obligation on the wife to promise her husband such obedience in an agreement. Yet I greatly fear that the philosophers who attribute some natural prerogative to the masculine sex generally either suffer from an ignorance of sacred history, which tells us about our first parents' original sin, or confuse the effects of common education, which is the true reason for the imperfection of the female sex, with the nature of the sex itself.

§111. Therefore, we shall choose a middle way and not believe that there is any reason in natural law why a wife should submit herself by means of an agreement in the proper sense to the power of her husband.

§112. The argument that the wife does not hold marital power, and therefore cannot transfer it to her husband in marriage, has already been sufficiently refuted by others.[20]

---

20. See Pufendorf, *Of the Law of Nature and Nations,* bk. VI, chap. i, §12.

§113. Indeed, the common principle that a person who does not have something cannot transfer it to another is only valid in rights that refer to things. For if you mean rights that refer to persons, such as power, then an infinite number of examples can be given.

§114. If, therefore, the husband does not by nature exercise power over the person of his wife, then it is even less the case that he has power by nature over the goods of his wife. That will depend on the agreement between the spouses and on positive laws.

§115. There is no less controversy over the question whether matrimony can be dissolved according to the law of nature. Here it seems two questions need to be separated from each other. First, whether the law of nature dictates that the essence of a marriage requires the contracting parties to agree that they want it to last until the end of their lives; then, assuming they have entered such an agreement, whether there can be just reasons that would allow one part to be granted a divorce against the will of the other, in spite of the agreement.

§116. Concerning the former, it is generally accepted by all nations that a momentary cohabitation for the sake of a single act of sexual intercourse is not considered marriage anywhere, because even if the persons involved in that single instance intended to produce a child, they cannot be certain to obtain the purpose of a marriage with this single act of physical intercourse. That requires a longer period of time and more frequent copulation.

§117. In addition, whichever society you look at, it normally does not deserve to be called a society, if it is only formed for the sake of a momentary fellowship. It is perhaps for that reason that Ulpian doubted whether he should allow a society among those who bought something by common consent and then divided it up among themselves immediately.[21]

---

21. See *Digest* 17.2.31ff.

§118. Yet it is not necessary to go to the other extreme. For it is not possible to argue that as conjugal society is not fleeting it must therefore be perpetual. Rather, if we take only natural law, then a society deserves to be called marriage even if the contracting parties separate after the child has been conceived, for they have obtained the purpose of that society.

§119. For it must not be believed that natural law binds humans to procreate forever. If there are certain cases, which we have listed above, in which it is clearly permissible not to enter such a society, there can also be cases in which someone meets the obligations of natural law if he produces one child. And so this too will be considered a marriage, even if it is formed only for that purpose.

§120. Hence, even if someone were under an unspecified obligation to produce more children, the law of nature nevertheless does not command that this has to be repeated with the same individual. Nothing prevents the man or the woman from concluding a new marriage with a different person, after this aim has been achieved in the first marriage.

§121. If it is permissible to withdraw from a society so quickly, then we must consider it to be all the more a case of marriage if the cohabitation of man and wife is uninterrupted until the child has been born, and even more so if this is the case until it has been brought up, and most of all if the marriage was entered into for life.

§122. Thus, according to natural reason these societies, formed in various ways, differ from each other in their degrees of perfection, but none is to be considered irrational.

§123. If we suppose that to be the case, then the man and the woman either decided how long they wanted to remain in this society when they first entered it, or they did not decide on it.

§124. If they did the former, I see no reason why it should not be permissible on the basis of natural reason alone for one spouse to withdraw once the purpose of the marriage has been fulfilled, even if this is against the will of the other.

§125. You may object that every pact includes the provision that one part cannot withdraw from it unless the other gives its consent or the agreement has been violated by the other party; therefore, it is contrary to natural law if one of the spouses withdraws from the other against this other person's will when the matrimonial agreement has not been violated in any respect and if he or she does so only to improve his or her own condition or because it pleases him or her to do so. But I would reply that this objection is not applicable because the spouse who withdraws from the other against the other's will does not withdraw from the agreement, but only from the society which he or she was never obliged to continue forever.

§126. If it should happen that the renunciation of this social bond caused harm to the other spouse, then the precept on avoiding harm to others requires the renouncing person to indemnify the other party, but it does not oblige him or her to refrain from the renunciation.

§127. Furthermore, although each spouse in marriage enjoys a right to physical contact with the other, and nobody can be deprived of a right against his or her will, the question is whether this right is perpetual or temporary and revocable.

§128. Finally, you may argue that marriages are not to be dissolved even by mutual consent, even if there is a very important reason, because it is indecent and harmful, and because the freedom to divorce cannot but severely undermine families and the public decorum in civil societies. I would reply that we have been concerned with what is just, not with what is decorous.

§129. Also, we are here concerned with explaining marriage in abstraction from the civil state. The interest of civil society, which civil laws need to take account of, must not be mixed with the purpose of conjugal society, which we are dealing with at the moment.

§130. Moreover, the same applies to the interest of the family, which is the society hoped for from marriage, but which is not the immediate primary purpose of marriage, although it is not yet clear in what respect the decorum of a family suffers from a divorce that is done with good grace.

§131. We must now examine the latter question: if a man has bound himself to a woman for the rest of his life, and she has bound herself to him, or if a particular period of time was fixed by some other means, could one party withdraw from this agreement for just reasons? There is no doubt that, if one spouse maliciously deserts the other or stubbornly and voluntarily denies the other what is owed in marriage, then this spouse, according to natural law, is freed from the obligation imposed by the agreement, because physical intercourse is necessary for obtaining the purpose of marriage. It is true in general that the damaged party acquires the right to withdraw from an agreement whenever its principal points have been infringed.

§132. The same reason suggests that if a woman has agreed not to have any children that are not her husband's, and, apart from having further children with him, not to admit further passengers on board the fully laden ship, then it is considered just grounds for divorce if the wife voluntarily and without coercion allows another man access to her body.

§133. People in all societies who enter agreements direct these toward the purpose of the society. Thus agreements based on natural law will include a tacit exception in case their purpose cannot be obtained. I would, therefore, believe that if we abstract from positive law, then the infertility or sterility of someone who in other respects is capable of copulation is sufficient grounds for divorce.

§134. Fertility is not in a person's power, which means that a sterile person is not to be considered guilty. However, infertility is to be considered an accident, and the consequences of an accident must normally be borne by the person most immediately affected by it. The sterile spouse, therefore, cannot demand that the other be deprived of achieving the purpose which he or she seeks in vain within that marriage and not be allowed to find it elsewhere.

§135. Moreover, besides the procreation of children, the persons entering marriage seek intimate and amicable company. According to natural law it is therefore permissible to end the ties of marriage because of intolerable manners and bad treatment. As uninterrupted and intimate cohabitation ceases, it is not necessary for procreation to continue.

§136. Generally speaking it is possible in an agreement consisting of several points to add a clause which states that, even if there is a deviation in one particular point, the parties will continue fulfilling the terms of the agreement in all other respects. So, even if the wife's troublesome behavior renders her unsuitable for continued cohabitation, she can continue fulfilling her obligation concerning the procreation of offspring. Yet it is not likely that someone whose company is intolerable will be up to performing this duty, or that her partner will not shun a body which houses such an off-putting host. Hardly anyone wishes to raise a child by a woman he dislikes. Therefore, when there is an agreement on physical contact and intimate company, these two must be judged to be mutually linked to such a degree that when one is broken the other appears to be broken as well.

§137. It is, therefore, contrary to natural law to separate spouses from the common table and bed because of intolerable manners and excessive ill-treatment and nevertheless keep the ties of marriage intact, by which they are prohibited from entering another marriage. That is, unless perhaps this separation is imposed for a certain time and as a punishment, in order to break stubbornness and in order to test more carefully whether there is any hope of an improvement in behavior.

§138. I come to the other point, which is a negative one and which we formulated above on the basis of the teachings concerning the purpose of conjugal society. From this we inferred that physical intercourse that is not done for the sake of creating offspring is not to be considered marriage.

§139. The purpose of such intercourse can be no other than the satisfaction of lust, as is clear from our conclusions above. Thus we have already slipped into discussing the extremely difficult question concerning the morality of lust, to the extent that this can be discussed within the limits of natural reason and in abstraction from divine revelation. We will make an effort to deal with this briefly, but succinctly.

§140. By lust we primarily mean a desire to get pleasure from an act of sexual intercourse.

§141. This will therefore be twofold: either the procreation of a child is not intended at all, or it is only accepted as an accidental outcome.

§142. In order to draw a more accurate distinction we shall call an act of lust of the former type whoring (a term to be used in a broad sense, including sodomy, rape, fornication, and other cases), while one of the latter type will be termed concubinage. We shall start by examining whoring.

§143. In order to prove the turpitude of whoring it is not enough to say that it does not serve the primary purpose of marriage. As we have shown above, the satisfaction of lust is also a purpose of marriage, albeit a secondary one. Rather, this argument [that whoring does not serve the primary purpose of marriage] only tells us that whoring is not marriage. It does not tell us that because whoring is not the same as marriage it is dishonest.

§144. It is obvious that a decorous and peaceful society could not exist among humans if all people believed that their organs of reproduction were destined only for the satisfaction of lust and applied them only to that end. But the question is whether this is a sufficient reason to prove that these forms of lust are universally prohibited by natural law. There are several reasons why I believe that this cannot be the case.

§145. For the reason for the prior argument is clearly based on the fact that if humans devoted themselves exclusively to the satisfaction of lust, they would sin against the precept we discussed above, which orders humans to enter marriage. But that danger need not be feared if a person only satisfies his lust on some occasions.

§146. Hence, we have already commented that this precept is indeterminate and general: it does not intend to impose a perpetual and continuous obligation, but one the effect of which sometimes ceases.

§147. We have derived this precept from the principle concerning the performance of the duties of humanity. If these duties ceased completely, then the peace of humankind would indeed be disturbed. But that would not be the case if their performance slackened temporarily.

§148. Thus, when you consider actions that are permitted or commanded by natural law, the following axiom seems to allow for many objections: "Whatever disturbs human society, if humans pursue it to the exclusion of everything else, is universally prohibited."

§149. So it is easy, for example, to regard the pleasure from food and drink, the profit from trade, playing at cards, etc., as indifferent matters, even if human society would without question suffer badly if humans devoted themselves exclusively to the pursuit of these pleasures.

§150. A defender of lust could easily turn our argument against us and describe procreation, which we have shown to be commanded [by natural law], as something despicable because the peace of humankind would be greatly disturbed if humans did nothing but procreate.

§151. The arguments that are commonly used to demonstrate the disgraceful nature of physical attraction toward animals or toward those of the same sex do not resolve all our doubts. It is argued that the other forms of lust are less sinful because in the case of ordinary lust the organs are not used for their natural purpose, while this unspeakable crime [sexual intercourse with animals or homosexual intercourse] is more despicable because in it the organs are used contrary to their natural purpose.

§152. We may not usually examine the truth of this reason because we are convinced of the validity of the conclusion. Yet it is still of great interest to the learned man to make sure that this true argument is not derived from false premises. This is so that he does not allow himself to be led astray from the true path of inquiry, because that would cause one absurd assumption to lead to several. It is also the case that he does not allow unprincipled people, who nowadays are willing to attack any truths whatsoever, to push him into a corner, forcing him (if he does not want to give up his previous opinion, which would not be seemly) to take flight from his ignorance by resorting to some meaningless distinctions of terms, which expose him to ridicule from those learned men who are impartial.

§153. Therefore, it has to be asked whether the use of organs contrary to nature or for ends other than those prescribed by nature is always a sin, and if that sin is as unspeakable as it is made out to be. The mouth and stomach, throat, and gullet are made to nourish man, and they direct us to take in food through the mouth, chew it, and send it down to the stomach. But is it therefore a crime to feed a person through clysters, though physicians recommend the use of clysters in severe illnesses? Or is it a sin against nature to nourish and restore a human being by infusing milk into his veins just because nature created other organs for nutrition and the creation of blood?

§154. The fabric of the human body is such that food ingested through the mouth and sent down to the stomach is expelled through the intestines. Is it therefore a crime to expel it through the mouth if it is necessary to vomit?

§155. Language is given to man to express his thoughts, hands for the sake of mechanical activities and arts. Does, therefore, someone sin against nature if he uses his hands instead of language to inform his fellow human being of his thoughts?

§156. Although some have a tendency to avoid these objections by replying that such examples are irrelevant, because they do not refer to sexual

love, their response is in fact rather obscure: they do not put forward a
clear and distinct reason for the disparity, to explain why this rule applies
to physical love but fails in all other cases.

§157. In order to do so, they usually appeal to the shame caused to man
and to human dignity, adding that the use of natural functions for an
unintended purpose (like those mentioned) is not to be considered a vice
because natural shame is not violated and involves nothing culpable if it
cannot be shown that human dignity is diminished as a result. They argue
that sexual crimes are another matter because these (including exhibition-
ism and incest) are offenses to shame or human dignity, as are the different kinds of whoring and polygamy.

§158. But this proof, which is based on shame and human dignity, seems
to me to make many assumptions and to affirm many opinions to be true
which we only accept as a result of habituation and persuasion by others,
rather than demonstration. If, therefore, you subject their hypotheses to
careful scrutiny, it is obvious they do not rest on such a firm foundation.
Thus it can easily be shown (to take this particular case) that vomiting is
contrary to natural shame and repugnant to human dignity.

§159. I fear, therefore, that the common reasons that are put forward against
whoring will not convince a pagan who has adopted the opinion of Terence, according to which it is not despicable for a young man to whore.[22]
It is rather to be feared that the respondent, who has not defended his position particularly well so far, turns from a respondent into an opponent.[23]

§160. "In what way," says he, "is the satisfaction of all lust contrary to reason? I know that this affection has been implanted in all humans. But how
can something be implanted in human nature and conflict with reason,
that is, the essence of human nature?

22. See Terence (Publius Terentius Afer; b. 193 or 183 B.C., d. 159 B.C.), "The Brothers," in Terence, *Terence*, vol. 2, ed. and trans. J. Barsby, Loeb Classical Library (Cambridge, MA: Harvard University Press, 2001).
23. The "respondent" was expected to defend the central arguments of a university
disputation against the criticisms of the "opponent" in a public debate.

§161. "There is no reason," he continues, "why you should say that the aim of this instinct is the procreation of children and therefore must be subordinated to it. You yourself admitted above that humans feel these stimuli very keenly, even if it is certain that sexual intercourse cannot lead to procreation, or even though civil reasons do not allow them to marry. As you admitted, in this latter case humans were not obliged to marry. Does a human being therefore act contrary to natural law if he follows a desire that is not peculiar to him and that cannot be the result of a bad education, but is common to all of humanity and even the most just of men, and if he represses his amorous frenzy by deriving some pleasure from something toward which nature impels him?"

§162. You may then argue that reason tells us this is despicable and we must not give in to it, because it often causes humans to lose control of themselves and to commit acts that are forbidden by natural law. But he will reply that these effects are to be attributed not so much to the passion itself and the inclination, but to the stubbornness with which man tried to repress this inclination. The argument, therefore, should be turned on its head, and the restraints on the urges of the passions should be relaxed, so that they cannot dethrone reason.

§163. "Thus the desire," he will argue, "to eat and drink is human, not prohibited by natural law, but if you do not provide the stomach with food and drink, hunger and thirst follow, which often drive people to commit equally great, if not greater, crimes.

§164. "Therefore," he will argue, "whoring is contrary to natural law if someone destroys the goods of his body or mind with it, if he inflicts humiliation or some other harm on another person, or if he violates agreements."

§165. In that case there is little to prevent him from going further and arguing that this is not only an indifferent and permissible, but an honest, action. What if he appeals to the duty of humanity in the case of a tender virgin, who is very ill because of a lack of sexual intercourse and in danger of losing her life? What if he appeals to the utility of the commonwealth, in whose interest it is to set up brothels in order that the purity of married women and virgins is subject to fewer dangers?

§166. He will finally add a question as a corollary,[24] whether we believe that the sexual intercourse of the husband with his pregnant wife is a sinful violation of reason. And on that basis he will want us to show why this action, even if it has only the satisfaction of lust as its purpose, deserves to be considered indifferent and other, similar actions do not.

§167. Here indeed others may believe whatever they want and consider me unworthy of the title of a philosopher. Yet I am compelled to confess that my reason, resting on all the rules of disputation and all principles of rational argument, gives up and does not know how to extricate itself from this labyrinth, unless Christian jurisprudence supplies it with an Ariadne's thread.

§168. You can therefore easily see what remains to be said about concubinage on the basis of the laws of nature. This usually stands for the long-term fellowship of a man and a woman, for the sake of the satisfaction of lust, but the generation of a child is not excluded. This [concubinage] differs from matrimony in the strict sense mainly with respect to its duration, because the latter is perpetual, while the former can be dissolved whenever it pleases the contracting parties. In the case of concubinage it is also assumed that it is entered mainly for the sake of habitual sexual intercourse. In the case of matrimony it is assumed that this is entered into mainly for the sake of producing children, even if the spouses in fact often mainly have the satisfaction of their lust in mind.

§169. Concerning the possibility of dissolving concubinage: we have said above that matrimony does not, according to natural law, require spouses to live together. It is clear that in this respect too the dictate of reason does not prove concubinage to be wrong.

---

24. Printed university disputations often had a list of "corollaria" at the end.

§170. But as far as the primary intention of satisfying lust is concerned, the partners in concubinage will commit a sin, because they turn the guidance of nature and its founder on its head. While the purpose of their intercourse is both procreation and the satisfaction of lust, they desire the former in a secondary sense and by accident, although they know from reason that it is the primary purpose of marriage.

§171. Since here the sin lies in the intention rather than the external action, it is also evident that, leaving aside revelation, this crime violates the first precept of divine jurisprudence in general and the duty of man toward God, rather than pertaining to natural jurisprudence in the strict sense, which mainly concerns the external actions of one person toward another.

§172. The term *concubinage* sometimes tends to be used for a secondary marriage, in which the wife or the children are not left with as many goods or provided with as much material support as their condition or status would otherwise have required. With the exception of those who know nothing about natural law, nobody doubts that this is not contrary to it.

§173. We have now said enough about the purpose of marriage. But in every society the persons involved as well as the purpose deserve to be considered. Therefore, it remains for us to consider the persons, but in such a way that we still keep both eyes fixed on the purpose of marriage, because it is a common saying of philosophers that the material of societies (for that is what they call persons) should be directed according to their end.

§174. So the primary thesis here is as follows: conjugal society requires persons who can produce offspring. It follows from this that this is the principal aim of marriage. In the previous chapter, however, we have already shown that the choice of persons in societies depends on this purpose.

§175. Therefore, a man and a woman are required, not two men and not two women, for these cannot produce a child.

§176. Unless you perhaps wanted to claim that women can conceive as a result of a strong imagination or without the sperm of a man, either of which is absurd.

§177. Furthermore, it is necessary for women and men to be capable of procreation. Therefore, infants who have not yet reached puberty are excluded.

§178. There is no marriage with a eunuch, who has either had his organ of reproduction removed or whose testicles have been cut off. The former is practiced in the Orient; the latter is more common in Europe.

§179. There is also no marriage with a woman who suffers from a physical defect that does not allow marital intercourse, because of the excessive narrowness of her vagina.

§180. As far as she and the oriental eunuchs are concerned, the matter is clear: they are capable of neither procreation nor the satisfaction of lust.

§181. Yet there have often been furious debates over European eunuchs: although they are unable to produce a child, they nevertheless are often such that they cannot be safely trusted with the custody of someone's wife, since they are highly promiscuous and pseudo-adulterers.[25]

§182. If we argue from reason, it seems to me evident from the line of argument above that the union of a eunuch with a woman is not to be considered marriage, because of the absence of the primary purpose.

§183. Yet some have argued the contrary, that they [European eunuchs] are capable of satisfying lust. Many others have doubted that, claiming that

---

25. On this, see Hieronymus Delphinus, *Eunuchi Conjugium, Die Capaunen-Heyrath* (Halle, 1685). See also Mary E. Frandsen, "*Eunuchi Conjugium:* The Marriage of a Castrato in Early Modern Germany," *Early Music History* 24 (2005): 53–124.

these dry sexual acts only stimulate lust further, but to me the opposite seems to be true.

§184. Let us therefore concede to the dissenters that this is so. Can they then produce a single example of a society that clearly lacks its proper primary purpose and is classified on the basis of its secondary purpose?

§185. Indeed, it is strange that they do not consider random whoring to be matrimony, since that too satisfies lust.

§186. It is even more ridiculous when they appeal to the fact that they provide mutual assistance, in running the household, for example, and taking care of bodily needs. As if it were a marriage when two men or two women formed a partnership for that purpose.

§187. It is another question whether the partnership of a eunuch with a woman must not be tolerated under natural law, just because it cannot be matrimony. Here we will have to repeat what we said above about lust in general. The resolution of the remaining issues will have to be postponed until the next chapter.

§188. There remain the impotent, the sterile, old men and women. Our customs permit them to marry, but we need to say something about this, especially as the patrons of eunuchs believe that their opinion is confirmed by these examples.

§189. They say that these people are allowed to marry, even though they never propagate and although old men are not even able to satisfy their lust. They can only obtain mutual assistance. Why then should eunuchs be banned from marrying, since they are not only able to offer mutual assistance, but also to provide the requisite pleasure?

§190. I confess that many have examined this kind of objection, especially as they saw that the common customs of nations allow marriage on the point of death, mainly in order to legitimate natural children. But there, too, it is impossible to obtain the procreation of a child or of any other aim of marriage because of the imminence of death.

§191. Some have tried to counter that objection by saying that consent just before death did not refer to a marriage that started from that instant in the present, but was only a declaration of affection, which was to be applied retrospectively, and created a presumption in favor of marriage [in previous years].

§192. But this reply seems to run counter to the common intention of nations, and, moreover, has the inconvenient consequence that he who begat children outside marriage, and was then made a eunuch by accident, can marry his concubine just before his death in order to legitimate his children. It [this reply] also cannot be applied universally to all marriages of this kind, since there are many of them, even where there are no children to be legitimated and with a woman with whom he had never before been together.

§193. Thus, to get rid of all these objections in one swoop, we declare briefly: these marriages of the impotent, the sterile, and old men and women are to be tolerated, because in all of them there is a hope that they can naturally produce a child.

§194. Impotent people are those who are prevented by some illness from being able to procreate immediately. But many do procreate once that obstacle has been removed.

§195. In sterile people the cause of sterility is hidden, and there are examples of sterile women who gave birth after they had been considered incurable by physicians.

§196. Concerning old men and women, even if physicians assign a certain number of years to men and women after which they cease to beget and conceive, this is determined on the basis of what usually tends to happens. Daily experience shows that children are born to old men.

§197. There is no reason to object that it is uncertain whether this was not done with the help of others. That goes against the presumption of a person's honesty until the contrary has been shown to be true. These conjectures are also supported by stories, based on experience, of old women who give birth. Why should that which can be hoped for in one sex not be a legitimate hope in the other sex?

§198. Yet it cannot be denied that young people or persons who are not very old are better able to fulfill the purpose of marriage. Therefore, it is not inappropriate if some civil laws forbid a woman to marry after the age of fifty and a man to do so after the age of sixty.

§199. Finally, in those marriages that are concluded just before death, there remains a hope that all aims of marriage can be obtained. We are not of course referring to that final moment, in which the soul leaves the body, but that time between life and death, in which humans, based on medical reasons, have lost hope that the sick person's health will be restored. There are so many people who recovered after the physicians had given up!

§200. The course of the argument leads us to the question whether the procreation of a child requires one man and one woman only, that is, whether polygamy is prohibited by natural law.

§201. This has been the subject of acrimonious debate ever since some fanatics desperately tried to defend the view that divine law commanded male polygamy and that Christian magistrates committed a grave sin if they did not permit this to their subjects.

§202. Here it has to be admitted that among various authors those who tried to suffocate this monstrous opinion by arguing from reason only provided it with an occasion to gather in strength and, with one great blow, to strike down these feeble attackers.

§203. Indeed, as we have shown elsewhere, male polygamy (one man being married to several wives) cannot be attacked on the basis of natural law, because there is no reason why it should directly disturb the sociality of humankind or prevent the begetting of children. If natural reason is left to its own devices, it would rather seem that polygamy helps to propagate humankind.

§204. The counterarguments that are put forward, concerning jealousy, domestic discord, the unkindness of stepmothers, which is continued in their offspring, and other domestic inconveniences—these have all been refuted several times by a variety of authors.

§205. If you want to add an a posteriori argument that will be valid against Christians to the previous a priori argument, then divine dispensation will provide a very good one: God in the Old Testament allowed the Jewish people, or at least certain fathers, to practice polygamy, and it was even considered one of the benefits conferred on David that God gave him several wives. For who would believe that God regarded something as a benefit which was contrary to human nature and banned by natural law?

§206. There is greater consensus among the learned that female polygamy, that is, the union of one woman with several men, is contrary to natural law, because it appears to conflict with (1) the procreation of offspring, (2) mutual assistance, (3) rule by the husband; also (4) because it only appears to serve the satisfaction of lust and (5) God never allowed it. If these reasons are at all valid, they will also be valid against having wives in common. Therefore, what we have to say should be extended to the community of wives, too.

§207. The solidity of these reasons, however, will in part be obvious from what has been said, and in part I have elsewhere shown it in individual cases in more detail.[26]

§208. On this basis it will not be difficult to respond to the secondary arguments. If female polygamy or the community of wives were allowed, then

26. See Thomasius, *De crimine bigamiae.*

many quarrels would break out between men over the attractive women. A pregnant woman would lack assistance, because none of the men would help her unless he knew she was pregnant with his child. That is impossible in this kind of community. Then the education of the child, which none of the men would want to undertake for the same reason, would be laborious and involve a lot of effort for the woman on her own, who would barely be able to manage. Finally, relatives would not be sufficiently distinct, and there could also be no patrimonies. And once these have been removed, a great part of the advantages that sustain and adorn human life would go under.

§209. But if we had nothing else to oppose to these arguments, it would be enough to point out that they refer to domestic inconveniences that can be easily remedied and are only the result of accident. And so we would have to repeat what is usually said in response to male polygamy.[27]

§210. I will not mention that the Stoics taught that wives should be held in common by the wise. Each [wise man] should have intercourse with the first woman that he met. For this would mean that all would be like fathers and love the offspring equally, and all suspicion of adultery and excessive zeal would be removed. I also will not mention that Plutarch believed it would very much conform to natural and civil reason if in some cases wives were held in common.[28]

§211. Now the arguments against female polygamy, especially the argument that it is not such a good means to obtain the goal of procreation and the propagation of the human race, show that it is barely permissible and closer to being prohibited than to being commanded. It is different with the marriage between one man and one woman, or with male polygamy.

27. See §204 in this chapter.
28. Thomasius is here drawing on Pufendorf, *Of the Law of Nature and Nations,* bk. VI, chap. i, §15. See also Diogenes Laertius, "Zeno," bk. VII, §131, p. 235, in Diogenes Laertius, *Lives of Eminent Philosophers,* and Plutarch, "Lycurgus," chap. xv, pp. 251–53, in Plutarch, *Lives,* trans. B. Perrin, vol. 1, Loeb Classical Library (London: Heinemann, 1914).

§212. If you want to examine the degrees of permissibility of these various kinds of union, and to define on the basis of unaided, natural reason which of these is to be considered the more decorous and perfect form of marriage, I greatly fear that male polygamy will be supported by most people. As I have said, the primary aim of marriage seems to be furthered more effectively by that than by monogamy, and domestic peace and quiet have been achieved perfectly well by nations using male polygamy. Finally, the jealousy of women generally presupposes some right acquired by consent. If, therefore, this acquisition ceases, this zeal will necessarily be greatly diminished, especially if the nation is such that the husbands are not excessively subservient to their wives, and the education of women is managed in such a way that their minds are not raised too high.

§213. On those grounds, monogamy is not to be regarded as being contrary to natural law, but reason will consider it to be placed in the middle between either kind of polygamy. Or, to speak more precisely, it will be related to the precept, as, for example, the number five is related to number seven, while male polygamy will be comparable to a six and female polygamy to a two.

§214. Yet at the same time the argument above depends on the resolution of the question whether it is permitted by natural law to enter matrimony with a woman who is already married to another or with a man who is already married to a woman. For if a man and a woman promise to live together forever and not to have physical intercourse with anyone else, the question undoubtedly has to be answered in the negative. Otherwise, it would be a violation of the precept of the law of nature, which says that promises must be kept.

§215. If such an agreement is lacking or one of the forms of polygamy is accepted, you will not be able within the limits of natural reason to come up with an argument that is suitable to convince anyone of the turpitude of such an action.

§216. You see, therefore, in what respect adultery is contrary to natural law. You may describe this, as the Romans did, as a violation of the marriage bed, or, as present-day jurists do, as a violation of conjugal faith. In either case the married person has violated the principle of natural law that promises must be kept. In the former this only applies to the woman, because among the Romans the man alone had the right to the marriage bed. In the latter it applies to both because of their mutual promise.

§217. An unmarried person who has an affair with the spouse of another sins against an innocent person, because this is a violation of the precept not to harm others.

§218. But if one of the partners agrees for the other to have physical intercourse with a third person, how do you want to show that there is nothing naturally repugnant about an intercourse of this kind? Indeed, both sides could renounce their right based on the agreement, unless a higher command stands in the way, which so far we have looked for in vain with the resources of reason.

§219. Hence it will be extremely difficult to demonstrate the despicability of bawdiness or its many different manifestations within the limits of that discipline [i.e., philosophy], which only follows natural reason.

§220. It remains to be seen whether persons between whom there is a blood relationship or something similar are by nature suited for marriage. Or whether incest is contrary to natural law.

§221. The belief that some people ought to abstain from marriage is seen to be common among all nations that have some sort of moral culture. Yet it is exceedingly difficult to assign a solid reason to this and one that clearly follows from the social nature of man, as all the other precepts do.

§222. Some here take refuge simply in the abhorrence felt by the human passions, claiming that all those who were not corrupted by a bad education or vicious habit sensed something within themselves that resisted such a union, and that this was a clear sign incest was prohibited by natural law.

§223. But others have already responded satisfactorily to these arguments.[29] Plutarch's argument about spreading friendship more widely by means of more extensive family relationships does not carry sufficient weight for that which happens contrary to it to be considered useless or illicit, even if Augustine adopted this opinion.[30]

§224. The best possible way to proceed is if we distinguish the different kinds of incest. For there is a difference between incest in cases of consanguinity and incest with other relatives. Each of the two takes place either in a direct or collateral line of descent.

§225. We must above all look at incest that is committed between blood relations in a direct line. For consanguinity is prior to wider family relations, but the direct line is the foundation of the collateral line.

§226. Socrates, that wise man, thought there was nothing wrong with such a marriage except for the difference in age, the result of which may be either sterility or a deformed offspring. But that seems a very poor argument.

§227. Others wanted to show the foulness of such marriages by saying that it led to confusion between the different words for friends. But I do not know why they want to judge things by their words and to forget the common axiom that words have been invented for the sake of things, not the other way round.

§228. Moreover, no law forbids a son to marry the mother of his stepmother, even if he thereby becomes father-in-law to his father and stepfather to his stepmother, and his stepmother becomes stepdaughter to her stepson and mother-in-law to her own mother, etc.

---

29. See Pufendorf, *Of the Law of Nature and Nations,* bk. I, chap. vi, §28, and Grotius, *The Rights of War and Peace,* bk. II, chap. v, §12.

30. Plutarch, "The Roman Questions," 108, in Plutarch, *Moralia,* vol. 4; Augustine, *The City of God,* bk. XV, chap. 16, p. 667.

§229. Those people, however, who insist categorically that natural law forbids marriages between ascendants and descendants, whatever the degree of difference between them, because of the common blood (which is certainly true in the closer degrees), only tighten the knot and do not untie it, for it is quite unclear how the physical community of blood can produce a moral effect.

§230. There remain two reasons which seem more substantial: the debt of reverence and natural shame. For the husband, who is the superior according to the law of marriage, cannot show the reverence toward his mother that nature requires, nor can the daughter show the requisite reverence to her father, for although she is the inferior in the marriage, matrimony leads to a society that excludes the necessity for such reverence.

§231. But there is no lack of possible responses. For if you separate reverence from shame, it does not seem so absurd for a mother to be married to a son who is his own master, since it is perfectly possible for a husband to show reverence to his wife because of her virtue, wisdom, or nobility. It is possible even more so for a daughter as wife to show reverence together with conjugal obedience toward her father and husband, if shame does not stand in the way.

§232. This assertion, however, can best be clarified through examples. Subjects owe their rulers greater reverence than children do their parents. In spite of that it does not seem contrary to natural law at all for a prince to marry a female subject and for a queen to marry a male subject, even if in either case the husband and wife retain the character of subjects, and so she is required to show reverence toward her husband, while he must do the same to the queen, his wife.

§233. Yet there was a time when I thought that reverence was the reason for the ban on marriages between relatives in a direct line, and that this principle could not be shaken by the example produced, because it was impossible to draw a conclusion from reverence based on man-made causes, and therefore capable of dispensation, and reverence that is immediately due on the basis of nature and therefore cannot be relaxed.

§234. But on closer examination this response does not get rid of the objection. This is not because it is not true that the reverence of subjects is based on human causes (which is the common opinion, about which more below), and therefore the reason for the reverence owed to the rulers is the same as that toward parents. Rather, the reason is that it does not seem to be entirely true that reverence toward parents cannot be relaxed.

§235. When we discuss paternal society we shall show that children must show reverence toward their parents as long as they are being educated by them, since there can be no obedience without reverence and without obedience there can be no education. Thus parents, being obliged to raise their children, cannot allow their reverence to slacken. But at the same time it will be clear that once the education is complete, the need for obedience ceases, and there remains only the reverence which is to be shown to parents in memory of the previous benefits. And since the parents only have a right to this reverence, without a concomitant obligation, I do not see why the parents cannot renounce this right and relax the demand for their children's reverence, especially as there is nothing despicable in familiar intercourse.

§236. Thus we often see a genteel father engage in friendly conversation with an adult son, who is endowed with sound judgment and good manners, talking to him with greater familiarity than you will find even among equals. And nevertheless nobody accuses them of a crime against right reason, not to mention the very frequent intimate conversations between mothers and their married daughters.

§237. As far as the marriage of a son with his mother is concerned, we have already shown that a wife does not owe reverence to her husband on the basis of natural law. So, even if we declared that filial reverence could not be relaxed, why should the mother in marriage not keep the right she already has to demand reverence?

§238. We will next examine shame which the jurist Paul already took notice of in his own age, when he said that it was a violation of shame to marry one's own daughter. And this is put forward as a general reason why marriages between persons related by birth or marriage are forbidden, or as a specific reason against the marriage between parents and their children.[31]

§239. It would take too much time to discuss the prior opinion. Therefore, we must only repeat here what we have stressed above when we were talking about whoring.

§240. As far as the latter is concerned, there is a twofold argument why we feel shame with respect to the genitals and the act of procreation: first, because these and the neighboring parts of the body eject ugly and fetid substances. Therefore, man's proud character, which longs for glory and grace, usually takes great care that these signs of weakness are not evident.

§241. Second, the passions have been corrupted by the fall and man's depraved lust likes to show itself with great force in those parts, but the linchpin of all decorum in human society is the regulation by sacred laws of the procreation of children. Nature was keen to preserve this dignity and invented shame, which led humans to cover these organs carefully, to prevent them from being constantly exposed to view and stimulating ever-ready lust. This made it possible to refrain from illicit venery to a greater degree. Even if it [sexual love] is legitimate, the tender sense of shame means it has to be performed in secret and without witnesses.

§242. This shame, it is said, is particularly strong in relation to those persons toward whom we owe some kind of reverence, or toward whom we need to display some kind of gravity, such as parents and children, so that he who is not ashamed to have physical intercourse with them is considered to be very brazen and a person for whom no sin is likely to be

31. See *Digest* 23.2.14.2.

too great. Because of this shame, therefore, it is argued, marriages between relatives in a direct line are considered prohibited.

§243. Yet aside from the fact that depraved lust, which is presented as the main foundation of shame, cannot really be demonstrated on the basis of reason, it seems that we must above all remember that the reason for the prohibition is sought in shame and reverence jointly.

§244. For just as we have discussed reverence separately from shame in some detail, so, if we speak about shame alone and leave aside reverence, it would seem to follow that no marriages are permitted at all, since all humans detect this shame within themselves and are therefore obliged to observe this shame among themselves.

§245. But even if you join shame and reverence, I fear that we will get the same response: that parents can relax this demand for reverence, and that we will again be faced with the example of the marriage of princes with their subjects.

§246. I would, therefore, prefer to accept the inadequacy of our powers of reasoning and to affirm that marriages between parents and children are not the subject of natural law, but of another, divine law.

§247. Therefore, it will be easy to judge concerning other persons with whom incest is committed. This incest is not covered by natural law, as others have already shown in greater detail, and as has already been accepted by many who have abandoned the previous opinion that marriages between brothers and sisters are also contrary to natural law.

§248. If we wanted to summarize what we have said so far, the definition of marriage, insofar as this is known from natural reason, is "a partnership of man and woman for the sake of procreation."

§249. The duties of spouses, however, are covered by this single precept: "Each spouse must do what prudence determines is necessary for the sake of procreation and, after that, the satisfaction of lust."

§250. The husband, therefore, will be obliged to sleep with the wife as much as is necessary for conception, and not to prevent conception through masturbation, and to extinguish the lust of the wife as much as he can while taking care not to cause harm to an unborn child.

§251. The duty of the wife is similar: to allow the husband physical inter-course not just for the sake of procreating children, but also to satisfy his lust.

§252. It is, therefore, a grave violation of their duty if either prevents conception by drinking something to cause sterility or brings about an abortion.

≈ CHAPTER III ≈

On the Positive Laws Concerning
the Duties of Marriage

§1. So far we have shown to what extent it is possible to teach the duties of marriage on the basis of natural reason alone. We must not be surprised, therefore, if we often see pagans being uncertain about how to derive their arguments, for which we as Christians can provide very clear reasons, and to see them appealing to some obscure law, which is unwritten, inborn, or something similar.

§2. Divine wisdom did not want man to enter this society, which is very natural and the seedbed of humankind, by following the guidance of reason alone, not even in the state of innocence. Marriage was established by God as soon as the first parents had been created, and it was reinforced by certain positive laws binding all humans, to which God, after the fall from grace, added others concerning the duties of spouses.

§3. Do not expect us, however, to inquire into the reason for this divine institution and to ask why God in that state of perfection added positive laws to the laws of nature: the humble reverence we owe toward the supreme God commands us to refrain from inquiring idly and with guilty curiosity into the reasons for God's deeds, which the Creator did not deign to reveal to us. It will be enough to contemplate with piety and devotion those laws which his benignity has added to those that have already been promulgated, to the extent that this is necessary for declarative, extensive, and restrictive interpretation.

§4. But we shall always take into account the requisites of divine positive law, as we defined them above. As far as the rabbinical traditions are concerned, we will not reject them out of hand, but will always subordinate them to the authority of Scripture.

§5. Divine laws are publicized in two ways, either explicitly in Scripture or by the fact that an institution is established by God. There is no doubt that the former type of divine law binds humankind. In the case of the latter it has to be supposed that (as the theologians demonstrate more fully) every divine institution is at the same time a divine law.

§6. There can be no doubt that the institution of marriage has the force of law. Our Savior, the best and authentic interpreter of the divine laws, often resolved matrimonial controversies on the basis of that original institution, as if on the basis of a law.

§7. Perhaps it is not inconvenient, therefore, if we present these divine laws in chronological order, beginning with those that accompanied the state of innocence and progressing from there to the laws that followed the fall from grace. Yet it is sometimes doubtful in which state of humankind they were promulgated, as we shall emphasize, and it is also to be feared that the students, for whom we are mainly writing this, will be confused if we follow a different method from that which we used in the previous chapter. We therefore thought it better to follow this order [which we used in the previous chapter], and to examine the degree to which the precepts of natural law have been supplemented by God and certain acts that are indifferent in terms of natural law have been commanded or forbidden by positive law.

§8. Therefore, concerning the command to enter matrimony, God repeated this in the first benediction, in the words "Be fruitful and increase in number." Like the subsequent words, "and subdue the earth,"[32] these

---

32. Genesis 1:28.

do not merely permit something to humans, but without doubt have an obligation linked to them.

§9. In that passage God, however, reiterated the law of nature, and, as everyone will agree, did not increase its obligation or want to restrict humans' liberty to an even greater degree than had been done by the dictate of reason. It necessarily follows that what we have added above by way of limitation and explanation to the precept on entering marriage is applicable here, too.

§10. Hence, I fear that the power and efficacy of the divine will may not be conveyed properly by saying that all humans should enter matrimony. For even if the dictate of reason on entering marriage binds all of humankind without exception, yet the precepts on performing the duties of humanity, to which we also refer the present command, are applied less strictly to all individual human beings. Even if, for example, humans in general are under an obligation to give alms, it would be absurd for someone to say that all humans had to give alms.

§11. Also, as all affirmative precepts require an appropriate occasion to be put into practice, it is crass to demand that this precept should carry such a strict obligation that he who is capable of procreation commits a mortal sin if he does not marry.[33]

§12. As if God wanted young men, who often know little more than boys, and are unsuitable to take on the role of a *paterfamilias,* to look for a wife, or [as if he wanted] those who can only guarantee a meager income to themselves and their dependents, to fill the state with beggars!

§13. This opinion perhaps takes its origin from the doctrine of the rabbis, who teach that because of this divine precept, "Be fruitful and increase in number," all men are required to marry a woman before completing their

---

33. Thomasius here refers to Johann David Schwertner (*praeses*) and Moses Schede (*respondens*), *De celebri sed flagitioso pseudo-politicorum axiomate: virum magnis in rebus civilibus versaturum tribus carere oportere: religione, uxore et pudore, a Boeclero in elogio Forstneri adnotato* (Leipzig, 1683).

twentieth year of age, unless someone devotes himself assiduously to the study of the law and therefore is immune to the sharper pangs of lust, or is incapable of procreation because of a lack of those organs which make us men.

§14. And this conjecture is heavily supported by the fact that people commonly add the same limitations as the rabbis: no person was allowed to evade marriage, unless this was by the command of a superior, that is, to follow a divine calling to practice sexual abstinence or because of impotence, as if the matter were settled as soon as these two limitations were observed.

§15. There is no doubt that impotent men are unsuitable for marriage, and the celibacy of those who have been awarded the gift of continence by God is to be considered not only permissible, but a very just act. Similarly, it is contrary to the whole practice of Christianity to say that all those sin who do not have the gift of continence and yet do not marry after puberty, or even after completing their twentieth year.

§16. For as the examples of those who marry before completing their twentieth year are very rare, it follows that enormous sins are being tolerated by all Christian princes, of whatever confession, and that theologians and preachers especially commit a grave sin because they do not persuade politicians that all young adults are to be compelled to enter matrimony no matter whether they have the means to sustain themselves and whether it is convenient or not.

§17. You cannot say that our people enjoy some prerogative before the Gentiles, and that all or at least most of those who abstain from matrimony have the gift of continence, since not only common life and marriages every day prove the opposite, but theologians commonly stress that the gift of continence today is to be regarded as extremely rare and must not be presumed.

§18. You will argue that the precept on entering marriage is affirmative and therefore obliges all humans capable of procreation to enter marriage;

and affirmative precepts like negative precepts are binding at all times and forever, that is, at all times and places. The only exception they allow is the contrary command of a superior.

§19. But this argument is false and can be refuted from the example of the divine law, according to which one must pray (because this concerns divine worship and there can be no superior precept). For even if the Apostle stressed that we must not cease praying, it would be absurd to conclude that we must pray at all times and places, so that a person would sin if he interrupts his prayers for some moments in order to refresh his body or perform some other, perfectly honest functions.

§20. I continue now with the consideration of matrimony, the purpose of which we have shown to be twofold: the procreation of offspring and the satisfaction of lust. Sacred history shows that the former was intended by God before the latter in the institution of marriage. It indicates that God created Eve for the sake of mutual assistance, because none of the beasts could give Adam any help.[34] That is, the beasts did not allow Adam to procreate, even if they might be sufficient to satisfy his lust.

§21. Yet it is difficult to say whether the satisfaction of lust was a secondary aim of marriage in the state of innocence. For there are those who think that lust was completely absent from the state of innocence.[35] Yet there are also those who believe that Adam, even had he remained in the state of innocence, would have felt great pleasure from sexual intercourse with a woman and would have slept with his wife when she was pregnant.[36]

§22. Here we seem to have to separate the physical meaning of lust, which consists in the pleasure of the erotic senses, from the moral meaning, which we have described above.

---

34. Genesis 2:18–22.
35. Thomasius here refers to Alberti, *Compendium,* chap. 10, §26.
36. Velthuysen, *Tractatus moralis.*

§23. The former is an indifferent act and was no more absent from the state of innocence than the pleasure of food and drink, or of other things that affect the human senses. For it is the result of the wonderful physical disposition and structure of the body, which was the same in the state of perfection as it is now, since the theologians have shown that original sin did not affect the natural substance of man.

§24. But in the latter sense it is a sin, and not the least part of original sin. It not only distracts humans from the true purpose of physical union, but is also to a great extent contrary to reason. Thus it could not be present in the original state of happiness.

§25. For our first ancestors never used food and drink purely for the sake of pleasure. Therefore, sexual intercourse would have served this purpose even less.

§26. In addition, in the present state of humankind the abundance of male seed, which is the result of luxury and intemperate eating and drinking, stimulates lust. In the state of innocence, however, there was no luxury at all.

§27. All these factors encourage the husband to sleep with his wife even when she is pregnant, and it is not probable that our first ancestors would have had intercourse after conception.

§28. After the fall from grace, however, God tolerated this [the satisfaction of lust] as a secondary purpose of marriage.

§29. We have added mutual assistance in domestic tasks to these two purposes. Undoubtedly this is not contrary to the divine institution [of marriage] after original sin. It is, however, strange to find among Christians people who believe that this is what was intended in the state of innocence when God said, "I will make an help meet suitable for him."[37]

37. Genesis 2:18.

§30. As if these words did not refer to the procreation of offspring, and as if Adam had wanted Eve's help in acquiring and keeping material goods, in governing servants, raising offspring, all of which tasks were unknown in the state of innocence.

§31. Universal positive law adds nothing new to what we have said in more detail above about consent that has been obstructed by fear, deceit, or error; it [universal positive law] leaves it to human laws to add more specific precepts for the sake of civil peace.

§32. This is the origin of the distinction between the essential and the accidental properties of marriage. Universal divine law knows no other essential features of marriage than those that contribute to the procreation of offspring.

§33. Hence it is that civil laws often vary in defining the essential features. Canon law denies that virginity is an essential quality, but our customs consider it to be a requisite. Without doubt this is based on the Mosaic forensic law, according to which a woman who pretends to be a virgin and is later discovered to have been deflowered, will not only be lawfully repudiated, but will be liable to punishment in addition.[38]

§34. What is also relevant here is that Hebrew civil laws had this particular rule with respect to fear: if a wife had been coerced by force or fear, then the marriage was invalid. But it was not the same, if the husband claimed to have been coerced, because he was not presumed to have been subject to force or fear to the same degree; he could also repudiate his wife at his pleasure if he was dissatisfied with the conditions of the marriage.

§35. I turn to the power of the husband, which I think we have shown cannot be demonstrated from the dictate of reason without the consent of the wife. But universal divine law adds the following precept here: "Let every wife be subject to her husband."

38. Deuteronomy 22:20–21.

§36. This law belongs to the punishments for the fall from grace. Scripture does not reveal anything similar to have been created by God in the state of innocence. Why therefore should we invent something like it?

§37. This is so especially as we showed at the beginning that the dictate of reason did not suggest God had wanted to subject Eve to Adam in the state of innocence. The common cause of power and subjection among humans is imperfection, which could not be predicated of Eve at that time.

§38. As you can see, this argument implies that the power of the husband cannot be demonstrated from reason, but not that it is contrary to it.

§39. Therefore, it will not matter at all if someone gives the example of angels, who do not suffer imperfection, but who nevertheless have some form of government and subjection among themselves, since Scripture applies titles describing their dominions and powers to them.

§40. We might say that there still is some doubt whether these names are only about order or whether they concern power as well. But a clearer response would be that the dictate of reason provides no grounds for assuming relationships of power between angels, but nor is it contrary to reason to do so. Therefore, since Scripture tell us so, we believe it rather than know it. But we cannot say anything similar about the power of the husband.

§41. We must not casually invent something in matters depending on divine revelation. It is possible, for example, that someone may wonder why the interpreters of Scripture generally declare that Eve was subject to her husband even before the fall, that her subjection after the fall was only increased as a way of punishing her, and that while previously she had submitted herself to the direction of her husband voluntarily, later she did so reluctantly and resentfully. Neither the text nor any weighty reason supports this interpretation.

§42. But the reason for this opinion seems to be a remarkable aberration from the rules of logical analysis. They have read what the Apostle [Paul] said, that it is not fitting for wives to command husbands. Two further reasons are added: that Adam was created prior to Eve, and that Eve, not Adam, was seduced by the serpent.[39]

§43. If you wanted to explain the doctrine of the Apostle on the basis of reason, you would come up with this paraphrase: it is not convenient for wives to command husbands, whether you look at the state of innocence or the postlapsarian state. For how could you pretend that the wife held such power in the state of innocence (assuming there was power in the state of innocence at all), since Adam had been created in complete freedom by God, and did nothing afterward to cause his Creator to deprive him of that and to subject him to Eve who had been made of his own flesh. If one of the spouses in the state of innocence was subordinated to the other, it would have been more appropriate for Eve to be subject to the rule of her husband, since she was created later and therefore did not enjoy full freedom before Adam. But following the fall from grace there is no reason why the wife should claim power over her husband. Rather she was compelled to acknowledge the rule of the husband as a punishment for the crime, because she had allowed herself to be seduced first, etc.

§44. But they have changed either the point of the debate or the argument of the Apostle, contrary to the rules of logic and the Apostle's intention. They have interpreted the reasons he [the Apostle] put forward against rule by the wife as if these had been meant to strengthen the rule of the husband: the latter argument was used to prove the power of the husband after the fall from grace, the former to prove it in the state of innocence. Their belief that the latter argument supported both claims [in the state of innocence and after the fall from grace] surely reinforced this explanation, which is why they believed this argument also applied to the first case [i.e., the state of innocence].

§45. But as our paraphrase shows, the Pauline argument is not pointless, even if it is not extended beyond our interpretation. It is therefore easy to reply to the objection by pointing out that it did not follow that the wife

39. 1 Timothy 2:11–14.

must not command the husband just because Adam was created before Eve—that is, unless this priority in time, which God points out to us, is to be judged to refer to power.

§46. You may want to insist further that the secret reason why Eve was not only not created before Adam, but not with him either is that she should not command him, nor be equal to him, but subjected to him. I would reply that this is a fallacy that begs the question, and that this argument is only capable of illustrating the power of the husband once it has been proved, not of actually proving it.

§47. Our opinion, therefore, remains unshaken that this precept only pertains to the situation after the fall from grace. But it will be a positive universal precept which is relevant to all wives, just as the punishment decreed for Adam affects all men.

§48. We conclude that this subjection was imposed on women by God, not to favor and reward the man, but as a disadvantage and punishment for the female sex, which God decreed should be put into practice by the husband. Therefore, it is not up to the husband to decide if he wants to leave the reins of domestic government to his wife on the basis of a conjugal agreement or by tacit connivance. They who do this sin no less than, for example, inferior magistrates, who do not inflict punishments on criminals and arrogate the right to grant mercy, which belongs to the legislator alone.

§49. Again, concerning the dissolubility of marriage, God did not want this decision to be left to human reasoning, but made it impossible by promulgating a positive law: marriage is an indissoluble society.

§50. This law was published through the institution of marriage. Moses does not state it explicitly, but it is concealed in the words used in establishing it: "Therefore a man will leave his father and mother and be united to his wife, and they will become one flesh."[40]

---

40. Genesis 2:24.

§51. We do not deny that various arguments, which are not even clumsy, can be found, if someone wanted to make a case for the permissibility of divorce, according to the rules of doctrinal interpretation. But all of these arguments are cut short with one blow, because our savior drew the following conclusion from these words, when he was disputing against the Pharisees: "Therefore they are not two but one flesh. Thus, what God joined, man may not separate."[41]

§52. For authentic interpretation, such as that of Christ, is not tied to the rules of doctrinal interpretation.[42]

§53. But just as positive laws are subordinated to limitations and dispensations of legislators, so the most merciful divine will grants a limitation for the law in question. Authors hold widely different opinions on this, to such an extent that already Augustine recognized this to be a particularly confused matter.[43]

§54. Indeed, when Moses in his forensic laws granted the Jews the right to dismiss their wives for dishonorable behavior, there immediately arose controversies over the meaning of that law since some believed that the husband was being forced to dismiss his wife in case of adultery, but others taught that he had only been granted the permission to do so.

§55. Again, the Sammaean School believed Moses had only meant adultery when he referred to dishonorable behavior, while the Hillelian interpreted the law as saying that the husband could dismiss the wife for any

---

41. Matthew 19:3–9.

42. Authentic interpretation (*interpretatio authentica*) is distinguished from doctrinal interpretation (*interpretatio doctrinalis*). The former is the interpretation of laws by the legislator, while the latter is a more limited degree of interpretation, which is permitted to those who apply the law, but do not create it.

43. Thomasius here refers to Strauch, *Institutionum juris publici specimen*, title 35; see also Selden, *Uxor Ebraica*, bk. 3, chap. 31, p. 447; Heinrich Linck (*praeses*) and Johann Eckhard Finck (*respondens*), *Usus divortiorum ex divino et humano hocque civili ac canonico iure* (Altdorf, 1686).

reason that caused him displeasure. The Jews later appear to have followed the second opinion to a greater extent than the first.[44]

§56. The Pharisees therefore appear to have had this dispute in mind when they asked Jesus whether it was allowed to divorce a wife, for whatever reason. And when Christ denied it and referred back to the first establishment of marriage, they appealed to the ancient law, arguing that Moses introduced the possibility of a dismissal.

§57. Yet Christ himself evidently approved the doctrine of the Sammaean School by stating that anyone who dismissed his wife (unless she was guilty of fornication) and took another committed adultery; he tacitly dismissed the other opinion by showing that Moses only permitted men to divorce their wives because of their hard-heartedness.

§58. There has been no less of a controversy over the interpretation of the words of Christ, since initially there were some who believed that the subject of the redeemer's discussion with the Pharisees applied only to Jews, but that Christians were not allowed to dismiss their wives, not even for adultery.[45]

§59. Others, however, believed this was allowed, but not commanded. There was no lack of those who defended the latter opinion, and Hieronymus and Augustine disagreed over this matter.[46]

§60. Moreover, others who have granted Christians the right to divorce on grounds of adultery have not been able to agree whether or not the husband can marry another during the lifetime of the adulteress.[47]

---

44. See Selden, *Uxor Ebraica,* bk. 3, chap. 20, pp. 328–29.

45. See also Pufendorf, *Of the Law of Nature and Nations,* bk. VI, chap. i, §23.

46. Thomasius is here drawing on Michael Havemann, *Gamologia synoptica, istud est Tractatus de jure connubiorum* (Frankfurt and Hamburg, 1672), bk. 3, title 6, nn. 3 and 4, pp. 402–3.

47. See Selden, *Uxor Ebraica,* bk. 3, chap. 31, p. 441.

§61. Finally, even if authors agree that Christ criticized the Hillelian opinion and therefore the acceptability of divorce, it is nevertheless disputable whether the term πορνεία (fornication) refers only to the crime of adultery or illicit sexual intercourse, or whether it includes other greater crimes, which tend to be described as fornication in sacred Scripture.

§62. To these you could also add the controversy over whether women also have the right to divorce [their husbands] in cases of adultery. Indeed, Justinus tells a story of a Christian wife who repudiated her impious and disgraceful husband in A.D. 150 on grounds of piety. The examples of Thecla and Fabiola are also discussed in this connection.[48]

§63. The law of Constantine the Great is no cause for uneasiness: he restricted the permission to divorce by declaring that the woman can repudiate her husband only on grounds of homicide, poisoning, and the desecration of graves, while the husband can repudiate his wife for being an adulteress, witch, or procuress. You see that adultery is not included among the causes for which a woman can dismiss her husband.[49]

§64. We must not, however, ignore the fact that when Constantine promulgated this law most of the Nicene fathers[50] were alive. They advised the emperor on all matters concerning Christianity, and he respected them so highly that he left all kinds of decisions almost exclusively to the judgment of the bishops.

§65. Also, we must not neglect to say that there was some doubt about how the opinion of Paul, who allowed malicious desertion as another rea-

---

48. Marcus Junianus Justinus was a Roman historian of the second or third century A.D. Thecla, a young noblewoman, renounced her fiancé after being converted to Christianity by the Apostle Paul. Fabiola (died ca. 400) was a Roman patrician married to a dissolute husband, whom she divorced. She then remarried and was subsequently widowed.

49. Theodosius, *Codex Theodosianus,* 2 vols., ed. Paul Kruger (Berlin: Weidmann, 1923–26), 3.16.1.

50. That is, the participants in the First Council of Nicaea (A.D. 325).

son for divorce besides adultery, could be reconciled with Christ.[51] In this matter, however, it is agreed that Christ speaks of the grounds on which divorce is possible, but Paul is not concerned with the grounds for divorce, but with protecting the liberty of an innocent spouse, who has been unjustly divorced by the other.

§66. These controversies show that it is not surprising if some of our highly authoritative jurists have defended the opinion that it is up to the ruler to define other justified causes for divorce apart from adultery and desertion though the case has to be dealt with in a court of law.

§67. Thus, Milton's opinion is not that flimsy and worthless, even if he is sometimes dismissed.[52] He defends the view that even according to the principles of Christian religion intolerable behavior, as well as unequal and incompatible minds, in the relations between spouses are sufficient grounds for divorce. Indeed, those who are perceived to be so ill suited to each other must be separated.

§68. What he [Milton] says concerning unequal minds[53] does not appear to merit lengthy discussion. I do not know what sort of idea he has of a woman who is suited to the genius of a wise and literate man, one who can become a companion in his studies, revive him with clever jokes when he is tired of his meditations, and lift his spirits with elegant little discourses whenever he is depressed. In that case, you will find very few marriages of wise men that could not be dissolved on those grounds.

§69. But it does seem possible to subscribe to his view on intolerable behavior, even if he does not defend it with reasons that are entirely just. For as we have just said, it is not yet decided among Christians whether Christ

---

51. 1 Corinthians 7:11.

52. See John Milton, *The Doctrine and Discipline of Divorce,* The Works of John Milton, vol. 3, part 2 (New York: Columbia University Press, 1931); Thomasius is here drawing on Pufendorf, *Of the Law of Nature and Nations,* bk. VI, chap. i, §24.

53. See Pufendorf, ibid.

in his disputation against the Pharisees was referring only to adultery or not [as a reason for divorce].

§70. Even if you agreed, you could still make a case on the basis of malicious desertion. Consistories sometimes equate this desertion with the stubborn refusal to perform the conjugal duty, and it has to be seen whether the intolerable behavior is regularly associated with the refusal of the conjugal debt, or whether the conjugal debt can be demanded from a person whose behavior is intolerable.

§71. But I do not wish to resolve a controversy that has been going for so many centuries. I continue rather with the morality of lust according to the doctrine of positive law, which adds this precept: "Avoid all sexual intercourse that is motivated only by lust."

§72. Here must be repeated what we showed a little earlier: lust in the state of innocence did not exist, but followed or accompanied original sin. Therefore, sexual intercourse that only serves to satisfy lust cannot but be sinful, because this is how sin is put into action. On this depends not only the indecency of simple whoring and illicit sexual intercourse, but especially that of bestiality.

§73. And so that no doubt would remain, God not only reckons sodomy of both kinds [i.e., sexual intercourse between men and between men and animals] to be a crime[54] with which the nations are said to have polluted themselves, indicating that this crime was forbidden from the very beginning, either by the original establishment of marriage or in other laws promulgated to Adam and Noah. He also often emphasizes that whorers and adulterers will not enter the kingdom of Heaven.

§74. And because the Apostle teaches that every man should have a wife in order to avoid whoring and vice versa,[55] and God wanted matrimony

---

54. A reference to Leviticus 18:22–23.
55. 1 Corinthians 7.

alone to be the remedy for the burning desire of lust, it follows that illicit sexual intercourse, in which the generation of a child is an unintended accident, and concubinage are forbidden by divine law.

§75. It must even be presumed that in the earliest times intercourse with a menstruating wife was prohibited, not only because the Gentiles were said to have polluted themselves with that crime, but also because this kind of intercourse does not normally lead to procreation and only does so accidentally. Here the reports of some are relevant that according to the laws of the Hebrews the father of a child that was born mutilated was stoned to death because it was assumed he had not abstained from intercourse with a menstruating woman.[56]

§76. We now turn to polygamy. We have shown that neither male nor female polygamy can be criticized on the grounds of natural law. It is another matter with positive universal law, which states that all forms of polygamy are prohibited because God in establishing marriage, which has the force of law, joined one man to one woman and therefore at the same time prohibited either kind of polygamy.

§77. But, you will say, if we extend the establishment of marriage to include the prohibition of polygamy, it would follow that humans must observe the other circumstances that were present at the time of the original establishment—for example, the fact that our first ancestors were naked, that the marriage was concluded in the open air and took place in God's presence, without the intervention of a priest, without the presence of parents and relatives, without guests, without music, without food and drink, without dowry and rings, etc., all of which we have in present-day marriages. Surely, you say, that would not only be ridiculous, but we would in some respects also sin against the dictate of right reason.[57]

56. See Ayrault, *Rerum iudicatarum Pandectae,* bk. II, title 4, chap. 8, p. 86.
57. Paragraphs 77–90 rest on Thomasius's earlier disputation *De crimine bigamiae* of 1685.

§78. To resolve this doubt, some tend to distinguish between the accidental and essential features of marriage. The argument based on the original establishment of marriage, therefore, was applicable to the essential features of marriage, that is, its substance, or the persons entering it, and its form, that is, the unbreakable bond between man and woman. It did not extend to the accidental features accompanying it, which were the basis for the objection. But we have already shown elsewhere that this response complicates the matter rather than cutting the knot.

§79. We would rather say that all circumstances of something established by God for humans are to be observed as law and to be considered essential, as long as it is apparent that God had a specific purpose that was relevant to the matter or did not remove these circumstances again afterward.

§80. It is thus clear that God created the first pair of ancestors in order that they propagate humankind through marriage. If, therefore, he had wanted to permit one woman to be joined to several men, or one man to several women, he would have created several men or several women, especially since the propagation of humankind, which is what the defenders of male polygamy mainly put forward as an argument, was more urgent then than it is now.

§81. I infer from this that God wanted this circumstance, the union of one man and one woman, to be something specific with respect to marriage, and that it, therefore, should be referred to its essential circumstances.

§82. The argument by the defenders of polygamy that God created only one pair of humans because he wanted all of humankind to be descended from one blood does not present any problems. This assertion is not incompatible with ours, since God could have had several reasons for doing something; moreover, this reason has a specific purpose with respect to marriage, which is sufficient for us. Therefore, I do not know whether they can develop any solid arguments from that.

§83. They may argue that this end would not have been obtained if God had created several women and joined them to Adam. Yet I fear that this opinion cannot be proved. To us the opinion of the physicians seems more convincing, who declare that the child is generated or indeed brought to life from the male seed only.[58] And in Scripture itself the following phrase is frequently used: a human being is generated from the blood of the man; and in jurisprudence, too, brothers who are descended from one father (but not from one mother) are for good reasons said to be related by blood.

§84. Concerning the examples of polygamy, everybody knows that our first parents were naked, but that is not relevant to matrimony in particular. If man had remained in the state of innocence, this would have applied to the blessed humans in heaven too. Yet after the fall God ordered our first parents to cover their nakedness and thereby abolished it.

§85. The fact that the first marriage was celebrated in open air again says nothing about marriage itself, since there were no buildings at that time and, in any case, location must normally be considered a contingent circumstance.

§86. God in our present times does not want to join humans in marriage himself. This is evident, because he does not converse with us the way he did with Adam.

§87. Finally, what is said about the priest, parents, guests, and other circumstances is no counterargument, since we have said only that none of the circumstances which were present at the first establishment of something by God are to be omitted by man; we did not say that none must be added. For other features may be introduced for the sake of observing decorum in human life, as long as the original circumstances are not removed by that.

§88. But what need is there for a more prolix controversy according to the rules of doctrinal interpretation? In his debate with the Pharisees which

---

58. That is, even if Adam had been married to several women, all his descendants would have been descended from one blood.

I referred to above, Christ himself, whose explanation must be considered an authentic interpretation, shows very clearly that both kinds of polygamy, male and female, are forbidden in the original establishment of marriage, by appealing to the establishment of marriage and saying: at the beginning it was not thus.[59]

§89. Although this debate [with the Pharisees] was not about polygamy, it is permissible to prove our thesis by arguing from Christ's statement. For if a woman whom a man had dismissed commits adultery by marrying another, a woman who takes another before she has been dismissed by her husband will be even more of an adulteress. And if a man who takes another woman after dismissing his previous wife (whether she is willing to be dismissed or not) is guilty of adultery, then he will be an even greater adulterer if he keeps his former wife and takes another in addition to her, whether this is in accordance with or against his former wife's will.

§90. The argument is so strong that it does not require further proof, although the aficionados of polygamy go to great lengths to refute it. This is why they suggest that the adultery, in the said passage by Christ, is not committed by marrying another person, but as a result of repudiating the previous spouse. However, others have already shown the emptiness of this falsehood.[60]

§91. It is easy to respond to the examples of male polygamy [that is, of one man having many wives]. Its permissibility is debated above all among the Jews. Those people who attack polygamy on grounds of natural law must either admit the possibility of dispensations in natural law or assert that God only tolerated polygamy, but did not approve of it.

§92. Yet neither explanation is convincing. We have shown that natural law does not allow dispensation.[61] The idea that God tolerated polygamy

59. See §§49ff in this chapter.
60. See Musaeus, *Dissertatio de quaestione controversa,* and Diecmann, *Vindiciae legis monogamicae,* which were responses to Lyser's *Discursus politicus de polygamia.*
61. See *Institutes,* bk. I, chap. ii, §98.

is (apart from other reasons) contradicted by the fact that God, when he listed the benefits he had conferred on David, included the fact that he had given him several wives. Not to mention the fact that we must not assume the patriarchs and other saintly men of the Old Testament to have lived in continual sin.

§93. Therefore, since it says nowhere that a special dispensation was made for their sake, I would suggest that God exempted the whole Jewish people from the observation of his universal positive law by means of a dispensation, but only until the advent of our Savior.

§94. But it is clear from what has been said that divine positive law extends the concept of adultery, the immorality of which we have derived by means of natural reason from the fact that it is contrary to the precept that we must keep promises and not harm others.[62]

§95. According to divine law it is also to be considered a case of adultery if someone wants to reserve the right of sexual intercourse with another man or woman by some formal agreement, or if this sexual intercourse takes place with the consent of the other spouse, because then it is a violation of the precept concerning the avoidance of lust and polygamy.

§96. At the same time it is obvious from the first establishment of marriage that the husband, as much as the wife, can commit adultery, even if he has an affair with an unmarried woman. Thus our commonly accepted definition of adultery as a violation of conjugal faith is very appropriate.

§97. Finally, the reason it is no secret why it was considered adultery among the Jews if someone slept with another man's wife but not if an unmarried woman slept with a married man is that polygamy was allowed to men. It is no surprise, therefore, that this definition of adultery was retained by the Romans, because they took their laws from the Greeks and

62. Ibid., bk. III, chap. ii from §216.

the Greeks drew heavily on the customs of the Jews via the philosophy of the barbarians.

§98. The following divine law, therefore, is derived from the prohibition of polygamy and lust: "Do not get involved in prostitution," that is, of the common kind, in particular that committed by spouses, and especially by the husband.

§99. Finally, we need to examine incest. Universal divine law has also prohibited this explicitly. We summarize its rule concerning incest as follows: "Refrain from sexual intercourse with parents and children, brothers and sisters, and those who take the place of parents and children and who are related to you in these respects."

§100. If there is any rule subject to many controversies, it is this one. To proceed in the requisite order, we show first that this rule is part of positive law, because we have shown above that the reprehensibility of incest cannot be shown from natural reason, even if it takes place between descendants within the same line.

§101. This rule does not concern either ceremonial or forensic law[63] because God said quite clearly that pagans violated these laws [on incest]. The law must therefore have been promulgated to them, too, either through Noah or Adam.

§102. It is of no interest to us whether the same prohibitions would have applied in the state of perfection and innocence. We consider this question a reflection of idle curiosity, since God, in his profound wisdom, did not reveal its solution to us. Yet we fear that those theorists who want to turn the state of innocence into the standard for the state of corruption will have to put a lot of effort into doing so if they want to use reasonable arguments and not human authority.

---

63. These are the two kinds of divine positive law promulgated to the Jews, but not to humankind as a whole.

§103. We have to examine what the law itself requires. God did not summarize this prohibition in one rule, as we have done, but instead listed several people who should abstain from marriage with each other. Hence, the disagreements over the persons who are not explicitly referred to in Scripture, but to whom the reason for the prohibition applies, as well as the disagreements over the reasons themselves.

§104. We assume that every law permits restrictive and extensive interpretation, in addition to declarative interpretation, if the reason of the law is clear and the legislator did not forbid extensive interpretation. This flows from what we have shown above in the chapter on interpretation.

§105. And then it is a self-evident postulate that we should give preference to the reason that the legislator himself referred to in his laws, rather than the reason supplied by the interpreters of the law. For the purpose of all interpretation is to form an idea of the will of the legislator. Where this is obscure, we need conjectures. Where the will is evident, conjectures have no place. Conjectures that do not conform to the mind of the legislator are not valid.

§106. The reasons that God provides for his laws are therefore to be preferred all the more to those that humans come up with, whatever their authority otherwise may be. Compared to divine wisdom they are all fools.

§107. If all those people who are responsible for judging legal cases relating to marriage had taken note of that and continued to take note of it now, there would quickly be an end to those copious mistaken claims based on the fundamental error that the rabbinical traditions are preferred to the word of God. There would also be a quick end to the disagreements that are common even among those who follow the same religion.

§108. Indeed, the ancient Jews claim two main reasons for the ban on certain marriages in Leviticus. One is based on natural shame, which does not permit parents to be mixed with their offspring, be it through themselves or through persons who are closely related to them by blood or marriage.

§109. The other reason is based on the fear that the daily and largely unobserved life together might provide an occasion for illicit intercourse and adultery, if such affairs could be confirmed by means of marriage. Hence, for example, they infer that marrying an aunt is forbidden, but not marrying the daughter of a brother, because young men regularly visit the houses of grandparents or even live in them together with their aunts, but they enter the houses of their brothers much more rarely and they do not enjoy as many rights there.

§110. Now, the rabbis themselves do not rely very much on these and other, even less weighty arguments, and they happily admit that the teachers of the traditions did not consider anything on this subject to be certain. It is then surprising that most of the Christians attribute more weight to these arguments than is just, as if some huge treasure of wisdom were concealed there.[64] But we must determine more clearly what they contain in the way of truth. For once these [arguments above] have been overturned, many conclusions that are incompatible with the true interpretation of divine law collapse automatically, especially those that, if you look at their foundations more carefully, are built exclusively or at least for the greatest part on this foundation.

§111. To begin with we note, in passing as it were, that the followers of the rabbis reject the reason that is common to all prohibitions, on which more soon. This reason has to be discussed in advance of the more particular rules, since in moral matters particular rules are limited by more general rules. Thus, two reasons were distinguished: one which referred to direct descent, and another which referred to descent in the collateral line.

§112. Concerning the former, the previous chapter has shown how strong the argument based on shame is if you want to prove that the union be-

---

64. See, for example, Grotius, *The Rights of War and Peace,* bk. V, chap. v, §14.

tween those descended from each other in the same direct line is by nature indecent.

§113. But we shall soon see whether God used this as a reason for justifying the law, based on his will, forbidding the union between parents and children.

§114. Thus, we shall add no more concerning the former case. In the latter case [that is, descent in the collateral line] it must not be dismissed by us so lightly because it contains a manifest absurdity, which is the origin of many errors, whether you consider it in itself, its application to persons mentioned in the prohibition, the conclusions that have been drawn concerning persons not mentioned in it, or, finally, the conclusions that ought to be drawn. Even aficionados of this reason undoubtedly consider it absurd.

§115. In itself it is acceptable as a subsidiary reason why God prohibited physical union between relatives by collateral descent, but only if it is subordinated to the general reason, which is derived from the proximity of blood and which has been repeated by God for the case of relatives by collateral descent,[65] in order to rule out any quibbling. This subsidiary, human reason is, however, often opposed to the reason given by God in such a way that the latter would have to give way to human reason: that is, these persons, it would follow, are not to be considered as being forbidden to enter a union if they do not see each other on a daily basis, even though there is the same familial relationship between them. Yet that is an attempt to correct divine wisdom, an absurdity that must not be condoned by any Christian.

§116. Hence the application of this rule works in the case of brothers and sisters, of whatever kind, whether they are true siblings or only half-siblings, because they live together and have contact with each other. But when we get to the paternal aunt and the maternal aunt, then the reason given by the rabbis begins to falter.

65. Leviticus 18:12–13.

§117. Concerning living together: if I am not mistaken, the authors on the customs of the Jews say that the agnate line enjoyed more than one prerogative before the cognate among the Hebrews (as among other nations). One of these, it was believed, was that after the death of the parents the unmarried daughters were raised by their brothers rather than their sisters. It was, therefore, more likely that young men lived with their paternal, rather than their maternal, aunts. So if God promulgated the prohibition of incest mainly because he was concerned about their daily social intercourse, then the difference between paternal and maternal aunt would have had to be taken into account to the same degree as that between the paternal aunt and the brother's daughter.[66]

§118. The Hebrews try to extricate themselves and look for new ways out of this difficulty by arguing that young men frequently visit the house of their grandparents—as if visiting the houses of the maternal and paternal grandparents in equal measure meant that the union with their maternal and paternal aunts was prohibited for the same reason. But let us see whether that is a remedy for the remaining absurdities.

§119. For a little later sexual intercourse with the paternal uncle's wife is prohibited.[67] Let us hear your reason, you lickspittle of the rabbis. Do you believe that the paternal uncle lived together with the wife in the grandfather's house, which you believe the brother's son visited so frequently? I do not think so. Or do you believe that the widow of the uncle spent time together with her father-in-law? This is even less likely, given the widespread dislike between mother-in-law and daughter-in-law. Or will you say finally that the brother's son frequently went to the uncle, although you do not believe that even brothers see each other that often?

---

66. That is, the fact that young men are more likely to be in the presence of their paternal than their maternal aunt should be reflected in the prohibition, just as the fact that they are more likely to be in the presence of their sister (i.e., the brother's daughter) is reflected in it.

67. Leviticus 18:14.

§120. The same reason applies to the prohibition concerning the brother's wife. For it is not possible to claim that she lives in her father-in-law's house; nor is there any need to fear that daily contact would lead to illicit sexual intercourse if one recalls what they themselves taught, namely, that access to brothers' houses was relatively rare and that they did not have the same rights there as in the grandparents' houses.

§121. But perhaps they try to look for a way out of their dilemma by pointing to the fact, which we mentioned above, namely, that brothers and sisters, following the death of their parents, were raised by their brothers and relatives on the father's side. Therefore, the marriage with the wife of the brother and of the paternal uncle was absolutely forbidden since it was not rare for the brother or son of the brother to be living there. Fine, I say, but if you look for so many escape routes in order to prove your reason for the persons included in the prohibition, beware that you do not provide me with an opportunity to show the absurdity which you commit when you derive conclusions concerning persons that are not mentioned there. For it is fair that you allow me the same liberty that you make use of, since I live with you in the Republic of Letters, in which all are equal.

§122. Let us begin with the daughter of the brother, who, you claimed, was allowed to marry the uncle. It is permissible to ask first what the grounds are for this argument that young men had less frequent access to the houses of the brothers than to the houses of the grandparents and that they did not have the same rights there. That is indeed contrary to the customs of all nations, and it cannot be shown from the histories that the Jews constituted an exception in that respect.

§123. I do know that children tend to be treated with greater indulgence by grandparents than by brothers, but this is only true with infants, or children who are very close to infancy. In adults, whom the legislator mainly has in mind, the matter is different. For even if they are perhaps treated more gently by the grandparents than by the parents, there is still no solid argument for saying that once they are grown-up they must lose interest in visiting their brothers' houses. I would even say that young men are more willing to visit regularly the family of their brother than that of the grandfather, because whatever the grandparents' degree of benevolence, this familiarity with them is combined with the great reverence owed to them, which takes its effect increasingly at that age. Yet there is no similar reason for showing such reverence to brothers, even if they are older, and where there is greater equality, there too is greater friendship, and a greater desire for society.

§124. And even if we granted them that paradoxical opinion, they will gain little by it. This is so, even if we use the argument that it is not uncommon for children of brothers to be educated by their uncles, and that therefore the daily contact between the uncle and his brother's daughter requires this prohibition.

§125. Or, if that argument is not considered acceptable, what about the fact that young girls as well as young men visit their grandfathers and grandmothers, and so have an opportunity of becoming familiar with their uncles? Or does it not happen frequently that grandparents raise the children of their son? Certainly nothing is more common than that grandmothers spoil their grandchildren excessively and like to see them frequently.

§126. The same can be applied, in its own way, to the daughter of the sister. I will not elaborate concerning other persons not mentioned here.

§127. If God had been referring to the daily and unobserved contact between certain persons in this law, then he would also have had to forbid the marriage between the children of two brothers or sisters, or at least that between the children of brothers, since these are often raised together by their grandparents or have some other opportunity for getting to know each other; or because, as we have said, if his father has died, the son of a brother is brought up by his uncle as his closest relative on his father's side. Thus, if marriage with the uncle's wife were prohibited because of the close familiarity with her, then there would be all the more reason to forbid marriage with the uncle's daughter. But it is clear from the following that these marriages are not banned by divine law.

§128. Let us therefore cast aside these reasons, which are not genuine, and stick to divine revelation. And since it is very clear on this matter, let us use revelation alone to demonstrate the law on incest that we have formulated above. Note that we have said that one should refrain from the conjunction of relatives. This not only prohibits matrimonial sexual intercourse [between relatives], but above all fornication, which is made worse by incest.

§129. Hence, God had a reason for prefixing his particular prohibitions with the general rule that nobody may have sexual intercourse with a woman who is closely related to him by blood.[68] He thereby wanted to indicate that humans should turn to this general law in cases of doubt, as a general principle for interpreting particular prohibitions.

§130. I say, "in cases of doubt." If the following, more specific laws obviously give a reason that has nothing to do with a close blood relationship, then the common principles of good interpretation dictate that we must rather adhere to these, and that these have to be extended to persons who are not closely related by blood.

§131. Yet this general reason will always mean that where there is the same, shared blood, there too the same prohibition applies, even with respect to persons who are not expressly mentioned. More specific reasons will indicate when there is a prohibition beyond that associated with a close relationship by blood. To put it briefly, an argument based on this general reason will confirm the applicability of the prohibition rather than deny it.

§132. Thus it will not be necessary for us to do what many others do and to discuss at great length the rules concerning the calculation of degrees of family relationships, because the principles passed on to us from God will show that the meaning of these prohibitions can be explained conveniently without referring to particular degrees of family relationship.

68. Ibid., 18:6.

§133. If you ask what the reason for this principle is, and why God wanted to ban certain marriages because of a close relationship by blood, I will reply that there is no need for us to inquire into this, because we are not interpreting human law, in which we commonly inquire into the utility of the commonwealth, which the prince must keep in mind when making his laws. We are interpreting divine law, and the desire to search into its reasons, when they are not revealed to us, is incompatible with the reverence that is owed to God.

§134. It is not even possible to identify the principle behind everything that is established by civil laws, let alone the reason for this principle. More often than not the law, even if it is harsh, has to be observed by the subjects because it is thus written. To an even greater degree do humans have to suppress their reason with respect to divine revelations, to avoid going too far. It is absolutely certain that God does everything with the greatest wisdom, even if we do not grasp the reasons behind his wisdom.

§135. And unless I am totally deceived, by adding the phrase "for I am Jehovah, your Lord" the omnipotent deity also wanted to cut short human curiosity, quite apart from everything else implied by it: we should not philosophize any further about the reason for this prohibition, but only consider that the supremely powerful and just God wanted it and let pious reverence suppress the prurient desire for further speculation.

§136. Now to proceed to particulars. I have said that intercourse between parents and children was prohibited. For we must start from consanguinity and from there move on to relationship by marriage, namely, the conjunction of related persons with the spouse of a relative. Among relatives the direct line takes precedence before the collateral. We, therefore, first need to look at parents and children, and it is with these that God, too, begins.

§137. He prohibits sexual intercourse with the father and the mother, and with the daughter of a son or daughter.[69] He gives this reason, with respect

69. Ibid., 18:7 and 10.

to the mother, that she is the mother and therefore must not be seen naked. With respect to the children he says that the nakedness of the parents is their own. Thereby, unless I am mistaken, the divine legislator wanted to indicate that the reverence owed to children by their parents, which never ceases, requires us to refrain from sexual intercourse with the parents. Father and mother continue to be father and mother even when the children are fully adult. They [the children] must abstain from incestuous intercourse out of shame, since it is considered a great violation of shame if someone is seen naked.

§138. But I see what you want to tell me. You remind me that in the previous chapter I rejected the arguments from reverence and shame for banning marriages between relatives in a direct line of descent. So it is. But I rejected them with the qualification that these reasons do not prove such marriages to be forbidden by the law of nature, without drawing on divine revelation. You should therefore have remembered that we are now concerned with positive laws, which command or forbid something that goes beyond reason and which are based on arguments that are not derived from a dictate of natural reason. A dictate that is not based on reason is not, however, automatically contrary to it.

§139. On the basis of this particular prohibition I formulate this first rule: "Divine law forbids all marriages between relatives in the same direct line of descent, in infinitum." Nobody doubts that they are forbidden. Thus it only has to be proved that this prohibition is valid in infinitum.

§140. I prove this first from the terms. The terms *father* and *mother,* as well as *daughter* and *son,* are used in either a wide or a strict sense in laws, also in the Hebrew tongue. In the latter sense the law applies only to parents and their immediate children. In the former sense all descendants are included. There is no compromise solution, up to the third or fourth degree perhaps, and excluding all others. It is therefore necessary for one of these meanings to be accepted as valid.

§141. The strict meaning, however, is not appropriate here. In part this is because all Christian interpreters agree that great-grandparents and great-

great-grandparents are covered by this prohibition. And in part this is because God's comment concerning the daughter's daughter shows that the term *father* necessarily includes the grandfather. It follows that God had in mind the broader meaning.

§142. I prove it, second, from the reason for the law, no matter whether you consider it according to our interpretation or stick closely to the literal meaning. For your grandmother, even if she is ten degrees removed from you, is your mother, because you are born of her blood; and the nakedness of your female descendant, even if this is in the tenth degree, is your nakedness, because she shares in your blood.

§143. Moreover, the further you ascend up the line of your ancestors, the greater the reverence you owe them, because all those who are in between owe them reverence, but you, on top of that, owe reverence to those who are in between. And the further down the line of descent you go, the greater is the reason for shame, which is the flip side of reverence.

§144. A few disagree with this rule.[70] They claim that beyond the great-grandmother and the great-granddaughter marriages between lineal descendants are not forbidden. But their argument is clumsy and, instead of the reason stated by God, is based on the physical mixture of the four temperaments or elements, or on the concept of participation in an identical essence or something similar.

§145. A better argument comes from those who say that marriages would be prohibited between lineal descendants ad infinitum, so that Adam, if he were resurrected, would not be able to marry anyone.

§146. But this objection is a curiosity rather than being capable of useful application. For Adam will not be resurrected for that purpose, and nowa-

---

70. Thomasius has in mind a work by T. H. Anglus, *Dux vitae sive statera morum ethico-politico-theologica* (Eleutheropolis, 1672), as well as the Catholic theologians Caesar Baronius (1538–1607) and Robert Bellarmine (1542–1621).

days it will not happen that an ancient great-great-great-grandmother wants to sleep with her great-great-great-grandson, or that the great-great-great-granddaughter has intercourse with her great-great-great-grandfather.

§147. I shall, therefore, leave aside lineal descent and move on to collateral descent, and first to brothers and sisters. God prohibited incest between these persons most clearly: you should not reveal the nakedness of your sister, who is the daughter of your father or mother, whether she is born at home or elsewhere.[71]

§148. That is the origin of the second rule: "In the case of collateral descent marriages are only forbidden between brothers and sisters." This proposition is demonstrated by the words of the divine law we have just referred to. The exclusion added to the law is derived from the fact that in collateral descent, following the brothers and sisters, there are the children of brothers and sisters, for whom no prohibition exists. And although there are great variations in human ecclesiastical law, even among Christians, concerning the permissibility of a marriage between cousins, nobody has defended the view that these marriages are contrary to divine law with the exception of Ambrose, who did not, however, provide any foundation for his assertion. Nor did he have one.[72]

§149. Moreover, brothers are either true brothers or half-brothers, and the latter are on either the mother's side or the father's side. Divine law is clear on the particular cases. A full sister is one who is born at home, a half-sister is one born outside the home, that is, from another marriage. A sister on the mother's side has the same mother as you do; one on the father's side, the same father.

§150. I would now move on to a different particular law if the repetition of the prohibition did not require some reflection. For God soon after

71. Leviticus 18:9.
72. Ambrose of Milan (A.D. 339–97) was one of the fathers of the church. Thomasius is here drawing on Robert Sharrock, *Judicia de variis incontinentiae speciebus* (Oxford, 1662), pp. 107–8.

added: "thy father's wife's daughter, begotten of thy father, she is thy sister, thou shalt not uncover her nakedness."[73] This is the translation given by Luther and nearly all the other versions. The usual exegesis of these words is that here again the marriage with a sister who is related by blood is prohibited.

§151. But there have been some, albeit few, who believe that this means something else, namely, that marriage is forbidden with a stepsister, whose mother gave birth to another child from my father.[74]

§152. They give two main reasons: first, that the common explanation is superfluous and leads to a tautology, since the sister who is related by blood has already been unambiguously banned in the previous passages. But the Holy Ghost is never guilty of tautologies.

§153. Second, they argue that in Holy Scripture the word is *Moledeth*, not *Muledeth*. The former is an active participle, the latter a passive participle. The usual versions, they say, have used the passive sense of the term, although the correct translation is more like the following: "You shall not dishonor the daughter of your father's wife (that is, your stepsister) after she (the stepmother) has given birth for your father to a child (a sister or brother whom you have in common with your stepsister) and so she (your stepsister, via this common sibling) has become your sister."

§154. As usual, many have tried to refute this dogma because of its novelty. But to be quite frank, I do not think they have responded satisfactorily to those two arguments.

§155. Most have tried to undermine this opinion on the ground that stepsisters are no relatives, whether by blood or marriage, and no family relationship by blood or marriage is created between them as a result of the

---

73. Leviticus 18:11.
74. These issues are discussed in Havemann, *Gamologia,* pp. 307ff.

birth of a sibling. This they prove easily from the definitions of cognate and affinal relatives, which are accepted in every legal system.

§156. But if I am not mistaken, that is a case of human laws setting up the norms by which divine law is to be interpreted, when it should rather be the other way round. Let us assume that marriages are banned by human law only if the two parties are related by blood or marriage. Are God's hands therefore bound, so that he cannot add a further prohibition to that?

§157. Indeed, human laws forbid marriages for other, civil reasons, apart from existing relationships by blood or marriage. Should not the same be allowed to God?

§158. But, you will say, the prohibition in question is discussed in the context of other prohibitions, in which God is continually concerned with prohibitions based on family relations, that is, consanguinity and affinal relationships. It would therefore be inappropriate to want to interpret this law as being about something else.

§159. I accept that. But I shall then point out to you that God himself stated quite clearly that in this case the family relationship (whether you wish to call it an affinal relationship, or consanguinity, or a mixture of both) is created by the birth of the common brother, in that she is related to my brother, and through him to myself. Thus she becomes my sister, because she is the sister of my brother.

§160. The fact that the laws are ignorant of this means of strengthening consanguinity and affinal relationships, and that *consanguinity* and *affinal relationship* are technical terms presents no obstacle. For here again a μετάβασις[75] is being committed. Let them talk as they wish within the limits of their discipline. Does God, the creator of speech, not have the power to extend the meaning of a term in his discipline to a case of which another discipline is ignorant?

75. The interference of one discipline in another.

§161. Thus it happens quite regularly that one expert uses a term in a different sense than another, who specializes in a different art.

§162. Indeed, quite often even those practicing a particular art use terms in different senses.

§163. Therefore, humans have erred when they denied any kinship in this case, though God evidently considered it to be such.

§164. The same reason for a prohibition will apply in a similar case: if my stepmother, who brings no stepdaughter into the marriage with my father, but bears children for my father, then marries another man after my father's death and gives birth to a daughter, I will not be able to marry her [the daughter].

§165. But if my stepmother did not give birth to a child from my father, I would be able to marry her daughter from a different husband, whom she married after the death of my father. This is possible even if the daughter was born after my stepmother became one flesh with my father, for the prohibition in divine law rests not on the union of flesh, but on the birth of the common sibling.

§166. Thus the marriage with the stepsister would be valid if the stepmother did not give birth to a child with my father, because then there would be no means of linking us.

§167. But what if in that case a common brother or sister is born after someone has already married his stepsister? Will the marriage that has been concluded according to the rules have to be rescinded because of the danger of incest? I do not think so.

§168. And here you will notice a difference between this prohibition and all others. In the other cases of incestuous marriage there has to be a divorce, because there all instances of sexual intercourse are incestuous. But here they are not.

§169. Indeed, in cases of incest the first instance of this intercourse is taken into account, to see if that is incestuous and if therefore all the others [that is, instances of intercourse] are to be considered as such. If not, then the others are not sinful either, even if some circumstance supervenes which would have rendered the union incestuous had it been present from the beginning.

§170. Thus, if your brother has sexual intercourse with your wife or your widow, then all the instances of intercourse are incestuous, because the first one was.

§171. But if you forgive the adultery and incest of your wife, you can continue to live with her without incest, even if she has become one flesh with your brother, because at the beginning your marriage was free of incest. It would have been incestuous if your brother had already had an affair with her at the time when you entered marriage with her. It is the same in all the other cases.

§172. Let us proceed to the unequal collateral line, which is particularly fertile ground for controversies and disagreements. We shall persist on our chosen path. God forbids seeing your paternal aunt's nakedness, because she is the closest blood relation of your father; likewise that of your maternal aunt, because she is the closest relation of your mother.[76]

§173. Hence I form the third rule: "In a collateral line marriages between different generations are prohibited only between those persons who take the place of parents and children, even if this is only on one side. This is the case ad infinitum [that is, no matter how many generations lie between]."

§174. The brothers and sisters of all my ancestors are said to take the place of my parents, all children of my brothers and sisters take the place of my children. Therefore, these persons are said to stand in a relation-

76. Leviticus 18:12–13.

ship of parents and children to each other, because they are the closest blood relations after the parents. When the parents die, it is to them that the burden of raising and maintaining the brothers' children usually passes.

§175. Even if God only mentioned the paternal and maternal aunts in his prohibition, the divine reason underlying it shows sufficiently clearly that God had in mind the parental and filial relationship. It is thus right to infer that any marriage with those people who are the closest collateral relatives of one's parents is forbidden.

§176. In the ascending collateral line, therefore, marriages are forbidden with the paternal and maternal uncles and with the paternal and maternal aunts. In the descending collateral line marriages with the son or daughter of a brother or sister are forbidden.

§177. This prohibition extends ad infinitum. For as we have suggested above, under this entire heading, the term *father and mother* is used in the broad sense, as standing for all members of the ascending line. If the term were to be understood strictly, God would undoubtedly have made that clear.

§178. Moreover, if you combine the divine reason based on the closeness of the relationship to the parents with the reason for banning marriages between members of the same direct line of descent, then it [the divine reason] has the effect that just as marriages between ascendants and descendants must cease for the sake of reverence and shame, so too the same reverence demands that the children of the brothers abstain from wedding their paternal uncles or aunts, etc., and the same shame before their maternal uncle or aunt means that matrimony with the children or grandchildren of their sister is banned.

§179. Because this reason is even stronger in the case of the brothers and sisters of grandparents, great-grandparents, and so on ad infinitum, the prohibition also necessarily extends ad infinitum.

§180. Finally, I said in the rule that this divine law is also concerned with brothers and sisters who are descended from only one of the two parents. Not only have the terms *brother* and *sister* above been employed in a broad sense, whence it is to be presumed that the meaning of the term is the same here; but the divine reason for this prohibition is also equally applicable to these [that is, brothers and sisters in the broad sense]. For they are the closest relatives of our parents, unless someone wanted to argue that in Saxon law half-brothers are regarded as more distant than full brothers. This is, however, quite unconvincing.[77]

§181. Among those who disagree some deny that marriages between a paternal uncle and his brother's daughter and between a sister's daughter and her maternal uncle are prohibited, some allow marriages between the brother's grandson or granddaughter and the sisters and brothers of their grandparents, while some believe that the prohibition in our rule pertains only to the full brothers and sisters of our parents.

§182. But the only foundation for all these opinions is the argument that a divine prohibition must not be extended to persons not mentioned in it, that prior to the Mosaic law marriages between two collateral lines were not forbidden, and that therefore this [Mosaic] law corrects and restricts the previous freedom and must therefore be regarded as a restrictive law, which does not permit an extensive interpretation on principle.

§183. We have not only refuted this belief in this chapter. When we talked about interpretation earlier, we also showed that it is wrong to consider laws that correct existing practice to be restrictive.

§184. The greater disagreement concerns the prohibition with respect to affinal relationships. There I said that no marriages are allowed between all those who are already related to each other by marriage. The words of the divine law are as follows: you shall not reveal the nakedness of your father's wife, because this is the nakedness of your father; you shall not

77. See Brunnemann, *De jure ecclesiastico tractatus posthumus,* pp. 618ff.

reveal the nakedness of your uncle's wife, because she is related to you by marriage; you shall not dishonor your daughter-in-law, for she is the wife of your son, and therefore you shall not reveal her nakedness; you shall not reveal the nakedness of your brother's wife, because it is your brother's nakedness; you shall not dishonor your wife and her daughter; and you shall not dishonor her son's daughter and her daughter's daughter, because they are of her flesh and such lying together is a crime.

§185. From these words I construct my final rule: "Those persons who are not allowed to marry one of two spouses because of consanguinity are also banned from marrying the other spouse because of their existing relationship by marriage."

§186. For this rule is quite evidently supported by the reasons that God added to this prohibition in the laws we reviewed. There is some variation in these reasons; at one point he argues that it is because of the nakedness of your father, at another that it is the nakedness of your brother; now he argues that it is because she is related to you by marriage, now that it is forbidden because she is the wife of your son, now that it is forbidden because she is the flesh (or closest relative) of your wife. In fact, however, these all end up saying the same.

§187. There are two kinds of relationship by marriage: one is to the blood relations of one's wife; the other is to the wives of one's own blood relations.

§188. The former kind is relevant to marriages between a man and his stepdaughter. Here the reason is that the stepdaughter is the closest relative of your wife; that is, just as your wife cannot become one flesh [with her daughter], so you who have become one flesh with your wife cannot join yourself with her [i.e., the stepdaughter's] flesh.

§189. The latter kind is relevant to the prohibition of marrying the stepmother or your brother's wife. There again the reason is the nakedness of your father and brother; that is, just as you cannot be joined in marriage to your forefathers or your sister, so too you cannot marry the woman who through a marriage with your father or your brother has become your mother or your sister respectively.

§190. The matter is more obvious in the reason that is used to argue against the marriage with your uncle's wife, who is related to you by marriage. Luther translated it as follows: "For she is your aunt." Or, as others have put it: "Because she is your father's sister." The meaning is as follows: just as you cannot enter marriage with an aunt, so you cannot marry your uncle's wife, who is regarded as your aunt because of her union with your uncle.

§191. Hence we conclude: between affinal relations in a direct line of descent marriage is prohibited ad infinitum. For just as the term *father* is common to all ancestors, so the term *son* stands for all descendants.

§192. Therefore, marrying a stepfather or stepmother (among your ascendants) and your stepson or stepdaughter (among your descendants) is forbidden, because their nakedness is that of your father or mother and that of your son or daughter. It is the same with your stepgrandfather and your stepgrandmother and their ancestors ad infinitum.

§193. On the other hand, unions with the brother-in-law, mother-in-law, stepson, or stepdaughter are prohibited because they are the blood relations of the husband or wife. And the same applies to the father-in-law's father and the son of the stepson ad infinitum.

§194. I do not believe that there has ever been any doubt about the prohibition concerning these persons, if we disregard those authors who argued that the prohibition on the basis of a blood relationship within the direct line of descent should not extend beyond the fourth generation, and who are therefore even less likely to accept a prohibition on the basis of an affinal relationship beyond the fourth degree.

§195. Moreover, we prove the following: in the collateral line marriages are prohibited between those persons whose relation to each other by marriage is like that between brother and sister.

§196. And these are, on the one side, the husband's brother and the brother's wife; on the other, the sister's husband and the wife's sister.

§197. About the former there is no doubt, given the explicit words of divine law.

§198. The latter, as is known, is the subject of a debate between theologians and jurists on the question whether someone can marry the sister of a deceased wife.[78] To spare you the tedium of reading through massive tomes, here are the main points.

§199. Those who assert the permissibility of such a marriage draw on the rabbinical doctrine and suggest that these laws are not applicable to persons who are not explicitly mentioned in them.

§200. They who consider such a marriage immoral opened the floodgates to controversy, because they searched for the proof of their claim in the express words of divine law, in which God set down that nobody must marry the sister of his wife and be intimate with her against the wife's will and during her lifetime.

§201. This is not to mention the fact that it was debated, with some reason, whether the "wife's sister" was her blood relation or simply a woman of the same tribe: in Mosaic law the term *brother* very often stood for any Jewish man. Here the full context shows, however, that this passage is principally concerned with polygamy.

§202. And therefore, it is argued, the meaning (if the term *sister* stands for any Jewish woman) is either that there had until then been a dispensation for male polygamy in the Old Testament, which was on condition

---

78. Thomasius is referring to a legal controversy in France over a man who obtained a dispensation that allowed him to marry the sister of his deceased wife: see *Journal du Palais, ou Recueil des principales decisions de tous les Parlemens,* part 9 (Paris, 1684), pp. 119–54.

that the husband did not take an additional wife against the will of his existing wife.

§203. Or (if *sister* stands for a blood relation of the wife) that male polygamy had been permitted until then, and that it had been permitted to take another wife against the will of the first wife as long as this new wife was not the sister of the existing wife.

§204. Since, therefore, everyone in defending a doctrine should make an effort at producing cogent reasons, however few there are, let us stick to the reason for the divine law. The brother-in-law cannot marry his wife's sister because she is of his wife's flesh or her closest relative. And the sister of the wife cannot marry her brother-in-law because his nakedness is also the nakedness of her sister.

§205. Thus we conclude: in different generations of a collateral line of descent marriages are forbidden between blood relations who take the place of parents and children, and with blood relations who stand in the relation of parents and children to the spouse.

§206. That is, marriages with the wives of the paternal or maternal uncle, the paternal great-uncle or maternal great-uncle, and so on ad infinitum are not valid; nor are marriages with the husbands of the paternal or maternal aunts, and so on ad infinitum valid in the descending line. And it is the same for marriages with the wife of the brother's or sister's son, etc., or those with the husband of a brother's or sister's daughter. The reason is that their nakedness is also the nakedness of your closest relatives.

§207. On the other hand, marriages with the paternal aunt, maternal aunt, paternal uncle, or maternal uncle and so on of your wife or husband are unlawful, as are those with the daughter or son of their brother or sister, etc. The reason, again, is that they are the closest relatives of your husband or wife.

§208. Those who disagree concede that marriage between the paternal uncle's wife and the son of the husband's brother is prohibited, but believe that marriage with the wife of the maternal uncle and the son of the husband's sister, similarly marriages between the husbands of paternal or maternal aunts and the daughters of the wife's brother or sister, are not forbidden.

§209. To an even lesser extent do they admit the extension of the prohibition if there are more generations between the two spouses. Hence they claim that marriages between the grandson of the husband's brother and the wife of the great-uncle are permitted.

§210. They state nothing new here, however, and only rely on reasons that have already been mentioned. There is thus no need to add anything to our reply.

§211. But we must not omit mentioning the well-known fact that canon law distinguishes between three degrees of affinal relationship, and the degree of affinal relationship changes whenever another person of a different sex is added through marriage to the person with the affinal relationship. The affinal relationship between the wife of the stepson and her husband's stepfather, for example, is of the second degree. And the same wife of the stepson stands in an affinal relationship of the third degree to that woman whom the husband's stepfather went on to marry at a later date.

§212. This variety of degrees is a fiction of canon law and has been invented to increase the wealth of the papacy. Divine law does not draw such distinctions and, as is clear above, there is no mention in divine law of a second or third degree of affinal relationship between people. It is, though, not to be condemned if the civil magistrates, within reasonable limits, extend the prohibition to the second degree of affinal relationship for the sake of public decorum, which is what our laws do.

§213. Thus, even if these [that is, our laws] do not permit marriages between the stepfather and the widow of the stepson or between the stepson and the widow of the stepfather, and although they are also condemned in Roman law, yet it cannot be concluded that this prohibition is derived from divine law, even though there has been no lack of learned men asserting this to be the case.[79]

§214. They did admittedly come up with a respectable argument for their opinion, namely, that their extensive interpretation drew on the same rules which we used in our argument: that the prohibition in divine law concerns people who are not mentioned in the law. We have inferred, for example, that marriages with the sister of the wife or with the wife of the uncle are forbidden, because either we have become one flesh with our wives, or other wives have become one flesh with our blood relations through sexual intercourse. Because there is an identical reason, we have thereby extended the words of the law to a case that was not explicitly covered by the law. So, too, do they derive their hypothesis from the fact that the same reason applies.

§215. They say that just as the stepfather undoubtedly cannot marry the stepdaughter, because the stepfather has become one flesh with the mother of the stepdaughter and the stepdaughter is the closest relative of the stepfather's wife, and just as the stepmother cannot marry the stepson, for the same reasons, so also is it impossible for the stepfather to enter marriage with the widow of a stepson, because this widow was one flesh with the stepson, and for the stepson to enter marriage with the widow of the stepfather, because she was one flesh with the stepfather. This union of the flesh through sexual intercourse has therefore had the effect that the stepson's widow is equivalent to a stepdaughter, while the widow of the stepfather is equivalent to a stepmother.

§216. We will not deny that this argument has some plausibility, but this can be easily rejected if only you pay careful attention to the nature of extensive interpretation. If it takes place, the extension can be made to a similar case that is not covered by the words of the law, as long as the

79. See Havemann, *Gamologia*, pp. 302–3.

reason remains the same. But if the law is extended to a case in which there is only a similar reason and not the same, then the interpretation is flawed.[80]

§217. We have, I think, consistently observed the rule of good interpretation in this chapter. We have, for example, said that one must refrain from marrying the wife's sister or the maternal uncle's wife, because it is evident that the same reason applies which God had in mind in the union of the flesh between spouses and in the close relationship between one spouse and his or her blood relations. There is thus no doubt that just as two brothers are kinsmen and the brother's wife is one flesh with her husband, so too are two sisters kinswomen and the husband of a sister is one flesh with his wife. Likewise, there is no doubt that just as the brother's son is related to the father's brother and the wife of the uncle has been united with the uncle, so too there is the same degree of proximity between the sister's son and the maternal uncle and the same union of flesh between the maternal uncle and his wife.[81]

§218. But in the argument of those who disagree with us it is not evident how the reason for this prohibition can be applied to the widow of the stepfather or stepson. For although the stepfather was one flesh with the mother of the stepson (from whom, as a close blood relation of the stepson, the prohibition is transferred to the stepfather, so that he cannot, for example, marry his stepdaughter), yet it is not at all evident, but actually very doubtful, whether the widow of the stepfather has become one flesh with the mother of the stepson, and, in the other case, whether the widow of the stepson is the closest blood relation of the stepfather's wife.

§219. Should you say that the doubt can be easily removed by arguing from a comparable case—for example, that just as the stepfather is one flesh with the mother of the stepson, so the widow of the stepfather is

---

80. See *Institutes,* bk. II, chap. xi, §89, on interpretation.
81. That is, he cannot marry his uncle's wife.

also of one flesh with the stepfather, and the stepson is thus a close blood relation of the stepfather's wife—my response is that it is obvious those who disagree with us have not applied the same reason of the legislator to a similar case, but rather extended the reason of the legislator to another, similar reason.

§220. God forbids the marriage between stepfather and stepdaughter because the nakedness of the stepfather is the nakedness of the stepdaughter's mother, and because the stepdaughter is the closest relative of the stepfather's wife. But the argument of the dissenters is as follows: the nakedness of the stepfather's widow is the same as the nakedness of the stepfather, and the nakedness of the stepson's widow is the nakedness of the person closest to the stepfather's wife. This differs from the first case, where God wanted to prevent marriage with the spouses of blood relations and the blood relations of spouses. But here what is being forbidden is the marriage with the spouses of relatives by marriage, and with those who are not related by blood to the spouses, but with the spouses of their blood relations.

§221. But, you will say, it is easy to show that this last reason is the same as the divine reason [for this rule]. The nakedness of the stepfather's widow is the nakedness of the stepfather himself, and the nakedness of the stepfather is the nakedness of the stepson's mother; therefore, the nakedness of the stepfather's widow is at the same time the nakedness of the stepson's mother, which divine law forbade the stepson to see. And because the nakedness of the stepson's widow is the nakedness of the stepson, and the stepson was the closest relative of the stepfather's wife, the widow of the stepson will also be the closest relative of the stepfather's wife. God thus forbade the stepfather to reveal her [i.e., the stepson's widow's] nakedness.

§222. But, I shall reply, that solution can easily be rejected because it does not proceed on the basis of the actual truth, but by using a fiction: in fact, the widow of the stepfather is not of one flesh with his previous wife, but only indirectly as a result of his two marriages.

§223. It is no use appealing to God and claiming that his reason [for the prohibition], when he says that the nakedness of the stepmother is that of the father, etc., concerns the fiction or the moral imputation.

§224. For the obstacle here is not only that a human fiction never has the same effect as the fiction of the legislator. We can also point out the common juristic principle that no fiction of a fiction is admissible. But this is precisely what occurred in this case.

§225. Since what we have said so far on these matters pertains to universal divine positive law, which binds all humans, it is quite clear how much power is left to human legislators with respect to marriage: they cannot forbid what God commanded, and they cannot allow what he prohibited. But with respect to intermediate things and actions they can, for the sake of good order and decorum, introduce specific rules for marital affairs.

§226. It would, therefore, be unjust if the legislator wanted to force all humans into marriage without considering their abilities and situations, and it would be a stupid law that forbade marriage to all citizens. There does, however, seem to be no reason why a civil law should not admit only celibate citizens to a certain public office, which they can fulfill far more conveniently than married people could—if, that is, the number of humans who are able to lead a chaste life is sufficient for that office. Thus it will be allowed to set down in a civil law the time, age, and condition of those to be joined in wedlock.

§227. Hence, it can be inferred from the above[82] that the Christian prince sins if he tries, by law, to subject husbands to the rule of their wives or even just to exempt wives from subjection to their husbands; at the same time another discussion above[83] shows why we suspend our judgment

82. See §48 in this chapter.
83. See §§67ff. in this chapter.

in the other controversy, whether a prince may admit other grounds for divorce, aside from malicious desertion and adultery.

§228. Moreover, the prince cannot publicly permit sexual intercourse that is only motivated by lust. For that reason it is contrary to divine law to have public brothels. It is another question whether the prince can punish harshly all lewd behavior and is obliged to inquire carefully into lewd behavior that is conducted in secret. That question is to be resolved on the basis of what we will say below in the chapter on punishments.

§229. Moreover, polygamy of either kind is incompatible with Christianity.

§230. Finally, concerning incest, the prince cannot grant dispensation in those cases that are forbidden by divine law, let alone introduce a law that is contrary to divine law on this matter. Thus even if the pope, as pseudo-representative of God, arrogates the power to grant dispensation in these matters, this power of dispensation has been called into doubt, not without reason, even by princes who follow the papal religion, especially in France.

§231. In those cases forbidden by God there is not only a duty to prevent the conclusion of a marriage but also to dissolve a marriage that has been concluded. This is clear not only from the words of the divine law, which demands that incestuous persons be extirpated, but can be proved above all from the nature of incest, since incest is sexual intercourse with a prohibited person. In an incestuous marriage there are as many acts of incest as there are acts of sexual intercourse. If the Christian prince, therefore, does not dissolve a marriage with a prohibited person, he de facto claims the right to grant dispensation from divine law.

§232. Thus it is not difficult to see what is to be thought of the opinion of some authors or the practice of certain courts where an incestuous marriage has been concluded, because the magistrates knew nothing of it, or permitted, because the magistrates were poorly informed or had been misled, and where it is then asserted that such spouses cannot be divorced once the marriage has been consummated or the wedding has been celebrated (the exception being a marriage between ascendants, because this would lead to greater scandal and the consciences of the spouses would suffer badly, etc.).

∞ CHAPTER IV ∞

On the Duties of Parents and Children

§1. Following conjugal society it is worth examining the society that exists between parents and children, commonly called paternal society. The purpose of conjugal society, as we have said, is the procreation of children. Paternal society is the result.

§2. There are great differences between authors over the derivation of the right of parents over children. Some appeal to the act of generation; others derive it from divine will; others again appeal to natural law and tacit consent.[84]

§3. There is similar disagreement over the prerogative of parents concerning the exercise of this right: some look mainly to the father; some grant the main role to the mother.

§4. To examine this question systematically, we must first search for the general difference between this society and all other natural societies, then inquire after its purpose. Once we have formed a correct view on these matters, any questions that occur can be resolved automatically. We will also always endeavor to separate natural law from positive law.

---

84. On these debates see Pufendorf, *Of the Law of Nature and Nations,* bk. VI, chap. ii.

§5. It is generally acknowledged that some form of society exists between parents and children, and no nation is so barbarous that it does not recognize it. It is also particularly worth noting that all other societies presuppose the consent of the persons living in them; even marriage [does] although it has been established by God. Only paternal society is entered into without direct and specific mutual consent.

§6. The parents have apparently given their consent to this society in some sense since they knowingly and willingly make an effort to procreate children and consent to marriage, the aim of which is the procreation of offspring. Yet this consent is immediately relevant only to married society, from which paternal society differs in kind. It is rash to derive the consent to paternal society from the consent to procreation as long as it has not been proved that procreation is the foundation of paternal society.

§7. The common rule that he who wants what comes first also wants its necessary consequences therefore will not be of any use here, because the question here is on what grounds paternal society has to be considered a necessary consequence of married society or the birth of a child.

§8. Even if we granted that there was consent on the part of the parents, it cannot be said that there is any society based on consent when there is no mutual consent, which is precisely what is lacking on the part of the children.

§9. Paternal society begins as soon as the offspring is born, but how can the infant consent when he is incapable of performing any act of a rational animal?

§10. The belief in some kind of tacit consent by the infants must collapse because we have shown above that there can be no tacit consent from someone who is unable to declare his consent explicitly.[85]

---

85. See *Institutes*, bk. II, chap. vi, §§30ff.

§11. Some do seek the foundation of the father's right in a tacit pact with the infants. They suggest that the infant's use of reason is hidden and he is therefore unable to promise expressly to his parents to perform the reciprocal duties, but he acquires no less of an obligation toward his parents as a result of their efforts than if he had given his express consent. (For it is presumed that if he who lacks the use of reason had had it at the time, and had realized that he would not have been able to preserve his life without the care of his parents and their power of command linked to this care, then he would willingly agree to this society and would have demanded a proper upbringing from them. This consent that is presumed to be based on reason has the effect of express consent, like the presumed consent in Roman law when the affairs of an absent person are conducted without his knowledge.)[86] Yet these people replace tacit consent with presumed consent, which, as we have shown, differs from tacit consent in many ways.[87]

§12. Among these is the fact that presumed consent is not a form of consent properly speaking.

§13. What contributes a lot to confirming our opinion is the fact that parallels are drawn here between the owner of a business, whose affairs are conducted in his absence, and children. For we have noted that the conduct of business affairs, with all quasi-contracts, does not belong to examples of tacit consent.

§14. Yet this fact also seems to show that paternal society cannot be derived from consent, because consent, whatever it is called, express or tacit, cannot properly constitute the origin of obligation unless this is with respect to actions that are free before consent is given. And it is not a matter of free choice either for the father or for the child to reject the rights and duties involved in the upbringing of the child.

86. See, for example, *Digest* 3.5.2.
87. See *Institutes,* bk. II, chap. vi, §§19ff.

§15. And I do not think that this argument can be undermined by objecting that there is no contradiction between something being based on a precept of natural law and something based on tacit consent, and saying that it is not left to human choice whether to obey God or not and that God nevertheless wanted to impose obedience on the faithful by a formal agreement.[88] So, too, a citizen is bound to do his military service for the commonwealth, and yet, when he is enlisted as a soldier, his consent and oath are added to it. Why then is it not possible to say that the tacit consent of the infant is understood to be present when the parent takes on the task of bringing him up? The effect of this is that he has no reason to complain that paternal rule was imposed on him against his will and in vain. Many arguments can be put forward against this objection.

§16. First, the origin of a right or obligation here does not refer to the first origin (which, as we have said above in the relevant passage, must always be found in a law), but to the immediate origin, which can sometimes, or even often, be derived from consent. In that respect there is clearly no contradiction if something is based on a precept of natural law and on tacit consent at the same time.

§17. But to be able to say that an obligation is immediately based on consent, this obligation must either have been clearly lacking before there was consent, or to have been lacking with respect to a certain person, or to have been insufficient.

§18. Thus, I am not bound to perform services for someone without giving my consent to this form of subjection. It is therefore correct to say that the obligation of the servant is based on consent.

§19. Thus, the obligation that exists between spouses owes its origin to consent: before they gave their consent either party was free to choose whom to marry, even if there might be a general obligation to enter marriage.

88. See Pufendorf, *Of the Law of Nature and Nations*, bk. VI, chap. i, §4.

§20. Thus, if a rich man promises a pauper one hundred thaler, the rich man is rightly said to be bound by his consent. There may have been an obligation to promise one hundred thaler before he gave his consent, but this obligation would have been imperfect.

§21. But if the force of an already existing obligation is only strengthened by the addition of consent, whether express or tacit, it does not seem possible, properly speaking, to attribute the origin of this obligation to consent (if we abstract from civil laws). Then consent is normally used only to signal the willingness to fulfill the obligation or to offer the other person greater security.

§22. If, for example, the two parties to a treaty only promise that which they were obliged to do anyway by natural law, then the obligation is not properly said to originate in that treaty, and these agreements will hardly deserve to be described as treaties.

§23. And if something has been promised before I confirm my promise with an oath, then the obligation in no way derives from the oath, but from the promise.

§24. It is the same with the examples listed. The faithful are subject to God before they make their promise, and citizens owe military duties to their commonwealth before they take their military oath. Therefore, promise or consent is added to these obligations, but the obligation does not derive its origin from that promise or consent.

§25. Therefore, assuming the tacit consent of the infant in paternal society does not appear necessary for saying that he has no reason to complain about the imposition of paternal rule on him against his [the infant's] will and in vain: children have no reason to complain, even if there is no tacit consent.

§26. For there are many obligations that bind humans against their will—all those, for example, that are derived from the absolute precepts listed in book 2. Nor does a superior require the consent of the subject to introduce an obligation.

§27. That the father's power over his son was not imposed in vain, however, will be shown shortly.

§28. For the purpose of paternal society is raising the offspring. Even if you added the power of the parents as another aim, the comparison of both aims soon reveals that raising the offspring is the primary purpose, while the power of the parents, with corresponding obedience on the part of the children, is the secondary aim.

§29. For that aim undoubtedly has to be considered primary which is being pursued at all times. It is the standard by which the other aim is measured, and once it has been achieved the society usually ceases to exist.

§30. But raising the offspring begins immediately after birth, before the children are capable of obedience. The power of the father is nothing other than a means without which it is impossible to raise the children. And once this education has been completed, paternal society is dissolved naturally.

§31. Therefore, the first precept in such a society directs the duty of parents toward their children: "Parents should raise their children."

§32. *Raising* here is nothing other than properly leading the child from first infancy to the maturity of body and mind.

§33. Therefore, it contains two parts, namely, nourishment, which pertains to the infant's body, and learning, which pertains to his mind.

§34. This precept flows from the law on performing the duties of humanity. I show this as follows.

§35. When infants are born, there can be no doubt that they are humans. Both modern and ancient philosophers have disagreed (and still disagree) a lot over the point in time when the infant in the uterus begins to be a human being. Some defend the view that souls are transferred from parents to children and look to the moment of conception; others, who believe in the infusion of souls,[89] state there is an unknown period of time before the fetus begins to be a living being. Others, such as the ancient Stoics, defended the view that the human soul was added in the moment of birth. Yet they all agree unanimously that recently born infants are to be regarded as humans.

§36. Because therefore they are humans, they necessarily share in those rights which humans have, insofar as their condition [as children] permits, and which are derived from the state of humanity in book 2.

§37. Therefore, there is a danger of violating the precept on avoiding pride if someone treats them with contempt. And although they are destitute of all goods of the mind and of fortune, as well as goods of the body, they can yet suffer injury with respect to them.

§38. Therefore, parents who kill their children or destroy other goods of their body not only violate the specific duty of parents, but that duty which all others also have toward their children and which they (the children) owe to all other humans as well. Their position as parents, however, makes it worse, since they should not only avoid harming their children but also promote their well-being as much as they can.

§39. Parents must not only observe negative precepts with respect to their children, but affirmative ones as well. The precept that agreements must be kept is not much use here, because infants, as we have said, are incapable of concluding such agreements unless other people represent them—in the commonwealth, for example, people such as tutors or guardians. But the precept on performing the duties of humanity deserves to be noted here in particular.

89. That is, infused by God externally rather than being transferred directly from parents to children.

§40. For it is certain that children will die of hunger, or that their life will not be that different from that of wild beasts, if nobody nourishes them or teaches them. It is necessary for other humans to promote their well-being, so that they do not just live, but live in accordance with reason.

§41. Normally, the duty to perform the duties of humanity binds all humans without distinction, but the upbringing of children involves costs and laborious efforts. It, therefore, cannot be reckoned among the common duties of humanity, but is a benefit. Moreover, there is a danger in delaying here, since children themselves cannot ask for the help of others, and it was therefore necessary that natural law determined certain people who should know immediately that they, before all others, had the duty to provide this benefit.

§42. Usually one person is under a greater obligation to provide benefits to another than someone else, and a close family relationship contributes a lot to augmenting the obligation. It follows automatically that parents need to take on this duty, because they have produced the child and are thus the closest relatives, and because it is mainly due to them rather than other humans that the children first came to life.

§43. Concerning the provision of nourishment there was no need for a corresponding duty for children, since their natural instinct impels them qua animals to accept it. The obligation they are under in that regard is part of the common duties of humanity toward themselves.

§44. It is different with learning. In adults this is hardly possible without discipline and the right of coercion; in children it is not possible at all without that. It follows that parents enjoy the right to direct the actions of their children using coercion.

§45. And this is the second precept, which explains the duty of children toward their parents in this society: "Children should obey their parents as long they live in this society [with their parents]."

§46. Obedience is a restriction of freedom, by means of which man detects an obligation on his part to regulate his actions (especially his external actions) according to the will of him who is the superior in that society.

§47. Obedience, like any obligation, is linked to the fear of punishment if something occurs that is contrary to the will of the superior. But there can be no fear among those who are intimately acquainted with each other. Thus this familiarity must sometimes be suppressed in paternal society. This suppression is called gravitas on the part of the parents and reverence on the part of the children.

§48. You see, therefore, that obedience and reverence are linked to each other, but not identical. Hence, there can be no obedience without reverence. But reverence can exist without obedience.

§49. Reverence in itself is an act by which someone freely and without being specifically commanded to do so declares in his external actions that the person in relation to whom he performs this act is considered by himself to be his superior.

§50. Since therefore superiority of power is different from the superiority based on an act of beneficence, on dignity, or on order, there are as many forms of reverence as there are forms of superiority. We thus have to take care that we do not confuse these forms of reverence with each other.

§51. But the children owe their parents obedience with reverence for as long as the paternal society is in existence. For that is as long as the power of parents over the actions of their children is effective.

§52. For paternal society is not indissoluble like conjugal society, no matter whether you look at natural law or universal positive law. Here the common rule applies: when the purpose ceases, the action ceases too, and thus the state consisting of several actions of that kind also ceases to exist.

§53. Therefore, paternal society must naturally expire when children are themselves capable of taking care of their livelihood and no longer need to be educated.

§54. I require both of these conditions to be fulfilled, for they are both properly necessary for founding paternal society.

§55. Hence, even if we assume that children are capable of taking care of their livelihood or have some other means of sustaining themselves, but leave much to be desired in the government of their own actions, it will be necessary for the society to continue because it is primarily the parents who hold the power of commanding them in this respect.

§56. On the other hand, children may be capable of directing their actions themselves but cannot provide for their own livelihood. It may seem at first that there is no need for parental power anymore, since its purpose no longer exists. Yet the person who confers a favor on me usually has the right to demand that I conform my actions to his will for the duration of the favor, by threatening to withdraw the favor. We, therefore, must grant this power to parents.

§57. In addition, we live in an imperfect state, in which human manners are perpetually being augmented or require augmentation. If we leave aside civil laws, the purposes and end of a good education cannot be defined in fixed rules. This must rather be left to the judgment and conscience of the father as the person who is by nature more prudent [than the child].

§58. Thus, it follows that in the state of nature the father could expel an indolent and disobedient son against his will from the family once he had reached maturity if the father had not neglected his duty to raise his children.

§59. The son, on the other hand, cannot normally withdraw from the society against the will of his father, unless he can prove the father's iniquity and his own virtues with convincing arguments.

§60. And even when paternal society ends, there still remains a perpetual debt of reverence on the part of the children because of the favors they have received, that is, nourishment and education, which cannot ever be undone once they have been conferred.

§61. But the power to command ceases. That is to be noted because several authors have confused the two.

§62. That is, children are bound at that time to honor their parents; to direct those actions that are of some concern to the paternal family in accordance with the advice and wishes of their parents, if possible; and to render them equivalent favors. If they neglect to do so, they commit a grave sin.

§63. Yet if they refuse to do so, the parents have no right to force their children to these actions. And if parents deny their consent without a good reason, then I believe children do not commit a sin if they proceed with actions that can no longer be delayed conveniently.

§64. It is clear from this that when we inquire about the duty of children toward their parents we usually distinguish two stages: one during which they are in the power of their parents; the other, when they are free from it. Others distinguish three stages: they subdivide the first into a period in which the children's judgment is not fully developed, and one in which their judgment is fully developed and they are adults, but part of the paternal family.

§65. This distinction is acceptable, but I am not sure it is very useful, since these two periods of fully developed and incompletely developed judgment differ only in the degree to which parents educate and command their children in them. This is greater in infants, whose tiniest actions require correction, than in adults. That is obvious.

§66. Based on the above we can easily resolve the specific controversies. (1) Which of the two parents has the main power over the children, mother or father? We reply that on the basis of natural law both have an equal right, because the foundation of this power is relevant to both unless the parents made a different agreement as part of their marriage.

§67. If you look at divine positive law, however, the father's role is clearly more important than that of the mother, since he has the power to direct the mother's actions in the interest of the family's utility.

§68. That is, unless the father orders something that has already been forbidden by divine law or the command of some other superior. Then the mother's command is to be preferred, which then, however, is not considered the mother's command specifically.

§69. (2) Does the father's power also extend to the goods of his children? Normally this is not the case, since the object of an education is the children's actions, rather than material goods, and nourishment is a burden [on the parents], not an entitlement or a means of acquisition.

§70. Parents will, therefore, take care that their children in their first infancy acquire what is useful to themselves; they will represent them in the acquisition and administration of goods. When the children have grown up, however, the parents will be able to prescribe rules of acquisition to them as long as the child is the owner in both cases.

§71. Parents are not strictly required by law to provide nourishment for their children if these have goods that are sufficient for their maintenance. Parents, therefore, will not sin if they subtract the costs of maintenance from their children's goods or derive some equivalent gain from the works and goods of their children.

§72. (3) Can parents fulfill their duty by means of someone else? They can, not only because the purpose of education and nourishment often cannot be obtained any other way. It is also so because it is considered morally equivalent if someone uses someone else to do what needs to be done, as long as the task does not require the particular expertise of the person who was originally responsible for it. That cannot be said to be the case here, because the creation of the child, as the foundation of the paternal obligation, does not impose a particular burden on parents before others.

§73. Therefore, parents not only are right to entrust the education of their child to suitable teachers, but can also give up the child to another for adoption if the child's well-being is served by it. And if there is no other means of nourishing the child, the parents can either pawn or sell him into tolerable servitude to prevent his dying from hunger. But this is only on condition that there is a right to get the child back in case the parents' fortunes improve or a relative wants to redeem him.

§74. But if parents are so inhumane as to expose and cast away their child, then the person who took care of him and raised him also succeeds to the rights of parenthood, so that the foster child owes his foster parent filial respect and obedience.

§75. (4) Do reverence and respect, which are perpetually owed to parents, depend more on the fact of procreation than on the benefit of an upbringing? Apart from the reasons others have produced, the comments above, together with what we have just said, show that we must pronounce in favor of upbringing.

§76. (5) Are children allowed to contract marriages against the parents' will? There we shall have to distinguish between children who live under the power of their parents and those who have left the paternal family. The former must, according to the law of obedience, ask for parental consent, and I believe a marriage to be automatically void without it, because this act is of the greatest importance and at the same time affects the parents' interests to a very high degree. Otherwise, they would be burdened against their will with the duty of feeding another person or be deprived against their will of their parental right.

§77. But if children have already separated from their parents, they violate the reverence they owe them by entering marriage without their parents' knowledge. The marriage itself, however, will not be invalid. And if the parents are asked for their consent and deny it without just reason, then the children can consummate the marriage without violating the respect due to their parents.

§78. Finally, if children who have already been brought up and are adult wish to enter marriage and are prepared to leave the paternal family, but the parents are being harsh and persnickety and refuse either to allow the children to leave or consent to their marriage, then the children will be able to act by themselves, while preserving their loyalty and reverence in all other matters.

§79. And yet, all the matters we have discussed in this chapter of the duty of parents and children must be understood in abstraction from civil laws. If these have established something different, do not believe that we have questioned that here or that it contradicts our view.

CHAPTER V

On the Duties of Lords and Servants

§1. We have shown in the first book that the master-servant relationship did not exist in the state of innocence.

§2. Even in the postlapsarian state there was no need for such a society, as long as the community of goods existed and there were no distinct claims of ownership. For need is the ultimate origin of such a society. But when goods are common to all, there can be no owner who aims to acquire something for himself rather than allowing others to have it. Nor can there be a servant who subjects himself to the ownership of another for the sake of receiving sustenance.

§3. But following the emergence of exclusive ownership [*dominium*] every head of household had to take care to acquire, administrate, and preserve the means necessary for sustaining his family. Other people, however, lacked these means and were incapable of acquiring them by their own ingenuity. It was, therefore, necessary that the former sought a servant and used him as a household tool, and that the latter looked around for a master from whom he could expect nourishment for his efforts.

§4. And so the purpose of the society formed by the master-servant relationship is, on the part of the master, the acquisition and preservation of material wealth; on the part of the servant it is his sustenance through nourishment.

§5. But even if mutual need impels humans to enter this master-servant relationship, it still normally requires mutual consent for its existence.

§6. But this purpose, which is intended by the master, shows that consent in the master-servant relationship by nature requires subjection on the part of the servant and the power to command on the part of the master.

§7. For the acquisition and preservation of goods vary in infinite ways, because of the infinite variety of circumstances. Therefore, these forms cannot be fixed in the formal agreement on which this society is based, but must be left to the future determination of one of the contracting parties, to be set out whenever there is a need for it.

§8. Since, therefore, the master is the principal cause there and the servant has the role of a tool, it is necessary that the master direct the actions of the servant.

§9. And (if you abstract from civil laws) he must do so using coercion, to the extent that this is necessary for obtaining this purpose, because without coercion the direction of these actions would be futile.

§10. This coercion usually cannot take the form of severe physical punishment, let alone punishment by death on the basis of the master's own authority, because the purpose of a society based on the master-servant relationship is not achieved through such punishments. These forms of punishment do not correct the servants' negligence in the performance of their work, nor do they improve their manners in accordance with decorum and tranquillity within the family.

§11. If the servant is guilty of a severe crime against someone outside the family, he can be expelled. And in the absence of a political commonwealth that is sufficient for the victim. If the crime was directed against the family itself, the master can adopt extreme measures to punish the servant, not as a servant but as an enemy.

§12. Thus, in sum, the duty of the servant is contained in this precept: "Perform the work you have promised to your master." That of the master is, "Pay your servant the agreed-upon wage."

§13. Moreover, depending on the degree of lack of ingenuity or of stupidity, a servant either tends to commit himself to perpetual servitude to a master or does so for a short and fixed period, sometimes even for particular labor services.

§14. In the latter case the agreed wage has to be paid and the work to be done. In the former the master must provide nourishment and whatever else is necessary for life, while the servant must do all the work given to him by the master and faithfully hand over to his master whatever are the fruits of this work.

§15. But in imposing labors the master must take account of the servant's strength and dexterity and not make harsh demands that exceed his powers.

§16. A servant, however, cannot be sold to another against his will, because he took this and no other master, and it is a matter of great interest to him which of the two masters he serves.

§17. In addition, he only consented to submit himself to his master's command and he still represents a person. Alienation, however, presumes ownership.

§18. Finally, alienation contributes nothing to achieving the aims of a society based on the master-servant relationship.

§19. It was a different matter with children since their society with the parents did not originate in consent. Also, in the case of children, it was often true that alienation served the purpose of that society and it did not matter to the children who brought them up.

§20. And all this is true in the society based on the master-servant relationship considered as a natural phenomenon. The manners of certain nations have introduced a different kind of servitude, that of captives in war, in which those whose lives were spared served in perpetuity in exchange for nourishment.

§21. Many people took to treating these servants more harshly because some of the animosity toward their former enemies still remained, and because these had intended to inflict grievous harm on us and our possessions. But as soon as mutual consent was established between such a victor and the defeated by virtue of being associated in one family, all previous hostility was considered to have been set aside.

§22. The master also does an injustice to such a servant who has been acquired in this way if he does not provide him the necessaries of life, or rages against him without reason, and even more if he kills him although he has not committed a crime worthy of such punishment.

§23. It is commonly accepted that servants who have been reduced to this condition by armed force can be transferred to whomever we like, like our other possessions, and can be traded like goods, so that the body of the servant is understood to be the property of the master.

§24. But there humanity reminds us that a servant is also human. And so we should never treat him as we do our other possessions, which we can use and abuse at whim, and destroy. When we decide to sell such a servant, we should not, if he does not deserve it, try to hand him over to those who will treat him inhumanely.

§25. Finally, it has been generally accepted that the offspring from parents who are servants are of the same servile status and belong to the master of the mother.

§26. This is defended with the argument that he whose property the body is also owns the fruit that is the product of this body, and that this offspring clearly was not going to be born if the master had used his right of war against the mother.[90]

§27. In addition, their parents do not own anything themselves and therefore have no means of nourishing their offspring unless from the goods of the master. Since, therefore, the master provided nourishment for such offspring long before his labor could be useful to him and the labor he receives after that does not greatly exceed the nourishment he has provided, this offspring will not be permitted to leave servitude against his master's will.

§28. Yet it is evident that since such servants born in the master's household have become servants through no fault of their own there is no pretext for treating them more harshly than perpetual wage-laborers.

§29. This servitude, however, is not as natural as the previous two forms, which are related to the common condition of human nature. But it is not contrary to reason, and indeed can be derived from the dictate of reason, if there is no other way I can safeguard myself against an enemy.

§30. It is, of course, permitted and exercised according to law, but not commanded. Therefore, those nations among whom this kind of servitude has become obsolete, as is the case among Christians, have not therefore committed sin.

§31. Yet even they [Christians] would not sin if they reintroduced this servitude, because this servitude does not violate either universal positive law or the rules of Christianity.

90. That is, killed her.

On the Duties of Those Living in a Commonwealth

§1. It would be easy to discuss the duties of those living in a commonwealth if there had not been such difficulties concerning the theory of such a civil society, without which these duties are discussed in vain. The reasons for these difficulties are the excessive adoration of the sayings of Aristotle, or rather of the sayings of his interpreters who have not properly understood him, as well as the eagerness to use arguments from everywhere to contradict those people who are believed to err; another reason is the explanation of passages from Scripture contrary to the rules of good interpretation and precepts of logic; and finally the idle, curious speculations of humans, who explore the state of innocence so thoroughly that they end up attributing I know not what kinds of societies to it, just because it seems nice to do so.

§2. We have shown in the first book that there were not going to be any commonwealths and civil societies in that state of perfection.[91] Hence I consider it a rhetorical trick that is suitable only for persuading the vulgar if someone claims that since the political community is the most perfect society it could not have been unbecoming to the most perfect state of humanity.[92]

---

91. See *Institutes*, bk. I, chap. ii, §37.
92. Thomasius has his orthodox Lutheran opponent Valentin Alberti in mind.

§3. For we have already discussed this doctrine of the Peripatetics concerning the political community as the most perfect human society, and I would surely offer the same reply to this frivolity as other people would if I argued that the most perfectly constructed buildings, most refined fare, most precious garments, and most wholesome medicines could not have been unbecoming to this state [of innocence].

§4. Let us see whether I can argue with the Peripatetics from common ground. We agree that the purpose of the political community is twofold. The principal and final end is εὐδαιμονία, that is, true civil happiness, not for one person, but for the entire people. The other, subordinate purpose is αὐτάρκεια, that is, the sufficiency of all external things and goods. I have already observed above that the legitimate measures to protect against violence pertain to happiness rather than sufficiency, since it is impossible to conceive of civil happiness without peace and common tranquillity.[93]

§5. We also agree in saying that the form of the political community is the commonwealth, that is, a relationship between those who command and those who obey, and between the supreme ruler and inferior magistrates.

§6. Hence, it seems that the definition of a political community flows automatically from its form and purpose. The political community is a natural society with a supreme power of command, for the sake of sufficiency and civil happiness.

§7. For we do not deny that the political community is a natural society, nor do we accuse Aristotle of being absurd when he said that man was by nature a political animal. But from this does not follow what the Aristotelian interpreters have postulated: that man is not only led toward political society by nature, but dragged into it, so that nature is the principal impelling cause for entering political society and all others, including need and fear, are to be regarded only as secondary and accidental causes.

93. See *Institutes,* bk. III, chap. i, §21.

§8. To take an example, the master-servant relationship is natural, even if humans invented it out of need.

§9. If some quality, therefore, is said to inhere in a creature by nature or a creature is said to be suited for something from birth, this phrase sometimes means that a thing is actually present in something by nature, without any prior action by itself or someone else. In that sense, for example, a fish is born to swim, a bird to fly, an oak tree to bear acorns.

§10. Sometimes, however, there is an aptitude or suitability in something to receive some sort of perfection, cultivation, or discipline which nature intended to be there, or certainly approves of as something that conforms to it and is not repugnant to it. In that sense a horse, for example, is naturally suited to trot majestically, which an ass cannot do, a parrot to chatter, a field to bring forth grain, a slope to bear vines, and humans to speak and learn various arts and sciences.

§11. Now we have shown that man is a political animal by nature in this latter sense and is driven toward political society not by some intrinsic natural instinct but by an extrinsic impulse. But we will not enter into an argument with Aristotle's disciples over the true meaning of that phrase, which could perhaps be explained quite conveniently in a way that supports our opinion. Our concern is with what Aristotle should have said, rather than with what he actually did say.

§12. We, therefore, declare that the principal cause that makes humans form political societies is not some intrinsic natural instinct, as in the case of marriage and paternal society, but the fear of external evils with which one human threatens another, while the lack of goods that are necessary to sustain life is the secondary cause.

§13. We prove the first as follows: if humans were made to set up commonwealths by some natural instinct, then they would have necessarily come into existence in the state of innocence, just like marriage and paternal society. But we have already proved that this is not the case.

§14. There is no reason for you to appeal to the corruption of human nature. If you meant the moral corruption of man and derived the political community from this instinct, it would follow that the desire for political society is sinful. If you look to the natural weaknesses, then I would have what I want, since need and fear are signs of these weaknesses.

§15. But why do we need many reasons? Our opinion can be supported on the basis of the purposes of political society. We have shown above[94] that the impulsive and final causes of an action are opposed to each other. Hence, whatever the Peripatetics may protest, fear is necessarily a primary impulsive cause for entering a political society, because it corresponds to its primary purpose, common tranquillity, while need is a secondary cause, because opposed to this is the sufficiency of all things as a secondary aim.

§16. Concerning fear, which is the main point of disagreement: if those who disagree declare that a political community can be conceived without it (which would be necessary, if fear were only a secondary cause), it would follow either that he who already lives peacefully would strive for a political society in vain, or that it is possible to desire a political community in which there is no peace.

§17. But their own [that is, the Peripatetics'] beliefs suggest that each of these two opinions is absurd. It is not only the case that when the purpose ceases, so does the relevant action, but a political community without a primary purpose is a nonbeing, since they [the Peripatetics] admit that the differences between societies reflect these societies' respective ends.

§18. Here, however, we must repeat something we taught in book 2, the distinction between different kinds of fear. Here we are not referring to that violent terror of the mind caused by the immediate threat of a grave evil, but distrust and an apprehension of future harm.

---

94. See *Institutes,* bk. II, chap. xi, §70.

§19. Thereby we parry the argument of certain people, who object that fear was far from being the cause of the establishment of political communities; they say that if humans had feared each other so much that they could not bear the sight of each other, and one person fled here, the other there, then humans would have remained separate forever.[95] For these people evidently use the term *fear* in the first sense and should have considered that fear can also refer to the precaution taken to make sure that there is no likely cause of fear.

§20. Those who follow the doctrine of Aristotle do not disagree with us that need is only the secondary cause of the political community. But contrary to the opinion of others, who believe that humans were led by need to associate in political communities, it has to be said that there is certainly no more miserable animal than man if individuals are left to themselves without any help from other humans. Yet it cannot be denied that once political communities were formed, human life became overrefined and subject to opulence and luxury. It also cannot be denied that before there were political communities, when humans acted separately in scattered families, the necessities of life were already adequately taken care of after the invention of agriculture and animal husbandry, viniculture, clothes production, and the other arts. Hence the heads of households who hold sufficient agricultural land, livestock, and servants lack nothing for leading a tolerable life, or if something is lacking it can easily be supplied through commercial exchange.

§21. This can be largely illustrated by a consideration of the human condition, in comparison with civil life, and by contemplating the state of nature and its inconveniences. The former will confirm that man does not by nature desire civil society; the latter will show why it was impossible to assuage that fear of suffering evil from other humans without a political community.

95. Pufendorf, *Of the Law of Nature and Nations,* bk. VII, chap. i, §7.

§22. Man is driven by inborn inclinations to want to be free from subjection to anyone and to want to do everything out of his own free will. He can barely, through fear of punishment, be brought to obey his rulers and to set aside his ferocity and his proclivity for the many vices, for which there are not even remotely similar examples in wild beasts.

§23. But he who becomes a citizen loses his natural liberty and subjects himself to the rule of another, who holds the right over life and death and at whose command many actions must be performed that one would shun otherwise. A good citizen, however, is one who promptly obeys the commands of his rulers and directs all his efforts toward the common good, even if this appears to contradict his own good.

§24. Moreover, natural law teaches that humans should refrain from inflicting injuries on anyone, though it does emphasize that they who cause injury to others will not remain unpunished. And yet reverence for this law cannot guarantee that humans live safely in the state of natural liberty, because there is a great mass of humans who do not care about anybody's right whenever there is a hope of personal gain. They trust in their own strength or circumspection and thereby hope to be able to repel or escape those whom they have harmed. Nor are the fear of God and the pangs of conscience perceived to have the power to constrain the malice of humans since many are concerned only with present threats, but do not care about future events and are moved only by that which is evident to the senses.

§25. If you insist that the nature of man should not be considered insofar as it is corrupt but in its perfect condition, I will reply that the dogma that all disciplines and sciences are to be taught according to the ideas of some utterly perfect condition, even if this no longer exists, has not only been exploded in book I.[96] You will also gain little by this objection because it has been made clear already that there were not going to be any commonwealths in the state of natural perfection, precisely because of this perfection.

96. See *Institutes,* bk. I, chap. iv, §§44 and 45.

§26. Now that we have examined the reason that leads humans to form civil society our next task is to investigate the reason why political communities were established. Here it is quite obvious that neither a particular location, nor arms, nor beasts could provide a sufficiently convenient and effective protection against the evils which human depravity threatens to inflict on individuals. That required other people, who are united—not a few, but a significant number of people, who did not come together suddenly and without proper consideration, or who were torn in different directions by differences of opinion, but people who agree concerning the means that are suitable to achieving the same purpose and who persist in this agreement.

§27. There are mainly two faults that stand in the way of achieving this aim when there are many people who are *sui juris* and do not depend on each other. One is the diversity of inclinations and of judgment, likewise the dullness of the mind and the obstinacy in defending one's own opinions tenaciously. The other is the torpor and reluctance to do what serves the common good but requires some effort. It is therefore necessary to resist these vices, the first by uniting the wills of all in perpetuity. This happens if every single person subjects his will to that of one person or one council. The second is resisted, however, if a power is established that can inflict a present evil that is immediately obvious to the senses on those who resist the common good. This is the case if each and every one obliges himself to apply his abilities in the way that this power wants him to.

§28. Where such a union of wills and abilities has been brought about, there a multitude of people comes to life as a single powerful body, namely, a political community.

§29. It is obvious from the above that the formation of a political community normally requires two agreements and one decree. The multitude of people who enter the first agreement when they are still in a state of natural liberty do so as individuals, because they want to form one perpetual community and become each other's co-citizens. It is necessary that each and every one consent to this, for he who does not consent remains outside the future political community.

§30. Following this agreement there has to be a decree concerning which form of government is to be introduced.

§31. Following this decree concerning the form of government there has to be another agreement, by which the person or persons are appointed on whom the government of this newly born political community is conferred. By the same agreement these persons bind themselves to take care of the common security and well-being, while all others bind themselves to obedience and subject their wills and abilities to his or their will and direction.

§32. But since political communities are categorized according to their form of government, we need to relate these types very briefly. The forms of government are either regular or irregular. Regular ones are those where supreme power is united in one person and extends itself undivided and unchallenged on the basis of a single will throughout all parts and affairs of the political community. Where this is not the case, we have an irregular form of government.

§33. There are three forms of regular government. Government is either conferred on one person, who is called a monarch, and the political community is then called a monarchy; or it is conferred on a group of people. This consists either of selected citizens or the most eminent citizens and is called an aristocracy, or of all heads of households or the people, which is a democracy.

§34. It is often the case that one form of government functions well in some places and poorly in others. It thus happens that some political communities are called healthy, others diseased and corrupt, even if there is no need to invent special forms or types of government because of these diseases, just as a healthy person does not differ from a sick person in kind.

§35. Some of these diseases with which political communities are infested adhere to people, others to the state itself. We are faced with human faults if those who are entrusted with the administration of power are unsuitable for this task, are negligent or corrupt, and if the citizens, who have the honor of obeying, are straining at the leash.

§36. There are also faults of the state when the laws or institutions of the political community are not adapted to the genius of the people or the region, or when they dispose the citizens to causing internal unrest or provoking the just hatred of neighboring states, or when they render them unfit to perform their proper functions, which are necessary for preserving the commonwealth, or when the fundamental laws are such that public affairs can be expedited only tardily and with great difficulty.

§37. Many people use particular terms to describe diseased commonwealths. A corrupt monarchy is termed a *tyranny,* a corrupt government by the few is called an *oligarchy,* and the corrupt form of the popular state an *ochlocracy,* though these terms are often used not so much to describe a diseased commonwealth, but to give vent to their passion or displeasure with the present state and its rulers.

§38. An irregular commonwealth is one in which the union that is the essence of the state is seen to be less than perfect. And this is not as a result of disease or some fault in the administration of the commonwealth, but as a result of law or custom that has been introduced legitimately.

§39. But there can be infinite ways of diverging from what is right, and it is therefore impossible to establish certain and definite types of irregular commonwealths. Yet their character can be grasped on the basis of one or the other example—say, if in one commonwealth the senate and the people both hold the supreme law in handling public affairs in such a way that neither is subject to the other; or if in a kingdom the power of the great men has increased so much that they are henceforth no more subject to the king than unequal allies are.

§40. Moreover, the description of the irregular commonwealth shows that if you apply here the earlier division of commonwealths, according to which some are healthy, others diseased, then irregular commonwealths have to be reckoned among the diseased, not because of some fault of the rulers, but because of a fault in their basic condition.[97]

§41. Indeed, it is commonly believed to be wicked and insulting if someone declares a particular commonwealth to be irregular and diseased, as if this were a sin against the reverence owed to the supreme powers and against the duty of a good citizen, who must have the highest regard for the commonwealth in which he lives and must never bring about or desire any change in it.

§42. But they do indeed argue sophistically, not to use a harsher term. First of all, to be ill is nothing shameful in itself or something that always implies some guilt on the part of the diseased. Often the weakness of the body's structure or particular circumstances that are beyond reproach, necessary, etc., are the causes of illnesses. The sedentary life of the learned, for example, is the cause of many illnesses.

§43. It is the same with diseased commonwealths: although certain faults are present in the state, these need not be imputed to the rulers or subjects. Not always, but in most cases some great necessity has introduced this disease into the state—the desire, for example, to restore peace and public tranquillity following some kind of unrest.

§44. We have said that the natural origin of the commonwealth is due to the free agreement and consent of those who enter it, and it therefore seems necessary to say that the faults of the state must also be imputed to the citizens themselves. Yet it is very rare for the first origin of some commonwealth to be known to us. But as far as the changes in a com-

97. Thomasius is contradicting Samuel Pufendorf's argument in his *De statu Imperii Germanici* published in 1667 under the pseudonym Severinus da Monzambano (see Samuel Pufendorf, *The Present State of Germany,* ed. M. Seidler [Indianapolis: Liberty Fund, 2007]). There Pufendorf had described the constitution of the Holy Roman Empire as irregular but denied that this meant it was also diseased. See Peter Schröder, "The Constitution of the Holy Roman Empire after 1648: Samuel Pufendorf's Assessment in his Monzambano," *Historical Journal* 42.2 (1999): 961–83.

monwealth are concerned, the will of one part of it is often not that free, but is heavily influenced by external disturbances. Indeed, one must not believe that the faults of a state were present from the beginning, immediately after the formation of the commonwealth. Rather, most of them have gradually crept into the commonwealth after its foundation.

§45. Thus, it is no sin against the reverence that is due to the commonwealth and the ruler to point out a disease. That is not in itself shameful. And so, too, not everyone who classifies something as diseased should be considered to be doing so out of insolence or to insult someone. In fact, in most cases he would sin and violate his duty if he concealed the disease.

§46. The physician and the medic offer a similar example in relation to the human body. They are not only blameless if they inform a person about a disease, but are accused of ignorance or malice if they claim a diseased body to be in perfect health.

§47. Now assume that the same reason applies to the doctor[98] and the counselor for the diseases of a commonwealth. The doctor would sin if he declared the commonwealth to be healthy when it is not. And he would sin not only when the prince asks for his opinion, but also when someone else asks whom he is obliged by some agreement or otherwise to tell the truth—just as a physician would sin who, when asked by a disciple, defended the view that a third person, who was ill, was actually in good health. The counselor would sin if he persuaded the prince, who asked him about measures to preserve the commonwealth, that no such measures were needed.

§48. Or do you seriously believe it to be the duty of a good citizen to tell a falsehood, that is, lie, to someone to whom he is obliged to tell the truth?

§49. Perhaps you put up with it if someone says these things in private and regard it a sin for someone to divulge his opinion in public. For the

98. That is, an academic teacher.

latter amounts to contempt for the commonwealth, since internal faults are rather to be concealed.

§50. As if it were prudent to hide what is evident to everyone and exposed to the knowledge of everyone in public laws! As if the physician were to be considered guilty of contempt and mockery for publicly drawing attention to the examples of people suffering from some dangerous diseases as long as these are diseases that are not the fault of the patients.

§51. Just as the axiom that every change in the commonwealth is ruinous is subject to an infinite number of limitations and elaborations, so the same is to be understood of a change in the persons of the rulers.

§52. But he who performs the role of the teacher does not intend to bring about change, but only draws attention to the disease, leaving its cure to others.

§53. It would be a sin against the rules of prudence and piety to diagnose the disease of the commonwealth and then advise removing the rulers— just as a physician who is as stupid as he is unjust, after diagnosing an illness, provides the patient with medicines that corrupt his brain, the seat of his soul.

§54. Just as a good physician must not use medicines to stir up malignant humidity in a body filled with impurities, to avoid destroying the whole person, but must rather provide medicines that strengthen the most vital parts of the body, so too will it often be the duty of the counselor to leave untouched a disease that is deeply rooted in a commonwealth and to direct his advice only toward preventing the evil from spreading.

§55. Yet it will not be safe to allow any private person to offer his advice spontaneously to the commonwealth, because it must be considered a fault (though quite a common one) if someone tries to do so, though it is a fault of imprudence rather than injustice. This is the same fault as that of him who offers medicines although he has not been called upon by the patient.

§56. But I fear that those who publicly criticize those who present commonwealths as irregular and diseased are unable to shed a similar fault. This is the fact that they have arrogated to themselves the defense of the honor and reverence owed to the commonwealth without being asked to do so—as if it were their personal duty to protect public tranquillity. The prince in the meantime says nothing and laughs at those armchair soldiers who invent enemies and attack them with straw swords.

§57. He who knows political controversies will not judge our digression to have been untimely. Let us continue. Systems of states are not to be confused with what we have reviewed so far concerning the forms of state. Systems are formed when several complete states are so connected by some peculiar tie, a common king or a perpetual treaty, that their collective forces can practically be regarded as the forces of one state.

§58. But beware of thinking that this division of the forms of a commonwealth is the same as that which is usually put forward. First, the discussion of systems of states is clearly being neglected. If you wanted to define them by comparing them with other states, you could perhaps call the former [that is, systems of states] composite commonwealths, the latter simple commonwealths.

§59. But do not think, second, that this distinction between simple and composite coincides with the common division of commonwealths into simple and mixed. For they call a mixed commonwealth what we term an irregular commonwealth, though the term *mixed commonwealth* is narrower than the term *irregular commonwealth*.

§60. Third, we consider an irregular commonwealth to be an example of a diseased commonwealth, but they praise the mixed commonwealth to the skies. We shall soon see how justified that is.

§61. Fourth, they regard this division of commonwealths into true and corrupt as a division into different species, but that is a flimsy argument.

§62. We have so far spoken about the constitution of a state. A state that has been constituted is conceived in the same way as a person. It is distinguished from all particular persons and known by a single name, and has its own rights and properties.

§63. Hence the state can be defined more fully as a moral composite person, whose will is encompassed in and united by the agreements between many people; it is held to be the will of all that it can use the powers and abilities of all individuals for the sake of common peace and security.

§64. It is not difficult to imagine how the will of the state is exercised whenever the government of the state lies with one man. But if this is wielded by a council of several citizens, then the decision of the majority of the council is held to represent the will of the state because there can be no other more convenient way of avoiding quarrels and dissent, unless it is expressly stated that a certain quota of council members must agree in order to represent the will of the whole.

§65. Once a state has been thus constituted, he on whom power has been conferred bears the title of ruler; all others are subjects or citizens, although the term *citizens* in its broad sense covers both orders.

§66. The power of the ruler in the state, however, is called in one word *majesty*. Those who defended the view that majesty was derived immediately from God have raised a storm in a teacup about this.[99]

§67. As often happens, when some false opinion has come up, the learned and the semi-learned try in equal measure to refute it, the former by attacking their adversaries with solid reasons, the latter with inept and ridiculous reasons. And so it happened that Machiavelli's book *The Prince* was read avidly, in which the author (either out of wickedness or with satirical intent) ordered that the prince should measure everything by the standard

99. Thomasius is referring to the Danish court preacher Hector Gottfried Masius, who published *Interesse principum circa religionem evangelicam* (Copenhagen, 1687).

of his own interest, but to do so craftily and secretly; the effect of this has been that among those who are opposed to this doctrine some have fallen into the opposite extreme. They are usually called the Monarchomachs and teach that the prince is bound to take care of public well-being to such an extent that if he acts otherwise he is obliged to render account to the people and even to be punished.

§68. But just as certain celebrated men have refuted these views roundly on the basis of genuine principles of politics, so too are there those who lapse into a new extreme: contrary to the beliefs of the Monarchomachs, they firmly believe that it is sound political science to defend with all their strength the theory that God is the immediate cause of majesty.

§69. Therefore, a certain part of the estates in France once demanded that this proposition be approved in public assemblies and confirmed by royal authority, as if without it there was no hope for public tranquillity in the kingdom. Nothing came of it, however, since the other orders showed that the well-being of France did not depend on it and that this controversy should be left to the lecterns of the schoolmen.

§70. In Germany, however, we do not recall any similar attempt, and we believe that the author of the following public doctrine indulged his passion rather than following the truth: that Germany and France would not be safe until there had been formal confirmation in solemn assemblies that God was the sole cause of majesty and that he who taught otherwise was to be punished by being sent into exile.[100]

§71. This silly bogey of some fictitious exile will not deter us from openly declaring our opinion on the cause of majesty. There are three principal opinions on that. One is that the people by their consent transfer power to their kings and thus bring forth majesty, and that God approved of this wholesome human institution.[101]

---

100. Horn, *Architectonica*, "Praefatio," p. 8 [no pagination].
101. See Grotius, *The Rights of War and Peace*, bk. I, chap. iv, §7, p. 358.

§72. The second is that of the eminent critics of the Monarchomach sect, namely, that God not only is the author and origin of majesty, but its immediate cause, not only in the first and ancient times of commonwealths, but even today whenever some prince succeeds to a kingdom, whether or not with the consent of the people, by just or unjust armed force.[102] For the consent of the people and the other means are indeed ways of acquiring majesty, but these ways are not the causes of the acquisition. The people, for example, may elect a prince, but once he has been chosen majesty is conferred on him immediately by God, etc.

§73. We hold the third opinion, which lies between the two: we argue that God first commanded humans to establish civil societies because the peace and tranquillity of humankind could not be maintained without them. In that sense God is correctly said to be the author of power in the state, or of majesty, and not to have approved it after the fact. So the origin of majesty pertains to God as author of natural law.

§74. But power that is produced directly in the state flows immediately from the kind of agreements by which the state grows together and which we have been explaining so far. This is when the people submit their powers and their will to the prince, and the prince accepts this subjection.

§75. And hence it is that one of the Apostles calls political power divinely ordained because he looks to its divine origins,[103] while another describes it as human because he is referring to its particular origin.[104]

§76. But perhaps you wish to know on what grounds those who make God the immediate cause of majesty defend their opinion? None at all, except for very feeble ones that a tyro could brush aside, which is why we shall not mention them.

---

102. See, for example, Horn, *Architectonica,* bk. II, chap. I, §x, pp. 192–93.
103. See Romans 13:1.
104. See 1 Peter 2:13.

§77. It was, therefore, necessary to compensate for the lack of reasons with the appearance of piety, by piling up many scriptural quotations which do testify to the divine origin of majesty but fail to prove its immediate derivation from God, except in the eyes of the vulgar and people unskilled in logic.

§78. The saying of the Apostle, "There is no power but of God" and "The powers that be are ordained of God,"[105] seemed to be extremely attractive to them. "For," they said, "is it not obvious that the Apostle here proves both our assertions, namely, that God is the origin of majesty and that he acknowledges no other cause of majesty apart from God? For he uses the particle *nisi* [except], which is exclusive and rules out all other causes apart from God. But the cause that is the sole cause is also necessarily the immediate cause."

§79. Thus they were close to boasting of having distinguished themselves by their close adherence to the rules of reasoning, since logical analysis teaches that an exclusive proposition contains two general propositions, one affirmative and the other negative.

§80. But the response to this sophistry is extremely easy. First, the context shows that the Apostle is here referring not only to that supreme power which is called majesty, but also to all subordinate powers which pertain to magistrates. Therefore, if in this phrase—there is no power but of God—he wanted to say that God is the immediate cause of that power about which he speaks it would have the absurd consequence that God is the immediate cause of the power of every magistrate, even the lowest. Not even those who disagree with us admit that.

§81. Hence, they commit a serious logical error which goes against the doctrine on equivalents and the principles concerning exclusive propositions when they regard the proposition "There is no power but of God" (which is the equivalent of: there is no power that is not from God, or all

105. Romans 13:1.

power comes from God) as an exclusive proposition—as if the Apostle had said power does not exist unless it is from God alone. For that would have been truly exclusive and the equivalent of this: power comes only, that is immediately, from God.

§82. The matter is so clear that it is embarrassing to add anything further, if some people had not many times created a great uproar about it. It may, therefore, be permitted to emphasize briefly that the Apostle added a clear paraphrase to the previous sentence in order to remove all doubt, since he immediately subjoins the statement "but where there is power, it comes from God," when otherwise he would have had to say, "where there is power, it comes from God alone." The truth of what has been said can also be illustrated with a similar example.

§83. Thus it is correct for me to say there is no man who is not from Adam (from God), but this proposition is not equivalent to the following: man does not exist, unless he is descended only from Adam (from God), which is also false.

§84. You see, therefore, that those who attack the Monarchomachs with these weapons defend a good cause badly. For just as they [the Monarchomachs] could be easily defeated without this fictitious argument, so too I am much mistaken if the Monarchomachs cannot turn these arguments against their critics.

§85. For when they declare that every prince, even he who acquires his kingdom by regicide, for example, is endowed with majesty directly by God, it follows from the common hypothesis of political theorists (which is that majesty has its place not only in a monarchy, but in an aristocracy and a democracy, too) that we would have to say the same about a people who unjustly overthrow their king and transform their monarchy into a democracy.

§86. The Monarchomachs therefore insist that although majesty is immediately from God that does not mean it is unjust for the people to depose and punish a king who abuses his divinely granted power. This is especially so since God, after the killing of the king, transfers majesty from him to the people. And they argue it is clear from this that killing a king is not unjust.

§87. This makes no sense unless the critics of the Monarchomachs wanted to make the absurd claim that God is not just the cause of sin, but (which is even worse) rewards sin as such.

§88. I do not see how they can extricate themselves from such a tight corner unless they seek refuge in meaningless distinctions or appeal to the vain bogey of their own authority by showing off their beard and their gown.[106]

§89. And even if the consent of the people, as we have said before, is required for the legitimate acquisition of political power, the ways in which this consent is elicited vary. Hence, orderly procedure demands that we briefly discuss the ways of acquiring political power.

§90. In discussing the means by which someone has acquired political power, it is normally assumed that he who acquires political power is different from those from whom or over whom it is acquired. In monarchies this difference is far more obvious than in an aristocracy or a democracy. We are therefore mainly concerned with monarchy and can then easily apply and adapt what we have said to aristocracy and democracy.

§91. Even if hereditary succession rarely takes place in an aristocracy and never in a democracy, and election also does not seem properly applicable to democracy, yet the distinction between violent and nonviolent means of acquiring power can be applied to either type.

§92. The nobles and the king may have been driven out by a rebellion and a democracy established, but even if the people expelled the king, it

---

106. That is, superficial signs of erudition.

cannot be said that they conferred political power on themselves by violent means, since in a democracy rulers and subjects are not distinguished physically, but only morally. They did, however, take power away from the king and the nobles by violent means, which here is sufficient.

§93. Monarchical political power is thus acquired either through violence or through the free consent of the people. Violence is either just or unjust. Whenever political power is acquired through either, it is usually called occupation, which must not be confused with that form of occupation through which things that have no owner are subjected to our ownership just by being seized physically.

§94. Political power is acquired through just violence, if someone has a just cause for waging war and with the help of arms and good fortune reduces a nation to the point that it is forced to subject itself to his command.

§95. Therefore, it is not true that he exercises political power over his defeated enemy immediately after victory and does not need to expect the consent of his subjects. For how would it be possible to move from the state of war to that of peace without an intervening agreement?

§96. Victors in a just war, however, do not need to flatter the defeated and gain their consent through bribery or entreaties, but can extract it by threatening extreme evils.

§97. And this is possible for two reasons: first, the victor could, if he wanted to make use of the full rigor of the law of war, deprive the defeated of their lives. Thus, when he allows them to suffer a smaller disadvantage, he even acquires a reputation for clemency.

§98. Second, he who goes to war with another whom he had previously harmed, and whom he refused to give satisfaction, wagers all his possessions on the fortunes of war. Thus he already agreed in advance, tacitly, to accept whatever condition the outcome of the war would assign to him.

§99. As far as an unjust invader is concerned, we first need to see whether he has by force turned a democracy into a monarchy or whether he has taken the place of a monarch who has been expelled.

§100. In the latter case the obligation to restore the previous monarch does not expire until the exiled king and his heirs, who had demanded the right to the kingdom, are extinct or they themselves consider their claim to be derelict.

§101. In the meantime, even if the conscience of the invader is not clear, the oath legally binds the subjects after they have given their consent, because they took this oath only after they had done everything that their previous king could demand of them.

§102. A people can be equally happy in a monarchy or a democracy, and as far as the prior case is concerned it seems highly probable that the desire for popular liberty may easily wane if this new king governs the commonwealth well. And that can be assumed if they are patient even for a moderate period of time and get used to him. In that way the fault in the means of acquisition is understood to have been purged.

§103. But if someone treats the citizens poorly after a violent change in the commonwealth, then his fault will not be purged by the passage of time, because long-lasting possession is here nothing other than the continual infliction of injury over a long period of time.

§104. The kingdom, however, is prepared for free consent of the people by means of an intervening election, by which the people, who are to be established or already have been established, of their own accord choose a particular man whom they believe to be a competent ruler. When the decree of the people has been communicated to him and he has accepted it, then the people promise obedience and political power is conferred on him.

§105. I said of their own accord, that is, if the people are not compelled by some superior force to transfer political power to him. That is the case, no matter whether the people transfer political power out of a desire to further their own convenience and out of some inner instinct, or whether they have been compelled to do so by some external necessity, such as fear of superior force threatened by another, hunger, etc. The usefulness of these different motives will, however, be evident when we come to the properties of political power.

§106. I said that the election is made by a people who are to be established or who have been established. The latter differs from the former in that it is undertaken after the previous king has died and thus is usually preceded by an interregnum.

§107. During an interregnum the political community may slide back into an imperfect condition, since the citizens are only connected to each other by the first agreement. The common name and the affection for the common fatherland, however, greatly support this agreement, and the fortunes of most of the citizens are closely linked to their country. These [fortunes] force good citizens to keep peace among themselves of their own accord and make it incumbent on them to set up a full political power all the more quickly. It does, however, contribute a lot toward avoiding the inconveniences that are liable to result from interregna if it is decided in advance who is to run the administration of the commonwealth when the throne is vacant.

§108. In some places there is a new election whenever a monarch has died. In others the kingdom is conferred on another person by law in such a way that it passes to others according to hereditary succession, without a new election. If the former is the case, it is called an elective monarchy; if the latter, hereditary.

§109. The right of succession, however, is established either by the authority of the king or that of the people, depending on whether the kingdom is patrimonial or usufructuary. More on this distinction soon.

§110. It is good if both [king and people] have declared their will. If they have not, this leads to very difficult controversies, because in the absence of an express will one needs to take recourse to the tacit will.

§111. It is not possible to come up with exact rules for this, not only because the human will, insofar as it shows any variation, certainly varies in infinite ways when it is concerned with the transfer of one's own goods. It is also difficult because one may want to take account of equity, and it is not easy to find an accepted form of intestate succession that does not rest on some kind of equity.

§112. And it is not a valid conjecture that in kingdoms the same form of succession must be observed as in the case of private property, since there is a huge difference between kingdoms and private possessions.

§113. In similar controversies that arise between princes it is easy to find conjectures opposed to other conjectures, since the foundation of conjecture is slippery. So, too, it only requires ingenuity to defend the rights of a particular prince in that matter. It is therefore no surprise if in an affair of this kind four or more very different parties have attempted to defend their rights in print. And if ever an axiom was true, the proverb "Blessed are those who are in possession" is true here.

§114. But if the controversies are to be judged according to what usually happens, we do not deny that famous men have preceded us and provided detailed rules. The authors who write about these questions usually tend to use them as a guideline.

§115. Political power in a state is called, in one word, majesty. We have already discussed its origin and the means of acquiring it. It is defined as the supreme power in directing the actions of citizens and in conducting matters of peace and war with those outside the commonwealth in the name of the state, in order to obtain the state's ends.[107]

§116. I say: *supreme power,* that is, one which in its exercise does not depend on any human being as a superior, but is exercised on the ba-

---

107. See Pufendorf, *Of the Law of Nature and Nations,* bk. VII, chap. vi, §1.

sis of its own judgment, so that its actions cannot be challenged by any superior.

§117. Hence it is also the case that the same political power is ἀνυπεύθυνον; that is, it is not obliged to justify itself before any mortal, in the sense of being subject to human punishments and coercion by a superior, if its actions are not approved by another.

§118. Related to this is the fact that the same supreme power is superior to all human laws and civil laws as such and is not normally bound by them. For these laws depend on the supreme power for their origin as well as their duration. Hence, it cannot be bound by the laws, for then it would be superior to itself.

§119. Moreover, the supreme nature of political power cannot be properly conceived if we do not believe a peculiar sanctity to be attached to it, so that it is not only a wicked sin to resist legitimate commands; their severity must also be patiently borne by citizens, the way that good children must bear the demands of parents. Yea, even when the ruler has inflicted the cruelest injuries, then individuals should rather save themselves by fleeing the country or putting up with the calamity, however great, rather than drawing the sword against him who may be harsh but is still the father of the fatherland.

§120. The Monarchomachs therefore attack this sanctity, but they are a foolish sect and have long ago been refuted by others. Their views inevitably undermine the supremacy of this power, so that the majesty that they grant kings is no such thing.

§121. Here the distinction between real and personal majesty is also relevant.

§122. With regard to the supremacy which is part of majesty, the politicians have asked whether it is possible to speak of a temporary monarch—that is, one whose power is limited to a certain and definite period of time, after which he has to become a private person again and can be compelled to do so by law.

§123. It seems to me that this question is to be affirmed, because being supreme and being temporary are not incompatible, and if the power of those princes who freely abdicate and adopt the life of a private person is truly to be considered majesty, there seems to be no reason why it should not be the same with those we are speaking about.

§124. Although these rulers can be forced by law to put down their office and just coercion is contrary to supremacy, this coercion does not take place until their power has ceased to be supreme.

§125. A temporary monarch is not bound thereby to justify himself before the people after he has laid down power. Nor is he subject to punishment for doing something badly. In that case his power is not ἀνυπεύθυνον, and therefore not supreme, but he is rather to be regarded as some kind of superior magistrate.

§126. A different controversy arises when we ask how to apply this to particular cases—for example, if you ask whether a Roman dictator held true majesty.[108] For there we need to adapt these principles to circumstances that have to be found out from histories. But that is not our purpose here.

§127. Moreover, the restriction of rule is not incompatible with its supremacy. Rather, in monarchies especially and in aristocracies it is possible to distinguish between absolute and limited rule.

§128. That monarch is said to hold absolute power who wields it on the basis of his own judgment, not according to the standard of specific and perpetual statutes, but as the present situation seems to require, and who

---

108. In ancient republican Rome a dictator was appointed for a limited period in times of emergency.

thus takes care of the commonwealth's well-being according to his own authority, as the times require.

§129. Because the judgment of one person, however, is not immune to errors and the will is easily turned toward evil, especially given such great freedom of action, it seemed advisable to some nations to circumscribe the exercise of the ruler's power within certain limits.

§130. This was done when, in bestowing the kingdom, they bound the king to observe certain laws concerning the administration of parts of political power. And whenever there were matters of supreme importance that could not be defined in advance, they wanted these to be undertaken only with the knowledge and consent of the people, or their assembled deputies, so that there should be less occasion for the king to deviate from the well-being of the kingdom.

§131. The laws that limit the power of the prince in this way are called fundamental laws, though it is entirely inappropriate to use the term *law* here, because they are rather to be described as agreements.

§132. Finally, a monarch with supreme power either has the power to alienate and divide the kingdom at will, or he lacks it.

§133. For the sake of distinction Grotius called the former kingdoms patrimonial, the latter usufructuary, because a usufructuary cannot alienate the thing in which he has a usufruct, while he who holds full patrimony can.[109]

§134. They who criticize this distinction by Grotius thus need to remind themselves that this terminology must not be extended beyond the common term, on which Grotius based the similarity. They must remember the common proverb that every simile is defective.

---

109. See Grotius, *The Rights of War and Peace,* bk. I, chap. iii, §§xi–xii. See also Barbeyrac's note 4 on p. 280.

§135. Though it is undeniable that it would be better to call the kingdoms of the latter type fideicommissary rather than usufructuary. Grotius does that from time to time.

§136. When it is asked a priori which kingdoms are to be considered usufructuary and which patrimonial, we must take the following view: if the people transferred their power of alienating [the kingdom] onto the king in a consensual agreement, then the kingdom must be patrimonial.

§137. Otherwise, a kingdom is to be considered patrimonial only if the king has acquired it by armed force or if he himself creates his own people, as in the case of Romulus, which is rare.

§138. Among the kingdoms that have been transferred to the king by free consent those are to be considered usufructuary in which the people did not want to have hereditary succession. That in itself made it clear that they did not want to grant the prince the right of alienation, since they did not even want the kingdom to be passed on to his progeny.

§139. In hereditary monarchies (or when it is unclear whether the kingdom is elective or hereditary) I would consider those to be usufructuary (and elective) where the people is moved only by an intrinsic instinct, as it were, and without serious external pressure to elect a king, whereas those where serious pressure from the outside impels the people to look for a king are patrimonial (and hereditary).

§140. If this question came up immediately after the transfer of the kingdom, then it must be assumed in the former case that the king would have accepted the kingdom without the power of alienating it and without the right of his heirs to succeed him; and in the latter that the people would have bowed to the king's demand for the power to alienate the kingdom and for the right of hereditary succession.

§141. For it is the usual practice in contracts that he who has less of an advantage from the contract prescribes laws to the other party, and that he who receives a greater benefit from the contract accepts conditions, even if they are harsh. But if the people choose a king without being forced to do so by any necessity, then it is in the interest of the king rather than the people; if serious necessity spurs on the people, it is in the interest of the people rather than the king.

§142. But majesty is exercised, as we have said in our definition, not only in relation to subjects, but in relation to equals outside the commonwealth. The elements of supreme power (which are commonly called regalia) can therefore be conveniently divided into internal regalia, which concern the first, and external, which concern the latter.

§143. The other division of regalia, into major and minor, is subject to many difficulties and is of greater use in resolving controversies in human law, to which it also owes its origin, than in natural jurisprudence, where minor regalia are required as much to obtain the ends of the commonwealth as major regalia are.

§144. The distinction of regalia that is based on the ends of the commonwealth is closer to the first distinction [into internal and external]. For these ends are advanced, first, if everything is conducted in a good and orderly fashion in the commonwealth and the citizens are protected from internal strife and, second, if they are defended from external force at the time of war.

§145. Therefore, either the regalia are directed primarily to one of those ways of promoting the ends of the commonwealth or they serve both.[110]

§146. In times of peace the main power of the ruler is legislation. Rulers use it to inform citizens of their will concerning matters that contribute to the well-being of the commonwealth, the will to which the citizens submitted themselves in the agreement establishing the political community.

---

110. That is, internal peace and external protection.

§147. Part of this is the power to use punishments. The intention is that citizens should be safe from damages and injuries which can be and often are inflicted by their fellow citizens. Without such a right legislative power would be in vain.

§148. Then there is judicial power, by which controversies over the correct application of laws to particular facts and illegal actions of citizens are resolved. Hence, this regalian right serves the legislative power and right of punishment.

§149. Now, the actions of individuals are governed by each person's opinion, but most tend to judge affairs as they are accustomed to and as they see them commonly judged, and very few can discern on their own what is true and honest. Thus it is useful for the state to proclaim publicly those doctrines that are in accordance with the true purpose and practice of political communities, and for the minds of citizens to be imbued with these doctrines from childhood onward. It is therefore the duty of the supreme power to employ people to teach such doctrines publicly—hence, the right to found schools and academies, as well as the right to regulate ecclesiastical affairs, narrowly understood.[111]

§150. But you must not believe that we are arguing for the precepts of religion to be directed according to the utility of particular commonwealths. That would be a dishonest interpretation of our words, since we speak of the common purpose of political communities.

§151. Its relationship to religion is as follows: if a religion is openly incompatible with the peace of the commonwealth, then it must be considered false, because God never wanted humans to be imbued with such beliefs and is not able to will that, because he is the author of commonwealths and could not have willed two mutually contradictory things.

---

111. The degree to which ecclesiastical affairs were subject to princely regulation was controversial. Orthodox Lutheran theorists accused Thomasius of "Caesaro-Papism," that is, of exaggerating the secular ruler's power in ecclesiastical affairs. See Ahnert, *Religion and the Origins of the German Enlightenment,* chap. 3.

§152. But there may be several ways of obtaining a purpose, and you cannot therefore reverse the argument and say, "This religion conforms to the purpose of a commonwealth, therefore it is true": for as we have shown above, for a religion to be true, it has to be revealed by God.

§153. The prince, therefore, who tolerates a false religion that is not contrary to the purpose of the state does not violate natural law and the duty of a good prince, but he does violate divine universal positive law and thus the duty of a good Christian. Theology, therefore, must here supply the defects of natural jurisprudence.

§154. The right of war and peace pertains to times of war, likewise the right to conclude treaties. The right to raise, arm, and form soldiers into units is also relevant here.

§155. The rights to establish magistrates and to impose taxes are equally relevant at both times.

§156. These parts of supreme power are naturally linked to each other in such a way that all these parts must be firmly held by one person or group for the state to have its proper form. If one or the other is missing, the state's power will be crippled and unsuitable to serve the purpose of the state.

§157. If they are divided, in that some powers are held by one person and others by another, the inevitable result will be an irregular and incoherent commonwealth. Not only will one power be useless or subservient to the other whenever there is disagreement. Given our corrupt condition there will also be a great danger of civil war if the united will that is the soul of the commonwealth is missing.

§158. All that is completely obvious, and yet there are some who try to justify a division of the parts of supreme power and invent mixed constitutions, which, if only they are well tempered, are supposed to produce the happiest commonwealth possible, if you can believe that.

§159. It is vain to appeal to the authority of Aristotle in support of mixed constitutions, since he is speaking about a very different kind of mixture, not that which is based on the division of the parts of supreme power.[112]

§160. It is not impossible for irregular or mixed commonwealths to exist, but where they do exist they must be reckoned diseased. The Peripatetics torture themselves in vain when they disagree so strongly with each other, trying to come up with a mixed form of government which they can claim is worth striving and hoping for.

§161. Having said that, we must now briefly explain the duty of rulers and of parents. The principles that the duty of supreme rulers is based on can be clearly gathered from the character and end of the states and from weighing up the parts of supreme power.

§162. Nobody, whatever condition he lives in, can fulfill his duty if he does not have an exact knowledge of his obligation. So, too, it is very much incumbent on the prince to observe this precept above all others: learn what pertains to the full knowledge of the duty of a good prince.

§163. Then the general law of the supreme rulers is this: the well-being of the people should be the supreme law. For power has been conferred on them to fulfill the purpose for which political communities were established. Hence, they must believe that nothing is to their private advantage that is not also to the advantage of the state.

§164. The exercise of the parts of supreme power must be directed toward this end. That is: citizens are to be imbued with good customs; suitable laws are to be passed and applied; judicious punishments are to be imposed; mutual injuries between citizens are to be forbidden; one must use suitable and honest ministers; taxes are to be imposed and collected properly; the opportunities for citizens to earn their living are to be

112. See Aristotle, *Politics,* bk. IV, chaps. 8 and 9.

encouraged; factions are to be prohibited; armed force is to be prepared against external invasions.

§165. The duty of subjects is either general or particular. The former originates in the common obligation by which they are subject to civil government. The latter, however, originates in the specific office and function that are imposed on each individual by the supreme power.

§166. General duty concerns either the rulers of the state, or the state as a whole, or fellow citizens.

§167. Hence, the first precept: "Be reverent, faithful, and obedient toward the rulers of the state."

§168. Second: "Hold nothing dearer than the well-being and safety of the whole state."

§169. Third: "Live in friendship and peace with your fellow citizens."

§170. Concerning particular duties the common precept is, "Do not aim for or take on an office in the commonwealth for which you know yourself to be unsuitable."

§171. Note the following with regard to all aspects of these duties: those who assist the rulers of a state with their advice; who are publicly constituted to perform sacred rites; who are publicly entrusted with the task of teaching the citizens about various matters; who are put in charge of jurisdiction; who are entrusted with military matters; who are enlisted as soldiers; on whose services the state draws in its external relations [e.g., diplomats]; who are in charge of collecting or dispensing the wealth of the state: these must direct all their actions toward preserving public peace, within and outside the state, and toward increasing the state's wealth, and they must be convinced that this is what they are doing when they observe the norm prescribed on this matter by rulers.

On the Duties of Citizens in States
Concerning Punishments

§1. We now need to examine the parts of supreme power one by one and see what has to be observed in each particular case. There are not such great or difficult controversies here, and everything that comes under this heading has already been fully and clearly explained by others.[113] Nothing remains for us to add to that and we can pass these matters by.

§2. Yet we cannot pass over the question of the infliction of punishments because there are many intricate questions in relation to it and the most outstanding intellects have toiled in vain to explain them.[114]

§3. There we shall soon need to separate the otiose questions from those which he who follows true wisdom and not its shadow need not be ashamed of.

§4. The question which kind of justice the imposition of punishments belongs to is in my opinion an otiose question. There are various opinions here. Some appeal to universal justice, others to commutative justice, others to distributive justice, others again to some third kind of particular

---

113. Thomasius has in mind Pufendorf, *Of the Law of Nature and Nations*, bk. VIII, chap. i.

114. See ibid., chap. iii.

justice which is what we believe. But what is the point of this? We have earlier rejected this whole division of justice as useless.[115]

§5. Concerning the other question, the intellect must be armed in advance with a distinct concept of punishment, because this term is subject to many ambiguities.

§6. There can be no doubt at all that punishments are something that happens to humans because of their crimes and against their will. It follows that we are not talking about a punishment which I agree to suffer, from which the Roman *stipulatio poenalis* derives its name.

§7. Among those punishments that are inflicted on people for their crimes, there are various kinds, whether you look at that which is inflicted on the offenders, the person inflicting it, or the intention of the person inflicting it.

§8. With respect to that which is inflicted on the offenders, (1) a punishment in the broad sense is one that includes the confiscation of the gain the guilty person actually has, whether this means the thing itself or its value or the gain this person has had if he has since consumed it, lost it, or given it away. Thus it is said: offenders are to be deprived of their gains as a punishment.

§9. (2) In the strict sense punishment only stands for the damage when the offender loses some good, but has not made any gain from the crime—be this good a good of fortune or of the body. Among the latter are included wealth and honor, among the former health (by which I do not mean absence of disease so much as absence of pain), sound limbs, and life. In that sense punishment is opposed to the restoration of damage.

115. See *Institutes*, bk. I, chap. i, §106.

§10. (3) In the strictest sense it stands for the infliction of physical harm or of disgrace. And so the payment of money as punishment is called a fine and is often opposed to punishment in the proper sense.

§11. With respect to the person inflicting it, (1) a punishment in the broad sense is that imposed by God on humans for certain crimes, whether this is done directly or through other humans. So diseases and other evils which we tend to regard as misfortune are termed punishments to the extent that God uses them to punish our crimes. So, likewise, injuries, conflagrations, or raids inflicted by humans are punishments to the extent that God uses these as instruments.

§12. (2) In the strict sense it stands for that which is inflicted by one human being on another, whether the person inflicting it is an equal or a superior. Thus revenge and punishment are often used interchangeably.

§13. (3) In the strictest sense it stands for that which is dictated by a superior to a subject who has committed a crime. And then punishment is opposed to revenge.

§14. Finally, you can classify punishments according to the purpose of the person inflicting them. To understand this purpose it must be noted that either the past or the future evil is taken into account.

§15. The past evil is either the harm inflicted on the injured person (which requires reparation) or it is the crime itself and the contempt of the superior it involves (which demands atonement).

§16. A future evil refers to the injured person and others who can be harmed again in this or a similar way and must be given security. Or it refers to the offender and those who could commit the same crime again or a similar crime and who must be corrected.

§17. Thus there are four purposes that they who punish offenders may have in mind: reparation, atonement, security, and correction. With regard to these punishment is either taken (1) in a broad sense that covers all these four purposes, including reparation.

§18. (2) In a strict sense, which is opposed to reparation and only includes the remaining three purposes—in such a way, however, that security and correction are the principal intention.

§19. (3) In the strictest sense, when it only stands for atonement.

§20. Now let us see which of these meanings is appropriate here. If we turn to the first category [that is, in relation to offenders], then the confiscation of the gain from the crime does not belong here since it is not a punishment properly speaking and belongs to the chapter in book 2 on avoiding harm to others. For that reason the law separates legal actions to obtain a thing from penal matters.

§21. Although the punishment that is caused to the goods of the body or to honor is undoubtedly a purer form of punishment than a fine, we still consider fines to be punishments.

§22. In the second category [that is, in relation to the person inflicting the punishment] the punishment in the broad sense has little to do with our plan here, because we are not dealing with the right of God over humans here, but only with the duties of humans toward each other, and because the discussion of divine punishments is a matter for theologians, not jurists.

§23. Punishment that is inflicted by an equal is not relevant here. We are currently explaining that part of majesty which regulates the relations between rulers and subjects in a state. Whatever one person inflicts on an equal because of a crime is revenge rather than punishment.

§24. In the third category a punishment for the sake of the reparation of damage is not punishment in the proper sense because this pertains to the chapter on avoiding harm to others.

§25. But a punishment the only purpose of which is atonement for a crime is a type of divine punishment, because man when punishing must never look to a past evil alone, but must also turn to some future good.

§26. Finally, the punishment that aims at security rather than correction is revenge rather than punishment.

§27. Thus of all the many meanings for the term *punishment* there remain from the first category that of punishment as the infliction of some evil and from the second that of a punishment that has correction as its main aim.

§28. On that basis we can define *punishment* as follows: it is an imposition of evil or pain, which a superior inflicts on an inferior against the latter's will and for the sake of the general correction of citizens.

§29. Others define it as an evil suffered that is inflicted because of an evil done.[116] Various people have raised objections to this definition: some say that the punishment sometimes consists in the action of the guilty person; others that not every crime is an action. But it is easy to reply to these, and all these objections can be avoided if you reformulate this definition and use the following brief and succinct phrase, as others have done: punishment is pain inflicted because of a crime.[117]

§30. Yet we do not want to have anything to do with this definition, because it fails to mention the person who inflicts the punishment and the purpose which the prince must keep in mind in punishments. These features render a punishment very different from revenge. The previous definition of punishment is, however, equally applicable to revenge.

---

116. Pufendorf, *Of the Law of Nature and Nations*, bk. VIII, chap. iii, §4; Grotius, *The Rights of War and Peace*, bk. II, chap. xx, §i.

117. Johann Christoph Becmann, *Meditationes politicae*, 3rd ed. (Frankfurt an der Oder, 1679), chap. XV, §ii, p. 206.

§31. Concerning the person who inflicts the punishment, it is known that Grotius attributed the power to inflict punishment to an equal, that is, to a person who was not guilty of a similar crime.[118] But that great man often means nothing by punishment other than verbal coercion. Perhaps he is misled by the fact that this coercion, like punishment in our sense, has correction as its aim. But what he means is in fact admonition rather than punishment, or it is punishment only in the most improper sense. He also believes that a person who throughout his life refrains from crimes acquires some superior right over another person, although in fact not any superiority will do: what is required is superiority of political power.

§32. Concerning the ends of punishments, there are many disagreements among the doctors, ancient and modern. But they all agree in saying that reparation and compensation for damage are not properly applicable here.

§33. As far as atonement, security, and correction are concerned two things need to be proved here: first, that among these purposes correction, not only that of the criminal but of citizens in general, is the primary purpose of proper punishment; second, that this purpose contains the others.

§34. We cannot prove the first in any better way than if we exclude the other purposes from the category of primary purpose. Concerning atonement, God as creator of man holds many rights over man that man does not have. Without doubt, the most powerful deity can reduce creatures to nothing without violating his own sanctity, so there is even less reason to doubt that he can make atonement alone the primary purpose of punishments that are inflicted on offenders.

§35. And indeed the purpose of eternal punishment is no other, because there will no longer be a need for security or correction in the afterlife.

---

118. Grotius, *The Rights of War and Peace*, bk. II, chap. xx, §iii.

§36. But that is not possible for humans, in part because we lack the rational capacity to conceive how God could intend this purpose without moral contradiction. Man is not the creator of man, nor is there between one human being and the other such an infinite distance in their respective beings as there is between God and man. And we have already emphasized above that there is no society of humans which is purely unequal: all are mixed.

§37. The supreme prince is also obliged to perform duties of humanity toward his subjects. It would therefore be inhumane if one man wanted to punish another only because of some past evil, especially if this person is penitent and asks for forgiveness for his deed.

§38. In addition, the right of punishment is one of the parts of majesty. But these, as we have shown, must be subordinated to the tranquillity of the commonwealth as a future good.

§39. We must not, therefore, be surprised that it is a vice and considered cruelty if man in punishments only looks toward past evil, but that it is not vice if God does so. For God is not man, and not everything that is inhumane implies a contradiction in God.

§40. Security and correction remain to be discussed. The prince is concerned about both in his punishments, as we shall soon explain; but he is concerned with correction to a greater degree than security, for we are here mainly looking for the purpose that distinguishes punishment from revenge—yet security is also a purpose of revenge.

§41. Indeed, correction implies security, but security does not imply correction.

§42. Thus, an equal protects only his liberty against an equal and the peace he himself enjoys. He has no interest whether the other people in this world are good or bad. But in the commonwealth the prince aims to make his citizens good by holding rewards and punishments before their eyes.

§43. Finally, correction is either that of the offender or of others who might commit a similar offense. The first is often intended, but the latter always is in punishments that are inflicted by the commonwealth, because the correction of the offender is part of the general correction, not vice versa. The effect is that all regalia take more account of common utility than that of individuals.

§44. This is evident from the example of capital punishments, in which the correction of the offender is not intended.

§45. General correction is the primary purpose of punishments, but it is quite clear that this includes atonement and security. If, for example, a murderer is beheaded, the purpose of the punishment is to set an example to other offenders and persuade them to refrain from sin. In that case, the citizens are assured that they are safe from such a crime, while the prince receives satisfaction for the contempt on the part of the offender, to the extent that this is possible.

§46. We shall soon show the difference between revenge and punishment. There are almost as many meanings of the term *revenge* as there are of *punishment,* because *revenge* and *punishment* are often used interchangeably by authors.

§47. I do not think it is easy to find the term *revenge* used by the ancient authors to describe an action that has the purpose of warding off an imminent injury. Among the moderns several have extended the term *revenge* to include that meaning, but I consider that inappropriate.

§48. There is also no doubt that we are not dealing here with divine revenge, about which theologians can tell us more. As far as human revenge is concerned, the way in which revenge differs from punishment will be clearest from its definition. Revenge in its proper sense is the imposition of an evil that is inflicted on an offender by an equal whom he has injured in the state of nature, so that in future the offender may beware of the injured party.

§49. Thus (1) punishment has its proper place in the civil state, revenge among those who live in a state of nature.

§50. (2) Punishment is inflicted by the ruler on the subject, while revenge takes place among equals.

§51. (3) The primary purpose of punishment is general betterment, while that of revenge is the security of the injured person. In a state of nature everyone must direct his actions in such a way that the common peace is not disturbed, but nobody has the power to direct the actions of others toward this end. That is why political power is required.

§52. Both punishment and revenge are such that they are not automatically either just or unjust. And hence punishment and revenge are divided into just and unjust. In both cases we have defined the just as the noblest analogous example.

§53. For as far as punishment is concerned, it incurs the charge of injustice if an equal wants to inflict it, or if a superior inflicts it out of pure pleasure because of the contempt shown to himself, etc.

§54. Revenge is unjust if in a political community with law courts an equal wants to revenge himself, or when an equal in the state of nature wants to take revenge primarily in order to achieve the correction of the offender or others, or the common security of others.

§55. But punishment in the proper sense is that which we (to use the terminology of political theorists) define elegantly and fittingly as medicinal punishment, because just as a physician applies medicines with the intention of restoring the health of an individual sick person, so too the prince in applying punishments must have in mind the rectitude of the moral body, that is, of the commonwealth when it suffers from moral illnesses.

§56. And indeed, if any moral doctrine can be illustrated by a medical simile, that of punishments certainly can. There is no question concerning punishments in which you cannot draw very appropriate parallels from the duty of a good physician to that of a punisher. That is, as long as you leave aside that difficult and intricate question, do humans have a duty with respect to punishments? That requires arguments found elsewhere.

§57. Yet that is already apparent: if we wanted to derive the right concerning punishments and answer the questions about it on the basis of the state of innocence, either *formaliter* or *normaliter*,[119] then it would be as inept as telling the physician who wanted to do his duty to turn back to that perfect state which was free of all illnesses and vices.

§58. We would even be creating a fiction that would hardly be fitting for a Christian person if we used the assumption that in the state of innocence all actions of the magistrate would have been directed toward the convenience of the subjects, just in order to contribute some conclusions to the debates over punishment. For we have already shown several times that in the state of innocence there would not have been any commonwealths.

§59. Let us turn to the matter at hand: the question whether there is a duty of man concerning punishments has to be divided into two parts. The first of these examines the duty of the punisher, the other the duty of the person to be punished.

§60. Concerning the former, I assert that the superior in a commonwealth is obliged to inflict the punishment. The truth of this assertion is crystal clear as soon as we have clarified to whom the superior is obliged and what the foundation of this obligation is.

---

119. Those parts of natural law that were applicable *formaliter* did not have to be adapted to the changed circumstances after the fall from grace, while those that were valid *normaliter* concerned rules for the particular corrupt state of humankind following the fall from grace (e.g., concerning slavery, which did not exist in the state of innocence). These terms were used by Thomasius's orthodox Lutheran adversary Valentin Alberti (1635–97), who argued that the principles of natural law had to be derived from the state of innocence, before original sin.

§61. The usual phrase is that punishment is owed to him who has committed a crime. But that phrase is clearly very awkward. For he to whom something is owed has a right to demand what is owed from the debtor. But who would say that the offender has a right with which he can demand that the magistrate inflict a punishment on him?

§62. But I do not believe this phrase means that criminals owe their punishment required by law to the magistrate. There is no example of a similar phrase by which an active quality is described in terms of something repugnant. I rather believe this phrase means that the magistrate owes it to others to inflict punishment on a criminal.

§63. For it is not valid to argue that the punishment is not owed to the offender and that therefore the superior is under no obligation to impose it. To whom therefore is he under an obligation? Clearly, to the commonwealth. Look for the proof in the preceding chapter, where we took the rule concerning the general duties of the supreme prince, that the well-being of the people should be the supreme law,[120] and derived from that the particular duty of the prince on properly regulating punishments. For without punishments for crimes there can be no public well-being.

§64. But determining public well-being in the commonwealth is the task of the prince, not of a private person. The prince also has no superior in the commonwealth, and the magistrate is inferior to the prince. It follows that the obligation of the prince is looser than that of the magistrate: that of the former is sometimes joined with the power to grant a pardon (on which more soon) and is imperfect, while that of the latter is perfect and without the power to grant forgiveness.

§65. It is no problem if you want to object that a superior has a right to inflict punishment and therefore cannot be under an obligation with

120. See *Institutes,* bk. III, chap. vi, §163.

respect to the exact same action without there being a contradiction. For that contradiction only seems to be there because these two predicates do not refer to the same thing. The superior holds a right in relation to the offender and all others who want to prevent him from taking this action. His obligation is in relation to God and the commonwealth.

§66. Thus the father has the right to coerce and correct the son and yet he is under an obligation toward God and the commonwealth to exercise this right. So, too, a public minister has the right to do what the prince has commanded him to do, but nonetheless is under an obligation to the prince to perform the action.

§67. And yet, if we turn to the other part of the question, you can firmly conclude from this objection that an offender is bound to receive a punishment, or the offender owes a punishment. For if the superior has the right in relation to the offender to inflict a punishment, then there is a corresponding obligation in the offender, because right and obligation are correlates. Neither of them can exist without the other.

§68. In its own way this right will even lead us to explain the obligation of the offender to suffer punishment. For since the superior has a right to inflict a punishment, the offender will certainly be obliged to suffer the punishment.

§69. But the phrase "to suffer punishment" is ambiguous. Even if we have defined punishment as the imposition of an evil or pain, the execution of the punishment implies several other antecedent actions immediately before the infliction of pain. Therefore, the punishment in this place is taken as the sum of all those actions that immediately inflict evil and those that immediately precede it.

§70. Antecedent actions are, for example, climbing a ladder leading to the gibbet, offering the neck to the executioner's sword or to the noose, or drinking poison.

§71. Actions that inflict pain directly and so fulfill the formal requirements of a punishment are either such that they are repugnant to the animal nature of man or such that they cause pain in man, insofar as he is a man and differs from beasts.

§72. Among the first category you should include those punishments that take away life and dissolve and destroy the structure and physical intactness of the parts of the body, internal and external.

§73. The latter are those that deprive a person of his wealth and honor, namely fines and infamy.

§74. Man senses an aversion in either case when punishment is inflicted on him in one of these two ways. In one case he senses it as a result of a physical and animal instinct, in the other as a result of the common inclination of humans to preserve their reputation and wealth. And yet this aversion is such that man using his right reason and preparing himself in the requisite manner can overcome it in either case, unless the pain is too sharp and lasting.

§75. Therefore, suffering a punishment means either not resisting a public power, when it inflicts pain itself, or not resisting a public power, but rather voluntarily performing the actions that immediately precede or accompany a punishment.

§76. The former meaning is not relevant here. For, as we have said, man may be capable by nature of bearing these punishments with patience, but such examples of human beings are extremely rare, so much so that legislators are usually not considered to have expected this degree of patient suffering from their subjects. When he imposes an obligation on his subjects, the prince must, unless supreme necessity and the utility of the commonwealth demand it, not demand that level of perfection of which an ideally perfect man is capable, but remind himself of human weakness. For such an obligation would be of no utility for the commonwealth and would not achieve the general purpose of punishment, common correction, so effectively if the offenders did not show some aversion when the punishment is actually executed. That is why punishments are often inflicted in the form of sharp and lasting pains, which not even the wise man of the Stoics or Epicurus would have been able to suffer patiently.

§77. Yet I think that the monetary fine must be excepted from this category of punishments, since there the above-mentioned reasons do not apply. This is suffering that does not require an extraordinary, but only an everyday kind of tolerance, nor is it used for correction like some remedy, but is the lowest degree of punishment.

§78. Thus, when we say that the offender is obliged to suffer a punishment, the meaning here is that he is obliged to perform the actions immediately preceding the punishment or accompanying it, which do not, however, immediately produce the pain itself, or that he is obliged to pay a monetary fine.

§79. The fact that the human appetite seems naturally to abhor those actions which it knows will certainly be followed by an evil causing pain does not pose a problem. There are many possible objections to that view, including the example of human vices. There is the well-known story of the man whose doctor had forbidden him to drink wine because he would go blind, and who nevertheless grabbed the glass greedily and exclaimed: "Farewell, dear eyesight."

§80. We must respond with a few words to the objections that learned men usually raise against our opinion. For first you might argue that we have said above that the commonwealth naturally owes its origin to agreements of the people with the king, but that it is in the nature of agreements that nobody can bind himself to do something impossible. To suffer death, wounds, or other bodily harm, however, and not resist the person inflicting these is impossible to man, since he flees these evils out of a natural necessity, as much as he can, and cannot do otherwise.

§81. But while we have said that it does not seem too great for human constancy to accept death without struggling against it, we have at the same time conceded that a person would not have wanted to bind himself to something like that by an agreement because such a thing in most cases is too much for the common constancy of mortals. Human laws, no less than agreements, must be made with an eye to human weakness.

§82. It is also said that you trust him who is bound by an agreement, yet those people who are led to their execution are put in chains or under guard. This is a sign that they do not appear sufficiently obliged to adhere to agreements about nonresistance. There are various possible replies to this.

§83. For, first, the point of the controversy is being changed here. It is asked whether someone can bind himself by an agreement to suffer a punishment. Another question is whether an offender is believed to be under a sufficient obligation as a result of an agreement [not to try to escape]. The first question is to be answered on the basis of the nature of agreements and of humans living in the state of corruption, but to the extent that this state is still morally sound; the latter concerns corrupt humans as such.

§84. Second, if someone wants to infer that because offenders are in chains they are unable to oblige themselves sufficiently by means of agreements, then there are many other examples like that. In general, those who are truly bound by means of agreements are not trusted absolutely and often aggressive precautions are taken to prevent their perfidy.

§85. Third, offenders are constrained by chains, not so much because of actions immediately preceding the punishment or accompanying it, but because of a natural tendency to flee from the actions that directly cause the pain.

§86. Furthermore, it is common to draw a distinction between the forms of concluding an agreement. Thus it is said that there are often agreements made of the following kind: kill me if I have not done this by the agreed-upon date (that is, you will have the right to impose capital punishment on me if I have not done this). But, it is argued, then to enter an agreement stating that if I have not done this I shall not resist him when he tries to kill me is unusual and useless, no matter whether the agreement is between two fellow citizens, between the political community and the citizen, or between two who live in natural liberty.

§87. For, it is said, fellow citizens cannot form such an agreement because in political communities the right to kill is not granted to a private person. There is no point for the political community to enter such an agreement with a citizen. It is enough that it can inflict punishments on those who cause harm if the individual citizens promise not to defend by force the person to be executed. Those who live in the state of natural liberty derive no benefit from such an agreement. For if you wish to kill someone in the pure state of nature, you have the right to do so, based on the state you are in. Hence there is no need for an agreement to be allowed to kill unless there was a previous agreement not to kill before a day determined in advance. Not even then does this agreement become fully effective, because if the promise has not been fulfilled by the agreed date, then the previous state of hostility returns, in spite of that agreement, and everything is allowed, including self-defense.

§88. It is true that if there is an agreement to kill me for failing to do something, then it is pointless to make another agreement that I shall not resist the person trying to kill me unless I have performed the agreed action—if "pointless" here is taken to mean "superfluous" and something that adds no new effect. As we have just said, the very fact that I transfer to another the right or the power to kill me on certain conditions implies a promise not to resist him when he exercises that right, because it would be ridiculous to have a right that cannot be exercised. Otherwise, this transfer of the power to kill would be similar to the invitation of someone who called his guests and then shut the door in their faces.

§89. The force of all agreements in the state of nature is such that they not only produce an intrinsic necessity to adhere to the terms of the agreement. They also give both sides the right to threaten the other with some evil in case of a refusal. And thus agreements are usually interpreted to mean the following: I promise I will do this for you, and if I don't you will have the power to compel me through the use of force and by inflicting some evil. It is useless and absurd to confirm this by adding to such agreements a promise not to resist the person inflicting this evil.

§90. If the person making the agreement has not been sufficiently reassured by the first part of the agreement, then he will not be reassured by the latter either. It would rather have to be solemnly confirmed by another penal agreement, as follows: if I resist you when you harm me, then you will have the power to punish me with some further evil. This shows that the second agreement adds nothing to the first. The first agreement already gives permission to punish its violation with an evil, and the second agreement is violated as easily as the first. What need, therefore, is there to prop up one agreement with another when it is no more difficult to break ten agreements than one?

§91. But if the meaning of the objection is that an agreement not to resist is useless because it has no effect and resistance is allowed in spite of it, then we will be happy to agree to the extent that fellow citizens are concerned as private persons who form agreements in this way. But we have a very different opinion concerning a pact that has been made between two persons living in a state of nature and one between the political community and a citizen.

§92. Concerning the former, the argument that humans in a state of nature live in a state of hostility smacks of a hypothesis that has long been exploded. We rather infer that every agreement implies an intrinsic necessity to fulfill what has been agreed, and hence also an agreement not to resist. It does not matter whether nonresistance was expressly promised, or the performance of something was promised to somebody, because this contains a tacit clause that the other must have the power to coerce me. For even that, I believe, which is tacitly contained in agreements adds to the intrinsic necessity to fulfill what has been agreed (which here happens as the result of nonresistance).

§93. The same should be said of the political community insofar as it enters an agreement with its future citizen. For at the time of the agreement he is still in a state of natural liberty and only a future citizen. Moreover, even if we regard such an agreement between the political community and the citizen to be superfluous, we cannot consider the effect of this agreement, the obligation not to resist, to be superfluous and useless in a political community.

§94. It has been said that it is sufficient for the political community to be able to inflict punishment on those who harm it if individual citizens promise not to try to defend by force the person condemned to death. But that will not provide much security for the prince, who thereby would be compelled to expose himself to danger by exacting a punishment from offenders.

§95. But perhaps those who disagree mean more than that and think that it is enough for the state if the individual citizens promise to join their forces against an offender condemned to death. Certainly the objection here is more polished, but not any more true. What if a huge multitude or great number of people have together committed an offense, which sometimes happens? Here the help of the other citizens against offenders who are convinced of the righteousness of their resistance is not as sufficient a remedy for restoring peace as if they [the offenders] lack this vain conviction and either resist more timidly or willingly submit themselves to punishments.

§96. If you then replied that according to our doctrine on these matters these offenders are not obliged to suffer willingly those actions that directly cause death or bodily harm, and that therefore peace in the commonwealth according to our hypothesis is not advanced effectively, I would respond that to achieve this happy state it is enough if all that the offenders do is not to resist the actions that precede the imposition of punishments, either directly or indirectly. Then the offender continues to disturb the common peace if he resists those who want to capture him with armed force and if he tries violently to free himself as the time of the execution approaches. When the sword cuts his neck and the noose strangles his throat, his resistance is not prejudicial to the commonwealth.

§97. Finally, it is also argued that a person cannot properly be said to be bound to some punishment because punishment means something that must be imposed on someone against his will and implies the aversion of this person's will, and that the things we are obliged to do must be such that we do them freely and willingly.

§98. It is often the case, even in matters other than punishment, that a person who earlier willingly entered an obligation later, out of malice, becomes reluctant to fulfill it, and that his will does not free him from this obligation. Yet the argument is that he must want it to be binding. But in the case of punishments there is no need for him to want it. He must not want it, since otherwise a punishment would not be a punishment and would not be a correction if it were not imposed against the person's will.

§99. We go along with all that if we are talking about the final actions linked to a punishment. These are inflicted against the will of the punished. Therefore, the offender is not under an obligation to suffer these willingly. In preceding and accompanying actions it is a different matter, because the definition of a punishment does not apply to these.

§100. It is now easy to judge which precepts cover the duty of citizens with respect to punishments. The duty of the offender is covered by a single precept: "Bear the punishment inflicted by a superior." Likewise, the only duty of a sick man is to apply the medicines prescribed to him by the physician.

§101. The duty of the prince who inflicts the punishment is covered by the general precept: "Punish offenders to the extent that this is necessary for the utility of the commonwealth." Likewise, the duty of the physician is to prescribe medicines to the patient to the extent that it is necessary for obtaining bodily health.

§102. From this general precept flow two particular ones. One concerns the actions that are to be punished, the other the form of punishment. The former is: "Punish actions that cause harm to the commonwealth and that can be corrected." The physician similarly does not prescribe medicines for every disorder, but only for that which produces a disease and can be remedied with medicines.

§103. Hence, merely internal actions are normally exempt from human punishments: the pleasurable contemplation of a sin, for example, a longing, a desire, or a resolution without effect. And this is so even if subsequently these come to the notice of someone else. Since such an internal action causes nobody any harm, it is in nobody's interest for anyone to be punished for it.

§104. Thus the physician normally does not apply medicines to suppress the internal inclination of a man toward excessive eating and drinking, if this person himself overcomes this inclination.

§105. It would also be too harsh to subject the tiniest lapses to human punishments. In our current condition we are not capable of avoiding these, however much we try.

§106. Thus, the physician does not immediately busy himself with correcting a moderate aberration from a regular lifestyle with medicines, even if it occurs repeatedly.

§107. Human laws also ignore many actions the opposite of which will be all the more splendid if they are not performed out of fear of punishment. This is true, for example, of the virtue of liberality and the duties of humanity. A physician similarly does not immediately apply medicines even if the aberration from the regular lifestyle is very great.

§108. And just as there are many very minor diseases where it is not worth the effort to bother the physician, so too are there many minor offenses where it is not worth the effort to bother the judges.

§109. Again, if a matter is very obscure, punishment must often be avoided, just as a physician must refrain from giving medicines if the symptoms of a disease are not clear.

§110. Hence, it is necessary to declare those vices of the mind that result from the common corruption of mortals to be incapable of correction by human punishment. These are so frequent that there would be nobody left to command if you wanted to punish these vices severely, even when they have not led to gross offenses: these are, for example, ambition, avarice, inhumanity, ingratitude, hypocrisy, envy, pride, irascibility, animosity, and similar vices.

§111. Similarly, the duty of the physician must never be extended to remedying the natural weakness of the human stomach, which is the cause of many illnesses, but it is enough for him to temper it, to prevent it from breaking out in disease.

§112. If an evil that has emerged and become obvious cannot be removed without undermining the entire political community (if, say, the number of sinners is so great that the state would be depopulated by executing them), then the prince will use punishments in vain, just as the physician would use medicines in vain if the disease is so inveterate and has struck such deep roots that it cannot be expelled without endangering the patient's life. But in either case it is sufficient if the prince and the physician use laws and medicines for the vice and the disease, respectively, to prevent it from spreading further.

§113. And yet what we have said so far is to be understood to apply in the normal and regular course of things. There may be circumstances when matters are different. So, for example, thoughts, if they become known, can sometimes be punished, for example, in the crime of lèse majesté. Thus, if necessity and the utility of the commonwealth require this, the prince can compel the performance of the duties of humanity with penal edicts, just as a physician sometimes uses medicines to get rid of an excessive inclination toward gluttony if he sees that it is the result of a faulty disposition. To an even greater degree does he often provide medicines for strengthening the stomach after there have been particularly dramatic aberrations from the regular diet.

§114. On the other hand, the rule may also fail to work in the case of those vices that do not seem subject to punishment because of the danger of incorrigibility if an equal or greater danger would result from omitting the punishment. Hence, there will be no lack of examples, for example, of several hundred people punished with death during a rebellion. Similarly the physician cuts off even the more important parts of the human body, even though that involves some danger to the patient's life, if there is a risk that the healthy part will be affected unless the diseased is cut away.

§115. It must not be believed that it is always necessary to demand a punishment whenever offenses have been committed that are capable of human punishment. But just as a good physician, apart from examining the disease, looks at the nature and constitution of the patient and does not, for example, immediately apply to a peasant suffering from a fever the same medicines that he would prescribe to a person with a weak constitution, so too will he examine other circumstances, for example, whether the disease persists or goes away by itself, whether there are any indications that it will go away by itself, etc. The prince too, who always considers punishments in the light of the utility of the commonwealth, weighs up similar circumstances.

§116. Among these circumstances are the following: if in a certain case the purposes of punishments do not seem necessary, or if forgiveness is likely to produce a greater benefit [for the commonwealth] than punishment, or if it seems possible to obtain the purposes of punishments more conveniently by some other means. Similarly, if he who has committed an offense draws attention to the outstanding services he or those linked to him have performed for the commonwealth, which deserve a specific reward; or if he is commended for something else remarkable, some rare skill, for example; or if there is a hope that he will clear himself of his offense with illustrious deeds, especially when he acted out of ignorance, even if he was not without blame for it; or if the particular reason for a law has ceased in the case of a particular deed.

§117. Therefore, it is clear that the paradox of the Stoics is false. They declared that it was never permitted to forgive or be lenient.[121] Their arguments can be easily refuted with the above.

§118. I come to the form of punishment where the following is taught: "Punish as much as is necessary for common correction." Natural law does not determine exactly the kind of punishment and how much punishment precisely must be inflicted for particular offenses. Natural law left it to the supreme civil power to define the nature and severity of punishments, and in doing so the supreme civil power must have nothing other than the utility of the commonwealth before its eyes, just as the physician has that of the body that is to be cured.

§119. Hence, it can (and usually does) happen that the same punishment is imposed on two unequal offenses. For the equality that judges are told to observe with respect to the defendants applies to those defendants who have committed the same type of offense: if the offense is then avenged in the case of one defendant, it cannot be forgiven in the case of the other, unless there is a very weighty reason. The physician likewise often applies one medicine to expel different illnesses.

§120. Although, therefore, it is impossible to establish very precise rules because of the infinite variety of circumstances, it is generally the case that the prince, when he imposes punishments, must take care that these punishments are proportionate to the offenses. That is, they must be such that they are sufficient to suppress the desire of mortals to commit sin. A physician also uses medicines that are proportionate to the disease.

---

121. See Johannes Stobaeus, *Florilegium,* ed. T. Gaisford (Oxford: Clarendon Press, 1823–24), vol. 2, T.46.50, p. 269.

§121. For that to be possible the severity of the crime itself must be judged and the guilty person must be considered, because a physician must also adapt the medicines he prescribes to the disease and the patient.

§122. The severity of a crime is judged from the object, the effect, and the frequency, just as the severity of a disease is judged on the basis of its location in the body, its symptoms, and its duration.

§123. From the object, because there is a sin insofar as the object is regarded as something noble and precious. Hence, those crimes that offend God are particularly serious. Then come those that offend rulers, followed by offenses against equals concerning their life, honor, goods, etc.

§124. From the effect, by considering whether much or little damage is done to the commonwealth as a result of it.

§125. And the frequency, if lighter punishments do not root out the evil. For then the common saying applies that as the crimes grow, so do the punishments.

§126. The guilty person must be considered in relation to the crime and the application of the punishment. So, too, does the physician often weigh up the proclivity of parts of the human body toward a certain disease and their receptiveness to treatment.

§127. The relation to the crime is judged from the viciousness of the intention. This, however, is determined from various indications—if, for example, he could have easily resisted the causes that drove him to commit the crime; or if there was some specific reason, apart from the general reason, that ought to have deterred the person from committing the crime; or where particular circumstances aggravate the deed; or if someone has a mind that is suitable to withstanding the enticements of sin. But it must also be considered whether someone was the first to do it, or whether he was seduced by the example of others, and whether he sinned once or several times and after being rebuked in vain.

§128. The aptitude to suffer pain is judged from the qualities that can increase and diminish the perception of the punishment. These are age, sex, status, wealth, strength, and similar things.

§129. It remains for us to show what divine law adds to the precepts of natural law in the doctrine of punishments. It adds, however, something to the precept that directs the duty of the prince concerning the form of punishment: "Use capital punishment to punish murder and other crimes specifically listed in divine law."

§130. For certain reasons God wanted to set down the punishments for certain crimes himself. Princes are obliged to obey him since he is the wisest being possible and the true interest of commonwealths is best known to him, and they are executors of the divine will in that respect. In the same way physicians would undoubtedly be under a similar obligation if God had revealed a medicine to humankind that was suitable to curing a particular kind of disease.

§131. Yet even God might not take into account the peace of humankind in a narrow sense but have in mind other reasons unknown to us, although it is certain that God, as founder of humankind and of the institution of commonwealths, never determined anything that is harmful to humankind.

§132. From this observation follow two conclusions. First, the prince normally has the right to pardon and to mitigate punishments if the utility of the commonwealth urges him to do so, even if this utility is only something hoped for and uncertain; but in crimes designated by divine law he cannot exercise the right of pardon and of mitigation in such cases without committing a sin, because an uncertain benefit for the commonwealth must give way to the clear expression of divine will.

§133. But if the prince cannot execute the punishment ordered by divine law without a most certain danger to the commonwealth, he will not sin if he omits it or defers it. The example of David with respect to Joab is relevant here.[122]

§134. Yet a difficulty arises in reviewing what belongs to these kinds of crimes. The express words of Scripture do not admit of any doubt concerning murder: God informed Noah and his children of his will that whoever has spilled human blood, his blood shall be spilled in turn.[123] These words not only contain a threat, but approbation, not a bare fact, but a right.

§135. By the other crimes I mean those that are listed in Leviticus with the declaration that the Gentiles polluted themselves with such detestable practices, and that he who performs these must be eradicated from his people.

§136. These are (1) all forms of incest discussed above, (2) sexual intercourse with a menstruating woman, (3), adultery, (4) the sacrifice of children to Moloch, and (5) sodomy.[124]

§137. Indeed, the doctors commonly disagree over adultery and most forms of incest and leave the determination of the punishment to the prince, but they neglect sexual intercourse with a menstruating woman. I also know that this is common practice among Christians. We do not, however, explain what happens, but what should happen according to God's wishes.

§138. The words of divine law, however, are clear and perspicuous: "For whosoever shall commit any of these abominations, even the souls that commit them shall be cut off from among their people."[125]

§139. These words cannot be considered a forensic law that concerns only the Jews, because it had previously been said that God eradicated

122. 1 Kings 2:32–34.
123. Genesis 9:6.
124. Leviticus 18 and 20.
125. Ibid., 18:29.

the Gentiles because of such crimes and that he wanted to extirpate the Israelites for the same reasons. God also does not say "your people," but "their people."

§140. And there is no reason to think that I am ignorant of Jewish history and do not know what the phrase "cut off from among their people" really means. It is well known what the rabbis invent concerning this extirpation and the excision, as well as the parallel phrases on carrying sin, on death without children, etc.[126] But it is also known that these fictions are devoid of all foundation and are incompatible with the context and parallel passages.

126. Ibid., 20:19–20.

CHAPTER VIII

On the Duties of Confederates

§1. A society of confederates is a society of several commonwealths that exists for the sake of a particular benefit.

§2. I say "of several commonwealths," for if two private persons come to an agreement for the sake of some benefit, that is an agreement or a contract, not a treaty. The same reason applies to an agreement between a prince and a private person, no matter whether of his own or another commonwealth.

§3. Even if a prince makes an agreement with another prince for the sake of some private benefit and not in the name of the commonwealth, it is an agreement rather than a treaty.

§4. But you will also remember that I called this a society of commonwealths, not an agreement. For even if a society of confederates always presupposes an agreement, or even if a treaty is a type of agreement between commonwealths, yet not every agreement between commonwealths produces a society, and so not every agreement between them is a treaty.

§5. Indeed, agreements between commonwealths can also occur with respect to some business that must be transacted immediately—for example, if one commonwealth sells something to the other. But treaties require a union of wills between two commonwealths that will persist for a longer period of time.

§6. But according to the common nature of treaties this is indefinite in that its duration is left to the agreement of the parties involved and does not require a perpetual union.

§7. I have finally said that treaties are formed for the sake of some particular benefit. Thereby a society of confederates differs from a system of states, which comes into being as a result of an undefined common utility and at the same time usually has a tendency toward perpetual union.

§8. Guiding such a society is this one precept: keep what has been promised in the treaty. And this is, so to speak, the conclusion from the general precept concerning keeping agreements, and cannot be otherwise, because we have said that treaties are a type of agreement. Hence, there is no reason to add anything to that.

§9. Unless, that is, [we add] the divisions between types of treaties and the differences between them and solemn promises. Treaties can be divided with respect to their subject matter into those that establish some mutual obligation that was already commanded previously by natural law and those that add something to the duties of natural law or only define them more precisely when they are undefined.

§10. The former either concern the general observation of the precepts of natural law and are just intended to strengthen friendship without the performance of a specified duty, or they concern a particular rule of natural law.

§11. And these either concern avoiding inflicting harm or just the exercise of simple humanity. This is where all those treaties belong that support the simple right of hospitality and trade, insofar as this is owed on the basis of natural law.

§12. The first and second of these three types barely deserve the name of treaties because they do not produce a new purpose that was not already there before the treaty. Hence, they are not so common today, though they were once not infrequent, because pagans were falsely convinced that it was permitted to embark on bandit raids on those who were not their confederates.

§13. The third type, however, which is entered into for the sake of the duties of humanity, makes it permissible after the alliance has been formed to take revenge for the violation of such a duty, something that was not allowed before the alliance came into existence.

§14. The alliances of the third kind, which are nobler than the other two, are either equal or unequal. The former are those that are the same for either side—not only if the same has been promised by either side (either in an absolute sense or relative to their respective resources), but also if they have been promised on equal conditions, so that neither party is in an inferior position to the other or subservient to the other.

§15. And these are entered into primarily for the sake of trade, a military alliance for giving mutual aid in an offensive or defensive war, or other things.

§16. Equal treaties concerning trade can be of various kinds. They can be made to ensure that citizens of either party need not pay any customs when they cross into the territory of the other or enter his ports, or that they never pay more than at the time the agreement is made, or no more than a certain quantity, or no more than citizens or other treaty parties do, etc.

§17. There is an equal military alliance if there is an agreement for either side to provide equal supplies of soldiers, ships, or other military matériel when either of them is invaded or wants to wage war against another power. Sometimes military aid is promised only for a particular war, or against certain enemies, or against all enemies with the exception of the allies of either confederate.

§18. Finally, equal treaties concerning other things are, for example, agreements not to have fortresses on the common border, not to defend or shelter subjects of the other, or, if they have been taken, to hand them over to the other, not to grant an enemy of the other right of way, and other stipulations like that.

§19. Yet this division of equal treatises can also be applied to unequal kinds, when either the mutual services are unequal or one party is inferior to the other. Unequal services are promised either by the worthier confederate or by the less worthy. The former occurs if the more powerful promises the other help and does not demand the same in return, or if he promises a greater proportion of his own resources than the other does. The latter is the case if an inferior confederate is obliged to render more than he receives from the other.

§20. Of the services that are rendered by the inferior confederate some are linked to a reduction of sovereign power—for example, if it has been agreed that the inferior confederate must not exercise part of this sovereign power without the consent of the superior confederate. Certain services, however, do not diminish sovereign power, even if linked to them is a transitory burden—one that can be fulfilled in a single act, once and for all. Examples are if one side is under an obligation under the terms of the treaty to pay subsidies for the army of the other, compensate for the costs of the war, pay a defined sum of money, raze walls, deliver hostages, surrender ships, weapons, etc.

§21. And not even all permanent burdens diminish sovereign power. Such are the obligation to consider the other party's friends and enemies as one's own, but not vice versa; being prohibited from building fortifications in certain locations, from sailing to certain places, etc. It is the same if one of the alliance partners is obliged to honor courteously the majesty of the other or to show some kind of reverence toward him and modestly to adapt himself to his wish.

§22. It is also common to divide alliances into real and personal. The latter are those that are entered into with respect to the person of the king himself and lapse with his death. The former are those that are not concluded so much with the king himself personally as with the commonwealth and the kingdom. They outlast the deaths of their authors.

§23. It is, however, clear from the definition of either type of alliance that this distinction does not pertain to all forms of government but mainly to a monarchy.

§24. In a democracy there is very little use for this distinction because the people do not perish, nor do they have a successor, but are, morally speaking, always the same. The same is to be said of an aristocratic constitution.

§25. Even if a democratic or aristocratic form of government is changed into a monarchy, the treaty persists. Although the commonwealth has been transformed, the people remain the same.

§26. As far as monarchy is concerned, I would regard this distinction to be the result of ambiguity, not a true division, because that which we have called a personal alliance is an agreement rather than a federation, according to what we have said above.[127]

§27. Thus there is no need for us to know the criteria that separate real from personal alliances, which are defined in various ways by different people.[128] For in doubtful cases a king is presumed to do what he does as a king, that is, as head of the commonwealth, and in doubtful cases, therefore, the agreements of kings are to be considered real alliances too, unless something else was expressly agreed or the nature of the matter indicates something different.

§28. Treaties differ from solemn promises, which is the proper term for those agreements that are entered into by an agent of the supreme power in matters concerning it, but without its explicit order. The supreme power is not bound by these, unless it ratifies them afterward, and if the agent has made an absolute promise that has not been ratified the supreme power will have to see how it renders satisfaction to those who have trusted the agent and been deceived by vain pacts.

127. See §3 in this chapter.
128. See Pufendorf, *Of the Law of Nature and Nations,* bk. VIII, chap. ix, §§7–8.

On Duties Toward Legates

§1. There remains the society of nations, in which as we have already said above no new purpose or new precepts are to be expected, only the application of the general precepts set out in the second book to two of the more important parts of the law of nations, those concerning legations and the right of burial.

§2. For there will be no need here to resort to some human positive law because as we have shown from the beginning the law of nations does not belong to positive law but is a form of natural law.

§3. Yet the subject matter itself tells us that when we are concerned with the society of nations we want to speak of the legates of different commonwealths, not of legates who connect the society of God with that of humans, or of those who link individual humans living in a single civil society, or individual humans in different commonwealths.

§4. We must, therefore, leave aside the titular legation of those who go to another commonwealth purely for the sake of private business, and who enjoy the favor and honor that go with the title of legate but are sent to the other commonwealth without any mandate.

§5. Again, among those who are sent from one commonwealth to the other, some either represent, by means of a legal fiction, the commonwealth or the prince they have been sent by, and they are called legates in the simple and strict sense; or they execute a public mandate without representing their commonwealth or prince.

§6. Examples nowadays are the people called agents, who are used in peacetime, while heralds, trumpeters, and drummers are used when there is a state of unrest or war.

§7. The former legates are, according to our customs, either temporary and extraordinary and are termed ambassadors; or they are perpetual and ordinary and are called residents.

§8. We shall discuss both kinds of legates, those who represent the prince and those who do not, but above all the former, because they are the nobler species.

§9. These can be considered in two ways, in relation to what they represent or in relation to their own person.

§10. And if you look at the connection that exists between a legate and his fellows, his family, and things, then he can be considered either in a completely physical sense, that is, in his own person alone, which does not exclude what he represents, or in a completely moral sense, and thus with regard to those things that are linked to him.

§11. Legates come either from a hostile or from a friendly prince. By the latter we also mean someone who is not an enemy and who declares war on certain conditions, just as the former is an enemy even if he puts forward plans for peace. You can say that the former is a legate in war, the latter a legate in peace.

§12. Finally, the legate can be considered in relation to the sender, or to him to whom he has been sent, or to him whose territory he travels through.

§13. The first relation is not relevant here, because the person who sent the legate lives with him in a civil society, not in the society of nations. The other two are relevant here, above all the second.

§14. The duty toward legates consists above all in two points: their admission and their inviolability. I take admission here in a broad sense that comprehends the right to be received and to be allowed to leave.

§15. The precept on being received is as follows: "Legates are not to be turned away without just cause."

§16. The basis for this is the precept on performing the duties of humanity. For commonwealths are linked to each other by various ties and by mutual duties, and in order to sustain these it is necessary for one commonwealth to signify its will to the other. But this cannot be conveniently done either through conversations between the princes themselves or in letters. It can, however, be done very conveniently through messengers. He who rejected legates without just cause would thus be sinning against the duties of humanity.

§17. I also extend this to those who are sent from one enemy to another. For in the midst of war humanity demands that we think of peace and hear the other side's proposals for peace.

§18. Our precept also applies to a third party, whose territories the legate travels across, insofar as this third party, too, is obliged to further the mutual duties of humanity. In this respect, however, the precept will apply in a greater degree to that legate who is sent by a friend than to that legate who comes from an enemy of the third party.

§19. It follows from the reason underlying this precept that the failure to receive a legate does not constitute a just cause for war unless extreme necessity has required this mission. As we have shown above, it is usually not possible to go to war because of a violation of the duties of humanity.

§20. Also, we have said "[they must not be turned away] without a just cause." But just as there are an infinite number of reasons that can excuse a person from the performance of the duties of humanity, so is it impossible to cover these just causes in fixed rules. Rather, these are to be left to each individual's own conscience and prudence.

§21. Examples are if it is certain that the legate has not come to talk about peace or public affairs, but in order to stir up unrest and incite the citizens to revolt; if he is not a legate, but a spy; if he has come to play for time, and by this delay intends to gain an advantage for his master and to harm him to whom he has been sent; if he has already tricked others in a similar way or is suspect for other reasons.

§22. But it is on the whole not a just cause if someone wants to turn away a legate because he comes from an armed enemy, because neither peace, nor an armistice, nor any other agreements between warring powers can be easily entered into without legates. Therefore, he who rejected legates on that pretext alone would remove all hope of reconciliation and restoring peace.

§23. I say "on the whole." But I would not immediately want to criticize the action of Pericles, on whose authority Melesippus, the legate of the Spartans, was sent away from Athenian soil on the grounds that he came from an armed enemy.[129] For it is no sin for someone in peacetime not to conclude a contract if it is not in his interest as much as the other side's, and to prescribe to another who wants to make an agreement certain conditions. And so, too, he who is the superior in a war will, all other things being equal, not commit a sin if he receives the legate of the other side wishing to discuss peace only on condition that he put down his weapons.

§24. Moreover, legates must on the whole not be turned away just because of their atheism or the stain of heresy, because the law of nations

129. Grotius, *The Rights of War and Peace*, bk. II, chap. xviii, §3.2, p. 904.

concerns the duties of nations as such, not insofar as they are Christian or pagan. There again, I would not want to criticize the action of Lysimachus for refusing to listen to Theodorus, who was called an atheist and had been sent to him by Ptolemy.[130] For it is normally up to the person I want to tell something to decide which messenger he wants to deal with.

§25. But this I believe it is true to say: there is every right to reject the continual legations of residents that are so common now. This is not so much because ancient custom, which was ignorant of them, proves that they are superfluous. For the duties of humanity are not based on necessity alone, but are also beneficial to others.

§26. The real reason is that such legations settle in one place in order to fish out the secrets of the other commonwealth, rather than for the sake of peace. Thus they are honest spies of what goes on in the other commonwealth. It would be miserable for princes if one could compel the other to put up with this espionage.

§27. As their admission, therefore, largely depends on the mere kindness of the person they are sent to, they can be turned away without breaking any law if it no longer seems convenient to permit them, as long as one is prepared to accept that one's own legates are treated the same way. For if someone refuses to admit residents but wants to impose his own on others, he clearly sins against the precept of preserving equality and avoiding pride.

§28. Those, on the other hand, who maintain that such legations cannot be expelled without some other just cause appeal to examples and the judgments of rulers and say that the consent of nations is deduced from these and thereby acquires its authority. Hence, it is argued, the nations gradually came to approve such legations by their mutual actions, allowed residents together with the other kinds of legates, and applied the same

130. Ibid., p. 905.

privileges of the law of nations to them. They then apparently must have bound themselves more tightly, so that what used to be an act of kindness and was based on the will of both sides was later transformed into mutual services that had the force of law.

§29. Hence, it is conceded that when this custom was first introduced kings and princes had more freedom and flexibility in deciding whether to admit legates.

§30. But in fact there is no need for such a full discussion, since the theorists who argue this presuppose that the law of nations is a form of human law, a view we have refuted at length above.

§31. In addition, the judgments of princes are here rightly suspect, since they cannot be judges in their own case and one prince has a greater interest in legations being admitted than another does.

§32. Yet I do not deny that here, as in any rejection of peacetime legates, one must proceed with great caution, to make sure the rejection does not cause an affront to the legate or the prince who sent him. For that would be a violation of the precept on avoiding pride and would be a just cause of war. The rejection is rather to be coupled with confirmations of lasting good will.

§33. I continue with the inviolability, by which I mean the debt that is owed to the legate and discharged by not injuring him.

§34. I here use the term *injury* in a broad sense, so that it includes an insult, and whether it is inflicted by causing something bad to happen to another person or by taking away a good he previously had.

§35. Although the term *injury* is otherwise applied to the violation of an innocent person, in the subject matter of legates it is taken in such a wide sense by authors that it is sometimes even extended to just force that is used against a harmful and criminal person.

§36. The result is the following precept concerning the inviolability of legates: "Do not injure innocent legates. Normally you must not even injure those who cause harm."

§37. But authors do not agree in explaining the real reason for this precept and clarifying its application. It seems to us that distinctions must be drawn (1) between innocent and harmful legates, (2) between legates in peacetime and legates in times of war, and (3) between him to whom the legate is sent and a third party.

§38. The inviolability of innocent legates in peacetime is undoubtedly supported by the common precepts of natural law on avoiding pride and not harming others. This applies to the prince who receives the legate and to any third party, for this kind of inviolability is owed to all humans. It is not specific to legates. Thus there is no need for us to resort here to the majesty of the prince who sends them to justify their protection against unjust force.

§39. And there is no doubt that if innocent legates have been sent by a friend and have been affronted or harmed, this can be justly avenged by war. The example of David's legates is relevant here.[131]

§40. Before an enemy's legates in wartime are admitted, their safety rests only on the precept concerning the performance of the duties of humanity. It is according to the rules for one enemy to harm another, but even if we leave aside any promise, the duty of humanity in the midst of war must incline both enemies to seek peace. In that case, therefore, the prince or a third party, or he to whom the legate was sent, does not violate the precept on not harming others, which is not observed between enemies anyway, if he does not admit the legate and kills him. He only violates the duties of humanity.

---

131. 2 Samuel 10.

§41. In doing so he does not provide a new cause for a just war but only confirms the old cause if it was just before.

§42. I say, "if it was just before." For if it previously was unjust, that is, if he who sent the legate caused an injury to the party to whom he sent the legate, I would not even consider the violation of the rights of the legate to transfer the justice of the war from one party to the other, unless perhaps the guilty party had sent the legate with conditions for peace, that is, offering compensation for the injury caused.

§43. Yet following their admission, the safety of the legates is also guaranteed by a pact in which the party he has been sent to and any third party promise not to injure him if he conducts himself innocently.

§44. But this pact is rarely explicit. It is usually to be counted among the tacit pacts and is to be inferred hence. As we have said, in war there can be no peace negotiations without intermediaries. Without the inviolability of legates, negotiations do not even begin, because nobody would readily take on the dangerous task of a legation, and the commonwealth could not in all honesty compel respected men (who are essential for a legation) to act as legates. The mission would either be unsuccessful, if the legate could be killed with impunity, or at least very difficult, if he could be harassed with impunity. In such circumstances, therefore, any rational person will conclude as follows: "he has admitted the legate; therefore he has promised him safety," because tacit pacts are often based on the principle that he who permits the end also permits the means necessary to achieving that end; in cases of doubt, however, they always argue, humans must interpret deeds as signs the way other humans do. A rational person is thus able to conclude that because the legate was admitted, therefore he was promised safety.

§45. I speak, however, of tacit, not presumed, pacts. I have discussed the difference between them at greater length in the second book. The obligation that follows the admission of the legate has no other origin than actual consent, and without consent no other law binds the princes to respect the legate's inviolability than that on performing the duties of humanity.

§46. This tacit pact will, therefore, have a new effect, such that if an innocent legate is harmed after he has been admitted, there is a just cause for war, or the just cause is at least transferred from the party that caused the harm to the prince of the legate who has been harmed, because agreements create a perfect right.

§47. It follows from the above that the legate in wartime can legally claim inviolability only after he has been admitted by the other prince. He will have no reason to complain if he has been forbidden to come and arrives nevertheless, except insofar as the duties of humanity bind the other prince.

§48. And even if the prince admits the legate in wartime on the express condition that he reserves the right to injure him, I should think that this injury only violates the imperfect right of the prince whose legate this is. For you would not be able to infer the tacit consent of the prince from the admission of the legate in this case because it is a common rule that we look in vain for tacit consent whenever the opposite is stated expressly.

§49. In addition, it can be deduced from what has been said previously that the legate, above all the legate in times of war, must signal his role to the other side in good time by sending ahead a servant or by some other sign accepted among the nations. Without such a sign the third prince or the party he is sent to will be justly ignorant and it will not be possible to say unambiguously that he has admitted the legate.

§50. Finally, the above also applies to the legate who is sent to end peace and declare war. According to the customs of nations the declaration of war is made by a messenger or legate, and there is a kind of tacit statement that war is waged in a rational fashion, that is with the intention of reaching a peace settlement. Those, on the other hand, who want to make it clear that they are waging a war without a chance for reconciliation will call the war ἀκήρυκτον, that is, unannounced. Add the fact that the legate performs this duty peacefully, that is, with innocent words, not aggressive arms. In that respect it is possible to salvage the opinion of Torquato Tasso that every legate is a man of peace.[132]

§51. So much on innocent legates. There remain the harmful legates, whose crimes can be considered in three ways. They either have themselves committed a crime without being commanded to do so by their prince, or have committed a crime on the prince's orders, or it is a question of imputing a crime to them that was committed by their prince alone.

§52. Concerning the first category there are the following questions. Which crimes deprive the legate of his protection? To what extent is he deprived of it? Or what punishments are legally permitted for his crimes?

§53. Concerning the former there are three opinions: one deprives the legate of the privilege of safety on the grounds of any crime, whatever shape or form; another opinion states that no crime can deprive him of this privilege; the third states that he can be deprived of it, but not for any crime.

§54. The first applies in the case of messengers who do not represent the person of the prince, for reasons that will be explained soon. It also applies to legates who are sent by the enemy, not only because he who causes harm to the other is thereby unable to appeal to the duty of humanity. It is also because the grounds on which we infer from the admission of a wartime legate the existence of a tacit pact to grant security are only valid in the case of innocent people, not those who are guilty.

§55. The second opinion is completely unjust, because it renders the condition of the prince meaner than that of the legate. It thus violates the

132. See Torquato Tasso, "Il messagiero," p. 437, in Torquato Tasso, *Dialoghi,* ed. E. Raimondi, vol. 3 (Florence: G. C. Sansoni, 1958).

precept on preserving equality, the source of all other duties man owes to man.

§56. Between these two extremes there lies a third opinion, that not every crime invalidates a legation's right to safety, but nor is it the case that no crime does. Not every crime does this: we do not want to reduce the legate to being one person in the crowd of common foreigners. But it is not the case that no crime has this effect, for we do not want to create an opportunity for any kind of misdeed.

§57. When, therefore, is a legate punished for a crime? Put briefly, if the crime is (1) manifest and (2) serious.

§58. As we have said, a person who is called a legate represents the person of his prince. Hence, he must not be forgiven for a crime that would not be condoned if his prince had committed it. What is not right for the legate is not right for the prince either.

§59. If the crime is not manifest, it will not be possible to punish the legate. He is not the subject of another, and thus there can be no judicial inquiry against him.

§60. If it is manifest and not serious, but minor, it is rather to be forgiven and ignored, because the prince would ignore it on the basis of the laws of friendship if something like that had been committed by the legate's prince.

§61. But here a new difficulty arises, that of defining minor and serious crimes. We cannot agree with the belief that a severe crime is one that the law of nature punishes with death, while a minor crime is one that is more lightly punished, because, as we have said above, the law of nature does not prescribe any particular punishment.

§62. Perhaps it will be more appropriate to say that those crimes are severe that have a tendency to disturb public affairs, that cause death among the prince's subjects with whom the legate is staying, or that cause great damage to their honor and material goods, especially if they are persons who are personally dear to the prince.

§63. Hence, it is quite clear which crimes I regard as minor. Among these I also include some crimes against the prince himself, for example, if the legate acts as a spy, if he shoots his mouth off and is impudent, and if he utters minor insults or threats against the prince.

§64. Though we rather like the opinion of those people who claim that a minor crime against a private person should be ignored, but if it is directed against the prince, the legate should be ordered to leave the territory and sent back without a reply.

§65. Concerning the question which measures can be taken against a legate who commits a severe and manifest crime, I distinguish between a crime that directly damages the status or dignity of the prince and one that harms a private person.

§66. In the former case the crime can be punished no matter whether he was unarmed or armed, that is, no matter whether he incited the subjects to revolt, took part in a conspiracy himself, or was present at the meetings of conspirators, whether he drew the sword together with rebels or enemies or armed his fellows against the state. It can be punished even by killing the legate, not as a subject but as an enemy, because not even the prince himself could expect any better treatment if he attempted anything comparable.

§67. It matters not if a conspiracy has so far been unarmed, unless we believe it to be a sin to overpower a sleeping enemy or forestall someone who has been caught making unambiguous preparations.

§68. Should such a legate escape unharmed, his prince can be requested to extradite him. Nor can he extricate himself if he offers to punish him, because the legate acted as an enemy. Enemies, however, are not punished by a third party but are coerced by him whose enemies they are. In addition, the purpose of punishments would be absent here.[133]

§69. If, however, he has harmed a private person by committing a severe crime, he need not immediately be considered an enemy of the prince to whom he has been sent. But just as his own prince would, if he had committed this, first have to be required to render satisfaction before it was possible to wage war against him, so too it is more than equitable for the same reason that the prince in whose territory he committed the crime sends him back to his prince with an appeal and demands that he be either handed over or punished by his own prince.

§70. Yet this has to be done so that his master has the choice whether to punish the legate or hand him over. For it would verge on contempt toward his master if the other prince wanted to punish the person who represented his master for the duration of his sojourn with the other and set aside this role only when he returned to his prince. Thus, the court for the location where the crime was committed is not responsible here, and so the injured party must either turn to the legate's own domestic law courts or at least act as if the legate had committed the crime after returning to his home territory.

§71. I said that the legate should be sent back. The prince in whose territory the crime was committed could keep the guilty person in chains until the other calls him away to be punished or renounces this subject, but returning the legate is not only more civil, but also seems to do more to strengthen peace.

§72. For this detention not only signals some mistrust toward the master of the legate, but verges on contempt toward the prince himself, whose person the legate represents. Moreover, he who does not normally have the right to punish does not have the right to arrest either.

---

133. That is, general correction (see bk. III, chap. vii, §28).

§73. Concerning the second category of crimes that are committed by legates by their prince's command, the same definitions that we have reviewed so far apply, because we have been considering the legate as a person representing his prince—unless perhaps you wanted to say that it would be imprudent to send back to his prince a legate who inflicts severe harm on a private person, because the prince, being an accomplice to this crime, will probably neither punish the legate nor hand him over.

§74. Therefore, I would think that the legate could be kept in chains until his master guarantees satisfaction for the injury inflicted by the legate as well as by himself.

§75. The common messengers, however, and those who do not represent their prince (trumpeters, for example) have no reason to complain if they are immediately killed for, say, verbal abuse that they utter at the command of their own master against the other party.

§76. But it is absurd that some people believe the legate can execute with impunity whatever the prince has commanded him to do, and that the crime is to be imputed only to the prince. On that basis the legate would be allowed to do more on foreign soil than his own prince would if he were there, while the prince would have less power in his own possessions than the head of household in his own family.

§77. Concerning the final category (if the legate's prince has committed a crime against the other prince without the knowledge of the legate) we need to make a distinction between what the injured party may do with respect to the legate and what he may do with respect to the prince who caused the injury.

§78. With respect to the prince who caused the injury it will be allowed to injure the legate to the extent that mutual offenses require compensation, not only in the actions of private persons but also in wars between princes.

§79. And yet, this license will be imperfect because it renders neither side secure in their conscience. Each side will be liable to the author of the law of nature for punishment, just as private persons cannot by mutual offenses compensate for the punishment that is to be inflicted by the prince.

§80. With respect to the legate, therefore, it has to be said that it is wrong to injure him, because the person of the prince, which he represents, grants him a privilege that must not be turned against him. It is also wrong because, to be accurate, the sins of the subjects must not normally be imputed to the prince, and those of the prince must not be imputed to his subjects.

§81. Hence, not only would a prince be cruel if he killed an innocent legate because the legate's master had done the same to his legate. I would even be reluctant to absolve from the stigma of cruelty those who killed trumpeters for carrying, say, letters full of verbal abuse, whose content they were not aware of.

§82. We have considered the inviolability of the legate in his own person, but we must not omit to examine those things which are linked to the legate, such as his companions and movable possessions.

§83. Companions are inviolable by association and hence to the extent that it seems fit to the legate. Thus if they have committed a rather more serious crime against private persons, the legate can be requested to surrender them.

§84. If he refuses to surrender them, they must not be taken by force, but the same procedure we have described in the case of a crime by the legate himself is applicable here.

§85. But what if the legate wants to punish his companions himself? It first needs to be determined whether the legate has jurisdiction over his own retinue. That, we believe, depends on the concession of the ruler with whom he is staying.

§86. On this concession it also depends whether refugees have the right to seek asylum in the house of the legate.

§87. Movable possessions are also regarded as accessories of the person of the legate. Therefore, they cannot be seized against the will of the legate as a security or to pay a debt, neither by the order of a judge nor by the hand of the king. For that would imply contempt for the legate's master.

§88. Therefore, if he is in debt and happens not to own any real estate in that place, he will have to be compelled in a friendly fashion to pay his debt, and if he resists, he who sent him has to be compelled. In extreme cases, therefore, those measures need to be taken that are usually taken in the case of debtors outside the territory.

On Duties Toward the Dead

§1. Plato declared that there were three kinds of justice, the first concerning the gods, another concerning humans, the third concerning the deceased. For those who perform sacred duties according to the laws and take care of sacred matters are devout and pious. Those, however, who return loans and deposits are just toward humans. But they who render the deceased their just due perform that third part of justice.[134]

§2. There is no doubt that this philosopher derived the duty toward the dead from the opinion that human souls are parts of the divine essence, that after they are separated from the body they continue to be involved in human affairs, and that the souls of more greatly honored people even become daemons, whose tombs are to be worshipped and adored. It is also known that the Romans regarded tombs as being under divine law.

§3. Hence it is not rare for the law on burying the dead to be called a divine law and νόμος δαίμονων [law of the daemons] by the Gentiles. In fact they had received the worship of sepulchers from the oracles.[135]

§4. We must ignore these pagan trifles and see whether the duties toward the dead can be derived from a different source. Usually the law concern-

---

134. See Plato, *The Laws*, 2 vols., trans. R. G. Bury, Loeb Classical Library (London: Heinemann, 1926), vol. 2, 927, p. 435.
135. See Grotius, *The Rights of War and Peace*, bk. II, chap. xix, §§1, 2, and 3.

ing burial is said to be part of the positive law of nations. But we do not acknowledge a positive law of nations. Others have derived the same from the precept of natural law concerning the duties of humanity. They do so, however, in such a way that they relate it to natural law mainly because it directs the duties of humans in the society of nations.

§5. But this does not seem accurate to us, because there is no doubt that humans living in civil society are as (and perhaps more) likely to bury their dead, and therefore the burial owed to the dead, if it is owed, is based on absolute precepts that must be followed in all societies, rather than the society of nations in particular.

§6. There is a common, rather confused argument, how the conclusion concerning the burial of the dead is derived from the precept concerning the duties of humanity. There tend to be all too great disagreements here; some appeal to humanity, others to mildness, pity, religion, piety, or justice; some assert that this duty was to be rendered not so much to man as to humanity, that is, not so much to the person as to human nature.

§7. To extricate ourselves from these troubled waters, we assume, first, that other humans are not under an obligation on the basis of natural law to the dead themselves. You may consider either the corpse or the soul separated from the body. The former, as an inanimate being, is not capable of any right or obligation. Reason on its own knows nothing of a separately existing soul. Whatever it does know it has from revelation. I say, "whatever it does know." I do not care about the arguments of the Scholastics who mix revelation with reason or use false and inept proofs in that matter.

§8. Thus, if there is an obligation to bury the dead, it exists in relation to other living humans.

§9. I presuppose, however, that burial is here understood to be the keeping of a human corpse in a specific location in the ground, so that it is not left as food to the birds and wild animals and is not devoured by the living.

§10. Again, it can be understood broadly to include the previous cremation of bodies, as was common among the Romans, or strictly, to exclude cremation, as is the practice among us Christians.

§11. Whichever way you consider burial, you will not be able to prove this duty from the precept of natural law that directs the duties of humans among each other.

§12. There are people who derive this debt from nature on the grounds that the body of man was made from earth and must be returned to earth, which is what God declared to Adam. In fact they draw on a reason that is not based on human nature but on divine revelation, since man on his own does not know what God told Adam; and even though there are similar sayings among pagans, we have already stressed a couple of times that the pagans derived a lot from their contacts with the Israelites.

§13. The same confusion is caused by those who believe that burial is owed to the dead because of the hope of resurrection. Here, too, the conclusion they draw does not follow. What do you think? Will humans devoured by cannibals or torn apart by wild beasts not be resurrected?

§14. It might be simpler to assert that since man is more excellent than all other animals it seems shameful to let other animals feast on his body, and that burial was invented to prevent this as far as possible. And even if there were no other injuries, the corpse would be mangled and disfigured, which would be completely contrary to human dignity. On that basis the conclusion appears to be demonstrated from the precept on performing the duties of humanity. Nevertheless, these reasons do not make these opinions probable, let alone prove them.

§15. For these arguments concerning the dignity of man are flawed from the beginning, since we have already rejected this method of demonstration based on human dignity or decency in our discussion of marriage, unless it rests on some specific precept of natural law. And so, too, many other arguments can be put forward which show that this dignity, whether real or false, is not taken care of by means of a burial.

§16. For why do you think it is less worthy for birds and quadrupeds to feast on a human cadaver than for worms to devour or fire to consume them? Are birds and wild beasts less worthy creatures than worms, fire, or earth? Or have only those nations that have embalmed their cadavers observed the law of nature? So Romans and Christians have not observed it?

§17. If the matter were to be resolved on the basis of the dignity of human nature, I would like to hear your reply to cannibals. They often boast and mock other nations, because they know no more worthy sepulcher than if they absorbed their dead into their own flesh and blood. And who does not commend the deed of Artemisia?[136]

§18. Moreover, should you want to compare burial in the broad and in the strict senses with each other, and ask whether it is more dignified for the cadaver to rot in the earth than to be reduced to ashes by fire, certainly fire is declared by many to be an element superior to earth.

§19. But perhaps divine positive law has given us a precept on burying the dead. It is not our task here to ask about particular positive laws whether they are forensic or ceremonial. There is no universal law [on burial]. Nor does God's declaration of the punishment whereby Adam must return to the dust from which he came make any reference to a command concerning burial.

§20. What then shall we say? We say that the burial practices of Christians are not contrary to natural law, and can be safely retained by them, be-

---

136. Queen Artemisia II of Caria (died ca. 350 B.C.) mixed the ashes of her dead husband, Mausolus, in her daily drink to become his living tomb. She erected the Mausoleum of Mausolus at Halicarnassus as a funeral monument to her husband.

cause they see in sacred history that from the very beginning of the world humans were buried in the earth.

§21. Yet other nations, who adopted other burial practices, have not sinned against universal divine laws.

§22. Even in the Christian world it is a matter for the prince to prescribe the form and ceremonies to be used in burials, and these can be changed without sin. And I mean this with regard not only to the laws expressly passed by the prince, but also to the ceremonies that have been introduced as customs by those who use them and with the tacit consent of the prince.

§23. Thus no matter whether a corpse is buried by day or by night, with or without an assembly, with or without a cortege, it cannot be said that there is any violation of the divine laws, if one argues with good reasons rather than passion.

§24. It is readily apparent that those who derive the right of burial from the law of nature or of nations argue in vain whether enemies and especially criminals are owed a burial.

§25. He who buries enemies does well, but it cannot be shown by any means that he who leaves them unburied has committed a sin. We do not care here for the testimonies of the Gentiles, whose false hypothesis we detected at the beginning [of this chapter].

§26. It is a matter for the prince to decide what happens to criminals. Some of them must be denied a burial as a warning to others, and neither divine law nor the law of nations is opposed to this power or prescribes any rules to the prince in determining this punishment.

§27. I do, however, regard it as clearly unjust if someone wants to go to war against another because of the denial of a burial, even if we conceded that some duty to bury the dead could be derived from the law of humanity. But the duties of humanity only produce an imperfect right.

§28. The fact that the Greeks in ancient times sometimes waged war on those grounds does not undermine our argument. We judge on the basis of reasonable argument, not examples.

§29. And this is not to mention the fact that the Greeks had perhaps been driven to this by the mistaken belief that the right to a burial derived from divine law and a precept of religion.

CHAPTER XI

On the Application of Divine Laws

§1. We said at the beginning that there are two parts of judicial jurisprudence, the interpretation of laws and their application. We have so far dealt with the skill of interpretation. It remains for us to say something about the skill of applying laws, but only very briefly.

§2. The interpretation of divine laws differs from the interpretation of human laws in many ways, but their application is the same in both cases.

§3. Application, however, is understood to be either a faculty of the intellect or a faculty of the will.

§4. If we understand it as a faculty of the intellect, it is the ability to apply the divine laws skillfully and fairly.

§5. Both are required in the advocate and the judge.

§6. For laws to be applied appropriately, we must examine all circumstances of the deed that is to be either defended or judged, even the smallest, because the smallest circumstance changes the applicability of the law.

§7. Even those circumstances that precede the deed and that follow it must be taken into account, to the extent that these are often of some importance to the deed itself.

§8. The means to finding these out is to read historians in the case of ancient deeds and to consult witnesses and documents for recent events.

§9. And by these means the advocate is not only able to understand the deed but can also point out the relevant circumstances to the judge or arbiter. He [the judge or arbiter] then decides whether these circumstances have been properly taken into account.

§10. That does not require some subtle prudence because it is very common to use a demonstration that is evident to the senses.

§11. Unless perhaps the proof has been conducted with contrived arguments, or the witnesses and the documents contradict each other.

§12. For then the judge must be furnished with the skill of sound reasoning, and experience in the discipline from which the argument is sought.

§13. But here a certain natural intellectual vivacity is required to extract what is true from what is false. Reading the histories of prudent judges is very conducive to that, as are the contemplation of human minds and also the instruction that those people who have written about the inquisitorial process give to judges on formulating the articles of the inquiry.

§14. If the proofs are extremely confused, then the decision in doubtful cases should be made in favor of the accused or the possessor.

§15. Others who have published texts on the duty and conscience of the judge or advocate have already explained in greater detail how these circumstances are applied fairly.

§16. Experience is requisite for the application of the laws to become a faculty of the will; a person must apply the divine laws frequently in an appropriate and fair fashion to the facts that occur.

§17. Yet one should not expect a legal defense or a sentence before the relevant parties have asked for it. There are many instances in ancient history, both sacred and profane, with which to exercise the mind. We have given an example in our dissertation on the Caudinian promise of the Romans.[137]

END OF THE THIRD BOOK

---

137. Christian Thomasius (*praeses*) and Carl von und zu Montzel (*respondens*), *De sponsione Romanorum Caudina* (Leipzig, 1684). The story of the *sponsio Caudina* is told in Livy's history of Rome, book IX, chaps. 2–9 (Livy, *Livy*, pp. 167–99). The Samnites had trapped a Roman army in a valley (the "Caudine forks") and forced the consuls leading the Roman army to accept a humiliating agreement to make peace. On their return to Rome the consuls argued that the Roman people were not bound by the terms of the peace, since this peace was not a treaty but merely a promise or guarantee (*sponsio*) that was binding only on the consuls. The consuls declared themselves willing to be handed over to the Samnites; however, the Roman people were free to renew the war against the Samnites without fear of divine sanctions that would follow from the violation of a treaty.

Selections from
Foundations of the Law of Nature and Nations

The Reason for This Work[1]

§1. In the *Institutes of Divine Jurisprudence* I defended the foundations on which the famous Pufendorf had constructed the law of nature and nations. I am not ashamed of that, nor do I regret it. For just as Grotius revived and began to purge this extremely useful discipline, which had been tainted and corrupted by dry scholasticism and which had been close to death, so it is evident that Pufendorf developed it in excellent ways and defended it vigorously against various adversaries. I have presented the essence of the arguments of either side in the first book of that treatise.[2]

§2. Yet Grotius could not remedy everything that had become corrupt in that discipline. If he had, there would have been no need for Pufendorf to examine many aspects [of natural law] more accurately. The corruption was so great that even following Pufendorf's careful scrutiny there remained a lot of questions to which others could apply their powers of

1. In the *Foundations* Thomasius revised his earlier natural law theory of the *Institutes,* and much of the *Foundations* was a paragraph-by-paragraph correction of particular points in the *Institutes.* Thomasius explained that he was led to write the *Foundations* after he had lectured on *prudentia legislatoria* (the prudence of a legislator) in a private *collegium* in 1702. There he had abandoned his earlier belief in a divine positive law that was binding on humans. This required him to rethink his earlier natural law theory. In 1703 he therefore gave a course of lectures that was the basis of the *Foundations.* These lectures, according to Thomasius, included paragraphs 1 to 25 of the introductory chapter, while paragraphs 26 to 31 were added in the first edition printed in Halle in 1705.

2. That is, Thomasius's *Institutes of Divine Jurisprudence.*

analysis. Thus, after many years of reflection, I shall try to see whether I can contribute something that will be useful and beneficial to young students.

§3. Both Grotius and Pufendorf include too many testimonies and references to the works of other authors—Grotius because he believed that these commonly accepted opinions[3] proved the law of nature itself, while Pufendorf did so for political reasons, because his detractors accused him of not having read the Greek and Latin authors.[4] Both deserve to be excused because they wrote at a time when all the learned were still steeped in the authority of the ancients.

§4. Yet this style of writing does students more harm than good. The mind is distracted rather than helped by such references. They only very rarely prove what they are meant to prove, since the ancients disagreed in infinite ways on moral matters. Moreover, most people nowadays are able and willing to examine what is said, rather than who said it. And this is so because the writings of Hobbes and Pufendorf on the duty of man and citizen are more to our taste than these purely ornamental commonplaces [*loci communes*]. Our present age is no longer ruled by the taste of Boecler,[5] because it is clearly no longer satisfied with seeing through the eyes of others.

§5. Until now I have also held this prejudice and, like Grotius and Pufendorf, searched for the essence of human nature in the opinions of others, though not as blindly as the Scholastics. I was more concerned with finding out what others said was relevant to human nature than with properly examining what each of us has within himself.

§6. Hence, while I confirmed much that had already been corrected by Grotius and Pufendorf, there still remained the fundamental error that is

3. The Latin term is *loci communes*. This is a term in rhetoric and refers to a passage of text held to be of general application.
    4. On this, see Hochstrasser, *Natural Law Theories in the Early Enlightenment,* chap. 2.
    5. Johann Heinrich Boecler (1611–72) was professor of law at Strasbourg.

relevant to all disciplines, which concerns the mutual relationship of the will and the intellect: this is the belief in the rule of the intellect over the will and the mistaken belief that necessarily results from it, that all humans have the same nature, just like all the other, lower forms of natural bodies. We have already rejected this error elsewhere,[6] and it is therefore quite evident that the whole system of moral philosophy needs to be rethought.

§7. Pufendorf argued that moral matters were capable of demonstration to the same degree as physics or mathematics, but he himself then opposed morality to nature in many ways, and in defining moral entities put too much emphasis on the role of imposition.[7] There is in fact a close connection between moral and natural matters, and moral principles can be demonstrated on natural grounds.

§8. Moreover, the term *law* is highly ambiguous and means various things in moral philosophy. We must above all carefully distinguish these various meanings of law. Yet I had so far omitted doing so because Grotius and Pufendorf had neglected to.

§9. This neglect, however, produced another error, which I had in common with Grotius and Pufendorf: I thought that divine law and human law were the same kind of law. I have, however, already shown elsewhere that divine law, insofar as it is understood as the law of nature and nations, is a broader kind of law, and that the definition [of law] really applies only to positive law in the strict and proper sense.[8]

§10. But since the main essential quality of law is punishment, this previous error led to another, that in the doctrine of punishments divine punishments were not separated from human punishments, but were

---

6. See Christian Thomasius, *Versuch von Wesen des Geistes.* Reprint of 1699 edition (Hildesheim: Georg Olms, 2004), chap. 7, especially thesis 179, p. 186.

7. "Imposition" referred to Pufendorf's belief that moral agents attached moral values to physical states of affairs, which otherwise were morally indifferent.

8. Christian Thomasius, *Observationes selectae ad rem litterariam spectantes* (Halle, 1700–1705), vol. 6, "Observatio 27," §§28ff.

considered together with divine punishments, as if there were no natural connection between vicious actions and their punishment.

§11. For the same reason internal obligation, which is the noblest form of obligation, was not distinguished from external obligation, and only the latter was presented as true obligation.

§12. Moreover, the difference between what is just, what is decorous, and what is honest could not be conceived without understanding the difference between these two kinds of obligation. Yet this difference is one of the central principles of moral philosophy, and the Scholastics almost to a man confused the just and the honest, or natural law and ethics; they never even thought about the decorous. I committed the same error, especially as Pufendorf mixes natural law and ethics, and whenever he discusses the sense of shame and decorum, he adopts the inadequate principles of Lambert van Velthuysen or at least produced no more solid principles.[9]

§13. In my *Institutes of Divine Jurisprudence* I pointed out the insufficiency of the common distinction of divine law into moral, ceremonial, and forensic, yet I did not avoid all the errors that resulted from this confused classification. The Scholastics wanted to strengthen the interest of the papal clergy and therefore referred many matters to the [divine] moral laws, which, in a legal sense, only bound the Jewish people, although other nations could include them in their rules of honesty and decorum.

§14. Thus the reasons that are usually given for this supposed morality and its universally binding character are not convincing and the inadequacy of these laws has become apparent in recent years in the legal controversies surrounding marriage. The defenders of the old Scholastic opinions, therefore, invented a new form of divine law between natural law and the particular Mosaic law and named it, conveniently, "universal divine positive law." Yet it has been impossible to find anyone who has explained the nature and essence of that divine law.

9. See Velthuysen (1622–85), *Epistolica dissertatio de principiis iusti et decori.*

§15. Therefore, the love of truth and sound argument led me to try to see whether it was possible to provide certain criteria for this universal law and apply them to its particular chapters. That is what I partly did in the first book of my *Institutes,* and partly in the third. And I do not remember anyone producing any counterarguments that would have undermined that aspect of my argument, or even caused me to be unsure. Rather, I found that many others I had not even mentioned were ploughing the same furrow.

§16. In the meantime, the more genuine examination of divine law in general also led me to realize that this universal positive law was a fiction, and while I was the first to place it on a stable foundation, I was also the first to tear it down again. That, however, required me to revise my *Institutes,* because many assertions there were based on this false foundation.

§17. The authors on natural law (which is, after all, written in the hearts of humans)[10] would have had to abstract from revelation and sacred Scripture, since nature and revelation are diverse principles and must not be confused, yet very few have observed this rule. Rather, it is common for authors on natural law to mix in a great heap of scriptural passages, though their intentions in doing so vary. The Scholastics want to tyrannize the consciences of humans under the pretext of piety; and since they cannot bind them by means of real reasons, they terrorize them by using the authority of false scriptural interpretations. Grotius wanted to undermine those erroneous interpretations of Scripture as much as he could by using his remarkable erudition;[11] and Pufendorf wanted to show that he taught nothing contrary to Scripture.

§18. I had the same intention as Pufendorf and therefore did not avoid using sacred Scripture, partly because I based this positive universal law mainly on Scripture and partly because a more thorough analysis of Scripture was required in order to examine the hypothesis of Pufendorf's

---

10. See Romans 2:15.

11. That is, he did not challenge the principle of using these scriptural passages in this kind of argument.

obstinate adversary,[12] who claimed that the fundamental principle of natural law had to be derived from the conformity and discrepancy with the state of innocence.

§19. I now experienced the same fate as Pufendorf: by appealing to Scripture I stirred up a hornets' nest, more than if I had refrained from doing so. Moreover, I myself had already undermined the idea of universal positive law, and the belief that the foundation of natural law had to be looked for in the state of innocence was as good as buried. The above-mentioned reason of natural law suggested that I should abstract from Scripture and the state of innocence, especially as this state of innocence has not only evidently been lost, but cannot be retrieved in this life either. Not to mention the fact that the purpose of Scripture is happiness in the afterlife, but moral philosophy and jurisprudence are entirely directed toward true happiness in this life.

§20. It is clear from the above why I shall refrain from referring to particular authors, Scripture, or the state of innocence in these reflections, and why I will not mention universal divine positive law with even one word. I will also make an effort to correct the remaining defects that I have pointed out above.[13]

§21. I also noticed that the principles I had demonstrated elsewhere concerning the nature of spirit, the essence of human nature, the differences in kind between humans, and the existence of spirits opposed to and in conflict with each other[14] displeased many, not so much because such persons dared to deny what I had shown, but because the technical terms I used in these assertions made them shudder. The main reason was that they immediately realized that my principles are incompatible with the opinions taught in schools and universities, although these are commonly regarded as articles of faith. I will therefore try to do something about this scandal.

---

12. A reference to the orthodox Lutheran theologian Valentin Alberti.
13. See §§5–12 in this chapter.
14. See Thomasius, *Versuch von Wesen des Geistes,* chap. 7.

§22. But we will achieve this if we abstract from logical and metaphysical terms, insofar as that is possible, and if the matter itself is presented in very perspicuous words that can be understood by anyone in general who just hears their sound or a brief description of them; also, nothing should be claimed or denied unless any human being who is not mired in prejudices can agree on the basis of common sense.

§23. I therefore do not care if you do not like the idea that the essence of humans consists in their will, that one human being is different in kind from the other, that humans are governed by opposing spirits, etc., as long as you clearly sense it to be true that the principle directing the actions of humans is not the intellect but the will, that individual human beings are naturally endowed with different, conflicting wills, and that even a single human being is driven by the will to desire now this, now something else that is opposed to his previous desire, etc.

§24. I shall also consider the moral nature of man according to the common sense of humankind, and show its close connection with the common nature of all other corporeal beings, what is otherwise, rather clumsily, described as man's physical nature. I shall thereby avoid the common mistake of opposing moral matters too strictly to physical matters, and I shall show at the same time that the moral nature of man is as susceptible to demonstration as his intellectual and corporeal nature.

§25. I shall finally explain the easily intelligible and perspicuous difference between the three categories of morality, namely, the honest, the decorous, and the just, insofar as this is evident from the common moral nature of humans. This difference will be of great use in resolving controversies that would otherwise be extremely difficult.

§26. [15]Some did not like the changes I made [to my previous theory], because I diverged from the common opinions which had received the approval of even the most famous men. But I ask them to consider, on the

---

15. According to Thomasius, this paragraph and the following ones were not delivered in the original lectures in 1703 but were added in the first printed edition in 1705.

other hand, that I resolved to follow common sense at all times; and that I prefer not to support opinions that require many subtle abstractions, but rather those whose truth one senses within oneself if one pays just a little more attention; and that I always made an effort to link conclusions to their principles and thus could not have emphasized principles that cannot be conveniently linked to conclusions whose truth is evident and widely accepted.

§27. Just as I leave everyone who does not approve of my ideas the freedom to continue on his well-trodden path, so I demand the same freedom for myself. I shall only place myself at a disadvantage by saying that I am prepared at the drop of a hat to change my opinion if I have been taught something better, yet will not be offended if those who disagree with me are prepared stubbornly to defend their own opinions.

§28. I shall therefore not resist if someone wants to teach me something better, but I do not promise that I shall change my opinion whenever someone is convinced that he has taught me something better. It is not enough that the physician is convinced that he has restored the health of the sick if the sick do not sense this themselves. Therefore, those who want to teach me something better should make sure first whether they themselves are in such a condition that they deserve to be considered teachers rather than pupils; whether they are free from passions and prejudices; whether they observe the rules of proper academic discussion and do not use fallacious arguments; whether they avoid fallacious conclusions, which lead to an absurdity when they are linked to their principles, rather than mine; whether a contradiction they want to demonstrate is really one or only seems to be so; etc.

§29. Above all, however, they should remember that I want to avoid any occasion for new controversy in a matter that does not require revelation but depends on everybody's everyday sense, and that therefore I only use reason. I do not contradict Scripture, but abstract from it. They should take into account that I am speaking about felicity, which is true felicity, but temporal and of this life; thus I do not contradict theologians speaking of eternal beatitude in a future life, one belonging to humans that are quite different from those living in this life, and thus a beatitude quite different from felicity in this life, even if perhaps some things may be assumed here which seem to be incompatible with what is taught in systems of theological doctrine. The physician teaches correctly that a virgin does not give birth and that a human being cannot be conceived without a male seed; and yet he does not contradict Scripture or the theologians, who teach on the basis of Scripture that Christ was conceived by a virgin without a male seed and was born without the loss of her virginity. Similarly, a jurist or philosopher will teach correctly that this or that cannot be done by humans without breaking the rules of justice and decorum, yet these actions may nevertheless not be contrary to the rules of divine sanctity and justice, which are above the standard of human rules.

§30. Finally, I ask all those who dislike my opinions for their novelty to think seriously about this passage from Seneca's *On the Happy Life,* chapters 1 and 2, before they get cross with me:

> Let us not follow the herds of our predecessors like sheep, and let us not continue to go where everyone has gone before, rather than where we should go. And there is nothing worse than allowing ourselves to be guided by common opinion, and to think that best which enjoys widespread approval and for which there are many examples; in that case we do not live according to reason, but by imitation. Look at those great crowds of people where one falls over the other. That is what happens when people are so tightly packed that one cannot fall without pulling another down onto the ground. The first are the cause of the ruin of the next lot. You see this happen all the time in real life. Nobody errs only for himself, but is the cause and author of error in others. For it is harmful to follow blindly what goes before, and since everybody would rather believe than judge, people never think deeply about life and just believe. This directs us and precipitates us toward disaster; we perish by following the examples of others, . . . [16] [And, as Seneca says a little later,] Since we are concerned with the happy life, there is no reason to reply as if it were a vote: this side seems to be the greater. That is the worse side, precisely

16. Seneca, "On the Happy Life," chap. 1, p. 101, in Seneca, *Moral Essays,* vol. 2.

because it is the opinion of the majority. Human affairs are not so well ordered, that what is better is approved by the majority. The support of a crowd is an argument for saying that the opinion is bad. Let us seek that which is the best thing to do, not what is most common, and that which secures our permanent happiness, not what has been commonly approved by the worst interpreters of truth. Among the common crowd, however, I include crowned heads, as well as those in work clothes.[17]

§31. If perhaps a pagan philosopher is not to your taste, here is a similar eloquent statement by a church father, book II, chapter 7, of the *Divine Institutes:*

In those matters that are the very point of life everybody should trust in himself and rest on his own judgment and his own senses in examining and weighing up the truth, rather than be deceived by blind belief in the errors of others, as if we lacked any rational faculties. God gave all people as much wisdom as was appropriate to each, so that they are able to investigate what they have not heard about, and to weigh up what they have heard. And it is not true that those who went before us were also superior to us in wisdom, which has been given to all in equal measure and therefore cannot be monopolized by our predecessors. Like the bright light of the sun it cannot be diminished, because just as the sun is the light for the eyes, so wisdom is the light for the human heart. Thus, since the desire to know, that is, to seek truth, is innate in all humans, those people deprive themselves of their wisdom who approve the ideas of the forefathers without any reflection and are led by others like sheep. They are mistaken if they believe that they cannot possibly know more than their ancestors [*majores*], because they themselves are called the descendants [*minores*], or that the ancestors could not have been misguided, since they are called *majores*.[18] What therefore prevents us from using their example? Just as they who had come up with false ideas transmitted them to posterity, so we, who have found something true, will transmit something better to posterity.[19]

17. Ibid., chap. 2, p. 103.
18. Lactantius is playing on the meaning of the Latin words *majores,* which means "the greater" as well as "ancestors," and *minores,* which means both "descendants" and "the lesser."
19. Lactantius, *Divine Institutes,* bk. II, chap. 7, pp. 136–37.

BOOK I

CHAPTER I

On the Moral Nature of Man

§1. That complete entity which is called "the world" consists of things, some of which are visible, while others are invisible, such as air, light, ether, etc. Visible things are called bodies; invisible things we shall call powers, faculties, qualities, etc.

§2. But just as the examples of air, light, and ether show that there are qualities that are destitute of any visible body, so too experience and common sense show that there is no visible body that is not endowed with an invisible power. There are, rather, many and various qualities that are all united with this visible body and influence it and other bodies.

§3. What is visible or tangible in bodies we call matter. What is invisible, however, and cannot be touched, we call its nature.

§4. Depending on the kind of influence this nature exercises, some bodies are heavenly and others terrestrial, some are solid and some are fluid, some are luminous, some are transparent, some are opaque, etc.

§5. Just as man is an example of a visible body, not an invisible power or quality, so he has many faculties in common with those other earthly bodies that are opaque and a mixture of solid and fluid (of which man is one example), and especially with mute living beings: e.g., life, locomotive power, the ability to procreate, digestion, which are usually attributed to the human body, together with visible matter.

§6. Those powers, however, that distinguish humans from the other bodies that are known to us, especially beasts, are called the human soul. You, therefore, have two general parts of man, the body and the soul or mind.

§7. But since man differs from all other bodies in terms of his power of understanding and willing, the human soul is commonly said to consist of two faculties, the understanding and the will.

§8. Moreover, the actual powers produce particular kinds of bodies and unite the particles of matter with each other in a specific structure and give them a certain shape. And these various shapes of bodies and the other properties that are evident to the senses are signs and indications of powers and qualities that distinguish the individual kinds of bodies from each other. And so it is with the human body, too.

§9. For either the human soul forms, in the mother's body, a shape that is different from other bodies, or at least this distinctive shape of the human body and its parts, internally and externally, indicates that the human soul has a different character and nature from the powers of other bodies.

§10. Here it is relevant to note that the head in humans is far greater in relation to the rest of the body than in any other kind of animal; that the amount of blood and animal spirits flowing from it is therefore greater, and secretion is also greater because of the erect stature; also, the vigor and movement [of blood and animal spirits] is greater because of the longer ascent to the head through the carotids; that man has his own plexus of nerves, that there is a connection between the pericardium and the diaphragm in the human body and, next to that, a link between the nerve of diaphragm and the plexus of nerves specific to man; that the desire for sexual intercourse is not limited in man to a particular season, but is virtually permanent; that man's face is an indicator of various passions and very different from the face of beasts; that he has hands that are suitable for doing infinite things of which beasts are incapable; that the joining of hand to arm and the structure of the feet are quite unique; that man walks upright, that he can speak, laugh, cry, sigh, and stimulate and signal many kinds of feelings by moving his eyes, etc.

§11. But man differs from other bodies with respect not only to the soul, but also to the shape of the body and its members, because these different shapes are also indications of different powers. It is therefore appropriate to look for the difference between man and the other bodies by examining the soul, that is, those specific powers the indications of which are those specific things in the human body that are perceived by the senses.

§12. Yet all powers are invisible and therefore cannot be immediately perceived by the senses, and therefore are not only said to be present when the signs of them are evident in the bodies, but they can also be conceived or defined only by the actions these signs cause in the things they influence—the power of the eye to see, for example, etc. It is the same with those specific powers that distinguish man from all the other bodies.

§13. Moreover, in the operations and actions of bodies the powers that lie behind them often act by means of other bodies and their powers. Therefore, it is not always possible to form conclusions from external signs about the power that first caused these; that power could be in another unknown or concealed place, and we will therefore require a careful examination to avoid being misled.

§14. Thus, the eyes of humans provide many indications of the human intellect and its varying acuteness among different humans, and of the passions of the human will. Yet accurately speaking, neither the intellect nor the will is located in the eyes.

§15. Man, however, is endowed with an intrinsic ability to inquire into the seats of his own powers and to feel them precisely where they are, that is, where they operate.

§16. Thus, he knows that the ability of understanding is not in the eye, but in the head, and the ability to will is not in the eye or the head, but in the heart. The operation of the intellect, which he feels in his head, is thought; that of the will, which he feels in his heart, is desire or love.

§17. Therefore, the intellect is an ability of the human soul to think in the head, and the will is the ability of the same soul to desire in the heart.

§18. The acts of the intellect, however, are thoughts about bodies or about powers. The former are called sense perceptions; the latter are the intellect strictly speaking or in the pure sense.[1]

§19. Sense perceptions of bodies are either of present or of absent bodies, which are either in the past or in the future. The sense perceptions of present bodies are called common sense, and they are not to be confused with the sensations that are usually called external senses, and that man has in common with beasts, such as vision, hearing, etc.

§20. The external or animal sensations are only of bodies and of states of bodies outside the seat of sense perception, but human sense perception or common sense also extends to the powers proper to man, or certainly to the operations that result from the powers in his own body.

§21. The external senses only have a simple, confused, and irrational perception or cognition, while human sense perception receives affirmation from the intellect concerning the thing that we sense.

§22. Human sense perception is an action proper to the intellect and not its instrument. Yet external sensation is a different power from both intellect and will, although it is the common stimulus of both.

§23. For there is nothing in the intellect in the strict sense which was not in the human senses before, either in itself or by virtue of its operations,

1. See §28 in this chapter.

and there is nothing in human sense perceptions that was not previously in the external senses. Thus there is no desire for that which is not known; all desire requires at the very least perception or cognition by the external senses.

§24. Thought which is concerned with past things or with their images that are imprinted on the mind by means of sensation either considers them just as they are offered to the senses, or divides and combines them. Either of the two can be called imagination, because it plays with images. In the common manner of speaking, however, the former is called memory, while the latter is called fantasy or imagination in the narrower sense.

§25. All present things become past things. Since future things are not yet present, however, and the intellect only starts with present things, it is necessary to judge of future events on the basis of present or past ones, by dividing or combining them. Hence, all contemplation of future events is a work of fantasy, not of memory or common sense.

§26. Yet all these forms of sensation that we have reviewed so far—that is, common sense, fantasy, memory—concern bodies. All bodies are, however, single entities. It is, therefore, clear that all thoughts about bodies, considered as wholes, are thoughts about individual entities and sensations.

§27. Now, as we have said that all bodies consist of matter and powers, but that matter cannot exist separately without powers, it is also clear that there can be no consideration, either in particular or in general, of matter as such in abstraction from everything else; that is only possible for powers.[2] Although the power that is common to all bodies, which makes them visible and gives them extension, is usually, though inaccurately, called matter, it is more precise to call it the nature of a body, since the power of bodies and their nature are synonyms.

2. In other words, according to Thomasius, powers can exist without matter, but matter cannot exist without powers.

§28. We either contemplate powers insofar as they are united with a body, or we abstract from this union. The former pertains to the senses. The latter is the contemplation of general truths. For since all general truths are formed by abstraction, and there is nothing in the world except bodies and powers, and matter cannot be abstracted from powers, it follows that abstraction is possible only in the case of powers. A power, therefore, should not be considered a particular entity, but something unifying or a unit. A unit, however, is an abstract, general concept.

§29. *Mathematics* examines the common power of all bodies, quantity. *Astronomy* examines the powers of heavenly bodies, *physics* the powers (united and separate) of terrestrial bodies, genuine *logic* the power of the human intellect in particular, *moral philosophy* that of the will. *Metaphysics* or natural theology examines the primary power of all powers.

§30. The different forms of thought are all the result of either inquiry or the formation of propositions. The former is called a question or suspension of judgment, the latter either affirmation or negation. Affirmation and negation are therefore actions of the intellect, not the will. And it is not possible to say what he thinks who thinks without either affirmation or negation or a question. Therefore, it is simply false to say that there is thought about a simple term, or it can be only a very confused thought and a shadow of thought rather than thought itself.

§31. There are two kinds of questions: does something exist? and what kind of thing is it? That is, either you can ask whether something constitutes or has a power, or you can ask what kind of power it constitutes or has.

§32. Moreover, there is either one thought or a plurality of thoughts. A series of several thoughts is called ratiocination or reflection; ratiocination often has a particular order or method.

§33. He who by means of ratiocination remembers many sensations is said to have an excellent memory; he who knows how to produce a chain of reasoning concerning various related powers is said to enjoy a sharp mind. He who quickly perceives the differences between powers is shown to have an outstanding judgment.

§34. I now continue by looking at the will. I have said that all volition is a longing in the heart. All longing is love. All love is a desire of uniting oneself with the object of this love. All desire is an impulse toward action. But as volition is an impulse in the heart, it differs from an impulse that is felt in other parts of the body, such as the urge to expel excrements or the itch in a sore.

§35. Even beasts will feel this impulse in their heart. Hence, this definition of the will is not yet sufficient. The impulse of beasts affects the locomotive powers of their bodies, but is not accompanied by thought. The impulse of the will, however, not only directs the locomotive power of the body, but also leads the intellect itself to think a lot about the loved object and the means of acquiring it and enjoying it. Therefore, the will is a longing of the heart that is always joined to thought in the intellect. Hence, if it is considered without regard to the power of thought, it is called sensitive appetite.

§36. Yet the will is not therefore a form of thought, whether you look at the impulse itself in the will or the thoughts in the intellect that are inspired by this impulse. For the feeling of the impulse in the heart is not the impulse itself, just as the feeling of pain in a sore foot is not the sore or the pain itself. And a thought caused by the will is not the will, since what impels and what is impelled are always distinct.

§37. In the meantime, the mutual relationship and coherence of intellect and will are clear from the above. The actions of the intellect are often moved without the action of the will. But the will always moves the intellect.

§38. Indeed, either the human powers are moved by other powers outside the human being, or one human power moves another.

§39. Powers outside the human being move not only the faculties of the human body, such as its power of locomotion, digestion, procreation, etc., but the thoughts themselves, especially sensual ones. They even move the will or appetite of man itself.

§40. Hence, the common saying that the will cannot be compelled is false. For while it would be stupid to ask about the visible coercion of something invisible, daily experience shows us that the invisible qualities of external powers can suppress or stimulate the will, that is, prevent it from acting or impelling it to do so.

§41. The powers of the human body can all stimulate the intellect. The intellect, on the other hand, does not command the locomotive power, or digestion, or the power of procreation, even if the moderation or excess of thoughts can either benefit or harm these faculties. But this moderation or excess does not come from the intellect iself, but from elsewhere.[3]

§42. And it is therefore false and contrary to common sense when it is generally taught that the thought of wanting to move my hand or foot, for example, has some locomotive force joined to it and is produced by the same. For experience shows that this kind of thought can exist without locomotion, and locomotive power in beasts and in humans shows that locomotion in beasts never involves thought, and in humans often does not do so either.

§43. The will has no power over digestion and the power of procreation; it is rather the case that these powers often influence the will in various ways. If the human body, however, is healthy and intact, then locomotive power is always, just as in beasts, subject to the impulse of the heart, even if this impulse does not always come from the human will, that is, even if it is not always joined to the thought that I move my members or want to move them. If, however, I want to move them—that is, if the impulse of the heart is joined to thought—I move them, and if I want to rest—

3. That is, from the will.

that is, if there is a desire in the heart for rest, joined to a corresponding thought—I rest.

§44. Locomotive power does not depend on the will in such a way that it receives its powers from it, but is distinct and separate from the will and, like all other powers in the world, has received its limits from the first and eternal quality and power, that is, God. Thus man cannot walk on air, [he cannot] move his foot counterclockwise and his hand clockwise at the same time, and, when he falls, he cannot direct his fall, etc.

§45. Moreover, the intellect has its own powers and can affirm and negate without the help of the will. The will, however, unless it is directly affected, has no such power over our sensations, except by physically obstructing our sensory organs.[4] The meditations of the pure intellect also have their duration and their limits, which do not depend on the will in any way. Therefore, the will is able to stimulate a train of thought, but if this develops momentum, the human will cannot order it to be silent. Hence, we often cannot sleep even if we want to, because the will cannot prevent the train of thoughts.

§46. But in determining what is good and bad for ourselves (if others are concerned, the intellect is freer), examining this good, and thinking about the means suitable to achieving it, the intellect is always subject to the impulse of the will. When the will seeks what is good or avoids what is bad, it is not being directed by the intellect. The will does not desire something because it seems good to the intellect, but it seems good to the intellect because the will desires it. Whether you consider sense perceptions or reflections, the truth of this will be apparent. If something is agreeable to the will, the intellect cannot perceive it as anything but agreeable, and if it is not agreeable to the will, the intellect cannot but perceive it as disagreeable. What is felt to be agreeable is felt to be good, and what is felt to be disagreeable is felt to be bad. Thus, the will prejudices the intellect and causes it to pay careful attention and think about the means of acquiring

4. The phrase "unless it is directly affected" is removed in later editions.

the object of the will's desire, and the intellect in considering these means cannot but regard the object of desire as something good.

§47. The common assertion that the intellect directs the will in matters of good and bad has been made partly because human nature was looked for in the books of other people, not in one's own senses; partly because the faculties of the intellect and the will were not properly distinguished; and partly because the Scholastics, for self-interested reasons, declared that the source of all felicity and misfortune was in the intellect, and hence came up with old wives' tales about human action and inculcated them as articles of faith into their students at the academies.[5]

§48. Intellect and will therefore both have their particular actions and passions.

§49. The intellect is said to act when it is impelled by the will to reflect on something, and is said to be passive when it is moved by things other than the will to think. Therefore, accurately speaking, the intellect is always passive and is never the first to move.

§50. The will is passive in relation to other things that stimulate it, but that does not include the intellect. It acts on the locomotive power of the other members, even on the head, that is, the locomotive power of the intellect.

§51. The intellect acts in the head, not outside it, and therefore every action of the intellect is immanent. To speak, that is, to communicate the actions of the intellect to another person, is an action of the body, while the desire to speak is an action of the will, not the intellect.

§52. Whenever the will acts, it acts outside the heart. It is therefore false to say that certain actions of the will are immanent because all are transeunt,

5. According to Thomasius, the Scholastics overemphasized the importance of the intellect. As a result, they defined morality and faith in terms of a correct intellectual understanding of philosophical and religious doctrines when the true foundation of virtue and religious faith was the reform and regeneration of the will.

unless by the term *immanent action* you mean internal actions. Yet that is not accurate, since all immanent action is internal, but not all internal actions are immanent.[6]

§53. The fact that choice is generally considered to be an immanent action of the will is because it was believed mistakenly and contrary to common sense that the will had an internal freedom, about which we shall say more below.

§54. The intellect, therefore, is never the faculty that first moves the other faculties, but the will is the first mover of the human soul, because it moves the intellect.

§55. Actions that are commanded by the will are said to be voluntary as well as spontaneous and morally imputable (because morals consist of a large number of consistent voluntary actions). All other actions are called involuntary, necessary, or even coerced.

§56. The will itself, however, is not a voluntary power, for otherwise there would be a will of the will, and this would be neither spontaneous nor moral. The will is itself a natural power and necessary, not voluntary. The will is called a moral power because it is the source of all morality.

§57. The moral nature of man, therefore, is a complex formed by the power of volition together with the powers that are subject to the will.

§58. Therefore, it is not right to oppose the moral nature of man to his physical nature, or to oppose it simply and absolutely to his rational or intellectual nature.

§59. For the term *physical human nature* is awkward, like speaking of "natural nature." It will not help if you excuse yourself by saying that it is called physical nature because it is the subject of physics. For moral

---

6. In later editions Thomasius removed the last section of this paragraph, from "unless" until the end, because, he said, internal and immanent actions here were synonyms.

nature, in its way, pertains to physics, because it depends on the will and is driven by it, and the discussion of the will is part of physics.

§60. Hence, it is clear that moral matters cannot be understood without natural [ones], because the former are conclusions based on the latter, and so moral philosophy is a subdivision of physics.

§61. But the rational nature of man is in a certain way opposed to its moral nature, to the extent that the thoughts of man do not depend on the will; and in a certain way they pertain to the moral nature of man, insofar as it is directed by the will.

§62. Human reason, therefore, is the property of the intellect alone, not the will; that is, the will of man is not itself rational, even if it is commonly called that, either because it is the first mover of the human soul and humans are called rational animals, or because the desire of beasts lacks all reason, while the human will, as we have said, is always joined to reason.

§63. Moral actions, however, are called either rational (to the extent that they conform to the reason of man when it is not driven by the will) or irrational (to the extent that they contradict it, even if they conform to the intellect insofar as it is directed by and passive in relation to the will). More on that later.

§64. For the intellect freely judges the nature of things as well as good and bad, whenever it is not driven by the will. It serves the will insofar as it is driven by it.

§65. The intellect, therefore, has its own freedom and servitude, either of which is not intrinsic, but extrinsic in relation to the will. Intrinsically, the intellect is neither free nor subservient, but a necessary power lacking all ability to choose.

§66. The will also has its own kind of freedom and servitude, but in a different respect. It is always free with regard to the intellect because it is never moved by it. Therefore, this freedom is again extrinsic. Intrinsically it has no freedom, that is, no power of choice.

§67. It serves other powers outside and within man, to the extent that they are welcome to the desire in the will and stimulate and incline it in a certain direction. It is not always understood that the will acts when it is stimulated by these powers, and hence the will is called free. But the will, too, is only free extrinsically, not intrinsically.

§68. But it is also evident that being intrinsically spontaneous and being intrinsically free are two totally different things. A spontaneous action is one that is commanded by the will and serves the will, but it is called free in the same respect as the will [that is, extrinsically].

§69. A spontaneous moral or voluntary action in man is that which comes from the will, as the prime moving principle of the human soul, and so man, as such, is called its author.

§70. And it is imputed to man because it is spontaneous, not because it is free. To impute is to call someone the author of an action, and the actions of humans that serve their desires are imputed to them.

§71. But because we have said that the will always has thought joined to it, spontaneous actions generally also require the intellect.

§72. Therefore, the first stirrings or impulses of the will are not imputed to man, because the will itself is not spontaneous, nor are sense perceptions, digestion, or the natural power of procreation; nor are the actions of other humans imputed, unless they are subject to the direction of the will, that is, the authority of another person; only the locomotive powers of my own body (including the head) and of any other body, insofar as it is directed by my will, are imputed.

§73. Moreover, since imputation is properly done by someone else and produces these peculiar moral effects, further discussion of imputation is to be set aside for now, until we have considered the nature of the will itself more distinctly.[7]

§74. All powers in this world are such that they support one thing and destroy another. In the former case they are united with each other, and it does not always matter if the forces of the two powers are equal or unequal. In the latter case there is a struggle between different powers; there the stronger faculty always overcomes the less powerful.

§75. Moreover, there is no power in the whole world except for the first and eternal power,[8] which does not need the help of another power in order to exist for any length of time. And there is no power, with the exception of the first power, that cannot be destroyed by another.

§76. No body, however, can exist without the preservation of its powers, and so that is called good which preserves the powers of a particular body, while that is called bad which destroys the powers of a body, because once the powers are destroyed, the body itself is destroyed, and when its powers are preserved, so is the relevant body.

§77. But the several powers of one body support each other and conspire to resist adverse powers. And so it is common to find impulses in bodies either to further the good of the body or to keep away evil. These impulses in relation to other bodies are called sympathy and antipathy.

§78. The union of powers with the body is called life, and its dissolution is death — even if the schools use this term more strictly because they deny that plants and trees have life.

§79. While there is life, the parts of the body which are the seats of the powers remain united with each other. Death dissolves the particles of the body and turns them to dust, but the powers fly away to join the powers that are separate from the body. It is not clear where exactly these are

7. This is discussed in bk. I, chap. vii, §§22ff. of the *Fundamenta*.
8. That is, God.

active, although it is certain that they are even less reduced to nothingness than the particles of the body.

§80. The body, therefore, is mortal, while its powers are immortal.

§81. Life, however, is the foundation of all other goods of the body. Therefore, the nature of the body is usually seen to be such that it has no power that desires its destruction, and that rather the powers of all bodies work together to prevent the death of the body.

§82. Thus, the sensitive appetite in all the beasts we know is very similar to the human will, for it pursues what is good and shuns what is bad.

§83. Yet the human will has this in common with the appetite of beasts, that it loves life and shuns death; and it loves life and fears death in a very confused and general way. That is, it bristles at those things that directly cause death and desires all means of preserving life. But the human will differs from the powers of other bodies and the appetite of beasts in that the human will desires many things that gradually destroy life and shuns many others that further the preservation of life.

§84. But since no power loves its opposite, those things that are desired by the will must necessarily preserve and increase the power of the will. In that respect, therefore, they are good, and those things that are shunned are repugnant to the will and therefore bad.

§85. Thus it is a peculiar feature of man that he has a primary power, whose goods often contradict the good of the whole.

§86. The good of the whole, however, must always be preferred to the good of a part, because the destruction of the whole would also mean the destruction of the parts.

§87. Thus the good of the whole is a true good, and the good of the part that destroys the whole is in fact an evil, though it appears to be a good.

§88. It is now clear that depending on the different interpretations, which are easily done, of the above, either is true: that the human will always desires what is good and that it often desires what is bad; that it always shuns what is bad and that it often shuns what is good.

§89. The impulse of the will toward something that is agreeable to itself is called longing, desire, love, hope; the impulse away from something hostile to oneself (as we have shown elsewhere, this results from the prior, not the prior from the latter)[9] is flight, horror, hate, fear. Each of the two impulses is called an affection because they are affections of the primary power of the human soul; they are also called passions of the soul because they are regularly stimulated by external things that are welcome or unwelcome to the soul, even if it has already been shown above that in regard to the intellect they are action, since they move themselves by their own force and are not stimulated by the other power of the human soul, namely, the intellect.

§90. Yet reason itself, or the human intellect, when it is free, that is, when it is not moved by the will and recognizes the difference between the true and the apparent good, is called right reason. But when it is under the influence of the will and believes an apparent good to be the real good, then it is called corrupt reason.

§91. Since the passions, however, move the blood in the heart so subtly that the motion of these passions can barely be perceived, even if someone pays great attention, it is often difficult to recognize the difference between right and corrupt reason. All passions have their intervals of rest, and there is thus no doubt that during this interval reason is free to judge correctly of good and evil. Yet human reason cannot trust itself as long as it cannot be certain when this interval occurs.

---

9. Christian Thomasius, *Ausübung der Sitten-Lehre*. Reprint of the 1696 edition (Hildesheim: Georg Olms, 1999), chap. 4, §§8–9, pp. 111–12. There, according to Thomasius, fear or hate of something can be defined as the desire for something else.

§92. Every human being, however, senses that according to the common proverb ("we are sharp-eyed concerning the affairs of others, but blind as moles concerning our own") the human intellect is disposed to judge the goodness or badness of other people's actions more accurately than its own. It does not take long to find the reason for that. For just as most of our actions are voluntary, our judgment concerning most of them is corrupt. But the actions of others do not normally depend on our will; therefore, the intellect here can retain its rectitude.

§93. Yet that does not mean everything is right there. It is often the case that the actions of others are directed by ourselves and become ours in that regard. We often approve the actions of others because they are agreeable to ours, but criticize them when they are contrary to ours. We often either love or hate those people whose actions we judge. That hate or love, however, often has such deep roots in our soul, and moves our intellect so subtly, that we not only fail to realize that it has been tainted by the passion, but persuade ourselves in good faith that we are free from all passion.

§94. Therefore, we require morality, a discipline that puts forward clear criteria of right and corrupt reason. There would be no need for that if human reason, as is commonly believed, enjoyed such rectitude that it could judge without difficulty true good and evil. Other natural bodies have no need for such a doctrine because their powers are not corrupt.

§95. But even if man could distinguish accurately between true and false good in the actions of others, what use is it to him if he does not apply this knowledge to his own conduct? Hence we require a system of morality to show us how man can put the doctrine of the true good into practice. Again, other natural bodies have no need of this because their powers do it spontaneously.

§96. Yet we must be very prudent here, since the common opinions that are almost universally received are based on a twofold error: first, that reason must prescribe a rule to the will and, second, that the will, which is free to do so, must follow the dictate of reason. Each of these two errors is contrary to common sense, as soon as you think about the nature of the human soul without prejudice.

§97. For if the will had to follow the intellect, the intellect would necessarily always be right. Yet they [who defend the primacy of the intellect] admit that the intellect is sometimes corrupt, in which case the will must not follow it. But the will does not have the power to judge whether the intellect is right or corrupt, since all judgment pertains to the intellect. Therefore, the will does not know whom to follow. Thus, if it does not know this, but follows the intellect nevertheless, it acts foolishly.

§98. Moreover, we have shown above that the understanding of good and bad by the intellect is corrupted by the will and is subject to its authority in moral matters, and the intellect does not exercise any power over the will (which they admit by saying that the will may be the king, but the intellect is the counselor). If therefore the will follows the intellect, it is futile to hope for any improvement. For how can the king be corrected by the counselor, whose advice is in all matters subject to the wishes of the king.

§99. Finally, if the will has no power of choice, then there is no doubt that the whole moral doctrine of the Scholastics collapses. The fact that the will does not have the power to choose, which the Scholastics attribute to it, will become even clearer if we first show the origin of that common error, the belief that there is only one kind of human will. This error is the result of the failure to examine human volition itself more deeply.

§100. The primary power is one and the same in all specific bodies of one genus or species. It directs their internal and external actions in a uniform fashion, and if you know the nature of one particular body, you can safely infer the nature and power of another of the same kind.

§101. The same observation applies to those natural bodies that are most similar to humans, namely beasts. If you have observed the actions of one fox, monkey, dog, etc., you know about all animals that have the same shape or carry the same external signs of their powers.

§102. Humans, however, are a very different matter. The wills of individual humans are rarely in harmony with each other. In most matters they differ greatly and are often sharply opposed to each other, so that one person does not want that which the other person wants or wants the exact opposite.

§103. This goes so far that there is no human being whose will is in complete harmony with the will of another person.

§104. But nor is there any person whose will is by nature opposed to the will of another person in every respect.[10]

§105. It is even the case that individual humans do not want the same thing forever. They often want different things, which are opposed to each other and incompatible. If they want something at one time, they may not want it at another, or they may want its opposite. Yes, even in one single moment they feel within themselves the anxiety of conflicting desires, which tear them hither and thither, so that for a long time they have no idea at all what they want.

§106. Just as we have noted above that the powers imprint the signs of their effects on the bodies, so too the truth of these assertions is clear from signs that are evident to the senses.

§107. For humans do not only see what pleases or displeases other humans by studying their voluntary actions, that is, their physical movements commanded by the will. The signs of intrinsic faculties or powers are also imprinted externally on the bodies of humans.[11]

§108. These signs are very unreliable if they depend only on the opinion of other humans and are not recognized by sense perception or reason.

---

10. This is a view Thomasius attributes to Thomas Hobbes.
11. Thomasius here has in mind laughter, tears, and an angry expression as signs of the passions.

Examples are chiromancy or physiognomy. They are reliable if they depend partly on sense perception, partly on ratiocination, as is the case with signs imprinted on the human face that are different from those signs that are associated with physiognomy.

§109. Man differs most from beasts in that the latter, if they are of the same kind, have a very similar face as well as the same members and structure, while humans have such dissimilar faces that it is considered a miracle if the faces of two humans are perfectly identical. I should think that there has never been such a complete identity of two faces that two humans could not be distinguished from each other if the others paid attention and were familiar with them.

§110. Yet the expression of human faces indicates their passions or affections, so that in some people the dominant passion concealed in their soul can be recognized by means of common sense, as surely as a concealed fire is revealed by its smoke.

§111. Thus the eyes of some infallibly reveal their lust, envy, gluttony, cruelty, cunning, etc.

§112. You can also find signs of humanity, pity, modesty, benevolence, etc., in the human face. But these are not as reliable; they require some reflection, because humans pretend and dissimulate. Reasoning, however, is necessary to distinguish the signs of genuine and pretended passions.

§113. In the meantime it should be noted that the visible signs of vicious passions do not deceive, whereas the signs of good passions often are deceptive. The reason will be evident below.

§114. We have equal need of reasoning or certainly of the attentive observation of several sensations when we study the signs of the faces of several people in whom there is no one dominant passion, because our intellect has some congenital knowledge of particular dominant passions, but not of mixed passions.

§115. Meanwhile, there is no doubt that the signs of mixed passions also appear in the face and that they can be recognized quite reliably by means of few, but careful, observations. Indeed, we see many wise people daily form an excellent judgment about the passions of another person at first sight.

§116. But the signs of the varying passions in one person are also evident. For there are not only signs of hope and joy at one time, and of fear and sadness at another, which can be variations in the passions of the same will. There may also be clear signs of lust at one time, and of avarice and envy at another, which are acts of volition that are divergent and conflict with each other.

§117. The Scholastics made the intellect the primary power of the human soul. It is therefore up to them to defend their opinion that man is the lowest species [*species infima*]. It is enough for us to have shown so far that the will is the primary power of the mind and that all humans differ with respect to their wills. We will not argue over terms; you can say that individual humans differ in kind or that they are the same in kind; as far as we are concerned either is permissible, as long as you accept that man is a special genus or species, whose individuals have different natures with regard to their wills.

§118. They, however, who attribute freedom of choice to every human have slid from this error into another one, the belief that all of humankind has one and the same nature. And because they observed that certain individual humans could omit certain actions without great difficulty, that is, without great resistance from their will, they thought that others could do this equally easily and just did not want to use their freedom. Moreover, because they attributed the same will to individual humans and yet noticed that the external actions of humans were often preceded by an internal struggle within the mind, and because no faculty of the mind could contradict itself, they either said that the intellect was struggling with the appetite, or invented some third entity, saying that the sensitive appetite struggled with the intellect, but the will was some kind of third faculty, which was free and could choose whether to follow the appetite or the intellect.

§119. It has been shown above that the intellect is purely passive in relation to the will and has no effect on the will, even if, left to itself, it sees and approves what is better,[12] that is, confirms that something is good. We have also shown that the sensitive appetite is part of the will itself or a generic term for the will; it has also been shown that the appetite of beasts does not destroy their lives but strives for their good. So, once it has been shown that individual humans do not have the same will, but wills that are opposed to each other, then this whole fairy tale, the common belief in the nature of the will and its freedom, just collapses.

§120. Above all, we must see whether we can relate these wills, which are indicated by the external actions of humans and of which individual humans are aware, to certain general types. Until these types are defined, they seem infinite in number. There is, however, no discipline or science of infinite things.

§121. All humans agree in that they want to live for a very long time, and if possible forever, and so all are horrified by death (unless they are led to desire the opposite by contrary passions that have been stimulated to an extreme degree).

§122. They also agree in wanting to spend their lives in the greatest happiness.

§123. They all agree in their desire to avoid an unhappy life.

§124. They agree in that they all avoid a life filled with pain and desire a pleasant life.

12. "[V]ideat meliora probetque": an allusion to Ovid, *Metamorphoses,* bk. 7, 20–21 ("video meliora proboque, deteriora sequor"). See Ovid, *Metamorphoses,* vol. 1, trans. J. F. Miller, 3rd ed., rev. G. P. Goold, Loeb Classical Library (Cambridge, Mass.: Harvard University Press, 1972).

§125. There is only this difference, that not all have the same idea of agreeableness and pain.

§126. They all agree that they desire food, drink, and when they are adults sexual intercourse with the other sex, that they want to have something of their own, preserve their extrinsic liberty, and not be esteemed less than other humans. And thus they all avoid the pains associated with hunger, thirst, and lack of sexual fulfillment, as well as those of extreme poverty, ignominy, and servitude.

§127. Yet they differ in that some seek their pleasure and indeed their happiness in the delights of food, drink, and venery, in one word, in the pleasures of the flesh. And thus they fear and avoid the least loss of such pleasure as something that is contrary to their very nature.

§128. Others, on the other hand, want to own everything and rest their pleasure and happiness in the ownership of material goods, which are capable of dominion, and on the other hand are very sad if others own something or if some of their property is taken away or destroyed.

§129. Finally, some think it their greatest happiness and pleasure if they command other humans and consider it the greatest misfortune not only if they must be subject to the command of others, but if others want to protect their own liberty and refuse to obey them.

§130. Moreover, experience and common sense teach that these three passions—lust, avarice, and ambition—rule all of humankind and that there is not a single person who is not governed by these three passions, though in different ways, because there is not one person in whom there is not a different mixture of these three wills.

§131. In some humans one of these three passions is more powerful than the other two and easily controls them, unless they are greatly stimulated by the powers of external things. In others the dominant passion is a mixture of two out of three passions, and the person often feels them struggling with each other within himself, so that he can barely discern which of the two dominates the other, even if one is always dominant and the third is easily controlled by the dominant passions unless it is greatly stimulated from the outside. In others all three passions rule in such a way that their powers are almost equal; then they sense the internal struggle at almost every time and are torn now this way, now that, unless one of them is greatly stimulated by external powers or is irritated in such a way that the other passion is not damaged as a result.[13]

§132. The fact that these three desires are not different motions that succeed each other naturally and that are directed by a single principle of volition, or that originate in various modifications of the intellect, is proved as follows. The intellect in all human beings is one and the same, and it cannot produce opposed and conflicting motions. For conflicting actions have different and conflicting principles or powers that immediately cause them. Not to mention the fact that it has already been shown that the intellect does not direct the appetite, but is directed by it when it comes to forming an idea of its own good.

§133. The same reason shows that voluntary actions that conflict with each other cannot originate in the same will.

§134. These motions of the will cannot originate in the general will and desire for a long and pleasant life, because they accelerate death noticeably or certainly sensibly affect life with many necessary evils.

§135. That these three wills are not only opposed to each other but in conflict is partly evident from their nature, and in part from their effects in individual humans as well as several different humans.

§136. Lust is opposed to property because it loves the community of goods and sharing them. It is hostile to the desire for power because it loves mutual complaisance.

---

13. Thomasius discusses these issues in his *Ausübung der Sitten-Lehre,* chap. 12 (on the mixtures of various main passions) and chap. 13 (on external signs of these passions).

§137. Avarice is the enemy of lust because it senses that lust resists its acquisition of property and wastes its own goods. It is hostile to the desire for power because this too dissipates goods and lets other people share in its ownership.

§138. Ambition is hostile to lust and avarice because it senses that each of the two impedes the acquisition of glory and power.

§139. Hence, it follows (and experience teaches) that ambitious, avaricious, and pleasure-seeking people are by their nature mutually repugnant to each other in their external affections.

§140. And it takes a blockhead not to see that the fear of disgrace, expenses, death, or disease conflicts with the desire for pleasure, that the fear of hard work and dangers conflicts with the desire for power, that the fear of ignominy and cares conflicts with the desire to be rich, and so on.

§141. The following doubt must, however, be removed. Hope and fear, joy and sadness, are contradictory affections, just as lust, ambition, and avarice are, and yet they can be derived from one will. The passion of lust, for example, may be full of hope, or fear, or joy, or sadness, depending on circumstances. The same applies to ambition and avarice. Why therefore can lust, ambition, and avarice, even if they are opposed to each other, not be derived from one source and so be considered rivulets of one will?

§142. Here we must first stress the following: that hope, fear, joy, and sadness are not primary affections, but only various effects, common to all, of these primary and mutually conflicting affections, as the following chapter will show. Hence, it is false that these four affections conflict with each other, since they are not in the heart at the same time and are not felt to be there at the same time; instead one succeeds the other. Yet when lust, ambition, and avarice are in conflict, they are felt at one and the same time.

§143. Thus, even if the conflicting passions are opposed to each other, not all opposites conflict with each other. And this opposition, which exists between hope, fear, joy, and sadness, is not an actual opposition between the actions of different wills or faculties, but only of concepts and definitions.

§144. It follows from the above that those things that are commonly attributed in the schools to choice and the freedom of the will are rather to be referred to the passions of the will and their coercion or necessity. If there is a struggle between different affections, the stronger power always wins. How this needs to be understood in more detail will be shown in the following chapter.

CHAPTER V

On the Law of Nature and Nations

§1. The term *right* is understood in various ways, mainly as a rule of actions or a power to act in relation to that rule—as Grotius puts it, either as a law or as the attribute of a person.

§2. There are as many meanings of the term *law* as there are different rules of moral actions. Therefore, law in a broad sense signifies legal opinions (*consilia*), the commands of kings and lords (*imperia*), paternal admonitions (a mixture of *imperium* and *consilium*), and the conditions of agreements (*pacta*).

§3. Law in the strict sense signifies the commands of rulers, lords, kings, and magistrates, and in the strictest sense the general commands of the rulers of a commonwealth. In either case it is distinct from a legal opinion and an agreement. Hence, at the same time, the difference of a law from advice and an agreement is evident.

§4. In the broad sense, therefore, the properties of a law are to recommend, exhort, prescribe, forbid, permit, punish, and compel.[14] In the strict sense the immediate property of a law is to prescribe and forbid, while the mediate properties that result from this are to impose punishments by means of magistrates, to compel judicially, and to declare those actions void that are against the laws.

14. This draws in part on *Digest* 1.3.7.

§5. For external fear, with which the laws threaten those who ignore them, is either the fear that an action will be futile, or the fear of suffering harm in something close to us, or the fear of punishment.

§6. Permitting is not a property of law, because he who permits does not prescribe a rule, unless this term includes the confirmation of a right belonging to someone else or the introduction of such a right. For if, for example, the father's power to command, the property rights of citizens, etc., are permitted by the laws, then others are prohibited from disturbing those who make use of their right. Yet in that case permission by the law is not a new action of the law, but is already included in the act of prohibition.

§7. It is therefore clear from the above that the controversy over prescriptive and permissive law is mainly quibbling over words.

§8. The effect and intention of law in either sense is obligation—external obligation if we take law in the strict sense, but also internal obligation if we take law in the broad sense, as is obvious from the more extensive discussion in the previous chapter.[15] Right and obligation are correlates, and it will, therefore, be clear from the teachings on correlates what right is in one sense, that is, when it is taken to be a power of acting in relation to a rule.[16]

§9. For just as obligation imposes a constraint on the will and its external freedom, so rights in this other sense emerge from a relaxation of the will and its external freedom, that is, from the removal of all impediments, or even support and assistance that are provided by the laws. Obligation instills fear, while a right gives grounds for hope or preserves it. Hence, obligation is said to be a passive moral quality and a right an active moral quality. Hence the rule that everybody can renounce his right, but not his obligation.

15. The title of the previous chapter was "On the Rules of Human Actions, Namely Advice and Command."
16. That is, as an attribute of a person.

§10. Obligation, however, and the right corresponding to an obligation are each referred to a rule, but in different ways. All obligation flows from a rule of action as the effect that is primarily intended by the person who prescribed the rule. Yet right is a secondary effect, which is intended indirectly, insofar as it is a correlate of obligation and insofar as it is sometimes newly introduced by human law.

§11. Hence, right is twofold. It is either what I have if I abstract from all human will, or it is what has its origin in a human law or agreement. We are said to have the first right by nature, previous to any human will, or from a rule of natural law. The second is derived from a rule based on human will or on human right. The former is called connate right, the latter acquired right.

§12. An example of connate law is the freedom and primeval community of goods. Political power and dominion are examples of the latter.

§13. Obligation is also either connate or acquired, but the definitions here are different. A connate obligation is one that humans have immediately from birth and which does not presuppose an act of will by the person who is being obligated. An acquired obligation presupposes such an act of will.

§14. Therefore, connate right and connate obligation, etc., do not always correspond to each other. For a son has a connate obligation toward his father, yet the right of the father is not connate but has been acquired through consent with the mother, but without consent of the child.

§15. Opposed to right and obligation is injury. He who makes use of his right does not injure anyone. Injury—that is, the denial of a right and an action contrary to an obligation—leads to an unjust action; a just action is what conforms to an obligation.

§16. It is, therefore, clear that right and the external obligation corresponding to right, as well as injustice, always presuppose two humans.

Therefore, nobody has properly speaking a right over himself, and nobody can do himself an injustice or be under an obligation toward himself. To a willing person no injury is done. And nobody can impose a law on himself.

§17. Therefore, all right is external, not internal, and the same needs to be said about the obligation corresponding to that right, that is, the external obligation.

§18. The reason for the kind of obligation that we have called internal is therefore different. For that does not always assume other people. Even if a human being is on his own, he is under an obligation to moderate his passions, because there would be a reasonable fear of harm if he acted contrary to this obligation. And on that account we are said to be under an obligation to ourselves, and are said to impose a law on ourselves (e.g., through vows), and everybody's closest obligation is to himself.

§19. *Obligation,* therefore, is a broader term than *right.* The subdivisions of right and of obligation thus are not the same.

§20. Therefore, obligation arises also from the rules of honesty, but these rules do not produce a right.

§21. Then does right arise only from the rules of justice as the terminology implies, or is it also based on the rules of decorum? Indeed, the rules of decorum also concern man in relation to other human beings. Yet nobody can be forced to perform the acts of decorum, and if he is forced, it is no longer a matter of decorum. Yet the obligation corresponding to right is always external, since it fears the coercion by other humans. Thus, right is not the product of the rules of decorum either.

§22. And hence it is clear that the meaning of right as a power to do something is not as widely accepted as the meaning of right as a law.

§23. Moreover, it is clear that Grotius's division of right into perfect and imperfect is not that helpful. For all right is perfect, and an imperfect right does not have injury as its opposite. An imperfect right extends no further than that which can be demanded from another on the basis of the rules of decorum, not of justice.

§24. The same reason applies to the division of obligation into perfect and imperfect. For there is no such thing as an imperfect obligation. And while internal obligation is more perfect than external, you cannot call one imperfect and the other perfect. Moreover, the rules of decorum and of honesty do not properly speaking put me under an obligation toward other humans, but toward myself.

§25. It flows from the above that the actions a person performs out of an internal obligation and on the basis of the rules of decorum and honesty are directed by virtue in general, and a person who practices these is called virtuous, not just. Those actions, however, which he performs on the basis of the rules of justice or of external obligation are directed by justice; if he performs these, he is called just.

§26. The right of all to everything thus collapses automatically,[17] because obligation, even if it can exist without a right, is yet no right itself, nor can right exist without obligation except in the exceptional case of supreme necessity.[18] Yet that right, by the very fact that it is a right of all to everything, does not have an obligation corresponding to it.

§27. The belief that all right is ultimately derived from agreement thus also collapses. For it has been shown here that there are connate rights, and in the previous chapter it has been observed that an agreement in itself does not create an obligation and, therefore, cannot by itself either produce or confirm a right.

§28. Right in either meaning is divided into natural law, the law of nations, and civil law, but the observations on each of these are not all the same. Therefore, I shall examine each of them in turn.

---

17. See Hobbes, *Leviathan,* chap. XIV, p. 91.

18. If, for example, I save myself from drowning by pushing another person off the plank to which I am clinging, that would be supreme necessity.

§29. Right in the sense of law is either natural or positive. The foundation of that division is the principle by which each of these two is known. The right of nature is known from the reasoning of an undisturbed mind, while positive law requires revelation and publication.

§30. Yet natural law is taken either in a broad sense, to the extent that it comprehends all moral precepts that are based on ratiocination, no matter whether they are rules of justice, honesty, or decorum; or in a strict sense, for the precepts of justice alone insofar as they are distinct from honesty and decorum.

§31. In the former sense, the principle by which natural law is known must be single, common to all humans, primary, and universally valid; if natural law is understood in the latter sense this principle can be secondary, special, and particular. If we neglect or omit this distinction, many useless but difficult disputes result concerning the principle of natural law.

§32. All positive right is human by virtue of its publication, which is an essential part of it; that is, it is publicized and revealed to others through the mediation of human beings. Whether these humans have this command immediately from God is something that philosophy does not know and leaves to theology to answer.

§33. Natural law, however, is written in the hearts of every person and does not require revelation by others or authority alone. Hence it is called divine, because it is derived from the author of all nature, including human nature, God.

§34. Yet beware of thinking that natural and positive law, divine and human law, are of the same kind. Natural law and divine law are more like advice than commands, but human law in the proper sense is always a rule based on command.

§35. Indeed, among humans law and advice are opposed to each other, and so law is taken to be the command not of a teacher, but of a ruler.

§36. But among humans the power of command is generally one of two kinds: paternal or lordly. The former mainly seeks to further the interest of the subject, the latter the self-interest of the ruler. Therefore, the former has more in common with advice than the latter. The power of the ruler, depending on the particular commonwealths, sometimes has more in common with paternal power, sometimes more with lordly power, but usually more with lordly power.

§37. Reason left to its own devices does not know that it must think of God as a king or lord, who wants to impose arbitrary punishments on those who have violated the precepts of natural law, because it sees that all those punishments, which are inflicted on the transgressors of natural law and are not under human control, are natural, and therefore are not punishments in the proper sense of the word.[19]

§38. Punishment is by its nature human and arbitrary, because every punishment is dictated by a human ruler. Natural law only dictates that sinners deserve to be punished. Moreover, among those who are governed only by the law of nature, war is the only means of coercion. There is no coercion through punishment in the state of nature. Grotius's idea of a punitive war has already been refuted.[20]

§39. Moreover, every punishment must be inflicted visibly, but the evils which God has ordained for the transgressors of natural law come secretly, in such a way that the connection of the evil with the sin is not evident, even if the evil itself is evident.

§40. In addition, the wise man conceives God as a teacher of natural law, rather than as a legislator. For natural law is a dictate of undisturbed reason when it is not distracted by the passions. But that is the task of the

19. By "arbitrary punishments" Thomasius means those punishments that are not the automatic, natural consequences of wrongdoing but are inflicted deliberately by a superior.

20. See Hugo Grotius, *Commentary on the Law of Prize and Booty,* ed. Martine Julia van Ittersum (Indianapolis: Liberty Fund, 2006), chap. viii, pp. 136–37.

teacher, to calm reason with his advice. Laws are published. The philosopher knows of no publication of natural law.

§41. Even if the wise man imagines God as a sort of human ruler, he thinks of him as a father rather than a lord, because it comes closer to the perfection of divine goodness for God to be seeking the good of humans rather than using the laws written on the human heart despotically to seek his own self-interest. The commands of a father, however, are advice rather than commands.

§42. Moreover, the conception of God as a father instills filial fear; that of God as a despot, however, instills servile fear. But we have already said above that the rational fear of God is filial, not servile.[21]

§43. Yet many people, because of their inborn stupidity, imagine God as some kind of despot and are incapable of a proper conception of God as long as they remain in that state. The wise man, however, must adapt himself to the capacities of the stupid when he prescribes rules to them. Hence, these points in treatises on natural law must be made gently, rather than being inculcated forcefully. We must wait until readers feel this truth in their hearts, rather than force them to argue over it.

§44. In the meantime, the wise man must not set aside this observation, nor must he put forward the common opinion as a foundation for his introduction to natural law, because the introduction must remove the mistaken ideas of the stupid. The common opinion, however, leads to countless errors.

§45. There is another difference between divine and human law, which can be perceived more clearly from the above. Human laws are often modified openly, and they are meant to be mutable. Yet natural law has never been changed because the natures of all things are perpetual and immutable. Indeed, reasoning cannot come up with likely reasons for thinking that God has changed or wanted to change natural law.

---

21. Thomasius makes this point in bk. 1, chap. ii, §§27–32, of *Foundations*.

§46. All doubts that are raised in this regard are derived from Scripture.[22] It is not the task of an introduction to natural law to respond to these, especially as it is not Scripture itself that has generated these doubts, which owe their origin rather to false interpretation by scholastic philosophy.

§47. In the meantime, natural law in the strict and in the broad senses are usually mixed up in this question. For even if natural law is never changed, the precepts of justice are by their nature more far-reaching and perpetual than those of honesty and decorum. Hence, the former are always the same, while the latter vary or at least allow for many qualifications.

§48. The rules of justice punish extremely evil acts, that is, those that are evil with regard to all humans. The rules of honesty concern extremely good acts, but the means of arriving at these rules vary, because there are also different ways of disregarding these rules. The rules of decorum concern various intermediate degrees of goodness and malice, which are almost infinite.

§49. The matter will become clearer in the following chapter.[23] Here this note can serve to explain the obscure opinion of the Scholastics that the negative precepts of natural law bind forever and at all times, while the affirmative precepts bind forever, but not at all times.

§50. The above comments also allow us to settle firmly that complex controversy[24] over the differences between natural and positive law with regard to the morality of human actions, with which both kinds of law are concerned.

§51. If God is conceived as a despotic legislator, who places humans under an external obligation, and if honesty and turpitude are considered synonyms for justice and injustice respectively, it is not true that there are ac-

---

22. Classical scriptural examples included God's command to sacrifice Isaac (Genesis 22) and the theft of the Egyptians' silver and gold (Exodus 3:22) by the Israelites.

23. The chapter to which Thomasius refers is "On the Principle of Natural Law and the Law of Nations, and the Principles of the Just, the Honest, and the Decorous."

24. See *Institutes,* bk. I, chap. ii, §§74ff.

tions that are honest or despicable by their nature and prior to the divine will. This has already been shown elsewhere.

§52. But if God is conceived as a father, adviser, and teacher, and if honesty and turpitude stand for goodness and malice or vice in general, rather than justice and injustice in particular, then it is true that those actions with which natural law in the broad as well as the strict sense is concerned are in themselves and by their moral nature good or bad with regard to all of humankind. But actions with which positive law as such is concerned are not perpetually good or bad on the basis of the nature of all humans.

§53. Although natural law provides the rule for positive law, this needs to be understood in different ways. Positive law cannot introduce any firm obligation on a subject that is contrary to natural law in the strict sense, which prohibits harming others. For we have already said that this [natural law in the strict sense] is universally binding. Yet positive law can on the basis of specific utility prohibit many things that are indifferent in terms of natural law, and add an extra support to natural law. Indeed, even in those matters that are already prohibited in natural law it can, for the sake of punishment, deprive another of life, reputation, or material goods, determine the nature of agreements, hinder the effects of keeping faith, etc.

§54. The general precepts of honesty are also universal. Therefore positive law cannot change anything here either. It can, however, add something to particular rules. Indeed, since these particular rules are to be derived from the variations in human nature which are not that obvious to the senses, it is useful for positive law to regulate many matters which it would otherwise be difficult to determine through reasoning alone. Hence the common saying that not all things are equally honest or despicable to all people.

§55. The same reason applies to the precepts concerning decorum. The search for good and bad means is more difficult, because these are not good or bad in an absolute sense but in relation to a greater good or a lesser evil. Hence, not all things are equally decorous or indecorous to all people. Therefore the decorous and the honest, as long as they are not contrary to right reason, are either natural or positive.

§56. From this also follows the need for positive law. Unless fools have begun to abandon their foolishness, they are hardly able to reflect seriously on the utility and agreeability of the true good, which is honest, decorous, and just at the same time, and to realize the burden and harm caused by true evil, which is despicable, indecorous, and unjust at the same time. And they are unable to do so even if they are every day encouraged by the advice of the wise to undertake such reflection. For since harm and usefulness have a necessary connection with the bad and the good, but one that is not so visible and palpable or immediate, the foolish are not adept at fearing what needs to be feared and at hoping where hope is required. Their stupidity deceives them and leads them to believe that they are clever enough to escape this inevitable harm, or they refuse to believe, because of their lack of experience, that they can achieve the necessary goods that accompany virtue and justice.

§57. Punishments in positive law are more palpable and visible and therefore more suitable to instilling fear in the foolish. The rewards of positive law are also more evident to the senses.

§58. Finally, the following needs to be noted. Natural law in the broad sense includes all of moral philosophy, that is, ethics and politics. For ethics teaches the principles of honesty, politics the principles of decorum. Natural law in the strict sense, which teaches the principles of justice and injustice, is thus clearly separated from ethics and politics.

§59. I continue with *right*, insofar as it describes a moral power related to a rule, or, as Grotius puts it, as an attribute of a person. *Right* in this sense is also either natural or positive. But here we are concerned with other definitions.

§60. We call *natural right* that which is the same among most humans known to us. For nobody knows the customs of all humans. And among those whom we know the term should be derived from the majority, rather than making an attempt to speak universally.

§61. *Positive right* is what varies among most humans we know.

§62. It would be accurate to say that *natural right* is a different kind of right than *positive right.*

§63. The effect of natural right in this sense is not the same as that of natural law. Natural law produces an obligation, which a person under such an obligation cannot renounce. Yet anyone can renounce a natural right, as explained above.

§64. Hence, natural law cannot be changed directly by positive law, but positive law can not only augment natural and positive right but even remove and diminish it, because either is by its nature permitted by natural law, not commanded or prohibited.

§65. There remains the law of nations. Here the vital question is aired, whether it is part of divine and natural law or a form of positive and human law. On the answer to that depends another question, whether it is mutable or immutable. If you resolve the ambiguity of the term *law of nations,* the matter will be clear.

§66. The law of nations is sometimes taken to be identical to natural law because all nations use it. Then it is quite clear that it is not a form of positive law or some form of natural law, but natural law itself and hence immutable.

§67. Sometimes it is taken to be that part of natural law that directs the actions of nations in relation to other nations. Then it is not natural law in its wider sense, but nevertheless a form of natural law and equally immutable. It is not human law, because the nations do not have a common legislator.

§68. Sometimes it is regarded as a positive law that is common to many nations. Then it is considered a form of positive law, but one that is usually derived from natural and positive principles. And according to this diversity it is partly mutable and partly immutable.

§69. Sometimes it is taken to be a personal faculty and attribute that is common to many nations. Then it is a form of natural law, but as mutable as natural right in this sense of the word.

§70. Finally it is understood as the customs of several nations with regard to decorum. Then it shares in natural law more than positive law. Yet it is still subject to mutation and variation, as we have noted above concerning decorum.

§71. The common distinction, however, which tends to be applied in this controversy, between cultured and barbarian nations, complicates matters rather than being of any use in resolving them.

§72. For who will determine which nation is cultured and which one is barbarous? Nations are equal to each other, and the term *barbarian* has its origin in the contempt of the Greeks, Romans, and those nations imitating them and stupidly despising other nations.

§73. Nowadays most nations are described as cultured, among whom many rites and ceremonies and pompous celebrations are widespread, which are falsely described as "decorum." It is clear that barbarian nations are inevitably more prudent and less vicious and stupid than cultured ones.

§74. This is illustrated by the opinion of Tacitus. The Romans considered themselves the most cultured nation, the Germans the most barbarian one. And yet, Tacitus praises the Germans, saying that among them good customs had greater force than good laws among the Romans.[25] And throughout the entire book he does his best to prove the truth of our assertion by going through all the customs of the Germans.

25. See Tacitus, *Germania,* ed. and trans. J. B. Rives (Oxford: Clarendon Press, 1999), chap. 19.2, p. 85.

§75. The opinion of others, who regard the law of nations as part of human law, can also be refuted very easily. They want to derive their opinion either from the nature of an agreement or from customary law.

§76. But the nations never formed an explicit agreement. And if they had formed one, then it is a precept of natural, not positive, law that agreements must be adhered to.

§77. It is not possible to suggest the possibility of a tacit agreement here. There is no evidence of a deed by the nations from which this tacit agreement could be proved. Nor is it possible that imitation alone can produce an obligation in matters that are freely chosen.

§78. It is not possible to use customary law to demonstrate the binding character of the law of nations. This is not so much because there is no superior among nations who could tacitly approve this customary law, but rather because it has already been shown elsewhere[26] that customary law produces a right of impunity and efficacy, but not an obligation.[27]

§79. Finally, there is no need to go on about the fact that natural law is understood by some in such a broad sense that it includes a natural instinct that man has in common with all other natural beings and is thus distinguished from the law of nations or that part of natural law that is specific to humans.[28] That particular meaning of natural law, which was typical of the Stoics and the jurists, has been widely refuted and is not used by anyone except poets and orators or pettifogging lawyers.

§80. For brutes and other physical bodies do not require a law, nor are they under any obligation. We have, however, said above that law, prop-

---

26. See Christian Thomasius (*praeses*) and Peter Herff (*respondens*), *Dissertatio inauguralis juridica, sistens conjecturas de jure consuetudinis et observantiae* (Halle, 1699).

27. That is, customary law gives legal sanction to an already existing state of affairs; it is not possible to claim a right by appealing to customary law.

28. See Justinian's *Institutes* 1.2.1–2.

erly speaking, is either a rule or a right, which has an obligation as its correlate.

§81. Hence, we do not need to spend a lot of time explaining the distinction between the primary and secondary laws of nature and nations, which has been invented only to rescue the opinion of Tribonian.[29]

29. Ibid., *Institutes* 1.2.

BIBLIOGRAPHY

I. Works by Christian Thomasius

Editions of the *Institutes of Divine Jurisprudence*

Institutiones jurisprudentiae divinae. Leipzig, 1688.

Göttliche Rechtsgelahrheit. Reprint of German edition (1709), with a preface by Frank Grunert. Hildesheim: Georg Olms, 2001.

Institutiones jurisprudentiae divinae. Reprint of 7th ed. (1730). Aalen: Scientia, 1994.

Editions of the *Foundations of the Law of Nature and Nations*

Fundamenta juris naturae et gentium. Halle, 1705.

Grundlehren des Natur- und Völkerrechts. Reprint of German edition (1709). Hildesheim: Georg Olms, 2003.

Fundamenta juris naturae et gentium. Reprint of 4th ed. (1718). Aalen: Scientia, 1979.

Other Works by Thomasius

Thomasius, Christian. *Ausübung der Sitten-Lehre.* Reprint of the 1696 edition. Hildesheim: Georg Olms, 1999.

———. *Christian Thomasius: Essays on Church and State.* Edited by Ian Hunter, Thomas Ahnert, and Frank Grunert. Indianapolis: Liberty Fund, 2007.

———. *De crimine bigamiae.* Leipzig, 1685.

———. *Einleitung zur Sittenlehre.* Halle, 1692.

———. *Introductio ad philosophiam aulicam* (1688). Edited by W. Schneiders and M. Schewe. Hildesheim: Georg Olms, 1993.

———. *Observationes selectae ad rem litterariam spectantes.* Halle, 1700–1705.

————. *Versuch von Wesen des Geistes.* Reprint of 1699 edition. Hildesheim: Georg Olms, 2004.

Thomasius, Christian (*praeses*), Georg Reichard Emme (*respondens*). *Philosophiam juris ostensam in doctrina de obligationibus et actionibus . . . sollenniter proponit Georg Reichard Emme.* Leipzig, 1682.

Thomasius, Christian (*praeses*), Peter Herff (*respondens*). *Dissertatio inauguralis juridica, sistens conjecturas de jure consuetudinis et observantiae.* Halle, 1699.

Thomasius, Christian (*praeses*), Carl von und zu Montzel (*respondens*). *De sponsione Romanorum Caudina.* Leipzig, 1684.

Thomasius, Christian (*praeses*), Peter Johann Oehnsen (*respondens*). *Disputatio juridica de filio sub conditione, si se filium probaverit, herede instituto, ad l. Lucius 83. de cond. & demonstr.* Leipzig, 1686.

Thomasius, Christian (*praeses*), Hieronymus Winckler (*respondens*). *Dissertatio juridica de servitute stillicidii, vom Trauff-Recht.* Leipzig, 1689.

II. Primary Sources by Other Authors

Works that are referred to only in the editor's introduction but not in the commentary on the text of Thomasius's *Institutes* or *Foundations* are marked with an asterisk (*).

Alberti, Valentin. *Compendium juris naturae orthodoxae theologiae conformatum et in duas partes distributum.* Leipzig, 1678.

————. *Compendium juris naturae orthodoxae theologiae conformatum et in duas partes distributum.* 2nd ed. Leipzig, 1696.

————. *Eros Lipsicus, quo Eris Scandica Samuelis Pufendorfi cum convitiis et erroribus suis mascule, modeste tamen repellitur.* Leipzig, 1687.

Ammianus Marcellinus. *Ammianus Marcellinus.* Translated by J. Rolfe. 3 vols. Loeb Classical Library. Cambridge, Mass.: Harvard University Press, 1971–72.

Anglus, T. H. (Thomas White). *Dux vitae sive statera morum ethico-politico-theologica.* Eleutheropolis, 1672.

*Anon. [Johann Friedrich Hombergk zu Vach]. *Dubia juris naturae.* Douai, 1719.

Apuleius. *The Golden Ass.* Translated by W. Adlington, revised by S. Gaselee. Loeb Classical Library. London: Heinemann, 1947.

Aristotle. *Aristotelis Ethicorum ad Nicomachum libri decem.* Helmstedt, 1660.

————. *Metaphysics.* 2 vols. Translated by Hugh Tredennick. Loeb Classical Library. London: Heinemann, 1933–36.

————. *Nicomachean Ethics.* Translated by H. Rackham. Loeb Classical Library. Cambridge, Mass.: Harvard University Press, 1947.

————. *On the Soul; Parva Naturalia; On Breath.* Translated by W. S. Hett. Loeb Classical Library. Cambridge, Mass.: Harvard University Press, 1995.

————. *Politics.* Edited by S. Everson. Cambridge: Cambridge University Press, 1990.

Augustine. *The City of God Against the Pagans.* Edited and translated by R. W. Dyson. Cambridge: Cambridge University Press, 1998.

————. *De Libero Arbitrio: The Free Choice of the Will.* Philadelphia: The Peter Reilly Company, 1937.

————. *The Greatness of the Soul; The Teacher.* Translated and edited by J. M. Colloran. Westminster, Md.: Newman Press, 1950.

————. *Sermons.* 11 vols. Translated and notes by E. Mill. Edited by J. E. Rotelle. Hyde Park, N.Y.: New City Press, 1990–97.

Ayrault, Pierre. *Rerum ab omni antiquitate iudicatarum Pandectae, recognitae a Philippo Andrea Oldenburgero.* Geneva, 1677.

Bayle, Pierre, ed. *Nouvelles de la République des Lettres.* Amsterdam, 1684.

Beckmann, Nicolaus, and Josua Schwartz. *Index quarundam novitatum, quas Dominus Samuel Puffendorff libro suo De jure naturae et gentium contra orthodoxa fundamenta Londini edidit.* N.p., 1673.

Becmann, Johann Christoph. *Meditationes politicae.* 3rd ed. Frankfurt an der Oder, 1679.

Beger, Lorenz (Daphnaeus Arcuarius). *Daphnai Arcuarii Kurtze, doch unpartheiisch- und gewissenhafte Betrachtung des in dem Natur- und Göttlichen Recht gegeründeten heyligen Ehstandes.* N.p., 1679.

Beverland, Adriaan. *Peccatum originale kat exochen sic nuncupatum.* Eleutheropolis, 1678.

Bochart, Samuel. *Geographiae sacrae pars prior Phaleg: seu de dispersione gentium et terrarum divisione facta in aedificatione turris Babel.* Caen, 1651.

Boecler, Johann Heinrich. *In Hugonis Grotii Jus belli et pacis commentatio.* Strasbourg, 1663–64.

Bohl, Samuel. *Tractatus contra matrimonium comprivignorum.* Rostock, 1637.

*Brucker, Johann Jacob. *Historia critica philosophiae.* Vol. IV. Leipzig, 1744.

Brunnemann, Johann. *De jure ecclesiastico tractatus posthumus.* Edited by S. Stryk. Frankfurt an der Oder, 1681.

Brunsmann, Johann. *Monogamia victrix: sive orthodoxa ecclesiae christianae sententia, de unius duntaxat eodem tempore concessis christiano nuptiis, a criminationibus vindicata quibusvis.* Frankfurt, 1678.

Buchholtz, Christoph Joachim. *Adsertio responsi iuris pro matrimonio principis cum defunctae uxoris sorore: Adversus argumenta Johannis Ottonis Taboris ICti & Michaelis Havemanni theologi.* Rinteln, 1659.

———. *Pro matrimonio principis cum defunctae uxoris sorore contracto.* Rinteln, 1651.

Calvinus, Justus. *Themis Hebraeo-Romana: Id est, iurisprudentia Mosaica, et iuris tum canonici, tum civilis, Romana, invicem collata, & methodice digesta.* Hanau, 1595.

Carpzov, Benedict. *Jurisprudentia ecclesiastica seu consistorialis.* Leipzig, 1649.

Carpzov, Johann Benedict. *Christi Thomaslection von der Jacobsleiter, bey Christlicher Leichbestattung des . . . Herrn Jacobi Thomasii, . . . in damahliger Leichpredigt . . . den 14. September, . . . Anno 1684. in der Pauliner-Kirchen erklaeret von Jo. Benedicto Carpzov.* Leipzig, ca. 1685.

Chemnitz, Bogislaw Philipp von (Hippolitus a Lapide). *Dissertatio de ratione status in Imperio nostro Romano-Germanico.* N.p., 1640.

Cicero, Marcus Tullius. *On Duties [De officiis].* Edited by M. T. Griffin and E. M. Atkins. Cambridge: Cambridge University Press, 1991.

———. *On Ends [De finibus bonorum et malorum].* Translated by H. Rackham. Loeb Classical Library. Cambridge, Mass.: Harvard University Press, 1999.

———. *Tusculan Disputations.* Translated by J. E. King. Loeb Classical Library. London: Heinemann, 1927.

Cumberland, Richard. *A Treatise of the Laws of Nature.* Edited by J. Parkin. Indianapolis: Liberty Fund, 2005.

Darmanson, Jean. *La beste transformée en Machine, diversée en deux dissertations prononcées à Amsterdam.* N.p., 1684.

Delphinus, Hieronymus. *Eunuchi Conjugium: Die Capaunen-Heyrath.* Halle, 1685.

Descartes, René. *Epistola Renati Descartes ad celeberrimum virum D. Gisbertum Voetium in qua examinantur duo libri, nuper pro Voetio Ultrajecti simul editi, unus de Confraternitate Mariana, alter de Philosophia Cartesiana.* Amsterdam, 1643.

———. *Meditationes de prima philosophia.* Paris, 1641.

———. *The Philosophical Works of Descartes.* 2 vols. Translated by E. S. Haldane and G. R. T. Ross. Cambridge: Cambridge University Press, 1982.

Diecmann, Johann. *Vindiciae legis monogamicae.* Stadae, 1678.

Diodorus Siculus. *Diodorus of Sicily.* 12 vols. Edited and translated by C. H. Oldfather. Loeb Classical Library. Cambridge, Mass.: Harvard University Press, 1933–67.

Diogenes Laertius. *Lives of Eminent Philosophers.* Vol. 2. Translated by R. D. Hicks. Loeb Classical Library. London: Heinemann, 1925.

Dorsche, Johann Georg. *Theologia moralis: Ex MSSto edita, & publicae sententiarum collationi in Academia Wittebergensi exposita.* Wittenberg, 1685.

Eckholt, Amadeus. *Compendiaria Pandectarum tractatio.* 2 vols. Leipzig, 1680.

Erasmus, Desiderius. *The Collected Works of Erasmus.* Edited by E. Fantham and E. Rummel, with the assistance of J. Ijsewijn. Vol. 29, pp. 77–123. Toronto, Buffalo, London: University of Toronto Press, 1989.

Eusebius, Desiderius. *Preparation for the Gospel.* Translated by E. H. Gifford. Eugene, Oregon: Wipf and Stock, 2002.

Feltmann, Gerhard. *Tractatus de polygamia.* Leipzig, 1677.

Gellius, Aulus. *The Attic Nights of Aulus Gellius.* Translated by J. C. Rolfe. Vol. 2. Loeb Classical Library. London: Heinemann, 1948.

Gerhard, Johann. *Methodus studii theologici.* Jena, 1620.

Gesenius, Friedrich (Christian Vigilis). *Ad Sincerum Warenbergium Suecum epistola seu dissertatio super polygamia simultanea.* Germanopolis, 1673.

Grotius, Hugo. *Commentary on the Law of Prize and Booty.* Edited by Martine Julia van Ittersum. Indianapolis: Liberty Fund, 2006.

———. *The Free Sea.* Edited by David Armitage. Indianapolis: Liberty Fund, 2004.

———. *The Rights of War and Peace.* Edited by Richard Tuck. 3 vols. Indianapolis: Liberty Fund, 2005.

*Gundling, Nicolaus Hieronymus. *Ausführlicher Discours über das Natur- und Völcker-Recht.* Frankfurt and Leipzig, 1734.

Havemann, Michael. *Adsertio responsi Mosis, contra matrimonium cum defunctae uxoris sorore.* Frankfurt and Bremen, 1660.

———. *Gamologia synoptica, istud est Tractatus de jure connubiorum.* Frankfurt and Hamburg, 1672.

Herodotus. *Herodotus.* Vol. 2. Translated by A. D. Godley. Loeb Classical Library. London: Heinemann, 1928.

Histoire Auguste [*Historia Augusta*]. Edited and translated by André Chastagnol. Paris: Laffont, 1994.

Hobbes, Thomas. *Leviathan.* Edited by R. Tuck. Cambridge: Cambridge University Press, 1996.

————. *On the Citizen.* Edited by R. Tuck and M. Silverthorne. Cambridge: Cambridge University Press, 1998.

Homer. *The Iliad.* Translated by A. T. Murray. Vol. 1. Loeb Classical Library. London: Heinemann, 1930.

Horace. *Satires, Epistles and Ars Poetica.* Translated by H. Rushton Fairclough. Loeb Classical Library. London: Heinemann, 1926.

Horn, Johann Friedrich. *Architectonica de civitate.* Editio Novissima. Leyden, 1699.

Horneius, Conrad. *Philosophiae moralis sive civilis doctrinae de moribus libri IV.* Frankfurt, 1634.

*Hume, David. *Treatise of Human Nature.* Oxford: Oxford University Press, 1978.

Josephus. *Josephus.* 10 vols. Translated by H. St. J. Thackeray. Loeb Classical Library. London: Heinemann, 1926–81.

Journal du Palais, ou Recueil des principales decisions de tous les Parlemens. Part 9. Paris, 1684.

Justinian. *Codex Justinianus.* Edited by Paul Krueger. Berlin: Weidmann, 1877.

————. *Digest.* Edited by Alan Watson. Philadelphia: University of Pennsylvania Press, 1998.

————. *Institutes.* Translated with an introduction by Peter Birks and Grant McLeod with Latin text by Paul Krueger. London: Duckworth, 1987.

Klenck, Jan. *Institutiones juris naturalis, gentium, et publici, ex Hugonis Grootii De jure belli ac pacis libris excerptae.* Amsterdam, 1665.

Kulpis, Johann Georg von. *Collegium Grotianum, super iure belli ac pacis: Anno 1682 in Academia Giessensi 15. exercitationibus primum institutum.* 2nd ed. Giessen, 1686.

Lactantius. *Divine Institutes.* Translated and edited by Anthony Bowen and Peter Garnsey. Liverpool: Liverpool University Press, 2003.

Linck, Heinrich (*praeses*), Johann Eckhard Finck (*respondens*). *Usus divortiorum ex divino et humano hocque civili ac canonico iure.* Altdorf, 1686.

Livy. *Livy.* Translated by B. O. Foster. Vol. 3. Loeb Classical Library. London: Heinemann, 1924.

Lucian. *Lucian.* Translated by A. M. Harmon. Vol. 1. Loeb Classical Library. London: Heinemann, 1913.

————. *Lucian.* Translated by A. M. Harmon. Vol. 5. Loeb Classical Library. London: Heinemann, 1936.

Luther, Martin. Luther's Works. Vol. 1: *Lectures on Genesis*, chapters 1–5. Edited by J. Pelikan. St. Louis, Missouri: Concordia, 1958.

Lyser, Johannes (Sincerus Warenberg). *Alethophili Germani discursus inter polygamum et monogamum de polygamia.* N.p., 1673.

―――. *Discursus politicus de polygamia.* Freiburg, 1674.

――― (Theophilus Alethaeus). *Polygamia triumphatrix, id est discursus politicus de polygamia.* Lund, 1682.

Martial. *Epigrams.* Vol. 1. Translated by W. C. A. Ker. Loeb Classical Library. London: Heinemann, 1930.

Martini, Jacob. *Partitiones et quaestiones metaphysicae, in quibus omnium fere terminorum metaphysicorum distinctiones accurate enumerantur & explicantur.* Wittenberg, 1615.

Masius, Hector Gottfried. *Interesse principum circa religionem evangelicam.* Copenhagen, 1687.

Maximus of Tyre. *The Philosophical Orations.* Edited and translated by M. S. Trapp. Oxford: Oxford University Press, 1997.

Melanchthon, Philipp. *Apologia Confessionis Augustanae* (1531). Translated into German and edited by Horst Georg Pöhlmann. Gütersloh: G. Mohn, 1967.

Milton, John. *The Doctrine and Discipline of Divorce.* The Works of John Milton, vol. 3, part 2. New York: Columbia University Press, 1931.

More, Thomas. *Utopia.* Edited by G. M. Logan and Robert M. Adams. Revised edition. Cambridge: Cambridge University Press, 2002.

Morhof, Daniel. *Dissertatio de paradoxis sensuum.* Kiel, 1676.

Musaeus, Johannes. *Dissertatio de quaestione controversa, an coniugium, primaeva eius institutione salva, inter plures, quam duos, esse possit?* Jena, 1675.

Osiander, Johann Adam. *Observationes maximam partem theologicae in libros tres De jure belli et pacis H. Grotii.* Tübingen, 1671.

―――. *Typus legis naturae.* Tübingen, 1669.

Ovid. *Metamorphoses.* Vol. 1. Translated by J. F. Miller. 3rd ed., revised by G. P. Goold. Loeb Classical Library. Cambridge, Mass.: Harvard University Press, 1972.

Pereira, Gomez. *Antoniana Margarita, opus nempe physicis, medicis ac theologis non minus utile, quam necessarium.* N.p., 1554.

Philastrius. *Diversarum hereseon liber.* Edited by F. Marx. Corpus Scriptorum Ecclesiasticorum Latinorum, vol. 38. Prague, Vienna, Leipzig: Tempsky, 1898.

Plato. *Cratylus; Parmenides; Greater Hippias; Lesser Hippias.* Translated by H. N. Fowler. Loeb Classical Library. London: Heinemann, 1926.

———. *The Laws.* 2 vols. Translated by R. G. Bury. Loeb Classical Library. London: Heinemann, 1926.

———. *The Republic.* Translated by T. Griffith. Edited by G. R. F. Ferrari. Cambridge: Cambridge University Press, 2008.

Plutarch. *Lives.* Translated by B. Perrin. Vol. 1. Loeb Classical Library. London: Heinemann, 1914.

———. *Moralia.* Vol. 4. Translated by F. C. Babbitt. Loeb Classical Library. London: Heinemann, 1936.

———. *Moralia.* Vol. 12. Translated by H. Cherniss and W. C. Helmbold. Loeb Classical Library. Cambridge, Mass.: Harvard University Press, 1957.

Pufendorf, Samuel. *Apologia pro se et suo libro, adversus autorem libelli famosi, cui titulus Index quarundam novitatum, quas Dominus Samuel Pufendorf libro suo De jure naturae et gentium contra orthodoxa fundamenta Londini edidit.* Germanopolis, 1674.

———. *De jure naturae et gentium libri octo.* Lund, 1672.

———. *De officio hominis et civis.* Lund, 1673.

———. *Elementa jurisprudentiae universalis.* The Hague, 1660.

———. *Of the Law of Nature and Nations.* Translated into English. Oxford, 1703.

———. *On the Duty of Man and Citizen.* Edited by J. Tully. Translated by M. Silverthorne. Cambridge: Cambridge University Press, 1991.

———. *The Present State of Germany.* Edited by M. Seidler. Indianapolis: Liberty Fund, 2007.

———. *The Whole Duty of Man, According to the Law of Nature.* Translated by Andrew Tooke. Edited by Ian Hunter and David Saunders. With *Two Discourses and a Commentary by Jean Barbeyrac.* Translated by David Saunders. Indianapolis: Liberty Fund, 2003.

Quintilian. *The Orator's Education.* Vol. 3. Edited and translated by D. Russell. Loeb Classical Library. Cambridge, Mass.: Harvard University Press, 2001.

Rachel, Samuel. *Dissertatio moralis de principiis actionum humanarum.* Helmstedt, 1660.

Rebhahn, Johann (*praes*), Johann Daniel Stalburger (*respondens*). *De interpretatione juris obscuri.* Strasbourg, 1671.

Repgow, Eike von. *The Saxon Mirror: A Sachsenspiegel of the Fourteenth Century.* Translated by M. Dobozy. Philadelphia: University of Pennsylvania Press, 1999.

Rondel, Jacques de. *La vie d'Epicure.* Paris, 1679.

Scherzer, Johann Adam. *Systema theologiae, 29 definitionibus absolutum.* Leipzig, 1680.

Schilter, Johann. *Manuductio philosophiae moralis ad veram, nec simulatam jurisprudentiam.* Jena, 1676.

Schlüter, Severin Walther. *Theologische Gedancken von der Polygynia, oder Von dem nehmen vieler Weiber.* Rostock, 1677.

*Schmauss, Johann Jacob. *Neues Systema des Rechts der Natur* (1754). Edited by M. Senn. Goldbach: Keip, 1999.

Schotanus, Christiaan. *Bibliotheca historiae sacrae per duas aetates & duo annorum milia, ab Adam ad Abraham.* Franeker, 1660.

Schwertner, Johann David (*praeses*), Moses Schede (*respondens*). *De celebri sed flagitioso pseudo-politicorum axiomate: virum magnis in rebus civilibus versaturum tribus carere oportere: religione, uxore et pudore, a Boeclero in elogio Forstneri adnotato.* Leipzig, 1683.

Seckendorff, Veit Ludwig von. *Christen-Stat.* Leipzig, 1685.

———. *Teutsche Reden.* Leipzig, 1686.

Selden, John. *De jure naturali et gentium iuxta disciplinam Hebraeorum.* London, 1640.

———. *On Jewish Marriage Law.* Translated with a commentary by J. Ziskind. Leiden: Brill, 1991.

———. *Uxor Ebraica.* London, 1646.

———. *Uxor Ebraica, seu de nuptiis et divortiis ex jure civili, id est, divino et Talmudico, veterum Ebraeorum, libri tres.* Editio nova. Frankfurt an der Oder, 1673.

Seneca, Lucius Annaeus. *Ad Lucilium epistulae morales.* Translated by R. M. Gummere. Vol. 3. Loeb Classical Library. London: Heinemann, 1953.

———. *Moral Essays.* Vol. 2. Translated by J. W. Basore. Loeb Classical Library. London: Heinemann, 1951.

———. *Moral Essays.* Vol. 3. Translated by J. W. Basore. Loeb Classical Library. London: Heinemann, 1935.

Sharrock, Robert. *Judicia de variis incontinentiae speciebus.* Oxford, 1662.

Sperling, Johann. *Physica anthropologia.* Wittenberg, 1647.

Stobaeus, Johannes. *Florilegium.* 4 vols. Edited by T. Gaisford. Oxford: Clarendon Press, 1822.

Strauch, Johannes. *Dissertationes undetriginta ad universum jus Justinianum privatum.* Frankfurt an der Oder, 1682.

———. *Institutionum juris publici specimen.* Frankfurt, 1683.

*Strube de Piermont, Frederic-Henri. *Ébauche des loix naturelles*. Amsterdam, 1744.

Sturm, Johann Christoph. *Philosophia eclectica*. Altdorf, 1686.

Tacitus. *Germania*. Edited and translated by J. B. Rives. Oxford: Clarendon Press, 1999.

Tasso, Torquato. *Dialoghi*. Edited by E. Raimondi. Vol. 3. Florence: G. C. Sansoni, 1958.

Terence. *Terence*. Edited and translated by J. Barsby. Vol. 2. Loeb Classical Library. Cambridge, Mass.: Harvard University Press, 2001.

Theodosius. *Codex Theodosianus*. 2 vols. Edited by Paul Kruger. Berlin: Weidmann, 1923–26.

Thomasius, Jacob. *Erotemata metaphysica pro incipientibus*. Leipzig, 1670.

———. *Orationes, partim ex umbone Templi Academici, partim ex Auditorii Philosophici cathedra recitatae, argumenti varii*. Leipzig, 1683.

———. *Physica*. Leipzig, 1670.

Thomasius, Jacob (*praeses*), Johann Jordan (*respondens*). *Dissertatio politico-oeconomica, de societate paterna*. Leipzig, 1654.

Thomasius, Jacob (*praeses*), Johann Adam Preunel (*respondens*). *Legatus inviolabilis*. Leipzig, 1667.

Uffelmann, Heinrich. *De jure quo homo homini in sermone obligatur liber unus*. Helmstedt, 1676.

Velthuysen, Lambert van. *Epistolica dissertatio de principiis iusti et decori, continens apologiam pro tractatu clarissimi Hobbaei, De cive*. Amsterdam, 1651.

———. *Opera omnia*. Rotterdam, 1680.

———. *Tractatus moralis de naturali pudore et dignitate hominis in quo agitur, de incestu, scortatione, voto caelibatus, conjugio, adulterio, polygamia et divortiis, etc*. Utrecht, 1676.

Virgil. *Virgil*. Translated by H. Rushton Fairclough, revised by G. P. Goold. Loeb Classical Library. Cambridge, Mass.: Harvard University Press, 1999.

Willis, Thomas. *De anima brutorum quae hominis vitalis ac sensitiva est exercitationes duae*. London, 1672.

Zeidler, Melchior. *Analysis posterior, sive De variis sciendi generibus et mediis eo perveniendi libri tres*. Königsberg, 1675.

Zeisold, Johannes. *Disputatio physica de notitiis naturalibus*. Jena, 1651–52.

Ziegler, Caspar. *In Hugonis Grotii De jure belli ac pacis libros, quibus naturae & gentium jus explicavit, notae et animadversiones subitariae*. Wittenberg, 1666.

III. Secondary Works

Ahnert, Thomas. "Enthusiasm and Enlightenment: Faith and Philosophy in the Thought of Christian Thomasius." In *Modern Intellectual History* 2.2 (2005): 153–77.

———. "Pleasure, Pain and Punishment in the Early Enlightenment: German and Scottish Debates." In S. Byrd, J. Hruschka, and Jan C. Joerden, eds., *The Development of Moral First Principles in the Philosophy of the Enlightenment,* pp. 173–87. Jahrbuch für Recht und Ethik, vol. 12. Berlin: Duncker and Humblot, 2004.

———. *Religion and the Origins of the German Enlightenment: Faith and the Reform of Learning in the Thought of Christian Thomasius.* Rochester, N.Y.: University of Rochester Press, 2006.

———. "Roman Law in Early Enlightenment Germany: The Case of Christian Thomasius' *De Aequitate Cerebrina Legis Secundae Codicis de Rescindenda Venditione* (1706)." *Ius commune* XXIV (1997): 153–70.

Boor, Friedrich de. "Die ersten Vorschläge des Christian Thomasius 'wegen Auffrichtung einer Neuen Academie zu Halle' aus dem Jahre 1690." In E. Donnert, ed., *Europa in der Frühen Neuzeit: Festschrift für Günther Mühlpfordt,* vol. 4. Weimar: Böhlau, 1997.

Dufour, Alfred. "Pufendorf." In J. H. Burns, ed. (with the assistance of Mark Goldie), *The Cambridge History of Political Thought, 1450–1700.* Cambridge: Cambridge University Press, 1991.

Frandsen, Mary E. "*Eunuchi Conjugium:* The Marriage of a Castrato in Early Modern Germany." *Early Music History* 24 (2005): 53–124.

Fulbrook, Mary. *Piety and Politics: Religion and the Rise of Absolutism in England, Württemberg and Prussia.* Cambridge: Cambridge University Press, 1983.

Grunert, Frank. *Normbegründung und politische Legitimität* (Frühe Neuzeit, 57). Tübingen: Max Niemeyer, 2000.

———. "Zur aufgeklärten Kritik am theokratischen Absolutismus: Der Streit zwischen Hector Gottfried Masius und Christian Thomasius über Ursprung und Begründung der summa potestas." In Friedrich Vollhardt, ed., *Christian Thomasius (1655–1728): Neue Forschungen im Kontext der Frühaufklärung* (Frühe Neuzeit, 37). Tübingen: Max Niemeyer, 1997.

Haakonssen, Knud. *Natural Law and Moral Philosophy: From Grotius to the Scottish Enlightenment.* Cambridge: Cambridge University Press, 1996.

Hinrichs, Carl. *Preußentum und Pietismus: Der Pietismus in Brandenburg-Preußen als religiös-soziale Reformbewegung*. Göttingen: Vandenhoeck & Ruprecht, 1971.

Hochstrasser, Tim. *Natural Law Theories in the Early Enlightenment*. Cambridge: Cambridge University Press, 2000.

Hunter, Ian. *Rival Enlightenments: Civil and Metaphysical Philosophy in Early Modern Germany*. Cambridge: Cambridge University Press, 2001.

————. *The Secularisation of the Confessional State: The Political Thought of Christian Thomasius*. Cambridge: Cambridge University Press, 2007.

Lieberwirth, Rolf. "Christian Thomasius (1655–1728)." In G. Jerouschek and A. Sames, eds., *Aufklärung und Erneuerung*. Hanau: Dausien, 1994.

————. "Die französischen Kultureinflüsse auf den deutschen Frühaufklärer Christian Thomasius." *Wissenschaftliche Zeitschrift der Universität Halle* 33 (1983).

Pott, Martin. "Christian Thomasius und Gottfried Arnold." In D. Blaufuss and F. Niewöhner, eds., *Gottfried Arnold (1666–1714)*. Wiesbaden: Harrasowitz, 1995.

Schneiders, Werner. *Naturrecht und Liebesethik: Zur Geschichte der praktischen Philosophie im Hinblick auf Christian Thomasius*. Hildesheim and New York: G. Olms, 1971.

Schröder, Peter. *Christian Thomasius zur Einführung*. Hamburg: Junius, 1999.

————. "The Constitution of the Holy Roman Empire after 1648: Samuel Pufendorf's Assessment in his Monzambano." *Historical Journal* 42.2 (1999): 961–83.

Vollhardt, Friedrich. *Selbstliebe und Geselligkeit*. Tübingen: Max Niemeyer, 2001.

Zimmermann, Reinhard. *The Law of Obligations: Roman Foundations of the Civilian Tradition*. Oxford: Clarendon Press, 1996.

INDEX

Abel and Cain, 56, 277–78
absolute monarchs, 504–5
accessories and accession, 284–85, 294–97
Acta Oettingensia, 18
actions, just and unjust, 82–84
Acts: 15:20, 151n58; 17:15–33, 51n90
Adam (biblical figure): dead, duty to, 562, 563; divine jurisprudence and, 44–45, 56, 91, 92, 99, 109, 140, 151; marriage in divine positive law and, 416, 418–21, 426, 428, 429, 432, 442; property and, 267, 269–70, 272, 273, 275, 277–78
adultery: compensation for, 194; in divine positive law, 422–25, 431–32; in natural law, 383, 384, 389, 404–5; punishment for, 537
Aeneid (Virgil), 319n112
affirmation, 586
affirmative versus negative precepts, 171–72
agents. *See* legates
agreements. *See* contracts
Alberti, Valentin: on commonwealths, 480n92; on derivation of natural law principles from prelapsarian state, 521n119, 576n12; fiction, use of, 56; Jacob Thomasius, eulogy of, 36–37; on marriage, 416n35; Thomasius's critique of, xiii–xviii
Albertus Magnus, 19

Alethaeus, Theophilus, 17
alienation, 477, 506
allies. *See* confederates
ambassadors. *See* legates
ambiguous terminology, 317–19
ambition, 603–6
Ambrose of Milan, 443
Ammianus Marcellinus, 249n49
Anglus, T. H., 442n70
animals. *See* beasts
Apologia (Pufendorf, 1674), 6, 38
application of divine and human laws, 566–68
Apuleius, 140n50
Arcuarius, Daphnaeus, 17
Ariadne (in Greek mythology), 396
aristocracies, 487, 488, 498, 543
Aristotle: authorities, citation of, 19; on civil societies/commonwealths, 480, 481, 482, 484, 510; on faculties or habits, 61n1, 64; on human rationality, 66; on innate ideas, 39–40; on intellect, 35–36; on law, 65; on marriage, 355; *Metaphysics,* 64n4; *Nicomachean Ethics,* xxi*n*38, 61n1, 78n13, 234n42, 355n3, 368n13; on passions, xxi*n*38; *Politics,* 261n56, 358n4, 359, 510n112; on property, 260; on right, 78; on societies, 355, 358, 359; on speech, 227; on supreme good, 130; on the soul, 156n4; on truth and lying, 234

This book is set in Adobe Garamond, a modern adaptation by Robert Slimbach of the typeface originally cut around 1540 by the French typographer and printer Claude Garamond. The Garamond face, with its small lowercase height and restrained contrast between thick and thin strokes, is a classic "old-style" face and has long been one of the most influential and widely used typefaces.

Printed on paper that is acid-free and meets the requirements of the American National Standard for Permanence of Paper for Printed Library Materials, z39.48–1992. ∞

Book design by Louise OFarrell
Gainesville, Florida
Typography by Newgen Publishing and Data Services
Austin, Texas
Printed and bound by
Sheridan Books, Inc.
Ann Arbor, Michigan